Marketing Strategy

A Decision-Focused Approach   Eighth Edition

Orville C. Walker, Jr.
James D. Watkins Professor of Marketing, Emeritus

University of Minnesota

John W. Mullins
Associate Professor of Management Practice in Marketing and Entrepreneurship

London Business School

 **McGraw-Hill Irwin**

MARKETING STRATEGY: A DECISION-FOCUSED APPROACH, EIGHTH EDITION

Published by McGraw-Hill/Irwin, a business unit of The McGraw-Hill Companies, Inc., 1221 Avenue of the Americas, New York, NY 10020. Copyright © 2014 by The McGraw-Hill Companies, Inc. All rights reserved. Previous editions © 2011, 2008, and 2006. No part of this publication may be reproduced or distributed in any form or by any means, or stored in a database or retrieval system, without the prior written consent of The McGraw-Hill Companies, Inc., including, but not limited to, in any network or other electronic storage or transmission, or broadcast for distance learning.

Some ancillaries, including electronic and print components, may not be available to customers outside the United States.

This book is printed on acid-free paper.

4 5 6 7 8 9 0 QVS/QVS 1 0 9 8 7 6 5

ISBN 978-0-07-802894-6
MHID 0-07-802894-9

Senior Vice President, Products & Markets: *Kurt L. Strand*
Vice President, Content Production & Technology Services: *Kimberly Meriwether David*
Editorial Director: *Paul Ducham*
Developmental Editor: *Sean M. Pankuch*
Director, Content Production: *Terri Schiesl*
Marketing Manager: *Donielle Xu*
Project Manager: *Mary Jane Lampe*
Cover Designer: *Studio Montage, St. Louis, Missouri*
Cover & Section Opener Image Credit: *Ingram Publishing/SuperStock*
Buyer: *Jennifer Pickel*
Media Project Manager: *Prashanthi Nadipalli*
Composition: *S4Carlisle Publishing Services*
Typeface: *10/12 Times New Roman*
Printer: *Quad/Graphics*

All credits appearing on page or at the end of the book are considered to be an extension of the copyright page.

Library of Congress Cataloging-in-Publication Data

Walker, Orville C.
    Marketing strategy : a decision-focused approach/Orville C. Walker, Jr., John W. Mullins.—8th ed.
      p. cm.
    Includes index.
    ISBN 978-0-07-802894-6—ISBN 0-07-802894-9   1.Marketing—Management.   I. Mullins, John W. (John Walker)   II. Title.
    HF5415.13.W249 2014
    658.8'02—dc23
                                                                        2012041227

The Internet addresses listed in the text were accurate at the time of publication. The inclusion of a website does not indicate an endorsement by the authors or McGraw-Hill, and McGraw-Hill does not guarantee the accuracy of the information presented at these sites.

www.mhhe.com

About the Authors

Orville C. Walker, Jr.

Orville C. Walker, Jr., is Professor Emeritus in the University of Minnesota's Carlson School of Management, where he served as the James D. Watkins Professor of Marketing and Director of the PhD Program. He holds a master's degree in social psychology from Ohio State University and a PhD in marketing from the University of Wisconsin–Madison.

Orville is the coauthor of three books and has published more than 50 research articles in scholarly and business journals. He has won several awards for his research, including the O'Dell award from the *Journal of Marketing Research,* the Maynard award from the *Journal of Marketing,* and a lifetime achievement award from the Sales Management Interest Group of the American Marketing Association.

Orville has been a consultant to a number of business firms and not-for-profit organizations, and he has taught in executive development programs around the world, including programs in Poland, Switzerland, Scotland, and Hong Kong. Perhaps his biggest business challenge, however, has been attempting to turn a profit as the owner-manager of a small vineyard in western Wisconsin.

John W. Mullins

John Mullins is Associate Professor of Management Practice in Marketing and Entrepreneurship at London Business School. He earned his MBA at the Stanford Graduate School of Business and, considerably later in life, his PhD in marketing from the University of Minnesota. An award-winning teacher, John brings to his teaching and research 20 years of executive experience in high-growth firms, including two ventures he founded, one of which he took public.

Since becoming a business school professor in 1992, John has published more than 40 articles in a variety of outlets, including *Harvard Business Review, Sloan Management Review,* the *Wall Street Journal,* the *Journal of Product Innovation Management,* and the *Journal of Business Venturing.* His research has won national and international awards from the Marketing Science Institute, the American Marketing Association, and the Richard D. Irwin Foundation. John is coauthor of *Marketing Strategy: A Strategic Decision-Making Approach,* 8th edition.

John's consulting, executive education, and case-writing regularly take him to destinations in Africa, India, and Latin America. John's best-selling trade book, *The New Business Road Test: What Entrepreneurs and Executives Should Do Before Writing a Business Plan,* is the definitive work on the assessment and shaping of market opportunities. John's newest trade book, coauthored with noted venture capital investor Randy Komisar and also a bestseller, *Getting to Plan B: Breaking Through to a Better Business Model,* has won widespread critical acclaim. It is reshaping the approach entrepreneurs and other innovators take to starting their new ventures.

Brief Table of Contents

Table of Contents

Preface

WHY THIS COURSE?

The best of the leading business schools and other executive education programs offer capstone or other elective courses in marketing whose strategic perspective challenges students to "pull it all together" and integrate what they have learned in earlier courses—including those in marketing and other disciplines—in making strategic marketing decisions. Whether called Marketing Strategy, Strategic Market Planning, Strategic Brand Management, or something else, such courses typically ask students to apply what they learn to decision making in case studies that bring alive real marketing situations. Many also ask students to complete a term-long project of some kind, such as the development of a marketing plan for a new or existing product or a new venture. We have written this text to serve exactly these kinds of case-based and project-based capstone and advanced elective courses.

WHY THIS BOOK?

Why did your instructor choose this book? Chances are that it was for one or more of the following reasons:

- Among your instructor's objectives is to give you the necessary tools and frameworks to enable you to be an effective contributor to marketing **decision-making,** whether as an entrepreneur or in an established firm. This book's focus on decision making sets it apart from other texts that place greater emphasis on *description* of marketing phenomena than on the strategic and tactical marketing *decisions* that marketing managers and entrepreneurs must make each and every day.

- Your instructor prefers a tightly written text whose strategic perspectives serve as a **concise foundation** around which a broader set of materials, such as case studies or supplementary readings that fit the specific theme of the course, are assembled. This text assumes student familiarity with—and thus does not repeat—the basics of buyer behavior, the 4 Ps, and other marketing fundamentals typically covered in earlier courses.

- Your instructor wants to use the most current and **web-savvy** book available. We integrate the latest new-economy developments into each chapter, and we devote an entire chapter—Chapter 11—to the development of marketing strategies for the new economy. In addition, we supplement the book with an interactive website to help you learn and to help your instructor choose the best case and other materials and in-class activities. Our goal—and probably that of your instructor, as well—is to make both the latest web-based tools as well as time-tested marketing principles relevant to those of you who will work in either old- or new-economy companies.

- Your instructor appreciates and believes you will benefit from the **real-world, global perspectives** offered by the authors of this book. Our combined entrepreneurial, marketing management, case-writing, and consulting experience spans a broad variety of manufacturing, service, software, and distribution industries and has taken us—and thereby you, the reader—around the world many times over.

As the reader will see from the outset in Chapter 1, marketing decision making is a critical activity in every firm, including start-ups—not just in big companies with traditional marketing departments. Further, it is not just marketing managers who make marketing decisions. People in nearly every role in every company can have a powerful influence on how happy its customers are—or are not—with the goods and services the company provides.

Stockbrokers must attract new customers. Accounting and consulting firms must find ways to differentiate their services from other providers so their customers have reasons to give them their business. Software engineers developing the next great internet or mobile application must understand how their technology can benefit the intended customer, for without such benefits, customers will not buy. Thus, we have written this book to meet the marketing needs of readers who hope to make a difference in the long-term strategic success of their organizations—whether their principal roles are in marketing or otherwise. In this brief preface, we want to say a bit more about each of the four distinctive benefits—bulleted previously—that this book offers its readers. We also point out the key changes in this edition compared to previous ones, and we thank our many students, colleagues, and others from whom we have learned so much, without whom this book would not have been possible.

A FOCUS ON DECISION MAKING

This eighth edition of *Marketing Strategy: A Decision-Focused Approach* retains the strategic perspectives that have marked the earlier editions, while providing, in each chapter, specific tools and frameworks for **making marketing decisions** that take best advantage of the conditions in which the firm finds itself—both internally, in terms of the firm's mission and competencies, and externally, in terms of the market and competitive context in which it operates.

This decision-focused approach is important to students and executives who are our readers, because in most advanced marketing management classes and executive courses, the students or participants will be asked to make numerous decisions—decisions in case studies about what the protagonist in the case should do; decisions in a course project, such as those entailed in developing a marketing plan; or decisions in a marketing simulation game.

Our decision-focused approach is also important to employers, who tell us they want today's graduates to be prepared to "hit the ground running" and contribute to the firm's decision making from day one. The ability to bring thoughtful and disciplined tools and frameworks—as opposed to seat-of-the-pants hunches or blind intuition—to marketing decision making is one of the key assets today's business school graduates offer their employers. This book puts the tools in the toolbox to make this happen. In the end, employers want to know what their new hires can *do,* not just what they *know.*

A CONCISE STRATEGIC FOUNDATION

This eighth edition serves as a **concise foundation** for a capstone or advanced elective course in marketing whose focus is on strategic issues. By combining this book with supplemental readings and/or cases, instructors can design a rich and varied course in which students learn experientially, as they focus on the various strategic decisions that define contemporary marketing theory and practice.

Because the book is concise, students learn the key strategic principles quickly, so they can devote most of their reading and prep time to the *application* of those principles to cases or a course project. The book's concise strategic focus also helps instructors build specialized elective courses—in Strategic Brand Management or in Marketing in the Socially Networked Economy, for example—that draw on supplemental readings to complete the thematic picture.

WEB-SAVVY INSIGHTS

Because this book has been written by authors from web-savvy institutions who work with web-savvy companies, it brings a realistic, informed, and **web-savvy perspective** to an important question many students are asking: "Have the advent of Internet, Facebook, and

Twitter, and the latest mobile apps changed all the rules?" Our answer is "well, yes and no." On one hand, today's digitally networked world has made available a host of new marketing tools—from blogs to tweets to e-mail marketing to delivery of digital goods and services over the Internet—most of which are available to companies in the so-called old and new economies alike. On the other hand, time-tested marketing fundamentals—such as understanding one's customers and competitors and meeting customer needs in ways that are differentiated from the offerings of those competitors—have become even more important in today's fast-moving world, as the many dot-com failures a few years ago attest.

Thus, throughout the book, we integrate examples of young entrepreneurial companies, high-tech, and no-tech—both successful and otherwise—to show how both yesterday's and today's marketing tools and decision frameworks can most effectively be applied.

A REAL-WORLD, GLOBAL PERSPECTIVE

Theory is important because it enhances our understanding of business phenomena and helps managers think about what they should do. It is in the *application* of theory—to the world of marketing practice—where we believe this book excels. Our decision focus is all about application. But we don't just bring an academic perspective to the party, important as that perspective is.

Both of us have successfully started and managed entrepreneurial companies—a vineyard in Orville's case and a fresh pasta company and an outdoor products company as part of the 20 years of executive experience with large companies and small ones that preceded John's academic career. In short, both of us have practiced the marketing lessons we preach, and we have the battle scars to prove it.

Both of us bring a rich variety of both domestic American and international consulting and executive education experience, with the latter ranging from Scotland to South Africa, from London to Lagos, from Hyderabad to Hong Kong and more. John's platform at London Business School, one of the world's most global institutions, keeps us in touch with the latest developments on the global business scene.

Both of us have contributed the fruits of our research to the growing body of knowledge in the marketing management, marketing strategy, new products, and entrepreneurship arenas.

The result of our collective and varied experience and expertise is a book marked by its real-world, global perspective. The book's many examples of real people from around the world making real strategic marketing decisions include examples of start-ups and high-growth companies as well as examples of larger, more established firms.

WHAT'S NEW IN THIS EDITION?

In this eighth edition of *Marketing Strategy,* we've gone to considerable lengths to address four key trends that are sweeping the world of marketing theory and practice, trends that are creating opportunities for well-educated graduates to bring new tools and ideas to their employers or to their own entrepreneurial ventures:

- The growing interest among students everywhere in learning what it will take to run their own companies, whether now—upon, or even before, graduation—or later in their careers.
- The growing importance of emerging markets such as India, China, Brazil, and Russia on the global economic stage and the growing realization in companies everywhere that business today is a global game.
- The increasing attention being given in many companies to issues concerning the measurement of marketing performance and the extent to which marketing activities and spending contribute to the creation of shareholder value.

- The changing nature of marketing research. These changes are being driven by two factors: the power of the Internet to make many kinds of research both less expensive and faster to carry out, and by a growing recognition that understanding customer desires in today's complex world requires more than an occasional customer survey.
- The growing ubiquity of social networks—Facebook, LinkedIn, Twitter, and the like—which provide powerful new communications tools for marketers of all kinds, whether companies with goods to sell or political organizations out to change the world.

We've addressed the first of these issues, students' growing interest in all things entrepreneurial, by adding more examples throughout the book of how entrepreneurial companies—not just large, established ones—are using the strategic tools and frameworks that this book brings to life. A new chapter-opening vignette on opportunities in the "app economy" should prove to be of interest to our many entrepreneurially minded readers. As the author team knows from personal experience, the entrepreneurial path is a long and difficult—but always exciting—one, and we'd like our readers who choose such a path to be well equipped for the journey.

Recent editions of this book have been known for their global perspective, and this edition is no exception. We have worked especially hard to add examples from fast-growing emerging economies like India, China, and Russia, and we've added two new global case vignettes—one on the emerging middle class in the developing world and another on Swedish appliance maker Electrolux's global strategy. We have also added a new section on positioning decisions in global markets in Chapter 6, and new material on some of the unique problems encountered in marketing across cultures, such as the discussion of stricter international bribery laws in Chapter 2.

To reflect the growing interest—some would say concern—about the **measurement of marketing performance,** we've added a new section to Chapter 13 to address the tools for analyzing and making the most of **search engine optimization** (SEO) and **search engine marketing** (SEM) techniques, two now essential arrows in every marketer's quiver that didn't even exist just a few editions ago. New technology that can bring up-to-the-minute performance data to managers' desktops is having profound effects on how today's most forward-thinking companies are run. Readers of this eighth edition should be equipped to contribute to the development of executive dashboards and other systems for measuring and tracking marketing performance.

Perhaps nothing, however, provides a greater opportunity for today's marketing graduates than the continuing rise of Internet penetration around the world and its growing importance for marketers—whether as a vehicle for promoting one's brand and building loyalty, a means of conducting marketing research, a way to disintermediate one's distribution channel and reach customers directly, or for other reasons. In this eighth edition, we've completely updated and revamped Chapter 11, which now focuses on the marketing implications of today's digitally and socially networked world. Though further innovations in this arena will no doubt have hit our readers' cell phones, laptops, and iPads by the time the ink is dry on this edition, Chapter 11 provides an underpinning to help students and faculty discuss why and how it's all happening, and to draw meaningful managerial implications for both marketers and aspiring entrepreneurs.

In addition to these more significant changes, every chapter has been refreshed, its examples updated, and the latest empirical evidence of what works and what doesn't incorporated. We've made a special effort to increase our coverage of recent conceptual developments and empirical findings in the academic literature as well as insights from the popular business press. However, the overall structure and flow of this eighth edition remains unchanged. Perhaps most importantly, its emphasis on strategic decision making remains intact. This book's decision-focused approach remains its key strength.

SPECIAL FEATURES

There are several special features we've used to call reader's attention to key concepts and examples, to make the book more readable and its key themes more engaging, and to direct both readers and instructors to additional resources to help make our marketing strategy subject matter come alive. These features include the following:

- Case vignettes: We open each chapter with a brief case vignette to illustrate how some of that chapter's key themes have been applied in a real company, chosen with the book's global focus clearly in mind.
- Strategic issues: We note in the margins key concepts or questions that are addressed more thoroughly in the adjacent text, to ensure that time-pressed readers don't overlook critical information or crucial questions they should ask.
- Global and Internet icons: We place icons in the margins to call the reader's attention to global examples as well as examples of how marketing strategy concepts are playing out in the Internet arena.
- Marketing plan exercises: Because many of our readers will be asked to prepare a marketing plan, whether on the job or as a class project, we highlight at the end of each chapter how that chapter's material might be effectively put to use in developing a marketing plan.
- Online learning center at **www.mhhe.com/walker8e:** We have placed a variety of supplemental materials for students and instructors on the book's website. To help students "crack tomorrow's case" or "pass the exam," the student resources include chapter quizzes and review material. Instructor resources include an instructor's manual, PowerPoint slides, and a test bank. In addition, we provide a list of recommended readings and cases to enable instructors to choose the most current and compelling materials in designing or updating a case-based or project-based course that's focused on marketing strategy or related issues

THANKS!

Simply put, this book is not solely our work—far from it. Many of our students, colleagues, and those we work with in industry have made contributions that have significantly shaped our perspectives on marketing decision making. We are grateful to all of them. We wish to give special thanks to Rebecca Quinn and Elizabeth Philp, both recent graduates of of London Business School. Rebecca's experience at social networking up-and-comer Wildfire has been hugely helpful in the extensive updating of Chapter 11. Without Elizabeth's research skills, the examples in this book and the references to current academic research would be fewer in number and far less compelling.

We would also like to thank the following reviewers for their outstanding comments: Chris Moberg, Ohio University; Robert M. Morgan, University of Alabama; Michael A. Petrochuk, Walsh University; and Karl S. Rutter, Columbia University.

We also thank a small army of talented people at McGraw-Hill/Irwin for their work that has turned our rough manuscript into an attractive and readable book. In particular, our editors, Laura Spell, Mary Jane Lampe, and Lori Bradshaw have been instrumental in giving birth to this edition. Without them, we'd probably still be writing!

Finally, we thank our parents, without whom, of course, neither of us would be here. To all of you we extend our love, our respect, and our gratitude for passing on to us your curiosity and your passion for learning. We therefore dedicate this book to Jeannette and Orville Walker, Sr., and to Alice and Jack Mullins.

Orville C. Walker, Jr.

John W. Mullins

Madison, Wisconsin, and London

Summer 2012

Introduction to Strategy

Chapter One

Market-Oriented Perspectives Underlie Successful Corporate, Business, and Marketing Strategies

Samsung—Changing Strategies to Build a Global Brand[1]

Samsung Electronics is the largest component of South Korea's largest *chaebol*—one of the giant family-controlled conglomerates that have been instrumental in building the country's economy over the last half century. Samsung's electronics unit started out in 1970 making cheap TV sets for the Sanyo label. Over time it morphed into a technically innovative company that was one of the pioneers in developing flat-screen displays, plasma TVs, multi-function cell phones, and other digital devices. But until the mid-1990s, the unit competed primarily by (a) producing technical components or low-cost manufactured products for firms with better-known brands, such as Dell, Hewlett-Packard, and General Electric and (b) selling me-too consumer products—such as TVs and microwave ovens—under the Samsung brand through discount chains such as Wal-Mart at very low prices.

Samsung's cost-driven competitive strategy worked well until 1996, but then several shocks in its market and competitive environments forced a major reevaluation. First, the global market for memory chips and other components Samsung supplied for other electronics brands softened due to increased competition and excess capacity. At about the same time, sales of Samsung's own branded products were also declining. As Yun Jong-yong—a company veteran who was brought in as CEO of the electronics unit—complained, Samsung could build a TV that was technically as good as a Sony, but because of the down-market image of the Samsung brand, its TVs sat at the back of the store or piled up in discount chains. Finally, the Asian financial crisis of 1997 made a major strategic shift essential for the unit's survival.

New Competitive and Marketing Strategies

Mr. Yun initiated an ambitious new competitive strategy aimed at developing and marketing technically superior products while building an image of Samsung as a stylish, high-quality brand commanding a premium price. The objective was to establish a unique competitive position using technical innovation and design to appeal to younger and relatively upscale customers around the world. "If we were to continue competing only on price," Mr. Yun argued, "the Chinese would slaughter us."

Technical Innovation and R&D

In order to implement its new competitive strategy, Samsung had to become a pioneer in developing new digital technologies. While Sony and other

3

rivals had a substantial lead in consumer electronics, that lead was rooted in the analog world. The digital world required new technical innovations. Consequently, the firm shifted substantial resources into R&D focused on technologies such as large-area LCDs, display drivers and chip sets, and mobile telephony. In the 2010 fiscal year it spent 9.1 trillion won ($7.9 billion)—about 6 percent of the unit's total revenue—on R&D. One quarter of the company's workforce—some 44,000 people—are engaged in R&D activities in more than 40 research centers around the world.

New Product Development and Design

But cutting-edge technology does not guarantee market success. It must be incorporated into products that deliver benefits that at least some segment of consumers will consider to be worth the price. Some of those benefits may be subjective—attractive styling, or a cool image. Therefore, new product development at Samsung usually involves a team of designers who collaborate closely with the firm's engineers, manufacturing people, and marketers. To ensure they stay in touch with consumer tastes in different countries, the firm's 450 designers are assigned to design centers in cities such as London, Tokyo, Shanghai, and San Francisco, and the company's market researchers run focus groups and user surveys in many markets around the world.

Marketing Programs to Build the Samsung Brand

Revamping Samsung's marketing efforts was also critical to the success of its new competitive strategy because even the most technically sophisticated and well-designed products are likely to fail unless potential customers know they exist, can acquire them easily, and think they are worth the money. Therefore, Eric Kim was recruited from outside the firm to head a global marketing effort for Samsung Electronics. One of his first moves was to reorganize the firm's distribution channels. Consistent with the strategic objective of establishing Samsung as a high-quality brand worthy of a premium price, many of the company's products were pulled out of low-priced discount chains and distributed through service-oriented electronics specialty stores and web retailers—such as Best Buy and Amazon.com—instead.

To ensure consistency in Samsung's marketing communications across world markets, Mr. Kim consolidated the firm's roster of advertising agencies from 55 down to a single global advertising group—British-based WPP. He then launched the firm's first brand-building campaign with fashion-forward TV commercials showing off the company's cool sense of style as well as the technical sophistication of its products.

The firm also makes extensive use of more contemporary promotional tools such as product placements, sponsorships, and internet advertising to strengthen its brand. For instance, Samsung provides both financial and technical support for a variety of sporting and cultural events in every major region of the world. It is a sponsor of the Olympics, Asian Games, and other international events, but it also supports regional and local events—such as the Montreal Jazz Festival and the Chelsea Football Club in the United Kingdom—as a means of staying close to local customers.

The Results

Samsung Electronics' revamped competitive strategy and the marketing programs designed to implement it have been a smashing success. According to studies by Interbrand (a brand consultancy), the global value of Samsung's brand increased by more than 200 percent over the first decade of the twenty-first century, overtaking Sony as the most valuable consumer electronics brand. And in spite of the fact that Apple's iPhone and iPad gate-crashed Samsung's position as the "cool designer" in the smartphone market, the brand's value increased another 20 percent in 2011. As a result, the unit's global revenues reached 165 trillion won (about $143 billion) in the 2011 fiscal year, and after-tax profits were 13.7 trillion won.

STRATEGIC CHALLENGES ADDRESSED IN CHAPTER 1

Samsung's experiences in the consumer electronics industry illustrate some important points about the nature of business strategy and the interrelationships among different levels of strategy in an organization, points that will recur as major themes throughout this book. They also demonstrate the importance of timely and accurate insights into customer desires, environmental trends, and competitors' actions in formulating successful strategies at every level.

Most firms, particularly larger corporations with multiple divisions or business units such as Samsung, pursue a hierarchy of interdependent strategies. Each strategy is formulated at different levels in the organization and deals with different sets of issues. For example, Samsung's decision to increase the resources devoted to R&D in order to become a pioneer in digital technology reflected the *chaebol*'s overarching **corporate strategy** which stressed engineering excellence and the organization's competencies in related product areas, such as semiconductors. This level of strategy provides direction concerning the organization's overall mission, the kinds of businesses it should be in, and its growth policies.

On the other hand, attempts to establish a unique competitive position for its products by using technical innovation and cool design to appeal to younger and relatively upscale customer segments around the world reflect Samsung Electronics' **business-level strategy.** This level of strategy primarily addresses how a business will compete in its industry in order to attain a sustainable advantage over its rivals.

Finally, interrelated functional decisions about how to divide the market into segments, which segments to target, what products to offer each target segment, what channels to use to distribute those products, what promotional tools and appeals to employ, and what prices to charge all reflect the **marketing strategies** for each of Samsung Electronics' various product-market entries.

Because a major part of the marketing manager's job is to monitor and analyze the needs and desires of potential customers, emerging challenges posed by competitors, and opportunities and threats related to trends in the external environment, they often play a crucial role in influencing strategies formulated at higher levels in the firm. While the need for a new competitive strategy at Samsung became obvious because of stagnating sales and declining profits, decisions about the content of those new strategies were influenced by information and analyses supplied by the firm's marketing and sales personnel.

Some firms systematically incorporate such market and competitive analyses into their planning processes. They also coordinate their activities around the primary goal of satisfying unmet customer needs. Such firms are *market-oriented* and follow a business philosophy commonly called the *marketing concept.* Market-oriented firms have been shown to be among the more profitable and successful at maintaining strong competitive positions in their industries over time. As we shall see later in this chapter, however, companies do not always embrace a market orientation—nor rely as heavily on inputs from their marketing and sales personnel—in developing their strategies. Some firms' strategies are driven more by technology, production, or cost concerns.

Strategic Issue

Each level of strategy must be consistent with—and therefore influenced and constrained by—higher levels within the hierarchy.

Regardless of their participation or influence in formulating corporate and business-level strategies, marketing managers' freedom of action is ultimately constrained by those higher-level strategies. The objectives, strategies, and action plans for a specific product-market are but one part of a hierarchy of strategies within the firm. Each level of strategy must be consistent with—and therefore influenced and constrained by—higher levels within the hierarchy. For example, not only the cool new digital products developed by Samsung, but also the retail outlets used to distribute them, their advertising appeals, promotional media, prices, and other aspects of their marketing programs were shaped by the unit's competitive strategy of establishing Samsung as a stylish, high-quality brand commanding a premium price.

These interrelationships among the various levels of strategy raise several questions of importance to marketing managers as well as managers in other functional areas and top executives. What do strategies consist of, and do they have similar or different components at the corporate, business, and functional levels? While marketing managers clearly bear the primary responsibility for developing strategic marketing plans for individual product offerings, what role do they play in formulating strategies at the corporate and divisional or business unit level? Why do some organizations pay much more attention to customers and competitors when formulating their strategies (i.e., why are some firms more market-oriented) than others, and does it make any difference in their performance? What specific decisions and analytical processes underlie the formulation and implementation of effective marketing strategies? These are the questions tackled in this chapter.

While our primary focus in this book is on the various analyses and program decisions that underlie the development of a sound marketing strategy for a good or service, that strategy and its various elements need to be periodically summarized and communicated to other people and functional departments in the organization. The marketing plan is an important tool for such communication. It spells out the objectives to be accomplished, the actions necessary to achieve those objectives, and the timing and locus of responsibility for each action. Consequently, the last section of this chapter briefly outlines the components and organizational framework of a formal marketing plan. Each of the plan's components will be examined in more detail in one or more future chapters, and each of those chapters will conclude with a detailed marketing planning exercise.

THREE LEVELS OF STRATEGY: SIMILAR COMPONENTS BUT DIFFERENT ISSUES

What Is a Strategy?

Although *strategy* first became a popular business buzzword during the 1960s, it continues to be the subject of widely differing definitions and interpretations. The following definition, however, captures the essence of the term:

> A **strategy** is a fundamental pattern of present and planned objectives, resource deployments, and interactions of an organization with markets, competitors, and other environmental factors.[2]

Our definition suggests that a strategy should specify (1) *what* (objectives to be accomplished), (2) *where* (on which industries and product-markets to focus), and (3) *how* (which resources and activities to allocate to each product-market to meet environmental opportunities and threats and to gain a competitive advantage).

The Components of Strategy

A well-developed strategy contains five components, or sets of issues:

1. *Scope.* The scope of an organization refers to the breadth of its strategic domain—the number and types of industries, product lines, and market segments it competes in or plans to enter. Decisions about an organization's strategic scope should reflect management's view of the firm's purpose or *mission*. This common thread among its various activities and product-markets defines the essential nature of what its business is and what it should be.

2. *Goals and objectives.* Strategies also should detail desired levels of accomplishment on one or more dimensions of performance—such as volume growth, profit contribution, or return on investment—over specified time periods for each of those businesses and product-markets and for the organization as a whole.

3. *Resource deployments.* Every organization has limited financial and human resources. Formulating a strategy also involves deciding how those resources are to be obtained and allocated across businesses, product-markets, and functional departments and activities within each business or product-market.

4. *Identification of a sustainable competitive advantage.* One important part of any strategy is a specification of *how the organization will compete* in each business and product-market within its domain. How can it position itself to develop and sustain a differential

advantage over current and potential competitors? To answer such questions, managers must examine the market opportunities in each business and product-market and the company's distinctive competencies or strengths relative to its competitors.

5. *Synergy.* Synergy exists when the firm's businesses, product-markets, resource deployments, and competencies complement and reinforce one another. Synergy enables the total performance of the related businesses to be greater than it would otherwise be: The whole becomes greater than the sum of its parts.

The Hierarchy of Strategies

Explicitly or implicitly, these five basic dimensions are part of all strategies. However, rather than a single comprehensive strategy, most organizations have a hierarchy of interrelated strategies, each formulated at a different level of the firm. The three major levels of strategy in most large, multiproduct organizations are (1) **corporate strategy,** (2) **business-level strategy,** and (3) **functional strategies** focused on a particular product-market entry. These three levels of strategy are diagrammed in Exhibit 1.1. In small

EXHIBIT 1.1 The Hierarchy of Strategies

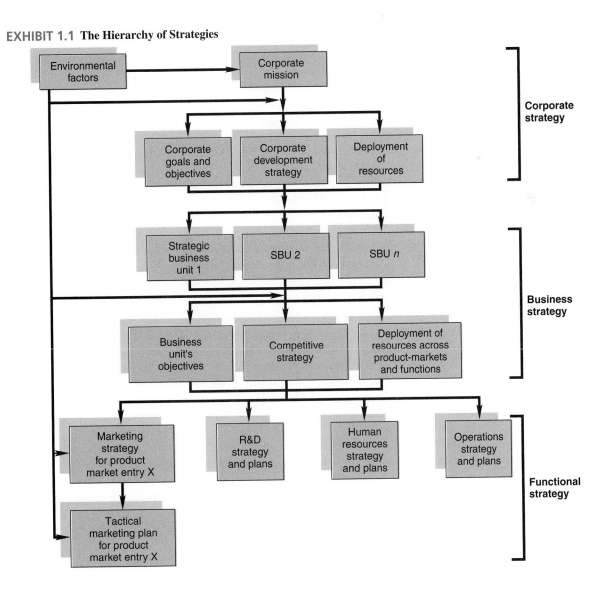

single-product-line companies or entrepreneurial start-ups, however, corporate and business-level strategic issues merge.

Our primary focus is on the development of marketing strategies and programs for individual product-market entries, but other functional departments—such as R&D and operations—also have strategies and plans for each of the firm's product-markets. Throughout this book, therefore, we examine the interfunctional implications of product-market strategies, conflicts across functional areas, and the mechanisms that firms use to resolve those conflicts.

Strategies at all three levels contain the five components mentioned earlier, but because each strategy serves a different purpose within the organization, each emphasizes a different set of issues. Exhibit 1.2 summarizes the specific focus and issues dealt with at each level of strategy; we discuss them in the next sections.

Corporate Strategy

At the corporate level, managers must coordinate the activities of multiple business units and, in the case of conglomerates, even separate legal business entities. Decisions about the organization's scope and resource deployments across its divisions or businesses are the primary focus of corporate strategy. The essential questions at this level include: What business(es) are we in? What business(es) should we be in? and What portion of our total resources should we devote to each of these businesses to achieve the organization's overall goals and objectives? Thus, when top-level managers at IBM decided to pursue future growth primarily through the development of consulting services and software rather than computer hardware a few years ago, they shifted substantial corporate resources—including R&D expenditures, marketing and advertising budgets, and vast numbers of customer service personnel—into the corporation's service and software businesses to support the new strategic direction.

Attempts to develop and maintain distinctive competencies at the corporate level focus on generating superior human, financial, and technological resources; designing effective organizational structures and processes; and seeking synergy among the firm's various businesses. Synergy can provide a major competitive advantage for firms where related businesses share R&D investments, product or production technologies, distribution channels, a common salesforce, and/or promotional themes.[3]

Business-Level Strategy

How a business unit competes within its industry is the critical focus of business-level strategy. A major issue in a business strategy is that of sustainable competitive advantage. What distinctive competencies can give the business unit a competitive advantage? Which of those competencies best match the needs and wants of the customers in the business's target segment(s)? For example, a business with low-cost sources of supply and efficient, modern plants might adopt a low-cost competitive strategy. One with a strong marketing department and a competent salesforce may compete by offering superior customer service.[4]

Another important issue a business-level strategy must address is appropriate scope: how many and which market segments to compete in and the overall breadth of product offerings and marketing programs to appeal to these segments. Finally, synergy should be sought across product-markets and across functional departments within the business.

EXHIBIT 1.2   Key Components of Corporate, Business, and Marketing Strategies

Strategy Components	Corporate Strategy	Business Strategy	Marketing Strategy
Scope	• Corporate domain—"Which businesses should we be in?"	• Business domain—"Which product-markets should we be in within this business or industry?"	• Target market definition • Product-line depth and breadth • Branding policies

	• Corporate development strategy
	    Conglomerate diversification (expansion into unrelated businesses)
	    Vertical integration
	    Acquisition and divestiture policies
		• Business development strategy
		    Concentric diversification (new products for existing customers or new customers for existing products)
			• Product-market development plan
			• Line extension and product elimination plans

Goals and objectives	• Overall corporate objectives aggregated across businesses
	    Revenue growth
	    Profitability
	    ROI (return on investment)
	    Earnings per share
	    Contributions to other stakeholders
		• Constrained by corporate goals
		• Objectives aggregated across product-market entries in the business unit
		    Sales growth
		    New product or market growth
		    Profitability
		    ROI
		    Cash flow
		    Strengthening bases of competitive advantage
			• Constrained by corporate and business goals
			• Objectives for a specific product-market entry
			    Sales
			    Market share
			    Contribution margin
			    Customer satisfaction

Allocation of resources	• Allocation among businesses in the corporate portfolio • Allocation across functions shared by multiple businesses (corporate R&D, MIS)	• Allocation among product-market entries in the business unit • Allocation across functional departments within the business unit	• Allocation across components of the marketing plan (elements of the marketing mix) for a specific product-market entry
Sources of competitive advantage	• Primarily through superior corporate financial or human resources; more corporate R&D; better organizational processes or synergies relative to competitors across all industries in which the firm operates	• Primarily through competitive strategy; business unit's competencies relative to competitors in its industry	• Primarily through effective product positioning; superiority on one or more components of the marketing mix relative to competitors within a specific product-market
Sources of synergy	• Shared resources, technologies, or functional competencies across businesses within the firm	• Shared resources (including favorable customer image) or functional competencies across product-markets within an industry	• Shared marketing resources, competencies, or activities across product-market entries

Marketing Strategy

The primary focus of marketing strategy is to effectively allocate and coordinate marketing resources and activities to accomplish the firm's objectives within a specific product-market. Therefore, the critical issue concerning the scope of a marketing strategy is specifying the target market(s) for a particular product or product line. Next, firms seek competitive advantage and synergy through a well-integrated program of marketing mix elements (primarily the 4 Ps of product, price, place, and promotion) tailored to the needs and wants of potential customers in that target market.

WHAT IS MARKETING'S ROLE IN FORMULATING AND IMPLEMENTING STRATEGIES?

The essence of strategic planning at all levels is identifying threats to avoid and opportunities to pursue. The primary strategic responsibility of any manager is to look outward continuously to keep the firm or business in step with changes in the environment. Because they occupy positions at the boundary between the firm and its customers, distributors, and competitors, marketing managers are usually most familiar with conditions and trends in the market environment. Consequently, they not only are responsible for developing strategic plans for their own product-market entries, but also are often primary participants and contributors to the planning process at the business and corporate levels as well.

The wide-ranging influence of marketing managers on higher-level strategic decisions is clearly shown in a survey of managers in 280 U.S. and 234 German business units of firms in the electrical equipment, mechanical machinery, and consumer package goods industries.[5] The study examined perceptions of marketing managers' influence relative to managers from sales, R&D, operations, and finance on a variety of strategic and tactical decisions within their businesses. Exhibit 1.3 summarizes the results.

EXHIBIT 1.3 **Influence of Functional Units over Various Business Decisions**

Decisions	Marketing	Sales	R&D	Operations	Finance
Business strategy decisions					
Strategic direction of the business	38	29**	11**	9**	14**
Expansion into new geographic markets	39	45**	3**	3**	10**
Choices of strategic partners	33	38*	7**	9**	12**
New product development	32	23**	29**	9**	7**
Major capital expenditures	13	11**	13	29**	35**
Marketing strategy decisions					
Advertising messages	65	29**	3**	1**	2**
Customer satisfaction measurement	48	35**	5**	8**	4**
Customer satisfaction improvement	40	37*	7**	10**	6**
Distribution strategy	34	52**	1**	6**	6**
Customer service and support	31	47**	5**	10**	7**
Pricing	30	41**	4**	9**	16**

The number in each cell is the mean of the amount of points given by responding managers to each function, using a constant-sum scale of 100. A *t*-test was performed to compare column 2 (mean of relative influence of marketing) with columns 3 through 6 (relative influence of sales, R&D, operations, and finance). Statistically significant differences with marketing are indicated by asterisks, where: * $p < .05$; ** $p < .01$.

Source: Reprinted with permission from *Journal of Marketing,* published by the American Marketing Association, Christian Homburg, John P. Workman Jr., and Harley Krohmer, "Marketing's Influence within the Firm," *Journal of Marketing* 63 (April 1999), p. 9.

The study found that, on average, marketing and sales executives exerted significantly more influence than managers from other functions on strategic decisions concerning traditional marketing activities, such as advertising messages, pricing, distribution, customer service and support, and measurement and improvement of customer satisfaction. Interestingly, though, the influence of sales executives was perceived to be even greater than that of marketing managers on some of these decisions. One reason—particularly in the industrial goods firms selling electronic equipment and machinery—may be that sales managers have more detailed information about customer needs and desires because they have direct and continuing contact with existing and potential buyers.

More surprisingly, marketing managers also were perceived to wield significantly more influence than managers from other functional areas on cross-functional, business-level strategic decisions. While the views of finance and operations executives carry more weight in approving major capital expenditures, marketing and sales managers exert more influence on decisions concerning the strategic direction of the business unit, expansion into new geographic markets, the selection of strategic business partners, and new product development.

Might the relative influence of the different functions become more similar as firms adopt more integrative organizational forms, such as cross-functional work teams? The study's results suggest not. Marketing's influence was not significantly reduced in companies that had instituted cross-functional structures and processes.

Variations in Marketing's Strategic Influence

Although marketing managers often have substantial influence on strategy formation at the corporate and business unit levels, the strength of that influence varies across organizations. For one thing, marketing managers may not play as pervasive a strategic role in other cultures as they do in the United States. For example, the study detailed in Exhibit 1.3 found that marketers' influence on both tactical and strategic issues was significantly lower in German firms. As one of the study's authors points out, "Germany has traditionally stressed technology and operations more than the softer, customer-oriented aspects central to marketing."[6]

Other variables appear to impact marketing's influence regardless of national culture. For instance, marketing managers tend to have greater strategic influence in firms that spend relatively heavily on R&D and that seek a competitive advantage based extensively on innovative product and service offerings. Similarly, marketing is more influencial in firms that have strong "customer-connecting" capabilities, especially when marketing has responsibility for the sales force.[7]

Market-Oriented Management

Another reason marketing managers do not play an equally extensive strategic role in every firm is because not all firms are equally market-oriented. Not surprisingly, marketers tend to have a greater influence on all levels of strategy in organizations that embrace a market-oriented philosophy of business.[8] More critically, managers in other functional areas of market-oriented firms incorporate more customer and competitor information into their decision-making processes as well.

Market-oriented organizations tend to operate according to the business philosophy known as the *marketing concept*. As originally stated by General Electric six decades ago, the **marketing concept** holds that the planning and coordination of all company activities around the primary goal of satisfying customer needs is the most effective means to attain and sustain a competitive advantage and achieve company objectives over time.

Thus, market-oriented firms are characterized by a consistent focus by personnel in all departments and at all levels on customers' needs and competitive circumstances in the market environment. They also are willing and able to quickly adapt products and

EXHIBIT 1.4 **Guidelines for Market-Oriented Management**

1. Create customer focus throughout the business.	9. Measure and manage customer expectations.
2. Listen to the customer.	10. Build customer relationships and loyalty.
3. Define and nurture your distinctive competence.	11. Define the business as a service business.
4. Define marketing as market intelligence.	12. Commit to continuous improvement and innovation.
5. Target customers precisely.	13. Manage culture along with strategy and structure.
6. Manage for profitability, not sales volume.	14. Grow with partners and alliances.
7. Make customer value the guiding star.	15. Destroy marketing bureaucracy.
8. Let the customer define quality.	

Source: Reprinted with permission from *Marketing Management,* published by the American Marketing Association, Frederick E. Webster Jr., "Executing the New Marketing Concept," *Marketing Management* 3, 1 (1994), p. 10.

functional programs to fit changes in that environment. Such firms pay a great deal of attention to customer research *before* products are designed and produced. They embrace the concept of market segmentation by adapting product offerings and marketing programs to the special needs of different target markets.

Market-oriented firms also adopt a variety of organizational procedures and structures to improve the responsiveness of their decision-making, including using more detailed environmental scanning and continuous, real-time information systems; seeking frequent feedback from and coordinating plans with key customers and major suppliers; decentralizing strategic decisions; encouraging entrepreneurial thinking among lower-level managers; and using interfunctional management teams to analyze issues and initiate strategic actions outside the formal planning process.[9] For instance, Samsung uses cross-functional teams of engineers, designers, marketers, market researchers, and process engineers to manage new product development projects and to adapt existing products to varying customer preferences in different markets around the world. These and other actions recommended to make an organization more market-driven and responsive to environmental changes are summarized in Exhibit 1.4.

Do Customers Always Know What They Want?

Some managers—particularly in high-tech firms—question whether a strong focus on customer needs and wants is always a good thing. They argue that customers cannot always articulate their needs and wants, in part because they do not know what kinds of products or services are technically possible. As Akio Morita, the late visionary CEO of Sony, once said:

> Our plan is to lead the public with new products rather than ask them what kind of products they want. The public does not know what is possible, but we do. So instead of doing a lot of marketing research, we refine our thinking on a product and its use and try to create a market for it by educating and communicating with the public.[10]

Others have pointed out that some very successful new products, such as the Chrysler minivan and Compaq's pioneering PC network server, were developed with little or no market research. On the other hand, some famous duds, such as Ford's Edsel, New Coke, and McDonald's McLean low-fat hamburger, were developed with a great deal of customer input.[11]

The laws of probability dictate that some new products will succeed and more will fail regardless of how much is spent on marketing research. But the critics of a strong customer focus argue that paying too much attention to customer needs and wants can stifle innovation and lead firms to produce nothing but marginal improvements or line extensions of products and services that already exist. How do marketers respond to this charge?

Although many consumers may lack the technical sophistication necessary to articulate their needs or wants for cutting-edge technical innovations, the same is not true for industrial purchasers. About half of all manufactured goods in most countries are sold to other organizations rather than individual consumers. Many high-tech industrial products are initiated at the urging of one or more major customers, developed with their cooperation (perhaps in the form of an alliance or partnership), and refined at customer beta sites.

As for consumer markets, one way to resolve the conflict between the views of technologists and marketers is to consider the two components of R&D. First there is basic research, and then there is development—the conversion of technical concepts into actual salable products or services. Most consumers have little knowledge of scientific advancements and emerging technologies. Therefore, they usually don't—and probably shouldn't—play a role in influencing how firms allocate their basic research dollars.

However, a customer focus is critical to development. Someone within the organization must have either the insight and market experience or the substantial customer input necessary to decide what product to develop from a new technology, what benefits it will offer to customers, and whether customers will value those benefits sufficiently to make the product a commercial success. The importance of a customer focus often becomes clear when a firm attempts to develop a variety of successful new product offerings from a single well-established technology, as illustrated by the travails of LEGO, the Swedish toy company, described in Exhibit 1.5.

EXHIBIT 1.5 *How LEGO Revived Its Brand*

Not many toy companies in the world have as much brand recognition as LEGO. Three generations of kids around the world have built cars, fire trucks, even entire cities, with the Swedish company's plastic bricks. But despite its widely known and respected brand, the firm's profits declined dramatically in the early to mid-2000s.

One reason for the decline was a loss of strategic focus. LEGO launched a kid's TV series, a set of action figures drawn from that series, and other products in highly competitive categories that were largely unrelated to the firm's popular bricks and where the firm had no experience or special expertise.

More critically, LEGO began foundering within its core product line as well. Top management had given free reign to the firm's designers to develop more imaginative creations for kids to build with LEGO bricks. The designers happily embraced their new freedom and developed many increasingly complex and artistic designs. Unfortunately, those complex designs incorporated thousands of new components, many of which were not interchangeable with those of other products in the line. As a result, parts inventories exploded and supply costs went through the roof. To make matters worse, many of the new designs did not appeal to the kids who are the

firm's ultimate consumers, and sales of the company's core products went downhill.

Paradoxically, the solution to LEGO's product design and profitability problems involved *reducing* the creative freedom of the firm's designers. Top executives decreed that new product development projects should be managed by *teams* involving marketing managers familiar with tastes, preferences, and purchase behaviors in different countries, manufacturing managers who could help control production and supply costs, market researchers who could test kids' reactions to various product prototypes, as well as designers.

While innovative product design is LEGO's primary competitive strength, the company has found that designers function most successfully when placed under some constraints, namely that the products being designed appeal to the customers who will use them. As Mads Nipper, LEGO's vice president of products and markets points out, "Children are . . . very demanding about what they want to buy. If your offer does not stack up, they will go somewhere else."

Source: Jay Greene, "How LEGO Revised Its Brand," www .businessweek/design.com, July 23, 2010. See also, Jay Greene, *Design Is How It Works* (New York: Portfolio/Penguin Group, 2010).

In the case of an innovative new technology, it often must be developed into a concrete product concept before consumers can react to it and its commercial potential can be assessed. In other cases, consumers can express their needs or wants for specific benefits even though they do not know what is technically feasible. They can tell you what problems they are having with current products and services and what additional benefits they would like from new ones. For instance, before Apple introduced the iPod, few consumers would have asked for such a product because they were unfamiliar with the possibilities of digitization and miniaturization in the electronics industry. But if a market researcher had asked whether they would buy a product smaller than a Sony Walkman that could store and play thousands of songs they could download from their computer without messing with cassette tapes or CDs, many probably would have said, "Certainly!"

A strong customer focus is not inconsistent with the development of technically innovative products, nor does it condemn a firm to concentrate on satisfying only current, articulated customer wants. More important, although firms can sometimes succeed in the short run even though they ignore customer desires, a strong customer focus usually pays big dividends in terms of market share and profit over the long haul. As one CEO pointed out, "I don't know how else you can sell in a consumer marketplace without understanding product design and usage. You have to know what the end user wants."[12]

Does Being Market-Oriented Pay?

Since an organization's success over time hinges on its ability to provide benefits of value to its customers—and to do that better than its competitors—it seems likely that market-oriented firms should perform better than others. By paying careful attention to customer needs and competitive threats—and by focusing activities across all functional departments on meeting those needs and threats effectively—organizations should be able to enhance, accelerate, and reduce the volatility and vulnerability of their cash flows.[13] And that should enhance their economic performance and shareholder value. Indeed, profitability is the third leg, together with a customer focus and cross-functional coordination, of the three-legged stool known as the marketing concept.

Sometimes the marketing concept is interpreted as a philosophy of trying to satisfy all customers' needs regardless of the cost. That would be a prescription for financial disaster. Instead, the marketing concept is consistent with the notion of focusing on only those segments of the customer population that the firm can satisfy both effectively *and* profitably. Firms might offer less extensive or costly goods and services to unprofitable segments or avoid them. For example, in recent years Samsung Electronics has resumed distributing some of its products through discount chains such as Walmart and Carrefour, but such low-price channels are largely reserved for the firm's older, no-frills models rather than its more stylish, cutting-edge new releases.

Substantial evidence supports the idea that being market-oriented pays dividends, at least in a developed economy such as the United States. A number of studies involving more than 500 firms or business units across a variety of industries indicate that a market orientation has a significant positive effect on various dimensions of performance, including return on assets, sales growth, new product success, customer equity, and market capitalization.[14] Even entrepreneurial start-ups appear to benefit from a strong customer orientation. One study of start-ups in Japan and the United States found that new firms that focused on marketing first, rather than lowering costs or advancing technology, were less likely to be brought down by competitors as their product-markets developed.[15]

Strategic Issue

A market orientation has a significant positive effect on various dimensions of performance, including return on assets, sales growth, and new product success.

Factors That Mediate a Firm's Market Orientation

Despite the evidence that a market orientation boosts performance, many companies around the world are not very focused on their customers or competitors. Among the reasons firms are not always in close touch with their market environments are these:

- Competitive conditions may enable a company to be successful in the short run without being particularly sensitive to customer desires.
- Different levels of economic development across industries or countries may favor different business philosophies.
- Firms can suffer from strategic inertia—the automatic continuation of strategies successful in the past, even though current market conditions are changing.

Competitive Factors Affecting a Firm's Market Orientation

The competitive conditions some firms face enable them to be successful in the short term without paying much attention to their customers, suppliers, distributors, or other organizations in their market environment. Early entrants into newly emerging industries, particularly industries based on new technologies, are especially likely to be internally focused and not very market-oriented. This is because there are likely to be relatively few strong competitors during the formative years of a new industry, customer demand for the new product is likely to grow rapidly and outstrip available supply, and production problems and resource constraints tend to represent more immediate threats to the survival of such new businesses.

Businesses facing such market and competitive conditions are often **product-oriented** or **production-oriented.** They focus most of their attention and resources on such functions as product and process engineering, production, and finance in order to acquire and manage the resources necessary to keep pace with growing demand. The business is primarily concerned with producing more of what it wants to make, and marketing generally plays a secondary role in formulating and implementing strategy. Other functional differences between production-oriented and market-oriented firms are summarized in Exhibit 1.6.

EXHIBIT 1.6   Differences between Production-Oriented and Market-Oriented Organizations

Business Activity or Function	Production Orientation	Marketing Orientation
Product offering	Company sells what it can make; primary focus on functional performance and cost.	Company makes what it can sell; primary focus on customers' needs and market opportunities.
Product line	Narrow.	Broad.
Pricing	Based on production and distribution costs.	Based on perceived benefits provided.
Research	Technical research; focus on product improvement and cost cutting in the production process.	Market research; focus on identifying new opportunities and applying new technology to satisfy customer needs.
Packaging	Protection for the product; minimize costs.	Designed for customer convenience; a promotional tool.
Credit	A necessary evil; minimize bad debt losses.	A customer service; a tool to attract customers.
Promotion	Emphasis on product features, quality, and price.	Emphasis on product benefits and ability to satisfy customers' needs or solve problems.

As industries grow, they become more competitive. New entrants are attracted and existing producers attempt to differentiate themselves through improved products and more efficient production processes. As a result, industry capacity often grows faster than demand, and the environment shifts from a seller's market to a buyer's market. Firms often respond to such changes with aggressive promotional activities—such as hiring more salespeople, increasing advertising budgets, or offering frequent price promotions—to maintain market share and hold down unit costs.

Unfortunately, this kind of **sales-oriented** response to increasing competition still focuses on selling what the firm wants to make rather than on customer needs. Worse, competitors can easily match such aggressive sales tactics. Simply spending more on selling efforts usually does not create a sustainable competitive advantage.

As industries mature, sales volume levels off, and technological differences among brands tend to disappear as manufacturers copy the best features of each other's products. Consequently, a firm must seek new market segments or steal share from competitors by offering lower prices, superior services, or intangible benefits other firms cannot match. At this stage, managers can most readily appreciate the benefits of a market orientation, and marketers are often given a bigger role in developing competitive strategies.[16] It is not surprising, then, that many of America's most market-oriented firms—and those working hardest to become market-oriented—are well-established competitors in relatively mature industries. Of course, a given industry's characteristics may make some components of a market orientation more critical for good performance than others. For example, in an industry dominated by large, dynamic competitors—as in the global automobile industry (e.g., Toyota, BMW, Ford, etc.)—being responsive to competitor actions may be even more important than a strong customer focus.[17] But the bottom line is that an orientation toward the *market*—competitors, customers, and potential customers—is usually crucial for continued success in global markets.

The Influence of Different Stages of Development across Industries and Global Markets

The previous discussion suggests that the degree of adoption of a market orientation varies not only across firms, but also across entire industries. Industries that are in earlier stages of their life cycles or that benefit from barriers to entry or other factors reducing the intensity of competition are likely to have relatively fewer market-oriented firms. For instance, in part because of governmental regulations that restricted competition, many service industries—including banks, airlines, physicians, lawyers, accountants, and insurance companies—were slow to adopt the marketing concept. But with the trend toward deregulation and the increasingly intense global competition in such industries, many service organizations are working much harder to understand and satisfy their customers.

Given that entire economies are in different stages of development around the world, the popularity—and even the appropriateness—of different business philosophies also may vary across countries. A production orientation was the dominant business philosophy in the United States, for instance, during the industrialization that occurred from the mid-1800s through World War I.[18] Similarly, a primary focus on developing product and production technology may still be appropriate in developing nations that are in the midst of industrialization.

International differences in business philosophies can cause some problems for the globalization of a firm's strategic marketing programs, but it can create some opportunities as well, especially for alliances or joint ventures. Consider, for example, The partnership between French automaker Renault-Nissan and the Russian car manufacturer AvtoVAZ discussed in Exhibit 1.7.

EXHIBIT 1.7   *Renault's Partnership with Russian Automaker AvtoVAZ Benefits Both Parties*

The AvtoVAZ car factory in the central Russian city of Togliatti is a decrepit, mile-long building where the company's Lada sedans are turned out by 40-year-old equipment. Nevertheless, the French carmaker Renault-Nissan recently paid $1 billion for a 25 percent stake in AvtoVAZ. Even after investing more millions to modernize the plant, Renault figures that Russia's low labor and energy costs will make the plant ideal for producing the Logan lineup of cars that the firm introduced in 2004. The no-frills Logan, starting at about $9,000, has become the world's most successful cheap car. Its partnership with AvtoVAZ should also help Renault appeal to Russian car buyers and capture a larger share of that country's growing market.

But AvtoVAZ will also benefit from the partnership, especially on the production side. The key reason the firm agreed to the deal with Renault was "the modern technology and know-how the company will provide us," according to Chairman Sergei Chemezov. The partnership may also encourage global auto parts suppliers to build new, more efficient plants near the AvtoVAZ factory.

Source: Based on material in Carol Matlack, "Renault's Ghosen Takes on a Russian Relic," www.businessweek.com, February 29, 2008, and Carol Matlack, "Carlos Ghosen's Russian Gambit," *BusinessWeek*, March 17, 2008, pp. 57–58. For more information about Renault's acquisitions and alliances, see the company website at www.renault.com.

Strategic Inertia

In some cases, a firm that achieved success by being in tune with its environment loses touch with its market because managers become reluctant to tamper with strategies and marketing programs that worked in the past. They begin to believe there is one best way to satisfy their customers. Such strategic inertia is dangerous because customers' needs and competitive offerings change over time. Thus, in environments where such changes happen frequently, the strategic planning process needs to be ongoing and adaptive. All the participants, whether from marketing or other functional departments, need to pay constant attention to what is happening with their customers and competitors.

Recent Developments Affecting the Strategic Role of Marketing

In the future, strategic inertia will be even more dangerous in many industries because they are facing increasing magnitudes and rates of change in their environments. These changes are rapidly altering the context in which marketing strategies are planned and carried out and the information and tools that marketers have at their disposal. These developments include (1) the increased globalization of markets and competition, (2) the growth of the service sector of the economy and the importance of service in maintaining customer satisfaction and loyalty, (3) the rapid development of new information and communications technologies, and (4) the growing importance of relationships for improved coordination and increased efficiency of marketing programs and for capturing a larger portion of customers' lifetime value. Some recent impacts of these four developments on marketing management are briefly summarized below and will be continuing themes throughout this book. We will also speculate from time to time about how these ongoing trends may reshape the tasks, tools, and techniques of marketing in the future. It is impossible to predict exactly how these trends will play out. Consequently, new business school graduates who both understand the marketing management process and are savvy with respect to one or more of these ongoing developments can play an important role—and gain a potential competitive advantage—within even the largest firms. Such newly minted managers can bring fresh perspectives and valuable insights concerning how these emerging trends are likely to impact their organizations' customers, competitors, and marketing strategies.

Globalization

International markets account for a large and growing portion of the sales of many organizations. But while global markets represent promising opportunities for additional sales growth and profits, differences in market and competitive conditions across country boundaries can require firms to adapt their competitive strategies and marketing programs to be successful. Even when similar marketing strategies are appropriate for multiple countries, international differences in infrastructure, culture, legal systems, and the like often mean that one or more elements of the marketing program—such as product features, promotional appeals, or distribution channels—must be tailored to local conditions for the strategy to be effective.

Increased Importance of Service

A service can be defined as "any activity or benefit that one party can offer another that is essentially intangible and that does not result in the ownership of anything. Its production may or may not be tied to a physical product."[19] Service businesses such as airlines, hotels, restaurants, and consulting firms account for roughly two-thirds of all economic activity in the United States, and services are the fastest-growing sector of most other developed economies around the world. Although many of the decisions and activities involved in marketing services are essentially the same as those for marketing physical goods, the intangible nature of many services can create unique challenges for marketers. We will discuss these challenges—and the tools and techniques firms have developed to deal with them—throughout this book.

As the definition suggests, services such as financing, delivery, installation, user training and assistance, and maintenance often are provided in conjunction with a physical product. Such ancillary services have become more critical to firms' continued sales and financial success in many product-markets. As markets have become crowded with global competitors offering similar products at ever-lower prices, the creative design and effective delivery of supplemental services have become crucial means by which a company may differentiate its offering and generate additional benefits and value for customers. Those additional benefits, in turn, can justify higher prices and margins in the short term and help improve customer satisfaction, retention, and loyalty over the long term.[20]

Of course, bad customer service can have the opposite effect. This is especially a danger when intense price competition pushes a firm to cut costs by reducing customer service and support. For instance, a few years ago Dell attempted to maintain its long-standing low-cost position in the personal computer industry by—among other things—reducing the number of technicians in its customer call centers and limiting each technician's training to only a few specialized problem areas. As a result, increasing numbers of customers spent 30 minutes or more on hold when they called Dell for help, and 45 percent were transferred at least once before they found a technician with the expertise to solve their problem. Consequently, Dell's customer satisfaction rating in the United States plummeted, and despite expensive attempts to improve service—including the use of independent retail outlets to sell and service Dell equipment—the firm's market share, profits, and stock price have still not fully recovered.[21]

Information Technology

The computer revolution and related technological developments are changing the nature of marketing management in two important ways. First, new technologies are making it possible for firms to collect and analyze more detailed information about potential customers and their needs, preferences, and buying habits, and about their competitors' offerings and prices. For instance, a recent study of chief marketing officers conducted by IBM across 19 industries in 64 different countries found that while 80 percent still relied on traditional marketing research and corporate benchmarking as their primary sources of market feedback, 26 percent said they are currently tracking blogs, 42 percent examine third-party reviews, and 48 percent are tracking customer reviews and ratings.[22] Thus, information technology is making it possible for many firms to identify and target smaller and more precisely defined market segments—sometimes segments consisting of only one or a few customers—and to customize product features, promotional appeals, prices, and financing arrangements to fit such segments.[23]

A second impact of information technology has been to open new channels for communications and transactions between suppliers and customers. As Exhibit 1.8 suggests, one simple way of categorizing these new channels is based on whether the suppliers and customers involved are organizations or individual consumers.

Global sales over the internet are growing so fast that solid estimates of their volume are hard to come by. However, internet revenues of manufacturers, wholesalers, retailers, and selected service firms amounted to over $3.4 trillion in the United States in 2009 (the most recent census data available at the time of this writing), and worldwide volume of about $8 trillion seems a reasonable guess for 2012.[24]

Roughly 80 percent of those sales were business-to-business transactions, such as those in the upper-left quadrant of Exhibit 1.8. Many high-tech firms such as Oracle Corp. and Cisco Systems, and even some more traditional companies such as Ford, conduct all or a large portion of their purchasing activities over the web. And many firms rely on their websites to communicate product information to potential customers, make sales, and deal with customer problems.

Perhaps even more important, though, new information and communications technologies are enabling firms to forge more cooperative and efficient relationships with their suppliers and distribution channel partners. For example, Procter & Gamble and 3M have formed alliances with major retailers—such as Kroger and Walmart—to develop automatic restocking systems. Sales information from the retailer's checkout scanners is sent directly to the supplier's computers, which figure out automatically when to replenish each product and schedule deliveries direct to each of the retailer's stores. Such paperless exchanges reduce mistakes and billbacks, minimize inventory levels, improve cash flow, and increase customer satisfaction and loyalty.

In contrast, internet sales from businesses to consumers (the upper-right quadrant in Exhibit 1.8) accounted for only about 8 percent of retail sales in the United states in

EXHIBIT 1.8   Categories of E-Commerce

	Business	Consumer
Business	**Business-to-Business (B2B)** Examples: • Purchasing sites of Ford, Oracle, Cisco • Supply chain networks linking producers and distribution channel members, such as 3M and Walmart	**Business-to-Consumer (B2C)** Examples: • E-tailers, such as E*Trade, Amazon, iTunes • Producers' direct sales sites, such as Dell, Ryanair, Sofitel Hotels • Websites of traditional retailers, such as Sears, Lands' End, Marks & Spencer
Consumer	**Consumer-to-Business (C2B)** Example: • Sites that enable consumers to bid on unsold airline tickets and other goods and services, such as Priceline	**Consumer-to-Consumer (C2C)** Examples: • Auction sites, such as eBay, QXL • Blogs praising/criticizing companies or brands

Source: Adapted from "A Survey of E-Commerce: Shopping Around the web," *The Economist,* February 26, 2000, p. 11.

2011—roughly $188 billion. However, consumer purchases over the internet continue to grow rapidly worldwide, particularly among younger buyers. In the United States for instance, 25 to 34 year olds already make more than a quarter of their purchases online, and new technologies—such as 4G phones and geolocation apps—will spur further growth. Consequently, online retail sales are forecast to exceed $270 billion by 2015.[25]

Also, web-based information is affecting consumer purchase patterns even when the purchases are made in traditional retail outlets. Among U.S. consumers with internet access, 78 percent report gathering information online before making a purchase. Most start their online search with a search engine like Google (58 percent), or by visiting a manufacturer's website (24 percent). But social media like Facebook, Twitter, and YouTube also impact people's decisions. About 30 percent of the respondents in a recent study said they used social media to help avoid brands their friends did not like, and 28 percent said they relied on their friends for news about hot new products or brands.[26]

Clearly, the web is presenting marketers with new strategic options—as well as new competitive threats and opportunities—regardless of what or to whom they are selling. Therefore, we will devote all of Chapter 11 to marketing strategies for e-commerce and discuss specific examples and their implications in every chapter.

Relationships across Functions and Firms

New information technologies and the ongoing search for greater marketing efficiency and customer value in the face of increasing competition are changing the nature of exchange between companies. Instead of engaging in a discrete series of arm's-length, adversarial exchanges with customers, channel members, and suppliers on the open market, more firms are trying to develop and nurture long-term relationships and alliances, such as the one between 3M and Walmart. Such cooperative relationships are thought to improve each partner's ability to adapt quickly to environmental changes or threats, to gain greater benefits at lower costs from its exchanges, and to increase the lifetime value of its customers.[27]

Similar kinds of cooperative relationships are emerging inside companies as firms seek mechanisms for more effectively and efficiently coordinating across functional departments the various activities necessary to identify, attract, service, and satisfy customers. In many firms, the planning and execution that used to be the responsibility of a product or marketing manager are now coordinated and carried out by cross-functional teams.

The Future Role of Marketing

In light of such changes, it is apparent that firms in most, if not all, industries will have to be market-oriented, tightly focused on customer needs and desires, and highly adaptive to succeed and prosper in the future. In turn, this suggests that the effective performance of marketing activities—particularly those associated with tracking, analyzing, and satisfying customers' needs—will become even more critical for the successful formulation and implementation of strategies at all organizational levels.

It is important to note, however, that such marketing activities may not always be carried out by marketing managers located in separate functional departments.[28] As more firms embrace the use of multifunctional teams or network structures, the boundaries between functions are likely to blur and the performance of marketing tasks will become everybody's business. Similarly, as organizations become more focused and specialized in developing unique core competencies, they will rely more heavily on suppliers, distributors, dealers, and other partners to perform activities—including marketing and sales tasks—that fall outside those areas of competence. All of this suggests that the ability to create, manage, and sustain exchange relationships with customers, vendors, distributors, and others will become a key strategic competence for firms in the future—and that is what marketing is all about.

FORMULATING AND IMPLEMENTING MARKETING STRATEGY—AN OVERVIEW OF THE PROCESS

This book examines the development and implementation of marketing strategies for individual product-market entries, whether goods or services. Exhibit 1.9 briefly diagrams the activities and decisions involved in this process, and it also serves as the organizational framework for the rest of this book. For that reason, it is important to note the basic focus of this framework and the sequence of events within it.

A Decision-Making Focus

The framework has a distinct decision-making focus. Planning and executing a marketing strategy involves many interrelated decisions about what to do, when to do it, and how. Those decisions are the primary focus of this book. Every chapter details either the decisions to be made and actions taken when designing and implementing strategies for various market situations or the analytical tools and frameworks you will need to make those decisions intelligently.

Analysis Comes First—The Four "Cs"

Exhibit 1.9 suggests that a substantial amount of analysis of customers, competitors, and the company itself should occur *before* designing a marketing strategy. This reflects our view that successful strategic decisions usually rest on an objective, detailed, and evidence-based understanding of the market and the environmental context. Of course, most marketing strategies never get implemented in quite the same way as they were drawn on paper. Adjustments are made, and new activities undertaken in response to rapid changes in customer demands, competitive actions, and shifting economic conditions. But a thorough and ongoing analysis of the market and the broader environment enables managers to make such adjustments in a well-reasoned and consistent way rather than by the seat of their pants.

The analysis necessary to provide the foundation for a good strategic marketing plan should focus on four elements of the overall environment that may influence its appropriateness and ultimate success: (1) the *company's* internal resources, capabilities, and strategies; (2) the environmental *context*—such as broad social, economic, and technology trends—in which the firm will compete; (3) the relative strengths and weaknesses of *competitors* and trends in the competitive environment; and (4) the needs, wants, and characteristics of current and potential *customers.* Marketers refer to these elements as the **4Cs.** They are the focus of a *market opportunity analysis* and are discussed in more detail following.

Integrating Marketing Strategy with the Firm's Other Strategies and Resources

A major part of the marketing manager's job is to monitor and analyze customers' needs and wants and the emerging opportunities and threats posed by competitors and trends in the external environment. Therefore, because all levels of strategy must consider such factors, marketers often play a major role in providing inputs to—and influencing the development of—corporate and business strategies. Conversely, general managers and senior managers in other functions need a solid understanding of marketing in order to craft effective organizational strategies.

Marketing managers also bear the primary responsibility for formulating and implementing strategic marketing plans for individual product-market entries or product lines. But as we have seen, such strategic marketing programs are not created in a vacuum. Instead, the marketing objectives and strategy for a particular product-market entry must

EXHIBIT 1.9 The Process of Formulating and Implementing Marketing Strategy

```
┌──────────────┐        ┌────────────────────────────────┐
│   External   │───────▶│ Corporate objectives and strategy│◀────┐
│ environment  │        │          (Chapter 2)           │     │
└──────────────┘        └────────────────────────────────┘     │
       │                          │                             │
       │                          ▼                             │
       │                ┌────────────────────────────────┐     │
       └───────────────▶│ Business-level objectives and strategy│◀──┤
                        │          (Chapter 3)           │     │
                        └────────────────────────────────┘     │
                                   │                            │
                                   ▼                            │
       ┌──────────────────────────────────────────────────┐   │
       │          Market opportunity analysis             │   │
       │   • Understanding market opportunities           │◀──┤
       │              (Chapter 4)                         │   │
       │   • Forecasting and market knowledge             │   │
       │              (Chapter 5)                         │   │
       │   • Customer analysis, segmentation, and         │   │
       │      targeting decisions  (Chapter 6)            │   │
       │   • Positioning decisions (Chapter 7)            │   │
       └──────────────────────────────────────────────────┘   │
                                   │                            │
                                   ▼                            │
       ┌──────────────────────────────────────────────────┐   │
       │  Formulating strategies for specific market situations│ │
       │   • Strategies for new market entries            │   │
       │              (Chapter 8)                         │   │
       │   • Strategies for growth markets                │   │
       │              (Chapter 9)                         │   │
       │   • Strategies for mature and declining markets  │   │
       │              (Chapter 10)                        │   │
       │   • Strategies for the new economy               │   │
       │              (Chapter 11)                        │   │
       └──────────────────────────────────────────────────┘   │
                                   │                            │
                                   ▼                            │
       ┌──────────────────────────────────────────────────┐   │
       │          Implementation and control              │   │
       │   • Implementing business and marketing strategies│──┘
       │              (Chapter 12)                        │
       │   • Controlling marketing strategies and programs│
       │              (Chapter 13)                        │
       └──────────────────────────────────────────────────┘
```

Strategic Issue

The marketing objectives and strategy for a particular product-market entry must be achievable with the company's available resources and capabilities and consistent with the direction and allocation of resources inherent in the firm's corporate and business-level strategies.

be achievable with the company's available resources and capabilities and consistent with the direction and allocation of resources inherent in the firm's corporate and business-level strategies. In other words, there should be a good fit—or internal consistency—among the elements of all three levels of strategy. Chapters 2 and 3 describe in more detail the components of corporate and business strategies and the roles marketers and other functional managers play in shaping the strategic direction of their organizations and business units.

Market Opportunity Analysis

A major factor in the success or failure of strategies at all three levels is whether the strategy elements are consistent with the realities of the firm's external environment and its own capabilities and resources. Thus, the first step in developing a strategic marketing plan—for a new venture, a new product, or an existing product or product line—is to undertake an analysis of the 4Cs, so that the nature and attractiveness of the market opportunity is well understood. Marketing managers in various line or staff positions—or entrepreneurs themselves, in start-up settings—typically carry out this responsibility.

Understanding Market Opportunities

Understanding the nature and attractiveness of any opportunity requires conducting an examination of the external environment, including the markets served and the industry of which the firm is a part. In turn, this examination involves a look at broad macro issues such as environmental trends that are driving or constraining market demand and the structural characteristics of the industry as a whole, as well as specific aspects of the target customers and their needs and of the particular firm and what it brings to the party. It's also necessary to examine the management team that will be charged with implementing whatever strategy is developed in order to determine if they have what it takes to get the job done. Chapter 4 provides a framework for examining these issues and dramatizes how different the attractiveness of one's market and one's industry can be, an insight that is easily (and often) overlooked.

Measuring Market Opportunities

Understanding the overall attractiveness of a market opportunity is one thing. Preparing an evidence-based forecast of the sales that can be achieved over the short and intermediate term is quite another and is a particularly difficult task for new products, especially those of the new-to-the-world variety. In Chapter 5, we outline several approaches to evidence-based forecasting, and we examine the factors that drive the pace at which innovations are adopted over time. We also briefly explore where to obtain the market knowledge required—the data to fill in the holes in one's understanding of any market opportunity—including sources both inside and outside the firm.

Market Segmentation, Targeting, and Positioning Decisions

Not all customers with similar needs seek the same products or services to satisfy those needs. Their purchase decisions may be influenced by individual preferences, personal characteristics, social circumstances, and so forth. On the other hand, customers who do purchase the same product may be motivated by different needs, seek different benefits from the product, rely on different sources of information about products, and obtain the product from different distribution channels. Thus, one of the manager's most crucial tasks is to divide customers into **market segments**—distinct subsets of people with similar needs, circumstances, and characteristics that lead them to respond in a similar way to a particular product or service offering or to a particular strategic marketing program. Chapter 6 examines dimensions for measurement and analytical techniques that can help managers identify and define market segments in both consumer and organizational markets.

After defining market segments and exploring customer needs and the firm's competitive strengths and weaknesses within segments, the manager must decide which segments represent attractive and viable opportunities for the company; that is, on which segments to focus a strategic marketing program. Chapter 6 discusses some of the considerations in *selecting a target segment.*

Finally, the manager must decide how to **position** the product or service offering and its brand within a target segment; that is, to design the product and its marketing program to emphasize attributes and benefits that appeal to customers in the target segment and at once distinguish the company's offering from those of competitors. Issues and analytical techniques involved in brand positioning decisions are discussed in Chapter 7.

Formulating Marketing Strategies for Specific Situations

The strategic marketing program for a product should reflect market demand and the competitive situation within the target market. But demand and competitive conditions change over time as a product moves through its life cycle. Therefore, different strategies are typically more appropriate and successful for different market conditions and at different life cycle stages. Chapter 8 examines some marketing strategies for introducing new goods or services to the market. Chapter 9 discusses strategies appropriate for building or maintaining a product's share of a growing market in the face of increasing competition. Chapter 10 considers strategies a manager might adopt in mature or declining markets. Chapter 11 explores how all of the preceding strategies might be influenced or modified by the rapidly evolving conditions being created by e-commerce.

Implementation and Control of the Marketing Strategy

A final critical determinant of a strategy's success is the firm's ability to implement it effectively. This depends on whether the strategy is consistent with the resources, the organizational structure, the coordination and control systems, and the skills and experience of company personnel.[29] Managers must design a strategy to fit the company's existing resources, competencies, and procedures—or try to construct new structures and systems to fit the chosen strategy. For example, Samsung's brand-building program would not have been so successful without its substantial investments in digital R&D, market research, and product design and the development of cross-functional product teams to encourage communication among the firm's engineers, designers, and marketers. Chapter 12 discusses the structural variables, planning and coordination processes, and personnel and corporate culture characteristics related to the successful implementation of various marketing strategies.

The final tasks in the marketing management process are determining whether the strategic marketing program is meeting objectives and adjusting the program when performance is disappointing. This evaluation and control process provides feedback to managers and serves as a basis for a market opportunity analysis in the next planning period. Chapter 13 examines ways to evaluate marketing performance and develop contingency plans when things go wrong.

The Marketing Plan—A Blueprint for Action

The results of the various analyses and marketing program decisions discussed previously should be summarized periodically in a detailed formal marketing plan.[30]

> A **marketing plan** is a written document detailing the current situation with respect to customers, competitors, and the external environment and providing guidelines for objectives, marketing actions, and resource allocations over the planning period for either an existing or a proposed product or service.

Although some firms—particularly smaller ones—do not bother to write their marketing plans, most organizations believe that "unless all the key elements of a plan are written down . . . there will always be loopholes for ambiguity or misunderstanding of strategies and objectives, or of assigned responsibilities for taking action."[31] This suggests that even small organizations with limited resources can benefit from preparing a written plan, however brief. Written plans also provide a concrete history of a product's strategies and performance over time, which aids institutional memory and helps educate new managers assigned to the product. Written plans are necessary in most larger organizations because a marketing manager's proposals usually must be reviewed and approved at higher levels of management and because the approved plan provides the benchmark against which the manager's performance will be judged. Finally, the discipline involved in producing a formal plan helps ensure that the proposed objectives, strategy, and marketing actions are based on rigorous analysis of the 4Cs and sound reasoning.

Because a written marketing plan is such an important tool for communicating and coordinating expectations and responsibilities throughout the firm, we will say more about it in Chapter 12 when we discuss the implementation of marketing programs in detail. But because the written plan attempts to summarize and communicate an overview of the strategic marketing management process we have been examining, it is worthwhile to briefly examine the contents of such plans here.

Marketing plans vary in timing, content, and organization across companies. In general, marketing plans are developed annually, though planning periods for some big-ticket industrial products such as commercial aircraft may be longer, and in some highly volatile industries such as telecommunications or electronics, they can be shorter. Plans typically follow a format similar to that outlined in Exhibit 1.10.

EXHIBIT 1.10   Contents of a Marketing Plan

Section	Content
I. Executive summary	Presents a short overview of the issues, objectives, strategy, and actions incorporated in the plan and their expected outcomes for quick management review.
II. Current situation and trends	Summarizes relevant background information on the market, competition and the macroenvironment, and trends therein, including size and growth rates for the overall market and key segments.
III. Performance review (for an existing product or service only)	Examines the past performance of the product and the elements of its marketing program (e.g., distribution, promotions, etc.).
IV. Key issues	Identifies the main opportunities and threats to the product that the plan must deal with in the coming year and the relative strengths and weaknesses of the product and business unit that must be taken into account in facing those issues.
V. Objectives	Specifies the goals to be accomplished in terms of sales volume, market share, and profit.
VI. Marketing strategy	Summarizes the overall strategic approach that will be used to meet the plan's objectives.
VII. Action plans	This is the most critical section of the annual plan for helping to ensure effective implementation and coordination of activities across functional departments. It specifies • The target market to be pursued. • What specific actions are to be taken with respect to each of the 4 Ps. • Who is responsible for each action. • When the action will be engaged in. • How much will be budgeted for each action.
VIII. Projected profit-and-loss statement	Presents the expected financial payoff from the plan.
IX. Controls	Discusses how the plan's progress will be monitored; may present contingency plans to be used if performance falls below expectations or the situation changes.
X. Contingency plans	Describes actions to be taken if specific threats or opportunities materialize during the planning period.

There are three major parts to the plan. First, the marketing manager details his or her assessment of the current situation. This is the homework portion of the plan where the manager summarizes the results of his or her analysis of current and potential customers, the company's relative strengths and weaknesses, the competitive situation, the major trends in the broader environment that may affect the product, and, for existing products, past performance outcomes. This section typically also includes forecasts, estimates of sales potential, and other assumptions underlying the plan, which are especially important for proposed new products or services. Based on these analyses, the manager also may call attention to several key issues—major opportunities or threats that should be dealt with during the planning period.

The second part of the plan details the strategy for the coming period. This part usually starts by detailing the objectives (e.g., sales volume, market share, profits, customer satisfaction levels, etc.) to be achieved by the product or service during the planning period. It then outlines the overall marketing strategy, the actions associated with each of the 4 Ps (the product, price, promotion, and "place" or distribution) necessary to implement the strategy, and the timing and locus of responsibility for each action.

Finally, the plan details the financial and resource implications of the strategy and the controls to be employed to monitor the plan's implementation and progress over the period. Some plans also specify some contingencies: how the plan will be modified if certain changes occur in the market, competitive, or external environments.

Marketing Plan Exercise

A common approach many instructors take in designing a course in marketing management is to focus the course around an application-oriented project, often done by small teams of students. Such a project allows students to actually apply what they learn, it adds a considerable amount of fun to the course, and it gives students some tangible output they can show prospective employers when they enter the job market. Perhaps the most common such marketing management project is the development of a marketing plan, either for a real company with real goods or services or for something entrepreneurial or hypothetical that the students themselves conceive.

From a student's perspective, such a project prepares marketing graduates to "hit the ground running" when they enter the job market, and it helps students who take nonmarketing jobs to better understand and appreciate marketing perspectives. When used in conjunction with decision-oriented cases, such an approach gives students two laps around the track for each element of the course: once when the course material in a given chapter is applied to a case and a second time when it is applied to the course project.

"But, we're only at Chapter 1!" you might say. "How do I go about doing what's necessary so that, by the end of the course, I can deliver a competently prepared marketing plan (or some similar assignment)?"

We briefly discussed the contents of a typical marketing plan for an existing product or product line at the end of Chapter 1. Here, we look at marketing plans for new products, where there are some extra challenges due to the lack of any history and the need to make lots of decisions from square one.

Thus, what follows is a more detailed set of guidelines for what each section of a good marketing plan entails. As you'll see, much of what you'll find here applies to marketing plans for existing businesses or product lines as well. You might think of this material as a road map for the project work you'll do in the course, if your course involves preparing a marketing plan or something similar. The fact that this outline looks slightly, but not fundamentally, different from the one in Exhibit 1.10 should be a clue to you that there's no single "right answer" to how a marketing plan should be assembled. Given the setting in which your project is to be carried out, we suggest you develop your own outline that best serves your context.

As you proceed through the book, you'll find at the end of every chapter an exercise that identifies how that chapter's learning contributes to the development of your marketing plan. If you do these exercises as you go along, you'll find that much of the work your marketing plan entails will get done as a result.

Outline: New Product Marketing Plan

1. Executive Summary
   - Summarize the product idea, its target market, and the results you forecast (sales, gross margin, and profit contribution) in not more than two pages.

2. The Product (Good or Service) or Business Idea
   - Identify the mission and SMART objectives (specific, measurable, attainable, relevant to your mission, and time-bound) of the business.
   - Briefly describe the product or service and its target market.
   - State your value proposition or a positioning statement that outlines the benefits your product, service, or business will provide to the target customer in order to differentiate your offering from currently available ones.

3. Market Analysis
   - Indicate who constitutes your overall market and the segment you will initially target (defined according to one or more of the following kinds of factors: demographic, geographic, and/or behavioral variables).
   - For this market overall and for your target segment:
     —Indicate their size and current and anticipated growth rate (measured if possible, in units, dollars, and number of potential customers).

     —Identify any unmet or poorly served needs that your new product or service will address.

     —.Identify relevant trends in any of the six macro trend categories that support or detract from the demand for your new product or service.
   - Identify the wants and needs your product serves. What benefits will you offer, and what product features will deliver them?

4. Competitor Assessment
   - Define the industry in which you will compete.
   - Assess the industry's five competitive forces.
   - Identify its critical success factors.
   - What direct and indirect competitors currently satisfy the needs of your proposed targets?
   - What competitive advantages and disadvantages will specific competitors have? Will you have?
   - What competitive responses to your entry are likely?

5. Marketing Strategy
   - What are your marketing objectives (SMART)?
   - What is your overall marketing strategy?
   - How will your offering be positioned?
   - Product decisions: features, augmented product, brand
   - Pricing decisions: pricing strategy, pricing specifics
   - Distribution decisions: channel structure, push or pull strategy
   - Promotional strategy: integrated marketing communications objectives and plan, copy platform, media plan, trade and consumer promotion plan, personal selling plan, public relations plan

6. Forecast and Budget
   - Provide one or more spreadsheets that detail your sales and gross margin forecast and marketing budget and the activities that will comprise it for 3–5 years, monthly for the first year. Indicate, by category of activity, all planned marketing spending for the execution of your marketing strategy, broken down into as many of the following categories as apply:
     —Advertising (creative and media expense)

     —Direct marketing (direct mail and/or telemarketing expense)

     —Internet marketing (website, banners, etc.)

     —Consumer promotion (discounts, samples, coupons, rebates, contests, etc.)

—Trade promotion (allowances/discounts to your distribution channels)

—Salesforce expenses (salary and fringes, sales materials, commission, travel)

—Public relations (nonpaid media)

—Customer service (inbound order taking, customer support, etc.)

—Other (sponsorships, events, etc.)

- Indicate, using appropriate measures, the level of effectiveness and efficiency you expect from each activity (reach, frequency, CPM, response rate, number of sales calls per week, close rate, duration of sales cycle, etc.). Provide appropriate *evidence* in a discussion that supports your contention that your planned marketing budget is sufficient to drive the sales you forecast.

7. Implementation and Control Plan
   - Provide an organizational chart for marketing people and functions.
   - Provide templates of strategic and/or operational control "dashboards" for key marketing management functions.

8. Contingency Plan
   - Identify what is likely to change or go wrong and what should be done if and when it does.

Discussion Questions

1. How are the basic business philosophies or orientations of a major consumer products firm such as General Mills or Nestlé and a small entrepreneurial start-up in a fast-growing, high-tech industry likely to differ? What are the implications of such philosophical differences for the role of marketers in the strategic planning processes of the two firms?

2. As the small entrepreneurial firm described in question 1 grows larger, its market matures, and its industry becomes more competitive. How should its business philosophy or orientation change? Why?

3. What role should marketing managers play in helping to formulate business-level (SBU) strategies in a large diversified firm such as General Motors? What kinds of information are marketers best able to provide as a basis for planning? Which issues or elements of business-level strategy can such information help to resolve?

Self-diagnostic questions to test your ability to apply the concepts in this chapter can be found at this book's website at **www.mhhe.com/walker8e.**

Endnotes

1. This case example is based on material found in "Samsung's Lessons in Design," *@issue: The Journal of Business and Design* 9, no. 1 (Fall 2003), pp. 25–31; "As Good as It Gets? Special Report: Samsung Electronics," *The Economist*, January 15, 2005, pp. 64–66; Moon Ihlwan, "Samsung's Rise in Digital TV," *www.businessweek.com*, October 4, 2007; "Losing Its Shine?" *The Economist*, February 9, 2008, p. 71; Cliff Edwards, "Samsung: Rethinking the Printer Business," *www.businessweek.com/innovation*, January 5, 2009; and the unit's 2010 Annual Report and 2011 Audited Financial Statements on the company's website at www.samsung.com.

2. For a summary of the definitions offered by a number of other authors, see Roger Kerin, Vijay Mahajan, and P. Rajan Varadarajan, *Contemporary Perspectives on Strategic Market Planning* (Boston: Allyn and Bacon, 1990), pp. 8–9. Our definition differs from some others, however, in that we view the setting of objectives as an integral part of strategy formulation, whereas they see objective setting as a separate process. Because a firm's objectives are influenced and constrained by many of the same environmental and competitive factors as the other elements of strategy, however, it seems logical to treat both the determination of objectives and the resource allocations aimed at reaching those objectives as two parts of the same strategic planning process.

3. However, although such corporate-level synergies often are used to justify mergers, acquisitions, and forays into new businesses, they sometimes prove elusive. For example, see Laura Landro, "Giants Talk Synergy but Few Make It Work," *The Wall Street Journal,* September 25, 1995, p. B1.

4. C. K. Prahalad and Gary Hamel, "The Core Competence of the Corporation," *Harvard Business Review* 68 (May–June 1990), pp. 79–91; and George S. Day and Prakash Nedungadi," Managerial Representations of Competitive Advantage," *Journal of Marketing* 58 (April 1994), pp. 31–44.

5. Christian Homburg, John P. Workman Jr., and Harley Krohmer, "Marketing's Influence within the Firm," *Journal of Marketing* 63 (April 1999), pp. 1–17.

6. Quoted in Katherine Z. Andrews, "Still a Major Player: Marketing's Role in Today's Firms," *Insights from MSI,* Winter 1999, p. 2.

7. Pravin Nath and Vijay Mahajan, "Marketing in the C-Suite: A Study of Chief Marketing Officer Power in Firms' Top Management Teams," *Journal of Marketing* 75 (January 2011), pp. 60–77; and Peter C. Verhoef, Peter S. H. Leeflang, Jochen Reiner, Martin Natter, William Baker, Amir Grinstein, Anders Gustafsson, Pamela Morrison, and John Saunders, " A Cross-National Investigation into the Marketing Department's Influence Within the Firm," *Journal of International Marketing* 19 (September 2011), pp. 59–86.

8. Peter C. Verhoef, et. al., "A Cross-National Investigation into the Marketing Department's Influence."

9. Frederick E. Webster Jr., "Executing the New Marketing Concept," *Marketing Management* 3 (1994), pp. 9–16; and George S. Day, "Creating a Superior Customer-Relating Capability," *Report #03–101* (Cambridge, MA: Marketing Science Institute, 2003).

10. Quoted in Gary Hamel and C. K. Prahalad, *Competing for the Future* (Cambridge, MA: Harvard Business School Press, 1994).

11. Justin Martin, "Ignore Your Customer," *Fortune,* May 1, 1995, pp. 121–26.

12. "The Right Stuff," *Journal of Business and Design* 2 (Fall 1996), p. 11.

13. Rajendra K. Srivastava, Tasadduq A. Shervani, and Liam Fahey, "Marketing, Business Processes, and Shareholder Value: An Organizationally Embedded View of Marketing Activities and the Discipline of Marketing," *Journal of Marketing* 63 (Special Issue 1999), pp. 168–79; and Thomas S. Gruca and Lopo L. Rego, "Customer Satisfaction, Cash Flow, and Shareholder Value," *Report #03–106* (Cambridge, MA: Marketing Science Institute, 2003).

14. For example, see John C. Narver and Stanley F. Slater, "The Effect of a Market Orientation on Business Profitability," *Journal of Marketing* 54 (April 1990), pp. 1–18; Bernard J. Jaworski and Ajay Kohli, "Market Orientation: Antecedents and Consequences," *Journal of Marketing* 57 (July 1993); Stanley F. Slater and John C. Narver, "Market Orientation, Performance, and the Moderating Influence of Competitive Environment," *Journal of Marketing* 58 (January 1994), pp. 46–55; Subin Im and John P. Workman, "Market Orientation, Creativity, and New Product Performance in High-Technology Firms," *Journal of Marketing* 68 (April 2004), pp. 114–32; Ahmet H. Kirca, Satish Jayachandran, and William O. Bearden, "Market Orientation: A Meta-Analytic Review and Assessment of Its Antecedents and Impact on Performance, *Journal of Marketing* 69 (April 2005), pp. 24–41; and V. Kumar and Denish Shah, "Expanding the Role of Marketing: From Customer Equity to Market Capitalization," *Journal of Marketing* 73 (November 2009), pp. 119–136.

15. Rohit Deshpande, Elie Ofek, and Sang-Hoon Kim, "Preempting Competitive Risk Via Customer Focus: Entrepreneurial Firms in Japan and the U.S.," *Report #03–114* (Cambridge, MA: Marketing Science Institute, 2003).

16. Stanley F. Slater and John C. Narver, "Market Orientation, Performance, and the Moderating Influence of Competitive Environment," *Journal of Marketing* 58 (January 1994), pp. 46–55; and John P. Workman Jr., "When Marketing Should Follow Instead of Lead," *Marketing Management* 2 (1993), pp. 8–19.

17. Charles H. Noble, Rajiv K. Sinha, and Ajith Kumar, "Market Orientation and Alternative Strategic Orientations: A Longitudinal Assessment of Performance Implications," *Journal of Marketing* 66 (October 2002), pp. 25–39.

18. E. Jerome McCarthy and William D. Perreault Jr., *Basic Marketing: A Global Managerial Approach,* 11th ed. (Burr Ridge, IL: Richard D. Irwin, 1993), chap. 2.

19. Philip Kotler and Gary Armstrong, *Principles of Marketing* (Englewood Cliffs, NJ: Prentice Hall, 1989), p. 575.

20. For examples, see Jena McGregor, "When Service Means Survival," *BusinessWeek,* March 2, 2009, pp. 26–30.

21. Brian Hindo, "Satisfaction Not Guaranteed," *BusinessWeek,* June 19, 2006, pp. 32–36; Arik Hesseldahl, "Dell's Disappointing Quarter," *www.businessweek.com/technology,* February 28, 2008; and Aaron Ricadela, "Dell: Scant Signs of Recovery," www.businessweek.com/technology, July 14, 2009.

22. Aaron Baar, "CMOs on Social Media: Do As I Say," www.mediapost.com, October 12, 2011.

23. For examples, see Faith Keenan, Stanley Holmes, Jay Greene, and Roger O. Crockett, "A Mass Market of One," *BusinessWeek,* December 2, 2002, pp. 68–72; and Anthony Bianco, "The Vanishing Mass Market," *BusinessWeek,* July 12, 2004, pp. 61–72.

24. "Summary of U.S. Shipments, Sales, Revenues, and E-commerce: 2000–2009," on the U.S. Census Bureau website at www.census.gov.

25. "Making It Click," *The Economist,* February 25, 2012, pp. 75–76.

26. Courtney Rubin, "Shoppers Combine Search, Social Media to Fuel Decisions," www.inc.com, February 25, 2011. Also see Jim Jansen, "Online Product Research," Pew Research Center's internet and American Life Project, www.pewinternet.org/reports/2010 (September 29, 2010).

27. Ravi S. Achrol and Philip Kotler, "Marketing in the Network Economy," *Journal of Marketing* 63 (Special Issue 1999), pp. 146–63.

28. Day, "Creating a Superior Customer-Relating Capability." Also see Son K. Lam, Florian Kraus, and Michael Ahearne, "The Diffusion of Market Orientation Throughout the Organization: A Social Learning Theory Perspective," *Journey of Marketing* 74 (September 2010), pp. 61–79.

29. George S. Day, "The Capabilities of Market-Driven Organizations," *Journal of Marketing* 58 (October 1994), pp. 37–52; and Stanley F. Slater, Eric M. Olson, and G. Thomas M. Hult, "Worried About Strategy Implementation? Don't Overlook Marketing's Role," *Business Horizons* 53 (2010), pp. 469–479 (archived online at www.sciencedirect.com).

30. For a more detailed discussion of formal marketing plans, see Donald R. Lehmann and Russell S. Winer, *Analysis for Marketing Planning,* 4th ed. (New York: Irwin/McGraw-Hill, 1997); and Marian Burk Wood, *The Marketing Plan: A Handbook,* 3rd ed. (Upper Saddle River, NJ: Prentice Hall, 2008).

31. David S. Hopkins, *The Marketing Plan* (New York: The Conference Board, 1981), p. 2.

Chapter **Two**

Corporate Strategy Decisions and Their Marketing Implications

Ryanair: Low Prices, High Profits—But Increasing Competition[1]

When the Ryan family launched Ryanair as Europe's first low-fare, no-frills airline in 1985, travelers wondered how the firm would ever make money offering €99 fares from Dublin to London when the cheapest flights available on British Airways or Aer Lingus cost more than twice as much. But the Irish company has grown into one of Europe's largest and most profitable airlines with more than 8,000 employees flying nearly one thousand different routes to 155 airports in 26 countries. Over the first decade of the twenty-first century, at a time when the global airline industry collectively lost nearly $50 billion, Ryanair earned healthy profits in 9 out of the 10 years. Most recently Ryanair made a net profit of €375 million on revenues of €3.6 billion in 2011.

From the beginning, the firm's executives have pursued a very straightforward corporate strategy, focusing exclusively on providing low-cost air transportation for consumers within the European Union, seeking a competitive advantage by offering the lowest fares of any airline operating in Europe.

Of course, a low-price competitive strategy can be profitable only when the firm's costs are also low. Therefore, all of Ryanair's functional activities and operating policies are designed with efficiency in mind. For instance, the firm owns rather than leases its airplanes, and nearly all 275 of those planes are Boeing 737s, thereby allowing standardization of maintenance activities and parts inventories. The company also concentrates its flights to and from underutilized regional airports such as Stansted outside of London and Charleroi south of Brussels. Such airports offer the company more favorable terms with respect to taxes, facilities fees, and ground handling charges than more popular and congested airports closer to major cities. The lack of congestion helps reduce turnaround times and thereby lowers costs by increasing utilization rates for planes and flight crews. It also helps Ryanair achieve the best on-time record of any European airline, 89 percent.

The firm's operating efficiencies have helped it successfully implement its low-price competitive strategy and hold its average fare below €35, substantially lower than even easyJet's, its strongest low-price competitor. Unfortunately, many of Ryanair's cost savings come at the expense of customer comfort and convenience. Not only do customers have to find their way to and from small airports far from the big cities, they have to carry and stow their own bags and do without meals, drinks, and other in-flight services. There is not much room for them to stretch out and relax during their flights since Ryanair carries 15 percent more seats per aircraft than traditional airlines. It is even difficult for customers to buy their tickets because the company pays no fees to computer reservation systems and no commissions to travel agents. Indeed, the company has instituted so many customer-unfriendly policies in its relentless pursuit of efficiency—like surcharges for such things as using its wheelchairs—that several newspapers, including *The Guardian,* have created reader competitions dedicated to describing Ryanair horror stories.

Advertising and promotion, however, are among the few areas where Ryanair has not tried to cut costs below its competitors. With the exception of the sales commissions mentioned previously, the company's marketing costs are about the same per passenger-kilometer as those of more traditional airlines. Even the most frugal flyers would not seek out Ryanair's cheap fares without being aware—and being frequently reminded—that they exist. The firm must also maintain an extensive web site and call center to facilitate the direct sale of tickets.

Although Ryanair's low-cost/low-price strategy has been very successful so far, there may be some turbulence on the company's horizon. For the past decade, the firm has relied on rapid growth, attained largely by adding new routes and more planes, to bring in new customers. But given that the company has adopted a more modest growth objective of 5 to 10 percent per year through 2015, the question is whether it can continue to generate enough repeat business from past customers to maintain its revenue stream and profitability. Clearly there is a sizable segment of customers who are willing to sacrifice comfort and convenience for low fares. But how large is that segment across the various countries that Ryanair serves, and how much comfort and convenience are those consumers willing to give up? While Ryanair's cost structure should enable it to make money at fares lower than the major airlines can match, some consumers may see those low fares as a poor value since they have to schlep their own bags and land at remote airports. And the number of such convenience-oriented consumers may increase if and when the European economies get stronger.

On the other hand, the double whammy of high fuel prices and slow economic growth have forced the full-service airlines to cut expensive customer services, but without being able to match Ryanair's low costs and cheap fares. In order to survive, those carriers are cutting flights to smaller cities, charging extra for baggage and snacks, and reducing the seats available for frequent flyers. With competition like that, maybe Ryanair's low-cost, no-frills flights will not be seen as such a bad value after all.

STRATEGIC CHALLENGES ADDRESSED IN CHAPTER 2

The corporate strategy crafted at the inception of Ryanair has provided a clear sense of direction and useful guidance for the firm's managers when developing competitive, marketing, and other functional strategies because it speaks to the dimensions of strategy we discussed in Chapter 1. First, it defines the overall mission and scope of the firm by clearly focusing on the price-conscious segment of airline passengers traveling within Europe. It also spells out goals and objectives for the company and specifies corporate development strategies for achieving those objectives. Specifically, the firm seeks to double its passenger volume—and revenues—in the next few years by increasing its flight frequency and market share on existing routes and by increasing the number of European cities it serves.

Ryanair's objectives and development strategy, in turn, influence the way it allocates its resources and leverages its competencies in order to maintain a competitive advantage. The firm is investing heavily in new planes to enable it to schedule more flights to more cities, and it spends substantial sums on advertising and promotion to help build customer awareness and market share. On the other hand, its operating policies are designed to maximize efficiency and limit costs so the company can profitably compete by offering the lowest fares in Europe.

The successful formulation of Ryanair's corporate strategy illustrates the importance of a detailed understanding of target customers, potential competitors, and the market environment when developing strategies at any level. As we pointed out in Chapter 1, marketers' close contact with customers and the external environment often means they play a crucial role in influencing strategies formulated at higher levels in the firm.

On the other hand, a well-defined corporate strategy also influences and constrains the strategic decisions that marketers and other functional managers can make at lower organizational levels. For instance, the firm's competitive strategy of offering the lowest fares of any airline operating in Europe obviously constrains managers' pricing decisions, and its cost-cutting policy of avoiding travel agent commissions forced it to be a pioneer in the direct marketing of tickets over the web.

In view of the interactions and interdependences between corporate-level strategy decisions and strategic marketing programs for individual product-market entries, this chapter examines the components of a well-defined corporate strategy in more detail: (1) the overall scope and mission of the organization; (2) company goals and objectives; (3) a source of competitive advantage; (4) a development strategy for future growth; (5) the allocation of corporate resources across the firm's various businesses; and (6) the search for synergy via the sharing of corporate resources, competencies, or programs across businesses or product lines. Exhibit 2.1 summarizes some of the crucial questions that need to be addressed by each of these six components.

Implications for Marketers and Their Marketing Plans

Although a market orientation—and the analytical tools that marketing managers use to examine customer desires and competitors' strengths and weaknesses—can provide useful

EXHIBIT 2.1 **Corporate Strategy Components and Issues**

Strategy Components	Key Issues
Scope, mission, and intent	• What business(es) should the firm be in?
	• What customer needs, market segments, and/or technologies should be focused on?
	• What is the firm's enduring strategic purpose or intent?
Objectives	• What performance dimensions should the firm's business units and employees focus on?
	• What is the target level of performance to be achieved on each dimension?
	• What is the time frame in which each target should be attained?
Source of competitive advantage	• What human, technical, or other resources or competencies available to the firm provide a basis for a sustainable competitive advantage?
Development strategy	• How can the firm achieve a desired level of growth over time?
	• Can the desired growth be attained by expanding the firm's current businesses?
	• Will the company have to diversify into new businesses or product-markets to achieve its future growth objectives?
Resource allocation	• How should the firm's limited financial resources be allocated across its businesses to produce the highest returns?
	• Of the alternative strategies that each business might pursue, which will produce the greatest returns for the dollars invested?
Sources of synergy	• What competencies, knowledge, and customer-based intangibles (e.g., brand recognition, reputation) might be developed and shared across the firm's businesses?
	• What operational resources, facilities, or functions (e.g., plants, R&D, salesforce) might the firm's businesses share to increase their efficiency?

insights to guide decisions concerning all elements of corporate strategy, they are particularly germane for revealing the most attractive avenues for future growth and for determining which businesses or product-markets are likely to produce the greatest returns on the company's resources. In turn, all six components of corporate strategy have major implications for the strategic marketing plans of the firm's various products or services. Together, they define the general strategic direction, objectives, and resource constraints within which those marketing plans must operate. We examine the marketing implications involved in both formulating and implementing these components of corporate strategy in the following sections. Finally, the Marketing Plan Exercise at the end of the chapter asks you to outline the corporate mission, growth strategy, and objectives which will underlie and constrain the plan you develop.

CORPORATE SCOPE—DEFINING THE FIRM'S MISSION

A well-thought-out mission statement guides an organization's managers as to which market opportunities to pursue and which fall outside the firm's strategic domain. A clearly stated mission can help instill a shared sense of direction, relevance, and achievement among employees, as well as a positive image of the firm among customers, investors, and other stakeholders.

To provide a useful sense of direction, a corporate mission statement should clearly define the organization's strategic scope. It should answer such fundamental questions as: What is our business? Who are our customers? What kinds of value can we provide to these customers? What should our business be in the future? For example, several years ago PepsiCo, the manufacturer of Pepsi-Cola, broadened its mission to focus on "marketing superior quality food and beverage products for households and consumers dining out." That clearly defined mission guided the firm's managers toward the acquisition of several related companies, such as Frito-Lay, Taco Bell, and Pizza Hut, and the divestiture of operations that no longer fit the company's primary thrust, like Wilson sporting goods.

More recently, in response to a changing global competitive environment, PepsiCo narrowed its scope to focus primarily on *package* foods (particularly salty snacks) and beverages distributed through supermarket and convenience store channels. This new, narrower mission led the firm to (1) divest all of its fast-food restaurant chains; (2) acquire complementary beverage businesses, such as Tropicana juices, Lipton's iced teas, and Gatorade sports drinks; and (3) develop new brands targeted at rapidly growing beverage segments, such as Aquafina bottled water.

PepsiCo's most recent mission continues to focus on packaged snacks and beverages sold through food retailers but also seeks "performance with purpose." That phrase essentially boils down to balancing the profit motive with the development of healthier, more nutritious snacks and drinks and striving for a net-zero impact on the environment. Consequently, PepsiCo has either acquired or partnered with a Bulgarian nut packager; an Israeli hummus producer; and Naked Juice, a California company that makes nutritional beverages such as smoothies.[2]

Market Influences on the Corporate Mission

Like any other strategy component, an organization's mission should fit both its internal characteristics and the opportunities and threats in its external environment. Obviously, the firm's mission should be compatible with its established values, resources, and distinctive competencies. But it should also focus the firm's efforts on markets where those resources and competencies will generate value for customers, an advantage over competitors, and synergy across its products. Thus, PepsiCo's new mission reflects (1) the firm's package goods marketing, sales, and distribution competencies; (2) its perception that substantial synergies can be realized across snack foods and beverages within supermarket channels via shared logistics, joint displays and sales promotions, cross-couponing, and the like; and (3) a corporate culture that believes the company should be an active player in solving some of the social problems—such as obesity and global warming—the world faces.

Criteria for Defining the Corporate Mission

Several criteria can be used to define an organization's strategic mission. Many firms specify their domain in *physical* terms, focusing on *products* or *services* or the *technology* used. The problem is that such statements can lead to slow reactions to technological or customer-demand changes. For example, Theodore Levitt argues that Penn Central's view of its mission as being "the railroad business" helped cause the firm's failure. Penn Central did not respond to major changes in transportation technology, such as the rapid growth of air travel and the increased efficiency of long-haul trucking. Nor did it respond to consumers' growing willingness to pay higher prices for the increased speed and convenience of air travel. Levitt argues that it is better to define a firm's mission as *what customer needs are to be satisfied and the functions the firm must perform to satisfy them.*[3] Products and technologies change over time, but basic customer needs tend to endure. Thus, if Penn Central had defined its mission as satisfying the transportation needs of its customers rather than simply being a railroad, it might have been more willing to expand its domain to incorporate newer technologies.

One problem with Levitt's advice, though, is that a mission statement focusing only on basic customer needs can be too broad to provide clear guidance and can fail to take into account the firm's specific competencies. If Penn Central had defined itself as a transportation company, should it have diversified into the trucking business? Started an airline? As the upper-right quadrant of Exhibit 2.2 suggests, the most useful mission statements focus on the customer need to be satisfied and the functions that must be performed to satisfy that need, and they are *specific* as to the customer groups and the products or technologies on which to concentrate. Thus, instead of seeing itself as being in the railroad business or as satisfying the transportation needs of all potential customers, Burlington Northern Santa Fe Railroad's mission is to provide long-distance transportation for large-volume producers of low-value, low-density products, such as coal and grain.

Social Values and Ethical Principles

An increasing number of organizations are developing mission statements that also attempt to define the social and ethical boundaries of their strategic domain. Some firms are actively pursuing social programs they believe to be intertwined with their economic objectives, whereas others simply seek to manage their businesses according to the principles of *sustainability*—meeting humanity's needs without harming future generations. For

EXHIBIT 2.2 **Characteristics of Effective Corporate Mission Statements**

	Broad	Specific
Functional Based on customer needs	Transportation business	Long-distance transportation for large-volume producers of low-value, low-density products
Physical Based on existing products or technology	Railroad business	Long-haul, coal-carrying railroad

Source: Adapted from *Strategy Formulation: Analytical Concepts,* 1st edition, by C. W. Hofer and D. Schendel, Thomson Learning, 1978.

example, Unilever has launched a variety of programs to help developing nations wrestle with poverty, water scarcity, and the effects of climate change. The firm's motives are at least as much economic as moral. Some 40 percent of the Dutch-British giant's sales and most of its growth now take place in developing nations, and Unilever food products account for about 10 percent of the world's tea, 30 percent of all spinach, and a large portion of all processed fish. As environmental regulations grow stricter around the world, the firm must invest in green technologies or its leadership in packaged foods, soaps, and other products could be imperiled. "You can't ignore the impact your company has on the community and the environment," points out CEO Patrick Cescau. These days, "it's also about growth and innovation. In the future, it will be the only way to do business."[4]

Unfortunately, many top managers are unsure about what kinds of social programs and principles best fit their organization's resources, competencies, and economic goals. In a recent McKinsey & Co. survey of more than 1,100 top global executives, 79 percent predicted at least some responsibility for dealing with future social and political issues would fall on corporations, but only 3 percent said they currently do a good job dealing with social pressures.[5] Thus, crafting mission statements that specify explicit social values, goals, and programs—with inputs from employees, customers, social interest groups, and other stakeholders—is becoming a more important part of corporate strategic planning.

The ethical principles a firm hopes to abide by in its dealings with customers, suppliers, and employees tend to be more straightforward and specific than the broader issues of social responsibility discussed above. Consequently, roughly two-thirds of U.S. firms have formal codes of ethics, and one in five large firms have formal departments dedicated to encouraging compliance with company ethical standards. At United Technologies, a global defense contractor and engineering firm, 160 business ethics officers monitor the firm's activities and relations with customers, suppliers, and governments around the world.[6]

Outside America, fewer firms have formal ethics bureaucracies. To some extent, this reflects the fact that in other countries governments and organized labor both play a bigger role in corporate life. In Germany, for instance, workers' councils often deal with issues such as sexual equality, race relations, and workers' rights.[7]

Ethics is concerned with the development of moral standards by which actions and situations can be judged. It focuses on those actions that may result in actual or potential harm of some kind (e.g., economic, mental, physical) to an individual, group, or organization.

Particular actions may be legal but not ethical. For instance, extreme and unsubstantiated advertising claims, such as "our product is far superior to Brand X," might be viewed as simply legal puffery engaged in to make a sale, but many marketers (and their customers) view such little white lies as unethical. Thus, ethics is more proactive than the law. Ethical standards attempt to anticipate and avoid social problems, whereas most laws and regulations emerge only after the negative consequences of an action become apparent.[8]

Why Are Ethics Important? The Marketing Implications of Ethical Standards

One might ask why a corporation should take responsibility for providing moral guidance to its managers and employees. Although such a question may be a good topic for philosophical debate, there is a compelling, practical reason for a firm to impose ethical standards to guide employees. Unethical practices can damage the trust between a firm and its suppliers or customers, thereby disrupting the development of long-term exchange relationships and resulting in the likely loss of sales and profits over time. For example, one survey of 135 purchasing managers from a variety of industries found that the more unethical a supplier's sales and marketing practices were perceived to be, the less eager were the purchasing managers to buy from that supplier.[9]

Strategic Issue

Unethical practices can damage the trust between a firm and its suppliers or customers, thereby disrupting the development of long-term exchange relationships and resulting in the likely loss of sales and profits over time.

Unfortunately, not all customers or competing suppliers adhere to the same ethical standards. As a result, marketers sometimes feel pressure to engage in actions that are inconsistent with what they believe to be right, such as paying bribes to win a sale from a potential customer or to ensure needed resources or services from suppliers and government agencies. Such dilemmas are particularly likely to arise as a company moves into global markets involving different cultures and levels of economic development where economic exigencies and ethical standards may be quite different. For example, in a recent survey of over 90,000 business people in 68 different countries, more than one-quarter of respondents reported paying a bribe in the past year. Bribes were most common in sub-Saharan Africa, where more than half of respondents had paid at least one, compared to 23 percent in Latin America, 19 percent in the Western Balkans and Turkey, 5 percent in the European Union and North America, and less than 1 percent in Denmark and Norway.[10]

Getting Caught Can Be Costly

Such inconsistencies in expectations and demands across countries and markets can lead to uncertainty among a firm's employees, and consequently to unethical—and possibly illegal—behavior. We have already seen that customers' perceptions of unethical behavior can damage their positive attitudes and loyalty toward the firm, and thereby reduce future sales revenues. But when employees are caught engaging in unlawful behavior—particularly bribery—by government regulators, fines and penalties can increase the costs dramatically. And those costs have been increasing in recent years as more countries pass strict laws against bribery—such as the Foreign Corrupt Practices Act in the United States and the Bribery Act in the United Kingdom—and as enforcement and fines have increased. For example, in 2009 American courts fined KBR, a construction firm, and Halliburton, its former parent, $579 million for paying bribes to obtain contracts in Nigeria. And they hit Siemens, a German conglomerate, with an $800 million fine, and the German authorities also fined Siemens a similar amount.[11]

Even when the fines imposed are not large, the negative publicity surrounding the exposure of unethical practices can raise doubts about future sales revenues and cash flows, thereby making investors more reluctant to commit funds and reducing the firm's market capitalization. A study of regulatory exposure of deceptive marketing practices in the pharmaceutical industry, for instance, found that the average capitalization loss following a Food and Drug Administration citation was about 1 percent. For a large firm like Pfizer, for example, that would mean a wealth loss of nearly $1 billion.[12]

A company can reduce such problems by spelling out formal social policies and ethical standards in its corporate mission statement and communicating and enforcing those standards. For example, Fluor—a multinational construction firm that earns more than half of its $17 billion revenue overseas—has a strict ethical policy against paying any bribes or kickbacks to win new projects. The firm puts all of its employees through online anticorruption training. Its executives also promote an open-door policy and a hot line for reporting bribe requests and suggesting ways around sticky situations, but employees receive zero tolerance and face tough penalties for any infractions. This dedication to high ethical standards and transparency helped make Flour the world's most admired engineering firm in *Fortune* magazine's survey in 2009.[13]

Unfortunately, it is not always easy to decide what a firm's ethical policies and standards should be. There are multiple philosophical traditions or frameworks that managers might use to evaluate the ethics of a given action. Consequently, different firms or managers can pursue somewhat different ethical standards, particularly across national cultures. Exhibit 2.3 displays a comparison (across three geographic regions) of the proportion of company ethical statements that address a set of specific issues. Note that a larger number of companies in the United States and Europe appear to be more concerned with the ethics

EXHIBIT 2.3 **Issues Addressed by Company Ethics Statements**

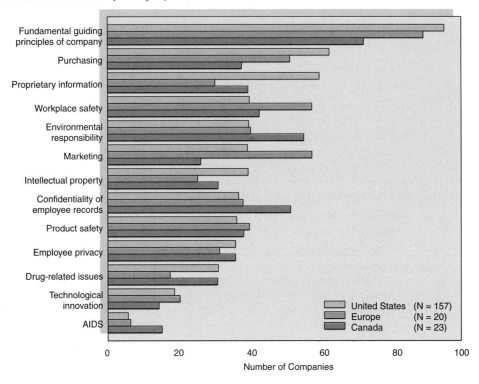

Source: Ronald E. Berenbeim, *Corporate Ethics Practices* (New York: The Conference Board, 1992). Reprinted by permission.

of their purchasing practices than those of their marketing activities. Comparing firms across regions, U.S. companies are more concerned about proprietary information. Canadian firms are more likely to have explicit guidelines concerning environmental responsibility, and European companies more frequently have standards focused on workplace safety. Since many ethical issues in marketing are open to interpretation and debate, we will examine such issues and their implications individually as they arise throughout the remainder of this book.

CORPORATE OBJECTIVES

Confucius said, "For one who has no objective, nothing is relevant." Formal objectives provide decision criteria that guide an organization's business units and employees toward specific dimensions and performance levels. Those same objectives provide the benchmarks against which actual performance can be evaluated.

To be useful as decision criteria and evaluative benchmarks, corporate objectives must be specific and measurable. Therefore, each objective contains four components:

- A *performance dimension* or attribute sought.
- A *measure or index* for evaluating progress.
- A *target or hurdle* level to be achieved.
- A *time frame* within which the target is to be accomplished.

EXHIBIT 2.4 **Common Performance Criteria and Measures That Specify Corporate, Business-Unit, and Marketing Objectives**

Performance Criteria	Possible Measures or Indexes
• Growth	$ sales Unit sales Percent change in sales
• Competitive strength	Market share Brand awareness Brand preference
• Innovativeness	$ sales from new products Percentage of sales from product-market entries introduced within past five years Percentage cost savings from new processes
• Profitability	$ profits Profit as percentage of sales Contribution margin* Return on investment (ROI) Return on net assets (RONA) Return on equity (ROE)
• Utilization of resources	Percent capacity utilization Fixed assets as percentage of sales
• Contribution to owners	Earnings per share Price/earnings ratio
• Contribution to customers	Price relative to competitors Product quality Customer satisfaction Customer retention Customer loyalty Customer lifetime value
• Contribution to employees	Wage rates, benefits Personnel development, promotions Employment stability, turnover
• Contribution to society	$ contributions to charities or community institutions Growth in employment

*Business-unit managers and marketing managers responsible for a product-market entry often have little control over costs associated with corporate overhead, such as the costs of corporate staff or R&D. It can be difficult to allocate those costs to specific strategic business units (SBUs) or products. Consequently, profit objectives at the SBU and product-market level are often stated as a desired *contribution margin* (the gross profit prior to allocating such overhead costs).

Exhibit 2.4 lists some common performance dimensions and measures used in specifying corporate as well as business-unit and marketing objectives. When specifying short-term business-level and marketing objectives, however, two additional dimensions become important: their relevance to higher-level strategies and goals and their attainability. Thus, we find it useful to follow the SMART acronym when specifying objectives at all levels: **s**pecific, **m**easurable, **a**ttainable, **r**elevant, and **t**ime-bound.

Enhancing Shareholder Value: The Ultimate Objective

In recent years, a growing number of executives of publicly held corporations have concluded that the organization's ultimate objective should be to increase its shareholders' economic returns as measured by dividends plus appreciation in the company's stock price.[14] To do so management must balance the interests of various corporate constituencies, including employees, customers, suppliers, debtholders, and stockholders. The firm's continued existence depends on a financial relationship with each of these parties. Employees want competitive wages. Customers want high quality at a competitive price. Suppliers and debtholders have financial claims that must be satisfied with cash when they fall due. Shareholders, as residual claimants, look for cash dividends and the prospect of future dividends reflected in the stock's market price.

If a company does not satisfy its constituents' financial claims, it ceases to be viable. Thus, a going concern must strive to enhance its ability to generate cash from the operation of its businesses and to obtain any additional funds needed from debt or equity financing.

The firm's ability to attain debt financing (its ability to borrow) depends in turn on projections of how much cash it can generate in the future. Similarly, the market value of its shares, and therefore its ability to attain equity financing, depends on investors' expectations of the firm's future cash-generating abilities. People willingly invest in a firm only when they expect a better return on their funds than they could get from other sources without exposing themselves to any greater risks. Thus, management's primary objective should be to pursue capital investments, acquisitions, and business strategies that will produce sufficient future cash flows to return positive value to shareholders. Failure to do so not only will depress the firm's stock price and inhibit the firm's ability to finance future operations and growth, but also it could make the organization more vulnerable to a takeover by outsiders who promise to increase its value to shareholders.

Given this rationale, many firms set explicit objectives targeted at increasing shareholder value. These are usually stated in terms of a target return on shareholder equity, increase in the stock price, or earnings per share. Recently, though, some executives have begun expressing such corporate objectives in terms of *economic value added* or *market value added (MVA)*. A firm's MVA is calculated by combining its debt and the market value of its stock and then subtracting the capital that has been invested in the company. The result, if positive, shows how much wealth the company has created.[15]

Unfortunately, such broad shareholder-value objectives do not always provide adequate guidance for a firm's lower-level managers or benchmarks for evaluating performance. For one thing, standard accounting measures, such as earnings per share or return on investment, are not always reliably linked to the true value of a company's stock.[16] As we shall see later in this chapter, tools are available to evaluate the future impact of alternative strategic actions on shareholder value, but those valuation methods have inherent pitfalls and can be difficult to apply at lower levels of strategy such as trying to choose the best marketing strategy for a particular product-market entry.[17]

Finally, there is a danger that a narrow focus on short-term financial, shareholder-value objectives may lead managers to pay too little attention to actions necessary to provide value to the firm's customers and sustain a competitive advantage.[18] In the long term, customer value and shareholder value converge; a firm can continue to provide attractive returns to shareholders only so long as it satisfies and retains its customers. But some managers may overlook this in the face of pressures to achieve aggressive short-term financial objectives and take cost-cutting actions that reduce product quality, weaken service, and lower customer value and satisfaction.

Strategic Issue

In the long term, customer value and shareholder value converge; a firm can continue to provide attractive returns to shareholders only so long as it satisfies and retains its customers.

The Marketing Implications of Corporate Objectives

Most organizations pursue multiple objectives. This is clearly demonstrated by a study of the stated objectives of 82 large corporations. The largest percentage of respondents (89 percent) had explicit profitability objectives: 82 percent reported growth objectives and 66 percent had specific market-share goals. More than 60 percent mentioned social responsibility, employee welfare, and customer service objectives, and 54 percent of the companies had R&D/new product development goals.[19] These percentages add up to more than 100 percent because most firms had several objectives.

Trying to achieve many objectives at once leads to conflicts and trade-offs. For example, the investment and expenditure necessary to pursue growth in the long term is likely to reduce profitability and ROI in the short term.[20] Managers can reconcile conflicting goals by prioritizing them. Another approach is to state one of the conflicting goals as a constraint or **hurdle.** Thus, a firm attempts to maximize growth subject to meeting some minimum ROI hurdle.

In firms with multiple business units or product lines, however, the most common way to pursue a set of conflicting objectives is to first break them down into subobjectives and then assign different subobjectives to different business units or products. Thus, subobjectives often vary across business units and product offerings depending on the attractiveness and potential of their industries, the strength of their competitive positions, and the resource allocation decisions made by corporate managers. For example, PepsiCo's managers likely set relatively high volume and share-growth objectives but lower ROI goals for the firm's SoBe Lifewater brand, which is battling for prominence in the growing vitamin-enhanced water category, than for Lay's potato chips, which hold a commanding 40 percent share of a mature product category. Therefore, two marketing managers responsible for different products may face very different goals and expectations—requiring different marketing strategies to accomplish—even though they work for the same organization. Unfortunately, such differences in objectives across product offerings at different life-cycle stages can sometimes result in a premature shift of marketing resources away from well-established brands toward the newer entrants. This can result in inadequate promotional support and a loss of market share, as has unfortunately been the case with PepsiCo's flagship Pepsi-Cola in recent years.[21]

As firms emphasize developing and maintaining long-term customer relationships, *customer-focused objectives*—such as satisfaction, retention, and loyalty—are being given greater importance. Such market-oriented objectives are more likely to be consistently pursued across business units and product offerings. There are several reasons for this. First, given the huge profit implications of a customer's lifetime value, maximizing satisfaction and loyalty tends to make good sense no matter what other financial objectives are being pursued in the short term. Second, satisfied, loyal customers of one product can be leveraged to provide synergies for other company products or services. Finally, customer satisfaction and loyalty are influenced by factors other than the product itself or the activities of the marketing department. A study of one industrial paper company, for example, found that about 80 percent of customers' satisfaction scores were accounted for by nonproduct factors, such as order processing, delivery, and postsale services.[22] Since such factors are influenced by many functional departments within the corporation, they are likely to have a similar impact across a firm's various businesses and products.

GAINING A COMPETITIVE ADVANTAGE

There are many ways a company might attempt to gain a competitive advantage over competitors within the scope of its competitive domain. In most cases, though, a *sustainable* competitive advantage at the corporate level is based on company resources, resources that other firms do not have, that take a long time to develop, and that are hard to acquire.[23] Many such unique resources are marketing related. For example, some businesses have highly developed information systems, extensive market research operations, and/or cooperative long-term relationships with customers that give them a superior ability to identify and respond to emerging customer needs and desires. Others have a brand name that customers recognize and trust, cooperative alliances with suppliers or distributors that enhance efficiency, or a body of satisfied and loyal customers who are predisposed to buy related products or services.[24]

But the fact that a company possesses resources that its competitors do not have is not sufficient to guarantee superior performance. The trick is to develop a competitive strategy for each division or business unit within the firm, and a strategic marketing program for each of its product-market entries, that convert one or more of the company's unique resources into something of value to customers. The firm must employ its resources in such a way that customers will have a good reason to purchase from it instead of its competitors. It needs to provide one or more superior benefits at a price similar to what competitors charge or deliver comparable benefits at lower cost. Then it needs to effectively communicate those benefits or cost savings so they will be accurately perceived by potential customers. As we saw in Chapter 1, For example, Samsung spent years developing technical R&D and product design expertise, which it employed effectively to launch a stream of very successful products aimed at upscale, high-margin market segments. The firm also underlook marketing actions aimed at building a brand image that communicates and reinforces its technical and design prowess, including extensive global advertising campaigns and a restructuring of its retail distribution channels to emphasize upscale specialty retailers.

Although one can conceive of a nearly infinite assortment of competitive strategies based on a firm's superior resources and capabilities, most can be classified into a few "generic" types. We devote Chapter 3 to a detailed discussion of these basic competitive strategies and their implications for marketing programs. For now, the key point is that those strategies are built—at least in part—on the firm's marketing-related resources and competencies. To the extent that a single corporate resource—such as a prestigious corporate brand or an excellent salesforce—might serve as the foundation for effective competitive and marketing strategies in more than one of a firm's business units or product lines, it may also produce synergy, as we shall see later.

CORPORATE GROWTH STRATEGIES

Often, the projected combined future sales and profits of a corporation's business units and product-markets fall short of the firm's long-run growth and profitability objectives. There is a gap between what the firm expects to become if it continues on its present course and what it would like to become. This is not surprising because some of its high-growth markets are likely to slip into maturity over time and some of its high-profit mature businesses may decline to insignificance as they get older. Thus, to determine where future growth is coming from, management must decide on a strategy to guide corporate development.

Essentially, a firm can go in two major directions in seeking future growth: **expansion** of its current businesses and activities or **diversification** into new businesses, either through internal business development or acquisition. Exhibit 2.5 outlines some specific options a firm might pursue while seeking growth in either of these directions.

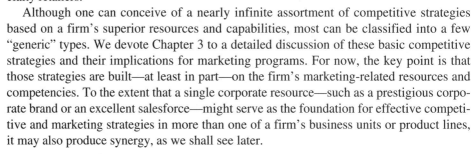

Strategic Issue

A firm can go in two major directions in seeking future growth: expansion of its current businesses and activities or diversification into new businesses.

EXHIBIT 2.5 Alternative Corporat e Growth Strategies

	Current products	New products

Current markets	Market penetration strategies
	
	• Increase market share
	
	• Increase product usage
	  Increase frequency of use
	  Increase quantity used
	  New applications
		Product development strategies
		
		• Product improvements
		
		• Product-line extensions
		
		• New products for same market

New markets	Market development strategies
	
	• Expand markets for existing
	  products
	  Geographic expansion
	  Target new segments
		Diversification strategies
		
		• Vertical integration
		  Forward integration
		  Backward integration
		
		• Diversification into related
		  businesses
		  (concentric diversification)
		
		• Diversification into unrelated
		  businesses
		  (conglomerate diversification)

Expansion by Increasing Penetration of Current Product-Markets

One way for a company to expand is by increasing its share of existing markets. This typically requires actions such as making product or service improvements, cutting costs and prices as Ryanair has done, or outspending competitors on advertising or promotions. Amazon.com pursued a combination of all these actions—as well as forming alliances with web portals, affinity groups, and the like—to expand its share of web shoppers, even though the expense of such activities postponed the firm's ability to become profitable.

Even when a firm holds a commanding share of an existing product-market, additional growth may be possible by encouraging current customers to become more loyal and concentrate their purchases, use more of the product or service, use it more often, or use it in new ways. In addition to its promotional efforts, Amazon.com spent hundreds of millions of dollars early in its development on warehouses, proprietary software, and other order fulfillment and customer service activities, investments that helped earn the loyalty of its customers. As a result, the vast majority of the firm's revenues around the world comes from repeat purchases, and Amazon was ranked as the world's best customer service organization in the annual J. D. Power-Business Week survey in 2009.[25] Other examples include museums that sponsor special exhibitions to encourage patrons to make repeat visits and the recipes that Quaker Oats includes on the package to tempt buyers to include oatmeal as an ingredient in other foods, such as cookies and desserts.

Expansion by Developing New Products for Current Customers

A second avenue to future growth is through a product-development strategy emphasizing the introduction of product-line extensions or new product or service offerings aimed at existing customers. For example, Arm & Hammer successfully introduced a laundry detergent, an oven cleaner, and a carpet cleaner. Each capitalized on baking soda's image as an effective deodorizer and on a high level of recognition of the Arm & Hammer brand. Similarly, Amazon has added a number of independent retail partners to the Amazon .com web site in order to expand the range of products its customers can purchase with one click.

Expansion by Selling Existing Products to New Segments or Countries

Perhaps the growth strategy with the greatest potential for many companies is the development of new markets for their existing goods or services. This may involve the creation of marketing programs aimed at nonuser or occasional-user segments of existing markets. Thus, theaters, orchestras, and other performing arts organizations often sponsor touring companies to reach audiences outside major metropolitan areas and promote matinee performances with lower prices and free public transportation to attract senior citizens and students.

Expansion into new geographic markets, particularly new countries, is also a primary growth strategy for many firms. For example, the strategic plan of Degussa, the large German specialty chemicals manufacturer, calls for greatly increased resources and marketing efforts to be directed toward China over the next few years. As Utz-Hellmuth Felcht—the chairman of the firm's management board—points out, the vast number of untapped potential customers for the firm's products means China offers greater promise for future sales growth than Western Europe and North America combined.[26]

Although developing nations represent attractive growth markets for basic industrial and infrastructure goods and services, growing personal incomes and falling trade barriers are making them attractive potential markets for many consumer goods and services as well. For instance, China is already the world's largest market for flat-panel TVs and will likely become the largest market for smartphones and other electronics products in the near future.

Even developed nations can represent growth opportunities for products or services based on newly emerging technologies or business models. For instance, although total retail sales in the United States will likely grow relatively slowly—if at all—over the next few years, internet sales are projected to grow 50 percent between 2012 and 2015. Therefore, many traditional retailers from Macy's to Marks and Spencer to Walmart are pursuing growth by trying to attract more online customers.[27]

Expansion by Diversifying

Firms also seek growth by diversifying their operations. This is typically riskier than the various expansion strategies because it often involves learning new operations and dealing with unfamiliar customer groups. Nevertheless, the majority of large global firms are diversified to one degree or another.

Vertical integration is one way for companies to diversify. **Forward vertical integration** occurs when a firm moves downstream in terms of the product flow, as when a manufacturer integrates by acquiring or launching a wholesale distributor or retail outlet. For example, most of Europe's fashion houses—like Ermenegeldo Zegna and Georgio Armani—own at least some of their own retail outlets in major cities in order to gain better control over their companies' merchandising programs and more direct feedback from customers. In recent years such integrated retail outlets have also been important for establishing a foothold in developing markets where independent retailers with a prestige image can be in short supply, such as China. Indeed, Zegna now earns 40 percent of its revenue from China.[28] **Backward integration** occurs when a firm moves upstream by acquiring a supplier.

Integration can give a firm access to scarce or volatile sources of supply or tighter control over the marketing, distribution, or servicing of its products. But it increases the risks inherent in committing substantial resources to a single industry. Also, the investment required to vertically integrate often offsets the additional profitability generated by the integrated operations, resulting in little improvement in return on investment.[29]

Related (or concentric) diversification occurs when a firm internally develops or acquires another business that does not have products or customers in common with its current businesses but that might contribute to internal synergy through the sharing of production facilities, brand names, R&D know-how, or marketing and distribution skills. Thus, PepsiCo acquired Cracker Jack to complement its salty snack brands and leverage its distribution strengths in grocery stores.

The motivations for **unrelated (or conglomerate) diversification** are primarily financial rather than operational. By definition, an unrelated diversification involves two businesses that have no commonalities in products, customers, production facilities, or functional areas of expertise. Such diversification mostly occurs when a disproportionate number of a firm's current businesses face decline because of decreasing demand, increased competition, or product obsolescence. The firm must seek new avenues of growth. Other, more fortunate, firms may move into unrelated businesses because they have more cash than they need in order to expand their current businesses or because they wish to discourage takeover attempts.

Unrelated diversification tends to be the riskiest growth strategy in terms of financial outcomes. Most empirical studies report that related diversification is more conducive to capital productivity and other dimensions of performance than is unrelated diversification.[30] This suggests that the ultimate goal of a corporation's strategy for growth should be to develop a compatible portfolio of businesses to which the firm can add value through the application of its unique core competencies. The corporation's marketing competencies can be particularly important in this regard.

Expansion by Diversifying through Organizational Relationships or Networks

Recently, firms have attempted to gain some benefits of market expansion or diversification while simultaneously focusing more intensely on a few core competencies. They try to accomplish this feat by forming relationships or organizational networks with other firms instead of acquiring ownership.[31]

Perhaps the best models of such organizational networks are the Japanese *keiretsu* and the Korean *chaebol*—coalitions of financial institutions, distributors, and manufacturing firms in a variety of industries that are often grouped around a large trading company that helps coordinate the activities of the various coalition members and markets their goods and services around the world. As we have seen, many Western firms, such as IBM, are also forming alliances with suppliers, resellers, and even customers to expand their product and service offerings without making major new investments or neglecting their own core competencies.

ALLOCATING CORPORATE RESOURCES

Diversified organizations have several advantages over more narrowly focused firms. They have a broader range of areas in which they can knowledgeably invest, and their growth and profitability rates may be more stable because they can offset declines in one business with gains in another. To exploit the advantages of diversification, though, corporate managers must make intelligent decisions about how to allocate financial and human resources across the firm's various businesses and product-markets. Three sets of analytical tools have proven useful in making such decisions: **portfolio models, value-based planning,** and **models that measure customer equity** to estimate the value of alternative marketing actions.

Portfolio Models

One of the most significant developments in strategic management during the 1970s and 1980s was the widespread adoption of portfolio models to help managers allocate corporate resources across multiple businesses. These models enable managers to classify and review their current and prospective businesses by viewing them as portfolios of investment opportunities and then evaluating each business's competitive strength and the attractiveness of the markets it serves.

The Boston Consulting Group's (BCG) Growth-Share Matrix

One of the first—and best known—of the portfolio models is the growth-share matrix developed by the Boston Consulting Group. It analyzes the impact of investing resources in different businesses on the corporation's future earnings and cash flows. Each business is positioned within a matrix, as shown in Exhibit 2.6. The vertical axis indicates the industry's growth rate, and the horizontal axis shows the business's relative market share.

The growth-share matrix assumes that a firm must generate cash from businesses with strong competitive positions in mature markets. Then it can fund investments and expenditures in industries that represent attractive future opportunities. Thus, the **market growth rate** on the vertical axis is a proxy measure for the maturity and attractiveness of an industry. This model represents businesses in rapidly growing industries as more attractive investment opportunities for future growth and profitability.

Similarly, a business's **relative market share** is a proxy for its competitive strength within its industry. It is computed by dividing the business's absolute market share in dollars or units by that of the leading competitor in the industry. Thus, in Exhibit 2.6 a

EXHIBIT 2.6 **BCG's Market Growth Relative Share Matrix**

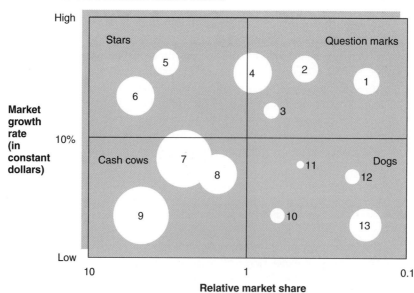

Source: Reprinted from *Long Range Planning,* Volume 10, pp. 9–15, Barry Hedley, "Strategy and the Business Portfolio," Copyright 1977, with permission from Elsevier.

business is in a strong competitive position if its share is equal to, or larger than, that of the next leading competitor (i.e., a relative share of 1.0 or larger). Finally, in the exhibit, the size of the circle representing each business is proportional to that unit's sales volume. Thus, businesses 7 and 9 are the largest-volume businesses in this hypothetical company, whereas business 11 is the smallest.

Resource Allocation and Strategy Implications

Each of the four cells in the growth-share matrix represents a different type of business with different strategy and resource requirements. The implications of each are discussed below and summarized in Exhibit 2.7.

- *Question marks.* Businesses in high-growth industries with low relative market shares (those in the upper-right quadrant of Exhibit 2.7) are called *question marks* or *problem children.* Such businesses require large amounts of cash, not only for expansion to keep up with the rapidly growing market, but also for marketing activities (or reduced margins) to build market share and catch the industry leader. If management can successfully increase the share of a question mark business, it becomes a star. But if managers fail, it eventually turns into a dog as the industry matures and the market growth rate slows.
- *Stars.* A *star* is the market leader in a high-growth industry. Stars are critical to the continued success of the firm. As their industries mature, they move into the bottom-left quadrant and become cash cows. Paradoxically, although stars are critically important, they often are net users rather than suppliers of cash in the short run (as indicated by the possibility of a negative cash flow shown in Exhibit 2.7). This is because the firm must continue to invest in such businesses to keep up with rapid market growth and to support the R&D and marketing activities necessary to maintain a leading market share.
- *Cash cows.* Businesses with a high relative share of low-growth markets are called *cash cows* because they are the primary generators of profits and cash in a corporation. Such businesses do not require much additional capital investment. Their markets are stable, and their share leadership position usually means they enjoy economies of scale

EXHIBIT 2.7 **Cash Flows across Businesses in the BCG Portfolio Model**

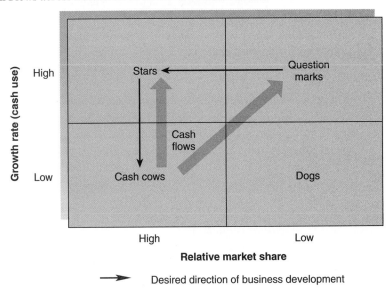

and relatively high profit margins. Consequently, the corporation can use the cash from these businesses to support its question marks and stars (as shown in Exhibit 2.7). However, this does not mean the firm should necessarily maximize the business's short-term cash flow by cutting R&D and marketing expenditures to the bone—particularly not in industries where the business might continue to generate substantial future sales.

- *Dogs.* Low-share businesses in low-growth markets are called *dogs* because although they may throw off some cash, they typically generate low profits, or losses. Divestiture is one option for such businesses, although it can be difficult to find an interested buyer. Another common strategy is to harvest dog businesses. This involves maximizing short-term cash flow by paring investments and expenditures until the business is gradually phased out.

Limitations of the Growth-Share Matrix

Because the growth-share matrix uses only two variables as a basis for categorizing and analyzing a firm's businesses, it is relatively easy to understand. But this simplicity helps explain its popularity, it also means the model has limitations:

- *Market growth rate is an inadequate descriptor of overall industry attractiveness.* Market growth is not always directly related to profitability or cash flow. Some high-growth industries have never been very profitable because low entry barriers and capital intensity have enabled supply to grow even faster, resulting in intense competition. Groupon and a host of other internet coupon sites currently face this dilemma.[32] Also, rapid growth in one year is no guarantee that growth will continue in the following year.

- *Relative market share is inadequate as a description of overall competitive strength.* Market share is more properly viewed as an outcome of past efforts to formulate and implement effective business-level and marketing strategies than as an indicator of enduring competitive strength.[33] If the external environment changes or the SBU's managers change their strategy, the business's relative market share can shift dramatically.

- *The outcomes of a growth-share analysis are highly sensitive to variations in how growth and share are measured.*[34] Defining the relevant industry and served market (i.e., the target-market segments being pursued) also can present problems. For example, does Pepsi-Cola compete only for a share of the cola market or for a share of the much larger market for nonalcoholic beverages, such as iced tea, bottled water, and fruit juices?

- *While the matrix specifies appropriate investment strategies for each business, it provides little guidance on how best to implement those strategies.* While the model suggests that a firm should invest cash in its question mark businesses, for instance, it does not consider whether there are any potential sources of competitive advantage that the business can exploit to successfully increase its share. Simply providing a business with more money does not guarantee that it will be able to improve its position within the matrix.

- *The model implicitly assumes that all business units are independent of one another except for the flow of cash.* If this assumption is inaccurate, the model can suggest some inappropriate resource allocation decisions. For instance, if other SBUs depend on a dog business as a source of supply—or if they share functional activities, such as a common plant or salesforce, with that business—harvesting the dog might increase the costs or reduce the effectiveness of the other SBUs.

Alternative Portfolio Models

In view of the preceding limitations, a number of firms have attempted to improve the basic portfolio model. Such improvements have focused primarily on developing more detailed, multifactor measures of industry attractiveness and a business's competitive strength and on making the analysis more future-oriented. Corporate managers must first select factors appropriate for their firm—such as industry size, competitive intensity, customer loyalty, R&D spending, and the like—and weight them according to their relative importance. They then rate each business and its industry on the two sets of factors. Next, they combine the weighted evaluations into summary measures used to place each business within one of the cells in the growth-share matrix.

These multifactor models are more detailed than the simple growth-share model and consequently provide more strategic guidance concerning the appropriate allocation of resources across businesses. They are also more useful for evaluating potential new product-markets. However, the multifactor measures in these models can be subjective and ambiguous, especially when managers must evaluate different industries on the same set of factors. Also, the conclusions drawn from these models still depend on the way industries and product-markets are defined.[35]

Value-Based Planning

As mentioned, one limitation of portfolio analysis is that it specifies how firms should allocate financial resources across their businesses without considering the competitive strategies those businesses are, or should be, pursuing. Portfolio analysis provides little guidance, for instance, in deciding which of two question mark businesses—each in attractive markets but following different strategies—is worthy of the greater investment or in choosing which of several competitive strategies a particular business unit should pursue.

Value-based planning is a resource allocation tool that attempts to address such questions by assessing the shareholder value a given strategy is likely to create. Thus, value-based planning provides a basis for comparing the economic returns to be gained from investing in different businesses pursuing different strategies or from alternative strategies that might be adopted by a given business unit.

A number of value-based planning methods are currently in use, but all share three basic features.[36] First, they assess the economic value a strategy is likely to produce by examining the cash flows it will generate, rather than relying on distorted accounting measures, such as return on investment.[37] Second, they estimate the shareholder value that a strategy will produce by discounting its forecasted cash flows by the business's risk-adjusted cost of capital. Finally, they evaluate strategies based on the likelihood that the investments required by a strategy will deliver returns greater than the cost of capital. The amount of return a strategy or operating program generates in excess of the cost of capital is commonly referred to as its **economic value added,** or EVA.[38] This approach to evaluating alternative strategies is particularly appropriate for use in allocating resources across business units because most capital investments are made at the business-unit level, and different business units typically face different risks and therefore have different costs of capital.

Discounted Cash Flow Model

Perhaps the best-known and most widely used approach to value-based planning is the discounted cash flow model proposed by Alfred Rappaport and the Alcar Group, Inc. In this model, as Exhibit 2.8 indicates, shareholder value created by a strategy is determined by the cash flow it generates, the business's cost of capital (which is used to discount future cash flows back to their present value), and the market value of the debt assigned to the business. The future cash flows generated by the strategy are, in turn, affected by six "value drivers": the rate of sales growth the strategy will produce, the operating profit margin, the income tax rate, investment in working capital, fixed capital investment required by the strategy, and the duration of value growth.

The first five value drivers are self-explanatory, but the sixth requires some elaboration. The duration of value growth represents management's estimate of the number of years

EXHIBIT 2.8 **Factors Affecting the Creation of Shareholder Value**

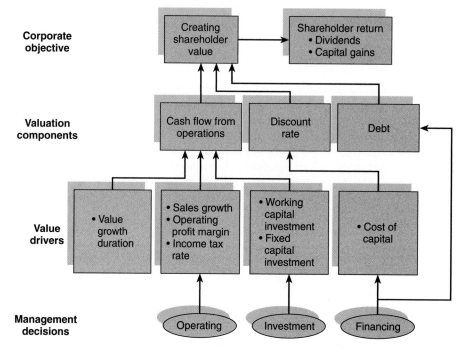

over which the strategy can be expected to produce rates of return that exceed the cost of capital. This estimate, in turn, is tied to two other management judgments. First, the manager must decide on the length of the planning period (typically three to five years); he or she must then estimate the residual value the strategy will continue to produce after the planning period is over. Such decisions are tricky, for they involve predictions of what will happen in the relatively distant future.[39]

Some Limitations of Value-Based Planning[40]

Value-based planning is not a substitute for strategic planning; it is only one tool for evaluating strategy alternatives identified and developed through managers' judgments. It does so by relying on forecasts of many kinds to put a financial value on the hopes, fears, and expectations managers associate with each alternative. Projections of cash inflows rest on forecasts of sales volume, product mix, unit prices, and competitors' actions. Expected cash outflows depend on projections of various cost elements, working capital, and investment requirements.

While good forecasts are notoriously difficult to make, they are critical to the validity of value-based planning. Once someone attaches numbers to judgments about what is likely to happen, people tend to endow those numbers with the concreteness of hard facts. Therefore, the numbers derived from value-based planning can sometimes take on a life of their own, and managers can lose sight of the assumptions underlying them.

Consequently, inaccurate forecasts can create problems in implementing value-based planning. For one thing, there are natural human tendencies to overvalue the financial projections associated with some strategy alternatives and to undervalue others. For instance, managers are likely to overestimate the future returns from a currently successful strategy.

Evidence of past success tends to carry more weight than qualitative assessments of future threats. Managers may pay too little attention to how competitive behavior, prices, and returns might change if, for example, the industry were suddenly beset by a slowdown in market growth and the appearance of excess capacity.

Strategic Issue

Some kinds of strategy alternatives are consistently undervalued. Particularly worrisome from a marketing viewpoint is the tendency to underestimate the value of keeping current customers.

On the other hand, some kinds of strategy alternatives are consistently undervalued. Particularly worrisome from a marketing viewpoint is the tendency to underestimate the value of keeping current customers. Putting a figure on the damage to a firm's competitive advantage from *not* making a strategic investment necessary to maintain the status quo is harder than documenting potential cost savings or profit improvements that an investment might generate. For example, a few years ago Cone Drive Operations, a small manufacturer of heavy-duty gears, faced a number of related problems. Profits were declining, inventory costs were climbing, and customers were unhappy because deliveries were often late. Cone's management thought that a $2 million computer-integrated manufacturing system might help solve these problems, but a discounted cash flow analysis indicated the system would be an unwise investment. Because the company had only $26 million in sales, it was hard to justify the $2 million investment in terms of cost savings. However, the financial analysis underestimated intangibles such as improved product quality, faster order processing, and improved customer satisfaction. Management decided to install the new system anyway, and new business and nonlabor savings paid back the investment in just one year. More important, Cone retained nearly all of its old customers, many of whom had been seriously considering switching to other suppliers.

Finally, another kind of problem involved in implementing value-based planning occurs when management fails to consider all the appropriate strategy alternatives. Since it is only an analytical tool, value-based planning can evaluate alternatives, but it cannot create them. The best strategy will never emerge from the evaluation process if management fails to identify it. To realize its full benefits, then, management must link value-based planning to sound strategic analysis that is rigorous enough to avoid the problems associated with undervaluing certain strategies, overvaluing others, and failing to consider all the options.

Using Customer Equity to Estimate the Value of Alternative Marketing Actions

A recent variation of value-based planning attempts to overcome some of the preceding limitations—particularly the inaccuracy of subjective forecasts and managers' tendency to overestimate or underestimate the value of particular actions—and is proving useful for evaluating alternative marketing strategies. This approach calculates the economic return for a prospective marketing initiative based on its likely impact on the firm's customer equity, which is the sum of the lifetime values of its current and future customers.[41] Each customer's lifetime value is estimated from data about the frequency of their purchases in the category, the average quantity purchased, and historical brand-switching patterns, combined with the firm's contribution margin. The necessary purchase data can be gotten from the firm's sales records, whereas brand-switching patterns can be estimated either from longitudinal panel data or survey data similar to that collected in customer satisfaction studies. Because market and competitive conditions, and therefore customer perceptions and behaviors, change over time, however, the underlying data needs to be updated on a regular basis—perhaps once or twice a year.

The impact of a firm's or business unit's past marketing actions on customer equity can be statistically estimated from historical data. This enables managers to identify the financial impact of alternative marketing "value drivers" of customer equity, such as brand advertising, quality or service improvements, loyalty programs, and the like. Once a manager calculates the implementation costs and capital requirements involved, it is then possible to estimate the financial return for any similar marketing initiative in the near future.

When dealing with organizational customers, an additional set of variables—characteristics of the interfirm relationship, such as trust, commitment, and the number and decision-making authority of contacts within the customer firm—can also impact customer equity and value over time. For example, increasing the number of contacts called upon within customer organizations experiencing relatively high employee turnover tends to increase the financial returns from those companies.[42] Therefore, alternative customer relationship management policies should be evaluated along with the other marketing "value drivers" when designing marketing strategies for organizational markets.

SOURCES OF SYNERGY

A final strategic concern at the corporate level is to increase synergy across the firm's various businesses and product-markets. As mentioned, synergy exists when two or more businesses or product-markets and their resources and competencies complement and reinforce one another so that the total performance of the related businesses is greater than it would be otherwise.

Knowledge-Based Synergies

Some potential synergies at the corporate level are knowledge-based. The performance of one business can be enhanced by the transfer of competencies, knowledge, or customer-related intangibles—such as brand-name recognition and reputation—from other units within the firm. For instance, the technical knowledge concerning image processing and the quality reputation that Canon developed in the camera business helped ease the firm's entry into the office copier business.

In part, such knowledge-based synergies are a function of the corporation's scope and mission—or how its managers answer the question: What businesses should we be in? When a firm's portfolio of businesses and product-markets reflects a common mission based on well-defined customer needs, market segments, or technologies, the company is more likely to develop core competencies, customer knowledge, and strong brand franchises that can be shared across businesses. However, the firm's organizational structure and allocation of resources also may enhance knowledge-based synergy. A centralized corporate R&D department, for example, is often more efficient and effective at discovering new technologies with potential applications across multiple businesses than if each business unit bore the burden of funding its own R&D efforts. Similarly, some argue that strong corporate-level coordination and support are necessary to maximize the strength of a firm's brand franchise and to glean full benefit from accumulated market knowledge, when the firm is competing in global markets.

Corporate Identity and the Corporate Brand as a Source of Synergy

Corporate identity—together with a strong corporate brand that embodies that identity—can help a firm stand out from its competitors and give it a sustainable advantage in the market. *Corporate identity* flows from the communications, impressions, and personality projected by an organization. It is shaped by the firm's mission and values, its functional competencies, the quality and design of its goods and services, its marketing communications, the actions of its personnel, the image generated by various corporate activities, and other factors.[43]

In order to project a positive, strong, and consistent identity, firms as diverse as Caterpillar, Walt Disney, and The Body Shop have established formal policies, criteria, and guidelines to help ensure that all the messages and sensory images they communicate reflect their unique values, personality, and competencies. One rationale for such corporate identity programs is that they can generate synergies that enhance the effectiveness and efficiency of the firm's marketing efforts for its individual product offerings. By focusing on a common core of corporate values and competencies, every impression generated by each product's design, packaging, advertising, and promotional materials can help reinforce and strengthen the impact of all the other impressions the firm communicates to its customers, employees, shareholders, and other audiences and thereby generate a bigger bang for its limited marketing bucks. For example, by consistently focusing on values and competencies associated with providing high-quality family entertainment, Disney has created an identity that helps stimulate customer demand across a wide range of product offerings—from movies to TV programs to licensed merchandise to theme parks and cruise ships.

Corporate Branding Strategy—When Does a Strong Corporate Brand Make Sense?

Before a company's reputation and corporate image can have any impact—either positive or negative—on customers' purchase decisions, those customers must be aware of which specific product or service offerings are sponsored by the company. This is where the firm's corporate branding strategy enters the picture. Essentially, a firm might pursue one of three options concerning the corporate brand:[44]

1. The corporate brand (typically the company's own name and logo) might serve as the brand name of all or most of the firm's products in markets around the world, as is the case with many high-tech (e.g., Cisco Systems, Siemens, IBM) and service (e.g., British Airways, Amazon.com) companies.
2. The firm might adopt a dual branding strategy where each offering carries both a corporate identifier and an individual product brand. Examples include Microsoft software products (e.g., Microsoft Windows, Microsoft Word, etc.) and Volkswagen automobiles.
3. Finally, each product offering might be given a unique brand and identity—perhaps even different brands across different global markets—whereas the identity of the source company is de-emphasized or hidden. This is the strategy pursued by Procter and Gamble, Unilever, and many other consumer package goods firms.

The question is when does it make sense to emphasize—and seek to gain synergy from—a strong corporate identity and brand name in a company's branding strategy. Surprisingly, this question has not been subjected to much empirical research.[45] However, some of the conditions favoring a dominant corporate brand are rather obvious. For instance, the corporate brand will not add much value to the firm's offerings unless the company has a strong and favorable image and reputation among potential customers in at least most of its target markets. Thus, the 3M Company features the 3M logo prominently on virtually all of its 60,000 products because the firm's reputation for innovativeness and reliability is perceived positively by many of its potential customers regardless of what they are buying.

A related point is that a strong corporate brand makes most sense when company-level competencies or resources are primarily responsible for generating the benefits and value customers receive from its various individual offerings. For example, many service organizations (e.g., Cathay Pacific, Disney, Marriot, etc.) emphasize their corporate brands. This is due, in part, to the fact that services are relatively intangible and much of their value is directly generated by the actions of company personnel and facilitated by other firm-specific resources, such as its physical facilities, employee training and reward programs, quality control systems, and the like.

Finally, an exploratory study based on interviews with managers in 11 Fortune 500 companies suggests that a firm is more likely to emphasize a strong corporate brand when its various product offerings are closely interrelated, either in terms of having similar positionings in the market or cross-product elasticities that might be leveraged to encourage customers to buy multiple products from the firm.[46] The study also found that firms with strong corporate brands tended to have more centralized decision-making structures where top management made more of the marketing strategy decisions. The obvious question, of course, is whether a firm's decision-making structure influences brand strategy, or vice versa. We will explore such organization design issues and their marketing strategy implications in more detail later in Chapter 12.

Synergy from Shared Resources

A second potential source of corporate synergy is inherent in sharing operational resources, facilities, and functions across business units. For instance, two or more businesses might produce products in a common plant or use a single salesforce to contact common customers. When such sharing helps increase economies of scale or experience-curve effects, it can improve the efficiency of each of the businesses involved. However, the sharing of operational facilities and functions may not produce positive synergies for all business units. Such sharing can limit a business's flexibility and reduce its ability to adapt quickly to changing market conditions and opportunities. Thus, a business whose competitive strategy is focused on new-product development and the pursuit of rapidly changing markets may be hindered more than helped when it is forced to share operating resources with other units.[47] For instance, when Frito-Lay attempted to enter the packaged cookie market with its Grandma's line of soft cookies, the company relied on its 10,000 salty-snack route salespeople to distribute the new line to grocery stores. The firm thought its huge and well-established snack salesforce would give its cookies a competitive advantage in gaining shelf space and retailer support. But because those salespeople were paid a commission on their total sales revenue, they were reluctant to take time from their salty-snack products to push the new cookies. The resulting lack of a strong sales effort contributed to Grandma's failure to achieve a sustainable market share.

As we shall see in Chapter 3, the type of competitive strategy a business unit chooses to pursue can have a number of implications for corporate-level decisions concerning organizational structure and resource allocation as well as for the marketing strategies and programs employed within the business.

<hr>

Marketing Plan Exercise

Write a draft mission statement for your company.

Identify which (if any) of the growth strategies identified in Exhibit 2.5 your plan will pursue, based on your still very preliminary thinking. Determine why that strategy does or does not make sense, compared to the other alternatives.

Set the objectives that your plan or project is intended to accomplish, measured in terms of sales and/or market share and profit contribution, over a specified time frame.

Discussion Questions

1. The Kelly Bottling Company, located in a large metropolitan area of some 5 million people, produced and marketed a line of carbonated beverages consisting mainly of flavored soft drinks (not including colas), soda water, and tonics. They were sold in different types of packages and sizes to a wide variety of retail accounts. How might such a company expand its revenues by pursuing each of the different expansion strategies discussed in Exhibit 2.5?

2. Which diversification strategy is illustrated by each of the following acquisitions? What synergies or benefits might each purchase produce?
   a. A packaged food company's acquisition of a fast-food company that features hamburgers and french fries.
   b. A large retailer's purchase of an interest in a company producing small appliances.
   c. A tobacco company's acquisition of a beer company.
   d. An oil company's acquisition of an insurance company.

3. Critics argue that the BCG portfolio model sometimes provides misleading advice concerning how resources should be allocated across SBUs or product markets. What are some of the possible limitations of the model? What might a manager do to reap the benefits of portfolio analysis while avoiding at least some shortcomings you have identified?

Self-diagnostic questions to test your ability to apply the concepts in this chapter can be found at this book's website at **www.mhhe.com/walker8e.**

Endnotes

1. This case example is based on material found in Andrea Felsted, "The Ryanair Advantage: Airport Charges and Maintenance," *Financial Times,* December 12, 2002, p. 19; "Lining Up for Profits," *The Economist,* November 12, 2005, pp. 71–73; Mark Scott, "Ryanair Faces Future Trouble," **www.businessweek.com/globalbiz,** June 6, 2008; Suzanne Kapner, "Flying the Unfriendly Skies," *Fortune,* July 7, 2008, p. 30; Felix Gillette, "The Duke of Discomfort," *Bloomberg Businessweek,* September 6, 2010, pp. 58–61; and Ryanair's 2011 annual report available at *www.ryanair.com.*

2. John A. Byrne, "PepsiCo's New Formula," *BusinessWeek,* April 10, 2000, pp. 172–84; Katrina Brooker, "The Pepsi Machine," *Fortune,* February 6, 2006, pp. 68–72; Betsy Morris, "The Pepsi Challenge: Can This Snack and Soda Giant Go Healthy?" *Fortune,* March 3, 2008, pp. 55–66; Beth Kowitt, "PepsiCo's Indra Nooyi: Niche Brands are the Future," www.fortune.cnn.com. October 5, 2010; and Duane Stanford, "At Pepsi, a Renewed Focus on Pepsi," *Bloomberg Businessweek,* February 6–February 12, 2012, pp. 25–26.

3. Theodore Levitt, "Marketing Myopia," *Harvard Business Review,* July–August 1960, pp. 455–56.

4. Pete Engardio, "Beyond the Green Corporation," *BusinessWeek,* January 29, 2007, p. 52. For additional examples, see Daniel Franklin, "Just Good Business," A Special Report on Corporate Social Responsibility," *The Economist,* January 19, 2008, pp. SR3–SR22.

5. Engardio, "Beyond the Green Corporation," p. 64.

6. "Good Grief," *The Economist,* April 8, 1995, p. 57; "Doing Well by Doing Good," *The Economist,* April 22, 2000, pp. 65–67; and Joseph Weber, "The New Ethics Enforcers," *BusinessWeek,* February 13, 2006, pp. 76–77.

7. "Doing Well by Doing Good," p. 66.

8. Robert A. Cooke, *Ethics in Business: A Perspective* (Chicago: Arthur Andersen, 1988).

9. I. Fredrick Trawick, John E. Swan, Gail W. McGee, and David R. Rink, "Influence of Buyer Ethics and Salesperson Behavior on Intention to Choose a Supplier," *Journal of the Academy of Marketing Science* 19 (Winter 1991), pp. 17–23.

10. Maria Ermakova and Chris Spillane, "Corruption Rises Over Three Years, More People Paid Bribes," www.bloomberg.com/news, December 10, 2010.

11. Ungreasing the Wheels, The Global Crackdown on Corporate Bribery," *The Economist,* November 21, 2009, pp. 68–69. Also see Dionne Searcey, "U.K. Law on Bribes Has Firms in a Sweat," www.WSJ.com/law, December 28, 2010; and James Surowiecki, "Invisible Hand, Greased Palm," *The New Yorker,* May 14, 2012, p. 44.

12. Martha Myslinski Tipton, Sundar G. Bharadwaj, and Diana C. Robertson, "Regulatory Exposure of Deceptive Marketing and Its Impact on Firm Value," *Journal of Marketing* 73 (November 2009), pp. 227–243.

13. Mina Kimes, "Fluor's Corporate Crime Fighter," *Fortune,* February 16, 2009, p. 26.

14. Alfred Rappaport, *Creating Shareholder Value: The New Standard for Business Performance* (New York: Free Press, 1986), chap. 1; and Shawn Tully, "America's Best Wealth Creators," *Fortune,* November 28, 1994, pp. 143–62.

15. Tully, "America's Best Wealth Creators," p. 143.

16. Bradley T. Gale and Donald J. Swire, "The Tricky Business of Measuring Wealth," *Planning Review,* March–April 1988, pp. 14–17, 47.

17. Patrick Barwise, Paul R. Marsh, and Robin Wensley, "Must Finance and Strategy Clash?" *Harvard Business Review,* September–October 1989, pp. 85–90; and George S. Day and Liam Fahey, "Putting Strategy into Shareholder Value Analysis," *Harvard Business Review,* March–April 1990, pp. 156–62.

18. "Debate: Duking It Out over EVA," *Fortune,* August 4, 1997, p. 232. For an approach that estimates the impact of various marketing actions on customer equity as a means of evaluating their financial returns, see Roland T. Rust, Katherine N. Lemon, and Valarie Zeithaml, "Return on Marketing: Using Customer Equity to Focus Marketing Strategy," *Journal of Marketing* 68 (January 2004), pp. 109–27; and Roland T. Rust, Tim Ambler, Gregory S. Carpenter, V. Kumar, and Rajendra K. Srivastava, "Measuring Marketing Productivity: Current Knowledge and Future Directions," *Journal of Marketing* 68 (October 2004), pp. 76–89.

19. Y. K. Shetty, "New Look at Corporate Goals," *California Management Review* 12 (Winter 1979), pp. 71–79; see also Robert S. Kaplan and David P. Norton, "Using the Balanced Scorecard as a Strategic Management System," *Harvard Business Review* 74 (January–February 1996), pp. 75–85.

20. Gordon Donaldson, *Managing Corporate Wealth* (New York: Praeger, 1984). See also Kaplan and Norton, "Using the Balanced Scorecard," and Rajendra K. Srivastava, Tasadduq A. Shervani, and Liam Fahey, "Marketing, Business Processes, and Shareholder Value: An Organizationally Embedded View of Marketing Activities and the Discipline of Marketing," *Journal of Marketing* 63 (Special Issue 1999), pp. 168–79.

21. Duane Stanford, "At Pepsi, a Renewed Focus on Pepsi."

22. Daniel P. Finkelman, "Crossing the 'Zone of Indifference,'" *Marketing Management* 2, no. 3 (1993), pp. 22–31. See also Jena McGregor, "Would You Recommend Us?" *BusinessWeek,* January 30, 2006, pp. 94–95; and Paul E. Farris, Neil T. Bendle, Phillip E. Pfeifer, and David J. Reibstein, *Marketing Metrics: 50+ Metrics Every Executive Should Master* (Philadelphia: Wharton School Publishing, 2006).

23. Jay B. Barney, "Firm Resources and Sustained Competitive Advantage," *Journal of Management* 17 (1991), pp. 99–120; and Margaret A. Peteraf, "The Cornerstone of Competitive Advantage: A Resource-Based View," *Strategic Management Journal* 14 (1993), pp. 179–92. Also see Shelby D. Hunt and Robert M. Morgan, "The Comparative Advantage Theory of Competition," *Journal of Marketing* 59 (April 1995).

24. George S. Day, "The Capabilities of Market-Driven Organizations," *Journal of Marketing* 58 (October 1994), pp. 37–52; George S. Day and Prakash Nedungadi, "Managerial Representations of Competitive Advantage," *Journal of Marketing* 58 (April 1994), pp. 31–44; and George S. Day, *Creating a Superior Customer-Relating Capability,* Report No. 03-101 (Cambridge, MA: Marketing Science Institute, 2003).

25. Heather Green, "How Amazon Aims to Keep You Clicking," *BusinessWeek,* March 2, 2009, pp. 34–40.

26. Interview with Mr. Utz-Hellmuth Felcht transcribed on Knowledge@Wharton, **www.knowledge.wharton.upenn.edu**, September 7, 2005.

27. "Making It Click," *The Economist,* February 25, 2012, pp. 75–76.

28. Clay Chandler, "China Deluxe: Armani, Mercedes, Dior, Cartier—Luxury Brands Are Rushing into China's Red-Hot Market," *Fortune,* July 26, 2004, pp. 148–56; and Carol Matlack and Eugene Tang, "Luxury Clothier Zegna's Marco Polo Moment," *BusinessWeek,* June 14, 2010, pp. 18–19.

29. Robert D. Buzzell and Bradley T. Gale, *The PIMS Principles: Linking Strategy to Performance* (New York: Free Press, 1987), chap. 8.

30. For a more comprehensive review of the evidence concerning the effects of diversification on firm performance, see Roger A. Kerin, Vijay Mahajan, and P. Rajan Varadarajan, *Contemporary Perspectives on Strategic Market Planning* (Boston: Allyn and Bacon, 1990), chap. 6.

31. For example, see Ravi S. Achrol and Philip Kotler, "Marketing in the Network Economy," *Journal of Marketing* 63 (Special Issue 1999), pp. 146–63.

32. Miguel Helft, "Meet the anti-Groupon," www.tech.fortune.cnn.com, April 30, 2012.

33. Robert Jacobson argues that market share and profitability are joint outcomes from successful strategies and, further, that management skills likely have the greatest impact on profitability. See "Distinguishing among Competing Theories of the Market Share Effect," *Journal of Marketing* 52 (October 1988), pp. 68–80.

34. Yoram Wind, Vijay Mahajan, and Donald J. Swire, "An Empirical Comparison of Standardized Portfolio Models," *Journal of Marketing* 47 (Spring 1983), pp. 89–99.

35. For a more detailed discussion of the uses and limitations of multifactor portfolio models, see Kerin, Mahajan, and Varadarajan, *Contemporary Perspectives on Strategic Market Planning,* chap. 3.

36. The discounted cash flow model is the approach focused on in this chapter. It is detailed in Alfred Rappaport, *Creating Shareholder Value: A New Standard for Business Performance* (New York: Free Press, 1986).

37. For a detailed discussion of the shortcomings of accounting data for determining the value created by a strategy, see Rappaport, *Creating Shareholder Value,* chap. 2.

38. For a more detailed discussion of EVA and some practical examples, see Shawn Tully, "The Real Key to Creating Wealth," *Fortune,* September 20, 1993, pp. 38–50; and Terrence P. Pare, "The New Champ of Wealth Creation," *Fortune,* September 18, 1995, pp. 131–32.

39. A more in-depth discussion of the forecasts and other procedures used in value-based planning can be found in Rappaport, *Creating Shareholder Value,* or Kerin, Mahajan, and Varadarajan, *Contemporary Perspectives on Strategic Market Planning,* chap. 9.

40. The limitations of value-based planning are discussed in more detail in George S. Day and Liam Fahey, "Putting Strategy into Shareholder Value Analysis," *Harvard Business Review,* March–April, 1990, pp. 156–62.

41. Rust, Lemon, and Zeithaml, "Return on Marketing: Using Customer Equity to Focus Marketing Strategy." Also see Verena Vogel, Heiner Evanschitzky, and B. Ramaseshan, "Customer Equity Drivers and Future Sales," *Journal of Marketing* 72 (November 2008), pp. 98–108; and V. Kumar and Denish Shah, "Expanding the Role of Marketing: From Customer Equity to Market Capitalization," *Journal of Marketing* 73 (November 2009), pp. 119–136.

42. Robert W. Palmatier, "Interfirm Relational Drivers of Customer Value," *Journal of Marketing* 72 (July 2008), pp. 76–89.

43. Wally Olins, *Corporate Identity* (Cambridge, MA: Harvard Business School Press, 1993).

44. For a more detailed typology of brand strategies or "architectures," see David A. Aaker and Erich Joachimsthaler, *Brand Leadership* (New York: Free Press, 2000).

45. For one recent exception, see Neil Morgan and Lopo L. Rego, "Brand Portfolio Strategy and Firm Performance," *Journal of Marketing* 73 (January 2009), pp. 59–74.

46. Gabriel J. Biehal and Daniel A. Sheinin, *Building Corporate Brands: An Exploratory Study,* Report 01–100 (Cambridge, MA: Marketing Science Institute, 2001). See also Aaker and Joachimsthaler, *Brand Leadership.*

47. Robert W. Ruekert and Orville C. Walker Jr., *Shared Marketing Programs and the Performance of Different Business Strategies,* Report 91–100 (Cambridge, MA: Marketing Science Institute, 1991).

Chapter Three

Business Strategies and Their Marketing Implications

Business Strategies and Marketing Programs at 3M[1]

The Minnesota Mining and Manufacturing Company, better known as 3M, began manufacturing sandpaper a century ago. Today it is the leader in dozens of technical areas from fluorochemistry to fiber optics. The firm makes more than 60,000 different products, which generated $29.6 billion in global sales in 2011. The company produced $6 billion in operating income.

As you might expect of a firm with so many products, 3M is organized into a large number of strategic business units (SBUs). The company contains 38 such SBUs or product divisions organized into six market sectors:

- The Industrial and Transportation Sector makes a variety of tapes, abrasives, adhesives, filters, and specialty chemicals for industrial applications ranging from electronics to aerospace to automobile manufacturing.
- The Health Care Sector markets a variety of medical, surgical, pharmaceutical, and dental products and services.
- The Consumer and Office Sector offers products for homes and offices, such as Post-it brand repositionable notes and Scotch brand tapes.
- The Electro and Communications Sector supplies connecting, splicing, and protective products for electronics and telecommunications markets.
- The Display and Graphics Sector is a world leader in the sales of films and reflective

materials for electronic displays, touch screens, commercial graphics, and traffic control.
- The Safety, Security, and Protection Services Sector markets a wide variety of products ranging from respirators for worker safety to cleaning supplies to fire protection products.

The corporation's growth strategy has focused primarily on internal new product development, emphasizing both improved products for existing customers and new products for new markets. One formal objective assigned to every business unit is to obtain at least 30 percent of annual sales from products introduced within the past four years. The company supports its growth strategy with a R&D budget of more than $1.5 billion, nearly 5.5 percent of total revenue.

The company also pursues growth through the aggressive development of foreign markets, and an additional organizational sector is responsible for coordinating the firm's marketing efforts across countries. In 2011, 3M attained $19.6 billion in sales—66 percent of its total revenue—from outside the United States.

Differences in customer needs and life-cycle stages across industries, however, lead 3M's various business units to pursue their growth objectives in different ways. The Industrial Tape Division within the Industrial and Transportation Sector, for example, operates in an industry where both the product technologies and the customer segments are relatively mature and stable. Growth in this group results from extending the scope of adhesive technology (for instance, attaching weather stripping to auto doors), product improvements and line extensions targeted at existing customers, and expansion into global markets.

In contrast, the firm's Drug Delivery Systems Division within the Health Care Sector develops new medical applications for emerging technologies developed in 3M's many R&D labs. It sells a variety of technologies for the delivery of medications that are inhaled or absorbed through the skin. Most of the unit's growth comes from developing new products, often through alliances with other pharmaceutical firms, aimed at new markets.

The competitive strategies of 3M's various business units also differ. For instance, the industrial tape unit is primarily concerned with maintaining its commanding market share in existing markets while preserving or even improving its profitability. Its competitive strategy is to differentiate itself from competitors on the basis of product quality and excellent customer service.

But the drug delivery systems unit's strategy is to avoid head-to-head competitive battles by being the technological leader and introducing a stream of unique new products. To be successful, though, the unit must devote substantial resources to R&D and to the stimulation of primary demand. Thus, its main objective is volume growth, and it must sometimes sacrifice short-run profitability to fund the product development and marketing efforts needed to accomplish that goal.

These differences in competitive strategy, in turn, influence the strategic marketing programs within the various business units. For instance, the firm spends little on advertising or sales promotion for its mature industrial tape products. However, it does maintain a large, well-trained technical salesforce that provides valuable problem-solving assistance and other services to customers.

In contrast, the pioneering nature of the drug delivery unit's technologies calls for more extensive promotion to attract potential alliance partners, develop awareness among prescribing physicians, and stimulate primary demand. Consequently, the unit devotes a relatively large portion of its revenues to advertising in technical journals aimed at the pharmaceutical industry, physicians, and other medical professionals.

Although different business and marketing strategies make sense for business units facing different market conditions, they pose a dilemma for top management. Can a variety of competitive strategies and marketing programs be consistent with, and effective under, a single corporate strategy or company policy? George Buckley had to address this issue when he took over as 3M's CEO in 2005. His predecessor had instituted a "six sigma" program throughout the firm. Six sigma is a quality control approach that uses rigorous statistical analysis to remove variability from a process—such as order fulfillment or product delivery—thereby reducing defects, improving quality, and lowering costs.

Six sigma's objectives and methods make good sense for mature businesses such as 3M's industrial tape unit where the product line is well established and improving quality and lowering costs are important means of maintaining profitability. But what about a business whose competitive strategy focuses on innovation and new product development, such as the drug delivery systems unit? As one management guru points out, "The more you hardwire a company for total quality management (e.g., six sigma), the more it is going to hurt breakthrough innovation. The mind-set that is needed, the capabilities that are needed, the metrics that are needed . . . for discontinuous innovation are totally different."

Consequently, CEO Buckley has made adjustments in the firm's corporate policies to accommodate some of the strategic differences across the firm's business units. For instance, while he has continued to pursue six sigma goals in 3M's mature businesses, he has loosened the reins a bit by deemphasizing the six sigma approach in the firm's research labs and some of its pioneering business units. He has also reemphasized some other company policies aimed at spurring creativity among the firm's scientists and engineers, such as allowing researchers to spend 15 percent of their time on whatever projects interest them. Consequently, a survey of global executives by Booz & Co. in 2011 ranked 3M as the third most innovative company in the world behind Google and Apple.

STRATEGIC CHALLENGES ADDRESSED IN CHAPTER 3

The situation at 3M illustrates that large firms with multiple businesses usually have a hierarchy of strategies extending from the corporate level down to the individual product-market entry. As we saw in Chapter 2, corporate strategy addresses such issues as the firm's mission and scope and the directions it will pursue for future growth. Thus, 3M's corporate growth strategy focuses primarily on developing new products and new applications for emerging technologies.

The major strategic question addressed at the business-unit level is: How should we compete in this business? For instance, 3M's industrial tape unit attempts to maintain its commanding market share and high profitability by differentiating itself on the basis of high product quality and good customer service. The drug delivery unit, on the other hand, seeks high growth via aggressive new product and market development.

Finally, the strategic marketing program for each product-market entry within a business unit attempts to allocate marketing resources and activities in a manner appropriate for accomplishing the business unit's objectives. Thus, most of the strategic marketing programs within 3M's drug delivery unit involve relatively large expenditures for marketing research and introductory advertising and promotion campaigns aimed at achieving sales growth.

One key reason for 3M's continuing success is that all three levels of strategy within the company have usually been characterized by good internal and external consistency, or **strategic fit.** The company's managers have done a good job of monitoring and adapting their strategies to the market opportunities, technological advances, and competitive threats in the company's external environment. The firm's marketing and sales managers play critical roles both in developing market-oriented strategies for individual products and in influencing and helping to formulate corporate and business-level strategies that are responsive to environmental conditions. At the same time, those strategies are usually internally compatible. Each strategy fits with those at other levels as well as with the unique competitive strengths and competencies of the relevant business unit and the company as a whole.

Strategic Issue

When there is a good fit between a business's competitive strategy and the strategic marketing programs of its various product or service offerings, the business will achieve better results.

Recent empirical evidence shows that when there is a good fit between a business's competitive strategy and the strategic marketing programs of its various product or service offerings, the business will achieve better results in terms of sales growth, market share, and profitability than when the two levels of strategy are inconsistent with one another.[2] Therefore, this chapter focuses on what marketing decision-makers can and should do to help ensure that the strategic marketing plans they develop are appropriate in light of the available resources and competitive thrust of the business that is their organizational home.

First, we briefly examine the strategic decisions that must be made at the business level, including how business units should be designed. We'll pay particular attention to the question of how a business might choose to compete. What generic competitive strategies might a business pursue, and in what environmental circumstances is each strategy most appropriate? We'll also explore whether the same kinds of competitive strategies are relevant for small, single-business organizations and entrepreneurial start-ups as for large multi-SBU firms such as 3M and whether technological shifts, such as the growth of e-commerce, are likely to give birth to new competitive strategies or make some old ones obsolete.

Next, we examine the interrelationships between different business competitive strategies and elements of the strategic marketing programs for the various products within the business. How does—or should—a particular competitive strategy influence or constrain marketing programs for the business's product offerings? What happens if the market positioning or specific marketing actions that would be most effective for appealing to a product's target customers do not fit very well with the competitive strategy of the larger business unit? For example, as some of the products made by the drug delivery unit at 3M—such as the inhalers they make for delivering asthma medications—become well established and mature, they may require marketing actions (e.g., more competitive pricing) that are not consistent with the aggressive product development strategy of the business unit. What should 3M and the marketing manager responsible for inhalers do under such circumstances?

Finally, the Marketing Plan Exercise at the end of the chapter asks you to identify the business-level competitive strategy that is being—or should be—pursued by the business unit or entrepreneurial start-up that houses your product-market entry. Why does that competitive strategy make sense given the capabilities and resources available? What does it imply for the marketing objectives, resources, and activities you will include in your marketing plan?

STRATEGIC DECISIONS AT THE BUSINESS-UNIT LEVEL

The components of a firm engaged in multiple industries or businesses are typically called **strategic business units (SBUs).** Managers within each of these business units decide which objectives, markets, and competitive strategies to pursue. Top-level corporate managers typically reserve the right to review and approve such decisions to ensure their overall consistency with the company's mission, objectives, and the allocation of resources across SBUs in its portfolio. However, SBU-level managers, particularly those in marketing and sales, bear the primary responsibility for collecting and analyzing relevant information and generating appropriate strategies for their businesses. Those managers are more familiar with a given SBU's products, customers, and competitors and are responsible for successfully implementing the strategy. The rationale for breaking larger firms into semiautonomous SBUs usually stems from a market-oriented desire to move strategic decision-making closer to the customers the business is trying to reach.

The first step in developing business-level strategies is for the firm to decide how to divide itself into SBUs. The managers in each SBU must then make recommendations about (*a*) the unit's objectives, (*b*) the scope of its target customers and offerings, (*c*) which broad competitive strategy to pursue to build a competitive advantage in its product-markets, and (*d*) how resources should be allocated across its product-market entries and functional departments.

How Should Strategic Business Units Be Designed?

Ideally, strategic business units have the following characteristics:

- *A homogeneous set of markets to serve with a limited number of related technologies.* Minimizing diversity across a SBU's product-market entries enables the unit's manager to better formulate and implement a coherent and internally consistent business strategy.

- *A unique set of product-markets,* in the sense that no other SBU within the firm competes for the same customers with similar products. Thus, the firm avoids duplication of effort and maximizes economies of scale within its SBUs.

- *Control over those factors necessary for successful performance,* such as production, R&D and engineering, marketing, and distribution. This does not mean a SBU should not share resources, such as a manufacturing plant or a salesforce, with one or more other business units. But the SBU should determine how its share of the joint resource is used to effectively carry out its strategy.

- *Responsibility for their own profitability.*

As you might expect, firms do not always meet all of these ideals when designing business units. There are usually trade-offs between having many small homogeneous SBUs versus large but fewer SBUs that corporate executives can more easily supervise.

What criteria should managers use to decide how product-markets should be clustered into a business unit? The three dimensions that define the scope and mission of the entire corporation also define individual SBUs:

1. *Technical compatibility,* particularly with respect to product technologies and operational requirements, such as the use of similar production facilities and engineering skills.
2. Similarity in the *customer needs* or the product benefits sought by customers in the target markets.
3. Similarity in the *personal characteristics* or behavior patterns of customers in the target markets.

Strategic Issue

When designing SBUs, the choice is often between technical/operational compatibility and customer homogeneity.

In practice, the choice is often between technical/operational compatibility on the one hand and customer homogeneity on the other. Frequently management defines SBUs by product-markets requiring similar technologies, production facilities, and employee skills. This minimizes the coordination problems involved in administering the unit and increases its ability to focus on one or a few critical competencies.

In some firms, however, the marketing synergies gained from coordinating technically different products aimed at the same customer need or market segment outweigh operational considerations. In these firms, managers group product-market entries into SBUs based on similarities across customers or distribution systems. For instance, 3M's medical products unit includes a wide range of products involving very different technologies and production processes. They are grouped within the same business unit, though, because all address health needs, are marketed to physicians and other health professionals, and can be sold through a common salesforce and distribution system.

Business-Unit Objectives

Companies break down corporate objectives into subobjectives for each SBU. In most cases, those subobjectives vary across SBUs according to the attractiveness of their industries, the strength of their competitive positions within those industries, and resource allocation decisions by corporate management. For example, managers may assign a SBU in a rapidly growing industry relatively high volume and share-growth objectives but lower ROI objectives than a SBU with a large share in a mature industry.

A similar process of breaking down overall SBU objectives into a set of subobjectives should occur for each product-market entry within the unit. Those subobjectives obviously must reflect the SBU's overall objectives, but once again, they may vary across product-market entries according to the attractiveness and growth potential of individual market segments and the competitive strengths of the company's product in each market. For example, when 3M's consumer products group first introduced its Scotch-Brite Never Rust soap pads—a new form of scouring pad that will never rust or splinter because it is made from recycled plastic beverage bottles—its objective was to capture a major share of the soap pad market from well-entrenched competitive brands such as SOS and Brillo. 3M wanted to maximize Never Rust's volume growth and market share even if the new line did not break even for several years. Consequently, the firm's top managers approved a major investment in a new plant and a substantial introductory advertising budget. At the same time, though, the consumer group maintained high profitability goals for its other established products—such as Scotch brand Magic Transparent Tape and Post-it brand notes—to provide the cash required for Never Rust's introduction and preserve the group's overall profit level.

Allocating Resources within the Business Unit

Once a SBU's objectives and budget have been approved at the corporate level, its managers must decide how the available resources should be allocated across the unit's various product-market entries. Because this allocation process is quite similar to allocating corporate resources across SBUs, many firms use similar economic value, value-based planning, or portfolio analysis tools for both. Of course, at the SBU level managers must determine the attractiveness of individual target markets, the competitive position of their products within those markets, and the customer equity and cash flows each product entry will likely generate rather than analyzing industry attractiveness and the overall competitive strengths of the firm.

Unfortunately, value-based planning is not a useful a tool for evaluating alternative resource allocations across product-market entries. This is because the product-market entries within a business unit often share the benefits of common investments and the costs of functional activities, as when multiple products are produced in the same plant or sold by the same salesforce. The difficulty of deciding what portion of such common investments and shared costs should be assigned to specific products increases the difficulty of applying a discounted cash flow analysis at the product-market level. As we shall see in Chapter 13, some firms have adopted activity-based costing systems in an attempt to resolve such problems,[3] but many difficulties remain. On the other hand, attempts to model the impact of various marketing initiatives on customer equity, as discussed in Chapter 2, are probably more appropriate at the product-market level than at the business level.[4]

HOW DO BUSINESSES COMPETE?

As mentioned, the essential strategic question at the SBU level is: How are we going to compete in this business? Thus, business strategies are primarily concerned with allocating resources across functional activities and product-markets to give the unit a sustainable advantage over its competitors. Of course, the unit's core competencies and resources, together with the customer and competitive characteristics of its industry, determine the viability of any particular competitive strategy.[5] The 3M drug delivery unit's strategy of gaining revenue growth via technological leadership and aggressive new product and market development, for instance, will continue to work only if the firm's R&D, engineering, and marketing competencies and resources continue to outweigh those of its competitors. Consequently, most SBUs pursue a single competitive strategy—one that best fits their market environments and competitive strengths—across all or most of the product-markets in which they compete. The question is: What alternative strategies are available to a business unit? What are the basic, or generic, competitive strategies most SBUs choose to pursue?

Generic Business-Level Competitive Strategies

Researchers have identified general categories of business-level competitive strategies based on overall patterns of purpose, practice, and performance in different businesses. Michael Porter distinguishes three strategies—or competitive positions—that businesses pursue to gain and maintain competitive advantages in their various product-markets: (1) *overall cost leadership;* (2) *differentiation*—building customer perceptions of superior product quality, design, or service; and (3) *focus,* in which the business avoids direct confrontation with its major competitors by concentrating on narrowly defined market niches.

Porter describes firms that lack a distinctive strategy as being "stuck in the middle" and predicts that they will perform poorly.[6]

Robert Miles and Charles Snow identified another set of business strategies based on a business's intended rate of product-market development (new product development, penetration of new markets).[7] They classify business units into four strategic types: *prospectors, defenders, analyzers,* and *reactors.* Exhibit 3.1 describes each of these business strategies briefly. As you can see, businesses pursuing a *prospector strategy* focus on growth through the development of new products and markets. 3M's drug delivery business unit illustrates this. *Defender businesses* concentrate on maintaining their positions in established product-markets while paying less attention to new product development, as is the case with 3M's industrial tape business unit. The *analyzer strategy* falls in between these two. An analyzer business attempts to maintain a strong position in its core product-market(s) but also seeks to expand into new—usually closely related—product-markets. Finally, *reactors* are businesses with no clearly defined strategy.

EXHIBIT 3.1 Definitions of Miles and Snow's Four Business Strategies

Prospector

- Operates within a broad product-market domain that undergoes periodic redefinition.
- Values being a "first mover" in new product and market areas, even if not all of these efforts prove to be highly profitable.
- Responds rapidly to early signals concerning areas of opportunity, and these responses often lead to new rounds of competitive actions.
- Competes primarily by stimulating and meeting new market opportunities but may not maintain strength over time in all markets it enters.

Defender

- Attempts to locate and maintain a secure position in relatively stable product or service areas.
- Offers relatively limited range of products or services compared with competitors.
- Tries to protect its domain by offering lower prices, higher quality, or better service than competitors.
- Usually not at the forefront of technological/new product development in its industry; tends to ignore industry changes not directly related to its area of operation.

Analyzer

- An intermediate type; makes fewer and slower product-market changes than prospectors but is less committed to stability and efficiency than defenders.
- Attempts to maintain a stable, limited line of products or services but carefully follows a selected set of promising new developments in its industry.
- Seldom a first mover, but often a second or third entrant in product-markets related to its existing market base—often with a lower cost or higher-quality product or service offering.

Reactor

- Lacks any well-defined competitive strategy.
- Does not have as consistent a product-market orientation as its competitors.
- Not as willing to assume the risks of new product or market development as its competitors.
- Not as aggressive in marketing established products as some competitors.
- Responds primarily when it is forced to by environmental pressures.

Source: Adapted from Raymond Miles and Charies Snow, *Organizational Strategy, Structure, and Process,* Copyright © 1978 McGraw-Hill; 2003 by the Board of Trustees of the Leland Stanford Jr. University. All rights reserved. Used with the permission of Stanford University Press, www.sup.org.

EXHIBIT 3.2   **Combined Typology of Business-Level Competitive Strategies**

Emphasis on new product-market growth

Heavy emphasis ◄──────────────────────► No emphasis

	Prospector	Analyzer	Defender	Reactor
Differentiation	Units primarily concerned with attaining growth through aggressive pursuit of new product-market opportunities	Units with strong core business; actively seeking to expand into related product-markets with **differentiated** offerings	Units primarily concerned with maintaining a **differentiated** position in mature markets	Units with no clearly defined product-market development or competitive strategy
Cost leadership		Units with strong core business; actively seeking to expand into related product-markets with **low-cost** offerings	Units primarily concerned with maintaining a **low-cost** position in mature markets	

Competitive strategy (vertical axis label)

Even though both the Porter and Miles and Snow typologies have received popular acceptance and research support, neither is complete by itself. For example, a *defender business unit* could pursue a variety of competitive approaches to protect its market position, such as offering the lowest cost or differentiating itself on quality or service. Thus, we have combined the two typologies in Exhibit 3.2 to provide a more comprehensive overview of business strategies. Exhibit 3.2 classifies business strategies on two primary dimensions: the unit's desired rate of product-market development (expansion) and the unit's intended method of competing in its established product-markets.

Each of our strategic categories could be further subdivided according to whether a business applies the strategy across a broadly defined product-market domain or concentrates on a narrowly defined segment where it hopes to avoid direct confrontation with major competitors (the focus strategy of Porter). Although this distinction is useful, it is more germane to a discussion of the business's target market strategy (as discussed in Chapter 6) than to its competitive strategy. Most businesses compete in a reasonably consistent way across all of their product-markets, whether their domain is broad or narrow.

Exhibit 3.2 describes only six business strategies, rather than the eight that one might expect. We view reactor and prospector business units as two homogeneous categories.

Evidence suggests that a substantial portion of businesses fall into the reactor category. One study, for instance, found that 50 out of 232 businesses examined could be classified as reactors.[8] By definition, however, such businesses do not have well-defined or consistent approaches either to new product development or to ways of competing in existing product-markets. In other words, reactors have no clear competitive strategy. Therefore, we will largely ignore them during the rest of this discussion.

Prospectors are also shown as a single strategic category in Exhibit 3.2 because the desire for rapid new product or market development is the overriding aspect of their strategy. There is little need for a prospector business to consider how it will compete in the new product-markets it develops because it will face little or no competition—at least not until those markets become established and other firms begin to enter.

Do the Same Competitive Strategies Work for Single-Business Firms and Start-ups?

Even small firms with a single business and only a few related product offerings or start-ups with a single product must decide how they will compete. Just like a SBU in a major corporation such as 3M, their competitive strategies should be tailored to their unique resources and competencies and aimed at securing a sustainable advantage over existing or potential competitors. Therefore, the same set of generic competitive strategies is just as appropriate for small firms as for business units within larger ones. For example, Pinkberry frozen yogurt shops have captured a significant portion of the upscale ice cream/gelato/frozen yogurt market in the United States with a differentiated defender strategy. They have successfully differentiated their stores by (1) hiring and training friendly enthusiastic store personnel, (2) offering more flavors and many more unique toppings than competitors, and (3) generating promotional buzz via celebrity endorsements. Their strategy enabled them to expand to 120 shops in only five years, even though the U.S. frozen dessert market is mature.

Impressively, too, Pinkberry has been able to generate substantial global sales by adapting their flavors and toppings to local cultures and tastes. For instance, they offer green tea–flavored yogurt in Asian shops, date and pistachio toppings in Kuwait, and Nutrella spread in Russia. By adjusting their differentiated defender strategy from country to country, the firm has been able to generate more than a quarter of its income from outside the United States, and that portion is expected to grow in the future.[9]

However, there is one important difference between single-business and multi-SBU organizations. In smaller single-business firms, the distinction between business-level competitive strategy and marketing strategy tends to blur, and the two strategies blend into one. Pinkberry's competitive strategy, for instance, is essentially the same as the market positioning of its stores: shops that offer high-quality frozen yogurt with a large variety of unique flavors and toppings, and fast, friendly customer service.

Strategic Issue

Although the taxonomy of competitive strategies is still relevant to entrepreneurial firms, in reality most of them—at least those that stand a reasonable chance of success—begin life as prospectors.

Another difference applies to entrepreneurial start-ups. Most start-ups do not have the resources to succeed by competing as a "me-too" competitor in a well-established and highly competitive product-market. By definition they do not have an established market position to defend. Therefore, while the taxonomy of competitive strategies is still relevant to entrepreneurial firms, in reality most of them—at least those that stand a reasonable chance of success—begin life as prospectors. They compete primarily by developing a unique product or service that meets the needs and preferences of a customer segment that is not being well served by established competitors.

The critical question for a start-up firm is: What happens when the new product matures and competitors arrive on the scene? Should the firm continue to focus on developing a stream of new products to stay a step ahead of the competition, even though such a strategy would mean paying less attention to its successful first entry? Should the firm switch to a defender strategy to leverage its initial success, even though that would mean competing head to head with other, probably bigger, competitors? Should the firm create two separate SBUs with different competitive strategies, even though it is small and resources are limited? These are the kinds of questions that arise when the market and competitive conditions facing a product entry change. The entry's marketing strategy should be adjusted in response to such changes, but that may make it less compatible with the overall competitive strategy of the business, which is typically harder to change in the short term. These and similar issues related to strategic change are examined in more detail later in this chapter.

Do the Same Competitive Strategies Work for Service Businesses?

What is a service? Basically, *services* can be thought of as **intangibles** and *goods* as **tangibles.** The former can rarely be experienced in advance of the sale, whereas the latter can be experienced, even tested, before purchase.[10] Using this distinction, a **service** can be defined as "any activity or benefit that one party can offer to another that is essentially intangible and that does not result in the ownership of anything. Its production may or may not be tied to a physical product."[11]

We typically associate services with nonmanufacturing businesses, even though service is often an indispensable part of a goods producer's offering. Services such as applications engineering, system design, delivery, installation, training, and maintenance can be crucial for building long-term relationships between manufacturers and their customers, particularly in consumer durable and industrial products businesses. Thus, almost all businesses are engaged in service to some extent.

Many organizations are concerned with producing and marketing a service as their primary offering rather than as an adjunct to a physical product. These organizations include public-sector and not-for-profit service organizations, such as churches, hospitals, universities, and arts organizations. The crucial question is this: To be successful, must service organizations employ different competitive strategies than goods manufacturers?

The framework we used to classify business-level competitive strategies in Exhibit 3.2 is equally valid for service businesses. Some service firms, such as Super 8 or Days Inn in the lodging industry, attempt to minimize costs and compete largely with low prices. Other firms, such as Marriott, differentiate their offerings on the basis of high service quality or unique benefits. Similarly, some service businesses adopt prospector strategies and aggressively pursue the development of new offerings or markets. For instance, American Express's Travel Related Services Division has developed a variety of new services tailored to specific segments of the firm's credit-card holders. Other service businesses focus narrowly on defending established positions in current markets. Still others can best be described as analyzers pursuing both established and new markets. For instance, Emirates, an airline whose competitive strategy is discussed in Exhibit 3.3, might best be described as a low-cost analyzer.

A study of the banking industry provides empirical evidence that service businesses actually do pursue the same types of competitive strategies as goods producers. The 329 bank CEOs who responded to the survey had little trouble categorizing their institution's competitive strategies into one of Miles and Snow's four types. Fifty-four of the executives reported that their banks were prospectors, 87 identified their firms as analyzers, 157 as defenders, and 31 as reactors.[12]

Do the Same Competitive Strategies Work for Global Competitors?

In terms of the strategies described in Exhibit 3.2, businesses that compete in multiple global markets almost always pursue one of the two types of analyzer strategy. They must continue to strengthen and defend their competitive position in their home country—and perhaps in other countries where they are well established—while simultaneously pursuing expansion and growth in new international markets.

When examined on a country-by-country basis, however, the same business unit might be viewed as pursuing different competitive strategies in different countries. For instance, although 3M's industrial tape group competes like a differentiated defender in the United States, Canada, and some European countries where it has established large market shares, it competes more like a prospector when attempting to open and develop new markets in emerging economies such as China and Mexico.

EXHIBIT 3.3 *Emirates Airline—Competing for Business Travelers while Building New Markets*

Habib Fekih was traveling the Mideast as a salesman for European plane manufacturer Airbus in 1985, the year Dubai's ruling family started a small airline called Emirates to shuttle Pakistani workers between Karachi and Dubai aboard two leased planes. "Nobody believed Emirates could be a successful airline," recalls Fekih, who now heads Airbus's Mideast subsidiary. "It was the joke of the day."

Emirates is a joke no longer. It has grown into the world's 10th largest airline, earning $492 million in profits in 2011 on sales of nearly $16 billion.

One important factor underlying Emirates's success is simply the geographic location of Dubai. It provides a convenient hub that has enabled Emirates to offer more convenient routes for business travelers shuttling between Europe or the United States and Asia. The rapid growth of many Asian economies in recent years has, in turn, generated increased demand and new customers for Emirates's flights.

Of course, many other airlines fly between Asia and the West, so Emirates has attempted to strengthen and defend its share of that market by offering good service with very low fares. Aggressive expansion via the purchase of new planes from Boeing and Airbus has made the company's fleet of 142 all wide body jets the youngest and most efficient of any airline. And when its recent order of 90 Airbus A380 superjumbo jets is delivered, it will be even more efficient. The A380's operating costs are 12 percent lower than the newest 747, and it carries about 500 passengers. Therefore, Emirates' cost per passenger mile is lower than any other intercontinental airline, and will be even lower in coming years. This allows the company to charge lower fares while still maintaining good service, expanding its routes to "secondary" airports like Manchester in the United Kingdom and Kolkata in India, and still make money. In other words, to implement a very successful low-cost analyzer strategy.

Source: Steve Rothwell and Andrea Rothman, "Emirates Wins with Big Planes and Low Costs," *Bloomberg Businessweek*, July 5, 2010, pp. 18–19; "Rulers of the New Silk Road," *The Economist*, July 5, 2010, pp. 75–77; and the Emirates Group's 2011–12 Annual Report on the firm's website, www.theemiratesgroup.com.

This suggests that a single SBU may need to engage in different functional activities (including different strategic marketing programs)—and perhaps even adopt different organizational structures to implement those activities—across the various countries in which it competes. For example, Huawei Technologies Co., located in Shenzhen, China, was able to compete very effectively in its home market as a low-cost analyzer. The company earned $2.4 billion in revenues in 2001 selling internet switches and routers patterned after the equipment manufactured by Cisco Systems and Alcatel, but at prices as much as 40 percent lower. However, only 10 percent of those revenues came from outside China. In order to compete more effectively in the developed markets of Europe and the Americas, Huawei had to expand its product line and develop new equipment with more innovative features and greater functionality. In other words, it had to compete more like a prospector in those markets. Consequently, the firm greatly increased its R&D spending and product development efforts. It also developed marketing programs geared to generating brand awareness and trial among potential customers. For the time being, Huawei relies heavily on alliances with established distributors and value-added resellers to develop and implement marketing programs in developed markets. For instance, the Vierling Group serves as Huawei's exclusive distributor in Germany, and the firm has also signed a distribution deal with IBM. As a result of these strategic adjustments, Huawei's revenues topped $32.3 billion in 2011, and nearly two-thirds of those sales came from outside of China.[13]

Will the Internet Change Everything?

Some analysts argue that the internet will change the way firms compete. The internet makes it easier for buyers and sellers to compare prices, reduces the number of middlemen necessary between manufacturers and end users, cuts transaction costs, improves the functioning of the price mechanism, and thereby increases competition.[14] One possible outcome of all these changes is that it will be harder for firms to differentiate themselves on any basis other than low price. All the business-level competitive strategies focused on differentiation will become less viable, whereas firms pursuing low-cost strategies will be more successful.

Although we agree that the internet has increased both efficiency and competitiveness in many product-markets, we doubt that competition will focus exclusively on price. For one thing, innovation is likely to continue—and probably accelerate—in the future. Unique new products and services will continue to emerge and provide a way for the innovator to gain a competitive advantage, at least in the short term. Thus, firms with the resources and competencies necessary to produce a continuing stream of new product or service offerings that appeal to one or more customer segments—that is, to effectively implement a prospector strategy—should be successful regardless of whether they are the lowest-cost producers in their industries. Amazon.com, the largest e-tailer as of early 2012, is generally not the lowest priced.

In addition, the internet is primarily a communications channel. Although it facilitates the dissemination of information, including price information, the goods and services themselves will continue to offer different features and benefits. As customers gather more information from the internet and become better informed, they are less likely to be swayed by superficial distinctions between brands. But if a firm offers unique benefits that a segment of customers perceives as *meaningful,* it should still be able to differentiate its offering and command a premium price, at least until its competitors offer something similar.

Strategic Issue

The internet will make it easier for firms to customize their offerings and personalize their relationships with their customers.

Finally, the internet will make it easier for firms to customize their offerings and personalize their relationships with their customers. Such personalization should differentiate the firm from its competitors in the customer's eyes and improve customer loyalty and retention. For instance, over the past few years, the internet has played a major role in developing logistical alliances among organizational buyers and their suppliers. Consumer goods and services firms, and even internet portals, also are using the internet's interactive capabilities to acquire and communicate information and build customer relationships. For example, about 40 percent of shoppers who buy clothing at Lands' End—both men and women—choose a customized garment tailored to their personal dimensions over the standard-sized equivalent, even though each customized garment costs more and takes longer to arrive. And customers who customize are more loyal to the company. Reorder rates for custom-clothing buyers are 35 percent higher than for buyers of Lands' End's standard items.[15]

HOW DO COMPETITIVE STRATEGIES DIFFER FROM ONE ANOTHER?

In Chapter 1, we said that all strategies consist of five components or underlying dimensions: scope (or breadth of strategic domain), goals and objectives, resource deployments, a basis for achieving a sustainable competitive advantage, and synergy. But the generic strategies summarized in Exhibit 3.2 are defined largely by their differences on only one dimension: the nature of the competitive advantage sought. Each strategy also involves some important differences on the other four dimensions—differences that are outlined in Exhibit 3.4 and discussed as follows. Those differences provide insights concerning the conditions under which each strategy is most appropriate and about the relative importance of different marketing actions in implementing them effectively.

EXHIBIT 3.4   How Business Strategies Differ in Scope, Objectives, Resource Deployments, and Synergy

Dimensions	Low-Cost Defender	Differentiated Defender	Prospector	Analyzer
• *Scope*	Mature/stable/well-defined domain; mature technology and customer segments	Mature/stable/well-defined domain; mature technology and customer segments	Broad/dynamic domains; technology and customer segments not well established	Mixture of defender and prospector strategies
• *Goals and objectives*				
Adaptability (new product success)	Very Little	Little	Extensive	Mixture of defender and prospector strategies
Effectiveness (increase in market share)	Low	Low	High	Mixture of defender and prospector strategies
Efficiency (ROI)	High	High	Low	Mixture of defender and prospector strategies
• *Resource deployment*	Generate excess cash (cash cows)	Generate excess cash (cash cows)	Need cash for product development (question marks or stars)	Need cash for product development but less so than do prospectors
• *Synergy*	Need to seek operating synergies to achieve efficiencies	Need to seek operating synergies to achieve efficiencies	Danger in sharing operating facilities and programs—better to share technology/marketing skills	Danger in sharing operating facilities and programs—better to share technology/marketing skills

Differences in Scope

Both the breadth and stability of a business's domain are likely to vary with different strategies. This, in turn, can affect the variables the corporation uses to define its various businesses. At one extreme, defender businesses, whether low-cost or differentiated, tend to operate in relatively well-defined, narrow, and stable domains where both the product technology and the customer segments are mature.

At the other extreme, prospector businesses usually operate in broad and rapidly changing domains where neither the technology nor customer segments are well established. The scope of such businesses often undergoes periodic redefinition. Thus, prospector businesses are typically organized around either a core technology that might lead to the development of products aimed at a broad range of customer segments or a basic customer need that might be met with products based on different technologies. The latter is the approach taken by 3M's drug delivery systems business. Its mission is to satisfy the health needs of a broad range of patients with new products developed from technologies drawn from other business units within the firm.

Analyzer businesses, whether low-cost or differentiated, fall somewhere in between the two extremes. They usually have a well-established core business to defend, and often their domain is primarily focused on that business. However, businesses pursuing this intermediate strategy are often in industries that are still growing or experiencing technological changes. Consequently, they must pay attention to the emergence of new customer segments and/or new product types. As a result, managers must review and adjust the domain of such businesses from time to time.

Differences in Goals and Objectives

Another important difference across generic business-level strategies with particular relevance for the design and implementation of appropriate marketing programs is that different strategies often focus on different objectives. SBU and product-market objectives might be specified on a variety of criteria, but to keep things simple, we focus on only three performance dimensions of major importance to both business-unit and marketing managers:

1. *Effectiveness.* The success of a business's products and programs relative to those of its competitors in the market. Effectiveness is commonly measured by such items as *sales growth* relative to competitors or *changes in market share.*
2. *Efficiency.* The outcomes of a business's programs relative to the resources used in implementing them. Common measures of efficiency are *profitability* as a percent of sales and *return on investment.*
3. *Adaptability.* The business's success in responding over time to changing conditions and opportunities in the environment. Adaptability can be measured in a variety of ways, but the most common ones are the *number of successful new products* introduced relative to competitors or the *percentage of sales accounted for by products introduced within the last five years.*

However, it is very difficult for any SBU, regardless of its competitive strategy, to simultaneously achieve outstanding performance on even this limited number of dimensions because they involve substantial trade-offs. Good performance on one dimension often means sacrificing performance on another.[16] For example, developing successful new products or attaining share growth often involves large marketing budgets, substantial up-front investment, high operating costs, and a shaving of profit margins—all of which reduce ROI. This suggests that managers should choose a competitive strategy with a view toward maximizing performance on one or two dimensions, while expecting to sacrifice some level of performance on the others, at least in the short term. Over the longer term, of course, the chosen strategy should promise discounted cash flows that exceed the business's cost of capital and thereby increase shareholder value.

As Exhibit 3.4 indicates, prospector businesses are expected to outperform defenders on both new product development and market-share growth. On the other hand, both defender strategies should lead to better returns on investment. Differentiated defenders likely produce higher returns than low-cost defenders, assuming that the greater expenses involved in maintaining their differentiated positions can be more than offset by the higher margins gained by avoiding the intense price competition low-cost competitors often face. Once again, both low-cost and differentiated analyzer strategies are likely to fall between the two extremes.[17]

Differences in Resource Deployment

Businesses following different strategies also tend to allocate their financial resources differently across product-markets, functional departments, and activities within each functional area. Prospector—and to a lesser degree, analyzer—businesses devote a relatively large proportion of resources to the development of new product-markets. Because such product-markets usually require more cash to develop than they produce short term, businesses pursuing these strategies often need infusions of financial resources from other parts of the corporation. In portfolio terms, they are "question marks" or "stars."

Defenders, on the other hand, focus the bulk of their resources on preserving existing positions in established product-markets. These product-markets are usually profitable; therefore, defender businesses typically generate excess cash to support product and market development efforts in other business units within the firm. They are the "cash cows."

Resource allocations among functional departments and activities within the SBU also vary across businesses pursuing different strategies. For instance, marketing budgets tend to be the largest as a percentage of a SBU's revenues when the business is pursuing a prospector strategy; they tend to be the smallest as a percentage of sales under a low-cost defender strategy. We discuss this in more detail later.

Differences in Sources of Synergy

Because different strategies emphasize different methods of competition and different functional activities, a given source of synergy may be more appropriate for some strategies than for others.

At one extreme, the sharing of operating facilities and programs may be an inappropriate approach to gaining synergy for businesses following a prospector strategy. To a lesser extent, this also may be true for both types of analyzer strategies. Such sharing can reduce a SBU's ability to adapt quickly to changing market demands or competitive threats. Commitments to internally negotiated price structures and materials, as well as the use of joint resources, facilities, and programs, increase interdependence among SBUs and limit their flexibility. It is more appropriate for such businesses to seek synergy through the sharing of a technology, engineering skills, or market knowledge—expertise that can help improve the success rate of their product development efforts. Thus, 3M's drug delivery systems business attempts to find medical applications for new technologies developed in many of the firm's other business units.

At the other extreme, however, low-cost defenders should seek operating synergies that will make them more efficient. Synergies that enable such businesses to increase economies of scale and experience curve effects are particularly desirable. They help reduce unit costs and strengthen the strategy's basis of competitive advantage. The primary means of gaining such operating synergies is through the sharing of resources, facilities, and functional activities across product-market entries within the business unit or across related business units. Emerson Electric, for instance, formed an "operating group" of several otherwise autonomous business units that make different types of electrical motors and tools. By sharing production facilities, marketing activities, and a common salesforce, the group was able to reduce the costs of both per-unit production and marketing.

DECIDING WHEN A STRATEGY IS APPROPRIATE: THE FIT BETWEEN BUSINESS STRATEGIES AND THE ENVIRONMENT

Because different strategies pursue different objectives in different domains with different competitive approaches, they do not all work equally well under the same environmental circumstances. The question is: Which environmental situations are most amenable to the successful pursuit of each type of strategy? Exhibit 3.5 outlines some major market,

EXHIBIT 3.5 **Environmental Factors Favorable to Different Business Strategies**

External Factors	Prospector	Analyzer	Differentiated Defender	Low-Cost Defender
Industry and market	Industry in introductory or early growth stage of life cycle; many potential customer segments as yet unidentified and/or undeveloped.	Industry in late growth or early maturity stage of life cycle; one or more product offerings currently targeted at major customer segments, but some potential segments may still be undeveloped.	Industry in maturity or decline stage of life cycle; current offerings targeted at all major segments; sales primarily due to repeat purchases/ replacement demand.	Industry in maturity or decline stage of life cycle; current offerings targeted at all major segments; sales primarily due to repeat purchases/ replacement demand.
Technology	Newly emerging technology; many applications as yet undeveloped.	Basic technology well developed but still evolving; product modifications and improvements—as well as emergence of new competing technologies—still likely.	Basic technology fully developed and stable; few major modifications or improvements likely.	Basic technology fully developed and stable; few major modifications or improvements likely.
Competition	Few established competitors; industry structure still emerging; single competitor holds commanding share of major market segments.	Large number of competitors, but future shakeout likely; industry structure still evolving; one or more competitors hold large shares in major segments, but continuing growth may allow rapid changes in relative shares.	Small to moderate number of well-established competitors; industry structure stable, though acquisitions and consolidation possible; maturity of markets means relative shares of competitors tend to be reasonably stable over time.	Small to moderate number of well-established competitors; industry structure stable, though acquisitions and consolidation possible; maturity of markets means relative shares of competitors tend to be reasonably stable over time.
Business's relative strengths	SBU (or parent) has strong R&D, product engineering and marketing research and marketing capabilities.	SBU (or parent) has good R&D, product engineering, and marketing research capabilities, but not as strong as some competitors'; has either low-cost position or strong sales, marketing, distribution, or service capabilities in one or more segments.	SBU has no outstanding strengths in R&D or product engineering; costs are higher than at least some competitors'; SBU's outstanding strengths are in process engineering and quality control and/or in marketing, sales, distribution, or customer services.	SBU (or parent) has superior sources of supply and/or process engineering and production capabilities that enable it to be low-cost producer; R&D, product engineering, marketing, sales, or service capabilities may not be as strong as some competitors.

technological, and competitive conditions—plus a business unit's strengths relative to its competitors—that are most favorable for the successful implementation of each generic business strategy. We next discuss the reasons each strategy fits best with a particular set of environmental conditions.

Appropriate Conditions for a Prospector Strategy

A prospector strategy is particularly well suited to unstable, rapidly changing environments resulting from new technology, shifting customer needs, or both. In either case, such industries tend to be at an early stage in their life cycles and offer many opportunities for new product-market entries. Industry structure is often unstable because few competitors are present and their relative market shares can shift rapidly as new products are introduced and new markets develop.

Because they emphasize the development of new products and/or new markets, the most successful prospectors are usually strong in, and devote substantial resources to, two broad areas of competence: first, R&D, product engineering, and other functional areas that identify new technology and convert it into innovative products and second, marketing research, marketing, and sales—functions necessary for the identification and development of new market opportunities.

In some cases, however, even though a prospector business has strong product development and marketing skills, it may lack the resources to maintain its early lead as product-markets grow and attract new competitors. For example, Minnetonka was the pioneer in several health and beauty-aid product categories with brands such as Softsoap liquid soap and Check-Up plaque-fighting toothpaste. However, because competitors such as Procter & Gamble and Colgate-Palmolive introduced competing brands with advertising and promotion budgets much larger than Minnetonka could match, the firm was eventually forced to change its strategy and concentrate on manufacturing products under licenses from larger firms.

Appropriate Conditions for an Analyzer Strategy

The analyzer strategy is a hybrid. On one hand, analyzers are concerned with defending—via low costs or differentiation in quality or service—a strong share position in one or more established product-markets. At the same time, the business must pay attention to new product development to avoid being leapfrogged by competitors with more technologically advanced products or being left behind in newly developing application segments within the market. This dual focus makes the analyzer strategy appropriate for well-developed industries that are still experiencing some growth and change as a consequence of evolving customer needs and desires or continuing technological improvements.

Automobile manufacturing is an example of such an industry. Competitors are relatively few and well established, the market is relatively mature except in emerging economies like China and India, but technology continues to advance. Recent changes in the industry's environment—such as rising fuel prices and concerns over the impact of auto emissions on global warming—have underscored the need for more efficient and ecologically friendly technologies. Thus, auto manufacturers around the world, including Toyota, Honda, and many others, are investing billions in a variety of different technologies to develop a new generation of cars, as discussed in Exhibit 3.6.

The actions of Toyota and Honda illustrate one problem with an analyzer strategy. Few businesses have the resources and competencies needed to successfully defend an established core business while generating revolutionary new products at the same time. Success on both dimensions requires strengths across virtually every functional area, and few businesses (or their parent companies) have such universal strengths relative to competitors. Therefore, analyzers are often not as innovative in new product development as prospectors. They may not be as profitable in defending their core businesses as defenders.

Appropriate Conditions for a Defender Strategy

A defender strategy makes sense only when a business has something worth defending. It is most appropriate for units with a profitable share of one or more major segments in a relatively mature, stable industry. Consistent with the "constant improvement" principles

EXHIBIT 3.6 *Analyzer Strategies in the Auto Industry*

Given that Toyota was already selling 300,000 of its Prius gas-electric hybrid cars annually by 2008, it was in the strongest position to respond to the double whammy of rising gas prices and growing concerns over the impact of exhaust emissions on global warming that caught the auto industry off guard that year. The firm's strategy, at least for the short term, was to rapidly expand its hybrid offerings and invest in R&D to further improve their efficiency. New hybrid models—including one in the firm's luxury Lexus line—were introduced in 2009 along with a lighter, more fuel-efficient version of the Prius.

Longer term, the company is eyeing plug-in electric cars. To that end, Toyota has created a special battery research division, complete with more than 100 engineers and technicians, and the firm has introduced a plug-in version of the Prius.

Honda also plans to beef up its hybrid offerings in the short term, but it also offers new clean-diesel engines, which are purportedly 25 percent more fuel efficient than gas engines, in its larger cars, including those that carry the luxury Acura brand.

For the longer term, Honda is focusing on fuel cell vehicles that run on liquid hydrogen and emit only water. In 2008 the firm began production on a fuel cell model called the FCX Clarity, which can go 280 miles on a tank of hydrogen and boast better fuel efficiency than comparable gas or hybrid cars. Honda hopes to have the technology ready for the mass market within 10 years. But since every Clarity currently costs an estimated $1 million to produce, cost reductions via economies of scale and experience will be critical for the car's future.

Many other auto companies are placing their bets on electric motors. Electric cars come in two varieties. Pure electric cars, like the Nissan Leaf and the Mitsubishi i-MiEV, can be driven for 100 miles or so before they need to be plugged in and recharged. Range-extenders, like the General Motors' Volt (introduced as the Ampera in Europe in 2010), can be recharged either by plugging into an outlet or by a small onboard gas engine. And all of the current competitors are nervously looking over their shoulders in anticipation of electric vehicles from China. The Chinese government is supporting electric car technology more than any other country. Beijing has already pledged over $17 billion for R&D, the installation of charging stations, customer subsidies, and the like.

Meanwhile, increasingly stringent regulations concerning fuel efficiency and emissions—particularly in the United States and Europe—have forced manufacturers to continue investing heavily in new designs and technology to improve the efficiency of their traditional gas and diesel-powered cars. But as those cars become more efficient, the relative superiority of the new hybrids and electric cars on "green" criteria will become smaller, and it will be harder for customers to justify paying a price premium.

Source: Ian Rowley, "Japan's New Green Car Push," www.businessweek.com July 2, 2008; "A Sparky New Motor," *The Economist,* October 9, 2010, pp. 89–90; Brian Dumaine, "China Charges into Electric Cars," *Fortune,* November 1, 2010, pp. 138–148; and "Revenge of the Petrolheads," *The Economist,* December 10, 2011, p. 73.

of total quality management, most successful defenders initiate process improvements, product improvements, or line extensions to help protect and strengthen their established positions. But they devote relatively few resources to basic R&D or the development of innovative new products. Thus, a defender strategy works best in industries where the basic technology is not very complex or where it is well developed and unlikely to change dramatically over the short term. For instance, Pillsbury's prepared-dough products SBU—now part of the General Mills Company—has pursued a differentiated defender strategy for years. The unit generates substantial profits from well-established refrigerated dough products such as Pillsbury Crescent rolls and Grands biscuits. But while it has introduced a number of line extensions over the years, most have been reconfigurations of the same basic dough-in-a-can technology, such as Soft Breadsticks.

Differentiated Defenders

To effectively defend its position by differentiation, a business must be strong in those functional areas critical for maintaining its particular competitive advantages over time. If a business's differentiation is based on superior product quality, those key functional areas include production, process engineering, quality control, and perhaps product engineering to develop product improvements. The effort to develop and maintain a quality differentiation can be worthwhile, though, because evidence suggests that superior product quality has a strong impact on a business's return on investment—an important performance objective for defenders.[18]

Regardless of the basis for differentiation, marketing is also important for the effective implementation of a differentiated defender strategy. Marketing activities that track changing customer needs and competitive actions and communicate the product offering's unique advantages through promotional and sales efforts to maintain customer awareness and loyalty are particularly important.

Low-Cost Defenders

Successful implementation of a low-cost defender strategy requires the business to be more efficient than its competitors. Thus, the business must establish the groundwork for such a strategy early in the growth stage of the industry. Achieving and maintaining the lowest per-unit cost usually means that the business has to seek large volume from the beginning—through some combination of low prices and promotional efforts—to gain economies of scale and experience. At the same time, such businesses must also invest in more plant capacity in anticipation of future growth and in state-of-the-art equipment to minimize production costs. This combination of low margins and heavy investment can be prohibitive unless the parent corporation can commit substantial resources to the business or unless extensive sharing of facilities, technologies, and programs with other business units is possible.

In recent years, some firms—particularly those in more developed economies—have tried to reduce their costs by outsourcing production and a few other corporate functions, such as customer call centers and human resources departments. However, outsourcing can lead to problems like reduced quality control and more complicated logistics that may raise the firm's costs in other areas. And because the efficiencies gained through outsourcing can be easily duplicated by competitors, it is not an effective way to build a *sustainable* low-cost advantage.[19]

The low-cost defender's need for efficiency also forces the standardization of product offerings and marketing programs across customer segments to achieve scale effects. Thus, such a strategy is usually not so effective in fragmented markets desiring customized offerings as it is in commodity industries such as basic chemicals, steel, or flour or in industries producing low-technology components such as electric motors or valves.

 Although low-cost defenders emphasize efficiency and low price as the primary focus of their competitive strategy, it is important to keep in mind that businesses pursuing other strategies should also operate as efficiently as possible given the functional activities necessary to implement those strategies. Some of the most effective businesses are those that work *simultaneously* to lower costs and improve quality and service.[20] Operating efficiency is likely to become even more critical as the internet makes it easier for customers to compare prices across alternative suppliers or to obtain low-price bids via "buyers' auction" sites, such as **www.MetalSite.com.**

HOW DIFFERENT BUSINESS STRATEGIES INFLUENCE MARKETING DECISIONS

Business units typically incorporate a number of distinct product-markets. A given entry's marketing manager monitors and evaluates the product's environmental situation and develops a marketing program suited to it. However, the manager's freedom to design such a program may be constrained by the business unit's competitive strategy. This is because different strategies focus on different objectives and seek to gain and maintain a competitive advantage in different ways. As a result, different functions within the SBU—and different activities within a given functional area, such as marketing—are critical for the success of different strategies.

There are, therefore, different key success factors inherent in the various generic business strategies. This constrains the individual marketing manager's freedom of action in two basic ways. First, because varying functions within the business unit are more important under different strategies, they receive different proportions of the SBU's total resources. Thus, the SBU's strategy influences *the amount of resources committed to marketing* and ultimately the budget available to an individual marketing manager within the business unit. Second, the SBU's choice of strategy influences both the kind of *market and competitive situation* that individual product-market entries are likely to face and the *objectives* they are asked to attain. Both constraints have implications for the design of marketing programs for individual products within a SBU.

Strategic Issue

The SBU's strategy influences the amount of resources committed to marketing and ultimately the budget available.

It is risky to draw broad generalizations about how specific marketing policies and program elements might fit within different business strategies. Although a business strategy is a general statement about how a SBU chooses to compete in an industry, that unit may comprise a number of product-market entries facing different competitive situations in various markets. Thus, there is likely to be a good deal of variation in marketing programs, and in the freedom individual marketing managers have in designing them, across products within a given SBU. Still, a business's strategy does set a general direction for the types of target markets it will pursue and how the unit will compete in those markets. It does have some influence on marketing policies that cut across product-markets. Exhibit 3.7 outlines differences in marketing policies and program elements that occur across businesses pursuing different strategies, and those differences are discussed as follows.

Product Policies

One set of marketing policies defines the nature of the products the business will concentrate on offering to its target markets. These policies concern the *breadth or diversity of product lines,* their *level of technical sophistication,* and the target *level of product quality* relative to competitors.

Because prospector businesses rely heavily on the continuing development of unique new products and the penetration of new markets as their primary competitive strategy, policies encouraging broader and more technically advanced product lines than those of competitors should be positively related to performance on the critical dimension of share growth. The diverse and technically advanced product offerings of 3M's drug delivery systems SBU are a good example of this.

Whether a prospector's products should be of higher quality than competitors' products is open to question. Quality is hard to define; it can mean different things to different customers. Even so, it is an important determinant of business profitability. Thus, Hambrick suggests that in product-markets where technical features or up-to-the-minute styling are key attributes in customers' definitions of quality, high-quality products may play a positive role in determining the success of a prospector strategy. In markets where the critical determinants of quality are reliability or brand familiarity, the maintenance of relatively high product quality is likely to be more strongly related to the successful performance of defender businesses, particularly differentiated defenders.[21]

Differentiated defenders compete by offering more or better choices to customers than do their competitors. For example, 3M's commercial graphics business, a major supplier of sign material for truck fleets, has strengthened its competitive position in that market by developing products appropriate for custom-designed signs. Until recently, the use of

EXHIBIT 3.7   **Differences in Marketing Policies and Program Components across Businesses Pursuing Different Strategies**

Marketing Policies and Program Components	Prospector	Strategy Differentiated Defender	Low-Cost Defender
Product policies			
• Product-line breadth relative to competitors	+	+	−
• Technical sophistication of products relative to competitors	+	+	−
• Product quality relative to competitors	?	+	−
• Service quality relative to competitors	?	+	−
Price policies			
• Price levels relative to competitors	+	+	−
Distribution policies			
• Degree of forward vertical integration relative to competitors	−	+	?
• Trade promotion expenses as percent of sales relative to competitors	+	−	−
Promotion policies			
• Advertising expenses as percent of sales relative to competitors	+	?	−
• Sales promotions expenses as percent of sales relative to competitors	+	?	−
• Salesforce expenses as percent of sales relative to competitors	?	+	−

Key: Plus sign (+) = greater than the average competitor.
Minus sign (−) = smaller than the average competitor.
Question mark (?) = uncertain relationship between strategy and marketing policy or program component.

film for individual signs was not economical. But the use of computer-controlled knives and a new Scotch-brand marking film produce signs of higher quality and at lower cost than those that are hand-painted. This kind of success in developing relatively broad and technically sophisticated product lines should be positively related to the long-term ROI performance of most differentiated defender businesses.

However, broad and sophisticated product lines are less consistent with the efficiency requirements of the low-cost defender strategy. For one thing, maintaining technical sophistication in a business's products requires continuing investments in product and process R&D. For another, broad, complex lines can lead to short production runs and larger inventories. Some of the efficiency problems associated with broader, more customized product lines may disappear, however, with continuing improvements in computer-assisted design and manufacturing, process reengineering, three-dimensional printing, and the like.[22]

Instead of, or in addition to, competing on the basis of product characteristics, businesses can distinguish themselves relative to competitors on the *quality of service* they offer. Such service might take many forms, including engineering and design services, alterations, installation, training of customer personnel, or maintenance and repair services. A policy of high service quality is particularly appropriate for differentiated defenders because it offers a way to maintain a competitive advantage in well-established markets.[23]

The appropriateness of an extensive service policy for low-cost defenders, though, is more questionable if higher operating and administrative costs offset customer satisfaction benefits. Those higher costs may detract from the business's ability to maintain the low prices critical to its strategy, as well as lowering ROI—at least in the short term. Further, one study of 71 SBUs pursuing a range of competitive strategies suggests that investments aimed at improving service efficiency and thereby reducing costs generally do not have as positive an impact on a unit's financial performance as service improvements aimed at increasing revenues via improved customer satisfaction and loyalty.[24]

Pricing Policies

Success in offering low prices relative to those of competitors should be positively related to the performance of low-cost defender businesses—for low price is the primary competitive weapon of such a strategy. However, such a policy is inconsistent with both differentiated defender and prospector strategies. The higher costs involved in differentiating a business's products on either a quality or service basis require higher prices to maintain profitability. Differentiation also provides customers with additional value for which higher prices can be charged. Similarly, the costs and benefits of new product and market development by prospector businesses require and justify relatively high prices. Thus, differentiated defenders and prospectors seldom adhere to a policy of low competitive prices.

Distribution Policies

Some observers argue that prospector businesses should show a greater degree of *forward vertical integration* than defender businesses.[25] The rationale for this view is that the prospector's focus on new product and market development requires superior market intelligence and frequent reeducation and motivation of distribution channel members. This can best be accomplished through tight control of company-owned channels. However, these arguments seem inconsistent with the prospector's need for flexibility in constructing new channels to distribute new products and reach new markets.

Attempting to maintain tight control over the behavior of channel members is a more appropriate policy for defenders who are trying to maintain strong positions in established markets. This is particularly true for defenders who rely on good customer service to differentiate themselves from competitors. Thus, it seems more likely that a relatively high degree of forward vertical integration is found among defender businesses, particularly differentiated defenders, whereas prospectors rely more heavily on independent channel members—such as manufacturer's representatives or wholesale distributors—to distribute their products.[26]

Because prospectors focus on new products where success is uncertain and sales volumes are small in the short run, they are likely to devote a larger percentage of sales to *trade promotions* than are defender businesses. Prospectors rely on trade promotion tools such as slotting allowances, quantity discounts, liberal credit terms, and other incentives to induce cooperation and support from their independent channel members.

Promotion Policies

Extensive marketing communications also play an important role in the successful implementation of both prospector and differentiated defender strategies. The form of that communication, however, may differ under the two strategies. Because prospectors must constantly work to generate awareness, stimulate trial, and build primary demand for new and unfamiliar products, high advertising and sales promotion expenditures are likely to bear a positive relationship to the new product and share-growth success of such businesses. The drug delivery SBU at 3M, for instance, devotes substantial resources to advertising in professional journals and distributing samples of new products, as well as to maintaining an extensive salesforce.

Differentiated defenders, on the other hand, are primarily concerned with maintaining the loyalty of established customers by adapting to their needs and providing good service. These tasks can best be accomplished—particularly in industrial goods and services industries—by an extensive, well-trained, well-supported, salesforce.[27] Therefore, differentiated defenders are likely to have higher salesforce expenditures than are competitors.

Finally, low-cost defenders appeal to their customers primarily on price. Thus, high expenditures on advertising, sales promotion, or the salesforce would detract from their basic strategy and might have a negative impact on their ROI. Consequently, such businesses are likely to make relatively low expenditures as a percentage of sales on those promotional activities.

WHAT IF THE BEST MARKETING PROGRAM FOR A PRODUCT DOES NOT FIT THE BUSINESS'S COMPETITIVE STRATEGY?

What should a marketing manager do if the market environment facing a particular product or service demands marketing actions that are not consistent with the overall competitive strategy of the business to which it belongs? What if, for example, the product's target market is rapidly becoming more mature and competitive, but it is housed in a prospector business unit that does not have the cost structure or the personnel to allow the aggressive pricing or excellent customer service that may be needed for the product to compete successfully? What if newly emerging technology demands that a mature product category undergo an innovative redesign even though the defender SBU does not have extensive R&D and product development capabilities?

If a business unit is focused on a single product category or technological domain—as is the case with 3M's industrial tape unit—the ideal solution might be for the whole SBU to change its strategy in response to shifting industry circumstances. As the product category matures, for instance, the SBU might switch from a prospector to an analyzer strategy and ultimately to one of the defender strategies.

The problem is that—as we shall see in Chapter 12—effective implementation of different business strategies requires not only different functional competencies and resources, but also different organizational structures, decision-making and coordination processes reward systems, and even personnel. Because such internal structures and processes are hard to change quickly, it can be very difficult for an entire SBU to make a successful transition from one basic strategy to another.[28] For example, many of Emerson Electric's SBUs historically were successful low-cost defenders, but accelerating technological change in their industries caused the corporation to try to convert them to low-cost analyzers who would focus more attention on new product and market development. Initially, however, this attempted shift in strategy resulted in some culture shock, conflict, and mixed performance outcomes within those units.

In view of the implementation problems involved, some firms do not try to make major changes in the basic competitive strategies of their existing business units. Instead, they might form new prospector SBUs to pursue emerging technologies and industries rather than expecting established units to handle extensive new product development efforts.

Similarly, as individual product-market entries gain successful positions in growing markets, some firms move them from the prospector unit that developed them into an existing analyzer or defender unit or even into a newly formed SBU better suited to reaping profits from them as their markets mature. For example, a number of innovative products developed at 3M, such as Post-it repositionable notes, have enjoyed sufficient success that new divisions were formed to concentrate on defending them as their markets matured.

EXHIBIT 3.8 *Jim Watkins Takes a Hike*

When he was a product manager at the Pillsbury Company in the early 1970s, James D. Watkins became convinced that microwave technology represented a major opportunity for the packaged food industry. Consequently, he developed a marketing plan that proposed the pioneering development and aggressive introduction of a line of microwavable food products, starting with microwave popcorn. However, the business unit he worked for—and the entire Pillsbury Company at that time—was focused on defending strong positions in established markets, largely through incremental line extensions and product improvements. In other words, it was pursuing more of an analyzer strategy. As a result, top management rejected Watkins's proposal as being too risky and requiring resources and capabilities that were in short supply.

Watkins subsequently quit Pillsbury, founded a new firm called Golden Valley Microwave, attracted venture capital, hired some food scientists to do the necessary R&D, and began to market ActII microwave popcorn through large mass merchandisers such as Wal-Mart. As Watkins had predicted in his original marketing plan, the availability of microwavable foods spurred a rapid increase in consumer demand for microwave ovens, which in turn increased demand for more microwavable foods. His new company grew rapidly, and a few years later he sold it to Conagra for many millions of dollars.

But don't be too critical of Pillsbury. Like a good analyzer, the company avoided playing the risky role of the pioneer, but it eventually responded to the growing potential of microwave technology and successfully launched its own line of microwavable foods, including popcorn.

Many successful entrepreneurial start-ups eventually reorganize into two or more business units, one to continue prospecting new products and markets and another to defend the firm's initial product offering as its market matures.

Finally, some firms that are technological leaders in their industries may divest or license individual product-market entries as they mature rather than defend them in the face of increasing competition and eroding margins. This approach is relatively common at firms such as 3M and DuPont.

Because the marketing manager responsible for a given product-market entry is usually most closely tuned in to changes in the market environment, he or she bears the responsibility for pointing out any mismatches between what is best for the product and the capabilities of the organizational unit to which it belongs. The marketer should develop a marketing strategy that makes the most sense in light of a detailed analysis of the available customer and competitive information and present a strong case for the resources necessary to implement the plan. If those resources are not available within the business unit or if the marketing strategy is inconsistent with the SBU's objectives or competitive strategy, top management faces a choice of moving the product to a more benign unit of the firm or rejecting the recommended strategy. If the strategy is rejected, the marketer will likely have to make compromises to the strategy to make it fit better with the competitive thrust of the SBU, even though an attractive opportunity may be lost. But if the marketer has great confidence in the recommended strategy, he or she might opt to quit the firm and pursue the opportunity elsewhere, as was the case with Jim Watkins, as discussed in Exhibit 3.8.

Marketing Plan Exercise

Using one or both of the Porter and the Miles and Snow frameworks, identify which type of business unit strategy your plan will pursue, based on your still very preliminary thinking. Identify the key capabilities and resources—marketing and otherwise—necessary to do so. Determine why that strategy does or does not make sense, compared to the other alternatives.

Discussion Questions

1. Compare and contrast the prospector and low-cost defender business strategies discussed in this chapter on each of the following strategic dimensions:
   a. Scope.
   b. Objectives.
   c. Deployment of resources.
   d. Sources of synergy.

2. The 3M Company's Industrial Tape SBU pursues a differentiated defender strategy in an industry where both the basic technologies and the customer segments are relatively mature and stable. Is the objective imposed by top management of obtaining 30 percent of sales from products introduced within the last four years an appropriate objective for such a SBU? What do you think top management hopes to accomplish by imposing such an objective on the Industrial Tape SBU? What are the potential disadvantages or dangers involved in imposing such an objective?

3. If you were the general manager of the 3M Industrial Tape SBU discussed in question 2, which objectives would you argue are most appropriate for your business unit in view of its strategy and its external environment? Why?

4. You are the marketing manager for a generic products division of a major pharmaceutical manufacturer. Your division uses the corporation's excess manufacturing capacity to produce generic prescription drugs—drugs whose patents have expired and can thus be manufactured by any company that wishes to produce them. Your division is a low-cost defender that maintains its position in the generic drug market by holding down its costs and selling generic products to distributors and pharmacies at very low prices. What are the implications of this business strategy for each of the 4 Ps in the strategic marketing program you would develop for your division?

Self-diagnostic questions to test your ability to apply the analytical tools and concepts in this chapter to marketing decision-making may be found at this book's web site at **www.mhhe.com/walker8e.**

Endnotes

1. Material for this opening case was obtained from *The 3M Company 2011 Annual Report* and other information found on the company's web site at *www.3m.com;* Jerry Useem, "Scotch Tape Plus Innovation Equals?" *Fortune,* August 12, 2002, pp. 127–32; Brian Hindo, "At 3M, A Struggle Between Efficiency and Creativity," *BusinessWeek-Indepth,* June 2007, pp. in8–in14; and, Will Daley, "3M Moves Most Capital Spending Outside U.S. for First Time," Bloomberg Businessweek Online, April 26, 2011, www.businessweek.com.

2. Stanley F. Slater and Eric M. Olson, "Marketing's Contribution to the Implementation of Business Strategy: An Empirical Analysis," *Strategic Management Journal* 22 (November 2001), pp. 1055–67; Eric M. Olson, Stanley F. Slater, and G. Tomas Hult, "The Performance Implications of Fit among Business Strategy, Marketing Organization Structure, and Strategic Behavior," *Journal of Marketing* 69 (July 2005), pp. 49–65; and, Stanley F. Slater, Eric M. Olson, and G. Thomas M. Hult, "Worried About Strategy Implementation? Don't Overlook Marketing's Role," *Business Horizons* 53 (2010), pp. 469–79.

3. For example, see Robin Cooper and Robert S. Kaplan, "Measure Costs Right: Make the Right Decisions," *Harvard Business Review,* September–October 1988, pp. 96–103; and Terrence P. Pare, "A New Tool for Managing Costs," *Fortune,* June 14, 1993, p. 124.

4. Roland T. Rust, Katherine N. Lemon, and Valarie Zeithaml, "Return on Marketing: Using Customer Equity to Focus Marketing Strategy," *Journal of Marketing* 68 (January 2004), pp. 109–27; and Verena Vogel, Heiner Evanschitzky, and B. Ramaseshan, "Customer Equity Drivers and Future Sales," *Journal of Marketing* 72 (November 2008), pp. 98–108.

5. C. K. Prahalad and Gary Hamel, "The Core Competence of the Corporation," *Harvard Business Review* 68 (May–June 1990), pp. 79–91.

6. Michael E. Porter, *Competitive Strategy* (New York: Free Press, 1980). Also see Michael E. Porter, *Competitive Advantage: Creating and Sustaining Superior Performance* (New York: Free Press, 1985).

7. Robert E. Miles and Charles C. Snow, *Organizational Strategy, Structure, and Process* (New York: McGraw-Hill, 1978). For another taxonomy of business-level competitive strategies that incorporates elements of both the Porter and Miles and Snow frameworks, see Michael Treacy and Fred Wiersema, *The Discipline of Market Leaders* (Reading, MA: Addison-Wesley, 1995).

8. Charles C. Snow and Lawrence G. Hrebiniak, "Strategy, Distinctive Competence, and Organizational Performance," *Administrative Science Quarterly* 25 (1980), pp. 317–35.

9. Leslie Patton, "Pinkberry Looks Abroad to Keep Its Cool," *Bloomberg Businessweek,* May 2, 2011, pp. 18–20.

10. Theodore Levitt, *The Marketing Imagination* (New York: Free Press, 1986), pp. 94–95.

11. Philip Kotler and Gary Armstrong, *Principles of Marketing* (Englewood Cliffs, NJ: Prentice Hall, 1989), p. 575.

12. Daryl O. McKee, P. Rajan Varadarajan, and William M. Pride, "Strategic Adaptability and Firm Performance: A Market-Contingent Perspective," *Journal of Marketing,* July 1989, pp. 21–35.

13. Bruce Einhorn, "The World's Most Influential Companies—Huawei," *Businessweek,* December 22, 2008, p. 51; and Huawei Technologies Co. 2011 Annual Report, www.huawei.com.

14. For examples, see Rajiv Lal and Miklos Savary, "When and How Is the internet Likely to Decrease Price?" *Marketing Science* 18 (Fall 1999), pp. 485–503; Paul Markillie, "A Perfect Market: A Survey of E-Commerce," *The Economist,* May 15, 2004, pp. 13–20; and Florian Zettlemeyer, Fiona Scott Morton, and Jorge Silva-Risso, "How the internet Lowers Prices: Evidence from Matched Survey and Automobile Transaction Data," *Journal of Marketing Research* 43 (May 2006), pp. 168–81.

15. Julie Schlosser, "Cashing In on the New World of Me," *Fortune,* December 13, 2004, pp. 244–50; Nanette Byrnes, "More Clicks at the Bricks," *BusinessWeek,* December 17, 2007, pp. 50–52; Nikolaus Franke, Peter Keinz, and Chritoph J. Steger, "Testing the Value of Customization: When Do Customers Really Prefer Products Tailored to Their Preferences?" *Journal of Marketing* 73 (September 2009), pp. 103–21; and "You Choose," *The Economist,* December 18, 2010, pp. 123–25.

16. Gordon Donaldson, *Managing Corporate Wealth* (New York: Praeger, 1984); and Spencer E. Ante, "Giving the Boss the Big Picture," *BusinessWeek,* February 13, 2006, pp. 48–50.

17. Donald C. Hambrick, "Some Tests of the Effectiveness and Functional Attributes of Miles and Snow's Strategic Types," *Academy of Management Journal* 26 (1983), pp. 5–26; and McKee, Varadarajan, and Pride, "Strategic Adaptability and Firm Performance."

18. Robert D. Buzzell and Bradley T. Gale, *The PIMS Principles: Linking Strategy to Performance* (New York: Free Press, 1987), chap. 6. Also see Roland T. Rust, Christine Moorman, and Peter R. Dickson, "Getting Return on Quality: Revenue Expansion, Cost Reduction, or Both? *Journal of Marketing* 66 (October 2002), pp. 7–24.

19. Peter Engardio, "The Future of Outsourcing," *BusinessWeek,* January 30, 2006, pp. 50–64; Rick Wartzman, "Insourcing and Outsurcing: The Right Mix," February 5, 2010 www.businessweek .com; David Whitford, "Where In the World Is Cheap Labor?" March 22, 2011 www.money.cnn .com and Peter Coy, Dexter Roberts, and Bruce Einhorn, "The Great Fall of China," *Bloomberg Businessweek,* May 7–13, 2012, pp. 6–8.

20. For example, see Ronald Henkoff, "Cost Cutting: How to Do It Right," *Fortune,* April 9, 1990, pp. 40–49.

21. Hambrick, "Some Tests of Effectiveness."

22. Anthony Bianco, "The Vanishing Mass Market," *BusinessWeek,* July 12, 2004, pp. 61–72; and "The Printed World," *The Economist,* February 12, 2011, pp. 77–79; Also see Paul Markillie, "A Third Industrial Revolution," *The Economist,* April 21, 2012, special report pp. 3–20.

23. Wolfgang Ulaga and Andreas Eggert, "Value-Based Differentiation in Business Relationships: Gaining and Sustaining Key Supplier Status," *Journal of Marketing* 70 (January 2006), pp. 119–36.

24. Roland T. Rust, Christine Moorman, and Peter R. Dickson, "Getting Return on Quality."

25. Miles and Snow, *Organizational Strategy, Structure, and Process;* and Hambrick, "Some Tests of Effectiveness."

26. Although Hambrick argues for the reverse relationship, data from his study of 850 SBUs actually support our contention that defenders have more vertically integrated channels than do prospectors. See Hambrick, "Some Tests of Effectiveness."

27. Leonard A. Schlesinger and James L. Heskett, "The Service-Driven Service Company," *Harvard Business Review* 69 (September–October 1991), pp. 71–81; and Ulaga and Eggert, "Value-Based Differentiation in Business Relationships."

28. Connie J. G. Gersick, "Revolutionary Change Theories: A Multilevel Exploration of the Punctuated Equilibrium Paradigm," *Academy of Management Review* 16 (1991), pp. 10–36; and Michael L. Tushman, William H. Newman, and Elaine Romanelli, "Convergence and Upheaval: Managing the Unsteady Pace of Organizational Evolution," *California Management Review* 29 (1986), pp. 29–44.

Section **Two**

Opportunity Analysis

Chapter Four

Understanding Market Opportunities

The Cellular Telephone Business: Increasing Competition in a Growing Market[1]

From London to Tokyo to Nairobi to Chicago,cell phones have become a "can't do without it" tool of time-pressed businesspeople, hip teenagers, rural farmers, fishermen in Africa, and just about anyone else who wants to stay in touch. The market for mobile telephone service has grown rapidly. In 1983, when the first cellular phone system began operations, it was projected that by 2000, fewer than 1 million people would subscribe. As a result of dramatic growth among both business and household users, however, by 2005, the number of cell phone users had reached more than 2 billion worldwide! By 2007, there were more cell phone subscriptions than people in the world's developed economies and by 2011, three-quarters of the world's 5 billion people had cell phone subscriptions. In the first quarter of 2012, more than 400 million cell phones were sold worldwide.

The continuing growth in demand for mobile voice and data services generates numerous opportunities in the cell phone manufacturing and cell phone service industries, among others. Prospective entrants and current players considering additional investments should consider, however, just how attractive these markets and industries really are.

The Mobile Telephony Market

By all accounts, the *market* for mobile telephony has been an attractive one. New features such as color screens, built-in cameras, and web browsers have attracted new users and encouraged existing users to upgrade their phones.

Given torrid growth on all fronts, most observers agree that the *market* for cell phone service and cell phones themselves has been attractive indeed, even though the market's torrid pace appears to be abating. But how attractive are the *industries* that serve this market?

Cell Phone Manufacturing

Rapid-fire advances from Nokia, BlackBerry, Apple, and many others brought countless new features to the market, driven by technological change that made all the new features and new uses possible. Nokia rocketed to world leadership in cell phones, leaving early and longtime leader Motorola in the dust. Nokia saw its global market share grow to 40 percent by 2007, based on its continuing strength in developed markets and its growing dominance of the market for low-priced handsets in the developing world. As industry analyst Neal Mawston noted, "Nokia has a world-class product portfolio and very few rivals can compete with that. They are now enjoying huge economies of scale that success conveys. Anybody who tries to get in a handset war with them is going to get hurt."

But in the turbulent mayhem that has characterized the global cell phone industry since its inception, Nokia's success did not last. The coming of Apple's touchscreen iPhone in 2007 took traditional competitors like Nokia and Motorola as well as other smartphone makers like BlackBerry's Research in Motion by storm. Google's Android operating system followed in 2008, opening the door to a plethora of cell phone makers who mimicked Apple's touchscreen interface. By early 2012, sales of Android phones overtook those of Apple, winning a 56 percent global market share. The top Android smartphone maker, Samsung, even topped Apple in sales, selling 38 million units in the first quarter of 2012. Together, Apple and Samsung won a stunning 49.3 percent share of the smartphone market, up from 29.3 percent a year earlier. Nokia, having largely missed the smartphone phenomenon, saw the price of its shares fall by 90 percent between 2007 and 2012.

The Chinese cell phone manufacturers, of course, were not sitting idly by. With growing demand for affordable smartphones in China driving their sales, four Chinese makers had moved into the top 12 globally by 2010. Over the first three quarters of 2011, Huawei's 4.47 million and ZTE's 3.03 million were approaching Apple's unit sales of 5.6 million smartphones in China alone.

This recent history in the hotly competitive cell phone manufacturing industry suggests that a rapidly growing market does not necessarily provide a smooth path to success. Growing markets are one thing, but turbulent industries serving those markets are quite another. Will Samsung or one of the Chinese makers trump Apple? Will Nokia, with its Lumia phones sporting Microsoft's new Metro user interface, make a comeback? Life is not easy if you're a cell phone maker!

Cell Phone Service Providers

In 2007, European leader Vodaphone bought into India's rapidly growing market by acquiring 67 percent of India's third-largest operator, Hutchinson Essar. CEO Arun Sarin was delighted. "We are going to learn as much from India as we are going to take from India," he crowed.

"Prices there are two-and-a-half cents a minute, and they make a 35 percent margin. How do you do that?"

Just two and a half years later, the price of a cell phone minute in India had collapsed to 1 U.S. cent. Sarin moved on and in came cost-cutter Vittorio Collao as Vodaphone's new CEO. Despite (or as a result of) the fact that India's cell phone operators installed in one year as much network capacity as Germany had built in the last 15 years, the pressure on prices and profits was relentless. Newcomer Uninor, a unit of Norway's Telenor, introduced a plan that offered calls for as little as 0.20 rupees per minute, about half of 1 U.S. cent.

In the more fully developed Western markets, consumer demand for faster 4G service and snazzier phones was swamping the service providers' networks and raising their costs. AT&T, the first provider to offer Apple's iPhone in the United States, plunged to dead last in some surveys of consumer satisfaction. Worse, from the providers' point of view, rapidly growing demand for Apple's iPad was chewing up bandwidth at 10 times the rate of early smartphones. Pricing plans that offered unlimited data were part of the problem. So will unlimited data plans go away? "I don't think you can have an unlimited model forever," says AT&T's John Stankey. "More people get drunk at an open bar than a cash bar."

Network Equipment Down, Too

Another industry that had raced to keep pace with the growing cell phone market—makers of network equipment like switches, towers, and more—also hit the skids. Longtime stalwarts Alcatel-Lucent and Nokia Siemens Networks were both running losses in 2010, in the face of waning demand for 3G technology and stiff competition from Ericsson and China's Huawei. They were hoping that orders for new 4G equipment would bail them out.

Thus, while the rapidly growing *market* for mobile telephone service has been an attractive one, the *industries* that serve this market face significant challenges.

STRATEGIC CHALLENGES ADDRESSED IN CHAPTER 4

As the examples of the cellular phone manufacturing and service industries show, serving a growing market hardly guarantees smooth sailing. Equally or more important are industry conditions and the degree to which specific players in the industry can, like Nokia or Apple, establish and sustain competitive advantage at least for a while. Thus, as entrepreneurs and marketing decision makers ponder an *opportunity* to enter or attempt to increase their share of a growing market like that for mobile phones, they also must carefully examine a host of other issues, including the conditions that are currently prevailing in the industry in which they would compete and the likelihood that favorable conditions will prevail in the future. Similarly, such decisions require a thorough examination of trends that are influencing market demand and are likely to do so in the future, whether favorably or otherwise.

Thus, in this chapter, we address the 4 Cs that were identified in Chapter 1 as the analytical foundation of the marketing management process. We provide a framework to help managers, entrepreneurs, and investors comprehensively assess the attractiveness of opportunities they encounter, in terms of the *company* and its people, the environmental *context* in which it operates, the *competition* it faces, and the wants and needs of the *customer* it seeks to serve. We do so by addressing the three questions crucial to the assessment of any market opportunity: How attractive is the market we serve or propose to serve? How attractive is the industry in which we would compete? Are the right human resources—in terms of people and their capabilities and connections—in place to effectively pursue the opportunity at hand?

Strategic Issue

How attractive is the market we serve or propose to serve? How attractive is the industry in which we would compete? Are the right resources—in terms of people and their capabilities and connections—in place to effectively pursue the opportunity at hand?

At the end of the chapter, the Marketing Plan Exercise outlines the secondary data you will need to gather in preparing a marketing plan, so that the market and competitive climate in which your product-market offering will compete is both well understood and properly documented. Without your having established such a foundation of evidence, readers of your plan will be unable to fully understand and buy into the marketing decisions your plan articulates.

We frame our discussion of opportunity assessment using the seven domains shown in Exhibit 4.1. As the seven domains framework suggests and the cellular telephony story shows, in today's rapidly changing and hotly competitive world it's not enough to have a large and growing market. The attractiveness of the industry is also important, as are the company's or entrepreneurial team's resources—human, financial, and otherwise. Before digging more deeply into the framework, however, we clarify the difference between two oft-confused terms: **market** and **industry.**

MARKETS AND INDUSTRIES: WHAT'S THE DIFFERENCE?

We define a *market* as being composed of individuals or organizations who are interested in and willing to buy a good or service to obtain benefits that will satisfy a particular want or need and have the resources to engage in such a transaction. One such market consists of college students who get hungry in the middle of the afternoon and have a few minutes and enough spare change to buy a snack between classes.

An *industry* is a group of firms that offer a product or class of products that are similar and are close substitutes for one another. What industries serve the student snack market? At the producer level, there are the salty-snack industry (makers of potato and corn chips and similar products); the candy industry; the fresh produce industry (growers of apples, oranges, bananas, and other easy-to-eat fruits); and others too numerous to mention. Distribution channels for these products include the supermarket industry, food service industry, coin-operated vending industry, and so on. Clearly, these industries differ and offer varying bundles of benefits to hungry students.

EXHIBIT 4.1 The Seven Domains of Attractive Opportunities

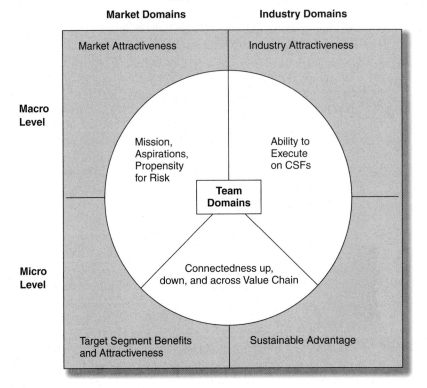

Source: John Mullins, *The New Business Road Test: What Entrepreneurs and Executives Should Do* Before *Writing a Business Plan* (London: FT/Prentice Hall, 2010).

Strategic Issue

Markets are composed of buyers; industries are composed of sellers. The distinction is often overlooked.

Thus, markets are composed of buyers; industries are composed of sellers. The distinction, often overlooked, is an important one because both markets and industries can vary substantially in their attractiveness, as we've seen in the cellular arena.

Further, sellers who look only to others in their own industry as competitors are likely to overlook other very real rivals and risk having their markets undercut by innovators from other industries. Should Kodak have been more concerned with Fuji, Agfa, and other longtime players in the film and photoprocessing industries, or should it have worried about Hewlett-Packard, Sony, and various online players whose digital technologies have made photography's century-old silver halide chemistry go the way of the buggy whip?[2] To add insult to injury, not only did digital cameras make film and conventional cameras obsolete, but the entry of smartphones that include cameras may soon make digital cameras obsolete.

ASSESSING MARKET AND INDUSTRY ATTRACTIVENESS

The seven domains framework enables marketers to answer two important questions, among others, in an evidence-based manner: How attractive is the market? How attractive is the industry? For a comparison of this approach to an older way of assessing the 4 Cs, see Exhibit 4.2.

EXHIBIT 4.2   *Why Not a SWOT?*

For many years, strategy textbooks have taught students to conduct a SWOT analysis that enumerates the strengths, weaknesses, opportunities, and threats faced by the firm in a particular market and industry setting. Doing so is useful, of course, but it fails to organize the output into answers to important strategic questions, such as those of market or industry attractiveness or the ability of the firm or its offering to achieve sustainable competitive advantage. The seven domains framework organizes similar information as a SWOT, and more, and does so in a manner that addresses such questions explicitly.

As Exhibit 4.1 shows, markets and industries must be assessed at both the macro and micro levels of analysis. But what do these levels really mean? On both the market and industry sides, the macro-level analyses are based on environmental conditions that affect the market or industry, respectively, as a whole, without regard to a particular company's strategy, target market, or its role in its industry. These external and often uncontrollable forces or conditions must be reckoned with in assessing and shaping any opportunity and, indeed, in developing any coherent marketing strategy.

At the micro level, the analyses look not at the market or the industry overall but at *individuals* in that market or industry, that is, specific target customers and companies themselves, respectively. We develop and apply the relevant analytical frameworks for the macro-level analyses first; then we address the micro-level analyses.

MACRO TREND ANALYSIS: A FRAMEWORK FOR ASSESSING MARKET ATTRACTIVENESS, MACRO LEVEL

Assessing market attractiveness requires that important ***macroenvironmental*** trends—or ***macro trends*** for short—be noticed and understood. The macroenvironment can be divided into six major components: demographic, sociocultural, economic, regulatory, technological, and natural arenas. The key question marketing managers and strategists must ask in each of these arenas is what trends are out there that are influencing demand in the market of interest, whether favorably or unfavorably.

The Demographic Environment

As the saying goes, demography is destiny. All kinds of things—from sales of music CDs to the state of public finances to society's costs of health care to the financing of pensions—are governed to a significant extent by demographic changes. While the number of specific demographic trends that might influence one marketer or another is without limit, there are currently four major global demographic trends that are likely to influence the fortunes of many companies, for better or worse: the aging of the world's population, the effect of the AIDS plague on demography, a rapidly growing middle class in emerging a countries, and increased levels of immigration.

Strategic Issue

Demography is destiny. All kinds of things are governed to a significant extent by demographic changes.

Aging

Exhibit 4.3 shows the projected increase in the portion of the population aged over 60 in several of the world's most developed countries. The chart shows that in Italy, for example, nearly half the population will be over 60 by the year 2040, according to current projections. Providers of health care, vacation homes, life insurance, and other goods and services have taken note of the graying of the world's population and are taking steps to develop marketing strategies to serve this fast-growing market.

EXHIBIT 4.3 **Aging Populations: % of the Population Aged over 60**

Chart showing % of population aged over 60 for US, Australia, Canada, UK, France, Germany, Sweden, Japan, Italy. Legend: 2000 (light), 2040* (dark). X-axis from 0 to 50. *Projection

Source: Norma Cohen and Clive Cookson, "The Planet Is Ever Greyer: But as Longevity Rises Faster than Forecast, the Elderly Are Also Becoming Healthier," *Financial Times,* January 19, 2004, p. 15.

Doing so, however, isn't always easy. Many people do not wish to be pigeonholed as elderly, and some who are getting older may not be very attracted to goods or services that remind them of their age. One marketer dealing with this challenge is Ferrari, whose average customer is nearing 50 and getting older with each passing year. "The profile of our customers means we have to pay attention to practicality and functionality without compromising the sportiness," says Giuseppe Bonollo, Ferrari's strategic marketing director. "The way the doors open on the Enzo, for example, allows part of the roof and part of the door undermolding to come away as well, making it easier to enter the car."[3]

The implications of the aging trend are not as clear-cut as they might appear. Surprisingly, perhaps, some 25 percent of the early buyers of Apple's iPhones—a "cool," cutting-edge product if there ever was one—were people over 50.[4] Further, there is evidence that today's elderly generation is both healthier and fitter than its predecessors. Thus, fears that health and other facilities will be swamped by hordes of ailing pensioners may be misplaced. "New data demolish such concerns," reports Raymond Tillis, professor of geriatric medicine at Manchester University in the United Kingdom. "There is a lot of evidence that disability among old people is declining rapidly."[5]

Aids

The death toll due to HIV/AIDS in Africa, the hardest hit region, was some 8 million from 1995 to 2000,[6] and the pandemic continues. At the end of 2010, it was estimated that some 34 million people were living with HIV worldwide, a 17 percent increase since 2001.[7] Across Africa, grandparents are raising an entire generation of children, since many parents have died.

Pharmaceutical companies and world health organizations are struggling to develop strategies to deal with the AIDS challenge, one that presents a huge and rapidly growing market, but one in which there is little ability to pay for the advanced drug therapies that offer hope to AIDS victims. But progress is being made: the rate of annual new HIV infections has fallen 21 percent between 1997 and 2010, owing in part to a substantial increase in access to antiretroviral therapy in Africa and elsewhere, especially in recent years.[8]

Growing Middle Class

In the emerging economies of Asia and Latin America, the pace of economic development in recent years has led to a rapid increase in the number of consumers deemed by demographers to be middle class. Though the definition of what constitutes middle class varies (for example, not living from hand to mouth, job to job, or season to season—as the poor do—is one definition), there is no dispute that their numbers have risen dramatically, to more than 50 percent of the world's total population by 2006.[9] Asia is now home to 60 percent of the world's middle class, compared to just 20 percent in 1980.[10]

We take a closer look at the implications of this trend in Chapter 6. For marketers, though, it is clear that no longer can we view emerging economies as consisting of a few rich people, alongside huddling masses of the poor. Even in the crowded, impoverished *favelas* of São Paolo, Brazil, and in rural villages in India, where there is little running water or electricity, satellite dishes are popping up on tin roofs. Marketers, take note (see Exhibit 4.4).

Increased Immigration

Not surprisingly, the increasing imbalance between the economic prospects for those living in more developed versus less developed countries is leading to increased levels of immigration. With the 2004 enlargement of the European Union from 15 to 25 countries, fears grew that some countries in the "old EU" would be swamped with immigrants from the accession countries in Eastern Europe, where per capita GDP is far less than the EU 15 average.[11] The recent economic turmoil in Europe may put an end to these fears, as high levels of unemployment in many parts of Europe make them lessattractive destinations than they once were.

In one sense, such immigration is nothing new, for melting pot countries such as the United States and the United Kingdom have for centuries welcomed immigrants to their shores. In the United States, many years of immigration from Mexico and Latin America have made the Sun Belt a bilingual region, and many now view Miami as the crossroads of Latin America. The implications for marketers seeking to gain market share among Hispanic Americans are obvious.

While immigration from the developing to the developed world continues at a high rate, there are also emerging signs that, at least among the better-educated portion of the diaspora in the West, growing numbers are returning to their homelands, where faster economic growth is creating economic opportunities that were absent years earlier.[12] Whether it is Asian doctors in Great Britain or engineers in California's Silicon Valley, many are taking what they've learned there to start new businesses in Mumbai, Bangalore, or Shanghai.

EXHIBIT 4.4 *Changing Assumptions and Mind-Sets*

It's not just a burgeoning middle class that is making marketers rethink how to better serve consumers in emerging markets. Such markets tend to have characteristics that differ from the traditional, mature markets on which many of our established marketing assumptions and strategies are based. These characteristics—including market heterogeneity, norms for socio-political governance, a chronic shortage of resources, unbranded competition, inadequate infrastructure, and more—can disrupt marketers' accepted perspectives and require a shift toward a truly global mind-set.

So must anything change? Competencies need to change, the marketing function needs greater transparency and governance, and talent must be sourced and developed on a global basis. These challenges make today an exciting time to enter the marketing profession, particularly for those who bring to their jobs a deep understanding of how consumers in emerging markets think and behave.

Source: Jagdish N. Sheth, "Impact of Emerging Markets on Marketing: Rethinking Existing Perspectives and Practices," *Journal of Marketing* 75 (July 2011), pp. 166–82.

The Sociocultural Environment

Sociocultural trends are those that have to do with the values, attitudes, and behavior of individuals in a given society. Cultures tend to evolve slowly, however, so some sociocultural trends can take a generation or more to have significant impact, as people tend to carry for a lifetime the values with which they grow up. Within this broadly stable pattern, however, sociocultural trends can and do exert powerful effects on markets for a great variety of goods and services. Two trends of particular relevance today are greater interest in *corporate social responsibility* by businesses and trends toward fitness and nutrition.

Corporate Social Responsibility

For years, the world's leading coffee marketers, including Kraft and Nestlé, resisted calls to pay premium prices for coffee grown in a sustainable manner, on farms that pay their workers a living wage and that respect the environment. In 2003, Kraft, running neck and neck with Nestlé for the number one spot in market share globally, reached agreement with the Rainforest Alliance, a nonprofit organization that seeks to improve the working, social, and environmental conditions in agriculture in the third world. The agreement called for Kraft to buy £5 million of Rainforest Alliance–certified coffee from Brazil, Colombia, Mexico, and Central America in 2004, paying a 20 percent premium to the farmers.[13]

Fast-forward to 2011. Fair trade coffee was becoming a big business, thanks to robust consumer demand. Some third-party certification groups, including Fair Trade USA, the national certification leader in the United States, adopted more inclusive policies that permitted large-scale producers into the game. Critics were furious, worrying that small farmer cooperatives—those whom fair trade is supposed to help—will soon get squeezed out.[14]

Fitness and Nutrition

Running. Working out. Fitness clubs. The South Beach and Atkins diets. These days, natural and organic foods are in. Sugar and cholesterol—at least the bad LDL cholesterol—are out. The implications of these sociocultural trends are playing out in grocery store produce departments, where entire sections are now devoted to organic produce; in the farming communities of North America and Europe, where fields formerly farmed with fertilizers are being transformed into organic ones; and on restaurant menus, where selections are being revamped to make them appeal to customers who have adopted new eating habits. The 20-ounce T-bone steak is a thing of the past, at least in some circles.

These trends are driving more than just the food business, however. Attendance at health and fitness clubs is booming. Sales of home exercise equipment are up, along with advice on how to purchase and use it to best advantage.[15]

The Economic Environment

Among the most far-reaching of the six macro trend components is the economic environment. When people's incomes rise or fall, when interest rates rise or fall, when the fiscal policy of governments results in increased or decreased government spending, entire sectors of economies are influenced deeply, and sometimes suddenly. As we write, with some Western economies struggling to bounce back from recession, and others—including Greece, Spain, and more—mired in severe downturns with bleak near-term prospects, the future of the developed economies appears to lie in the factories of exporters or in the purses and wallets of their—or China's or India's—shoppers.

The implications of trends like these in consumer spending can be dramatic for marketers, to be sure, but they can be far subtler than one might imagine. Take robust economic health,

Strategic Issue

Take robust economic health, for example. It's good for everyone, right?

for example. It's good for everyone, right? Not if you're the operator of a chain of check-cashing outlets or pawn shops, which thrive when times are tough and people need to turn unwanted assets into cash quickly. Or what about discount airlines? Shouldn't they be thriving in a troubled economic environment? Ryanair, Europe's largest airline by passenger count, announced that it would cut its capacity—grounding 80 of its 300 jets—for its winter season beginning in October 2011. "It's the first time ever that we'll go negative on traffic," CEO Michael O'Leary said in an interview. "We take delivery of 50 aircraft this winter so instead of running around trying to open up new bases and routes in November and December we'll sit them on the ground. There will still be strong growth next summer but trying to open up new routes with high oil prices is stupid in the winter."[16] The hundred-dollar price per barrel of oil has forced even the discounters like Ryanair and Southwest to raise prices, and cash-strapped travelers are finding other ways to get around (see Exhibit 4.5).

Whether the current economic difficulties in Europe are resolved smoothly or not—as we write, the pessimists appear to hold the upper hand—it seems abundantly clear that the world's wealth is moving inexorably eastward and south, to the rapidly growing markets of Asia and Latin America, including the **BRIC countries** and others. Marketers everywhere must face the fact that the so-called **emerging markets** are no longer just seen as sources of low-cost commodities and labor. Rather, they are where any growth in demand must come from. Asia is already the largest market for many product categories, including cars (35 percent of global demand in 2009) and mobile phones (43 percent). In **purchasing-power-parity** terms, three of the world's four biggest economies (China, Japan, and India) are already in Asia, and more than half of global GDP growth over the past decade has come from Asia.[17] Tomorrow's business leaders will need truly global perspectives to make the most of these changes. Doing so is not always easy, however (see Exhibit 4.6).

The Regulatory Environment

In every country and across some countries—those that are members of the EU, for example—there is a *regulatory environment* within which local and multinational firms operate. As with the other macro trend components, political and legal trends, especially those that result in *regulation* or *deregulation,* can have powerful impact on market attractiveness, as we've just seen in the example of retailing in India (Exhibit 4.6), where barriers to foreign direct investment are helping retailers like Easy Day and Pantaloon grow.

EXHIBIT 4.5 *No Pat-Downs on Megabus*

Long distance discount bus operators like Mega-bus and BoltBus, with their easy internet booking, free WiFi, streetside pickup, and power outlets on board, are winning customers like Chicago's Bobbie Joe Crail. "The bus can be inconvenient," says Crail, "but it's so much cheaper to string bus trips together than to fly." A study by Chicago's DePaul University reports that curbside carriers, at current capacity, eliminate 11 million gallons of fuel consumption annually and take 24,000 cars off the road.

Professor of transportation Joseph Schwieterman at DePaul is not surprised. "It's not just high fuel prices—it's

the hassle factor at the airports that has left many fliers disenchanted." On Megabus, passengers don't have to take their shoes off unless they want to, and there's no security pat-down either!

Sources: Brian Burnsed, "Suddenly It's Cool to Take the Bus," *BusinessWeek* European Edition, September 29, 2008, p. 64; Ben Austen, "The Megabus Effect," *Bloomberg Businessweek,* April 17, 2011, pp. 63–67. For more on Megabus or Boltbus, see *www.megabus.com* or *www.boltbus.com/default.aspx.*

EXHIBIT 4.6 *Modern Retailing in India? Good Luck!*

Western retailers, as well as Indian entrepreneurs, have been salivating for years at the prospect of transforming India's nineteenth-century retailing industry, in which only 7 percent of the country's $435 billion in retailing volume is done in chain stores, compared to about 20 percent in China and 35 percent in Brazil. Easy Day, whose modern supermarkets would be at home most anywhere in the west, is one example of a company trying to do just that. A government-imposed ban on **foreign direct investment** by multi-brand chains like America's Walmart or France's Carrefour would appear to pave Easy Day's road to runaway success.

For Easy Day, though, adapting to a bewildering and sometimes conflicting abundance of local rules, the more than 20 officially recognized local languages, 14 main types of cuisine, and three main religions whose dietary strictures carry considerable weight, is the easy part. Much more difficult are the challenges entailed in dealing with a lack of cool-chain storage and distribution, potholed roads, sky-high prices for property, a plethora of state-by-state taxes (and delays) levied on goods that move across and sometimes within state boundaries, and—perhaps most important—populist public policies that protect small shop-owners.

Will India's retailing industry make it into the twentieth century—never mind the twenty-first—any time soon? Pantaloon's Kishore Biyani, thinks progress has been made. "Indians are learning to come to consumerism," he says. With supermarkets, specialty stores, and mass-merchandise megastores in 73 cities and predicted sales of $4 billion in 2012, Pantaloon's parent company Future Group is the country's largest and most successful retailer, with volume two-and-one-half times its nearest competitor. But as one observer of India's retailing landscape puts it, highlighting the tension, "Customers are taking to choice and consumption like ducks to water. It is the politicians' mind-set that needs to change."

Source: *The Economist,* "Send for the Supermarketers," April 16, 2011. For more on Pantaloon or Easy Day, see www.pantaloonretail.in or www.easydayindia.com.

The power of deregulation to influence market attractiveness is now well-known. Government, business, and the general public throughout much of the world have become increasingly aware that overregulation protects inefficiencies, restricts entry by new competitors, and creates inflationary pressures. In the United States, airlines, trucking, railroads, telecommunications, and banking have been deregulated. Markets have also been liberated in western and eastern Europe, Asia, and many developing countries. Trade barriers are crumbling due to political unrest and technological innovation.

Deregulation has typically changed the structure of the affected industries as well as lowered prices, creating rapid growth in some markets as a result. For example, the period following deregulation of the U.S. airline industry (1978–1985) gave rise to a new airline category—the budget airline. The rise of Southwest and other budget airlines led to lower fares across all routes and forced the major carriers to streamline operations and phase out underperforming routes. A similar story has followed in the European market, where discount airlines Ryanair, Wiz, easyJet, and others have made vacation destinations places to fly to rather than drive to.

Perhaps surprisingly, then, a trend of ***reregulation*** is taking hold, especially in Europe and the United States, as a result of a perceived failure of the global financial services industry to self-regulate its practices, seen as a key cause of the 2007–2008 financial meltdown, the effects of which are still playing out.[18] Whether this reregulation trend will gather steam—or spread to other industries, such as taxing products that lead to obesity—may depend, in part, on the speed at which the European and American economies recover. With things still getting worse—not better—in some countries as we write, marketers appear headed for an era in which public policy-makers will play an increasing regulatory role.

The Technological Environment

In the past three decades, an amazing number of new technologies has created new markets for such products as video recorders, compact disks, ever-more-powerful and ever-smaller computers, smartphones, new lightweight materials, and genetically engineered drugs. Technological progress is unlikely to abate.

Technology can also change how businesses operate (banks, airlines, retail stores, and marketing research firms), how goods and services as well as ideas are exchanged, how crops are grown, and how individuals learn and earn as well as interact with one another. Consumers today enjoy check-free banking, the death of the invoice, and ticketless air travel.

Many of these innovations are the result not only of changes in computing systems, but also of reduced costs in communicating (voice or data). For example, the cost of processing an additional telephone call is so small it might as well be free. Distance is no longer a factor—it costs about the same to make a trans-Atlantic call as one to your next-door neighbor. If you place the call on Skype, it can cost nothing at all!

New developments in telecommunications and computing have led to the rapid convergence of the telecommunications, computing, and entertainment industries. Music-hungry consumers have been downloading music from legal and illegal sites, thereby hammering the music industry and have forced the industry to change the way it distributes music. But things appear to be looking up (see Exhibit 4.7).

What's next? Some observers say the digitization of manufacturing will bring on the third industrial revolution, following mechanization of the British textile industry in the eighteenth century and Henry Ford's invention of mass production in the twentieth. The cost of producing smaller batches with wider variety is falling dramatically, and ***mass customization***—where things are designed on a computer and "printed" layer by layer on a 3D printer—may be the wave of the future. Perfectly fitted hearing aids and highly specialized parts for military jets are but two of the product categories for which this incredible future is here now.[19] Savvy marketers and entrepreneurs who follow technological trends are able to foresee new and previously unheard of applications such as these and thereby place themselves and their firms at the forefront of the innovation curve, sometimes earning entrepreneurial fortunes in the process.

Strategic Issue

Savvy marketers and entrepreneurs who follow technological trends are able to foresee new and previously unheard of applications, sometimes earning entrepreneurial fortunes in the process.

In addition to creating attractive new markets, technological developments are having a profound impact on all aspects of marketing practice, including marketing communication (ads on the web or via e-mail), distribution (books and other consumer and industrial

---

EXHIBIT 4.7 *The Music Industry Brightens*

Technology, which has made life very difficult for the music industry for more than a decade, is, perhaps surprisingly, the source of a growing market for music. The Nielsen SoundScan report for the first half of 2011 heralded the first rise in album sales in the United State in seven years. Lady Gaga's May 2011 release, "Born this Way," sold a million copies in its first week alone. But it's the newer music distribution mechanisms that are making much of the difference. Revenues from new music-streaming websites such as Spotify, other direct-to-consumer sales, advertising revenue from YouTube and other sites, and concert royalties have driven overall

music revenue 50 percent higher since 2006, while driving recording costs (an ordinary laptop is all you need) and distribution costs lower.

"The internet has allowed for a lot more diversity in music," says Britain's Anna Calvi, whose growing popularity has been driven in part by videos posted on YouTube. "It is a healthy part of the artistic process is to be able to show your work, and this is now possible for everyone."

Source: Andrew McKie, "Music Industry Sighs No More," *The Wall Street Journal European Edition*, August 5, 2011, p. W8. For more on Spotify, see *www.spotify.com*.

goods bought and sold via the web), packaging (use of new materials), and marketing research (monitoring supermarket purchases with scanners or internet activity with digital "*cookies*"). For example, a recent study has shown that social networks influence consumer decisions about staying with or leaving service providers. In particular, highly connected customers are more likely to defect from a service provider in response to others in their network doing the same.[20] We explore these kinds of changes and others in the ensuing chapters in this book.

The Natural Environment

Everything ultimately depends on the natural environment, including marketing. Changes in the earth's resources and climate can have significant and far-reaching effects. The world's supply of oil is finite, for example, leading automakers to develop new hot-selling hybrid gas-electric vehicles such as the Toyota Prius, which can go more than 50 miles on a gallon of gas. The skyrocketing price of oil has caused demand for gas-guzzling sport utility vehicles to plummet.[21]

In general, discussion of the problems in the natural environment has stressed the threats and penalties facing business throughout the world. But business can do a number of things to turn problems into opportunities. One is to invest in research to find ways to save energy in heating and lighting. Another is to find new energy sources such as wind farms and hydroelectric projects. In virtually every corner of the clean-tech and green-tech arenas, entrepreneurs and marketers are looking for ways to save the planet and deliver shareholder returns at the same time. And, in response to growing consumer concern in Britain about environmental issues, a growing number of marketers, including Tesco, the United Kingdom's largest supermarket chain, have begun adding *carbon footprint labels* to some of their products.[22]

Businesses have also seen opportunities in developing thousands of *green products* (those that are environmentally friendly) such as phosphate-free detergents, tuna caught without netting dolphins, organic fertilizers, high-efficiency LED lighting, recycled paper, and clothes made from 100 percent organic cotton and colored with nontoxic dyes. DuPont, long synonymous with petrochemicals, is reinventing itself as an eco-conscious company. More than $5 billion of its $29 billion in revenue comes from sustainable products, including a new corn-based fiber called Sorona, which can be used to make clothing, carpet, and other products.[23] There is a growing recognition that creating a more sustainable natural environment is an important job, one to which today's newly educated marketers can contribute (see Exhibit 4.8).

EXHIBIT 4.8 *Clean-Tech, Green-Tech, Sustainability and You*

Fuel-efficient cars are once again in favor, Tesla's electric cars are cool (*www.teslamotors.com*), and solar energy is hot. Clean-tech and green-tech investment funds have sprung up in Silicon Valley, London, Mumbai, and seemingly everywhere else to invest in companies that hope to create a more sustainable future. Green-tech outfits like Spain's T-Solar (*www.tsolar.com*), U.S. green energy producer Ameresco (*www.amerescosolar.com*), and the renewable unit of the Italian utility Enel (*www.enel.com*) have raised capital in hot IPOs.

Business school students, too, are getting in on the sustainability game. Business plan competitions for socially and environmentally friendly ventures, like the Global Social Venture Competition held annually at the Haas School of Business at the University of California, Berkeley, and fed from a network of business schools around the world, now motivate students to think in triple bottom-line terms, rather than solely about profit. Social returns, environmental returns, and economic returns: Wouldn't the world be a better place if we had more of all three?

Sources: Mark Scott and Alex Morales, "A Gold Rush in Green Technology," *Bloomberg Businessweek* European Edition, April 25, 2010, p. 24; the Global Social Venture Competition website at *www.gsvc.com*.

Trends in the natural environment are creating opportunities for companies like Du-Pont. On the other hand, if global warming continues, it may play havoc with markets for winter vacationers, snowmobiles, and other products and services whose demand depends on the reliable coming of Old Man Winter. Other natural trends, such as the depletion of natural resources and fresh groundwater, may significantly impact firms in many industries serving a vast array of markets. Tracking such trends and understanding their effects is an important task.

YOUR MARKET IS ATTRACTIVE: WHAT ABOUT YOUR INDUSTRY?

As we saw at the outset of this chapter, consumers and businesspeople have become hooked on cell phones, and the market for mobile communication has grown rapidly. By most measures, this is a large, growing, and attractive *market*. But are cell phone manufacturing and cellular services attractive *industries?* An industry's attractiveness at a point in time can best be judged by analyzing the five major competitive forces, which we address in this section.

Porter's Five Competitive Forces[24]

Five competitive forces collectively determine an industry's long-term attractiveness—rivalry among present competitors, threat of new entrants into the industry, the bargaining power of suppliers, the bargaining power of buyers, and the threat of substitute products (see Exhibit 4.9).

Strategic Issue

Five competitive forces collectively determine an industry's long-term attractiveness.

This mix of forces explains why some industries are consistently more profitable than others and provides further insights into which resources are required and which strategies should be adopted to be successful. A useful way to conduct a five forces analysis of an industry's attractiveness is to construct a checklist based on Porter's seminal work.[25]

The strength of the individual forces varies from industry to industry and, over time, within the same industry. In the fast-food industry, the key forces are rivalry among present competitors (for example, Wendy's versus Burger King versus McDonald's) as well as the threat posed by substitute products (fast casual outlets such as Chipotle and Panera, salad bars, and frozen meals, for example).

Rivalry among Present Competitors

Rivalry occurs among firms that produce products that are close substitutes for each other, especially when one competitor acts to improve its standing or protect its position. Thus, firms are mutually dependent: What one firm does affects others and vice versa.

EXHIBIT 4.9 The Major Forces That Determine Industry Attractiveness

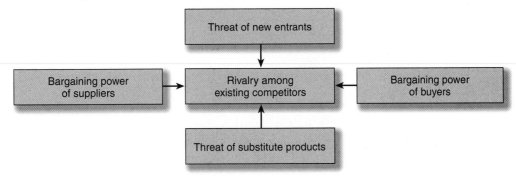

Ordinarily, profitability decreases as rivalry increases. Rivalry is greater under the following conditions:

- *There is high investment intensity; that is, the amount of fixed and working capital required to produce a dollar of sales is large.* High intensity requires firms to operate at or near capacity, thereby putting strong downward pressure on prices when demand slackens. Thus, high-investment–intensity businesses are, on average, much less profitable than those with a lower level of investment. Consider the airline industry, in which many of the largest airlines have fallen into (and sometimes exited from) bankruptcy. As the noted investor Warren Buffett observed, the entire airline industry has not made a dime for investors in its century of existence.[26]

- *There are many small firms in an industry or no dominant firms exist.* The restaurant industry is a good example.

- *There is little product differentiation*—for example, gasoline, major appliances, TV sets, and passenger-car tires.

- *It's easy for customers to switch from one seller's products to those of others* (low switching cost for buyers).

The greater the competitive rivalry in an industry, the less attractive it is to current players or would-be entrants. Consider cell phone service. The cellular service industry is capital intensive. Though there are several dominant firms whose products are differentiated through rapid technological change, such as faster 4G networks, consumers' switching costs to change cell phone service providers or handsets are low. Thus, rivalry among service providers, never mind for cell phone manufacturers, is brutal.

Threat of New Entrants

A second force affecting industry attractiveness is the threat of new entrants. New competitors add capacity to the industry and bring with them the need to gain market share, thereby making competition more intense. For cellular telephone operators, license requirements and the huge cost of obtaining bandwidth in government auctions make threat of entry into the cellular service industry relatively low in most countries. The less the threat of new entrants, the greater will be an industry's attractiveness, so this is good news for cellular operators. Entry is more difficult under the following conditions:

Strategic Issue

The greater the threat of new entrants, the less will be an industry's attractiveness.

- *When strong economies of scale and learning effects are present,* since it takes time to obtain the volume and learning required to yield a low relative cost per unit. If existing firms are vertically integrated, entry becomes even more expensive. Also, if the existing firms share their output with their related businesses, the problem of overcoming the cost disadvantage is made even more difficult.

- *If the industry has strong capital requirements at the outset.*

- *When strong product differentiation exists among current players.*

- *If gaining distribution is particularly difficult.*

At least one study suggests, however, that establishing entry barriers may be overrated as a mechanism for sustaining one's competitive advantage.[27] Entry barriers may well deter me-too entries, but they are less likely to deter more innovative entries. The results of this study suggest that a combination of effectively managing innovation cycles while building entry barriers through cost advantages or proprietary technologies can enhance incumbents' ability to sustain competitive advantage over time. Nokia was able to do so in mobile-phone manufacturing in this way for quite some time.

Bargaining Power of Suppliers

The bargaining power of suppliers over firms in an industry is the third major determinant of industry attractiveness. It is exercised largely through increased prices or more onerous terms and conditions of sale. Its impact can be significant, particularly when there is a limited number of suppliers serving an industry. Their power is increased under the following conditions:

- *If the cost of switching suppliers is high.*
- *If prices of substitutes are high.*
- *If suppliers can realistically threaten forward integration.*
- *When the supplier's product is a large part of the buyer's value added*—as is the case with aluminum cans, where the cost of aluminum is a large part of the value added.

In recent years, the bargaining power of suppliers in many industries has changed dramatically as more companies seek a partnership relationship with their suppliers. What was once an arm's-length adversarial relationship has turned into a cooperative one resulting in lower transaction costs, improved quality derived primarily from using a supplier's technological skills to design and manufacture parts, and decreased transaction time in terms of inventory replenishments through just-in-time procurement systems.

The greater the bargaining power of the key suppliers to an industry, the less will be the overall attractiveness of the industry. The newly discovered power that governments worldwide have exerted by auctioning bandwidth for new cellular services has raised their bargaining power as suppliers of bandwidth to the cellular services industry, thereby reducing the attractiveness of this industry.

Bargaining Power of Buyers

An industry's customers constantly look for reduced prices, improved product quality, and added services and thus can affect competition within an industry. Buyers play individual suppliers against one another in their efforts to obtain these and other concessions. This is certainly the case with some large retailers such as Walmart and Carrefour in their dealings with their suppliers.

The extent to which buyers succeed in their bargaining efforts depends on several factors, including these:

- *The extent of buyer concentration,* as when a few large buyers that account for a large portion of industry sales can gain concessions. Automakers' power over suppliers of tires is a good example.
- *Switching costs that reduce the buyer's bargaining power.*
- *The threat of backward integration,* thereby alleviating the need for the supplier.
- *The product's importance to the performance of the buyer's product*—the greater the importance, the lower the buyer's bargaining power.
- *Buyer profitability*—if buyers earn low profits and the product involved is an important part of their costs, then bargaining will be more aggressive.

The greater the power of the high-volume customers served by an industry, the less attractive will be that industry. One attractive dimension of the cellular phone service industry is that its customers have relatively little power to set terms and conditions for cellular phone service. Buyers are numerous and not very concentrated, and their cell phone costs are typically not of great importance or expense, relatively speaking.

Strategic Issue

The greater the power of the high-volume customers served by an industry, the less attractive will be that industry.

Threat of Substitute Products

Substitutes are alternative product types (not brands) produced by *other* industries that perform essentially the same functions, such as plastic bottles versus aluminum cans, digital photography over silver-halide film, and the faxing or e-mailing of documents versus overnight express delivery. Substitute products put a ceiling on the profitability of an industry by limiting the price that can be charged, especially when supply exceeds demand. Thus, in food-packaging, aluminum cans are substitutes for plastic bottles and conversely, and each constrains the prices that can be charged by the other.

A Five Forces Analysis of the Cellular Phone Service Industry

A useful way to summarize a five forces industry analysis is to construct a chart like that shown in Exhibit 4.10. There, we summarize one analyst's judgment of the favorability of the five forces for the European cellular phone service industry in the year 2012. This analysis indicates that, consistent with the preceding discussion, compared to earlier in the industry's history when there were fewer players (thus, less rivalry), no threatening substitutes on the horizon, and a cozier relationship with governments to provide bandwidth, the industry in 2012 was probably less attractive than some industries, for which four or five of the forces might be favorable.

Thus, marketers who must decide whether to enter or continue to invest in this industry must make a judgment as to whether the rapid growth of the *market—a favorable* **environmental context**—is sufficient to offset the deteriorating attractiveness of the *industry—the not-so-favorable* **competitive situation**. Given this mixed outlook, strategists would consider

EXHIBIT 4.10   **Five Forces Analysis of the European Cell Phone Service Industry in 2012**

Five Forces	Score	Rationale
Rivalry among present competitors	Rivalry is high leading to high customer churn: unfavorable	Products are differentiated through new features and services; customer switching costs are low.
Threat of new entrants	Threat of new entrants is low: moderately favorable	While rapid pace of technological change may bring new entrants based on new technologies (e.g., packet switching, satellites), new service providers must purchase a bandwidth license by spending billions.
Supplier power	Supplier power is high: moderately unfavorable	Governments in developed markets have raised the price of additional bandwidth through auctions.
Buyer power	Buyer power is low: very favorable	Even large customers have little power to set terms and conditions in this industry.
Threat of substitutes	Threat of substitutes is high: moderately unfavorable	PDAs, tablet computers, and laptops using Wi-Fi networks to access the web could cannibalize expected sales of 3G and 4G wireless network cell phones.

Overall conclusion: Only two of the five forces are favorable, while three are unfavorable. Thus, the cellular phone service industry, at least in the European market, is not very attractive at this time. In emerging markets, supplier power and threat of substitutes are often more favorable, since governments are more welcoming of telecom development, and substitutes are not likely to enter anytime soon. Thus industry attractiveness is brighter therein.

other factors, including the degree to which they believe they are likely to be able to establish and sustain competitive advantage. We further develop this theme later in this chapter.

CHALLENGES IN MACRO-LEVEL MARKET AND INDUSTRY ANALYSIS

In order to analyze the attractiveness of one's market or industry, one must first identify, of course, exactly which market or industry is to be analyzed. On the market side and recalling that markets consist of customers—whether individual consumers, trade customers like retailers, or business users in B2B markets—the challenge often lies in sizing the relevant market. Markets can (and should) be measured in various ways—in numbers of qualified potential customers (those that are potentially willing and able to buy), in units consumed of a class of goods or services, in terms of value (the aggregate spending on a class of goods or services) and so on. It is informative to measure market size and growth rates in customer numbers as well as in unit and value terms.

Strategic Issue

Markets can be measured in various ways—in numbers of qualified potential customers or in terms of value.

On the industry side, there's the question of how narrowly or broadly to define one's industry. Are Ball, a maker of aluminum beverage cans, and AMCOR, a maker of plastic beverage bottles, in the same industry (the packaging industry) or different industries (aluminum containers and plastic packaging)? Are Ford and Mack truck in the same industry (automotive) or different industries (autos and trucks)? There are no simple answers here, but a good way to identify the most suitable definition of the industry you are in is to consider whether the kinds of key suppliers, the processes by which value is added, and the kinds of buyers are the same for your company and other companies whose industry you may consider yourself a part of. If two or all three of these value chain elements are similar, it's probably appropriate to say you are all in the same industry. If two or more of them are different, you probably are in different industries, as is the case for Ball and AMCOR, where many of the customers are the same, but key suppliers (aluminum versus petroleum-based plastics) and value-adding processes (aluminum cans and plastic bottles are made very differently) differ. Thus, a five forces analysis of the aluminum can industry would consider the threat of substitutes from the plastic, glass, and paper packaging industries. For an approach to strategic thinking that avoids the constraints of traditional industry definitions, see Exhibit 4.11.

EXHIBIT 4.11   *Competing in Blue Oceans*

Chan Kim and Renée Mauborgne argue that one way out of today's hotly contested industry spaces defined by conventional boundaries is to develop what they call blue oceans, previously unknown market spaces as yet undiscovered by existing competition. Rather than focusing on "beating the competition," they argue, managers should focus more of their strategic efforts on finding markets where there is little competition—blue oceans—and then take steps to exploit and protect these oceans.

Their research found that companies that were effective in creating blue oceans never used the competition as a benchmark. Instead, they made competition irrelevant by creating a huge leap in value for both the company and for the new buyers it served. Henry Ford's Model T automobile created a blue ocean, an automotive industry that barely existed at the time. So, too, did Federal Express in overnight package delivery, Cirque du Soleil in circus (or is it theater?), and CNN in news broadcasting.

A key tenet of all these companies is that they rejected the notion that there must be a trade-off between value and cost, an inherent assumption that's all too frequent in strategic circles. Rejecting the tired strategic logic of red oceans—overcrowded industries where companies seek ways of beating one another—can lead, they found, to rapid, profitable, and often uncontested growth for a decade or more.

Source: W. Chan Kim and Renée Mauborgne, "Blue Ocean Strategy," *Harvard Business Review*, October 2004. For more on Blue Ocean Strategy, see *www.blueoceanstrategy.com*.

EXHIBIT 4.12 *Safaricom Outruns the Data*

In October 2000, Michael Joseph, the newly arrived CEO of Safaricom, was pondering how best to relaunch Safaricom's mobile phone service in Kenya. Safaricom had taken over the formerly government-owned cell phone operation, which had only 15,000 high-priced cell phone lines serving the business and government elite. Joseph wondered if there was enough buying power to enable his company to target the mass market in Kenya. The secondary data were not encouraging, since there were only 10 land-based telephone lines per 1,000 people in Kenya and only 26 televisions per 1,000. GDP per capita was a paltry $360, according to government figures. He gambled that the data were wrong and there was more buying power in Kenya than the figures foretold. Joseph's gamble paid off. Safaricom's launch was a hit from the start, and by 2006, more than 5 million Kenyans had cell phones, nearly one in every six Kenyans. By 2011, 25 million Kenyans, more than 60 percent of the total population, had cell phones.

Sources: Charles Mayaka, "Safaricom (A)," United States International University, 2005; Kachwanya, Mobile Monday—Kenya, "Kenyan Mobile Phone Penetration Is Now over 63%," June 7, 2011, *http://mobilemonday.co.ke/2011/kenyan-mobile-phone-penetration-is-now-over-63/*. For more on Safaricom, see *www.safaricom.co.ke*.

Information Sources for Macro-Level Analyses

In the developed economies, there is an endless supply of information about macro trends and industry forces, including the popular and business press, the internet, supplier and customer contacts, and so on. In emerging economies, however, such information is more difficult to find and can, in many cases, be misleading (see Exhibit 4.12). Thus, gathering relevant data is not difficult, but it does take time and effort. A good place to start is with trade associations and trade magazines, both of which typically track and report on trends relevant to the industries they serve. Most local, state, and federal governments provide demographic data easily accessible at their websites, such as *www.census.gov* in the United States. Government sources and the business press are good places to look for economic trends and data from Eurostat, the statistical office of the European Union (*www. europa.eu.int/ comm/eurostat*). Almost all sources of information are now readily available on the web. A list of some of the most useful sources of secondary data for macro-level market and industry analyses is provided in Exhibit 4.13.

The key outputs of a competent macro trend analysis for any market should include both quantitative and qualitative data. Quantitative data should provide evidence of the market's size and growth rate, for the overall market as well as for key segments. Qualitative data should include trends that will likely influence these figures in the future, whether favorably or unfavorably.

UNDERSTANDING MARKETS AT THE MICRO LEVEL

A market may be large and growing, but that does not mean customers will buy whatever it is that is proposed to be offered if a particular opportunity is pursued. Most new products, including those targeted at large and growing markets, fail because not enough customers buy them. A colorless version of Pepsi-Cola—without the caramel coloring—test-marketed unsuccessfully by Pepsi in the 1990s is but one of thousands of examples that capable marketers have brought to market with little success.

Thus, in assessing market opportunities at the micro level, one looks individually at customers—whether trade customers or end consumers or business users—to understand the attractiveness of the target segment itself. While we devote an entire later chapter to market segmentation and targeting (Chapter 6), it's worthwhile to take a brief look at the relevant issues for opportunity attractiveness here.

EXHIBIT 4.13   Some Information Sources for Market and Industry Analysis

Type of Information	Library Sources	Internet Sources
To find trade associations and trade magazines	*Gale Directory of Publications; Encyclopedia of Associations; UK Trade Association Forum; European Trade Associations*	www.gale.com www.taforum.org
Information on specific companies	*Hoover's Online Business; Ward's Business Directory; Dun and Bradstreet Million Dollar Directory; Moody's Industrial Manual*	www.hoovers.com www.sec.gov/edgarhp.htm www.dnbmdd.com/mddi
U.S. demographic and lifestyle data	*Lifestyle Market Analyst*	www.census.gov
Demographic data on a specific region or local trade area in the United States	Sourcebook of County Demographics; Sourcebook of Zip Code Demographics; Survey of Buying Power in Sales and Marketing Management	
International demographics and world trade	*Predicasts F&S Index* United States, Europe, and International	www.instat.com www.stat-usa.gov www.cia.gov/cia/publications/factbook/index.html www.i-trade.com ec.europa.eu/eurostat
Macro trends	*Statistical Abstract of the United States; Business Periodicals Index*	www.unescap.org/stat/ (Asia) www.stat-usa.gov
E-commerce	*Red Herring magazine*	www.thestandard.com www.ecommercetimes.com www.comscore.com www.emarketer.com
Proprietary providers of research reports		www.forrester.com www.gartner.com
Market share information	*Market Share Reporter*	www.scarborough.com
Average financial statements by industry	*Annual Statement Studies*, Risk Management Association, formerly, Robert Morris and Associates	www.rmahq.org/RMA/Rmauniverse/productsandservices/RMAbookstore/statementstudies/default.htm

Given the rate of change on the web, some of the preceding internet addresses may change, and some print sources may add websites.

Source: Adapted from pp. 27, 63, 124, and 158 from *Find It Fast,* 4th ed., by Robert I. Berkman. Updated July 2009. Some URLs may have changed.

Opportunities are attractive at the micro level on the market side (see Exhibit 4.1) when the market offering meets most or all of the following tests.[28]

- *There's a clearly identified source of customer pain, for some clearly identifiable set of target customers, which the offering resolves.* Thus, customer need is established.
- *The offering provides customer benefits that other solutions do not.* Thus, customers are likely to buy *your* solution!
- *The target segment is likely to grow.*
- *There are other segments for which the currently targeted segment may provide a springboard for subsequent entry.*

For most companies and most goods or services, meeting the first two of these tests is all about delivering what Patrick Barwise and Seán Meehan call **generic category benefits**—the basics that customers expect a good marketer to provide in a particular product category.[29] Often, doing so involves effective implementation—something some companies are not very good at—rather than a fancy strategy.

So, can an opportunity in a market that's stagnant or declining at the macro level be an attractive one? The answer is an emphatic yes! Starbucks transformed a boring and stagnant American market for coffee into a growth machine. Nike did likewise in athletic shoes. Deliver what the customer wants and needs—that others don't deliver effectively—and promote it successfully, and the world will beat a path to your door.

On the flip side, what about me-too products, mere knock-offs of others that are already successful? While there's often room for imitators and followers in fast-growing markets, as we'll see in Chapter 9, even they typically need to do something different—better, faster, or cheaper—in order to win a meaningful share of the market.

UNDERSTANDING INDUSTRIES AT THE MICRO LEVEL

We've seen that, on the market side (see Exhibit 4.1), a particular opportunity may look attractive at the macro level but quite unattractive at the micro level—or vice versa, of course. Does the same pattern hold on the industry side of the picture?

On the industry side, the key micro-level question to ask is whether whatever competitive advantage there might be as a result of the benefits offered to the target market—the market side, micro-level assessment, as we've just seen—can be sustained over a significant period of time. Nobody wants to enter a market with something new, of course, only to have competitors quickly follow and steal your thunder? Thus, entering a market without a source of sustainable competitive advantage is a trap!

Let's briefly examine how one can develop and sustain competitive advantage. To do so, we'll look, at the micro level, at the company itself rather than the broader industry of which it is a part, which we examined earlier at the macro level. Opportunities are attractive at the micro level on the industry side when the company itself meets most or all of the following tests.[30]

- *It possesses something proprietary that other companies cannot easily duplicate or imitate.* Patents, at least defensible ones, can provide this, as can a well-known brand.
- *The business has or can develop superior organizational processes, capabilities, or resources that others would find it difficult to imitate or duplicate.* In the 1970s, before the Gap stores became a fashion brand in their own right, they sold only Levi-Strauss merchandise, most of which was also available in department stores. Gap's competitive advantage was that its systems ensured that virtually every item in its huge assortment of Levi's was in stock in every size every day, something other stores simply found too difficult to match in the days prior to bar codes and point-of-sale cash registers. Other stores had piles of Levi's, but often seemed to be out of the customer's size. As Gap's early advertising proclaimed, "Four tons of Levi's, in just your size!"
- *The company's business model is economically viable*—unlike the many dot-com businesses that went bust at the dawn of the millennium!

A considerable body of research by strategic management and marketing scholars has examined the issue of competitive advantage through what has become known as the resource-based view of the firm. In general, this literature argues that gathering resources that are valuable, rare, and inimitable by others (a tall order, at least in the long run) provides the best path toward competitive advantage. As we've previously noted, patents,

EXHIBIT 4.14   *Sustainable Competitive Advantage in the Internet World*

Yahoo! wasn't the world's first web portal. The iPod wasn't the first MP3 player that could download tunes or play music on the go. Facebook wasn't the world's first social network. All three companies ate another then-dominant company's lunch. So is sustainable competitive advantage a myth in today's internet world?

The Wharton School's Kartik Hosanagar argues it is not. "To get consumers to switch, you cannot be as good or slightly better. You have to be much, much better along dimensions that matter to consumers." Unfortunately, incumbents can often replicate new features with the expertise and equipment they already have in house, counters Hosanagar's Wharton colleague Eric Clemons. When Google+ introduced new features in social networking, Facebook simply copied them. In turn, Google+ will probably match whatever Facebook does next, even copying what Facebook's acquisition of Instagram brings them for a whole lot less—maybe

$999 million less—than Instagram's $1 billion price tag, says Clemons.

The one weapon that some think can work is patents. Even here, though, companies' troves of patents—for which others sometimes pay handsomely, as in Google's recent acquisition of Motorola Mobility for its large mobile telecom patent portfolio—seem better suited to keeping lawyers busy, or your competitor's lawyers (Apple's?) off your back, than for actually deterring competitive moves.

So will competitive advantage be sustainable for long in the new internet or mobile venture that you have been working on? Don't count on it. But if your technology or your implementation is good enough or innovative enough, as Instagram's was, maybe somebody will buy you before somebody else eats your lunch.

Source: Knowledge@Wharton, "King of the Hill: Can Established Tech Companies Be Bested?" April 25, 2012, *http://knowledge .wharton.upenn.edu/article.cfm?articleid=2989.*

brands, and superior capabilities or processes can deliver competitive advantage, at least for some period of time. Another source of sustainable competitive advantage, according to a recent study, is a genuine focus on getting to know both one's customers and competitors and widely sharing the information that results within the organization.[30] For a discussion of sustainable competitive advantage in today's internet world, see Exhibit 4.14. Should you enter an industry—like social networks or mobile apps—where sustainable advantage is going to be difficult to come by? Facebook's Mark Zuckerberg did, and he's done pretty well. But we're not all Mark Zuckerberg.

THE TEAM DOMAINS: THE KEY TO THE PURSUIT OF ATTRACTIVE OPPORTUNITIES

Opportunities are only as good as the people who will pursue them. Thus, even if some combination of market and industry factors renders an opportunity attractive at first blush, there remain some crucial questions:

- *Does the opportunity fit what we want to do?*
- *Do we have the people who can execute on whatever it takes to be successful in this particular industry?*
- *Do we have the right connections?* As the saying goes, "It's not what you know, it's who you know."

These three questions address the remaining three of the seven domains in our opportunity assessment framework.

MISSION, ASPIRATIONS, AND RISK PROPENSITY

These days, every company has a mission statement, and every entrepreneur has a pretty good idea of what she wants to do—software, a mobile app, running a retail shop, or whatever. Similarly, everyone has some idea about what size opportunity is deemed attractive. For some companies, if an opportunity lacks the potential to reach, say, $100 million in sales, it's too small. For some entrepreneurs who wish to run lifestyle businesses, if an opportunity will require more than 20 people to pursue it, it's too big. Finally, everyone and every company has views on how much risk is acceptable. Are we prepared to bet the ranch, mortgage the house, or risk a shortfall in the progression of our ever-increasing quarterly earnings that we deliver to Wall Street?

Notwithstanding the merits of a particular opportunity in market and industry terms, it must also measure up to the expectations of the people who will pursue it, or they'll say, "No, this one's not for us." Most airline caterers probably will not pursue opportunities in fast-food despite their ability to source meals in a consistent—if not the tastiest—manner. Most large companies will not pursue opportunities to serve very small niche markets. It's not worth their time and attention to do so. Many entrepreneurs—or at least their spouses—are unwilling to mortgage the house. Whatever the tests for a given individual or company, they must be met if an opportunity is to be deemed attractive.

ABILITY TO EXECUTE ON THE INDUSTRY'S CRITICAL SUCCESS FACTORS

Strategic Issue

In most industries, there are a small number of critical factors that tend to separate the winners from the also-rans.

In every industry, there's variation in performance. Some firms outperform others in their industry year after year. In most industries, in addition to hard-to-imitate elements that are firm specific, there are also a small number of critical factors that tend to separate the winners from the also-rans. These few factors are that industry's critical success factors, or CSFs for short. As the saying goes in retailing, there are three such factors in that industry: location, location, and location.

How might one's CSFs be identified? There are two key questions to ask:

- *Which few decisions or activities are the ones that, if gotten wrong, will almost always have severely negative effects on company performance?* In retailing, location is such a factor. Good customer service, for example, while important, is not a CSF, since there are many retailers whose customer service is nothing special—or downright nonexistent—but whose performance in financial terms is quite good.

- *Which decisions or activities, done right, will almost always deliver disproportionately positive effects on performance?* Again, in retailing, location qualifies. Certain high-traffic locations can be licenses to print money, no matter how well or poorly the business is run.

Thus, to assess opportunities, one must identify the industry's few CSFs, which generally do not include money, which in some industries may be table stakes—something you must have, but which generally does not lead to competitive advantage (see Exhibit 4.15). Then one must ask a simple question: Do we have on our team—or can we attract—the competencies and capabilities necessary to deliver what's called for by our industry's CSFs?[31] If that's not the case, the team itself may be a risk factor for the opportunity under consideration. For some, that's a risk they are willing to take, as Mark Zuckerberg and many other entrepreneurs have done. For most entrepreneurs, however, a team that has not shown the ability to deliver on the industry's CSFs will have a more difficult time raising capital, and is likely to raise it—if at all—on more onerous terms.

CONNECTEDNESS: IT'S *WHO* YOU KNOW, NOT *WHAT* YOU KNOW

The familiar saying holds true in assessing opportunities, as well as in other arenas, but for a different reason. Despite the insights to be gleaned from the seven domains, reality dictates that there will remain considerable uncertainty about just how attractive a particular

EXHIBIT 4.15 *Is Cash a Critical Success Factor?*

What about money, the reader may ask? Aren't the financial resources needed to pursue the opportunity just as important as the people? Most entrepreneurs and most venture capital investors would argue that the money is actually the easy part. If you have an opportunity to serve an attractive market, in an attractive industry, that's consistent with the kinds of things the people involved want to do, and with a team that can show they've done

it before with the same CSFs, finding the money is not very difficult. The same holds true for prying money loose from the corporate coffers in established organizations.

Source: John W. Mullins, *The New Business Road Test: What Entrepreneurs and Executives Should Do Before Writing a Business Plan* (London: Prentice Hall/FT, 2010). For more on John Mullins and his books, see *http://faculty.london.edu/jmullins/*.

opportunity really is. Can we really deliver what we promise? Will customers really buy? Will macro trends change course, for better or worse? Will the structural characteristics of the industry change, favorably or otherwise? Will an unanticipated competitor arrive on our doorstep, or will a new market suddenly open up?

Any or all of these things can happen, and the people who are the best connected—up the value chain, to insightful suppliers with a broad view of what's happening in their customer markets; down the value chain, to customers who can tell you about their changing needs; and across the value chain, among fellow players in your own industry who face the same challenges you do— are the ones who will first see the winds of change shifting direction. In turn, they'll be the ones who are best placed to change strategy before others know the winds have changed. Put simply, networks count!

Strategic Issue

Having a well-connected team in place enhances the attractiveness of the opportunity itself because the team is more likely to be able to ride out the inevitable winds of change.

Having a well-connected team in place enhances the attractiveness of the opportunity itself because the team is more likely to be able to ride out the inevitable winds of change. Because experienced investors understand this dynamic, they are more likely to fund entrepreneurs who are well connected in particularly valuable ways: a rolodex of prospective customers, key supplier relationships, and so on.

A recent study found that connections are important in emerging markets like China, too. A survey of 241 Chinese firms found that business relationships and political relationships both have a positive effect on performance, with business relationships more beneficial in a rapidly changing environment and political relationships more beneficial when the environment is stable.[32]

PUTTING THE SEVEN DOMAINS TO WORK

In the words of noted investor Warren Buffett, "When a management with a reputation for brilliance takes on a business with a reputation for bad economics, it's the reputation of the business that remains intact."[33] If you or your company choose unattractive opportunities to pursue, you'll face tough sledding, no matter what you learn from the rest of this book. Thus, it's worth keeping the lessons of this chapter in mind as you learn about the rest of the task of developing compelling marketing strategies in succeeding chapters.

It's also worth noting that the seven domains are not additive. A simple checklist on which you score each domain and sum the scores won't do, for an opportunity's strength on some domains—especially at the micro level—can outweigh weaknesses on others. Starbucks has done quite nicely in what was a boring and stagnant coffee market when it got started.

Finally, it's worth noting that opportunities don't just sit there; they change and may be further developed. Damaging flaws found in the opportunity assessment process are there to be mitigated or remedied by various means.[34] Thus, the seven domains provide a useful and integrative lens through which to examine the fundamental health of a business and the opportunities it has chosen to pursue at any stage in its products' life cycles, a topic to which we devote considerable attention in Chapters 8, 9, and 10, where we explore the various strategies that are best suited to different stages in the development of markets.

To close this chapter, we wrap up with a brief look at a tool for coping with the reality of the changing world around us, and we consider the perils of swimming against the changing tide.

ANTICIPATING AND RESPONDING TO ENVIRONMENTAL CHANGE

Critical changes in macroenvironmental conditions often call for changes in the firm's strategy. Such changes can be proactive or reactive, or both. To the extent that a firm identifies and effectively deals with key trends before its competitors do, it is more likely to win and retain competitive advantage. In any case, management needs systems to help identify, evaluate, and respond to environmental events that may affect the firm's longer-term profitability and position. One such approach uses an opportunity/threat matrix to better assess the impact and the timing of an event, followed by the development of an appropriate response strategy. This approach is discussed as follows.

Impact and Timing of Event

In any given period, many environmental events that could have an impact on the firm—either positively or negatively—may be detected. Somehow, management must determine the probability of their occurrence and the degree of impact (on profitability and/or market share) of each event. One relatively simple way to accomplish these tasks is to use a 2 × 2 dimensional *opportunity/threat matrix* such as that shown in Exhibit 4.16. This example contains four potential environmental events that the high-speed access division of a large European telecommunications company might have identified as worthy of concern in 2012. The probability of each occurring by the year 2017 was rated, as was the impact on the company in terms of profitability or market share. The event likely both to occur by 2017 and to have the greatest impact appears in the upper left-hand box. At the very least, such an event should be examined closely, including estimating with as much precision as possible its impact on profitability and market share.

EXHIBIT 4.16   Opportunity/Threat Matrix for a European Telecommunications Company in 2012

Level of Impact on Company*	Probability of Occurrence (2017)	
	High	Low
High	4	1
Low	2	3

1. Wireless communications technology will make networks based on fiber and copper wires redundant.

2. Cloud technology will provide for the storage and accessing of vast quantities of data at affordable costs.

3. Consumers will move most of their TV viewing from televisions to personal computers.

4. Voice-over-internet Protocol (VoIP) will become the dominant force in the telecommunications industry.

*Profits or market share or both

The opportunity/threat matrix enables the examination of a large number of events in such a way that management can focus on the most important ones. Thus, events such as number 4 in the exhibit with a high probability of occurring and having a high impact should be closely monitored. Those with a low probability of occurrence and low impact, such as number 3 in the exhibit, should probably be dropped, at least for the moment. Events with a low probability/high impact (number 1) should be reexamined less frequently to determine whether the impact rating remains sound.

SWIMMING UPSTREAM OR DOWNSTREAM: AN IMPORTANT STRATEGIC CHOICE

Fitness is a social trend. The graying of the world population is a demographic one. Global warming and increased attention to sustainability are trends related to our natural environment. All these trends influence the fortunes of some companies, but not others. As we have seen, the influence of macro trends like these can be pervasive and powerful. In general, life is better swimming downstream, accompanied by favorable trends, than upstream, running counter to such trends.

Like mosquitoes or cooling breezes on a humid summer evening, trends will always be present, whether marketing managers like them or not. The question is what managers can do about them. For some trends, marketers and other managers can do little but react and adapt.

Strategic Issue

Like mosquitoes or cooling breezes on a humid summer evening, trends will always be present, whether marketing managers like them or not. The question is what managers can do about them.

In the 1990s, manufacturers of products sold in spray containers were required to find new propellants less harmful to the ozone layer. Governments concerned about global warming mandated this change. For other trends, such as the shift toward or away from casual dress in the workplace, favorable moves can be reinforced through effective marketing. Similarly, sometimes, unfavorable ones can be mitigated. But doing these things requires that important trends be noticed and understood.

The seven domains framework introduced in this chapter sets the market and competitive context—the 4 Cs—for the marketing decisions to be addressed in the remainder of this book. Such decisions cannot be made in a vacuum; for without a deep understanding of the context in which one goes to market, one simply cannot develop effective strategies that take into account the market and competitive realities. Gaining such an understanding requires information, of course. We deal with the challenges in gathering such information through marketing research and its use in forecasting in the next chapter.

Marketing Plan Exercise

For the market offering on which your marketing plan or consulting project is based, use internet and other available secondary resources to conduct macro-level market and industry analyses. Your analyses should include a macro trend analysis encompassing all relevant macro-trend categories and should uncover *quantitative* data that provides evidence of the size and growth rate of the overall market, as well as qualitative data regarding the five forces. You should also identify, if you can, the few critical success factors that apply in your industry.

Your analyses should meet the following tests:

- The source for each item of data or each trend should be cited, with a reference list at the end. Trade associations and/or trade magazines should typically be among the citations.
- Your macro-trend analysis should cover any of the six macro-environmental categories that are relevant and should prioritize their importance to your business.
- Your evidence of market size and growth rate should, ideally, indicate market size using multiple measures, such as number of potential customers, aggregate revenue of the market, and aggregate units of the good or service consumed by the market.

- Your five forces analysis should draw evidence-based conclusions as to the favorability of each of the five forces and of the overall attractiveness of your industry.
- You should draw summary conclusions about the attractiveness of the overall market and the industry at the macro level.
- Critical success factors should be just a few and might be inferred from trade magazine articles for the industry in question.

Discussion Questions

1. You are an entrepreneur who has developed a packaging technology that instantly chills single-serving containers of cold beverages such as beer, carbonated drinks, and fruit juices. The customers of such packaging, therefore, would be beverage-makers. You are not certain whether your technology is patentable. Using the seven domains framework, assess this opportunity and describe any strategic decisions you could make to maximize the opportunity's attractiveness.

2. Drinking water pollution (contamination) has become a serious problem in many countries. What problems and opportunities does this present for what consumer and industrial goods?

3. Taking into account the five competitive forces, what do you think lies ahead for the worldwide automotive industry?

4. The president of a large manufacturer of household appliances (such as dishwashing machines, refrigerators, washers, and dryers) that are manufactured and sold in the United States, Japan, Mexico, and Europe has asked you to develop a system for monitoring and evaluating the impact of major environmental trends on the company's strategies and programs. Briefly describe your proposed system in terms of how you would organize your scanning activities, identify important environmental issues, and evaluate the impact of each issue.

Additional self-diagnostic questions to test your ability to apply the analytical tools and concepts in this chapter to strategic decision making may be found at the book's website at **www.mhhe.com/walker8e.**

Endnotes

1. Information on the cellular telephone business in the 21st century comes from the following sources: Moon Ihlwan, "Asia Gets Hooked on Wireless," *BusinessWeek*, June 19, 2000, p. 109; Stephen Baker, "The Race to Rule Mobile," *BusinessWeek* International Edition, February 21, 2000; Stephen Baker, "Smart Phones," *BusinessWeek* International Edition, October 18, 1999; "Online Overseas," *New York Times*, June 7, 2000, p. H8; Steve Frank, "Darling to Dog to . . .," *The Wall Street Journal Sunday*, June 18, 2000; Bea Hunt, "Basking in 3G's Rays," *Financial Times*, February 14, 2005, FTIT Review, p. 1; Andy Reinhardt, "Cell Phones for the People," *BusinessWeek*, November 14, 2005, p. 65; Kevin J. O'Brien, "For Cellphone Makers, the Fight Is for Second Place," *International Herald Tribune*, February 13, 2008, p. 13; Andrew Parker and Paul Taylor, "Mobile Businesses Send out Differing Signal," *Financial Times*, February 15, 2010, p. 18; Roben Farzad, "AT&T's iMess," *Bloomberg Businessweek*, February 15, 2012, pp. 34–40; Joe Leahy, "A Tough Call," *Financial Times*, May 25, 2010, p. 13; "The Lex Column," *Financial Times*, September 19, 2010, p. 18; "Not Just Talk," *The Economist*, January 29, 2011, pp. 65–66; Edmond Lococo, "China Unicom's Smart Call on Cheap Phones," *Bloomberg Businessweek*, January 30, 2012, pp. 24–25; Reuters Helsinki, "Nokia Defends Ground Plans for a Turnaround," *The Economic Times Hyderabad*, May 4, 2012, p. 18; John P. Mello Jr., "Mobile Phone Sales Sink for First Time in Three Years," *Gartner*, *http://www.pcworld.com/printable/article/id,255692/printable.html*; May 16, 2012.

2. Amy Yee, "Banishing the Negative: How Kodak Is Developing Its Blueprint for a Digital Transformation," *Financial Times*, January 26, 2006, p. 15.

3. Dan Roberts, "The Ageing Business: Companies and Marketers Wrestle with Adapting Their Products to Older Consumers' Demands," *Financial Times*, January 20, 2004, p. 19.

4. Francesco Guerrera and Jonathan Birchall, "Boom Time," *Financial Times*, December 6, 2007, p. 13.

5. Norma Cohen and Clive Cookson, "The Planet Is Ever Greyer: But as Longevity Rises Faster Than Forecast, the Elderly Are Also Becoming Healthier," *Financial Times*, January 19, 2004, p. 15.

6. Martin Wolf, "People, Plagues, and Prosperity: Five Trends that Promise to Transform the World's Population within 50 Years," *Financial Times*, February 27, 2003, p. 17.

7. "UN Aids World AIDS Day Report 2011," p. 6, *www.unaids.org.*

8. "UN AIDS Day Special Report," 2011, p. 6, *www.unaids.com.*

9. John Parker, "Burgeoning Bourgeoisie," *The Economist*, February 14, 2009, p. 5.

10. ibid.

11. *The Economist*, "A Club in Need of a New Vision," April 29, 2004.

12. *The Economist,* "Weaving the World Together," November 19, 2011, pp. 76–78.

13. Sara Silver, "Kraft Blends Ethics with Coffee Beans," *Financial Times*, October 7, 2003, p. 106.

14. Dave Gram, "Fair Trade Movement Faces Crossroad," May 31, 2012, *http://metronews.ca/news/world/244957/fair-trade-movement-faces-crossroad/.*

15. Liz Neporent and Michele Bibbey, "The Ten Tricks of Buying Home Exercise Equipment," *www.ivillage.co.uk/dietandfitness/getfit/cardio/articles/ 0,,254_157720.00.html.*

16. Steve Rothwell, "Ryanair's First-Ever Capacity Reduction Marks End of Discount-Airline Boom," Bloomberg, at *http://www.bloomberg.com/news/2011-05-23/23/ryanair-expects-similar-profit-this-year- on-fuel-slower-traffic-growth-html.*

17. *The Economist*, "East or Famine," February 27, 2010, pp. 77–78.

18. Justin Fox, *Time,* "The Re-regulation of the American Financial System," February 25, 2009, *http://business.time.com/2009/02/25/the-re-regulation-of-the-american-financial-system/*

19. *The Economist,* "The Third Industrial Revolution," April 21, 2012, p. 13; *The Economist,* "A Third Industrial Revolution," Special Report, April 21, 2012, pp. 1–16.

20. Irit Nitzan and Barak Libai, "Social Effects on Customer Retention," *Journal of Marketing* 75 (November 2011), pp. 24–38.

21. David Welch, "GM: Live Green or Die," *BusinessWeek* European Edition, May 26, 2008, pp. 36–41.

22. *The Economist,* "Following the Footprints," Technology Quarterly, June 4, 2011, pp. 13–15.

23. Nicholas Varchaver, "Chemical Reaction," *Fortune* European Edition, April 2, 2007, pp. 41–44.

24. Michael Porter, *Competitive Strategy* (New York: Free Press, 1980).

25. For an example of such a checklist, see John W. Mullins, *The New Business Road Test*, chap. 13 (London: Prentice Hall/FT, 2010).

26. "Airlines and the Canine Features of Unprofitable Industries," *Financial Times*, September 27, 2005, p. 23.

27. Jin K. Han, Namwoon Kim, and Hong-Bumm Kim, "Entry Barriers: A Dull-, One-, or Two-Edged Sword for Incumbents? Unraveling the Paradox from a Contingency Perspective," *Journal of Marketing* 65 (January 2001), pp. 1–14.

28. For more detail on micro-market attractiveness, see Mullins, *The New Business Road Test*, chap. 2.

29. Patrick Barwise and Seán Meehan, *Simply Better: Winning and Keeping Customers by Delivering What Matters Most* (Cambridge, MA: Harvard Business School Press, 2004).

30. V. Kumar, Eli Jones, Rajkumar Venkatesan, and Robert P. Leone, "Is Market Orientation a Source of Sustainable Competitive Advantage or Simply the Cost of Competing?" *Journal of Marketing* 75 (January 2011), pp. 16–30.

31. Mullins, *The New Business Road Test*, chap. 5.

32. For the classic articles on competencies and capabilities, see George S. Day, "The Capabilities of Market-Driven Organizations," *Journal of Marketing* 58 (October 1994), pp. 37–52; and C. K. Prahalad and Gary Hamel, "The Core Competence of the Corporation," *Harvard Business Review* 68 (May–June 1990), pp. 79–91.

33. Shibin Sheng, Kevin Zheng Zhou, and Julie Juan Li, "The Effects of Business and Political Ties on Firm Performance: Evidence from China," *Journal of Marketing* 75 (January 2011), pp. 1–15.

34. Quoted in Herb Greenburg, "How to Avoid the Value Trap," *Fortune*, June 10, 2002, p. 194.

35. For more on how crucial flaws may be mitigated or resolved, see Mullins, *The New Business Road Test*, chap. 9.

Measuring Market Opportunities: Forecasting and Market Knowledge

Intel's Secret Weapon[1]

Genevieve Bell has a radical idea. Bell, the only female among Intel's roster of top technical talent dubbed Intel Fellows, and Director of Intel's User Experience Group, thinks the world would be a better place if we can better understand how people would like to use technology, rather than tossing technology that people don't really want into the market at an alarming pace. Bell was given her own lab at Intel in 2010, an event that may change Intel, or even the future of technology itself.

"Imagine," says Bell, "If we were willing to take on board the ways in which PCs don't work and applied that to other technologies such as our refrigerators or televisions. If your fridge said, "I'm terribly sorry, you cannot have that cold milk until I've rebooted myself and downloaded new drivers!" or your TV said, "You cannot watch the end of the cricket match because I am defragging my hard drive," we would all go insane."

Bell's Charter at Intel

In Bell's view, her charter at Intel is straightforward, "To provide insights and inspire innovation." Her team of social scientists, interaction designers and human factors engineers is charged with setting research directions, leading new product strategy and definition, and driving consumer-centric product innovation and thinking across the company. All this is everyday work for this wiry-haired woman

who as a very small girl used to kill things—frogs and the like—growing up in an aboriginal community in Australia's outback.

Why is there a role like Bell's at Intel today? "I joined Intel in 1998," she recalls, "There was a collective sense in Intel's senior management that they didn't know what was going to happen when PCs became mass market. They knew they had market research, they knew they had the skills to size markets and how to survey people, and a little bit of usability work was going on even then, but I think the sense of what was missing was this notion about what was motivating people, what did they care about and was there an opportunity if you understood the things to drive new uses of technology."

"For many years thereafter, a part of every presentation I gave, every class I taught, every meeting I attended was explaining what an anthropologist was, what ethnography was, what was user centered design and why it was going to be a useful tool at Intel." In her 13 years at Intel, Bell has fundamentally changed how the company envisions, plans, and develops its product platforms.

How Do Anthropology and Ethnography Work?

Bell and her team spend their time hanging out wherever they can find users of technology—people on holiday, people in their workplace, people at home with their families in every corner of the planet. "At Intel, we try to start with people first—we ask questions about who they are and what they care about, we also ask questions about technology: What do you love about it, how does it frustrate you, what do you hate about it, what can't you live without?"

One of the key tools in the modern anthropologist's toolkit is the digital camera. Says Bell, "We can now put digital cameras in the hands of our research participants. There is nothing like the film a five-year-old takes of its own home—you realize that electrical outlets are everywhere and furniture is really badly designed." Seeing the world as it really is and though other people's eyes is what anthropologists do that traditional market researchers often miss.

What is Bell Learning about Generation X?

One of the questions Bell and her team are sometimes asked is whether today's Generation X—who seem to be digitally connected all the time—are somehow different from their parents' generation. "I don't think it's as easy as we sometimes think," says Bell. "We fall into the trap of assuming that what you are and what you do at 16 is what you will do for the rest of your life. I don't know why we believe that because we were all 16 once, and we mostly don't behave now as we did then."

In a study of early adopters of social networking technology, Bell spoke to a young woman who had just had a baby and was no longer blogging as much. "Have you ever tried to breast-feed a baby and use a laptop?" the woman asked. "It's just not going to happen. It is much easier to go back to watching television. It doesn't demand so much when I have this other thing I'm trying to do!"

Can Bell's Work Make a Difference?

Bell, who brings to her craft a doctorate in anthropology from Stanford University, has become one of the world's leading thinkers on the mash-up of humanity and technology. She has worked tirelessly to get Intel chip designers to not simply build ever-faster chips and market them everywhere. The internet, in many parts of the world, means text on a cell phone, so Intel's speedy but pricey Celeron chips are not very relevant in some markets. Intel's cheaper and less power-hungry Atom chips are a better way to go. "Genevieve and her team make us engineers think differently," says Stephen Pawlowski, who leads Intel's chip architecture research team. "We intend to use Bell's expertise heavily as we focus on emerging growth markets."

Perhaps if Bell has her way, one day we'll all be using PCs that actually start when we ask them to start, and stop when we are done. Or if she fails in her quest, Apple will continue its inroads into the PC, smartphone, and other consumer electronics markets with its legendary skills at doing what Bell hopes Intel can do. And the rest of us will continue to be subservient to the products we buy, rather than masters of them.

As Bell puts it, "Anthropology continues to be a really important way to bring voices into the technology realm that really need to be there. Ruth Benedict, an early anthropologist, had a great line—"The role of the anthropologist is to make the world safe for people." Let's hope people like Benedict and Bell prevail!

STRATEGIC CHALLENGES ADDRESSED IN CHAPTER 5

Entrepreneurs and managers in established firms like Intel need to develop knowledge about their market and industry and synthesize that knowledge into tangible plans that their organizations can act on. These plans can take many forms. For entrepreneurs a business plan may be needed to raise the necessary capital to start the venture. For new product managers in established firms, marketing plans must be developed to win support and resources to permit the product's launch. In organizations of all kinds, annual budgets are prepared to guide decision making for the coming year. These decisions determine staffing, investments in productive capacity, levels of operating expense, and so on. In almost every case, these planning and budgeting activities begin with a sales forecast. Once a sales figure is agreed to, the various activities and investments needed to support the planned sales level are budgeted.

Thus, in Chapter 5, we deal with some key issues that enable managers and entrepreneurs to bring life to their dreams. First, we address the challenges in estimating **market potential** and **forecasting** sales, for both new and existing products or businesses. We provide a menu of evidence-based forecasting methods, each of which is useful in some situations, but not others, and we discuss their limitations. We also examine the process by which innovative new products diffuse into the market over time, a source of insight into the particularly difficult task of forecasting sales of innovative new products.

Strategic Issue

We provide a menu of evidence-based forecasting methods, each of which is useful in some situations, but not others.

Next, we address several systematic sources of information—internal record systems, marketing databases, competitive intelligence systems, and systems that organize and track information about client contact—that keep marketers in touch with what's going on in the marketplace. Designing such systems effectively is crucial for marketers, who need to be well-informed about the market and competitive context that we've dealt with in the previous chapters of this book.

Finally, and very briefly, we touch on marketing research, where data is gathered about a particular marketing challenge or situation. In this part of the chapter, we assume the reader has already learned the basics of planning and conducting marketing research, which we do not cover here. Making strategic marketing decisions based on hunches—instead of more carefully thought-out research inquiries, even modest ones done quickly—can be a risky proposition indeed. Thus we probe some of the common pitfalls that users of marketing research will encounter, and we identify some of the questions such users should ask.

In the Marketing Plan Exercise at the end of the chapter, we suggest an approach for planning the marketing research that must underpin a marketing plan, so that the output of that research delivers relevant qualitative and quantitative data as well as an evidence-based sales forecast that's likely to pass muster.

EVERY FORECAST IS WRONG!

We know of no manager who has ever seen a forecast that came in *exactly* on the money. Most forecasts turn out too high, some too low. Forecasting is an inherently difficult task because no one has a perfect crystal ball. The future is inherently uncertain, especially in today's rapidly changing markets. Consumer wants and needs shift, buffeted by the winds of ever-changing macro trends. Competitors come and go. New technologies from Intel and others sweep away old ones. Some forecasts are based on extensive and expensive research, others on small-scale inquiries, and still others on uninformed hunches. As we have seen, however, forecasting plays a central role in all kinds of planning and budgeting in all kinds of businesses and other organizations. Given the stakes and the risks entailed in being *very* wrong with a forecast, some effort to prepare an **evidence-based forecast,** instead of a wild guess, is almost always called for, even if time and money are scarce. So forecast we must. But how?

A FORECASTER'S TOOL KIT: A TOOL FOR EVERY FORECASTING SETTING

Before choosing a method to prepare a forecast, one first must know what is to be estimated or forecasted. First, there's the size of the potential market, that is, the likely demand from all actual and potential buyers of a product or product class. An estimate of **market potential** often serves as a starting point for preparing a sales forecast, which we explore in more detail later in this chapter.

Such estimates are particularly crucial for aspiring entrepreneurs, where levels of risk and uncertainty are especially high. Such was the case for two business school graduates who set out to build a pay telephone business, African Communications Group (ACG), in Tanzania in the early 1990s, before the wave of cell telephone development washed across sub-Saharan Africa. Monique Maddy and Come Laguë knew that, to obtain the financing they would need and to obtain the necessary licenses, they would have to prepare a credible business plan. They also knew that among the most critical elements of any business plan was the sales forecast. Not only would the sales numbers serve as a starting point from which most of the other numbers in the plan would be developed, but they would serve as a key litmus test for prospective investors.

If the sales forecast was well supported and credible, Maddy and Laguë believed the rest of the pieces would fall into place. The secondary data they gathered convinced them that the market and industry were sufficiently attractive. But coming up with hard numbers for market potential and sales revenue was another story altogether.

For starters, they knew that prospective investors would want to know how large the potential market for telephone services would be in the coming years, measured perhaps in several ways: in numbers of telephone users, in numbers and/or minutes of calls, and in dollars or Tanzanian shillings. This market was composed of those consumers who were likely to have both the willingness and ability to buy and would use a phone card or one of ACG's other services at one of ACG's pay phones. There was also the size of the currently **penetrated market,** those who were actually using pay phones in Tanzania at the time of the forecast. Investors would also want to know these figures—the size of the potential and penetrated markets for the market segments Maddy and Laguë intend to serve, their **target market.** They would also need a **sales forecast,** in which they predicted sales revenues for ACG for five years or so. How might Maddy and Laguë do these things?

Established organizations employ two broad approaches for preparing a sales forecast: top-down and bottom-up. Under the top-down approach, a central person or persons take the responsibility for forecasting and prepare an overall forecast, perhaps using aggregate economic data, current sales trends, or other methods we describe shortly. Under the bottom-up approach, common in decentralized firms, each part of the firm prepares its own sales forecast, and the parts are aggregated to create the forecast for the firm as a whole. For an example of how managers at Gap Inc. retailing divisions combine both methods to forecast next-year sales, see Exhibit 5.1.

Strategic Issue

Established organizations employ two broad approaches for preparing a sales forecast: top-down and bottom-up.

The bottom-up logic also applied to Maddy and Laguë's task. They could break their anticipated demand into pieces and sum the components to create the summary forecast. These pieces could be market segments, such as small retailers, mobile businesspeople, consumers, and so on, or product lines, such as revenue from phone cards or individual pay phones, voice-mail fees, pager fees, and the like.

Using the bottom-up approach presented numerous advantages. First, this approach would force them to think clearly about the drivers of demand for each market segment or product line and thus better understand the real potential of their business and its parts. Second, they would be forced to make explicit assumptions about the drivers of demand in each category, assumptions they could debate—and support with evidence gathered from their research—with prospective investors and which they could later verify as the business unfolds. Third, such an approach facilitated "what if" planning. Various combinations of market segments and/or product lines could be combined to build a business plan that looked viable.

What forecasting methods, or tools, could Maddy and Laguë choose from? There are numerous evidence-based methods for estimating market potential and forecasting sales and we examine their merits and limitations in the following sections. An all-too-common

EXHIBIT 5.1   *Forecasting Next Year's Sales at Gap*

At international retailer Gap Inc., forecasting sales for the next year for each of its key brands—Gap, Banana Republic, and Old Navy—is an important process that drives a host of decisions, including how much merchandise to plan to buy for the coming year. Both top-down and bottom-up approaches are used.

At Old Navy, for example, each merchandiser generates a forecast of what level of sales his or her category—women's knit tops, men's jeans, and so on—can achieve for the next year. Group merchandise managers then provide their input and sum these numbers to create a total forecast from a merchandising perspective. A second bottom-up forecast is generated by the store operations organization, summing stores and groups of stores. Simultaneously, a top-down figure is prepared at headquarters in California, using macroeconomic data,

corporate growth objectives, and other factors. The three forecasts are then compared, differences debated, and a final figure on which to base merchandise procurement and expense budgets is determined. Though the effort to prepare such a forecast is considerable, the broad involvement in the process helps to ensure both knowledgeable input to the forecast as well as subsequent commitment to "make the numbers." Most important, Old Navy finds that the different processes together with the ensuing discussion lead to substantially better forecasts.

Source: Marshal L. Fisher, Ananth Raman, and Anna Sheen McClelland, "Rocket Science Retailing Is Almost Here: Are You Ready?" *Harvard Business Review*, July–August 2000. For more on Gap, see *www.gap.com.*

method, not evidenced-based—the SWAG method (Silly Wild-@*# Guess)—is not condoned here, though there is little else to support some forecasts!

Statistical Methods

Statistical methods use past history and various statistical techniques, such as multiple regression or time series analysis, to forecast the future based on an extrapolation of the past.[2] This method is typically not useful for ACG or other entrepreneurs or new product managers charged with forecasting sales for a new product or new business, since there is no history in their venture on which to base a statistical forecast.

In established firms, for established products, statistical methods are extremely useful. When Michelin, the tire manufacturer, wants to forecast demand for the replacement automobile tire market in Asia for the next year, it can build a statistical model using such factors as the number and age of vehicles currently on the road in Asia, predictions of GDP for the region, the last few years' demand, and other relevant factors to forecast market potential as well as Michelin's own replacement tire sales for the coming year. Such a procedure is likely to result in a more accurate forecast than other methods, especially because Michelin has years of experience with which to calibrate its statistical model.

As with all forecasting methods, statistical methods have important limitations. Most important of these is that statistical methods generally assume that the future will look very much like the past. Sometimes this is not the case. US WEST (now CenturyLink), the regional Bell telephone company serving the Rocky Mountain and Northwest regions of the United States, ran into trouble when its statistical models used to predict needs for telephone capacity failed to allow for rapidly increasing use of the internet, faxes, and second lines for teenagers in American homes. Suddenly, the average number of lines per home skyrocketed, and there was not enough physical plant—cable in the ground, switches, and so on—to accommodate the growing demand. Consumers had to wait, sometimes for months, to get additional lines, and they were not happy about it!

Similarly, if product or market characteristics change, statistical models used without adequate judgment may not keep pace. When tire manufacturers produce automobile tires that last 80,000 miles instead of 30,000 to 50,000 miles, the annual demand

Strategic Issue

Statistical methods generally assume that the future will look very much like the past. Sometimes this is not the case.

for replacement tires is reduced. If automobile manufacturers were to change the number of wheels on the typical car from four, the old statistical models would also be in trouble. For example, many large-capacity pickup trucks sold in the United States feature six wheels.

Observation

Another method for preparing an evidence-based forecast is to directly observe or gather existing data about what real consumers do in the product-market of interest. Maddy and Laguë conducted a study of pay phone use in Tanzania to find out how many minutes per day the typical pay phone was used. Their study showed that an average of 150 three-minute calls were made per day at the 60 working pay phones then provided by other companies in Dar es Salaam. Revenue for most pay phones fell into the US $100 to $150 range.[3]

Like statistical methods, **observation-based forecasting** is attractive because it is based on what people actually *do*. If behavioral or usage data can be found from existing secondary sources—in company files, at the library, or on the internet—data collection is both faster and cheaper than if a new study like the one Maddy and Laguë conducted must be designed and carried out. For new-to-the-world products, however, observation is typically not possible, and secondary data are not available, since the product often does not yet exist, except in concept form. Had there been no pay phones in Tanzania or a similar country, observation would not have been possible. Market tests and concept tests, which we discuss later in this section, are two ways to get real purchase data about new-to-the-world products.

Surveys or Focus Groups

Another common way to forecast sales or estimate market potential is to conduct surveys or focus groups. These methods can be done with various kinds of respondents, and in today's internet age, are increasingly done online. Consumers, after being shown a statement of the product concept (a **concept test**) or a prototype or sample of the product, can be asked how likely they are to buy, creating a **survey of buyers' intentions.** Buyers can also be asked about their current buying behavior: what they currently buy, how often, or how much they use. Salespeople can be asked how much they are likely to sell, completing a **survey of salesforce opinion.** Experts of various kinds—members of the distribution channel, suppliers, consultants, trade association executives, and so on—can also be surveyed.

As part of their research in Dar es Salaam, Maddy and Laguë surveyed pay phone customers to find out more about them. A whopping 65 percent were using a pay phone because they lacked access to another working phone—good news for the ACG concept! Sixty-three percent were business customers, 20 percent were students or teachers, and 17 percent were other nonbusiness customers. Business customers spent an average of US$10 per week for 14 pay phone calls, and nonbusiness customers spent US$6 per week for 12 calls.[4] By combining these data with demographic data on the Tanzanian population, Maddy and Laguë now had what they needed to prepare an evidence-based, bottom-up forecast of market potential, market segment by market segment.

Surveys and focus groups possess important limitations, however. For one, what people *say* is not always what people *do.* Consumer surveys of buyer intention are always heavily discounted to allow for this fact. For one common approach to doing so, see Exhibit 5.2. Second, the persons who are surveyed may not be knowledgeable, but if asked

EXHIBIT 5.2   *A Survey of Buyers' Intentions: What People Say Is Not What They Do*

When Nestlé's refrigerated foods division in the United States was considering whether to acquire Lambert's Pasta and Cheese, a fresh pasta company, it wanted to forecast the likely first-year sales volume if the acquisition were completed. To do so, Nestlé used a concept test in which consumers were asked, among other things, how likely they were to try the fresh pasta product. The results were as shown in the first two columns in the following table.

Purchase Intent	% Response	Rule of Thumb Reduction for Forecasting Purposes	Percentage of Market Deemed Likely to Actually Buy
Definitely would buy	27%	Multiply by .8	27% × .8 = 21.6%
Probably would buy	43%	Multiply by .3	43% × .3 = 12.9%
Might or might not buy	22%	Count as zero	
Probably or definitely would not buy	8%	Count as zero	
Totals	100%		21.6% + 12.9% = 34.5%

Even though 70% of consumers surveyed indicated they were likely to buy, Nestlé's experience indicated that these "top two box" percentages should be cut sharply: "definitely" responses were reduced by 20%, while "probably" responses were reduced by 70%; and "maybe" responses were considered as "no." These adjustments, shown in columns three and four, reduced the 70% figure by more than half, to 34.5%. Most consumer product manufacturers who employ concept tests use similar rules of thumb when interpreting purchase intent data for forecasting purposes because they have learned that what people say they will buy exceeds what they will actually buy. Similar logic is useful in a variety of forecasting situations.

Source: Marie Bell and V. Kasturi Rangan, "A Survey of Buyers' Intentions: What People Say Is Not What They Do" from *Nestlé Refrigerated Foods: Contadina Pasta and Pizza,* case no. 9-595-035. Boston: Harvard Business School, 1995. Copyright © 1995 by the President and Fellows of Harvard College. Reprinted by permission. see *www.nestle.com*.

for their opinion, they will probably provide it! Third, what people imagine about a product concept in a survey may not be what is actually delivered once the product is launched. If consumers are asked if they will buy an "old world pasta sauce with homemade flavor," they will surely provide a response. Whether they will actually *like* the taste and texture of the sauce that the lab develops is another story!

In general, statistical and observational methods, where adequate data or settings are available in which to apply them, are superior to survey methods of forecasting because such methods are based, at least in part, on what people have *actually done* or bought (e.g., the number of old cars actually on the road or the length of pay phone calls in Tanzania), while survey methods (Are you likely to buy replacement tires this year? How often are you likely to use a pay phone?) are based on what people *say,* a less reliable indicator of their future behavior.

Analogy

 An approach often used for new product forecasting where neither statistical methods nor observations are possible is to forecast the sales or market potential for a new product or product class by **analogy.** Under this method, the product is compared with similar historical data that *are* available. When Danone, the leading marketer of yogurt in Europe, plans to introduce a new flavor, its managers look at the sales history of earlier introductions to forecast the sales for the newest flavor. This method is also used for new-to-the-world high-technology products, for which product prototypes are often either not available or extremely expensive to produce. Rather than conduct surveys to ask consumers about their likelihood to buy a product they can hardly imagine (What would someone have said in 1978 about his or her likelihood to buy a personal computer?), forecasters consider related product introductions with which the new product may be compared.

Indeed, Apple, in developing its now wildly successful music business, had a number of available analogs with which to shed light on the likely demand for paid downloading of music from iTunes and for the demand for a user-friendly portable device—the iPod—on which to play it. First, Napster, the free peer-to-peer music-sharing site, was all the rage with consumers (though not with the music publishing industry, which eventually convinced the courts that Napster was illegal). Second, the Sony Walkman had sold more than 300 million units, proving there was vibrant demand for a portable music player. The use of analogs like these, as well as anti-logs—previous examples one explicitly decides *not* to copy—is a useful approach for many entrepreneurs as they mold their initial ideas into more refined versions that will actually work.[5]

As always, there are limitations. First, the new product and its pricing are never exactly like that to which the analogy is drawn. Downloaded music from Napster was free, but Apple planned to ask consumers to pay for their tunes. What price should Apple charge, and with free downloads available, would customers be willing to pay anything at all? Second, market and competitive conditions may vary from when the analogous product was launched. Such conditions must be taken into account.

Judgment

While we hesitate to call this a forecasting method of its own, since capable and informed judgment is required for *all* methods, sometimes forecasts are made *solely* on the basis of experienced **judgment,** or intuition. Some decision makers, even effective ones, are intuitive in their decision processes and cannot always articulate the basis for their judgments. Said a footwear buyer at Nine West Group, an international manufacturer and retailer of shoes and fashion accessories, "Trend forecasting is a visceral thing that cannot be trained. I rely on my sense of color and texture, but at times I cannot explain why I feel a certain way . . . . I just know."[6] Those with sufficient experience in a market they know well may be quite accurate in their intuitive forecasts. Unfortunately, it is often difficult for them to defend their forecasts against those prepared by evidence-based methods when the two differ. Nonetheless, the importance of experienced judgment in forecasting, whether it is used solely and intuitively or in concert with evidence-based methods, cannot be discounted.

Experiments and Market Tests

Market tests of various kinds are the last of our six commonly used forecasting methods. Used largely for new consumer products, market tests such as **experimental test markets** may be done under controlled experimental conditions in research laboratories or in live **test markets** with real advertising and promotion and distribution in stores.

Use of live test markets has declined over the past few decades for two reasons. First, they are expensive to conduct because significant quantities of the new product must be produced and marketing activities of various kinds must be paid for. More importantly, in today's data-intensive environment, especially for consumer products sold through supermarkets and mass merchants, competitors can buy the data collected through scanners at the checkout and learn the results of the test market without bearing the expense. More diabolically, competitors can engage in marketing tactics to mislead the company conducting the test by increasing sampling programs, offering deep discounts or buy-one-get-one-free promotions, or otherwise distorting normal purchasing patterns in the category. Experimental test markets, on the other hand, are still commonly used.

The coming of the internet has made possible a new kind of market test: an offer directly to consumers on the web. Offers to chat rooms, interest groups, or e-mail lists of current customers are among the common approaches. Use of such techniques has increased due to companies' ability to carry out such tests quickly and at low cost. We explore these and other internet marketing strategies in greater detail in Chapter 11.

Other Mathematical Approaches: Chain Ratios and Indices

Two additional mathematically-driven approaches to forecasting are the chain ratio calculation or the use of indices. See Exhibit 5.3 and Exhibit 5.4 for examples applying these mathematical calculations to arrive at sales forecasts. Both approaches begin with an estimate of market potential (the number of households in the target market in Exhibit 5.3; the national market potential for a product category in Exhibit 5.4). The market potential is then multiplied by various fractional factors that, taken together, predict the portion of the overall market potential that one firm or product can expect to obtain. In Exhibit 5.3, which shows the more detailed of the two approaches, the factors reflect the appeal of the product to consumers, as measured by marketing research data and the company's planned marketing program.

Other quantitative methods, especially useful for new products, have also been developed. These include conjoint analysis,[7] a method to forecast the impact on consumer demand of different combinations of attributes that might be included in a new product, and methods to mathematically model the diffusion of innovation process for consumer durables,[8] discussed in the next section.

EXHIBIT 5.3 *Chain Ratio Forecast: Trial of Fresh Pasta*

Once Nestlé's research on fresh pasta had been completed (see Exhibit 5.2), it used the chain ratio method to calculate the total number of households who would try their fresh pasta. The chain ratio calculation went like this

Research Results for:	Data from Research	Chain Ratio Calculation	Result
Number of households in target market	77.4 million		
Concept purchase intent: adjusted figure from Exhibit 5.2	34.5% will try the product	77.4 million × 34.5%	26.7 million households will try *if aware*
Awareness adjustment: based on planned advertising level	48% will be aware of the product	26.7 million × 48%	12.8 million households will try *if they find product at their store*
Distribution adjustment: based on likely extent of distribution in supermarkets, given the introductory trade promotion plan	The product will obtain distribution reaching 70% of U.S. households	12.8 million × 70%	9.0 million will try the product

Similar chain ratio logic is useful in a variety of forecasting settings.

Source: Marie Bell and V. Kasturi Rangan, "Chain Reaction Forecast: Trial of Fresh Pasta," from *Nestlé Refrigerated Foods: Contadina Pasta, and Pizza,* case no. 9-595-035 (Boston: Harvard Business School Publishing, 1995). Copyright © 1995 by the President and Fellows of Harvard College. Reprinted by permission. For more on Nestlé, see *www.nestle.com*

EXHIBIT 5.4 *Estimating Market Potential Using Indices*

In many countries there are published indices of buying behavior, including the "Annual Survey of Buying Power" published by *Sales and Marketing Management* in the United States. The Buying Power Index (BPI) is a weighted sum of a geographical area's percentage of national buying power for the area, based on census income data (weight = .5), plus the percentage of national retail sales for the area (weight = .3), plus the percentage of national population located in the area (weight = .2). If this calculation comes to 3.50 for a given state or region, one might expect 3.5% of sales in a given category (toys, power tools, or whatever) to come from that geographical area.

Category development indices (CDIs) are similar indices that report the ratio of consumption in a certain category (for instance, restaurant sales) to population in a defined geographical area. Trade associations or trade magazines relevant to the category typically publish such indices. Ratios greater than 1.0 for a particular geographic area (perhaps, metropolitan Chicago) indicate that the area does more business than average (compared to the country as a whole) in that category. **Brand development indices** (BDIs) compare sales for a given *brand* (for example, Pizza Hut restaurants) to population. Companies that use BDI indices typically calculate them for their own use. The ratio of the BDI to the CDI for a given area is an indicator of how well a brand is doing, compared to its category overall, in that area. These various indices are useful for estimating market potential in defined geographic areas. They are, however, crude numbers, in that they do not consider differences in consumer behavior from region to region. The CDI or BDI for snowmobiles in Minnesota (with its freezing winters) is far higher than in balmy Texas, for example. Attempting to rectify this imbalance by increasing the snowmobile advertising budget in Texas would be difficult!

RATE OF DIFFUSION OF INNOVATIONS: ANOTHER PERSPECTIVE ON FORECASTING

Before entrepreneurs or established marketers invest in the development and introduction of an innovation, they want to know how rapidly the innovation is likely to be adopted by the target market. The faster the adoption rate, the faster will be the rate at which the innovative new product's sales ramp up. **Diffusion of innovation** theory seeks to explain the adoption of an innovative product or service over time among a group of potential buyers. Lack of awareness and limited distribution typically limit early adoption. As positive word about the product spreads, the product is adopted by additional consumers. Diffusion theory is useful to managers in predicting the likely adoption rate for new and innovative goods or services. As we noted in the preceding section, it has also led to various modeling approaches for predicting the sales of consumer durables.[9]

Strategic Issue

Diffusion theory is useful to managers in predicting the likely adoption rate for new and innovative goods or services.

The Adoption Process and Rate of Adoption

The **adoption process** involves the attitudinal changes experienced by individuals from the time they first hear about a new product, service, or idea until they adopt it. Not all individuals respond alike; some tend to adopt early, some late, and some never. If plotted on a cumulative basis, the percentage of people adopting a new product over time resembles an S curve. Although the curve tends to have the same shape regardless of the product involved, the length of time required differs among products—often substantially.

The time dimension is a function of the rate at which people in the target group (those ultimately adopting) move through the five stages in the adoption process. Generally, the speed of the adoption process depends heavily on the following factors: (1) the risk (cost of product failure or dissatisfaction), (2) the relative advantage over other products, (3) the relative simplicity of the new product, (4) its compatibility with previously adopted ideas, and behavior, (5) the extent to which its trial can be accomplished on a small-scale basis, and (6) the ease with which the central idea of the new product can be communicated.[10] Other factors, while less important, are also at work, particularly at the individual level, including the growing influence of social media. People who are better connected in social networks tend to adopt earlier, due to their earlier exposure to an innovation. People who serve as hubs in social networks may even provide clues to the future success of innovations.[11]

Thought should also be given to the legitimacy of the new product in the eyes of its stakeholders. Legitimacy may come from associations with established firms, the success of historical product launches or hiring a well-known name in the field.[12] Some new products move quickly through the adoption process (a new breakfast cereal), while others take years.

The rate at which an innovative new product category passes through the adoption process is also a function of the actions taken by the product's marketers. Thus, the diffusion process may be faster when there is strong competition among competitors, when they have favorable reputations, and when they allocate substantial sums to R&D (to improve performance) and marketing (to build awareness). Early cell telephones scored high on most of the key adoption factors.

Adopter Categories

Early adopters differ from later adopters. If we use time of adoption as a basis for classifying individuals, five major groups can be distinguished: innovators, early adopters, early majority, late majority, and laggards. See Exhibit 5.5 for an illustration and Exhibit 5.6 for the approximate size and characteristics of each group.[13] Because each category comprises individuals who have similar characteristics and because individuals differ substantially across categories, these adopter groups can be considered market segments. Thus, one would use a different set of strategies to market a new product to the early adopter group than to market it to the late majority group. For a discussion of the challenges in transitioning marketing efforts from group to group, see Exhibit 5.7.

Implications of Diffusion of Innovation Theory for Forecasting Sales of New Products and New Firms

Optimistic entrepreneurs or new product managers sometimes wax euphoric about the prospects for the innovations they plan to bring to market. They naively forecast that their innovations will capture 10 or 20 percent of the market in its first year. How likely is it that a truly innovative new product, even a compellingly attractive one, will win all of the innovators plus most of the early

EXHIBIT 5.5 **Diffusion of Innovation Curve**

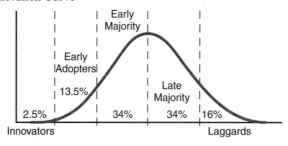

EXHIBIT 5.6 *Size and Characteristics of Individual Adopter Group*

- **Innovators** represent the first 2.5 percent of all individuals who ultimately adopt a new product. They are more venturesome than later adopters, more likely to be receptive to new ideas, and tend to have high incomes, which reduces the risk of a loss arising from an early adoption.

- **Early adopters** represent the next 13 to 14 percent who adopt. They are more a part of the local scene, are often opinion leaders, serve as vital links to members of the early majority group (because of their social proximity), and participate more in community organizations than do later adopters.

- The **early majority** includes 34 percent of those who adopt. These individuals display less leadership than early adopters, tend to be active in community affairs

(thereby gaining respect from their peers), do not like to take unnecessary risks, and want to be sure that a new product will prove successful before they adopt it.

- The **late majority** represents another 34 percent. Frequently, these individuals adopt a new product because they are forced to do so for either economic or social reasons. They participate in community activities less than the previous groups and only rarely assume a leadership role.

- **Laggards** comprise the last 16 percent of adopters. Of all the adopters, they are the most "local." They participate less in community matters than members of the other groups and stubbornly resist change. In some cases, their adoption of a product is so late it has already been replaced by another new product.

EXHIBIT 5.7 *Crossing the Chasm: A Difficult Transition in the Diffusion Process*

In Geoffrey Moore's classic book on the marketing of high-technology products, Moore explores the challenges of crossing the "chasm," as he calls it, in the diffusion process between the early adopters and the early majority. For many high-tech products, innovators and early adopters have quite different needs from early majority customers. They are often willing to adopt a revolutionary new product that is not yet very user-friendly or whose product features have not yet been fully developed. Their own technical skill enables them to adapt such a product to their needs and resolve some of the uncertainties inherent in the product's perhaps still-unclear potential. Their

self-perception as an innovator gives them comfort in trying new products before others do. Early majority buyers, on the other hand, typically require easier-to-use products, whose benefits are clearly defined, and for which there is proof that the product will perform. Taking a product from the first group of buyers to the second is a difficult challenge, one that is compounded by the fact that buyers in the innovator and early adopter groups are not likely to associate or talk with buyers in the early majority group.

Sources: Geoffrey A. Moore, *Crossing the Chasm* (New York: HarperCollins, 1991).

adopters in its first year on the market? History suggests that such penetration levels are rare at the outset. More typically, first-year penetration levels include some but not all of the innovators, well under 2.5 percent of those who, it is hoped, will ultimately adopt!

A good way to estimate how quickly an innovation is likely to move through the diffusion process is to construct a chart that rates the adoption on the six key factors influencing adoption speed, as shown in Exhibit 5.8. An innovation that is risky for the prospective user to try or buy, has little competitive advantage, is complex or incompatible with current user behavior, and for which it is difficult or expensive to try or to understand its benefits is likely to face tough sledding, regardless of the attractiveness of the market. Personal robots, introduced in the early 1980s with great fanfare, were such an innovation. Thus, introducing a new product that delivers no real benefits or lacks competitive advantage into *any* market, regardless of its high-tech profile, is likely to be an unpleasant experience!

EXHIBIT 5.8   **Comparison of Rate of Adoption of Cellular Phones and Early Personal Computers for Home Use**

Adoption Factor	Cell Phones		Home Computers	
Risk	+/−	Moderate risk: Cell phones were given away to attract early adopters who agreed to one year's usage.	−	An expensive investment wasted, if it turned out not to be useful.
Relative advantage	+	Enabled people to make and receive phone calls from anywhere—in the car or at the beach!	−	It was not clear, in the early days of personal computing, what the advantages of a PC were in the home.
Relative simplicity	+	Early cell phones were easy to use.	−	Early PCs were inordinately complex to use.
Compatibility with current behavior	+	Just like making or receiving a phone call at home or office.	−	Lots of learning required to use.
Ease of small-scale trial	+/−	Easy to demonstrate, but contracts required.	+/−	One could visit a store for hands-on trial but couldn't understand the "bits, bytes, and RAM."
Ease of communication of benefits	+	"Make or receive calls anywhere" is easy to understand.	−	Benefits were not clear, thus not communicable.

Key: + Favorable for rapid adoption

       − Unfavorable for rapid adoption

CAUTIONS AND CAVEATS IN FORECASTING

Psychological Biases in Forecasting

To a varying degree, the effectiveness of all of the forecasting methods we've just reviewed is often undermined by excessive optimism on the forecaster's part, especially in new product or new venture settings. Forecasters often fall prey to what Dan Lovallo and Daniel Kahneman call the planning fallacy, a tendency to make decisions based on delusional optimism rather than on a rational weighting of possible gains and losses and the probabilities thereof.[14] A solution they espouse, based on the systematic use of multiple analogs, is discussed in Exhibit 5.9.

Common Sources of Error in Forecasting

Several sources of potential error in forecasts should be recognized. First, forecasters are subject to anchoring bias, where forecasts are perhaps inappropriately "anchored" in recent historical figures, even though market conditions have markedly changed, for better or worse.[15]

Second, capacity constraints are sometimes misinterpreted as forecasts. Someone planning to open a car wash that can process one car every seven minutes would probably be amiss in assuming sufficient demand to actually run at that rate all the time. A restaurant chain that is able to turn its tables 2.5 times each night, on average, must still do local market research to ascertain how much volume a new restaurant will really generate. Putting similar 80-table restaurants in two trade areas with different population makeup and density, with different levels of competition, may result in vastly different sales levels.

Another source of error in forecasting is incentive pay. Bonus plans can cause managers to artificially inflate or deflate forecasts, whether intentionally or otherwise.

EXHIBIT 5.9 *Managing the View through Your Rose-Colored Glasses*

Even in new product and new venture settings, virtually nothing is completely new. Many similar products or ventures have undoubtedly preceded yours. Even in the theatre, there are only 36 literary plots: Leonard Bernstein's *West Side Story* is an adaptation of Shakespeare's *Romeo and Juliet*, set in New York's Harlem in the 1950s. Dan Lovallo and Daniel Kahneman argue that the overoptimistic, rosy view can be mitigated by systematically assembling a class of similar projects, laying out the distribution of actual outcomes of those projects from best to worst, and then positioning the current project in that distribution. The resulting forecast will be far more accurate. This "outside view," as they call it, is much more likely to yield realistic estimates because it bypasses the cognitive and organizational biases that tend to hype the more typical "inside view" that's based on the project itself.

Sources: John Mullins and Randy Komisar, *Getting to Plan B: Breaking Through to a Better Business Model*, Boston: Harvard Business Press, 2009; and Dan Lovallo and Daniel Kahneman, "Delusions of Success," *Harvard Business Review*, July 2003.

"Sandbagging"—setting the forecast or target at an easily achievable figure in order to earn bonuses when that figure is beaten—is common.

Finally, unstated but implicit assumptions can overstate a well-intentioned forecast. While 34.5 percent of those surveyed (after adjustments, as shown in Exhibit 5.2) may indicate their willingness to buy a new grocery product, such as fresh pasta, for such a forecast to pan out requires that consumers actually are *made aware* of the new product when it is introduced and that the product *can actually be found* on supermarket shelves. Assumptions of **awareness** and **distribution coverage** at levels less than 100 percent, depending on the nature of the planned marketing program for the product, should be applied to such a forecast, using the chain ratio method (see Exhibit 5.3).

In today's fast-changing world that is becoming harder and harder to predict, these common sources of error in forecasting are only the beginning of the challenge that forecasters must address. In their new book, *Future Ready; How to Master Business Forecasting,* Steve Morlidge and Steve Player argue that, in many companies, today's forecasting culture—based on a command-and-control mind set, an annual budget-driver schedule, and a predict and comply approach—has simply gone wrong (See Exhibit 5.10).[16]

Keys to Good Forecasting

A key goal of good forecasting is to identify the full range of possibilities about the future, not some illusory set of certainties that are, in fact, not certain at all.[17] There are two important keys to improve the credibility and accuracy of a set of forecasts of sales and market potential. The first of these is to make explicit the **assumptions** on which the forecast is based. This way, if there is debate or doubt about the forecast, the *assumptions* can be debated, and data to support the assumptions can be obtained. The resulting conversation is far more useful than stating mere opinions about whether the forecast is too high or too low. For ACG, the combination of observational and survey forecasting methods enabled Maddy and Laguë to articulate the assumptions on which their revenue forecasts were based and to support those assumptions with data. Their evidence-based forecast was instrumental in their obtaining US$3.5 million in start-up capital to get their venture off the ground.[18]

Strategic Issue

There are two important keys to improve the credibility and accuracy of forecasts of sales and market potential.

The second key to effective forecasting is to use multiple methods. But there are so many methods. How should one choose? Do you have historical data? Use one or more statistical methods. No such data? Find some suitable analogies. Are there similar products in the market already? Find some customers to observe as they use or buy them. Is your concept well defined or your prototype ready to show? Conduct a survey of buyer

EXHIBIT 5.10 *Mastering Forecasting*

Let's face it. It is nigh on impossible to predict the future. The world is too complex and too dynamic to do so with any confidence. So what is a forecaster to do? Morlidge and Player offer six pragmatic suggestions about what to do and how to do it, as shown in the table below.

Issue	What to Stop Doing	What to Start Doing
Purpose	Stop using the budget process and accounting structure to drive your forecasts	Start recognizing the distinction between targets (what you hope will happen) and forecasts (what you think will happen) and the gap between them
Time	Stop producing forecasts on the accounting department's timetable	Start producing rolling forecasts, and update them based on the rate of change of the variables that drive your decisions
Models	Stop relying on a single approach	Start using different types of models and approaches in combination
Measurement	Stop measuring the quality of your forecasts informally	Start routinely measuring forecast error to find biases, rather than focusing on accuracy
Risk	Stop forecasting single-point outcomes	Start assessing alternative potential outcomes
Process	Stop treating forecasting as an optional exercise	Start building forecasting into the fabric of your managerial processes

Source: Steve Morlidge and Steve Player, *Future Ready: How to Master Business Forecasting* (Chichester, West Sussex, UK: John Wiley and Sons, Ltd, 2010). For more on Steve Morlidge, see *http://www.satoripartners.co.uk/About_Me.html.*

intentions. Can you produce some product or deliver the service, at least on a trial basis? Try an experimental market test of one kind or another. Do you have early adoption data? Model the diffusion process. And so on.

Thus, the best way to forecast, as we saw in Exhibit 5.1, is to employ multiple methods. If the results of two or more forecasting methods converge on similar results, that will build your and others' confidence in what the forecasts say. If not, you'll be well-placed to ask yourself some probing questions about the assumptions on which the various forecasts are based and why the forecasts from different approaches differ, perhaps using the approach suggested in Exhibit 5.9. Ultimately, however, any forecast is almost certainly wrong. Contingency plans should be developed to cope with the reality that ultimately unfolds.

WHY DATA? WHY MARKETING RESEARCH?

In the first portion of this chapter, we provided several approaches to forecasting, each of which requires that data be collected. Similarly, the first four chapters of this book provided frameworks for gaining a better understanding of market and competitive conditions and of what buyers in a given market want and need—what we call **market knowledge.**[19] Obtaining market knowledge also requires data, and so far we've provided little discussion of exactly how one might best find the necessary data. Without relevant and timely data, market knowledge is generally incomplete and often ill-informed, based perhaps on hunches or intuition that may or may not be correct. For an example of how Starbucks uses qualitative marketing research to systematically tap into its customers' ideas and suggestions, see Exhibit 5.11.

As should be clear to the reader by now, without adequate market knowledge, marketing decisions are likely to be misguided. Products for which there is little demand may

EXHIBIT 5.11 *Starbucks Listens, "Splash Sticks" Are the Result*

In January 2008, Starbucks founder Howard Schultz returned to his former CEO role, in an effort to reinvigorate the company following a string of disappointing performance figures. One of the first things Schultz did was to launch an online listening post, MyStarbucksIdea.com, in order, as Schultz put it, to instill what he calls "a seeing culture" into the company. It quickly became clear that Starbucks customers weren't reticent. More than 10,000 of them wanted something to plug the hole in the lid on their take-out coffee that would prevent spilling. The result? Starbucks' new reusable "splash stick" does just that.

The Starbucks system and others like it, such as Dell's IdeaStorm.com, are powered by new "Ideas" software from Salesforce.com. "It's like a live focus group that never closes," says Marc Benioff, Salesforce's chairman and CEO. The Starbucks website is backed by 48 specially trained "idea partners" who host the online discussions that ensue. They also act as advocates for customers' ideas so they get a fair hearing inside the company. Chris Bruzzo, Starbucks' chief technology officer, says the purpose of MyStarbucksIdea.com was to "open up a dialogue with customers and build up this muscle inside our company." MyStarbucksIdea.com is but one manifestation of how online tools are reshaping the practice of marketing research and leading to a better understanding of what customers want.

Source: Jeff Jarvis, "The Buzz from Starbucks Customers," *BusinessWeek* European Edition, April 28, 2008. For more on Starbucks, see *www.starbucks.com*.

be introduced, only to subsequently fail. New markets may be entered, despite market or industry conditions that make success unlikely. Attractive product-markets may be overlooked. Products may be marketed to the wrong target market, when consumers in another market segment would like the product better. Pricing may be too high, reducing sales, or too low, leaving money on the table. Advertising and promotion monies may be poorly spent. Second-best distribution channels may be chosen. These outcomes are all too common. Most often, they result from ill-formed or underinformed marketing decisions. Thoughtfully designed, competently executed marketing research can mitigate the chances of such unpleasant outcomes.

Thus, in the remainder of this chapter, we address some of the challenges of obtaining market knowledge to support strategic decision making, including the development of systems to track pertinent market information inside and outside the firm, as well as the design and implementation of more targeted studies intended to collect information about a particular marketing problem. We begin by discussing the principal kinds of **market knowledge systems** used in companies large and small, and we show how such systems can improve the timeliness and quality of marketing decisions.

CUSTOMER RELATIONSHIP MANAGEMENT: CHARTING A PATH TOWARD COMPETITIVE ADVANTAGE

Marketing is rapidly becoming a game where information, rather than raw marketing muscle, wins the race for competitive advantage. There are four commonly used market knowledge systems on which companies rely to keep pace with daily developments: internal records regarding marketing performance (in terms of sales and the effectiveness and efficiency of marketing programs), marketing databases, competitive intelligence systems, and systems to organize client contact. Taken together, these systems lie at the heart of the systematic practice of **customer relationship management** (CRM). Effective use of CRM is likely to result in happier, higher-volume, more loyal customers. Few of these systems that made modern CRM possible existed in their current form until developments in data processing and telecommunications made them cost-effective.

Strategic Issue

Marketing is rapidly becoming a game where information, rather than raw marketing muscle, wins the race for competitive advantage.

Internal Records Systems

Every Monday morning, each retail director at the headquarters of Nine West Retail Stores, a leading operator of shoe specialty stores, receives the "Godzilla Report," a tabulation of detailed sales and inventory information about the fastest-selling items in Nine West stores from the prior week.[20] By style and color, each director learns which items in his or her stores are selling fast and need to be reordered. A similar report provides information about all other styles currently in Nine West's stores, so that slow sellers can be marked down or transferred to stores where those styles are in higher demand. Additional reports aggregate sales information by style and color; by merchandise category (e.g., dress or casual); by store, area, or region; and for various time periods. The information provided by these reports constitutes the backbone of Nine West's decision making about which shoes to offer in which of its stores. Imagine how much more difficult the retail director's job would be without today's point-of-sale systems to collect and report such data! Imagine the potential advantage Nine West has over shoe retailers who lack such information.

Every marketer, not just retailers, needs information about "what's hot, what's not." Unfortunately, accounting systems generally do not collect such data. Typically, such systems just track dollars of revenue, with no information about *which* goods or services were sold. Thus, marketers need **internal records systems** to track what is selling, how fast, in which locations, to which customers, and so on. Providing input on the design of such systems so that the right data are provided to the right people at the right time is a critical marketing responsibility in any company. But what constitutes critical marketing information varies from company to company and industry to industry.

Strategic Issue

Every marketer, not just retailers, needs information about "what's hot, what's not." Unfortunately, accounting systems generally do not collect such data.

Nine West retail directors need to know which styles and colors are selling, in which stores, at what rate. Walmart believes its key suppliers need to know its store-by-store item and category sales data, so it provides password-protected online access to such data to some suppliers. Telemarketers need to know which callers are producing sales, at what times of day, and for which products. Marketers of kitchen gadgets through infomercials on late-night television need to know which ads on which stations in which cities are performing, in order to place media spending where it will be most productive. Companies selling their wares to industrial markets through outside salesforces need to know not only which products are selling to which customers, but also which salespeople are selling how much, at what margins and expense rates, and to whom. The salesforce, too, needs information about status of current orders, customer purchasing history, and so on.

For those charged with developing or updating internal record systems in their companies, we provide, in Exhibit 5.12, a series of questions to help marketing decision makers specify what internally generated sales data are needed, when, for whom, in what sequence, and at what level of aggregation. The answers to these questions should drive the design of such systems as well as the design and formatting of their output.

Marketing Databases Make CRM Possible

In the technology boom of the late 1990s, several companies launched extensive and expensive projects to help them better manage customer relationships through enhanced use of customer data. Although many large-scale CRM projects have failed to show an adequate return on investment, CRM has proved to be very successful in managing marketing campaigns and in serving customers more effectively and more efficiently.

EXHIBIT 5.12 Designing an Internal Records System for Marketing Decision Makers

Questions to Ask	Implications for a Chain Footwear Retailer	Implications for an Infomercial Marketer of Kitchen Gadgets
What information is key to providing our customers with what they want?	Need to *know* which shoes sell, in which stores and markets, at what rate	Need to *know* which gadgets sell, in what markets, at what rate
What regular marketing decisions are critical to our profitability?	Decide which shoes and shoe categories to buy more of, which to buy less of or get rid of, in which stores and markets to sell them	*Decide* on which specific TV stations, programs, and times of day to place infomercials for which gadgets
What data are critical to managing profitability?	Inventory turnover and gross margin	Contribution margin (gross margin less media cost) per gadget sold
Who needs to know?	Buyers and managers of merchandise categories	Media buyers, product managers
When do they need to know for competitive advantage?	For hottest sellers, need to know before competitors, to beat them to reorder market. For dogs, need to know weekly, to mark them down.	Need to know daily, for prior night's ads, to reallocate media dollars
In what *sequence* and at what *level of aggregation* should data be reported?	Sequence of report: hot sellers first, in order of inventory turnover Aggregation: by style and color for buyers, by category for merchandise managers	Sequence of report: hot stations and programs first, in order of contribution margin per gadget sold Aggregation: By stations/programs for media buyers, by gadget for product managers

The purpose of CRM is to develop a unified and cohesive view of the customer from every touch point within the company, whether by telephone, over the web, by mail, or in person, and, in so doing, to increase profitability and shareholder value. CRM, when implemented successfully, is a cross-functional process that requires coordination and broad-based strategic thinking. The goal of most CRM efforts is to profitably win a growing share of key customers' business while finding lower-cost but effective ways of serving less valuable customers. A key element in such efforts is the use of marketing databases, often in conjunction with call centers where many customer contacts occur.

Databases created for CRM purposes typically capture information about most or all of the following for each customer.[21]

- Transactions: Complete transaction detail, including dates, items purchased, and prices paid.
- Instances of customer contact: Whether sales calls, call center inquiries, service requests, or whatever, a CRM system should capture the detail of each and every customer contact with the company.
- Customer demographics: Relevant descriptive data to facilitate market segmentation and target marketing are crucial.
- Customer responses: A CRM system should capture linkages between marketing activities and customer action. Did the customer respond to an e-mail? A direct mail shot? A face-to-face sales call?

Many companies have become quite sophisticated about using marketing databases. Catalog marketers such as Lands' End and L. L. Bean, based in the United States, know who are their best customers and what categories they tend to buy. Online marketers such as Amazon use "cookies," electronic signatures placed at a customer's personal computer, so they not only keep track of what each customer has bought, but also recognize the customer when he or she logs on to their site. Airlines track members of their frequent flyer programs and target some with special promotions. Supermarket chain Tesco in the United Kingdom uses its loyalty cards to track and analyze customer buying patterns and to offer customers coupons and incentives tailored to their buying behavior. Tesco uses its analysis in deciding product placement on shelves, managing coupon campaigns, tailoring product portfolios to individual stores, and much more.[22] The use of sophisticated loyalty cards by large retailers has now gone global (see Exhibit 5.13).

Strategic Issue

Designing marketing databases that take effective advantage of customer data that companies are in a position to collect requires that several major issues be considered.

Designing marketing databases that take effective advantage of customer data that companies are in a position to collect requires that several major issues be considered: the cost of collecting the data, the economic benefits of using the data, the ability of the company to keep the data current in today's mobile society, and the rapid advances in technology that permit the data to be used to maximum advantage.

Collecting information, then storing and maintaining it, always costs money. If a company wants to know more about the demographics and lifestyles of its best customers, in addition to their purchasing histories, it must obtain demographic and lifestyle data about them. Doing so is more difficult than it sounds; many people are unwilling to spend much time filling out forms that ask nosy questions about education, income, whether they play tennis, and what kind of car they drive. The cost of collecting such information must be weighed against its value. What will be done with the information once it is in hand? Marketers planning to build their own databases need also to consider several increasingly important ethical issues, as discussed in Ethical Perspective 5.1.

EXHIBIT 5.13 *Loyalty Cards Go Global*

Many of us have wallets full of so-called loyalty cards, the reward cards that retailers, airlines, and other merchants give us to keep us coming back for more. While keeping us coming back is one important goal, "[t]he real value-added is the data," says Rupert Duchesne, the CEO of Aimia, a Canadian firm. Aimia, a $2.2 billion multinational company, runs multimerchant programs across Europe and the Middle East, including the Nectar card, the United Kingdom's largest loyalty program with 18 million subscribers. Nectar cardholders earn points on their supermarket shopping (from Sainsbury, the United Kingdom's number two supermarket retailer), on their airline tickets (from Expedia and easyJet), and much more.

By mining the data for its member merchants, Aimia enables them to offer targeted discounts and other promotions to their customers. Aimia is now taking on its next challenge, teaming up with the Tata Group, India's largest family-run conglomerate, to offer Nectarlike loyalty solutions for India's highly fragmented retail industry. In an industry where less than 7 percent of retail volume is done by chain retailers, Aimia will need many member merchants to take part.

Will Indian consumers soon become the loyalty-program junkies that many consumers are in the West? Many skeptical Indians consider such programs to be plots, "To make them buy things they don't want," says Suhel Seth, a marketing observer in India. But even Seth thinks that the trust Indians have in the Tata brand will give Tata and Aimia a good chance to succeed.

Source: "Spies in Your Wallet," *The Economist*, November 5, 2011, p. 85.

Ⓔ Ethical Perspective Ethical Issues in Database Marketing, Internet Marketing, and Marketing Research

5.1

New technologies relating to the gathering and use of information about consumers and their behavior, interests, and intentions raise a host of legal and ethical questions. These new technologies have the potential to harm individuals when such information "is used without their knowledge and/or consent, leading them to be *excluded from* or *included in* activities in such a way that they are harmed economically, psychologically, or physically." Examples include the improper disclosure of a person's credit rating, denying medical insurance to an individual based on confidential information, and a person's being placed on target lists for direct mail and telemarketing. The depth of privacy concerns varies from country to country, a critical issue for internet marketers, given their global reach.

Ethical issues in marketing research stem, in large part, from the interaction between the researcher and respondents, clients, and the general public. For instance, respondents should not be pressured to participate, should have the right to remain anonymous, and should not be deceived by fake sponsorship.

Client issues involve the confidentiality of the research findings and the obligation to strive to provide unbiased and honest results regardless of client expectations. The public is very much involved when they are exposed to a sales solicitation disguised as a marketing research study or issuing from data obtained from "volunteer surveys" using write-ins or call-ins.

In discussing the reliability of, and ethical issues involved with, marketing research studies, a *Wall Street Journal* article noted that many studies "are little more than vehicles for pitching a product or opinion." An examination of hundreds of recent studies indicated that the business of research has become pervaded by bias and distortion. More studies are being sponsored by companies or groups with a financial interest in the results. This too often leads to a bias in the way questions are asked.

Because of shortages in time and money, sample sizes are being reduced to the point that, when groups are further broken into subgroups, the margin of error becomes unacceptable—assuming a probability sample was used. In addition to sample size, the way the sampling universe is defined can bias the results. Thus, in a Chrysler study showing that people preferred Chrysler's cars to Toyota's, a sample of only 100 respondents was used in each of two tests, and none owned a foreign car. Thus, the respondents may well have been biased in favor of U.S. cars.

In addition to the preceding problems, subjective sampling procedures are often used, data analysis may be flawed, or only the best conclusions are reported. Frequently researchers are hired whose views on the subject area being researched are known to be similar to those of the client. In an attempt to regulate the marketing research industry, several codes of conduct and ethics have been developed. For the United States these include published codes by the American Marketing Association, the American Association for Public Opinion Research, the Marketing Research Association, and the Council of American Survey Research Organizations. In the United Kingdom, the Market Research Society has developed an ethical Code of Conduct that all members are required to adhere to. Similar organizations have developed localized guidelines in other countries. For one such listing of organizations in other countries, see the British Market Research Association website at *www.bmra.org.uk.*

Sources: Paul N. Bloom, Robert Adler, and George R. Milne, "Identifying the Legal and Ethical Risks and Costs of Using New Information Technologies to Support Marketing Programs," in *The Marketing Information Revolution,* Robert C. Blattberg, Rashi Glazer, and John D. C. Little, eds. (Boston: Harvard Business School Press, 1994), p. 294; Cynthia Crossen, "Studies Galore Support Products and Positions, But Are They Reliable?" *The Wall Street Journal,* November 14, 1991, pp. A1 and A8; and Thomas E. Weber, "Europe and U.S. Reach Truce on Net Privacy, but What Comes Next?" *The Wall Street Journal,* June 19, 2000, p. B1.

Building or accessing marketing databases is but a small part of any effective CRM effort, however. Implementing such an effort requires four key steps:[23]

- Gaining broad-based organizational support for creating and adopting a CRM strategy.
- Forming a cross-functional CRM team with membership from all functions that have customer contact.

- Conducting a needs analysis that identifies both customer and business needs.
- Developing a CRM strategy to guide implementation.

One of the things that some CRM efforts make possible is segmenting markets according to the lifetime value of customers, rather than by more traditional means. **Customer lifetime value** (CLV) refers to the margins that a customer generates over a lifetime less the cost of serving the customer. Calculating CLV is not a trivial task; it requires both historical purchasing data and forecasting of future customer purchases which, as we've seen, is always somewhat tenuous. Nevertheless, research conducted by Deloitte Consulting found that companies that use CLV metrics are 60 percent more profitable than firms that do not.[24] Other research has focused on the long-run value of customers that have been acquired through referral programs, and found them to be at least 16 percent higher than comparable, nonreferred customers.[25]

The rapid rise in so-called two-sided markets—in which one set of customers who pay little or nothing (Google search users, for example) are essential to attract a completely different and more lucrative set of customers (advertisers who buy ads that are delivered in response to Google searches)—has led to an even more vexing challenge than the calculation of customer lifetime value in a conventional sense. This challenge is to figure out the value of both kinds of customers: those who search (and are not asked to pay), in Google's case, and those who pay, the advertisers.

Marketing academicians and marketers themselves are beginning to address this and similar kinds of problems, using sophisticated models that help marketers decide on which set of customers to spend marketing dollars, when, and in what pattern over time.[26] Well-educated marketing graduates with an affinity for web analytics are well placed to make meaningful contributions to their employers or to start new kinds of businesses themselves to address complex issues like these. But complex algorithms are not always beneficial. One study found that single-variable models or simple heuristics were as effective as more complex models.[27]

Why CRM Efforts Fail

Unfortunately, there have been many instances of CRM installations that were unsuccessful, sometimes dramatically so. All of us have experienced infuriating occasions where wading through endless levels of telephone prompts and poorly trained or soulless customer service representatives has damaged or destroyed, rather than enhanced, the customer relationship the company sought to build. Research by Bain & Co. suggests that there are four major pitfalls to watch out for:[28]

- Implementing CRM without first developing a strategy.
- Putting CRM in place without changing organizational structure and/or processes.
- Assuming that more CRM is better.
- Failure to prioritize which customer relationships are most worth investing in.

Client Contact Systems

One good starting point for developing CRM capabilities in companies having limited resources is to put in place salesforce automation software. Such software helps companies disseminate real-time product information to salespeople to enable them to be more productive and more able to satisfy customer needs. Such software also allows companies to effectively capture customer intelligence from salespeople, keep track of it for use on later sales calls, and even transfer it to other salespeople in the event of a salesperson leaving the company. Several low-cost software applications that run on PCs are available. Sage ACT and GoldMine are two of the best-known programs in this arena, and Salesforce.com (see *www.salesforce.com* for a free trial) offers a web-based product. These programs keep track of clients' names, addresses, phone and fax numbers, and so on—along with all kinds of personal tidbits, such as their spouse's and children's names and the kind of wine the client likes to drink—and they also provide an organized way to make notes about each contact with the customer.

CRM is a topic about which whole chapters—even entire books—have been written, so we've just scratched the surface with our treatment here. There are a couple of good websites for those interested in learning more about CRM. One is *www.crmdaily. com*, which provides daily updates on the latest happenings in the CRM field. Another is *www.1to1 .com*, the website of the Peppers and Rogers group, a leading consultancy in this arena.

Competitive Intelligence Systems[29]

In today's fast-paced business climate, keeping up with competitors and the changing macroenvironment is no easy task. Competitive intelligence (CI) is a systematic and ethical approach for gathering and analyzing information about competitors' activities and related business trends. It is based on the idea that more than 80 percent of all information is public knowledge. The most important sources of CI information include companies' annual and other financial reports, speeches by company executives, government documents, online databases, trade organizations, as well as the popular and business press. The challenge is to find the relevant knowledge, analyze it, and share it with the decision makers in the organization, so they can use it. The critical questions that managers setting up a CI system should ask are:

- How rapidly does the competitive climate in our industry change? How important is it that we keep abreast of such changes?
- What are the objectives for CI in our company?
- Who are the best internal clients for CI? To whom should the CI effort report?
- What budget should be allocated to CI? Will it be staffed full- or part-time?

In companies that operate in industries with dynamic competitive contexts, the use of full-time CI staff is growing.

MARKETING RESEARCH: A FOUNDATION FOR MARKETING DECISION MAKING

We now turn very briefly to the **marketing research** task: the design, collection, analysis, and reporting of research intended to gather data pertinent to a *particular* marketing challenge or situation. The word *particular* is very important. Marketing research is intended to address carefully defined marketing problems or opportunities. Research carried out without carefully thought-out objectives usually means time and money down the tubes! Some marketing problems commonly addressed through marketing research include tracking customer satisfaction from unit to unit or year to year (**tracking studies**); testing consumer responses to elements of marketing programs, such as prices or proposed advertising campaigns; and assessing the likelihood that consumers will buy proposed new products.

Strategic Issue

Research carried out without carefully thought-out objectives usually means time and money down the tubes!

The steps in the marketing research process are shown in Exhibit 5.14. As this exhibit shows, the marketing research process is fraught with numerous opportunities for error. That's why it's so important that all who play influential roles in setting strategy for their firms or who use marketing research results for decision making be well-informed and critical users of the information that results from market research studies.

EXHIBIT 5.14   Steps in the Marketing Research Process: What Can Go Wrong?

Steps	What Frequently Goes Wrong?
1. Identify managerial problem and establish research objectives.	Management identifies no clear objective, no decision to be made based on the proposed research.
2. Determine data sources (primary or secondary) and types of data and research approaches (qualitative or quantitative) required.	Primary data are collected when cheaper and faster secondary data will do. Quantitative data are collected without first collecting qualitative data.
3. Design research: type of study, data collection approach, sample, etc.	These are technical issues best managed by skilled practitioners. Doing these steps poorly can generate misleading or incorrect results.
4. Collect data.	Collector bias: hearing what you want to hear.
5. Analyze data.	Tabulation errors or incorrect use or interpretation of statistical procedures may mislead the user.
6. Report results to the decision maker.	Some users do not really want objective information—they want to prove what they already believe to be true.

It is beyond the scope of this book, however, to instruct the reader in how to design marketing research studies. For those wishing to read more on this topic, numerous textbooks and websites on marketing research are available.

WHAT USERS OF MARKETING RESEARCH SHOULD ASK

The steps identified in Exhibit 5.14 make clear where many of the potential stumbling blocks are in designing and conducting marketing research. The informed and critical user of marketing research should ask the following questions, ideally before implementing the research or if necessary subsequent to its completion, to ensure that the research is unbiased and the results are trustworthy.

1. What are the objectives of the research? Will the data to be collected meet those objectives?
2. Are the data sources appropriate? Is cheaper, faster secondary data used where possible? Is qualitative research planned to ensure that quantitative research, if any, is on target?
3. Are the planned qualitative and/or quantitative research approaches suited to the objectives of the research? Qualitative research is generally better for deep insights into consumer behavior, while quantitative research is better for measurement of a population's attitudes and likely responses to products or marketing programs.
4. Is the research designed well? Will questionnaire scales permit the measurement necessary to meet the research objectives? Are the questions on a survey or in an interview or focus group unbiased? ("Isn't this a great new product? Do you like it?") Do the contact method and sampling plan entail any known bias? Is the sample size large enough to meet the research objectives?
5. Are the planned analyses appropriate? They should be specified *before* the research is conducted.

In the remaining chapters in this book, we shall return from time to time to the marketing research topic and show how marketing research informs not only market and competitive analysis and customer understanding, but also the design and implementation of marketing programs.

Marketing Plan Exercise

Prepare a detailed plan for conducting the primary research required to complete your project. The research plan needs to do three things:

- Precisely spell out the research objectives the research is intended to meet.
- Design the research to get you there. Identify your methods, your sample, and any statistics (means, etc.) you will employ. Prepare drafts of questionnaires, guides for focus group sessions or in-depth interviews, plans for how you will conduct observational research, and so forth.
- Describe how the combination of your secondary research and your planned primary research will lead to your estimate of target market size and your sales forecast for your marketing plan. Precisely spell out the mathematics that will do this, connecting it to specific secondary data or specific answers to questions or observations from your primary data.

Your research design should clearly identify and satisfy your research objectives, and appropriate qualitative and/or quantitative research should be competently designed, using what you learned in previous coursework or any supplementary readings necessary.

Discussion Questions

1. Given that absolute market potential almost always exceeds actual industry sales, why do marketers bother to make potential estimates? Discuss four decisions that a marketer of industrial grinding machinery might make based on such potential estimates.

2. To more effectively allocate promotion expenditures and sales efforts, the marketing manager for a company marketing frozen food entrées would like to know the relative market potential for their products in every county in the United States. What variables would you include in a multi-factor index for measuring relative potential? Explain your rationale for including each variable. Where might you find up-to-date information about each of the variables in your index?

3. Suppose you are the product manager responsible for General Electric's line of trash compactors. After many years, the product has yet to gain acceptance by many consumers. Use the diffusion of innovation theory discussed in the text to explain why trash compactors have achieved such poor market penetration. What does this imply concerning the shape of the rest of the trash compactor's life-cycle curve? What actions might you consider taking to increase the market penetration for this product?

Additional self-diagnostic questions to test your ability to apply the analytical tools and concepts in this chapter to strategic decision making may be found at the book's website at **www.mhhe.com/walker8e.**

Endnotes

1. This material is drawn from Stephen Prentice, "Intel's Genevieve Bell: An Anthropologist at the Cutting Edge of Technology and Society: A Gartner Fellows Interview," April 23, 2010; Rob Enderle, "Intel's Secret Weapon," *TG Daily, http://www.tgdaily.com/hardware-opinion/50438-genevieve-bell-intel; http://www.gartner.com/displaydoument?id1358720*; Mike Magee, "Intel's Genevieve Bell Drank Water out of Frogs," TechEye, *http://www.techeye.net/chips/*; Michael V. Copeland, "Intel's Cultural Anthropologist," *Fortune* European Edition, September 27, 2010, pp. 16–17; Intel, "Mobile Etiquette Mishaps Are Running Rampant," *Hoteliers,* March 17, 2011, *http://www.4hoteliers.com/4hots_nshw.php?mwi8403*; and the Intel website at *http://www.intel.com/pressroom/kist/bios/gbell.htm.*

2. Kenneth D. Lawrence, Ronald K. Klimberg, and Sheila M. Lawrence, *Fundamentals of Forecasting Using Excel* (New York: Industrial Press, 2009).

3. Anita M. McGahan, *African Communications Group (Condensed)* (Boston: Harvard Business School Publishing, 1999).

4. McGahan, *African Communications Group (Condensed).*

5. For more on analogs and antilogs and their use in developing evidence-based forecasts and business models, see John Mullins and Randy Komisar, *Getting to Plan B: Breaking Through to a Better Business Model* (Boston: Harvard Business Press, 2009).

6. Colin Welch and Ananth Raman, *Merchandising at Nine West Retail Stores* (Boston: Harvard Business School Publishing, 1998).

7. For more on conjoint analysis, see Vithala Rao, *Applied Conjoint Analysis* (New York: Springer Publishing, 2009).

8. See Frank M. Bass, "A New Product Growth Model for Consumer Durables," *Management Science,* January 1969, pp. 215–27; and Trichy V. Krishnan, Frank M. Bass, and V. Kumar, "Impact of a Late Entrant on the Diffusion of a New Product/Service," *Journal of Marketing Research,* May 2000, pp. 269–78.

9. Ibid.

10. Everett M. Rogers, *Diffusion of Innovations* (New York: Free Press, 1983).

11. Jacob Goldenburg, Sangman Han, Donald R. Lehmann, and Jae Weon Hong, "The Role of Hubs in the Adoption Process," *Journal of Marketing* 73 (March 2009), pp. 1–13.

12. Raghunath Singh Rao, Rajesh K. Chandy, and Jaideep C. Prabhu, "The Fruits of Legitimacy: Why Some New Ventures Gain More from Innovation Than Others," *Journal of Marketing* 72 (July 2008), pp. 58–75.

13. Rogers, *Diffusion of Innovations.*

13. Dale O. Coxe, *African Communications Group* (Boston: Harvard Business School Publishing, 1996).

14. Dan Lovallo and Daniel Kahneman, "Delusions of Success," *Harvard Business Review,* July 2003.

15. Amos Tversky and Daniel Kahneman, "Judgment under Uncertainty," *Science* 185 (1974), pp. 1124–31.

16. Steve Morlidge and Steve Player, *Future Ready: How to Master Business Forecasting* (Chichester, West Sussex, UK: John Wiley and Sons, Ltd, 2010).

17. Paul Saffo, "Six Rules for Effective Forecasting," *Harvard Business Review,* July–August 2007.

19. Li and Calantone define market knowledge as "organized and structured information about the market." See Tiger Li and Roger J. Calantone, "The Impact of Market Knowledge Competence on New Product Advantage: Conceptualization and Empirical Examination," *Journal of Marketing,* October 1998, pp. 13–29.

20. Welch and Raman, *Merchandising at Nine West Retail Stores.*

21. Russell S. Winer, "A Framework for Customer Relationship Management," *California Management Review* 43 (*Summer 2001*), pp. 89–105.

22. "Marketing—Clubbing Together," *Retail Week,* November 8, 2002.

23. For more on this topic, see V. Kumar and Werner J. Reinartz, *Customer Relationship Management* (Hoboken, NJ: John Wiley & Sons, 2006).

24. Sudhir Kale, "CRM Failure and the Seven Deadly Sins," *Marketing Management* 13 (April 2004), pp. 42–46.

25. Philipp Schmitt, Bernd Skiera, and Christophe Van den Bulte, "Referral Programs and Customer Value," *Journal of Marketing* 75 (January 2011), pp. 46–59.

26. For one such approach, see Sunil Gupta and Carl F. Mela, "What Is a Free Customer Worth?" *Harvard Business Review,* November 2008, pp. 102–109.

27. Markus Wubben and Florian V. Wangenheim, "Instant Customer Base Analysis: Managerial Heuristics Often 'Get It Right'," *Journal of Marketing* 72 (May 2008), pp. 82–93.

28. Darrell K. Rigby, Frederick F. Reichfeld, and Phil Schafter, "Avoid the Four Perils of CRM," *Harvard Business Review,* February 2002, pp. 101–9.

29. Information in this section comes from the Society of Competitive Intelligence Professionals website at *www.scip.org.*

Chapter Six

Targeting Attractive Market Segments

The Developing World's Emerging Middle Class[1]

For many years, in the eyes of Western marketers, there were only two market segments in the developing world—the very rich (of which there were not very many, but they had plenty of money to spend)—and everyone else, all very poor. With the 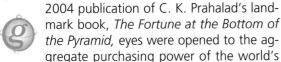 2004 publication of C. K. Prahalad's landmark book, *The Fortune at the Bottom of the Pyramid,* eyes were opened to the aggregate purchasing power of the world's poorest citizens, often defined as those earning less than $2 per day. Prahalad called attention to what a few companies had already figured out, that if you packed shampoo in single-portion sachets, poor consumers could and would buy it, even though the large economy size bottle sold in the west was completely irrelevant.

Today, a new reality is emerging all over the developing world. Rapid economic development has spawned a large and growing middle class, one with discretionary spending power and a plethora of unmet needs that local and foreign marketers are just starting to serve. But targeting the developing world's new middle class isn't as simple as following the old division between rich and poor, for this new group is a heterogeneous one, whose composition varies from country to country.

The New Middle Class: Who and How Large?

There are two common approaches to defining this new middle class, which sits just above the poor in Prahalad's pyramid: in absolute terms without

regard to local conditions or in relative terms, wherein what's "middle" is defined more locally. Central to the middle class notion is a reasonable amount of income that is discretionary—perhaps one-third, according to Diana Farrell of the National Economic Council in the United States—which goes to goods and services other than food and shelter. Most of the time, this means holding a steady job with salary and some benefits or running a small business whose employees go beyond the immediate family.

If one defines middle class as those having incomes greater than Brazil's average income and less than Italy's—roughly between $12 and $50 per person per day—the middle class population in emerging markets was about 250 million in 2000 and 400 million in 2005. But such an approach omits very large numbers of people in India and China who are clearly middle class but don't earn $12 per day. Martin Ravallion of the World Bank uses a range of $2 to $13 at 2005 purchasing-power parity prices, above the accepted poverty line in the developing world but below the American one. By his definition, India's middle class population rose from 147 million to 264 million from 1990 to 2005 and China's from 174 million to 806 million. The middle class in emerging markets globally nearly doubled over that period, from 1.4 billion to 2.6 billion. It now accounts for more than half of the developing world's population, up from one-third in 1990.

Shasi Thanoor, an Indian commentator, argues that the middle class is a category that is "more sociological than logical." It is, of course, an income category, but it's also a set of attitudes, even a mindset. And new kinds of spending patterns, too. These households spend proportionately less on food and housing, so they have money to spend on private education, health care, motorcycles, modern kitchens, air conditioners, and more. McKinsey believes that India's middle class will reach 580 million people by 2025. For marketers, this phenomenon holds powerful implications in market segmentation terms.

Targeting India's New Middle Class

Consider Dinaz Vervatwala, owner of a growing chain of fitness studios in India's fast-growing high-tech hot spot, Hyderabad. Vervatwala pioneered the aerobics industry in Hyderabad in 1993, opening her first fitness studio to serve upscale women in the posh Banjara Hills neighborhood. Hyderabad has grown rapidly in recent years, and her business has grown with it. The growth of high-tech industries in Hyderabad—from software to business process outsourcing and more—has created a new market of fitness customers having a blend of Indian and Western attitudes and aspirations.

As we write, there are four Dinaz's Fitness Studios in Hyderabad (*www.dinazs.com*), employing more than 50 people in total, each the product of a range of important marketing decisions. What socioeconomic level should Vervatwala target? What level of service do customers want, and what price will they pay for it? Where should new stores be located? Should she continue to target women, or should she expand her sights to include men (so far, not the case)? Each of these decisions required Vervatwala to think clearly about not just the growing market that was readily apparent, but about the market segments within it that she wanted to target, where to find them and how best to serve them.

Targeting: One Ingredient in Marketing Success

As Dinaz Vervatwala foresaw, Hyderabad's rapid growth has created a growing middle class of customers she was eager and willing to serve. But it's not just fitness studios that are growing in India. By 2007, India had more cell phone users than America. China had twice as many. In banking, ICICI, a large Indian bank, added 4 million new customers in 2008, most of them previously unbanked and living in India's second and third tier cities, where much of the growth in India's middle class is taking place. But bricks and mortar weren't a part of the bank's effort. ICICI's mobile phone banking innovations and vigorous cost-cutting reduced its transaction costs to levels far below those of its competitors.

Market segmentation decisions are not confined to small entrepreneurial companies like Dinaz's, of course. In March 2011, Vikram Pandit, CEO of CitiBank, announced that CitiBank, attracted by the explosion in trade and capital flows within and into emerging market countries like Brazil, China, and India, planned to become the world's "largest emerging markets financial services company." CitiBank already earns more than half its profits from developing countries.

Some observers argue that Asia, in particular, has reached a tipping point. The Chinese already buy more cars and more cell phones than Americans and will soon surpass them in computers, too, not to mention numerous other categories where the same thing is happening. Targeting attractive market segments in these rapidly growing markets and developing marketing strategies that are tailored to serve the chosen segments is what good marketers, whether entrepreneurs like Dinaz Vervatwala or bankers like those at ICICI and CitiBank, do.

STRATEGIC CHALLENGES ADDRESSED IN CHAPTER 6

Targeting the most attractive market segments is an issue that arises for marketers everywhere, not just in emerging economies. Different groups of customers—different market segments—have different wants and needs, both tangible and intangible. Fitness *aficionadas* may measure their progress by stepping on the scale, but the real benefits that Dinaz

Vervatwala offers—overall appearance, energy, and attitude—are more difficult to quantify. In virtually any market, if different segments can be clearly identified, specific goods or services with specific marketing programs can be developed to meet the physical needs of the customer (pounds lost or kept at bay, muscles finely toned, endurance enhanced) as well as the emotional needs that consumers attach to their favorite pursuits (looking good in the clubs or at work).

In Chapter 6, we draw on the foundation of market knowledge and customer understanding established in the first five chapters to introduce what are probably the most important and fundamental tools in the marketer's tool kit: **market segmentation** and **target marketing.** Together with differentiation and brand positioning, which we address in Chapter 7, these tools provide the platform on which most effective marketing programs are built. Learning to apply these tools effectively, however, requires addressing several important questions. Why do market segmentation and target marketing make sense? Why not sell the same fitness services—or bank accounts, automobiles, or whatever—to everyone? How can potentially attractive market segments be identified and defined? Finally, how can these segments be prioritized so that the most attractive ones are pursued? Answering these questions should enable an entrepreneur, a venture capital investor in Silicon Valley or Hyderabad, or a marketing manager in a multinational firm to decide which market segments should be targeted and provide insight into which investments should be made.

In the Marketing Plan Exercise at the end of this chapter, we encourage those working on marketing plans to use this chapter's lessons to clearly identify the market segment(s) you will target, the benefits you'll offer to customers in that segment, and the key features of your goods or services that will deliver these benefits.

DO MARKET SEGMENTATION AND TARGET MARKETING MAKE SENSE IN TODAY'S GLOBAL ECONOMY?

Market segmentation is the process by which a market is divided into distinct subsets of customers with similar needs and characteristics that lead them to respond in similar ways to a particular product offering and marketing program. Target marketing requires evaluating the relative attractiveness of various segments in terms of market potential, growth rate, competitive intensity, and other factors, along with the firm's mission and capabilities to deliver what each segment wants, in order to choose which segments it will serve. A recent cross-industry study demonstrated the importance of choosing one's market segments carefully. By focusing marketing effort on the most important customers, where important is defined by customer satisfaction, customer loyalty and share of wallet, higher average customer profitability and return on sales is realized.[2]

Brand positioning entails designing product offerings and marketing programs that can establish an enduring competitive advantage in the target market by creating a unique brand image, or position, in the customer's mind. Dinaz Vervatwala founded her first fitness studio in part because she saw a market segment—women in Banjara Hills—whose needs were not being fully met. She chose to target this segment because fitness training was growing in popularity and because she had particular knowledge and expertise she could bring to the party. She positioned her fitness studios as the ones that were focused on women only, without any ogling males anywhere nearby.

These three decision processes—market segmentation, target marketing, and positioning—are closely linked and have strong interdependence. All must be well considered and implemented if the firm is to be successful in managing a given product-market relationship. No matter how large the firm, however, its resources are usually limited compared with the number of alternative market segments available for pursuit. Thus, a firm must make choices. Even in the unusual case where a firm can afford to serve all market segments, it must determine the most appropriate allocation and deployment of its marketing effort *across* segments. In East Africa, for example, to reach rural villages. Coca-Cola relies on more than 13,000 small distributors—many of whom use pushcarts and hand trucks—to reach local mom and pop retailers.[3] By tailoring its promotion and distribution methods by market and market segment, Coke's sales in Africa surpassed $550 million in 2009.[4] But are all these analyses and conscious choices about which segments to serve and how best to serve them really necessary?

Most Markets Are Heterogeneous

Because markets are rarely homogeneous in benefits wanted, purchase rates, and price and promotion elasticities, their response rates to products and marketing programs differ. Variation among market segments in product preferences, size of and growth in demand, media habits, and competitive structures further affect the differences and response rates. Thus, markets are complex entities that can be defined (and segmented) in a variety of ways. As New York–based trend tracker Tom Vierhile notes, "what consumers really appear to hunger for are products that fit their unique needs, wants, and desires. They want products that talk just to them. . . . and appeal just to them on an emotional level."[5] The critical issue for marketers is to find an appropriate segmentation scheme that will facilitate target marketing, positioning, and the formulation and implementation of successful marketing strategies and programs.

Today's Market Realities Often Make Segmentation Imperative

Market segmentation has become increasingly important in the development of marketing strategies for several reasons. First, population growth in many developed countries has slowed, and more product-markets are maturing. This sparks more intense competition in existing markets as firms seek growth via gains in market share and encourages companies to find new markets they've not served previously. Often, as they search for faster-growing markets, their attention turns to the developing world, where the enormous diversity in demographic profiles and market conditions makes careful market segmentation and targeting essential. Nokia, for example, has targeted the fast-growing Indian market, where a majority of the population lives in rural areas. In doing so, it's had to adapt the design of its cell phones, adding dust-proof keypads and eliminating other features to make its phones affordable to India's low-income masses. When Nokia's researchers discovered that many cell phones in India were used by more than one person, Nokia developed handsets with multiple address books.[6] By developing products uniquely suited to the Indian market and various segments therein, Nokia has become the market leader.[7] Whether Nokia can retain its lead in India as the smartphone revolution takes hold there remains to be seen.

Second, such social and economic forces as expanding disposable incomes, higher educational levels, and more awareness of the world have produced customers with more varied and sophisticated needs, tastes, and lifestyles than ever before. This has led to an outpouring of goods and services that compete with one another for the opportunity of satisfying some group of consumers.

Third, there is an increasingly important trend toward microsegmentation in which extremely small market segments are targeted. For a discussion of how one company built itself into a multimillion-dollar business while serving a very small niche, see Exhibit 6.1. This trend has been accelerated in some industries by new technology such as computer-aided design, which has enabled firms to mass-customize many products as diverse as

EXHIBIT 6.1   *Can Under Armour Become Another Nike?*

Kevin Plank did not set out to create a cult around athletic underwear—he simply wanted a comfortable T-shirt to wear under his football pads that would wick moisture away from his skin and protect him from heat exhaustion during practice. After hunting through all the sporting goods shops, Kevin realized that there was not a single product on the market that met his needs. He set out to create one. In March 1996, just before graduation, Kevin had some T-shirts sewn up in Lycra and found that he had solved a common problem for all of his teammates.

Under Armour, the company that was soon born in his grandmother's basement, made its first sale of 200 shirts for $12 apiece to the football team at Georgia Tech. Kevin ended his company's first year with sales of $17,000. Under Armour was marketed by word-of-mouth from happy, satisfied customers and grew with sales to athletic teams in colleges. The company got its big break due to a product placement in the Oliver Stone football movie *Any Given Sunday*. Buzz from the movie and a first-time ad in *ESPN Magazine* during the movie

premiere boosted Under Armour sales to $1.35 million in 1999. Under Armour's sales in 2001 drove triple-digit growth in its category and led industry peers at *Sporting Goods Business* to recognize the company as "Apparel Supplier of the Year." Under Armour's sales soared to U.S.$55 million in 2002 and more than $400 million in 2006 and more than $850 million in 2009.

The underserved niche market segment that Kevin Plank discovered and his success have not gone unnoticed. Ironically, recent entrants to this segment are Nike and Reebok. Will Under Armour be able to withstand the competitive heat? Kevin Plank's reaction? "I'll never let them see me sweat."

Source: Company website: *www.underarmour.com*; Elaine Shannon, "Tight Skivvies; They're What Everyone's Wearing This Season. Here's Why," *Time*, January 13, 2003, p. A1; and Stanley Holmes, "Under Armour May Be Overstretched," *BusinessWeek European Edition*, April 30, 2007, p. 65. "Matt Townsend, "Under Armour's Daring Half-Court Shot," *Bloomberg Businessweek*, European Edition, November 1–7, 2010, pp. 24–25. For more on Under Armour, see *www.underarmour.com*.

T-shirts and coffee mugs, even designer jeans and cars. Mass customization websites such as CaféPress and Zazzle in the United States and Spreadshirt in Europe now make it possible for consumers to order T-shirts and other custom-designed products in quantities of one or one thousand, with almost instant delivery. No longer must everyone at the company picnic wear exactly the same T-shirt, since companies like these let everyone choose their own style, size, and color, and even the slogan. Customized products have been shown to generate greater appeal for customers than products designed for specific segments, particularly in terms of purchase intention, willingness to pay, and positive attitude towards the product.[8]

Finally, many marketing organizations have made it easier to implement sharply focused marketing programs by more sharply targeting their own services. For example, many new media have sprung up to appeal to narrow interest groups. In the United Kingdom, these include special interest magazines, such as *Wanderlust* and *Autocar;* radio stations with formats targeted to different demographic groups, such as classical music, rock, country, and jazz, not to mention chat shows of various kinds; and cable TV channels, such as Sky Sport and the Discovery Channel. Also, more broad-based magazines, such as *Time,* in the United States, and *The Economist* and *Hello* in Britain, offer advertisers the opportunity to target specific groups of people within their subscription base. An advertiser can target specific regions, cities, or postal codes, or even selected income groups.

HOW ARE MARKET SEGMENTS BEST DEFINED?

There are three important steps in the market segmentation process:

- **Identify a homogeneous segment that differs from other segments.** The process should identify one or more relatively homogeneous groups of prospective buyers with regard to their wants and needs and/or their likely responses to differences in the

Strategic Issue

There are three important steps in the market segmentation process.

elements of the marketing mix—***the 4 Ps*** (product, price, promotion, and place). For Dinaz Vervatwala, women were targeted even though most other fitness clubs in India targeted men and women.

- **Specify criteria that define the segment.** The segmentation criteria should measure or describe the segments clearly enough so that members can be readily identified and accessed, in order for the marketer to know whether a given prospective customer is or is not in the target market and in order to reach the prospective customer with advertising or other marketing communication messages. Like most retailers, whether of goods or services, Vervatwala targets well-defined trading areas in placing new studios.
- **Determine segment size and potential.** Finally, the segmentation process should determine the size and market potential of each segment for use in prioritizing which segments to pursue, a topic we address in more detail later in this chapter. In most developed countries, detailed demographic data showing what kind of people live where is readily available.

Given these objectives, what kinds of segmentation criteria, or descriptors, are most useful? Segmentation decisions are best made in one of three ways: based on *who* the customers are, based on *where* they are, or based on *how they behave* relevant to the market in question. The three approaches apply in both consumer and organizational markets. We examine each of these approaches as follows.

Who They Are: Segmenting Demographically

While firm demographics (age of firm, size of firm, industry, etc.) are useful in segmenting organizational markets, we usually think of demographics in terms of attributes of individual consumers, as shown in Exhibit 6.2. Some examples of demographic attributes used to segment consumer markets are as follows:

- *Age.* Since mobile phone penetration has reached saturation levels in most of Europe and the United Kingdom, some mobile service providers have focused their attention on the 55–65 and 65-plus segments to improve usage and penetration. These segments' high disposable incomes and their ability to devote time to new habits are seen as a lucrative market opportunity.

EXHIBIT 6.2 Some of the More Commonly Used Demographic Attributes*

Demographic Descriptors	Examples of Categories
Age	Under 2, 2–5, 6–11, 12–17, 18–24, 25–34, 35–49, 50–64, 65 and over
Sex	Male, female
Household life cycle	Young, single; newly married, no children; youngest child under 6; youngest child 6 or over; older couples with dependent children; older couples without dependent children; older couples retired; older, single
Income	Under $15,000, $15,000–24,999; $25,000–74,999, etc.
Occupation	Professional, manager, clerical, sales, supervisor, blue collar, homemaker, student, unemployed
Education	Some high school, graduated high school, some college, graduated college
Events	Birthdays, graduations, anniversaries, national holidays, sporting events
Race and ethnic origin	African American, Anglo-Saxon, Asian, Hispanic, Italian, Jewish, Scandinavian

*Others include marital status, home ownership, and presence and age of children.

EXHIBIT 6.3 *LEGOs for Girls?*

For more than 50 years, boys everywhere have been developing their spatial and fine-motor skills by building things—from cars to police stations to spaceships and more—with LEGOs. But Peggy Orenstein, author of *Cinderella Ate My Daughter,* wasn't happy that LEGOs simply didn't appeal to girls. "The last time I was in a LEGO store, there was this little pink ghetto over in one corner," she says. "Is this the best you can do?"

LEGO Group CEO Jørgen Vig Knudstorp, a father of two daughters and two sons, wasn't happy, either. In late 2011 and early 2012, LEGO launched an ambitious effort, Lego Friends, with five new main characters aimed at girls aged 5 and up. To develop Lego Friends, LEGO undertook an extensive research effort in Germany, Korea, the United Kingdom, and the United States to better understand girls and their play. Using mostly cultural

anthropology embedded in family settings, rather than focus groups, LEGO's research team was able to discern some important differences between girls' and boys' play. Boys tended to see their LEGO figures as third persons while girls tended to see them as avatars in their own image. Girls loved role-play, too.

Will LEGO's new strategy to conquer the girls' segment work? It's too early to tell. But Knudstorp is satisfied that girls will no longer be left out. "I don't have any illusions that the girls' business will be bigger than the boys' business, but at least for those who are looking for it, we have something to offer."

Source: Brad Wieners, "Lego Is for Girls," *Bloomberg Businessweek* European edition, December 19, 2011, pp. 68–73. For more on LEGO, see *www.lego.com.*

- *Sex.* The Danish toy maker LEGO has recently embarked on an ambitious effort to encourage girls, never LEGO's market, to build and play with LEGOs (see Exhibit 6.3).[10] As many marketers are discovering, however, thinking about all men or all women as a single market segment is usually naive. Understanding segments within the male population, for example, can bring out insights previously missed.[11]

- Among women, sharply targeted segmentation schemes can often deliver attractive results. A plethora of juice-based dietary cleansing brands targeting the urban get-thin-quick segment has emerged in recent years. New York's Organic Avenue and BluePrint Cleanse, Los Angeles-based Cooler Cleanse and iZo Cleanze are among them. We get "a *lot* of mommies," reports BluePrint co-founder Erica Huss Jones. But Dr. Michael D. Gershon of Columbia University's Department of Anatomy and Cell Biology is less than enthralled. There's "nothing but danger associated with cleansing", he says. "It is a practice to be condemned.[12]

- *Income.* Higher-income households purchase a disproportionate number of expensive cars and theater tickets, and other luxury items. Nokia's former subsidiary, Vertu, offers an ultra-exclusive mobile telephone and services built around the phone, targeting the same customers who buy luxury watches and custom-made cars. In 2012, Nokia sold Vertu in order to focus its efforts on reviving its troubled core mobile phone business.[13]

- *Occupation.* The sales of certain kinds of products (e.g., work shoes, automobiles, uniforms, and trade magazines) are tied closely to occupational type. The increase in the number of working women has created needs for specialized goods and services including financial services, business wardrobes, convenience foods, automobiles, and special-interest magazines.

- *Education.* There is a strong positive correlation between the level of education and the purchase of travel, books, magazines, insurance, and high-end photographic equipment.

- *Race and ethnic origin.* More and more companies are targeting ethnic segments via specialized marketing programs. In the United States, car companies have found ways to cater to the needs of the multicultural segment, which was estimated to comprise 32 percent of the U.S. population in 2010. Macy's, the American department store chain, has developed a training program for minority suppliers to help it better serve its growing number of Hispanic, African American, and Asian shoppers. Bill Hawthorne, Macy's senior vice president for diversity strategies, embraces the market segmentation challenge he faces. "There are differences, that is the beauty of diversity. Let's celebrate those. And let's figure out as a retailer how to merchandise that."[14]

Demographic descriptors are also important in the segmentation of industrial markets, which are typically segmented in two stages. The first, *macrosegmentation,* divides the market according to the characteristics of the buying organization using such attributes as age of firm, firm size, and industry affiliation (SIC code in the United States). The international counterpart of SIC is the trade-category code.

The second stage, *microsegmentation,* groups customers by the characteristics of the individuals who influence the purchasing decision—for instance, age, sex, and position within the organization. International markets are often segmented in a similar hierarchical fashion, starting with countries, followed by groups of individuals or buying organizations.

Where They Are: Segmenting Geographically

Different locations or regions vary in their sales potential, growth rates, customer needs, cultures, climates, service needs, and competitive structures, as well as purchase rates for a variety of goods. For example, more pickup trucks are sold in the Southwest United States, more vans in the Northeast, and more diesel-fueled cars in Europe. More and more advertisers are taking advantage of geographic media buys in order to efficiently reach the market segments they target.

Nestlé, in order to reach the 800,000 Brazilians who live in the Amazon River basin, chartered a boat stocked with more than 300 of its brands, including Nescafé instant coffee, Maggi soups and seasonings, and Leche Ideal, Nestlé's fortified powdered milk. Says Nestlé Brazil CEO Ivan Zurita, "We're going to pick up the customer where he is."[15]

Geographic segmentation is used in both consumer and organizational markets and is particularly important in retailing and many services businesses, where customers are unwilling to travel very far to obtain the goods or services they require. Thus, one way to segment retail markets is by distance or driving time from a particular location. The area included within such a geographically defined region is called a **trade area.**

Geodemographic Segmentation

Marketers targeting emerging markets in the developing world must pay particular attention to market segmentation within the geographic regions they target. Virtually every developing country contains a small segment of extremely wealthy people, a rapidly growing but perhaps relatively small middle class, and large numbers of people who are poor by Western standards. The first two of these demographic groups are most often found in the cities, while many poor live either in rural areas or in urban slums. Treating the people of any developing country as a single market segment is not likely to bring success.

In emerging and developed markets alike, many segmentation schemes involve *both* demographic and geographic factors. Thus, retailers usually want to know something about the people who live within, perhaps, a two-mile or five-mile radius of their proposed new store. Neiman Marcus, the upscale department store, might target one demographic group within a given trade area, and Walmart, a discounter, might target another. Claritas (*www.claritas.com*) and others offer low-cost reports based on census data that show the demographic profile of the population residing within any given radius of a particular street corner or shopping center location in the United States. These reports are useful in assessing the size and market potential of a market segment defined by a particular trade area. Geodemographics also attempts to predict consumer behavior by making demographic, psychographic, and consumer information available at the block and zip code or postal code levels. Claritas's PRIZM service classifies all U.S. households into 66 demographically and behaviorally distinct clusters, each of which, in turn, is assigned to one of 14 social groups and 11 life stage groups.[16] Claritas, now part of Nielsen, offers datasets for other countries as well.

How They Behave: Behavioral Segmentation

There is no limit to the number of insightful ways successful marketers have segmented markets in behavioral terms. Kevin Plank of Under Armour initially targeted college and university athletic teams. Mountain bike makers Specialized and Gary Fisher target bicyclists who wish to ride on single-track trails or back-country terrain. Europe's easyJet airline originally targeted leisure travelers. Gatorade's original target market consisted of athletes who needed to replenish water and salts lost through perspiration. This simple segmentation scheme created a whole new category of "sports beverages," which grew to include entries from Coke (Powerade) and Pepsi (All Sport), though Gatorade still dominates the category. This onetime niche market has grown into a multibillion-dollar market in the United States alone.

These examples all demonstrate the power of highly specific behavioral descriptors in defining sharply focused market segments, based not on *who* the target consumers are or *where* they live, but based on what they *do*. In virtually every consumer and organizational market there are segments like these just waiting to be identified and targeted by insightful marketers. Behavioral attributes can take many forms, including those based on consumer needs; on product usage patterns; on more general behavioral patterns, including lifestyle, which often cuts across demographic categories or varies within them; and, in organizational markets, on the structure of firms' purchasing activities and the types of buying situations they encounter. We examine some of these forms next.

Consumer Needs

Customer needs are often expressed in **benefits sought** from a particular product or service. Different individual customers have different needs and thus attach different degrees of importance to the benefits offered by different products. In the end, the product that provides the best bundle of benefits—given the customer's particular needs—is most likely to be purchased. For an example of how targeting a distinct set of consumer needs has taken a late entrant to the top of the car rental industry, see Exhibit 6.4.

Since purchasing is a problem-solving process, consumers often evaluate product alternatives on the basis of desired characteristics and how valuable each characteristic is to the consumer—**choice criteria.** Marketers can define segments according to these different choice criteria in terms of the presence or absence of certain characteristics and the importance attached to each. Firms typically single out a limited number of benefit segments to target. Thus, for example, different automobile manufacturers have emphasized different benefits over the years, such as Volvo's safety versus Jaguar's styling, quickness, and status.

In organizational markets, customers consider relevant benefits that include product performance in different use situations. For example, high-powered arrays of disk storage and servers are bought because they meet the high-speed computational requirements of a small group of customers such as governments, universities, and research labs. Other considerations in the purchase of industrial products/services include on-time delivery, credit terms, economy, spare parts availability, and training.

Product Usage and Purchase Influence

In addition to highly specific behavioral attributes such as those just discussed, there are more general product-related attributes as well. They include product usage, loyalty,

EXHIBIT 6.4   *Enterprise Rent-a-Car: Targeting Pays Off*

In 1963, Jack Taylor added car rentals to his small automobile leasing business. Taylor's strategy was to serve a completely different target market than the majors, Hertz and Avis, and provide replacement cars for people involved in accidents or breakdowns and those who were grounded while their cars were being serviced. Serving this market required a completely different sort of service—delivering the car to the customer, for example—than the majors provided. "This stuff is a lot more complicated than handing out keys at the airport," says Andy Taylor, Jack's son and now chairman and CEO. The business grew steadily, if unexceptionally, until the 1990s, when the younger Taylor stepped on the gas and cruised past Hertz and Avis to take the number one spot in the U.S. market, with a fleet of 500,000 vehicles and more than $6 billion in revenue for the privately held company. Canada and Europe followed and Enterprise now serves the United Kingdom, Ireland, and Germany, as well as North America. While Enterprise now serves target segments beyond the car-replacement market, its clear focus on a narrowly defined segment that the majors had ignored provided the beachhead and an impregnable foundation on which the company was able to grow. Equally important, the strong customer service culture and decentralized decision making that were crucial to the initial strategy have become the lynchpin of the company's wider success. Enterprise measures each of its branches each month in terms of both profitability and customer service (two questions are asked of each customer: Are you satisfied with our service? Would you come back?), and no one gets promoted from branches that have below-average customer service scores, no matter how strong their financial performance. Enterprise has found that customers who answer "completely satisfied" on question one are three times more likely to come back.

Clear targeting. Exceptional customer service. It's a combination that's kept Enterprise rolling for nearly 50 years.

Source: Simon London, "Driving Home the Service Ethic," *Financial Times*, June 3, 2003. For more on Enterprise Rent-a-Car, see *www.enterprise.com*.

---

purchase predisposition, and purchase influence, all of which can be used to segment both consumer and industrial markets. **Product usage** is important because in many markets a small proportion of potential customers makes a high percentage of all purchases. In organizational markets, the customers are better known, and heavy or large users (often called *key accounts*) are easier to identify.

For Coca-Cola, differences in product usage rates provide clues to where its growth prospects are most attractive. North Americans bought $2.6 billion worth of Coke in 1989, and just $2.9 billion in 2009. So Coke is looking elsewhere for growth, like Kenya, for example, where annual per capita consumption is just 39 servings, compared to 665 servings in Mexico, whose people guzzle more Coke than those anywhere else. Coke provides refrigerated coolers to the mom and pop *dukas* where Kenyans shop, and even prescribes exactly how they should be stocked: half-liter bottles of Coke at the top, Fanta in the middle, and large bottles at the bottom.[17]

Market segmentation based on sources of **purchase influence** for the product category is relevant for both consumer and organizational markets. Many products used by various family members are purchased by the wife, but joint husband–wife decisions are becoming more common. Children's products, prescription drugs, and gifts are clearly influenced by a variety of family members. In organizational markets, several individuals or units with varying degrees of influence participate in buying decisions.

Lifestyle

Segmentation by lifestyle, or psychographics, segments markets on the basis of consumers' activities, interests, and opinions—in other words, what they do or believe, rather than who they are in a demographic sense. From such information it is possible to infer what types of products and services appeal to a particular group, as well as how best to communicate with individuals in the group. Even among demographic groups that might at first glance seem homogeneous, behavioral segmentation based on lifestyle is identifying new target markets for savvy marketers (see Exhibit 6.5).

EXHIBIT 6.5   *Marketing to Baby Boomers: Rethinking the Rules*

By 2006, more than half the baby boomers in the United States—those born between 1946 and 1964—had turned 50 or older. With combined spending power of more than $1 trillion per annum among the 50- to 60-year-olds alone, this growing market simply cannot be ignored. What marketers are discovering, though, is that these aging customers aren't all the same. Demographic segmentation just won't do. Behavior is the key. Consumers aged 50+ buy a quarter of all Vespa motor scooters in the United States. Better still for Vespa, with boomers' empty-nester spending power, they tend to buy the top-of-the-line models. But that doesn't mean all boomers are fantasizing about their younger days. Indeed, wrinkles and gray hair are in among many boomers, along with healthier diets and lifestyles to help them age gracefully.

But are these consumers counting their days until they can retire to the shuffleboard court or bingo parlor? Hardly. As a result, Del Webb, the retirement-community division of Pulte Homes Inc., is changing the way it markets its properties, with more emphasis on the varied and active lifestyles that many of tomorrow's retirees will lead. "We have to keep up with residents," says David G. Schreiner, vice president for active-adult business development at Del Webb. "The War Generation was far more predictable and con sistent, but this generation gives you a bunch of paradoxes."

Source: Louise Lee, "Love Those Boomers," *BusinessWeek*, October 24, 2005. For more on Vespa's and Del Webb's marketing to baby boomers, see *www.vespa.com* and *www.delwebb.com*.

Strategic Business Insights, formerly a division of the Stanford Research Institute (SRI) has created a U.S. segmentation service (called VALS 2), which builds on the concept of self-orientation and resources for the individual. *Self-orientation* is based on how consumers pursue and acquire products and services that provide satisfaction and shape their identities. In doing so, they are motivated by the orientations of principle, status, and action. Principle-oriented consumers are motivated by abstract and idealized criteria, while status-oriented consumers shop for products that demonstrate the consumer's success. Action-oriented consumers are guided by the need for social or physical activity, variety, and risk-taking. *Resources* include all of the psychological, physical, demographic, and material means consumers have to draw on. They include education, income, self-confidence, health, eagerness to buy, intelligence, and energy level—on a continuum from minimal to abundant.

Based on these two dimensions, VALS 2 defines eight segments that exhibit distinctive behavior and decision making—actualizers, fulfillers, achievers, experiencers, believers, strivers, makers, and strugglers. Claritas and similar commercial organizations identify each of the respondents as to their VALS type, thereby permitting a cross-classification of VALS type with the product usage and personal information collected by such companies. Thus, users can determine what each VALS segment bought, what their media habits are, and similar data. The VALS system has been further developed in Europe and Asia. Those interested in the VALS segmentation scheme can complete a short survey on the VALS website (log onto *www.strategicbusinessinsights.com/vals/presurvey.shtml*) and discover the VALS segment to which they belong.

Strategic Issue

Those interested in the VALS segmentation scheme can complete a short survey on the VALS website and discover the VALS segment to which they belong.

Organizational Behavioral Attributes

Purchasing structure and buying situation segmentation attributes are unique to organizational markets. **Purchasing structure** is the degree to which the purchasing activity is centralized. In such a structure the buyer is likely to consider all transactions with a given supplier on a companywide or global basis, to emphasize cost savings, and to minimize risk. In a decentralized situation, the buyer is apt to be more sensitive to the user's need, to emphasize product quality and fast delivery, and to be less cost-conscious. Some marketers segment their markets accordingly and target customers whose purchasing structure is similar (companies who buy centrally from one location to meet their global needs, for example).

The **buying situation** attribute includes three distinct types of situations: straight rebuy, a recurring situation handled on a routine basis; modified rebuy, which occurs when some element, such as price or delivery schedule, has changed in a client–supplier relationship; and a new buying situation, which is likely to require the customer gathering considerable information and evaluating alternative suppliers. Business-to-business marketers seeking new customers often find the buying situation to be a useful way to decide which new customers to target.

Innovative Segmentation: A Key to Marketing Breakthroughs

At the beginning of this section, we identified three steps in the market segmentation process:

- Identify a homogeneous segment that differs from others.
- Specify criteria that define the segment.
- Determine segment size and potential.

Skilled marketers, such as the creators of Under Armour athletic wear, LEGO toys, and Enterprise Rent-a-Car, know that following this process to an insightful and innovative market segmentation scheme is often the key to marketing breakthroughs. Often, combinations of different attributes are used to more precisely target an attractive segment: perhaps some behavioral dimension together with a carefully defined demographic profile within some geographic region. Generally, it is useful to know the demographic profile of the target market to be pursued, even if the driving force behind the segmentation scheme is geographical and/or behavioral in nature, because understanding the demographic profile of a target market enables the marketer to better choose targeted advertising media or other marketing communication vehicles.

As several examples in this section have shown, at the foundation of many a marketing breakthrough one often finds an insightful segmentation scheme that is sharply focused in a *behavioral* way. Marketers with superior market knowledge are probably more likely to generate the insights necessary to define market segments in these innovative and meaningful ways. Sometimes these insights are counterintuitive, even surprising (see Exhibit 6.6).

Strategic Issue

At the foundation of many a marketing breakthrough one often finds an insightful segmentation scheme that is sharply focused in a behavioral way.

EXHIBIT 6.6 *Illiterate Consumers: A Segment Worth Targeting?*

Some 21–23 percent of United States consumers simply do not have the basic language and numeracy skills that are necessary to effectively navigate today's typical retail shopping environment. In many developing countries, the proportion of consumers who are functionally illiterate is even higher. But these groups have surprising purchasing power, controlling $380 billion in spending in the United States alone in 2003. Because these consumers do not assimilate information in the same way literate consumers do, however, various kinds of marketing efforts—from price promotions, to retail signage, to the packaging of "new and improved" products, most of which are words- and numbers-based—are wasted on, or even misleading to, this consumer population. Such tactics may even cause these consumers to switch away from the brands being promoted. Some marketers are addressing this opportunity, however, and have found ways to better meet these consumers' needs. Employee training to help reduce customers' possible losses of self-esteem (what happens if they don't have enough money at checkout), the use of pictorial information alongside word information, and other measures can make these consumers both loyal and profitable.

Source: Madhubalan Viswanathan, José Antonio Rosa, and James Edwin Harris, "Decision Making and Coping of Functionally Illiterate Consumers and Some Implications for Marketing Management," *Journal of Marketing* 69 (January 2005), pp. 15–31.

CHOOSING ATTRACTIVE MARKET SEGMENTS: A FIVE-STEP PROCESS

Most firms, not even Coca-Cola, no longer aim a single product and marketing program at the mass market. Instead, they break that market into homogeneous segments on the basis of meaningful differences in buyer behavior or in the benefits sought by different groups of customers. Then they tailor products—such as Coca-Cola, Coke Zero, Coke Light, and Diet Coke—and marketing programs to the particular desires and idiosyncrasies of each segment. *But not all segments represent equally attractive opportunities for the firm.* To prioritize target segments by their potential, marketers must evaluate their future attractiveness and their firm's strengths and capabilities relative to the segments' needs and competitive situations.

Strategic Issue

Most firms no longer aim a single product and marketing program at the mass market.

Within an established firm, rather than allowing each business unit or product manager to develop an approach to evaluate the potential of alternative market segments, it is often better to apply a common analytical framework across segments. With this approach, managers can compare the future potential of different segments using the same set of criteria and then prioritize them in order to decide which segments to target and how resources and marketing efforts should be allocated. One useful analytical framework managers or entrepreneurs can use for this purpose is the **market attractiveness/competitive position matrix.** As we saw in Chapter 2, managers use such models at the corporate level to allocate resources across businesses, or at the business-unit level to assign resources across product-markets. We are concerned with the second application here.

Exhibit 6.7 outlines the steps involved in developing a market attractiveness/competitive position matrix for analyzing current and potential target markets. Underlying such a matrix is the notion that managers can judge the attractiveness of a market (its profit potential)

EXHIBIT 6.7 **Steps in Constructing a Market Attractiveness/Competitive Position Matrix for Evaluating Potential Target Markets**

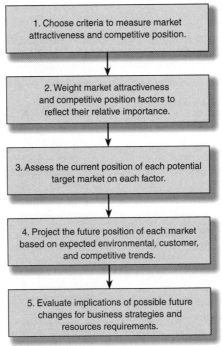

1. Choose criteria to measure market attractiveness and competitive position.

2. Weight market attractiveness and competitive position factors to reflect their relative importance.

3. Assess the current position of each potential target market on each factor.

4. Project the future position of each market based on expected environmental, customer, and competitive trends.

5. Evaluate implications of possible future changes for business strategies and resources requirements.

by examining market, competitive, and environmental factors that may influence profitability. Similarly, they can estimate the strength of the firm's competitive position by looking at the firm's capabilities or shortcomings *relative* to the needs of the market and the competencies of likely competitors. By combining the results of these analyses with other considerations, including risk, the mission of the firm, and ethical issues (see Ethical Perspective 6.1), evidence-based conclusions about which markets and market segments should be pursued can be reached.

The first steps in developing a market-attractiveness/competitive-position matrix, are to identify the most relevant variables for evaluating alternative market segments and the firm's competitive position regarding them and to weight each variable in importance. Note, too, that Exhibit 6.7 suggests conducting a forecast of future changes in market attractiveness or competitive position in addition to, but separately from, an assessment of the current situation. This reflects the fact that a decision to target a particular segment is a strategic choice that the firm will have to live with for some time.

Step 1: Select Market Attractiveness and Competitive Position Factors

An evaluation of the attractiveness of a particular market or market segment and of the strength of the firm's current or potential competitive position in it builds naturally on the

Strategic Issue

Both market and competitive perspectives are necessary.

kind of opportunity analysis developed in Chapter 4. Managers can assess both dimensions on the basis of information obtained from analyses of the environment, industry and competitive situation, market potential estimates, and customer needs. To make these assessments, they need to

---

Ⓔ Ethical Perspective Eat Chocolate, Get Fit?   6.1

In 2003, Cadbury, the British confectionery company, launched a "Sports for Schools" promotion, emulating an earlier and very successful promotion that Tesco, the leading grocer in the United Kingdom, had run called "Computers for Schools." Cadbury offered to buy fitness equipment for schools in exchange for tokens obtained through consumer purchases of Cadbury confectionery.

Following howls of protest in the media, in which the program was characterized as a perverse incentive for children to eat more of a product widely considered to be associated with child obesity, a growing problem in the United Kingdom and elsewhere, Cadbury withdrew the program.

As the U.K.'s Food Commission calculated, "Cadbury's wants children to eat 2 million kilograms of fat (more than 4 million pounds)—to get fit." According to the Food Commission's calculations, a netball that sold for £5 in sporting goods stores would require consumer tokens from £38 worth of Cadbury products. These £38 worth of products would, in turn, involve consuming more than 20,000 calories and over 1,000 grams of fat. In targeting children and families with this promotion, Cadbury

overlooked or misunderstood consumers' rising concerns over child obesity.

Empirical research by Craig Smith and Elizabeth Cooper-Martin indicates that ethical concerns such as those that arose here are particularly likely to arise over targeting strategies where the target market is perceived as vulnerable and where the products concerned are, in any sense, perceived to be harmful. Thus, it's not necessarily the products themselves that lead to ethical concerns, but targeting and market segmentation decisions to which insufficient ethical consideration is given. As Smith and Cooper-Martin note, "Marketing managers should be alert to public disquiet over the ethics of certain targeting strategies," especially when consumer vulnerability and product harm enter the equation.

Sources: N. Craig Smith, "Out of Leftfield: Societal Issues as Causes of Failure of New Marketing Initiatives," *Business Strategy Review,* Summer 2007; and N. Craig Smith and Elizabeth Cooper-Martin, "Ethics and Target Marketing: The Role of Product Harm and Consumer Vulnerability," *Journal of Marketing* 61 (July 1997), pp. 1–20. For more on Cadbury's, now a division of Kraft, see *www.cadbury.co.uk.*

establish criteria, such as those shown in Exhibit 6.8, against which prospective markets or market segments can be evaluated. Both market and competitive perspectives are necessary.

Market Attractiveness Factors

As we saw in Chapter 4, assessing the attractiveness of markets or market segments involves determining the market's size and growth rate and assessing various trends—demographic, sociocultural, economic, political/ legal, technological, and natural—that influence demand in that market. An even more critical factor in determining whether to *enter* a new market or market segment, however, is the degree to which *unmet customer needs,* or needs that are currently not being well served, can be identified. In the absence of unmet or underserved needs, it is likely to be difficult to win customer loyalty, regardless of how large the market or how fast it is growing. "Me-too" products often face difficult going in today's highly competitive markets.

Competitive Position Factors

As we showed in Chapter 4, understanding the attractiveness of the industry in which one competes is also important. Entering a segment in a way that would place the firm in an unattractive industry or increase its exposure therein may not be wise. Of more immediate and salient concern, however, is the degree to which the firm's proposed product will be sufficiently *differentiated* from its competitors, given the critical success factors and product life-cycle conditions already prevalent in the category. Similarly, decision makers need to know whether their firm has or will be able to acquire the resources it will take—human, financial, and otherwise—to effectively compete in the new segment. Simply put, most new goods or services need to be either better from a consumer point of view or cheaper than those they hope to replace. Entering a new market or market segment without a source of sustainable competitive advantage is often a trap.

EXHIBIT 6.8 **Factors Underlying Market Attractiveness and Competitive Position**

Market Attractiveness Factors

Customer needs and behavior
- Are there unmet or underserved needs we can satisfy?

Market or market segment size and growth rate
- Market potential in units, revenue, number of prospective customers
- Growth rate in units, revenue, number of prospective customers
- Might the target segment constitute a platform for later expansion into related segments in the market as a whole?

Macro trends: Are they favorable, on balance?
- Demographic
- Sociocultural
- Economic
- Political/legal
- Technological
- Natural

Competitive Position Factors

Opportunity for competitive advantage
- Can we differentiate?
- Can we perform against critical success factors?
- Stage of competing products in product life cycle: Is the timing right?

Firm and competitor capabilities and resources
- Management strength and depth
- Financial and functional resources: marketing, distribution, manufacturing, R&D, etc.
- Brand image
- Relative market share

Attractiveness of industry in which we would compete
- Threat of new entrants
- Threat of substitutes
- Buyer power
- Supplier power
- Competitive rivalry
- Industry capacity

Step 2: Weight Each Factor

Next, a numerical weight is assigned to each factor to indicate its relative importance in the overall assessment. Weights that Under Armour's Kevin Plank might have assigned to the major factors in Exhibit 6.8 are shown in Exhibit 6.9. Some users would rate each bullet point in Exhibit 6.8 independently, assigning a weight to each one.

The task of weighting the factors—as well as determining them in the first place—gets more complicated as companies reach out to new and different markets, like the growing middle class in the developing world. Both the scores and the weights placed on different factors may differ in emerging versus developed markets, for example, and the factors and their weights may differ across markets where a category is relatively mature versus nascent. Macro trends are generally more favourable for Coca-Cola in emerging markets with growing middle classes, for example, than in North America or western Europe, where both population growth and Soft drink consumption have been relatively flat or down.

Step 3: Rate Segments on Each Factor, Plot Results on Matrices

This step requires that evidence—typically both qualitative and quantitative data—be collected to objectively assess each of the criteria identified in Step 1. For Under Armour the assessment of the various factors might have looked as shown in Exhibit 6.9. While more detailed evidence than we discuss here should have been, and no doubt was, gathered, Kevin Plank might have reached the following conclusions:

Market Attractiveness Factors

- Unmet needs for wicking underwear for athletic teams have been identified and are well understood. Score: 9.
- The athletic team segment is small, but easily identified and reached and might lead to other segments in the future. Score: 7.
- Macro trends are largely favorable: Sports are "in," the number of people in athletically active demographic groups is growing, and niche brands for other athletic pursuits (e.g., Patagonia for outdoor enthusiasts), have been successful. Score: 9.

Competitive Position Factors

- Opportunity for competitive advantage is modest: Proposed garments will be differentiated, but are easily imitated; Under Armour, as a new firm, has no track record. Score: 6.

EXHIBIT 6.9 **Assessing the Athletic Underwear Market Segment at Under Armour's Inception**

	Weight	Rating (0–10 Scale)	Total
Market-attractiveness factors			
Customer needs and behavior: unmet needs?	.5	9	4.5
Segment size and growth rate	.2	7	1.4
Macro trends	.3	9	2.7
Total: Market attractiveness	**1.0**		**8.6**
Competitive-position factors			
Opportunity for competitive advantage	.4	6	2.4
Capabilities and resources	.2	5	1.0
Industry attractiveness	.4	5	2.0
Total: Competitive position	**1.0**		**5.0**

- Resources are extremely limited, though the founder knows the athletic community. Score: 5.
- Five forces are mixed: Entry barriers are very low (unfavorable), buyer power and supplier power are low (favorable), there is little threat of substitutes (favorable), and rivalry among existing firms is modest. Score: 5.

Mere armchair judgments about each criterion are not very credible and run the risk of taking the manager or entrepreneur into a market segment that may turn out not to be viable. It is especially important to undertake a detailed analysis of key competitors, especially with regard to their objectives, strategy, resources, and marketing programs. Similarly, compelling evidence that a proposed entry into a new segment will satisfy some previously unmet needs, and do so in a way that can bring about sustainable competitive advantage, is called for. Both qualitative and quantitative marketing research results are typically used for this purpose. Once these assessments have been made, the weighted results can be plotted on a **market attractiveness/competitive position matrix** like the one shown in Exhibit 6.10.

Strategic Issue

Compelling evidence that a proposed entry into a new segment will satisfy some previously unmet needs, and do so in a way that can bring about sustainable competitive advantage, is called for.

Step 4: Project Future Position for Each Segment

Forecasting a market's future is more difficult than assessing its current state. Managers or entrepreneurs should first determine how the market's attractiveness is likely to change over the next three to five years, if not longer. The starting point for this assessment is to consider possible shifts in customer needs and behavior, the entry or exit of competitors, and changes in their strategies. Managers must also address several broader issues, such as possible changes in product or process technology, shifts in the economic climate, the impact of social or political trends, and shifts in the bargaining power or vertical integration of customers.

For example, **Eons.com,** a social networking site for U.S. baby boomers, was banking on expectations that today's baby boomers will remain active as they pass the age of 50. Jeff Taylor, Eons's founder (who was founder and CEO of the job site **Monster.com**), says people in previous generations may have "dried up like a raisin" as they got older, but not today's baby boomers. "They're pumping up life, having fun on the flip side of 50," he says.[18] Many 50-plus consumers have been using cell phones, the internet, and other

EXHIBIT 6.10 **Market-Attractiveness/Competitive-Position Matrix, for Under Armour at Inception**

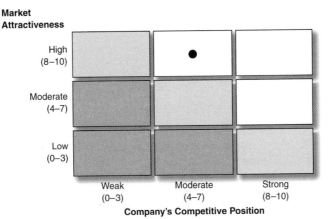

● = Market attractiveness and competitive position for Under Armour at inception

high-tech gadgets for two or three decades, so Taylor figured that his target market would be internet-savvy. Unfortunately for Eons, many baby boomers joined their younger children on Facebook, thereby obviating the need for a social network of their own. Eons was unceremoniously sold in 2011.[19]

Once they have determined any changes likely to occur in market attractiveness, managers must next determine how the business's competitive position in the market is likely to change, assuming that it responds effectively to projected environmental changes but the firm does not undertake any initiatives requiring a change in basic strategy. The expected changes in both market attractiveness and competitive position can then be plotted on the matrix in the form of a vector to reflect the direction and magnitude of the expected changes. Anticipating such changes may be especially important in today's internet age and in today's increasingly integrated and competitive global economy.

Step 5: Choose Segments to Target, Allocate Resources

Managers should consider a market segment to be a desirable target only if it is strongly positive on at least one of the two dimensions of market attractiveness and potential competitive position and at least moderately positive on the other. In Exhibit 6.10, this includes markets positioned in any of the three cells in the upper right-hand corner of the matrix. However, a business may decide to enter a market that currently falls into one of the middle cells under these conditions: (1) managers believe that the market's attractiveness or their competitive strength is likely to improve over the next few years; (2) they see such markets as stepping-stones to entering larger, more attractive markets in the future; or (3) shared costs or synergies are present, thereby benefiting another entry.

Under Armour used its growth in the apparel category and its retailer relationships to expand the range of its apparel and, more recently, to enter the market for athletic footwear. However, both its 2008 entry into the cross-trainers category and its 2009 entry into running flopped. Undeterred, Under Armour launched its Micro G basketball shoe in October 2009, taking on Nike and its firmly entrenched 95 percent share in the basketball category. Will Under Armour be able to successfully migrate from its original niche underwear segment into footwear? Nike does not seem worried. Says Nike spokesman Derek Kent, "We thrive on competition of any kind. We expect to further expand our leadership position."[20]

The market attractiveness/competitive position matrix offers general guidance for strategic objectives and allocation of resources for segments currently targeted and suggests which new segments to enter. Thus, it can also be useful, especially under changing market conditions, for assessing markets or market segments from which to withdraw or to which allocations of resources, financial and otherwise, might be reduced. Exhibit 6.11 summarizes one observer's generic guidelines for strategic objectives and resource allocations for markets in each of the matrix cells.

DIFFERENT TARGETING STRATEGIES SUIT DIFFERENT OPPORTUNITIES

Most successful entrepreneurial ventures target narrowly defined market segments at the outset, as did Dinaz Vervatwala and Kevin Plank, for two reasons. One, doing so puts the nascent firm in position to achieve early success in a market segment that it understands particularly well. Second, such a strategy conserves precious resources, both financial and otherwise. But segmenting the market into narrow niches and then choosing one niche to target is not

EXHIBIT 6.11 Implications of Alternative Positions within the Market Attractiveness/Competitive Position Matrix for Target Market Selection, Strategic Objectives, and Resource Allocation

Competitive Position

Market Attractiveness	Weak	Moderate	Strong
High	Build selectively: • Specialize around limited strengths • Seek ways to overcome weaknesses • Withdraw if indications of sustainable growth are lacking	DESIRABLE POTENTIAL TARGET Invest to build: • Challenge for leadership • Build selectively on strengths • Reinforce vulnerable areas	DESIRABLE POTENTIAL TARGET Protect position: • Invest to grow at maximum digestible rate • Concentrate on maintaining strength
Moderate	Limited expansion or harvest: • Look for ways to expand without high risk; otherwise, minimize investment and focus operations	Manage for earnings: • Protect existing strengths • Invest to improve position only in areas where risk is low	DESIRABLE POTENTIAL TARGET Build selectively: • Emphasize profitability by increasing productivity • Build up ability to counter competition
Low	Divest: • Sell when possible to maximize cash value • Meantime, cut fixed costs and avoid further investment	Manage for earnings: • Protect position • Minimize investment	Protect and refocus: • Defend strengths • Seek ways to increase current earnings without speeding market's decline

Sources: Adapted from George S. Day, *Analysis for Strategic Market Decisions* (St. Paul: West, 1986), p. 204; and S. J. Robinson, R. E. Hitchens, and D. P. Wade, "The Directional Policy Matrix: Tool for Strategic Planning," *Long Range Planning* 11 (1978), pp. 8–15.

always the best strategy, particularly for established firms having substantial resources. Three common targeting strategies are **niche-market, mass-market,** and **growth-market** strategies.

Niche-Market Strategy

This strategy involves serving one or more segments that, while not the largest, consist of a sufficient number of customers seeking somewhat-specialized benefits from a good or service, as Dinaz's Fitness Studios and Under Armour did.

Nestlé did just this in launching its exclusive—and pricey, at 10 times the price per cup compared to buying unground beans at the supermarket—Nespresso brand of coffee, packed in single-serve capsules for high-end consumers who would like to enjoy an espresso or cappuccino at home. Nespresso has become a $3 billion business, growing at more than 20 percent annually.[21] Such a strategy is designed to avoid direct competition with larger firms that are pursuing the bigger segments. Unfortunately, overall coffee consumption is down in some countries, as four-dollar lattes have become less fashionable in the distressed global economy. For an example of an American bank pursuing a niche market strategy in a services business, see Exhibit 6.12.

Mass-Market Strategy

A business can pursue a mass-market strategy in two ways. First, it can ignore any segment differences and design a single product-and-marketing program that will appeal to the largest number of consumers. The primary object of this strategy is to capture sufficient volume to gain economies of scale and a cost advantage. This strategy requires

EXHIBIT 6.12 *PNC Bank Targets Generation Y*

When it comes to banking, the members of Generation Y—those aged 18–34, by PNC Financial Services' definition, including many of the readers of this book—have different needs from their parents' generation. The most important of these differences, banking-wise, is that they tend to be clueless about how to manage their money. Some, in this debit card day and age, don't even know how to balance a checkbook because they rarely write checks. As Michael Ley, the PNC executive who led a project to target these customers says, "This group understands how to research online, but they said, 'We need help helping ourselves.'"

PNC decided that Gen Y was worth targeting, so they developed a new online product called the "Virtual Wallet." Virtual Wallet consists of three accounts: "Spend," "Reserve," and "Growth," all linked together with a user-friendly interface. What sets Virtual Wallet apart from other banks' products is features such as getting account balances by text message. Colleen Rohlf, a 24-year-old teacher from Pittsburgh, doesn't have to

worry any more about exactly how much money is in her account and doesn't have to worry about going online to find out. "I always know how much money I have," she says.

PNC likes this target market because it tends to hold higher balances than others and because Virtual Wallet customers rarely call customer service or show up in a branch office, keeping handling costs down. By late 2008, PNC had signed up more than 20,000 Virtual Wallet customers, of which 70 percent fell into the Gen Y demographic. With an average of 130 new customers signing on daily, PNC expected to break even in about two years, a year less than a conventional brick-and-mortar branch would take. As Gen Y grows up, PNC plans to add additional user-friendly tools for loans, investments, and other financial services.

Source: Burt Helm, "User-Friendly Finance for Generation Y," *BusinessWeek*, European Edition, December 8, 2008, p. 66. For more about PNC Bank, see *www.pnc.com*.

substantial resources, including production capacity, and good mass-marketing capabilities. Consequently, it is favored by larger companies or business units or by those whose parent corporation provides substantial support. For example, when Honda first entered the American and European motorcycle markets, it targeted the high-volume segment consisting of buyers of low-displacement, low-priced cycles. Honda subsequently used the sales volume and scale economies it achieved in that mass-market segment to help it expand into smaller, more-specialized segments of the market.

A second approach to the mass market is to design separate products and marketing programs for the differing segments. This is often called **differentiated marketing.** Marriott and Europe's Accor do this with their various hotel chains. Although such a strategy can generate more sales than an undifferentiated strategy, it can also increase costs in product design, manufacturing, inventory, and marketing, especially promotion.

Growth-Market Strategy

Most companies would probably prefer to make life simple and sell more or less identical products wherever they go. In fact, some do. Boeing, whose largest markets for passenger jets are now in India and China, sells more or less the same planes there that they sell elsewhere. Automakers like Ford and Toyota design cars on global platforms. An Apple iPod is an iPod wherever you go. But for most companies, segmenting global markets presents similar, if not more daunting, challenges compared to segmenting their home markets.[22]

Businesses pursuing a growth-market strategy often target one or more fast-growth segments, even though these segments may not currently be very large. It is a strategy often favored by smaller companies to avoid direct confrontations with larger firms while building volume and share. Most venture capital firms invest only in firms pursuing growth-market strategies because doing so is the only way they can earn the 30 percent to 60 percent annual rates of return on investment that they seek for portfolio companies.

VC-backed Zynga, the multiplayer online gaming company whose games are played by more than 120 million users, hitched its wagon to fast-growing Facebook, whose user base has grown at a torrid pace. Founded in 2007, privately held Zynga's revenues were thought to have surpassed $450 million in 2010. "Only a few companies are so privileged to get the rocket-ship growth that Zynga has," crowed Reid Hoffman, cofounder of LinkedIn and a Zynga director and investor.[23] In December 2011, Zynga IPO'd, but perceptions of overly rich valuations of Zynga, Facebook, Groupon, and other tech IPOs drove the stock to less than half of its offering price by June 2012.[24] Thus, despite the excitement that growth-market strategies can generate, they are far from certain to deliver strong long-term financial performance.

A growth-market strategy usually requires strong R&D and marketing capabilities to consistently identify and develop products appealing to newly emerging user segments, plus the resources to finance rapid growth. One problem, however, is that fast growth, if sustained, attracts large competitors. The acquisition of Playfish by longtime gaming leader Electronic Arts may give Zynga a run for its money and compound its difficulties.[25] The goal of the early entrant is to have developed an enduring competitive position via its products, service, distribution, costs, and its brand by the time competitors enter. In the online world, however, such positions can be fleeting.

GLOBAL MARKET SEGMENTATION

One traditional approach to global market segmentation in the developed world was to view a country as a single segment comprising all consumers. As we have seen earlier in this chapter, this approach is seriously flawed because it relies on country variables rather than consumer behavior, assumes homogeneity *within* the country segment, and ignores the possibility of the existence of homogeneous groups of consumers *across* country segments.

Strategic Issue

One traditional approach to global market segmentation has been to view a country as a single segment comprising all consumers. This approach is seriously flawed.

More and more companies are approaching global market segmentation by attempting to identify consumers with similar needs and wants reflected in their behavior in the marketplace in a range of countries. This intercountry segmentation enables a company to develop reasonably standardized programs requiring little change across local markets, thereby resulting in scale economies. Star TV's launch of a Pan-Asian satellite television service broadcasting throughout Asia in English and Chinese is an example of such a strategy. By 2011, Star reached more than 400 million viewers in 53 Asian countries.[26]

There are many reasons—beyond mere ambitions to grow—why companies expand internationally with sharply targeted strategies. Some companies go international to defend their home position against global competitors who are constantly looking for vulnerability. For example, Caterpillar, through a joint venture with Mitsubishi Heavy Industries, has for more than 30 years made a substantial investment in Japan to deny its Japanese competitor, Komatsu, strength at home, thereby taking away its profit sanctuary. Had Cat not been successful in doing so, Komatsu would have been able to compete more aggressively with Cat, not only in the United States, but also in other major world markets.

Another reason a firm may go overseas and target a specific country is to service customers who are also engaging in global expansion. In recent years Japanese automobile companies that have created U.S. and other overseas manufacturing facilities have encouraged their parts suppliers to do the same. Firms also enter overseas markets to earn foreign exchange and, in some cases, are subsidized by their governments to do so. Others, like Coca-Cola, ramp up their international growth when opportunities for growth in their home markets falter.

Whatever the motivation, though, the challenges entailed in crossing borders are always tricky. Companies that "go global" need to decide when to standardize their offerings, and when to tailor them to local needs in what remains a highly diverse global marketplace. In a recent study, even something as subtle as the difference in culture between European Americans and Asian Americans, for example, provoked different reactions to an exclusive deal. European Americans had high levels of responsiveness in relation to the deal whereas Asian Americans reacted negatively and preferred discounts that were more widely available.[27] Says Singapore-based brand strategist Martin Roll, "Contrary to many predictions, the flattening of the world has not flattened unique cultural and national characteristics, or the idiosyncratic preferences of customers."[28] The need for marketers to hone their skills at segmenting markets and targeting those they see as the most attractive appears not to be going away any time soon.

Marketing Plan Exercise	Identify the primary target market for the good(s) or service(s) to be marketed using demographic, geographic, and/or behavioral descriptors. Identify the key benefits the product(s) deliver(s) to the target market and the features that deliver these benefits. Prepare a market attractiveness/competitive position matrix for the segment.

Discussion Questions	1. Extensive market segmentation is a relatively recent phenomenon. Until about the middle of the 20th century many firms offered a single basic product aimed at the entire mass market (such as Coca-Cola or Levi jeans). But in recent years many firms—including industrial goods manufacturers and services producers as well as consumer products companies—have begun segmenting their markets and developing different products and marketing programs targeted at different segments. Which environmental changes have helped spark this increased interest in market segmentation? What advantages or benefits can a firm gain from properly segmenting its market?
	2. Exactly what is the relationship between market segmentation, target marketing, and positioning? What damage will be done to a company's target marketing and positioning efforts if markets are incorrectly or not effectively or insightfully segmented?
	3. Can market segmentation be taken too far? What are the potential disadvantages of oversegmenting a market? What strategy might a firm pursue when it believes that the market has been broken into too many small segments?
	4. What is the difference between a *growth-market* targeting strategy and a *niche* targeting strategy? What capabilities or strengths should a business possess to implement a growth-market targeting strategy effectively?

Additional self-diagnostic questions to test your ability to apply the analytical tools and concepts in this chapter to strategic decision making may be found at the book's website at **www.nihhe.com/ walker8e.**

Endnotes	1. Information to prepare this section was taken from John Parker, "Burgeoning Bourgeoisie" special report, *The Economist,* February 24, 2009, pp. 3–6; "Who's in the Middle?" "Burgeoning Bourgeoisie" special report, *The Economist,* February 24, 2009, p. 4; and the Dinaz's Fitness Studios website at *www.dinazs.com.* David Pilling, Kathrin Hille, and Amy Kazmin, "Stroll to a New Status." *Financial Times,* January 5, 2011, p. 11; Donal Griffin, "Pandit Stakes Citi's Future on Emerging Markets," *Bloomberg Business week* European Edition, March 21–27, 2011, pp. 49–50.

2. Christian Homburg, Mathias Droll, and Dirk Totzek, "Customer Prioritisation: Does It Pay Off, and How Should It Be Implemented?" *Journal of Marketing* 72 (September 2008), pp. 110–30.

3. Duane D. Stanford, "Coke's Last Round," *Bloomberg Businessweek*, November 1–7, 2010, pp. 54–61.

4. Marc Gunther, "The World's New Economic Landscape," *Fortune* European Edition, July 26, 2010, pp. 81–82.

5. Shelley Emling, "Buyers Want It to Be All About Me," *International Herald Tribune,* January 21–22, 2006, p. 16.

6. Gunther, "The World's New Economic Landscape."

7. Jack Ewing, "First Mover in Mobile," *BusinessWeek*, European Edition, May 14, 2007, p. 60.

8. To see the vast array of customized products that such websites offer, see *www.cafepress.com, www.zazzle.com, or www.spreadshirt.com.*

9. Nikolaus Franke, Peter Keinz, and Christoph J. Steger, "Testing the Value of Customization: When Do Customers Really Prefer Products Tailored to Their Preferences?" *Journal of Marketing* 73 (September 2009), pp. 103–21.

10. Brad Wieners, "Lego Is for Girls," *Bloomberg Businessweek* European Edition, December 19, 2011, pp. 68–73.

11. Nanette Byrnes, "Secrets of the Male Shopper," *BusinessWeek,* European Edition, September 4, 2006, pp. 45–51.

12. Gillian Reagan, "Nothing Tastes as Good as Skinny Feels," *Bloomberg Businessweek* European Edition, February 21–27, 2011.

13. Jeff Blagdon, "Nokia Sells Vertu Luxury Phone Arm to EQT, Keeps 10 Percent Stake," The Verge, June 14, 2012, at http://www.theverge.com/2012/6/14/3084531/nokia-vertu-sale-eqt

14. Cotten Timberlake, "At Macy's, the Many Colors of Cash," *Bloomberg Businessweek* European Edition, January 16, 2012, pp. 21–22.

15. Gunther, "The World's New Economic Landscape."

16. See *www.claritas.com.*

17. Stanford, "Coke's Last Round."

18. Laura Petrecca, "Tech Giants Target Older Users—and Their Cash," *USA Today*, November 30, 2007, p. 5A.

19. Kyle Alspach, "Shutdown Rumors Swirl about Eons.com," *Boston Business Journal,* May 24, 2012, *http://www.bizjournals.com/boston/blog/startups/2012/05/rumors-swirl-about-eonscom-social .html.*

20. Matt Townsend, "Under Armour's Daring Half-Court Shot," *Bloomberg Businessweek* European Edition, November 1–7, 2010, pp. 24–25.

21. Tom Mulier, "Nestlé's Recipe for Juggling Volatile Commodity Costs," *Bloomberg Businessweek* European Edition, March 21–27, 2011.

22. Gunther, "The World's New Economic Landscape."

23. Douglas MacMillan, "Zynga and Facebook, It's Complicated," *Bloomberg Businessweek* European Edition, April 26–May 2, 2010, pp. 47–48.

24. Stephen Russolillo, "Zynga Shares Rally Again; Analyst Thinks Selloff Is Overdone," *WSJ Blogs Market Beat,* June 18, 2012, *http://blogs.wsj.com/marketbeat/2012/06/18/ zynga-shares-rally-again-analyst-thinks-selloff-is-overdone/.*

25. MacMillan, "Zynga and Facebook, It's Complicated."

26. STAR TV website at *www.startv.com/corporate/about/index.htm.*

27. Michael J. Barone and Tirthankar Roy, "Does Exclusivity Always Pay Off? Exclusive Price Promotions and Consumer Response," *Journal of Marketing* 74 (March 2010), pp. 121–32.

28. Gunther, "The World's New Economic Landsape" p. 82.

Chapter **Seven**

Differentiation and Brand Positioning

A Sustainable Retailer? Marks & Spencer Says "Yes" in Tangible Ways[1]

In 2007 Marks & Spencer (M&S), the venerable operator of department and food stores in the United Kingdom and abroad, announced plans to become the world's most sustainable retailer. It would, said CEO Sir Stuart Rose, "meet 100 specific commitments, including pledges on reducing waste, sustainable sourcing, energy efficiency, and more."

If nothing else, M&S's so-called Plan A program, which was subsequently increased by an additional 80 commitments, is notable not only for its specificity, but for both its breadth and its depth. Says current CEO Marc Bolland, Plan A is "an integral part of our business (and) an integral part of our brand." Nearly everyone talks about sustainability these days, of course. But for many observers, the commitment of M&S is real. M&S has "really stuck to it, even through the recession," says Robert Jones of international brand consultant Wolff Olins. "I think that is admirable. In the green expert community it is seen as genuine, and not as greenwash."

How M&S Does it

M&S does many of the usual things, from using less energy in its stores and its fleet (down 20 percent), reducing packaging (down 19 percent in its food business and 35 percent in general merchandise), even sending its food waste to anaerobic digestion plants, which turn it into energy, instead of to landfills. But it has also developed numerous approaches for bringing its suppliers and its customers into the sustainability game.

Take the manufacture of men's suits, for example. In June 2012, M&S introduced what it called the world's "most sustainable suit." Made from organic Australian wool (apparently British sheep can't compete with the softness and the overall quality of their counterparts Down Under), with linings made from recycled pop bottles, zippers of recycled polyester, and even reclaimed stray buttons, the suit sells for a mere £349 (about $550).

Or consider children's clothing. In 2012, M&S committed to making its entire line of children's wear with completely traceable materials. A new line of sustainable clothing was scheduled for launch in late 2012. Says Krishan Hundal, who heads sourcing and technology at M&S, "In years to come we expect all (general merchandise) products to have complete traceability."

To push its supply chain toward greater sustainability, M&S put in place financial incentives for its buying teams and created a £50 million ($80 million) fund on which suppliers can draw to institute new ways of working.

Customers, Too

M&S wants to prod its customers into making more sustainable choices, too. In 2011, a survey of British consumers found that 74 percent had thrown away unwanted clothes in the past year. One in five had done so after wearing an item just once. M&S responded with a "Shwopping" promotion, in which it encouraged consumers to bring in an old item for recycling or reuse when buying a new one. Half a million garments were collected in the campaign's first six weeks. The goal is to help stop the estimated 1 billion garments that end up in landfills each year and recycle as many garments, some 350 million, as M&S sells each year.

Marks & Spencer's Progress and Goals

By 2012, some 90 of the original 100 commitments had already been achieved, and the Plan A program generated £105 million ($168 million) profit contribution in 2011 alone. While some sceptics note that becoming carbon neutral, as M&S did in 2011 for the first time by buying carbon credits to offset its emissions, doesn't exactly solve the carbon problem, its progress on its 180 commitments seems tangible and real.

The company's goal is that, by 2020, all M&S products will have at least one sustainable attribute. Such a plan requires clear targets, new metrics for measuring progress, and transparent reporting, not to mention a genuine commitment from top management on down. As CEO Bolland, who brings more than 20 years of brand marketing experience to his new role, puts it, Plan A is "a strong point of difference," that helps M&S stand out from its many competitors. "It is an essential part of our DNA and fundamental to our plans to become an international, multi-channel retailer."

STRATEGIC CHALLENGES ADDRESSED IN CHAPTER 7

The success of a brand offered to a given target market often depends on how well it is positioned within that market segment—that is, how well it performs *relative to* competitive offerings and to the needs of the target audience. **Brand positioning** refers to both the place a brand occupies in customers' minds relative to their needs and competing brands and to the marketer's decision making intended to create such a position. Thus, positioning comprises both competitive *and* customer considerations.

Brand positioning is basically concerned with differentiation. Ries and Trout, who popularized the concept of positioning, view it as a creative undertaking whereby an existing brand in an overcrowded marketplace of similar brands can be given a distinctive position in the minds of targeted prospects. While their concept was concerned with an existing brand, it is equally applicable for new brands.[2] While typically thought of in relation to the marketing of consumer goods, it has equal value for industrial goods and for services, which require essentially the same procedure as consumer goods. Because services are characterized by their intangibility, perishability, consumer participation in their delivery, and the simultaneous nature of their production and consumption, they are generally more difficult for marketers to position successfully.

In Chapter 7, we take the final step in preparing the foundation on which effective marketing strategies are based. Drawing on decisions made about target markets, as discussed in Chapter 6, we address the critical question: "How should a business position its product offering—whether goods or services—so customers in the target market perceive the offering as providing the benefits they seek, thereby giving the product an advantage over current and potential future competitors?" For Marks & Spencer, sustainability is the company's answer to creating a distinctive positioning in the crowded retailing industry in which it competes.

Strategic Issue

The brand positioning decision is a strategic one, with implications not only for how the firm's goods or services should be designed, but also for developing the other elements of the marketing mix.

As we shall see, the brand positioning decision is a strategic one, with implications not only for how the firm's goods or services should be designed, but also for developing the other elements of the marketing mix. Pricing decisions, promotion decisions, and decisions about how products are to be distributed all follow from and contribute to the effectiveness of the positioning of the product in its competitive space. Thus, the material in this chapter provides a foundation for virtually all of the strategic decision making that follows in the balance of this book.

For readers who are tasked with preparing marketing plans, the Marketing Plan Exercise at the end of this chapter suggests that you apply the various tools and techniques—from positioning statements to value propositions to perceptual maps to value curves—to the offering for which you are preparing your marketing plan. Putting these tools to work in a practical setting will bring them to life and provide a solid foundation upon which your marketing strategy can be constructed.

DIFFERENTIATION: ONE KEY TO CUSTOMER PREFERENCE AND COMPETITIVE ADVANTAGE

Why do customers prefer one product, whether a good or a service, over another? In today's highly competitive markets, consumers have numerous options. They can choose from dozens of best-selling novels to take along on an upcoming vacation. They can buy the novel they choose from an online merchant such as Amazon.com, from large chain booksellers such as Barnes and Noble or their online counterparts, from book clubs, from a local bookstore, or in some cases from their nearby supermarket or mass merchant. They can download it digitally to their Kindle or smartphone. They can even borrow the book at their local library and not buy it at all! Whether it's goods such as books or services such as libraries, consumers make choices such as these nearly every day. In most cases, consumers or organizational customers choose what they buy for one of two reasons: what they choose is *better,* in some sense, or *cheaper.* In either case, the good or service they choose is, in some way, almost always *different* from others they could have chosen.

Differentiation is a powerful theme in developing business strategies, as well as in marketing. As Michael Porter points out, "A company can outperform its rivals only if it can establish a difference that it can preserve. It must deliver greater value to customers or create comparable value at a lower cost, or both."[3] Most of the time, differentiation is why people buy. They buy the latest John Grisham novel because they know it will be a page-turner, different from the last Grisham they read, and hard to put down. They buy it from Amazon .com because they know Amazon will have it in stock and its one-click ordering system takes only a minute. Or they buy it from the megastore because it's fun to browse there or from their local bookseller because they feel good about supporting their local merchants. They buy it at the supermarket because it's convenient.

Strategic Issue

Most of the time differentiation is why people buy.

All these book-selling strategies are different, and they appeal to different consumers (i.e., different market segments) at different points in time, for different book-buying purposes. If these strategies did not vary, consumers would have no reason to use some of them, and they would buy their books where they were cheapest or most convenient, though even in such a case, the cheaper pricing or greater convenience would still constitute differences.

Differentiation among Competing Brands

As we saw in Chapter 6, customers in one market segment have wants and needs that differ in some way from those of customers in other segments. Brand positioning allows the marketer to take advantage of and be responsive to such differences and position particular goods and services to better meet the needs of consumers in one or more of these segments. These differences are often physical. The trays in which Marks & Spencer packs its apples are now made of recycled paper pulp instead of polystyrene, and can be recycled or composted. But differences can also be perceptual, as when athletic footwear and apparel, for example, benefit from endorsements by Roger Federer, Kobe Bryant, or other famous athletes. Deciding whether to use physical or perceptual positioning—or both—is a key responsibility that today's brand managers hold. Package design can be used to create perceptions of sophistication, for example, and can help consumers see the product as either belonging to a set of competitive products or standing out from that set.[4] Creating *both* physical and perceptual differences, using all the elements of the marketing mix—product, pricing, promotion, and distribution decisions—is what effective brand positioning seeks to accomplish.

PHYSICAL POSITIONING

One way to assess the current position of a brand relative to competitors is on the basis of how various brands compare on some set of objective physical characteristics. In many cases, a physical positioning analysis can provide useful information to a marketing manager, particularly in the early stages of identifying and designing new product offerings. Sometimes, physical differences provide the basis for entirely new product lines, even new companies, as the example of Geox shoes in Exhibit 7.1 demonstrates.

Despite being based primarily on technical rather than on market data, physical comparisons can be an essential step in undertaking a positioning analysis, which sets the foundation for brand positioning decisions. This is especially true with the competitive offerings of many industrial goods and services, which buyers typically evaluate largely on the basis of such characteristics. In addition, physical positioning contributes to a better marketing/R&D interface by determining key physical product characteristics; helps define the structure of competition by revealing the degree to which the various brands compete with one another; and may indicate the presence of meaningful product gaps (the lack of products having certain desired physical characteristics), which, in turn, may reveal opportunities for a new product entry, such as Mario Polegato's breathable shoes.

Limitations of Physical Positioning

A simple comparison of only the physical dimensions of alternative offerings usually does *not* provide a complete picture of relative positions because, as we noted earlier, positioning ultimately occurs in customers' minds. Even though a brand's physical characteristics, package, name, price, and ancillary services can be designed to achieve a particular

---

EXHIBIT 7.1   *Your Feet Want to Breathe*

More than 20 years ago, Mario Moretti Polegato was out hiking under the hot summer sun on a business trip to Reno, Nevada. In an effort to relieve the discomfort of his sweaty feet, Polegato poked holes in the soles of his shoes. "Why doesn't anyone make shoes that can breathe?" he wondered. After trying unsuccessfully to sell his idea of breathable shoes to Nike and Adidas, he decided to strike out on his own. Polegato founded Geox in 1995, starting with children's shoes and later adding adult styles. Customers responded. In 2007, his Milan-listed company sold 21 million pairs of shoes, some $1.2 billion worth, everything from rhinestone-studded but breathable sandals fit for a night on the town to earthy moccasins to a new line of athletic footwear. Thousands of tiny holes in the sole of every Geox shoe let air in but keep water out.

In Polegato's view, most athletic shoe makers focus on performance and competitive advantage. The Geox mind-set—it's all about comfort—is different. He says, "Feet have to breathe."

Source: Jennifer L. Schlenker, "Geox Takes on the Goliaths of Sport," *BusinessWeek*, European Edition, April 14, 2008, p. 58. For more on Geox see *www.geox.com*.

position in the market, customers may attach less importance to some of these characteristics than, or perceive them differently from, what the firm expects. Also, customers' attitudes toward a product are often based on social or psychological attributes not amenable to objective comparison, such as perceptions of the product's aesthetic appeal, sportiness, or status image (for example, in the United States, French wine from Bordeaux has traditionally been thought of as expensive or as an accompaniment to French food). Consequently, **perceptual positioning analysis**—whether aimed at discovering opportunities for new product entries or evaluating and adjusting the position of a current offering—is critically important.

PERCEPTUAL POSITIONING

Consumers often know very little about the essential physical attributes of many of the brands they buy, especially household products. The same is true for many services. Even if they did, they might not understand the physical attributes well enough to use them as a basis for choosing between competitive offerings. (For the major differences between physical and perceptual product positioning analyses, see Exhibit 7.2.) Many consumers do not want to be bothered about a product's physical characteristics because they are not buying these physical properties but rather the benefits they provide. While the physical properties of a product certainly influence the benefits provided, a consumer can typically evaluate a product better on the basis of what it *does* than what it *is*. Thus, for example, a headache remedy may be judged on how quickly it brings relief, a toothpaste on the freshness of breath provided, or a vehicle on how comfortably it rides.

Some marketers have begun positioning their products around lifestyles, instead of performance, in hopes of positioning their brand as a means of self-expression. A recent study argues that such a positioning strategy may inadvertently expose the brand to competition from other unrelated product categories, which may also be available to fulfill self-expressive needs.[5]

The evaluation of many goods and services is subjective because it is influenced by factors other than physical properties, including the way products are presented, our past experiences with them, and the opinions of others. Thus, physically similar products may be perceived as being different because of different histories, names, and advertising campaigns. For example, Sri Lankan tea producer Dilmah positions its teas in the same way wine has been positioned for years (see Exhibit 7.3).

EXHIBIT 7.2   Comparison of Physical and Perceptual Positioning Analyses

Physical Positioning	Perceptual Positioning
• Technical orientation	• Consumer orientation
• Physical characteristics	• Perceptual attributes
• Objective measures	• Perceptual measures
• Data readily available	• Need for marketing research
• Physical brand properties	• Perceptual brand positions and positioning intensities
• Large number of dimensions	• Limited number of dimensions
• Represents impact of product specs	• Represents impact of product specs and communication
• Direct R&D implications	• R&D implications need to be interpreted

EXHIBIT 7.3 *Not Your Ordinary Cup of Tea*

"What's grown on that field," says the Dilmah Group's Dilhan Fernando, "will differ drastically from what's grown over here." Fernando and his brother Malik think it's high time for a revolution in the way tea is blended and marketed. Their Ceylon teas, as they call them, harking back to Sri Lanka's colonial heritage, are positioned like fine wine, with elegant packaging extolling the subtly distinctive flavors of teas grown on a single hillside.

In the declining and still relatively fragmented global tea industry, which has lost $70 billion in sales to coffee in recent years, Dilmah has risen out of nowhere. Founded in the midst of Sri Lanka's civil war in 1988, it now ranks as the third-largest stand-alone tea brand, behind Unilever's Lipton and Associated British Foods' Twinings and about even with Tetley, owned by India's Tata Group.

The multinational players scoff at Dilmah's success. "The wine analogy is fairly ridiculous," says John Cornish, Twinings' international marketing director. But William Gorman, executive chair of Britain's Tea Council, says, "Dilmah is a very interesting company. This is an industry that has been incredibly slow to innovate, and Dilmah has shown it how."

With Starbucks having acquired Tazo Tea in 1999 and other boutique brands also making headway, Dilmah's positioning strategy may be just the ticket to turning tea's sales trend around. With a growing number of chic Dilmah T-bars now open in countries where the majors have limited clout—65 bars and rising, in places such as Poland, Kazakstan, and the United Arab Emirates—the Fernando brothers are making sure they don't leave distribution and brand awareness to chance.

Source: Eric Ellis, "Vintage Ceylon," *Fortune,* International Edition, June 25, 2007, pp. 22–24. For more on Dilmah, see *www.dilmahtea.com.*

LEVERS MARKETERS CAN USE TO ESTABLISH BRAND POSITIONING

Customers or prospective customers perceive some physical as well as other differences between goods or services within a product category, of course. Marketing decision makers seeking to win a particular position in customers' minds will seek to endow their brand with various kinds of attributes, which may be categorized as follows:

- *Simple physically based attributes.* These are directly related to a single physical dimension such as quality, power, or size. While there may be a direct correspondence between a physical dimension and a perceptual attribute, an analysis of consumers' perception of products on these attributes may unveil phenomena of interest to a marketing strategy. For instance, two cars with an estimated gasoline mileage of 23.2 and 25.8 miles per gallon may be perceived as having similar gasoline consumption.

- *Complex physically based attributes.* Because of the presence of a large number of physical characteristics, consumers may use composite attributes to evaluate competitive offerings. The development of such summary indicators is usually subjective because of the relative importance attached to different cues. Examples of composite attributes are the speed of a computer system, roominess of a car, and a product or service being user-friendly.

- *Essentially abstract attributes.* Although these perceptual attributes are influenced by physical characteristics, they are not related to them in any direct way. Examples include the sexiness of a perfume, heritage of a fine cognac, and prestige of a car. All of these attributes are highly subjective and difficult to relate to physical characteristics other than by experience.

- *Price.* A brand's price may imply other attributes, such as high or low quality. Discount airlines like Southwest, Brazil's Azul, and Ireland's Ryanair are careful to ensure that the low-priced image they seek does not imply a low level of safety, too.

The importance of perceptual attributes with their subjective component varies across consumers and product classes. Thus, it can be argued that consumers familiar with a given product class are apt to rely more on physical characteristics and less on perceptual attributes than consumers who are less familiar with that product class. It can also be argued that while perceptual positioning is essential for many consumer goods, such is not necessarily the case for many industrial goods.

Even though there is probably considerable truth in these statements, perceptual attributes must be considered in positioning most products. One reason is the growing similarity of the physical characteristics of more and more brands. This increases the importance of other, largely subjective dimensions. Consider, for example, whether Nike's Zoom Kobe VI basketball shoes would have sold as well without basketball star Kobe Bryant's endorsement and his presence in their ads.

Strategic Issue

Perceptual attributes must be considered in positioning most brands.

PREPARING THE FOUNDATION FOR MARKETING STRATEGIES: THE BRAND POSITIONING PROCESS

Positioning a new brand in customers' minds or repositioning a current brand involves a series of steps, as outlined in Exhibit 7.4. These steps are applicable to goods and services, in domestic or international markets, and to new and existing brands. Thus, when we say "brand" in the rest of this chapter and those that follow, we include both existing goods and services and planned new products—goods or services—that do not yet exist. We do not suggest that the determinant product attributes and the perceptions of consumers of various competitive offerings will remain constant across countries or other market segments; in fact they are likely to vary with most products. After managers have selected a relevant set of competing offerings serving a target market (Step 1), they must identify a set of critical or determinant product attributes important to customers in that target market (Step 2).

Step 3 involves collecting information from a sample of customers about their perceptions of the various offerings, and in Step 4 researchers analyze this information to determine the brand's current position in customers' minds and the intensity thereof (does it occupy a dominant position), as well as those of competitors.

Managers then ascertain the customers' most preferred combinations of determinant attributes, which requires the collection of further data (Step 5). This allows an examination of the fit between the preferences of a given target segment of customers and the current positions of competitive offerings (Step 6). Finally, in Step 7, managers write a concise statement that communicates the positioning decision they have reached. A discussion of these steps in the positioning process takes up most of the remainder of this chapter.

Step 1: Identify a Relevant Set of Competitive Products

Positioning analyses are useful at many levels: company, business unit, product category, and specific product line or brand. At the company or business unit level, such analyses are useful to determine how an entire company or business unit is positioned relative to its competitors. Even countries can be thought of as having brand positions in the marketplace. Unfortunately for Chinese manufacturers, a string of toy recalls for safety reasons, incidents of poisonous pet foods, and other scares mean that the words "Made in China" do not ring with confidence in some consumers' ears. Positioning that says "cheap" in the mind of the consumer is not what quality and globally oriented Chinese companies such as personal computer manufacturer Lenovo and brewer Tsingtao want to hear.[6]

At the product category level, the analysis examines customers' perceptions about types of products they might consider as substitutes to satisfy the same basic need. Suppose,

EXHIBIT 7.4 **Steps in the Positioning Process for Goods and Services**

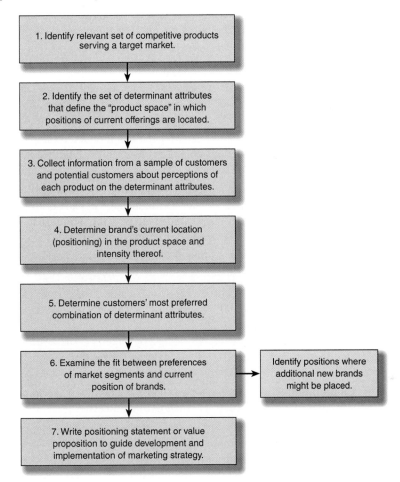

for example, a company is considering introducing a new instant breakfast drink. The new product would have to compete with other breakfast foods, such as bacon and eggs, breakfast cereals, and even fast-food drive-throughs. To understand the new product's position in the market, a marketer could obtain customer perceptions of the new product concept relative to likely substitute products on various critical determinant attributes, as we describe in Steps 3 and 4 of the positioning process (see Exhibit 7.4).

A positioning analysis at the product or brand level can be helpful to better understand how various brands appeal to customers, to position proposed new products or brands or reposition current ones, and to identify where new competitive opportunities might be found. The new supplement-fortified "relaxation beverage," Just Chill, presents itself as a clear alternative to the likes of Red Bull, coffee, and the increasingly overcrowded energy drink category. Will an overstimulated public go for Just Chill? Its retail distribution is confined mainly to Southern California and a few online retailers as we write. But, as Just Chill creator Max Baumann says, "People don't need more energy drinks or caffeine; they need something to chill them out."[7]

Strategic Issue

Marketers who omit important substitute products or potential competitors risk being blindsided by unforeseen competition.

At whichever level the positioning analysis is to be done, the analyst's choice of competing products (or product categories or firms) is critical. Marketers who omit important substitute products or potential competitors risk being blindsided by unforeseen competition. Just ask Kodak or Fuji who their key competitors are today!

Step 2: Identify Determinant Attributes

Positioning, whether for goods or services, can be based on a variety of attributes—some in the form of surrogates that imply desirable features or benefits as a positioning base. Some common bases are the following.[8]

- **Features** are often used in physical product positioning and, hence, with industrial products. An example of emphasizing features with a consumer good is U.S. high-end home appliance maker Jenn-Air's claim; "This is the quietest dishwasher made in America." Amazon.com has a unique "1-click" ordering system.

- **Benefits,** like features, are directly related to a product. Examples here include Volvo's emphasis on safety, Toyota's emphasis on reliability, and Norelco's promising a "close and comfortable shave."

- **Parentage** includes who makes it ("At Fidelity, you're not just buying a fund, a stock, or a bond—you're buying a better way to manage it") and prior products ("Buying a car is like getting married. It's a good idea to know the family first—followed by a picture of the ancestors of the Mercedes-Benz S class model").

- **Manufacturing process** is often the subject of a firm's positioning efforts. An example is Jaeger-LeCoultre's statement about its watches; "We know it's perfect, but we take another 1,000 hours just to be sure."

- **Ingredients** as a positioning concept is illustrated by some clothing manufacturers' saying their shirts are made only of organic cotton.

- **Endorsements** are of two types—those by experts ("Discover why over 5,000 American doctors and medical professionals prescribe this Swedish mattress"—Tempur-Pedic) and those via emulation as with Kobe Bryant wearing Nike shoes.

- **Comparison** with a competitor's product is common ("Tests prove Pedigree is more nutritious than IAMS, costs less than IAMS, and tastes great, too"—Pedigree Mealtime pet food).

- **Proenvironment** positioning seeks to portray a company as a good citizen ("Because we recycle over 100 million plastic bottles a year, landfills can be filled with other things, like land, for instance"—Phillips Petroleum, part of Conoco Phillips).

- **Price/quality** is used in cases such as Walmart successfully positioning itself as the lowest-price seller of household products.

Theoretically, consumers can use many attributes to evaluate competing brands, but the number actually influencing a consumer's choice is typically small, partly because consumers can consider only attributes of which they are aware. The more variables used in positioning a given brand, the greater the chance of confusion and even disbelief on the part of the consumer. The positioning effort must be kept as simple as possible and complexity should generally be avoided at all costs. Marks & Spencer's focus on sustainability is a good example. Even marketers of bottled water are seeking to differentiate and better position their products (see Exhibit 7.5).

In using one or more attributes as the basis of a brand's positioning effort, it is important to recognize that the importance attached to these attributes often varies. For example, while the brands of soap or shampoo provided by a hotel may be an attribute that some consumers use in evaluating hotels, most are unlikely to attach much importance to this when deciding which hotel chain to patronize. Bedding, however, is another story, as specialty linens maker Anichini has found. Its exquisite bedding helps luxury boutique hotels and resorts like the Bacara Resort in Santa Barbara, California stand out from the sameness of the ubiquitous—and in some people's minds, boring—chain hotels.[9] Even an important attribute may not greatly influence a consumer's preference if all the alternative brands are perceived to be about equal on that dimension. Deposit safety is an important attribute in

EXHIBIT 7.5 *Can You Position Bottled Water?*

The growth category called bottled water has suddenly come to a screeching halt. Growth in the United States in 2008 slowed to 2 percent, down from near-double-digit rates earlier. Environmental concerns are the driver, at least in part. The energy costs and pollution that the bottled products generate are far higher compared to plain old tap water, which arrives in your home or workplace much more efficiently. The slump is expected to turn into a full-fledged downturn in 2009, as budget-squeezed customers turned to the tap.

Big players such as Coca-Cola, PepsiCo, and Nestlé are jostling for position to reverse the decline. "But it's all just water," you might say. Not so fast. They are scrambling to offer products that put something in the bottle other than just plain water. Coke's Dasani has introduced a flavored version called Dasani Essence.

Pepsi's SoBe Lifewater added stevia, a new all-natural sweetener. Other companies are focused on refillable bottles, a bit better environmentally, at least at the margin. Meanwhile water filter manufacturers, such as Clorax's Brita and Procter & Gamble's PUR, are enjoying healthy sales increases.

Who will prosper in this shakeout? It's too soon to tell, but positioning one bottled water as fundamentally different from another is a stern test of these companies' marketing prowess or, as some observers lament, an indicator of consumer marketing run amok.

Source: Christopher Palmeri and Nanette Byrnes, "Coke and Pepsi Try Reinventing Water," *BusinessWeek*, European Edition, March 2, 2009, p. 58.

banking, but most consumers perceived all banks to be about equally safe, at least until the recent financial crisis. Consequently, for banks, deposit safety has not been a **determinant attribute:** It does not play a major role in helping customers to differentiate among the alternatives and to determine which bank they prefer.

Marketers should rely primarily on determinant attributes, whether benefits or features, in defining the product space in a positioning analysis. The question is: "How can a marketer find out which product dimensions are determinant attributes?" Doing so typically requires conducting some kind of marketing research. This brings us to Step 3.

Step 3: Collect Data about Customers' Perceptions for Brands in the Competitive Set

Having identified a set of competing brands, the marketer needs to know what attributes are determinant for the target market and the product category under consideration. He or she also needs to know how different brands in the competitive set are viewed on these attributes. Typically, this market knowledge is developed by first conducting qualitative research, perhaps interviews or focus groups, to learn which attributes are determinant. Sometimes, participants in such studies are engaged through online brand communities on Facebook or other internet sites. Assuming that such consumers are loyal or committed brand users, however, is probably not a safe assumption to make.[10] Then quantitative research follows, perhaps a survey of consumers about their perceptions, to gather data on how competing brands score on these attributes. Later in this chapter, we discuss several statistical and analytical tools that are useful at this step of the positioning process.

Step 4: Analyze the Current Positions of Brands in the Competitive Set

Whether the positioning process is directed at a new brand not yet introduced or repositioning one that already exists, it is important to develop a clear understanding of the positioning of the existing brands in the competitive set (see Step 1). There are two useful tools for doing so. One is the **positioning grid,** also called a **perceptual map.** The other is the **value curve.** The positioning grid provides a visual representation of the positions of various products or brands in the competitive set in terms of (typically) two determinant attributes. Where more than two attributes are to be considered in a positioning analysis, multidimensional grids, or multiple grids, are produced. Alternatively, a value curve, which comprises more than just two dimensions, can be generated, as we describe further below.

But not all brands exist in the awareness of most consumers. A brand that is not known by a consumer cannot, by definition, occupy a position in that consumer's mind. Often the awareness set for a given product class is three or fewer brands. Thus, many if not most brands have little or no position in the minds of many consumers. Consider coffee bars, which, in recent years, have become ubiquitous in cities worldwide. In London, three major chains dominate—Starbucks, Coffee Republic, and Caffé Nero—each with its own ambience and image with consumers. There are also several smaller chains and numerous independents, most of which are largely unknown—thus with no clear positioning—to most Londoners.

With consumers having so many coffee bars to choose from already—often several shops within a few hundred feet of each other on any busy street—for a new coffee bar entrant to be successful, it must adopt a clear positioning in consumers' minds to give consumers a reason to switch. Determining the attributes on which the brand's positioning will be based is a key outcome of the positioning process and a driver of the marketing communication strategy, as well as the marketing strategy overall, that will ultimately be developed. Without clear guidance about the intended position of the brand, advertising agencies, salesforces, and others charged with building the awareness and recognition of the product in the marketplace will be ill-equipped to do their jobs.

Building a Positioning Grid

An example of what can be done with data gathered in Step 3 is found in Exhibit 7.6, which shows the results obtained from a classical study that portrays how a sample of consumers positioned a number of women's clothing retailers in the Washington, D.C., area. Respondents rated the various stores on the two determinant attributes of value and fashionability. Some stores, such as Nordstrom and Kmart, occupy relatively distant positions from one another, indicating that consumers see them as very different. Other stores occupy positions comparable to one another (Neiman Marcus, Saks) and thus are considered relatively alike, meaning the intensity of competition between these stores is likely to be considerably greater than for those that occupy widely divergent positions.

The store positioning shown in Exhibit 7.6 also provides useful information about possible opportunities for the launching of a new store or the repositioning of an existing one. Positioning for a new store could be done by examining the positioning map for empty spaces (competitive gaps) where no existing store is currently located. There is such a gap in the upper-right quadrant of the "value/fashionability" map in Exhibit 7.6. This gap may represent an opportunity for developing a new entry or repositioning an old one that is perceived to offer greater fashionability than Nordstrom at a lower price. Of course, such gaps may exist simply because a particular position is either (1) impossible for any brand to attain because of technical constraints or (2) undesirable since there are few prospective customers for a brand with that set of attributes. It is important that positioning grids be built on a foundation of well-designed marketing research, rather than naive hunches. Several software tools have been developed for designing positioning studies and analyzing the results, some of which we identify in Exhibit 7.7.

Building a Value Curve

Given that crafting strategies involves making choices—choices about what *not* to do, as well as what to do—another useful tool for positioning decisions is the value curve.[11] Value curves indicate how products within a category compare in terms of the level—high or low—of as many attributes as are relevant. Thus, unlike perceptual maps, which are most easily viewed in just two dimensions, value curves are multidimensional.

EXHIBIT 7.6 Perceptual Map of Women's Clothing Retailers in Washington, D.C.

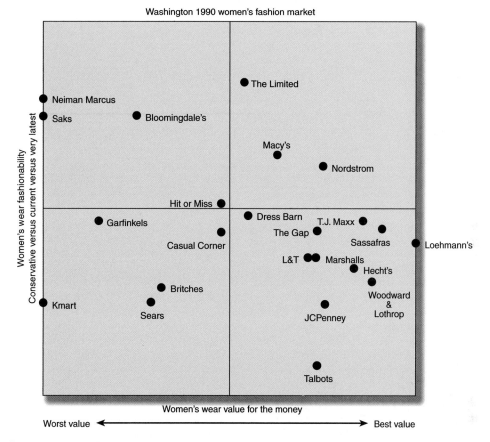

Source: Adapted from Douglas Tigert and Stephen Arnold, "Nordstrom: How Good Are They?" *Babson College Retailing Research Reports,* September 1990, as shown in Micheal Levy and Barton A. Weitz, *Retailing Management* (Burr Ridge, IL: Richard D. Irwin. 1992), p. 205.

Sometimes, value is best delivered by eliminating or reducing the level of some attributes, especially those not really desired or appreciated by the target customer, and increasing the level of others, the ones the customer really wants. Let's imagine that in addition to the data shown on the perceptual map in Exhibit 7.6, we have data about several other variables for three stores: Neiman Marcus, Sears, and J.C.Penney. We could build value curves for the three retailers by plotting these hypothetical data as shown in Exhibit 7.8.

The value curves show that, among other things, Sears and J.C.Penney choose to compete by reducing their level of customer service, ambience, category depth, and fashionability, presumably in order to deliver increased value for money. Neiman Marcus offers higher levels of customer service, ambience, category depth, and fashionability, presumably because the target customer it seeks to serve is willing to pay for these attributes.

Marketing Opportunities to Gain a Distinct Position

Strategic Issue

Competing head-on against the leaders on the basis of attributes appropriated by larger competitors is not likely to be effective.

In situations where one or a limited number of brands dominate a product class (or type) in the minds of consumers, the main opportunity for competitors generally lies in obtaining a profitable position within a market segment *not* dominated by a leading brand. Competing head-on against the leaders on the basis of attributes appropriated by larger competitors is not likely to be effective.

EXHIBIT 7.7 *Software Tools for Positioning Decision Making*

Software tools useful for making positioning decisions include applications that identify important determinant attributes, as well as statistical applications that can plot positioning grids from market research data.

Conjoint analysis: As we mention in Step 5 of the positioning process, it is important to learn which key attributes are important to consumers. Conjoint analysis is one tool for doing so. Conjoint analysis determines which combination of a limited number of attributes consumers most prefer. The technique is helpful for identifying appealing new product designs and important points that might be included in a product's advertising. Although it can provide some insights about consumer preferences, it cannot provide information about how consumers perceive the positioning of existing products in relation to product dimensions. Conjoint analysis is one way to narrow down a set of product attributes to those most important to consider in product design and positioning decisions. Most often, it is used with physical attributes, not perceptual ones. Several widely used conjoint analysis applications are available from Sawtooth Software, Inc. (*www.sawtoothsoftware.com*).

Factor analysis and discriminant analysis: Factor analysis and discriminant analysis are two statistical techniques useful in constructing positioning grids based on actual marketing research data. They are included in most broad-based statistical packages, such as SPSS MR (*www.spss.com/spssmr*). To employ factor analysis, the analyst must first identify the salient attributes consumers use to evaluate products in the category under study. The analyst then collects data from a sample of consumers concerning their ratings of each product or brand on all attributes. The factor analysis program next determines which attributes are related to the same underlying construct ("load" on the same factor). The analyst uses those underlying constructs or factors as the dimensions for a product space map, and the program indicates where each product or brand is perceived to be located on each factor.

Discriminant analysis requires the same input data as factor analysis. The discriminant analysis program then determines consumers' perceptual dimensions on the basis of which attributes best differentiate, or discriminate, among brands. Once again, those underlying dimensions can be used to construct a product space map, but they are usually not so easily interpretable as the factors identified through factor analysis. Also, as with factor analysis, the underlying dimensions may be more a function of the attributes used to collect consumer ratings than of the product characteristics that consumers actually consider to be most important.

Multidimensional scaling: Unlike the other techniques in which the underlying dimensions identified depend on the attributes supplied by the researcher when collecting data, multidimensional scaling produces dimensions based on consumer judgments about the similarity of, or their preferences for, the actual brands. These underlying dimensions are thought to be the basic dimensions that consumers actually use to evaluate alternative brands in the product class. Multidimensional scaling programs that use data on similarities construct geometrically spaced maps on which the brands perceived to be most similar are placed close together. Those that use consumer preferences produce joint space maps that show consumer ideal points and then position the most- preferred brands close to those ideal points.

Unfortunately, the underlying dimensions of the maps produced by multidimensional scaling can be difficult to interpret. Also, the dimensions identified are only those that already exist for currently available brands. This makes the technique less useful for investigating new product concepts that might involve new characteristics. Finally, the technique is subject to statistical limitations when the number of alternative brands being investigated is small. As a rule, such techniques should be applied only when at least eight or more different products or brands are being examined.

 A better option is to concentrate on an attribute prized by members of a given market segment. Toyota, with its traditional baby-boomer customer base getting older, launched its Scion brand in 2004, targeted at American youth. Instead of transitional mass marketing, the Scion team used edgy internet-based marketing, including making virtual Scions available for virtual purchase on Second Life, a website that was then growing in popularity with the younger set.[12] Scion's hip, youthful image has helped the new brand score with its Generation Y target market.

Constraints Imposed by an Intense Position

Although marketers should generally seek a distinctive and intense position for their brands, attaining such a position imposes constraints on future strategies. If shifts in

EXHIBIT 7.8 **Value Curves for Neiman Marcus, J.C.Penney, and Sears**

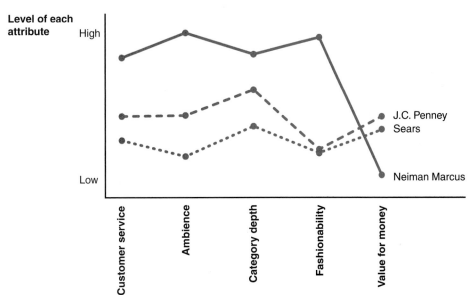

the market environment cause customers to reduce the importance they attach to a current determinant attribute, marketers may have difficulty repositioning a brand with an intensely perceived position on that attribute. Repositioning carries with it the threat of alienating part or all of the product's current users regardless of success with its newly targeted group. Success in its repositioning efforts may well ensure losing its current group of users, as Talbots, the women's apparel retailer, found when it sought a younger customer base in 2011. As Lazard Capital Markets analyst Jennifer Davis observed, "For many years, younger women in their 30s and 40s saw Talbots as their mother's store. If they want to save themselves, they need to make up their minds about who their audience is."[13]

Another concern is the dilution of an existing intense position as a result of consolidation. For example, British Leyland was formed through a series of mergers involving a number of British car manufacturers. For years, the company did not have a clear identity because it was new and manufactured a variety of brands, including Rover, Triumph, and Austin-Morris. Most Europeans had difficulty spontaneously recalling any British car manufacturer since once-strong brand names such as Austin and Morris had lost their identity and meaning. Following a long series of divestitures, buyouts, and reorganizations, British Leyland's successor company, MG Rover, went bankrupt in 2005. While there's little doubt that high-cost manufacturing contributed to the company's demise, a lack of clear positioning for many of its brands was surely a contributing factor.[14]

Another danger associated with an intensely positioned brand is the temptation to overexploit that position by using the brand name on line extensions and new products. The danger here is that the new products may not fit the original positioning and the brand's strong image is diluted. For example, for many years, the Holiday Inn Group offered travelers the choice of staying in Holiday Inn, Holiday Inn Express, Holiday Inn Select, or Holiday Inn Garden Court, each of which operated at a different price point and service offering. Such a diverse offering bearing a single brand can be very confusing to consumers.

Limitations of Product Positioning Analysis

The analysis depicted in Exhibit 7.6 is often referred to as *product positioning* because it indicates how alternative products or brands are positioned relative to one another in customers' minds. The problem with this analysis is that it does not tell the marketer which positions are most appealing to customers.[15] Thus, there is no way to determine if there is a market for a new brand or store that might locate in an "open" position or whether the customers in other market segments prefer brands or stores with different attributes and positions. To solve such problems, it is necessary to measure customers' preferences and locate them in the product space along with their perceptions of the positions of existing brands. This is called a **market positioning analysis.** We deal with this issue in Step 5.

Step 5: Determine Customers' Most Preferred Combination of Attributes

There are several ways analysts can measure customer preferences and include them in a positioning analysis. For instance, survey respondents can be asked to think of the ideal brand within a category—a hypothetical brand possessing the perfect combination of attributes (from the customer's viewpoint). Respondents could then rate their ideal product and existing products on a number of attributes. An alternative approach is to ask respondents not only to judge the degree of similarity among pairs of existing brands, but also to indicate their degree of preference for each. In either case, the analyst, using the appropriate statistical techniques, can locate the respondents' ideal points relative to the positions of the various existing brands on the product space map.

Another method of assessing customers' preferences and trade-offs among them is a statistical technique called *conjoint analysis.*[16] Customers are surveyed and asked their preferences among various real or hypothetical product configurations, each with attributes that are systematically varied. By analyzing the resulting data, the marketer can learn which of several attributes are more important than the others. These results can then be used in positioning analyses such as those described here.

Whichever approach is used, the results will look something like Exhibit 7.9, which shows a hypothetical cluster of ideal points for one segment of women's clothing consumers. As a group, this segment would seem to prefer Nordstrom over any other women's clothing retailer on the map.

There are, however, several reasons not all customers in this segment are likely to prefer Nordstrom. First, the ideal points of some customers are actually closer to Macy's than Nordstrom. Second, customers whose ideal point is equidistant between the two stores may be relatively indifferent in their choice of which store to patronize. Finally, customers sometimes may patronize stores somewhat further away from their ideal—particularly when buying low-involvement, nondurable goods or services—to assess the qualities of new stores, to reassess older stores from time to time, or just for the sake of variety.

Using price as one dimension of a positioning grid, or as a key dimension on which a brand is positioned, is typically not very useful unless price is a key driver of the marketing strategy. This is the case for two reasons. First, price is easily imitable by competitors. Unless the firm has a clear cost advantage over its competitors, by virtue of its processes, buying power, or other sources of efficiency, using low price as a basis for positioning can be a fast road to a price war that no one (except consumers) will win.

Strategic Issue

Using price as one dimension of a positioning grid is typically not very useful.

Second, claims that one's brand—whether a good or a service—is low-priced are sometimes not very credible because so many marketers make such claims. It is often better to position around more enduring differentiators and let price speak more subtly for itself.

EXHIBIT 7.9 **Perceptual Map of Women's Clothing Retailers in Washington, D.C., Showing the Ideal Points of a Segment of Consumers**

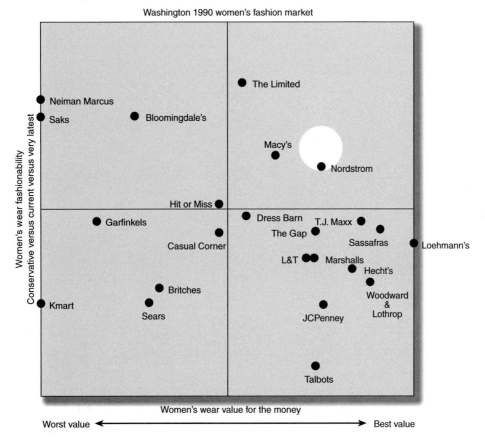

Source: Adapted from Douglas Tigert and Stephen Arnold, "Nordstrom: How Good Are They?" *Babson College Retailing Research Reports,* September 1990.

Walmart, an exception, has been able to sustain its low-price positioning in the United States because its costs and its prices on many items, compared to its chief competitors, actually are lower.

Step 6: Consider Fit of Possible Positions with Customer Needs and Segment Attractiveness

An important criterion for defining market segments is the difference in the benefits sought by different customers. Because differences between customers' ideal points reflect variations in the benefits they seek, a market positioning analysis can simultaneously identify distinct market segments as well as the perceived positions of different brands. When customers' ideal points cluster in two or more locations on the product space map, the analyst can consider each cluster a distinct market segment.[17] For analytical purposes, each cluster is represented by a circle that encloses most of the ideal points for that segment; the size of the circle reflects the relative proportion of customers within a particular segment.

Exhibit 7.10 groups the sample of Washington, D.C. respondents into five distinct segments on the basis of clusters of ideal points.[18] Segment 5 contains the largest proportion of customers; segment 1, the smallest.[19] By examining the preferences of customers in different segments along with their perceptions of the positions of existing brands, analysts can learn much about (1) the competitive strength of different brands in different

EXHIBIT 7.10   Perceptual Map of Women's Clothing Retailers in Washington, D.C., Showing Five Segments Based on Ideal Points

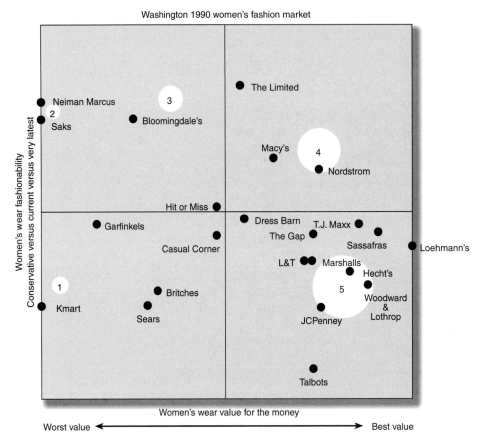

Source: Adapted from Douglas Tigert and Stephen Arnold, "Nordstrom: How Good Are They?" *Babson College Retailing Research Reports,* September 1990.

segments, (2) the intensity of the rivalry between brands in a given segment, and (3) the opportunities for gaining a differentiated position within a specific target segment.

Step 6 not only concludes the analysis portion of the positioning process and crystallizes the decision about the positioning a brand should hold, but it also can uncover locations in the product space where additional new brands could be positioned to serve customer needs not well served by current competitors. Thus, as Exhibit 7.4 suggested, a side benefit of the positioning process is recognition of underserved positions where additional new products might be placed.

Step 7: Write Positioning Statement or Value Proposition to Guide Development of Marketing Strategy

The final decision about where to position a new brand or reposition an existing one should be based on both the market targeting analysis discussed in Chapter 6 and the results of a brand positioning analysis. The position chosen should match the preferences of a particular market segment and should take into account the current positions of competing brands.

It should also reflect the current and *future* attractiveness of the target market (its size, expected growth, and environmental constraints) and the relative strengths and weaknesses of competitors. Such information, together with an analysis of the costs required to acquire and maintain these positions, allows an assessment of the economic implications of different market positioning strategies.

Most successful products are positioned based on one or, at most, two determinant attributes, whether physical or perceptual. Using more attributes simply confuses customers. Domino's Pizza in the United States, in its early days, focused its positioning solely on its fast delivery, since that was the principal dimension on which it established its competitive advantage. While there are many things Domino's could have said about the pizza itself, it chose to focus its positioning on its key point of differentiation: fast delivery. Later, when fast delivery became common in the pizza industry, Domino's added a heat retention device to its delivery containers and added a second positioning attribute: hot. Papa John's, a later entrant in the pizza business, positions its offering around a single attribute, the quality of its pizza, with its promotional phrase "Better ingredients. Better pizza."

Strategic Issue

Most successful products are positioned based on one or, at most, two determinant attributes.

Where there are no real product differences, as in so-called **me-too products,** or no differential benefits to the user, not only is success hard to achieve, but also ethical issues may arise. For an example of ethical issues involving positioning in the pharmaceutical industry, see Ethical Perspective 7.1.

Once the desired positioning for the product has been determined, it's a good idea to write it down so those charged with developing and implementing the marketing strategy have a clear understanding of what is intended for the product and where it will fit in its competitive set. Two approaches are commonly used for doing so. In the classical approach, a **positioning statement** is written. A more recent approach, one adopted by a growing number of firms, involves writing a **value proposition** for the product.

Writing a Positioning Statement or a Value Proposition

A positioning statement is a succinct statement that identifies the target market for which the product is intended and the product category in which it competes and states the unique benefit the product offers. An example of a positioning statement that reflects Volvo's marketing strategy in the United States is shown in Exhibit 7.11.

A value proposition is similarly explicit about what the product does for the customer (and sometimes, what it does not do) and typically also includes information about pricing relative to competitors. Both positioning statements and value propositions should

---

Ⓔ Ethical Perspective Positioning in the Pharmaceutical Industry—An Ethical Quagmire

7.1

Under constant and ever-increasing pressure to perform, the pharmaceutical industry is frequently cited for practices that are ethically questionable. An article in the British journal *The Lancet* provided an assessment of advertisements in Spanish medical journals in 1997 for antihypertensive (drugs used to treat high blood pressure) and lipid-lowering (i.e., cholesterol-lowering) drugs. The advertisements studied in a six-month period (264 different ads for antihypertensives and 23 different ads for lipid-lowering drugs) made a total of 125 referenced claims. After excluding the 23 claims that did not have published data, the researchers found that in 44 percent of the cases, the published data did not support the statements made in the ads. This study is a note of caution for doctors who prescribe medicines based on the evidence of reported research on drugs.

Is such marketing really in the best long-term interests of the shareholders?

Source: Pilar Villanueva, Salvador Peiró, Julián Librero, and Inmaculada Pereiró, "Accuracy of Pharmaceutical Advertisements in Medical Journals," *The Lancet,* January 4, 2003.

EXHIBIT 7.11   Positioning Statement and Value Propositions for Volvo Automobiles in the United States

Positioning Statement	Value Propositions
For upscale American families, Volvo is the automobile that offers the utmost in safety.	• Target market: Upscale American families • Benefits offered: Safety • Price range: 20% premium over similar cars

generally reflect a **unique selling proposition (USP)** that the product embodies. In this sense, they reflect the basis on which the marketer intends to win competitive advantage by differentiating the product from others in its competitive space.

The notion of the USP has been oversold, however, since in many product categories, especially mature ones, customers are more interested in the degree to which particular products meet their already well-established needs rather than the degree to which they differ from others. Newness and differentiation are not always what the customer wants! We address this issue later in this chapter.

A value proposition is another way to clearly and succinctly state a product's positioning. In its shortest form, a value proposition typically looks like this:

- Target market
- Benefits offered (and not offered)
- Price range (relative to competitors)

Exhibit 7.11 also provides a value proposition for Volvo. More fully developed value propositions sometimes identify the best competing alternatives available to the customer and specify the benefits, in measurable terms, that the customer can expect to receive by using the proposed product. Detailed value propositions such as these are particularly helpful in positioning industrial goods and services, where quantifiable customer benefits are often essential to make the sale.

Strategic Issue

It is important that the positioning statement or value proposition states benefits that the user of the product will obtain, rather than features or attributes of the product itself.

It is important that the positioning statement or value proposition states **benefits** that the user of the product will obtain, rather than **features** or attributes of the product itself or vague or ambiguous platitudes about high quality or excellent service. By *benefits,* we mean the resulting measurable end-use consequences that the user will experience through the use of the product, in comparison to others.

The marketer generally writes positioning statements and value propositions for use internally and by others, such as advertising agencies engaged to develop the marketing strategy. They are short and succinct and are typically *not* written in catchy consumer language, though catchy **slogans** and **tag lines** for communication with customers often follow. They are most commonly written for a product line or a brand, as is the case in our Volvo example, but sometimes for a single product or for a business as a whole. For products, they play several important roles. They provide direction for R&D and product development about what kind of attributes should be built into the product (side-door airbags, for example, in Volvo's case). They provide direction for those who create advertising campaigns about what the focus of those campaigns should be (for example, Volvo's ads almost always focus on safety, even though Volvo could say other things about its cars). The value proposition also provides direction for pricing decisions.

Thus, in a very real sense, the positioning statement or value proposition constitutes the foundation upon which the marketing strategy is built. More broadly, when used at the business level, as they sometimes are, these statements articulate the strategic direction toward which the company's activities in all arenas should be directed. Promising a certain sort of positioning, or value, to the target market is one thing. Delivering it is another. Clear and concise positioning statements and value propositions can play important roles in effectively executing the intended strategy.

THE OUTCOME OF EFFECTIVE POSITIONING: BUILDING BRAND EQUITY

Brand equity is the term marketers use to refer to the value created by establishing customer preference for one's brand. It reflects how consumers feel, think, and act toward the brand, and it has implications for the prices and profits the brand can achieve in the marketplace and for the market capitalization of the company owning the brand.[20] When companies create differences between their brands and other brands, differences that consumers view as meaningful, brand equity is the result. Effective positioning decisions that lead to effective marketing programs are critical to this process.

Consider Procter & Gamble, arguably one of the world's most successful marketers over the past century. Its market capitalization of $180 million in 2011 is due in large part to the brand equity it has built for its portfolio of brands in the more than 140 countries in which it does business. As P&G's global marketing officer James Stengel notes about consumers, "They want to trust something. People really do care what's behind the brand, what's behind the business. They care about the values of a brand and the values of a company. We can never be complacent about that. Businesses and brands that are breaking records are those that inspire trust and affection and loyalty by being authentic, by not being arrogant, and by being empathetic to those they serve."[21]

In India, for example, P&G sells shampoo one sachet at a time, rather than in the giant economy-size bottles found in American showers, reflecting Indian consumers' limited purchasing power. In North America, P&G has turned its trusted detergent brand, Tide, into a growth machine by adding innovative new cleaning products such as the Tide Stain Stick that people can carry with them.[22]

Managing Brand Equity

While brand positioning decisions are crucial in large companies such as P&G and to the development of new brands, whether goods or services, in entrepreneurial start-ups, there are two ongoing issues that are essential if whatever brand value that's been built is to be maintained and grown: brand reinforcement and brand revitalization.

Some companies have maintained strong brands for many decades—for example, P&G's Tide, Crest, and Pampers, Wrigley's gum, Coca-Cola, Disney, and numerous others. Other brands with substantial brand equity are more recent phenomena—including Nike, Dell, Apple, and Google, all of which made *Bloomberg BusinessWeek's* 2011 list of the 100 best global brands.[23] All of these companies, young and old, nurture and protect their brands, ensuring that the products that bear their brands stand for something consistent and that marketing messages reinforce the brand strategy and personality.

Sometimes, however, market conditions or marketing mistakes make it necessary to revitalize a brand that has lost its lustre. The emergence of new competitors or changes in consumer tastes and preferences can affect a brand's fortunes, sometimes for the worse. Repositioning a brand can be extremely difficult, however (see Exhibit 7.12).

Additionally, rebranding can sometimes help marketers achieve a more unified approach in their marketing efforts. Federated Stores, a collection of U.S. department stores operating under a variety of hundred-year-old brands of their long-departed

---

EXHIBIT 7.12 *J.C.Penney Makeover Not Making It*

Retailing whiz Ron Johnson, who in earlier career roles collaborated with up-and-coming product designers to develop Target's "cheap chic" persona and with Steve Jobs to create Apple's ultra-cool and immensely profitable retailing strategy has taken on his biggest challenge yet, that of remaking the venerable but tired J.C.Penney department store chain. To put it bluntly, six months into the job as Penney's CEO, it was not going well. Same-store sales, off 19 percent in the first three months of 2012, and profitability were plummeting.

J.C.Penney had trained its customers to ignore anything offered at regular price—less than 1 percent of all Penney merchandise was sold at regular price—and wait for a promotional event. When Johnson took away the promotions in favor of an everyday "fair and square" pricing strategy, customers simply waited for the next sale, which, under the new strategy, never came. Apparently, they're still waiting.

Johnson's struggles to remake J.C.Penney illustrate just how difficult it can be to reposition a brand that becames known for one thing and make it known for another. His vision is to create a new shopping environment with 100 in-store boutiques selling goods made specifically for J.C.Penney by the likes of Martha Stewart, Jonathan Adler, and Vivienne Tam. But first, says Johnson, he had to fix the coupon-driven pricing model. "We wouldn't have had access to many of our new brands and design partners without implementing a new pricing model," he says.

So what has gone wrong? Marketing consultant Martha Guidry says that J.C.Penney's attempt to get rid of coupons and promotions was a good idea but that Penney failed to make it relevant to the consumer. "It would have been really easy for them to have said, 'Fair and Square pricing is a sale price every day,' and I think people would've gotten it, but they didn't communicate it that way," she said. Will Johnson's repositioning of J.C.Penney eventually work? Stay tuned.

Sources: Susan Berfield with Sapna Meheshwari, "J.C.Penney vs. the Bargain Hunters," *Bloomberg Businessweek* European edition, May 28, 2012; and Drew Bowling, "The Trials and Tribulations of J.C.Penney's 'Fair and Square' Strategy, June 29, 2012, *Web-ProNews* at *http://www.webpronews.com/the-trials-tribulations-of-j-c-pennys-marketing-strategy-2012-06*. For more on J.C.Penney, see *www.jcpenney.com*.

---

founders—from Wanamakers in Philadelphia to Marshall Field in Chicago—was unable to build a coherent nationwide marketing strategy. "Since we weren't a national brand, I couldn't even advertise during the Macy's Thanksgiving Day Parade," says Federated CEO Terry Lundgren.[24] Federated was printing 16 different shopping bags, running 16 different catalogs, and buying merchandise locally in 16 different regions across the United States.

Despite a lot of push-back from local managers, Lundgren thought there was an opportunity to take advantage of the Macy's parade and put the Macy's brand on most of the Federated stores. Converting more than 600 stores from their former nameplates and creating a centralized hut localized strategy took nearly five years, but has delivered impressive results. Same-store sales were up 4.6 percent and Macy's nearly doubled its operating profit in 2010 over 2009. Says Lundgren of the rebranding decision, "If we hadn't made that decision a few years ago, the external environment would have forced it on us. It was the right choice.[25]

As we have seen in this chapter, brand positioning is much more than a one-time exercise. It's an ongoing, never-ending process, one in which the best marketers keep abreast of market and competitive changes in order to maintain and grow the brand equity they have built. Positioning decisions, important as they are, only set the foundation for the development and implementation of effective marketing programs, however. It is those marketing programs whose job is to deliver on the brand promise. Developing and implementing marketing programs and strategies is the focus of much of the remainder of this book. Before turning to those issues, we wrap up our work on positioning by addressing positioning decisions in global markets, and we address a few caveats to which attention should be given along the way.

POSITIONING DECISIONS IN GLOBAL MARKETS

As many industries have undergone consolidation in recent years, the consolidators have found themselves managing a plethora of brands. Nowhere is the phenomenon more prevalent than in the beer industry, where beers were traditionally brewed locally and marketed for local appeal. Take Anheuser-Busch InBev's Budweiser beer, for example. AB InBev now wants to turn Budweiser, long a mass-market leader in the United States, into a global brand—the "American Dream in a bottle," says Chris Burggraeve, AB InBev's chief marketing officer.[26] AB InBev has rolled out Bud as a premium brand in Russia and Brazil. In China, the world's largest beer market by volume, Bud has garnered a third of the premium market, which accounts for some 3 percent of sales, since its launch in 2010.[27]

Making a beer into a premium brand outside of its home base is nothing new for beer marketers. Guinness and Heineken are both popularly priced products in their home countries Ireland and the Netherlands, respectively, but are sold with premium positioning elsewhere. Stella Artois, known as the drink of choice for hooligans in Britain, was recently launched as a sophisticated ale in Argentina.[28] Brahma, a leading Brazilian mass-market brand, has been successful in Europe with its premium positioning as "Brazil in a bottle," even in the vodka-loving Ukraine.[29]

For another example, consider the ice cream industry, worth some $74 billion in annual sales, dominated by giants such as Nestlé and Unilever, which together control about a third of the global market. But upstart General Mills has taken its niche Häagen-Dazs brand into cultlike status in markets from France to China, a far cry from its merely upscale image in the United States. "It is a jewel of a brand for us," says General Mills CEO Ken Powell. "It's highly differentiated, beautifully positioned across markets—and with lots of growth opportunities." Häagen-Dazs did $100 million in sales in China in 2010 and, as a super-premium product, it generates among the highest margins among all General Mills brands. Unlike in other countries, about 80 percent of Häagen-Dazs sales in China come from its shops, rather than from the supermarket freezer. But retail will grow, says Powell. "You start in the shops to build a brand image. As you get traffic and people recognize the brand, you start advertising and putting the product in retail outlets."[30]

Over time, as the globalization of most media make it possible for consumers to understand what's available elsewhere and see how it is positioned, marketers will have to be careful that marketing messages in one part of the world don't conflict with established positioning in another. But the potential for taking brands upscale when they leave home is one that marketers in industries other than beer and ice cream could probably emulate.

SOME CAVEATS IN POSITIONING DECISION MAKING

We noted earlier in this chapter that it's generally desirable to identify a unique selling proposition that clarifies how the product is differentiated from others. A book by Patrick Barwise and Seán Meehan argues, however, that contrary to conventional wisdom, buyers only rarely look for uniqueness. They argue that the degree to which a brand can grow to dominate its category is a reflection of how many users in the category believe it delivers the main category benefits.[31] They say the infinitesimal differentiators that some marketers worry so much about make little real difference. Thus, they argue that marketing strategists should focus their efforts on delivering the benefits that matter most to the target customer—even if other competitors do so as well—and not worry so much about inventing trivial differences that don't really matter.

A second caveat is the question of whether, if one is to differentiate, the focus should be on features—tangible attributes of the good or service itself, such as Volvo's side-door airbags and other safety features—or the benefits the features deliver—safety, in Volvo's case. At the end of the day, customers buy what they buy, whether goods or services, in order to obtain certain benefits. They could care less about features for their own sake. Thus, it's the benefits that matter.

But words are cheap, for marketers as well as for politicians' election-year promises. To be credible in telling the benefits story, marketers must back up their words with features that actually deliver the benefits that are promised. The challenge for marketing strategists is to keep benefits as the focus of the value proposition and at the top of everyone's mind—copywriters, salespeople, everyone who sells in one way or another—but find a way to credibly support and effectively communicate the benefits that are claimed. Doing so is far more difficult than it sounds, which is why so many ads and so many salespeople talk about features instead of benefits.

Marketing Plan Exercise

Write a positioning statement and a value proposition for the product(s) to be marketed. Construct one or more perceptual maps or a value curve to clarify its positioning versus competitors.

Discussion Questions

1. Given the challenges inherent in repositioning a fast-food chain, how would you further update the Subway product line and advertising campaign in light of current macro trends?
2. What is meant by a *determinant attribute* for a given product? Explain why the identification of such attributes is so important. What would be an example of a determinant attribute for each of the following products and services?
   a. A cruise line
   b. A laptop computer
   c. French wine
   d. Women's sportswear
   e. A hospital
   f. A liberal arts college
   g. A tractor
3. Should positioning be based on product features or benefits? Why? Under what circumstances should features be the focus of an advertising campaign?
4. In terms of positioning strategy, what is the rationale for the fact that Nabisco offers many different brands within the cracker category, each of which is perceived as being only slightly different from the others? What are the advantages and limitations of such a strategy?

Additional self-diagnostic questions to test your ability to apply the analytical tools and concepts in this chapter to strategic decision making may be found at the book's website at **www.mhhe.com/walker8e.**

Endnotes

1. The Marks & Spencer story has been sourced from Andrea Felsted, "A Green Blueprint," *Financial Times Boldness in Business,* March 17, 2011, pp. 18–21; Will Nichols, "M&S Goes Carbon Neutral as Sustainability Savings Stack Up," *BusinessGreen,* June 7, 2012, at *www.businessgreen.com/print_article/bg/news/2182619/-goes-carbon-neutral-sustainability-savings-stack; BusinessGreen* staff, "M&S: Britons Wasting £91m of Clothes That Have Been Worn Just Once," *BusinessGreen,* June 18, 2012, at *www.businessgreen.com/bg/news/2184971/-britons-wasting-gbp91m-clothes-worn;* "'Shwopping' Helps M&S Capture Half a Million Items," June 19, 2012, at *www.letsrecycle.com/news/latest-news/textiles/2018shwopping2019-helps-m-s-capture-half-a-million-items;* Will Nichols,

"Children's Clothes to Be M&S' First 'Fully Traceable' Range," *BusinessGreen,* June 19, 2012, at *www.businessgreen.com/print_article/bg/news/2185464/childrens-clothes-traceable-range;* Tamsin Blanchard, "Marks & Spencer Launch the World's 'Most Sustainable Suit,'" *The Telegraph,* June 19, 2012, at *http://fashion.telegraph.co.uk/columns/tamsin-blanchard/TMG9340870/Marks-and-Spencer-launch-the-worlds-most-sustainable-suit.html;* Petah Marian, "UK: M&S Boss Sees Shoppers at Centre of Sustainability Push," *Just-Style,* June 20, 2012, at *www.just-style.com/news/ms-boss-says-consumers-need-to-be-at-centre-of-sustainability-push_id114703.aspx;* and Lynn Beavis, "M&S: Doing the Right Thing Leads to Change for the Better," *The Guardian Sustainable Business,* June 20, 2012, at *www.guardian.co.uk/sustainable-business/best-practice-exchange/marks-and-spencer-change-better.*

2. Al Ries and Jack Trout, *Positioning: The Battle for Your Mind* (New York: Warner Books, 1982).

3. Michael Porter, "What Is Strategy?" *Harvard Business Review,* November–December 1996, p. 62.

4. Ulrich R. Orth and Keven Malkewitz, "Holistic Package Design and Consumer Brand Impressions," *Journal of Marketing* 72 (May 2008), pp. 64–81.

5. Alexander Chernev, Ryan Hamilton, and David Gal, "Competing for Consumer Identity: Limits to Self-Expression and the Perils of Lifestyle Branding," *Journal of Marketing* 75 (May 2011), pp. 66–82.

6. Dexter Roberts, "China's Brands: Damaged Goods," *BusinessWeek,* European Edition, September 24, 2007, p. 47.

7. Adam Baer, "The Big Chill," *Hemispheres,* April 2011, pp. 50–52.

8. Adapted from C. Merle Crawford and C. Anthony Di Benedetto, *New Products Management* (Burr Ridge, IL: McGraw-Hill/Irwin, 2008).

9. See the company's website at *www.anichini.com.*

10. Scott A. Thompson and Rajiv K. Sinha, "Brand Communities and New Product Adoption: The Influence and Limits of Oppositional Loyalty," *Journal of Marketing* 72 (November 2008), pp. 65–68.

11. For more on strategy making as choices, see Constantinos C. Markides, *All the Right Moves: A Guide to Crafting Breakthrough Strategy* (Cambridge, MA: Harvard Business School Press, 2000). For more on value curves, see W. Chan Kim and Renée Mauborgne, "Value Innovation: The Strategic Logic of High Growth," *Harvard Business Review* (January–February, 1997), pp. 103–12.

12. Roland Jones, "Can Toyota's Scion Keep Its Edge?" *www.msnbc.msn.com/id/17688646l,* March 21, 2007.

13. Ashley Lutz, "How Talbots Got the Girl—And Lost the Woman," *Bloomberg Businessweek* European Edition, June 20, 2011, pp. 25–26.

14. Lindsay Brooke, "Mini: The Real Story," *Automotive Industries,* April 2002. For more on BL's history, see also "British Leyland Motor Corporation," *http://en.wikipedia.org/wiki/British_Leyland.*

15. Existing brands' attractiveness can be inferred from current sales volumes and market shares. The position occupied by the share leader is obviously more appealing to a greater number of customers than are the positions occupied by lesser brands.

16. For more on conjoint analysis, see Vithala Rao, *Applied Conjoint Analysis* (New York: Springer Publishing, 2009).

17. When using preference data to define market segments, however, the analyst should also collect information about customers' demographic characteristics, lifestyle, product usage, and other potential segmentation variables. This enables the analyst to develop a more complete picture of the differences among benefit segments. Such information can be useful for developing advertising appeals, selecting media, focusing personal selling efforts, and designing many of the other elements of a marketing program that can be effective in appealing to a particular segment.

18. The size of the individual circles in Exhibit 7.10 is fictitious and designed for illustrative purposes only.

19. The map in Exhibit 7.10 shows five distinct preference segments but only one set of perceived product positions. The implication is that consumers in this sample were similar in the way they perceived existing brands but different in the product attributes they preferred. This is the most common situation; customers tend to vary more in the benefits they seek than in how they perceive available products or brands. Sometimes, however, various segments may perceive the positions of existing brands quite differently. They may even use different determinant attributes in assessing these positions. Under such circumstances, a marketer should construct a separate market-positioning map for each segment.

20. Kevin Lane Keller, *Strategic Brand Management,* 3rd ed. (Upper Saddle River, NJ: Prentice Hall, 2008).

21. Geoff Colvin, "Selling P&G," *Fortune,* International Edition, September 17, 2007, p. 82.

22. Ibid., pp. 81–87.

23. "100 Best Global Brands," *Bloomberg Businessweek*, November 29, 2011.

24. Terry Lundgren, "Hard Choices," *Bloomberg Businessweek,* November 29–December 5, 2010, p.104.

25. Macy's Inc 2010 Annual Report at *http://www.macysinc.com/Investors/vote/2010_ar.pdf.*

26. Clementine Fletcher, "This Bud's for You, Emerging Markets," *Bloomberg Businessweek* European Edition, October 3, 2011, pp. 26–27.

27. Ibid.

28. Ibid.

29. Roger Bennett, "Gained in Translation," *Bloomberg Businessweek* European Edition, April 2, 2011, p. 85.

30. David A. Kaplan, "General Mills' Global Sweet Spot," *Fortune* European Edition, May 23, 2011, pp. 94–100.

31. Patrick Barwise and Seán Meehan, *Simply Better: Winning and Keeping Customers by Delivering What Matters Most* (Cambridge, MA: Harvard Business School Press, 2004).

Formulating Marketing Strategies

Chapter **Eight**

Marketing Strategies for New Market Entries

Canon, Inc.—Success That Is Hard to Copy[1]

Even before the global economic slump starting in 2008 and the devastating earthquake and tsunami of 2011, Japan's economy had suffered through four recessions during the 1990s and the early years of this century. Consequently, many Japanese manufacturers—even some of the largest global competitors—struggled to remain profitable and survive. However, a few firms not only survived, but also grew and prospered in spite of the difficult domestic market environment. Canon, Inc. is one of those stellar performers. From 2000 on, the company delivered seven straight years of record annual sales and profits and averaged a 16 percent return on equity. Unfortunately, the worldwide recession of 2008 brought that string of performance records to an end, but Canon still managed to earn an operating profit of $4.75 billion on net sales of $45 billion in 2011.

How has Canon managed to wring so much money out of its copiers, printers, and cameras when other Japanese electronics firms have floundered? For one thing, Fujio Mitarai, the firm's CEO, has been willing to adopt some Western cost-cutting practices he learned during the 23 years he worked for Canon in America. First, he narrowed the company's strategic scope by concentrating on a few product markets where the firm had an established market presence and superior technological capabilities, while abandoning other businesses where it had a weaker competitive position, such as personal computers and liquid-crystal displays. Mr. Mitarai also scrapped the assembly lines in all 29 of Canon's Japanese plants, replacing them with small work teams—or "cells"—of about six employees who do the work of about 30 workers under the old system. These self-managed cells have not only reduced Canon's labor costs, but have also enabled the firm to cut its inventory of component parts by 30 percent and to close 20 of its 34 warehouses.

But a sharper market focus and increased manufacturing efficiency are not sufficient to explain the firm's strong performance. Other Japanese electronics firms have copied such cost-cutting actions without duplicating Canon's results. A second important strategic thrust underlying Canon's success is a heavy emphasis on developing and marketing a stream of new products, product improvements, and line extensions in order to sustain a leading share position in its core businesses.

As a first step toward implementing this product development strategy, the company plows nearly 8 percent of its total revenues back into product R&D. Some of that investment is targeted at continued improvement of Canon's offerings in businesses where it already holds a dominant market share. For instance, Canon's technical leadership has enabled it to maintain a 60 percent share of the global market for the core engines used to power laser printers, including printers developed through an alliance with Hewlett-Packard. In other cases, Canon's development efforts focus on innovative new-to-the-world products, such as the development of a digital radiography system or an advanced diagmatic imaging technology which the firm hopes will enable detection of metabolic changes in patients and thus facilitate early diagnosis of disease. Sometimes the firm simply modifies existing products or technologies to better serve new application segments, such as developing a wide-format bubble-jet printer for use in the commercial printing industry.

Of course, it is one thing to develop a bunch of new products on the cutting edge of technology, but making potential customers aware of those new products and their benefits—and actually generating sales revenues—requires effective and well-funded marketing and sales efforts as well. Consequently, Canon has restructured its global sales and marketing organization in recent years to decentralize decision-making and make its marketing plans better adapted to local market conditions. This is particularly critical because the firm earns more than 80 percent of its sales revenues in markets outside of Japan. For example, the company established Canon Europe Ltd. in the United Kingdom to help coordinate regional marketing efforts and strengthen its sales network in the European Union, which is now the company's largest market in terms of revenue.

STRATEGIC CHALLENGES ADDRESSED IN CHAPTER 8

Canon's success illustrates several important points about new product and market development. First, both sales growth and cost cutting can help improve profits. But although it is often easier to cut costs in the short term, revenue growth—particularly growth generated by the development of innovative new products—can have a bigger impact on a firm's profitability and shareholder value over the long haul. This point is confirmed by a study of 847 large corporations conducted by Mercer Management Consulting. The authors found that the compound annual growth rate in the market value of companies that achieved higher-than-average profit growth but lower revenue growth than their industry's average—companies that increased profits mostly by cutting costs, in other words—was 11.6 percent from 1989 to 1992. By contrast, companies that achieved higher-than-average profits as the result of higher-than-average revenue growth saw their market value jump at an annual rate double that—23.5 percent.[2]

Canon's history also illustrates that new product introductions can involve products that differ in their degree of newness from the perspective of the company and its customers. Some of the products developed by the firm, such as its first office copier, presented a new technical challenge to the company but did not seem very innovative to potential customers who viewed the copiers merely as simpler and cheaper versions of Xerox's machines. But some of the firm's new product introductions—such as its digital radiology system—were truly innovations that were new to potential customers and the company alike.

This chapter examines marketing strategies and programs appropriate for offerings that are *new to the target customers*. Our primary focus is on programs used by the pioneer firm—or first entrant—into a particular product-market. Being the pioneer gains a firm a number of potential competitive advantages, but it also involves some major risks. Some pioneers capitalize on their early advantage and maintain a leading market share of the product category, earning substantial revenues and profits, well into the later stages of the product's life cycle.

Strategic Issue

Being the pioneer gains a firm a number of potential competitive advantages, but it also involves some major risks.

Other pioneers are less successful. Although Canon has pioneered some new product categories, for instance, it has not always ended up as the share leader in those categories as they grew and matured. In some cases, this was a consequence of Canon's strategy of withdrawing from markets where it could not sustain superior technical expertise, as in the case of liquid-crystal displays. But in other cases, followers have overtaken the pioneer by offering better products, superior customer service, or lower prices. This leads to an interesting strategic question: Is it usually better for a firm to bear the high costs and risks of being the pioneer in hopes of maintaining a profitable position as the market grows or to be a follower that watches for possible design or marketing mistakes by the pioneer before joining the fray with its own entry? We examine this question later in this chapter.

Not all pioneers are intent on remaining the overall share leader as the market grows. Some adopt a niche market strategy geared to making substantial profits from specialized market segments where they will face fewer large competitors. Others—like Canon—try to stay one jump ahead of the competition by introducing a constant stream of new products and withdrawing from older markets as they become more competitive. Which strategy is best? It depends on the firm's resources and competencies, the strength of likely future competitors, and characteristics of the product and its target market. Therefore, we will examine some alternative strategies that might be adopted by a pioneer and the situations where each makes most sense.

If you are working on the Marketing Plan Exercise and if your plan involves the introduction of a new product or service that is unfamiliar to potential customers, you will be asked to detail your strategy as the category's pioneer. As mentioned previously, you will need to justify that strategy in terms of your business's competencies and resources, potential customer characteristics, segments, and choice criteria, and an analysis of potential future competitors, how soon they are likely to enter the market and their relative strengths and weaknesses.

But even a successful pioneering firm's marketing strategy must change and adapt as its product moves through a life cycle from introduction to rapid growth, maturity, and ultimately, decline. Consequently, we begin this chapter with a brief overview of the product life cycle, the market and competitive changes that typically occur at each of its stages, and their implications for marketing strategy. Chapters 9 and 10 will then further elaborate the strategic options available to market pioneers and followers as their markets grow and then mature. How should the pioneer adjust its strategy to maintain its position as market leader when new competitors arrive on the scene? What marketing programs might those late-arriving followers employ to successfully challenge an entrenched market leader?

SUSTAINING COMPETITIVE ADVANTAGE OVER THE PRODUCT LIFE CYCLE

The product life cycle is concerned with the sales history of a product or product class. The concept holds that a product's sales change over time in a predictable way and that products go through a series of five distinct stages: introduction, growth, shakeout, maturity, and decline (see Exhibit 8.1). Each of these stages provides distinct opportunities and threats, thereby affecting the firm's strategy as well as its marketing programs. Despite the fact that many new products do not follow such a prescribed route because of failure, the concept is extremely valuable in helping management look into the future and better anticipate what changes will need to be made in strategic marketing programs.

Strategic Issue

The PLC concept is extremely valuable in helping management look into the future and better anticipate what changes will need to be made in strategic marketing programs.

At the beginning (the **introductory stage**), a new product's purchase is limited because many members of the target market are unaware of its existence; also, the product often lacks easy availability. As more people learn about the product and it becomes more readily available, sales increase at a progressively faster rate (the **growth stage**). Growth

EXHIBIT 8.1   **Generalized Product Life Cycle**

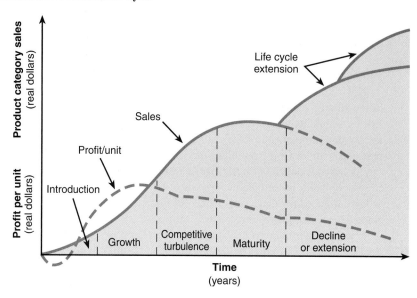

slows as the number of buyers nears the maximum and repeat sales become increasingly more important than first-time sales. As the number of both buyers and their purchases stabilizes, growth becomes largely a function of population growth in the target market. At the end of the growth period—just before the advent of maturity—the **shakeout** or **competitive turbulence stage** occurs. This is characterized by a decreasing growth rate that results in strong price competition, forcing many firms to exit the industry or sell out. The **mature stage** is reached when the net adoption rate holds steady—that is, when adopters approximate dropouts. When the latter begin to exceed new first-time users, the sales rate declines, and the product is said to have reached its final or **decline stage.**

Many products do not go through the product life cycle curve shown in Exhibit 8.1 because a high percentage are aborted after an unsatisfactory introductory period. Other products seemingly never die (Scotch whiskey, automobiles). The shape of the life cycle curve varies considerably between and within industries but is typically described as S-shaped.

Fads, such as pet rocks and hula hoops, enter suddenly, experience strong and quick enthusiasm, peak early, and enter the decline stage shortly thereafter. Thus, even when successful, their life cycle is unusually short and is typically depicted in the form of an inverted V.[3]

Market and Competitive Implications of Product Life-Cycle Stages

The various stages of the product life cycle present different opportunities and threats to the firm. By understanding the characteristics of the major stages, a firm can do a better job of setting forth its objectives and formulating its strategies as well as developing its action plans, as briefly summarized in Exhibit 8.2.

Introductory Stage

There is a vast difference between pioneering a product class and a product type. The former is more difficult, time-consuming, expensive, and risky, as, for example, when the telephone was introduced versus the introduction of the cellular phone. The introductory period, in particular, is apt to be long, even for relatively simple product classes such as

EXHIBIT 8.2   Expected Characteristics and Responses by Major Life Cycle Stages

	Stages in Product Life Cycle				
Stage Characteristics	**Introduction**	**Growth**	**Shakeout**	**Mature**	**Decline**
Market growth rate (constant dollars)	Moderate	High	Leveling off	Insignificant	Negative
Technical change in product design	High	Moderate	Limited	Limited	Limited
Segments	Few	Few to many	Few to many	Few to many	Few
Competitors	Few	Many	Decreasing	Limited	Few
Profitability	Negative	High	Low	High for market-share leaders	Low
Firm's Normative Responses					
Strategic marketing objectives	Stimulate primary demand	Build share	Build share	Hold share	Harvest
Product	Improve quality	Continue quality improvements	Rationalize	Concentrate on features	No change
Product line	Narrow	Broad	Rationalize	Hold length of line	Reduce length of line
Price	Skimming or penetration	Reduce	Reduce	Hold or reduce selectively	Reduce
Channels	Selective	Intensive	Intensive	Intensive	Selective
Communications	High	High	High	High to declining	Reduce

packaged food products. Because product type and subtype entries usually emerge during the late-growth and maturity stages of the product class, they have shorter introductory and growth periods. Once the product is launched, the firm's goal should be to move it through the introductory stage as quickly as possible. Research, engineering, and manufacturing capacity are critical to ensure the availability of quality products. Where service is important, the firm must be able to provide it promptly (as in postpurchase service and spare parts availability).

Marketing Mix in the Introductory Stage

The length of the product line typically should be relatively short to reduce production costs and hold down inventories. Efforts to establish competitive advantage are typically focused on differentiating the new product or product line from solutions customers previously employed to satisfy the targeted want or need.

The firm's pricing is strongly affected by a variety of factors: the product's value to the end user; how quickly it can be imitated by competitors; the presence of close substitutes; and the effect of price on volume (elasticity) and, in turn, on costs. Basic strategy choices involve skimming and penetration. **Skimming** is designed to obtain as much margin per unit as possible. This enables the company to recover its new product investments more quickly. Such a strategy is particularly appropriate in niche markets and where consumers are relatively insensitive to price, as was the case in the sale of cellular phones to business executives early in the product life cycle. **Penetration pricing** enables the firm to strive for quick market development and makes sense when there is a steep experience curve, which lowers costs; a large market; and strong potential competition.

The importance of **distribution** and channel intermediaries varies substantially from consumer to industrial goods. The latter are often sold direct, but with few exceptions consumer goods use one or more channel intermediaries. Product availability is particularly important with consumer goods because of the large amounts spent on promotion to make consumers aware of the product and to induce usage. Distribution is easier if the company uses the same channels for its other products and has a successful track record with new product introductions.

During the introductory period, **promotion** expenditures involving advertising and salesforce are a high percentage of sales, especially for a mass-market, small-value product. Some dot-coms have spent themselves to failure for promotional purposes. For industrial goods, personal selling costs are apt to be much higher than advertising costs.

The communications task at the outset is to build awareness of the new product's uniqueness, which is typically an expensive undertaking. Further, the promotional expenditures (such as in-store displays, premiums, coupons, samples, and off-list pricing) required to obtain product availability and trial are substantial. For industrial products, the time required to develop awareness of the product's uniqueness is often extensive due to the number of people in the buying center and the complexity of the buying systems.

However, not every company introducing a new product or service, especially cash-strapped entrepreneurial ventures, can afford extensive promotional campaigns aimed at building brand awareness and distribution channels. Luckily, the internet is providing such firms with a number of alternative promotional tools that are much less costly. For example, companies such as Nantucket Nectars in the United States and Innocent Drinks in the United Kingdom have relied on quirky public relations efforts, internet ads, word of mouth on social networking sites such as Facebook, and blogs to build their brands' identities—particularly among niche segments of younger consumers—and slowly build distribution in small-scale and specialty retail outlets. Such efforts generated sufficient customer demand over time that some big retail chains became interested in carrying their products.[4]

Growth Stage

This stage starts with a sharp increase in sales. Important product improvements continue in the growth stage, but at a slower rate. Increased brand differentiation occurs primarily in product features. The product line expands to attract new segments, offering an array of prices and different product features. During the latter part of the growth stage, the firm—especially the dominant one—makes every effort to extend growth by adding new segments, lowering costs, improving product quality, adding new features, and trying to increase product usage among present users.

Marketing Mix Changes

Although the *product line* expands to attract new market segments, the quest for competitive advantage shifts to differentiation from other entrants in the product class. *Prices* tend to decline during the growth period, and price differences between brands decrease. The extent of the decline depends on cost-volume relationships, industry concentration, and the volatility of raw material costs. If growth is so strong it outpaces supply, there is little or no pressure on price; indeed, it may enable sellers to charge premium prices.

During this period, sellers of both industrial and consumer goods strive to build a channel or a direct sales system that provides maximum product availability and service at the lowest cost. If this can be accomplished, rivals are placed at a disadvantage, even to the extent of being excluded from some markets. This is particularly the case with some consumer goods for which the number of intermediaries in any one market is limited. A brand must attain some degree of distribution success in advance of the mature stage because channel members then tend to drop less successful brands.

Promotion costs (advertising and personal selling) become more concerned with building demand for a company's brand (selective demand) than demand for the product class or type (primary demand). Firms strive to build favorable attitudes toward their brand on the basis of its unique features. Communications are also used to cultivate new segments. Even though promotion costs remain high, they typically decline as a percentage of sales.

Shakeout Stage

The advent of this period is signaled by a drop in the overall growth rate and is typically marked by substantial price cuts. As weaker competitors exit the market, the stronger firms gain share. Thus, major changes in the industry's competitive structure occur. During shakeout, the firm must *rationalize* its product line by eliminating weaker items, emphasize creative promotional pricing, and strengthen its channel relationships. The personal computer industry has been mired in a global price war in recent years as it adjusted to slowing growth, and several firms have dropped out of the retail computer market. To a considerable extent, what happens during the shakeout is predetermined by how well the brand has been positioned in relation to its targeted segments, its distribution system, and its relative costs per unit.

Marketing Mix Changes

In addition to entering into more direct *price* competition, firms make every effort to maintain and enhance their *distribution* system. Channel intermediaries use this downturn in industry sales growth to reduce the number of products carried and, hence, their inventories. Weaker competitors often have to offer their intermediaries substantial inducements to continue stocking all or even part of their line. *Promotion costs* may increase, particularly for low-share firms, as companies attempt to maintain their distribution by offering customers buying incentives.

Mature Stage

When sales plateau, the product enters the mature stage, which typically lasts for some time. Most products now on the market are in the mature stage. Stability in terms of demand, technology, and competition characterizes maturity. Strong market leaders, because of lower per-unit costs and the lack of any need to expand their facilities, should enjoy strong profits and high positive cash flows. But there is always the possibility of changes in the marketplace, product, channels of distribution, production processes, and nature and scope of competition. The longer the mature stage lasts, the greater the possibility of change. If the firm does not respond successfully to a change but its competitors do, then a change in industry structure may occur.

Marketing Mix Changes

Because of technical maturity, the various brands in the marketplace become more similar; therefore, any significant breakthroughs by R&D or engineering that help to differentiate the product or reduce its cost can have a substantial payout. One option is to add value to the product that benefits the customer by improving the ease of use (voice-activated search with smartphones), by incorporating labor-saving features, or by selling systems rather than single products (e.g., by adding extended service contracts). Increasingly, *service* becomes a way of differentiating the offering. *Promotion* expenditures and *prices* tend to remain stable during the mature stage. But the nature of the former is apt to change;

media advertising for consumer goods declines and in-store promotions, including price deals, increase. The price premium attainable by the high-quality producer tends to erode. The effect of experience on costs and prices becomes smaller and smaller. Competition may force prices down, especially when the leading competitors hold similar shares. For consumer goods, distribution and in-store displays (shelf facings) become increasingly important, as does effective cost management.

Decline Stage

Eventually most products enter the decline stage, which may be gradual (canned vegetables/ hot cereals) or extremely fast (some prescription drugs). The sales pattern may be one of decline and then petrification as a small residual segment still clings to the use of the product (tooth powder versus toothpaste). Products enter this stage primarily because of technologically superior substitutes (computers over typewriters) or a shift in consumer tastes, values, and beliefs.

As sales decline, costs increase, and radical efforts are needed to reduce costs and the asset base. Even so, if exit barriers are low, many firms vacate the market, which increases the sales of remaining firms, thereby delaying their exit. Stronger firms may even prosper for a time. If the curve is a steep decline followed by a plateau, then some firms can adjust. If the firm is strong in some segments vacated by its competitors, then it may experience a sufficient increase in market share to compensate for loss of sales elsewhere.

Marketing Mix Changes

Marketing expenditures, especially those associated with *promotion,* usually decrease as a percentage of sales in the decline stage. *Prices* tend to remain stable if the rate of decline is slow, there are some enduring profitable segments and low exit barriers, customers are weak and fragmented, and there are few single-product competitors. Conversely, aggressive pricing is apt to occur when decline is fast and erratic, there are no strong unique segments, there are high exit barriers, a number of large single-product competitors are present, and customers have strong bargaining power. For consumer goods, marketing activity centers on distribution—persuading intermediaries to continue to stock the item even though they may not promote it. For industrial products, the problem may center around maintaining the interest of the salesforce in selling the item.

Strategic Implications of the Product Life Cycle

The product life-cycle model is a framework that signals the occurrence of opportunities and threats in the marketplace and the industry, thereby helping the business better anticipate change in the product's strategic market objective, its strategy, and its marketing program. As Exhibit 8.3 indicates, there is a strong relationship between the market and industry characteristics of each stage, the entry's market share objectives, and the level of investment, which, in turn, strongly affect cash flow and profit.

Introductory and Growth Stages

Because the introduction of a new product requires large investments, most firms sustain a rather sizable short-term loss. As the product moves into the growth stage, sales increase rapidly; hence, substantial investments continue. Profitability is depressed because facilities have to be built in advance to ensure supply. The firm with the largest share during this period should have the lowest per-unit costs due to scale and learning effects. If it chooses to decrease its real price proportionate to the decline in its costs, it dries up the investment incentives of would-be entrants and lower-share competitors. The innovating firm's share is likely to erode substantially during the growth stage. Nevertheless, it must still make large investments; for even though it is losing share, its sales are increasing. New entrants

EXHIBIT 8.3 **Relationship of Strategic Market Position Objective, Investment Levels, Profits, and Cash Flow to Individual Stages in the Product Life Cycle**

Stages in the Product Life Cycle				
Stage	**Strategic Market Objective**	**Investments**	**Profits**	**Cash Flow**
Introduction	For both innovators and followers, accelerate overall market growth and product acceptance through awareness, trial, and product availability	Moderate to high for R&D, capacity, working capital, and marketing (sales and advertising)	Highly negative	Highly negative
Growth	Increase competitive position	High to very high	High to moderate	Negative
Shakeout	Improve/solidify competitive position	Moderate	Low to moderate	Low to moderate
Mature	Maintain position	Low	High	Moderate

and low-share sellers are at a substantial disadvantage here. They must not only invest to accommodate market growth, but also to gain market share.

Mature and Declining Stages

As the product enters the mature stage, the larger-share sellers should be able to reap the benefits of their earlier investments. Given that the price is sufficient to keep the higher-cost sellers in business, that growth investments are no longer needed, and that most competitors may no longer be striving to gain share, the leader's profitability and positive cash flow can be substantial. But the leader needs to continue making investments to improve its product and to make its manufacturing, marketing, and physical logistics more efficient. The generalized product life cycle model portrays a profitability peak during the latter part of the growth stage. But one study of over 1,000 industrial businesses found that despite declining margins, overall profitability did not decline during maturity mainly because less money was spent on marketing and R&D.[5]

Limitations of the Product Life-Cycle Framework

The product life-cycle model's major weakness lies in its normative approach to prescribing strategies based on assumptions about the features or characteristics of each stage. It fails to take into account that the product life cycle is, in reality, driven by market forces expressing the evolution of consumer preferences (the market), technology (the product), and competition (the supply side).[6] In other words, the length of the life cycle and the market and competitive conditions at each stage can vary substantially across different product and service offerings. As we shall see, then, there's usually more than one viable strategy a marketing manager might pursue at each stage, and the best choice—as always—depends on the specific situation in the marketplace.

NEW MARKET ENTRIES—HOW NEW IS NEW?

A survey of the new product development practices of 700 U.S. corporations conducted by the consulting firm Booz, Allen & Hamilton found that the products introduced by those firms over a five-year period were not all equally "new." The study identified six categories of new products based on their degree of newness as perceived by both the company and the target customers. These categories are discussed as follows and diagrammed in Exhibit 8.4, which also indicates the percentage of new entries falling in each category

EXHIBIT 8.4   **Categories of New Products Defined According to Their Degree of Newness to the Company and Customers in the Target Market**

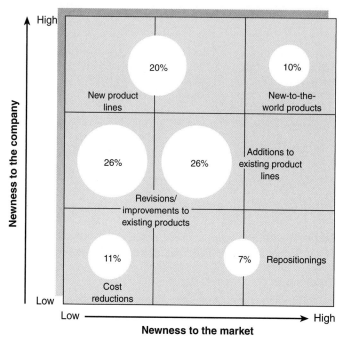

Source: New Products Management for the 1980s (New York: Booz, Allen & Hamilton, 1982). Reprinted by permission.

during the five-year study period. Notice that only 10 percent of all new product introductions fell into the new-to-the-world category.[7]

- *New-to-the-world products*—True innovations that are new to the firm and create an entirely new market (10 percent).

- *New product lines*—A product category that is new for the company introducing it, but not new to customers in the target market because of the existence of one or more competitive brands (20 percent).

- *Additions to existing product lines*—New items that supplement a firm's established product line. These items may be moderately new to both the firm and the customers in its established product-markets. They also may serve to expand the market segments appealed to by the line (26 percent).

- *Improvements in or revisions of existing products*—Items providing improved performance or greater perceived value brought out to replace existing products. These items may present moderately new marketing and production challenges to the firm, but unless they represent a technologically new generation of products, customers are likely to perceive them as similar to the products they replace (26 percent).

- *Repositionings*—Existing products that are targeted at new applications and new market segments (7 percent).

- *Cost reductions*—Product modifications providing similar performance at lower cost (11 percent).

A product's degree of newness—to the company, its target customers, or both—helps determine the amount of complexity and uncertainty involved in the engineering, operations, and marketing tasks necessary to make it a successful new entry. It also contributes to the amount of risk inherent in those tasks.

Introducing a product that is new to both the firm and target customers requires the greatest expenditure of effort and resources. It also involves the greatest amount of uncertainty and risk of failure because of the lack of information and experience with the technology and the target customers.

Products new to target customers but not new to the firm (such as line extensions or modifications aimed at new customer segments or repositionings of existing products) are often not very innovative in design or operations, but they may present a great deal of marketing uncertainty. The marketing challenge here—as with new-to-the-world products—is to build **primary demand,** making target customers aware of the product and convincing them to adopt it.[8] We investigate this marketing problem in this chapter.

Finally, products new to the company but not to the market (such as new product lines, line extensions, product modifications, and cost reductions) often present fewer challenges for R&D and product engineering. The company can study and learn from earlier designs or competitors' products. However, these products can present major challenges for process engineering, production scheduling, quality control, and inventory management. Once the company introduces such a product into the market, its primary marketing objective is to build selective demand and capture market share, convincing customers the new offering is better than existing competitive products. We discuss marketing programs a firm might use to accomplish these objectives later in Chapter 9.

OBJECTIVES OF NEW PRODUCT AND MARKET DEVELOPMENT

The primary objective of most new product and market development efforts is to secure future volume and profit growth. This objective has become even more crucial in recent years due to rapidly advancing technology and more intense global competition. A steady flow of new products and the development of new markets, including those in foreign countries, are essential for the continued growth of most firms.

However, individual development projects also may accomplish a variety of other strategic objectives. When asked what strategic role was served by their most successful recent new entry, the respondents in the Booz, Allen & Hamilton survey mentioned eight different strategic objectives. Exhibit 8.5 lists these objectives and the percentage of respondents that mentioned each one. The exhibit also indicates which objectives focused on external concerns (e.g., defending market share) and which were driven by a desire to improve or build upon the firm's internal strengths. Most respondents indicated their new entry helped accomplish more than one objective.

Exhibit 8.6 shows that different types of new entries are appropriate for achieving different strategic objectives. For example, if the objective is to establish a foothold in or preempt a new market segment, the firm must introduce a product that is new to that market, although it may not be entirely new to the company. On the other hand, if the objective is to improve cash flow by adding another cash generator, simple line extensions or product modifications—particularly those that reduce unit costs—may do the trick.

A business's objectives for its new entries influence the kind of entry strategy it should pursue and the marketing and other functional programs needed to implement that strategy. For instance, if a business is pursuing a prospector strategy and its objectives are to maintain a position as a product innovator and to establish footholds in a variety of new product-markets, it should attempt to be the pioneer in as many of those markets as possible. As we saw in Chapter 3, successful implementation of such a strategy requires the business to be competent in and devote substantial resources to R&D, product engineering, marketing, and marketing research.

On the other hand, if the business is concerned primarily with defending an already strong market share position in its industry, it may prefer to be a follower. Usually entering

EXHIBIT 8.5   Strategic Objectives Attained by Successful New Market Entries

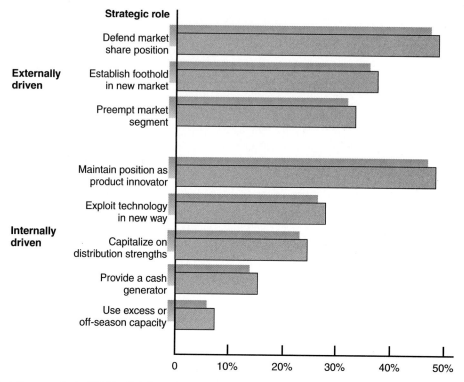

Source: New Products Management for the 1980s (New York: Booz, Allen & Hamilton, 1982), p. 11. Reprinted by permission.

EXHIBIT 8.6   Types of New Market Entries Appropriate for Different Strategic Objectives

Objective	New Entry
Maintain position as a product innovator	New-to-the-world products; improvements or revisions to existing products
Defend a current market-share position	Improvements or revisions to existing products; additions to existing product line; cost reductions
Establish a foothold in a future new market; preempt a market segment	New-to-the-world products; additions to existing product line; repositionings
Exploit technology in a new way	New-to-the-world products; new product line; additions to or revision of existing product line
Capitalize on distribution strengths	New-to-the-world products; new product line; additions to or revisions of existing product line
Provide a cash generator	Additions to or revisions of existing product line; repositionings; cost reductions
Use excess or off-season capacity	New-to-the-world product; new product line

new product-markets only after an innovator, a follower relies on superior quality, better customer service, or lower prices to offset the pioneer's early lead. This strategy usually requires fewer investments in R&D and product development, but marketing and sales still are critical in implementing it effectively. A more detailed comparison of these alternative new market entry strategies is the focus of the next section of this chapter.

MARKET ENTRY STRATEGIES: IS IT BETTER TO BE A PIONEER OR A FOLLOWER?

With products such as Word, Excel, and PowerPoint, Microsoft holds a leading share of most office application software categories. But in most of those categories, the firm was not the pioneer. Lotus 1-2-3 was the leading spreadsheet for many years, and WordPerfect and other programs led the word processing category. But as a follower, Microsoft developed improved product designs offering better performance, and it had superior financial resources to aggressively promote its products. Microsoft's Windows also held a commanding share of the operating systems market, a position the firm could leverage to convince personal computer manufacturers to bundle its applications software with their machines.

On the other hand, some of the software industry's pioneers have not fared so well in the marketplace. Lotus, for example, experienced financial difficulties and was ultimately acquired by IBM. Although we have stressed the competitive importance of growth via the introduction of new products, the important strategic question is whether it always makes sense to go first. Or do *both* pioneer and follower market entry strategies have some particular advantages under different conditions?

Pioneer Strategy

Conventional wisdom holds that although they take the greatest risks and probably experience more failures than their more conservative competitors, successful pioneers are handsomely rewarded. It is assumed competitive advantages inherent in being the first to enter a new product-market can be sustained through the growth stage and into the maturity stage of the product life cycle, resulting in a strong share position and substantial returns.

Some of the potential sources of competitive advantage available to pioneers are briefly summarized in Exhibit 8.7 and discussed as follows.[9]

1. *First choice of market segments and positions.* The pioneer has the opportunity to develop a product offering with attributes most important to the largest segment of customers or to promote the importance of attributes that favor its brand. Thus, the pioneer's brand can become the standard of reference customers use to evaluate other brands. This can make it more difficult for followers with me-too products to convince existing customers that their new brands are superior to the older and more familiar pioneer. If the pioneer has successfully tied its offering to the choice criteria of the largest group of customers, it also becomes more difficult for followers to differentiate

EXHIBIT 8.7   Potential Advantages of Pioneer and Follower Strategies

Pioneer	Follower
• First choice of market segments and positions; influence on customer choice criteria	• Ability to take advantage of pioneer's positioning mistakes
• Pioneer defines the rules of the game	• Ability to take advantage of pioneer's product mistakes
• Distribution advantages	• Ability to take advantage of pioneer's marketing mistakes
• Economies of scale and experience	• Ability to take advantage of latest technology
• High switching costs for early adopters	• Ability to take advantage of pioneer's limited resources
• Possibility of positive network effects	
• Possibility of preempting scare resources	

their offerings in ways that are attractive to the mass-market segment. They may have to target a smaller peripheral segment or niche instead.

2. *The pioneer defines the rules of the game.* The pioneer's actions on such variables as product quality, price, distribution, warranties, postsale service, and promotional appeals and budgets set standards that subsequent competitors must meet or beat. If the pioneer sets those standards high enough, it can raise the costs of entry and perhaps preempt some potential competitors.[10]

3. *Distribution advantages.* The pioneer has the most options in designing a distribution channel to bring the new product to market. This is particularly important for industrial goods where, if the pioneer exercises its options well and with dispatch, it should end up with a network of the best distributors. This can exclude later entrants from some markets. Distributors are often reluctant to take on second or third brands. This is especially true when the product is technically complex and the distributor must carry large inventories of the product and spare parts or invest in specialized training and service.

   For consumer package goods, it is more difficult to slow the entry of later competitors by preempting distribution alternatives. Nevertheless, the pioneer still has the advantage of attaining more retail outlets and shelf-facings at the outset of the growth stage. By quickly expanding its product line following an initial success, the pioneer can appropriate still more shelf space, thereby making the challenge faced by followers even more difficult. Since many retailers are reducing the number of brands they carry in a given product category to speed inventory turnover and reduce costs, it is becoming more difficult for followers with unfamiliar brands and small market shares to gain extensive distribution.[11]

4. *Economies of scale and experience.* Being first means the pioneer can gain accumulated volume and experience and thereby lower per unit costs at a faster rate than followers. This advantage is particularly pronounced when the product is technically sophisticated and involves high development costs or when its life cycle is likely to be short with sales increasing rapidly during the introduction and early growth stages.

   As we shall see later, the pioneer can deploy these cost advantages in a number of ways to protect its early lead against followers. One strategy is to lower price, which can discourage followers from entering the market because it raises the volume necessary for them to break even. Or the pioneer might invest its savings in additional marketing efforts to expand its penetration of the market, such as heavier advertising, a larger salesforce, or continuing product improvements or line extensions.

5. *High switching costs for early adopters.* Customers who are early to adopt a pioneer's new product may be reluctant to change suppliers when competitive products appear. This is particularly true for industrial goods where the costs of switching suppliers can be high. Compatible equipment and spare parts, investments in employee training, and the risks of lower product quality or customer service make it easier for the pioneer to retain its early customers over time.

   In some cases, however, switching costs can work against the pioneer and in favor of followers. A pioneer may have trouble converting customers to a new technology if they must bear high switching costs to abandon their old way of doing things. Pioneers in the development of music CDs, for instance, faced the formidable task of convincing potential buyers to abandon their substantial investments in turntables and LP record libraries and to start all over again with the new technology. Once the pioneers had begun to convince consumers that the superior convenience, sound quality, and durability of CDs justified those high switching costs, however, demand for CDs and CD players began to grow rapidly, and it was easier for followers to attract customers.

6. *Possibility of positive network effects.* The value of some kinds of goods and services to an individual customer increases as greater numbers of other people adopt the product and the network of users grows larger. Economists say that such products exhibit **network externalities** or **positive network effects.** Information and communications technologies, such as wireless phones, computer software, e-mail, and many social internet sites such as Facebook and Twitter, are particularly likely to benefit from network effects.[12] For instance, the value of eBay as an auction site increases as the number of potential buyers and sellers who visit and trade on the site increases. If the pioneer in such a product or service category can gain and maintain a substantial customer base before competing technologies or providers appear on the market, the positive network effects generated by that customer base will enhance the benefits of the pioneer's offering and make it more difficult for followers to match its perceived value. Recent research suggests that the positive impacts of such network effects on pioneer survival and economic success are enhanced when the new products involved are relatively radical and technologically advanced.[13]

On the other hand, for the digital new products and services most likely to benefit from positive network effects, some of the other potential first mover advantages may not be as relevant. For instance, because of the relatively modest fixed costs and low marginal costs of producing digitized information products such as software and music, pioneers are unlikely to benefit from substantial economies of scale.[14]

7. *Possibility of preempting scarce resources and suppliers.* The pioneer may be able to negotiate favorable deals with suppliers who are eager for new business or who do not appreciate the size of the opportunity for their raw materials or component parts. If later entrants subsequently find those materials and components in short supply, they may be constrained from expanding as fast as they might like or be forced to pay premium prices. For example, Apple was able to absorb more than half the entire production of Toshiba's innovative 1.8-inch hard disk, a crucial component of Apple's iPod digital music player. As a result, competitors had difficulty matching the small size and simplicity of the iPod for several years until Toshiba was able to expand production capacity and other producers—such as Hitachi—developed similar hard drives.[15]

Not All Pioneers Capitalize on Their Potential Advantages

There is some evidence to suggest that the preceding advantages can help pioneers gain and maintain a competitive edge in new markets. For instance, some research has found that surviving pioneers hold a significantly larger average market share when their industries reach maturity than firms that were either fast followers or late entrants in the product category.[16]

On the other hand, some pioneers fail. They either abandon the product category, go out of business, or get acquired before their industry matures. One study, which took these failed pioneers into account and averaged their performance together with that of the more successful survivors, found that pioneers overall did not perform as well over the long haul as followers.[17] However, a more recent study suggests that—in industrial goods industries, at least—pioneers have substantially better ten-years survival rates than followers.[18]

Of course, survival, volume, and market share are not the only dimensions on which success can be measured. Unfortunately, there is little evidence concerning the effect of the timing of a firm's entry into a new market on its ultimate profitability in that market or the value generated for shareholders.[19]

In view of the mixed research evidence, it seems reasonable to conclude that although a pioneer may have some *potential* competitive advantages, not all pioneers are successful at capitalizing on them. Some fail during the introductory or shakeout stages of their industries' life cycles. Those that survive may lack the resources to keep up with rapid growth or the competencies needed to maintain their early lead in the face of onslaughts by strong followers.[20]

Follower Strategy

In many cases, a firm becomes a follower by default. It is simply beaten to a new product-market by a quicker competitor. But even when a company has the capability of being the first mover, the preceding observations suggest there may be some advantages to letting other firms go first into a product-market.[21] Let the pioneer shoulder the initial risks while the followers observe their shortcomings and mistakes. Possible advantages of such a follower strategy are briefly summarized in Exhibit 8.7 and discussed as follows.

1. *Ability to take advantage of the pioneer's positioning mistakes.* If the pioneer misjudges the preferences and purchase criteria of the mass-market segment or attempts to satisfy two or more segments at once, it is vulnerable to the introduction of more precisely positioned products by a follower. By tailoring its offerings to each distinct segment, the follower(s) can successfully encircle the pioneer.

2. *Ability to take advantage of the pioneer's product mistakes.* If the pioneer's initial product has technical limitations or design flaws, the follower can benefit by overcoming these weaknesses. Even when the pioneering product is technically satisfactory, a follower may gain an advantage through product enhancements. For example, the iPhone's sleek design, innovative software, and functionality enabled Apple to capture a substantial share of the global mobile phone market from well-established competitors such as Nokia—the cellular phone pioneer—and other early entrants like Motorola, and Samsung.

3. *Ability to take advantage of the pioneer's marketing mistakes.* If the pioneer makes any marketing mistakes in introducing a new entry, it opens opportunities for later entrants. This observation is closely related to the first two points, yet goes beyond product positioning and design to the actual execution of the pioneer's marketing program. For example, the pioneer may fail to attain adequate distribution, spend too little on introductory advertising, or use ineffective promotional appeals to communicate the product's benefits. A follower can observe these mistakes, design a marketing program to overcome them, and successfully compete head-to-head with the pioneer.

    Marketing mistakes can leave a pioneer vulnerable to challenges from later entrants even in product categories with substantial positive network effects. For example, Microsoft's Windows operating system was not the first user-friendly system on the market. However, Microsoft promoted and priced Windows very aggressively, it formed alliances with original equipment manufacturers (OEMs) in the personal computer industry to encourage them to install Windows on their machines, and it engaged in extensive licensing and cooperative agreements with other software developers. All these actions helped Windows capture a commanding share of the operating systems market, which in turn generated tremendous positive network effects for Windows and made it difficult for alternative systems to compete (perhaps *too* difficult, from the U.S. Justice Department's and European Union antitrust officials' perspectives).

4. *Ability to take advantage of the latest technology.* In industries characterized by rapid technological advances, followers can possibly introduce products based on a superior, second-generation technology and thereby gain an advantage over the pioneer. The pioneer may have difficulty reacting quickly to such advances if it is heavily committed

to an earlier technology. Thus, Canon expects its new diagmatic imaging technology to give it an advantage in the medical imaging market that major competitors such as General Electric will have trouble matching.

5. *Ability to take advantage of pioneer's limited resources.* If the pioneer has limited resources for production facilities or marketing programs or fails to commit sufficient resources to its new entry, followers willing and able to outspend the pioneer experience few enduring constraints.

Determinants of Success for Pioneers and Followers

Our discussion suggests that a pioneering firm stands the best chance for long-term success in market-share leadership and profitability when (1) the new product-market is insulated from the entry of competitors, at least for awhile, by strong patent protection, proprietary technology, substantial investment requirements, or positive network effects or (2) the firm has sufficient size, resources, and competencies to take full advantage of its pioneering position and preserve it in the face of later competitive entries. Evidence suggests that organizational competencies, such as R&D and marketing skills, not only affect a firm's success as a pioneer, but also may influence the company's decision about whether or not to be a pioneer in the first place. Firms that perceive they lack the competencies necessary to sustain a first-mover advantage may be more likely to wait for another company to take the lead and to enter the market later.[22]

McDonald's is an example of a pioneer that has succeeded by aggressively building on the foundations of its early advantage. Although the firm started small as a single hamburger restaurant, it used the franchise system of distribution to rapidly expand the number of McDonald's outlets with a minimum cash investment. That expansion plus stringent quality and cost controls, relatively low prices made possible by experience-curve effects, heavy advertising expenditures, product line expansion aimed at specific market segments (such as Egg McMuffin for the breakfast crowd), and expanded hours to serve night-shift workers and early risers have all enabled the firm to maintain a commanding share of the fast-food industry.[23]

On the other hand, a follower will most likely succeed when there are few legal, technological, or financial barriers to inhibit entry and when it has sufficient resources or competencies to overwhelm the pioneer's early advantage. For example, given Procter & Gamble's well-established brand name and superior advertising and promotional resources, the company was able to quickly take the market share lead away from pioneer Minnetonka, Inc., in the plaque-fighting toothpaste market with a reformulated version of Crest.

A study conducted across a broad range of industries supports these observations.[24] The author's findings are briefly summarized in Exhibit 8.8 and discussed as follows. The author found that, regardless of the industry involved, pioneers able to maintain their preeminent position well into the market's growth stage had supported their early entry with one or more of the following marketing strategy elements:

- *Large entry scale*—Successful pioneers had sufficient capacity, or could expand quickly enough, to pursue a mass-market targeting strategy, usually on a national rather than a local or regional basis. Thus, they could expand their volume quickly and achieve the benefits of experience-curve effects before major competitors could confront them.

- *Broad product line*—Successful pioneers also quickly add line extensions or modifications to their initial product to tailor their offerings to specific market segments. This helps reduce their vulnerability to later entrants who might differentiate themselves by targeting one or more peripheral markets. This point gains further support from a study

EXHIBIT 8.8 Marketing Strategy Elements Pursued by Successful Pioneers, Fast Followers, and Late Entrants

These marketers . . .	are characterized by one or more of these strategy elements:
Successful pioneers	• Large entry scale • Broad product line • High product quality • Heavy promotional expenditures
Successful fast followers	• Larger entry scale than the pioneer • Leapfrogging the pioneer with superior: product technology product quality customer service
Successful late entrants	• Focus on peripheral target markets or niches

of over 2,000 manufacturing businesses that found that market pioneers have a higher probability of engaging in further product development than either fast followers or late entrants, but that they tend to emphasize product improvements and line extensions rather than radical innovations.[25]

• *High product quality*—Successful pioneers also offer a high-quality, well-designed product from the beginning, thus removing one potential differential advantage for later followers. Competent engineering, thorough product and market testing before commercialization, and good quality control during the production process are all important to the continued success of pioneers.

• *Heavy promotional expenditures*—Successful pioneers had marketing programs characterized by relatively high advertising and promotional expenditures as a percentage of sales. Initially the promotion helps to stimulate awareness and primary demand for the new product category, build volume, and reduce unit costs. Later, this promotion focuses on building selective demand for the pioneer's brand and reinforcing loyalty as new competitors enter.

The same study found that the most successful fast followers had the resources to enter the new market on a larger scale than the pioneer. Consequently, they could quickly reduce their unit costs, offer lower prices than incumbent competitors, and enjoy any positive network effects. Some fast followers achieved success, however, by leapfrogging earlier entrants. These followers won customers away from the pioneer by offering a product with more sophisticated technology, better quality, or superior service.[26] Indeed, a recent study of competitors in high-tech markets indicates that market share leadership in such markets tends to accrue to the firm with the highest quality product regardless of whether it was a pioneer or a follower, even when there are substantial network effects.[27]

Finally, some late entrants also achieved substantial profits by avoiding direct confrontations with more established competitors and by pursuing peripheral target markets. They often offer tailor-made products to smaller market niches and support them with high levels of service.[28]

Followers typically enter a market after it is in the growth phase of its life cycle, and they start with low market shares relative to the established pioneer. Consequently, our discussion in Chapter 9 of marketing strategies for low-share competitors in growth markets is germane to both fast followers and later entrants. Before focusing on strategies for followers, however, we first examine strategies that might be successfully employed by the first entrant in a new product-market.

STRATEGIC MARKETING PROGRAMS FOR PIONEERS

Strategic Issue

Success of a pioneering strategy depends on the nature of the demand and competitive situation the pioneer encounters in the market and on the pioneer's ability to design and support an effective marketing program.

The preceding discussion suggests that the ultimate success of a pioneering strategy depends on the nature of the demand and competitive situation the pioneer encounters in the market and on the pioneer's ability to design and support an effective marketing program. It also depends on how the pioneer defines *success*—in other words, the objectives it seeks to achieve. Thus, a pioneer might choose from one of three different types of marketing strategies: mass-market penetration, niche penetration, or skimming and early withdrawal. Exhibit 8.9 summarizes the primary objectives of each strategy and the circumstances favoring their use. Although specific conditions may favor a given strategy, they do not guarantee its success. Much still depends on how effectively a firm implements the strategy. Also, it is highly unlikely that all the listed conditions will exist simultaneously in any single product-market.

Mass-Market Penetration

The ultimate objective of a mass-market penetration strategy is to capture and maintain a commanding share of the total market for the new product. Thus, the critical marketing task is to convince as many potential customers as possible to adopt the pioneer's product quickly to drive down unit costs and build a large contingent of loyal customers before competitors enter the market.

Mass-market penetration tends to be most successful when entry barriers inhibit or delay the appearance of competitors, thus allowing the pioneer more time to build volume, lower costs, and create loyal customers, or when the pioneer has competencies or resources that most potential competitors cannot match. Relevant competencies include product engineering, promotional and channel management skills, and the financial and organizational resources necessary to expand capacity in advance of demand. In some cases, though, a smaller firm with limited resources can successfully employ a mass-market penetration strategy if the market has a protracted adoption process and slow initial growth. Slow growth can delay competitive entry because fewer competitors are attracted to a market with questionable future growth. This allows the pioneer more time to expand capacity.

Mass-market penetration is also an appropriate strategy when the product category is likely to experience positive network effects. Since the value of such products increases as the number of users grows, it makes sense for the pioneer to quickly capture and maintain as large a customer base as possible.

Niche Penetration

Even when a new product-market expands quickly, however, it still may be possible for a small firm with limited resources to be a successful pioneer. In such cases, though, the firm must define success in a more limited way. Instead of pursuing the objective of capturing and sustaining a leading share of the entire market, it may make more sense for such firms to focus their efforts on a single market segment. This kind of **niche penetration** strategy can help the smaller pioneer gain the biggest bang for its limited bucks and avoid direct confrontations with bigger competitors.

A niche penetration strategy is most appropriate when the new market is expected to grow quickly and there are a number of different benefit or applications segments to appeal to. It is particularly attractive when there are few barriers to the entry of major competitors and when the pioneer has only limited resources and competencies to defend any advantage it gains through early entry.

Some pioneers may intend to pursue a mass-market penetration strategy when introducing a new product or service, but they end up implementing a niche penetration strategy

EXHIBIT 8.9 **Marketing Objectives and Strategies for New Product Pioneers**

	Alternative Marketing Strategies		
Situational Variables	**Mass-Market Penetration**	**Niche Penetration**	**Skimming: Early Withdrawal**
Primary objective	• Maximize number of triers and adopters in *total market*. • Maintain leading share position in *total market*.	• Maximize number of triers and adopters in *target segment*. • Maintain leading share position in *target segment*.	• Recoup development and commercialization costs as soon as possible. • Withdraw from market when increasing competition puts pressure on margins.
Market characteristics	• Large potential demand. • Relatively homogeneous customer needs. • Customers likely to adopt product relatively quickly; short diffusion process.	• Large potential demand. • Fragmented market; many different applications and benefit segments. • Customers likely to adopt product relatively quickly; short adoption process.	• Limited potential demand. • Customers likely to adopt product relatively quickly; short adoption process. • Early adopters willing to pay high price; demand is price inelastic.
Product characteristics	• Product technology patentable or difficult to copy. • Substantial network effects; value increases with growth of installed customer base. • Components or materials difficult to obtain; limited sources of supply. • Complex production process; substantial development and/or investment required.	• Product technology offers little patent protection; easily copied or adapted. • Limited or no network effects. • Components or materials easy to obtain; many sources of supply. • Relatively simple production process; little development or additional investment required.	• Product technology offers little patent protection; easily copied or adapted. • Limited or no network effects. • Components or materials easy to obtain; many sources of supply. • Relatively simple production process; little development or additional investment required.
Competitor characteristics	• Few potential competitors. • Most potential competitors have limited resources and competencies; few sources of differential advantage.	• Many potential competitors. • Some potential competitors have substantial resources and competencies; possible sources of differential advantage.	• Many potential competitors. • Some potential competitors have substantial resources and competencies; possible sources of differential advantage.
Firm characteristics	• Strong product engineering skills; able to quickly develop product modifications and line extensions for multiple market segments. • Strong marketing skills and resources; ability to identify and develop marketing programs for multiple segments; ability to shift from stimulation of primary demand to stimulation of selective demand as competitors enter. • Sufficient financial and organizational resources to build capacity in advance of growth in demand.	• Limited product engineering skills and resources. • Limited marketing skills and resources. • Insufficient financial or organizational resources to build capacity in advance of growing demand.	• Strong basic R&D and new product development skills; a prospector with good capability for continued new product innovation. • Good sales and promotional skills; able to quickly build primary demand in target market; perhaps has limited marketing resources for long-term market maintenance. • Limited financial or organizational resources to commit to building capacity in advance of growth in demand.

instead. This is particularly likely when the new market grows faster or is more fragmented than the pioneer expects. Facing such a situation, a pioneer with limited resources may decide to concentrate on holding its leading position in one or a few segments, rather than spreading itself too thin developing unique line extensions and marketing programs for many different markets or going deep into debt to finance rapid expansion. Of course, when a small firm with limited resources is successful at capturing a substantial share of one or a few niche segments, it can become a very attractive candidate for acquisition by larger competitors. Note, for example, Facebook's purchase of Instagram and a number of other web-based startups in recent years. Unfortunately, such acquisitions don't always turn out well for either the acquiring firm nor for the sales and market-share growth of the acquired brand. One reason startup acquisitions are often disappointing is that large industry leaders don't have the institutional know-how or the appropriate organization structure and culture to take advantage of them. Large companies generally require large infrastructure, and that means layers of management processes, departments, and committees; not to mention potential differences in strategic goals, revenue targets, and the like.[29]

Skimming and Early Withdrawal

Even when a firm has the resources to sustain a leading position in a new product-market, it may choose not to. Competition is usually inevitable, and prices and margins tend to drop dramatically after followers enter the market. Therefore, some pioneers opt to pursue a **skimming** strategy while planning an early withdrawal from the market. This involves setting a high price and engaging in only limited advertising and promotion to maximize per-unit profits and recover the product's development costs as quickly as possible. At the same time, the firm may work to develop new applications for its technology or the next generation of more advanced technology. Then when competitors enter the market and margins fall, the firm is ready to cannibalize its own product with one based on new technology or to move into new segments of the market.

The 3M Company is a master of the skimming strategy. According to one 3M manager, "We hit fast, price high (full economic value of the product to the user), and get the heck out when the me-too products pour in." The new markets pioneered by the company are often smaller ones, and the firm may dominate them for only about five years or so. By then, it is ready to launch the next generation of new technology or to move the old technology into new applications. For instance, within two years of 3M's introduction of the first water-activated casting tape for setting broken bones, eight other firms had introduced similar products. But since the company's R&D people had been working on a replacement version all along, it was able to drop the old product and introduce a technically superior tape that was stronger, easier to use, and commanded a premium price.[30]

As Exhibit 8.9 indicates, either small or large firms can use strategies of skimming and early withdrawal. But it is critical that the company have good R&D and product development skills so it can produce a constant stream of new products or new applications to replace older ones as they attract heavy competition. Also, since a firm pursuing this kind of strategy plans to remain in a market only short term, it is most appropriate when there are few barriers to entry, the product is expected to diffuse rapidly, and the pioneer lacks the capacity or other resources necessary to defend a leading share position over the long haul.

Marketing Program Components for a Mass-Market Penetration Strategy

As mentioned, the crucial marketing task in a mass-market penetration strategy is to maximize the number of customers adopting the firm's new product as quickly as possible. This requires a marketing program focused on (1) *aggressively building product awareness and motivation to buy* among a broad cross-section of potential customers and (2) *making it as*

Strategic Issue

The crucial marketing task in a mass-market penetration strategy is to maximize the number of customers adopting the firm's new product as quickly as possible.

easy as possible for those customers to try the new product, on the assumption that they will try it, like it, develop loyalty, and make repeat purchases.

Exhibit 8.10 outlines a number of marketing activities that might help increase customers' awareness and willingness to buy or improve their ability to try the product. This is by no means an exhaustive list, nor do we mean to imply that a successful pioneer must necessarily engage in all of the listed activities. Marketing managers must develop programs combining activities that fit both the objectives of a mass-market penetration strategy and the specific market and potential competitive conditions the new product faces.

Increasing Customers' Awareness and Willingness to Buy

Obviously, heavy expenditures on advertising, introductory promotions such as sampling and couponing, and personal selling efforts all can increase awareness of a new product or service among potential customers. This is the critical first step in the adoption process for a new entry. The relative importance of these promotional tools varies, however, depending on the nature of the product and the number of potential customers. For instance, personal selling efforts are often the most critical component of the promotional mix for highly technical industrial products with a limited potential customer base, such as Canon's new wide-format bubble jet printer. Media advertising, internet ads and videos, PR campaigns, and sales promotion are usually more useful for building awareness and primary demand for a new consumer good among customers in the mass market. In either case, when designing a mass-market penetration marketing program, firms should broadly focus promotional efforts to expose and attract as many potential customers as possible before competitors show up.

Firms might also attempt to increase customers' willingness to buy their products by reducing the risk associated with buying something new. This can be done by letting customers try the product without obligation, as when car dealers allow potential customers to test-drive a new model or when software developers allow customers to download a trial version and use it free for 30 days. Liberal return policies and extended warranties can serve the same purpose.

Finally, a firm committed to mass-market penetration might also broaden its product offerings to increase its appeal to as many market segments as possible. This helps reduce its vulnerability to later entrants who could focus on specific market niches. Firms can accomplish such market expansion through the rapid introduction of line extensions, additional package sizes, or product modifications targeted at new applications and market segments.

Increasing Customers' Ability to Buy

For customers to adopt a new product and develop loyalty toward it, they must be aware of the item and be motivated to buy. But they also must have the wherewithal to purchase it. Thus, to capture as many customers in as short a time as possible, it usually makes sense for a firm pursuing mass-market penetration to keep prices low (penetration pricing) and perhaps offer liberal financing arrangements or easy credit terms during the introductory period.

Pioneers introducing new information or communications technologies tend to be particularly aggressive in pricing their offerings for two reasons. First, as we have seen, such products often can benefit from positive network effects if enough customers can be induced to adopt them quickly. Second, the variable costs of producing and distributing additional units of such products is usually very low, perhaps even approaching zero. For instance, the costs of developing a new software product are high, but once it is developed,

EXHIBIT 8.10   Components of Strategic Marketing Programs for Pioneers

Strategic Objectives and Tasks	Alternative Marketing Programs		
	Mass-Market Penetration	**Niche Penetration**	**Skimming: Early Withdrawal**
Increase customers' awareness and willingness to buy	• Heavy advertising to generate awareness among customers in mass market; broad use of mass and digital media.	• Heavy advertising directed at target segment to generate awareness; use selective media relevant to target.	• Limited advertising to generate awareness, particularly among least price-sensitive early adopters.
	• Extensive salesforce efforts to win new adopters; possible use of incentives to encourage new product sales.	• Extensive salesforce efforts focused on potential customers in target segment; possible use of incentives to encourage new product sales to target accounts.	• Extensive salesforce efforts, particularly focused on largest potential adopters; possible use of volume-based incentives to encourage new product sales.
	• Advertising and sales appeals stress generic benefits of new product type.	• Advertising and sales appeals stress generic benefits of new product type.	• Advertising and sales appeals stress generic benefits of new product type.
	• Extensive introductory sales promotions to induce trial (sampling, couponing, quantity discounts).	• Extensive introductory sales promotions to induce trial, but focused on target segment.	• Limited use, if any, of introductory sales promotions; if used, they should be volume-based quantity discounts.
	• Move relatively quickly to expand offerings (line extensions, multiple package sizes) to appeal to multiple segments.	• Additional product development limited to improvements or modifications to increase appeal to target segment.	• Little, if any, additional development within the product category.
	• Offer free trial, liberal return, or extended warranty policies to reduce customers' perceived risk of adopting the new product.	• Offer free trial, liberal return, or extended warranty policies to reduce target customers' perceived risk of adopting the new product.	• Offer free trial, liberal return, or extended warranty policies to reduce target customers' perceived risk of adopting the new product.
Increase customers' ability to buy	• Penetration pricing; or start with high price but bring out lower-priced versions in anticipation of competitive entries.	• Penetration pricing; or start with high price but bring out lower-priced versions in anticipation of competitive entries.	• Skimming pricing; attempt to maintain margins at level consistent with value of product to early adopters.
	• Extended credit terms to encourage initial purchases.	• Extended credit terms to encourage initial purchases.	• Extended credit terms to encourage initial purchases.
	• Heavy use of trade promotions aimed at gaining extensive distribution.	• Trade promotions aimed at gaining solid distribution among retailers or distributors pertinent for reaching target segment.	• Limited use of trade promotions; only as necessary to gain adequate distribution.
	• Offer engineering, installation, and training services to increase new product's compatibility with customers' current operations to reduce switching costs.	• Offer engineering, installation, and training services to increase new product's compatibility with customers' current operations to reduce switching costs.	• Offer limited engineering, installation, and training services as necessary to overcome customers' objections.

copies can be made and distributed over the internet for next to nothing. These two factors mean that it often makes sense for pioneers in such product categories to set their price very low to initial customers—perhaps even to give away trial copies—in hopes of quickly building a large installed base, capturing more value from later customers with higher prices, and maximizing the lifetime value of their customers by selling them upgrades and enhanced versions of the product in the future.[31]

Another factor that can inhibit customers' ability to buy is a lack of product availability. Thus, extensive personal selling and trade promotions aimed at gaining adequate distribution are usually a critical part of a mass-market penetration marketing program. Such efforts should take place before the start of promotional campaigns to ensure that the product is available as soon as customers are motivated to buy it.

A highly technical new product's incompatibility with other related products or systems currently used also can inhibit customers' purchases. It can result in high switching costs for a potential adopter. The pioneer might reduce those costs by designing the product to be as compatible as possible with related equipment. It also might offer engineering services to help make the new product more compatible with existing operations, provide free installation assistance, and conduct training programs for the customer's employees.

The preceding actions are suited not just to the marketing of products; most are essential elements of mass-market penetration strategies for new service, retail, and even e-commerce web sites as well. The marketing actions of an e-tailer such as Amazon.com, discussed in Exhibit 8.11, provide a textbook example of the elements of, as well as some the risks inherent in, a mass-market penetration strategy.

Additional Considerations When Pioneering Global Markets

Whether the product-market a pioneer is trying to penetrate is domestic or foreign, many of the marketing tasks appropriate for increasing potential customers' awareness, willingness, and ability to buy the new product or service are largely the same. Of course, some of the tactical aspects of the pioneer's strategic marketing program—such as specific product features, promotional appeals, or distribution channels—may have to be adjusted to fit different cultural, legal, or economic circumstances across national borders. For Bausch & Lomb to develop the Chinese market for contact lenses, for instance, it first had to develop an extensive training program for the country's opticians and build a network of retail outlets, actions that were unnecessary in more developed markets.

Unless the firm already has an economic presence in a country via the manufacture or marketing of other products or services, however, a potential global pioneer faces at least one additional question: What mode of entry is most appropriate? There are three basic mechanisms for entering a foreign market: exporting through agents (e.g., using local manufacturers' representatives or distributors), contractual agreements (e.g., licensing or franchise arrangements with local firms), and direct investment.

Exporting is the simplest way to enter a foreign market because it involves the least commitment and risk. It can be direct or indirect. The latter relies on the expertise of domestic international middlemen: **export merchants,** who buy the product and sell it overseas for their own account; **export agents,** who sell on a commission basis; and **cooperative organizations,** which export for several producers—especially those selling farm products. Direct exporting uses foreign-based distributors and agents or operating units (i.e., branches or subsidiaries) set up in the foreign country.

Contractual entry modes are nonequity arrangements that involve the transfer of technology or skills to an entity in a foreign country. In **licensing,** a firm offers the right to use its intangible assets (e.g., technology, know-how, patents, company name, trademarks) in exchange for royalties or some other form of payment. Licensing is less flexible and

EXHIBIT 8.11   *Amazon's Mass-Market Penetration Strategy*

Founded in 1994 by Jeff Bezos as the first online bookstore, Amazon.com (www.amazon.com) has employed many of the marketing tactics we have listed as possible components of a mass-market penetration strategy. In the early days, the firm spent heavily on various promotional tools to attract buyers and build a base of loyal customers. In the late 1990s, the firm was spending an average of more than $50 for each new customer it attracted. The money was spent on banner advertising and alliances with other sites and web portals, traditional media advertising, special consumer promotions, and an "associates" program through which sites that offer a link to Amazon get a cut of any sales they referred. As Amazon has built its customer base and increased public awareness, its acquisition costs per customer have declined substantially.

In the early years, many of Amazon's inventory storage and order fulfillment functions were outsourced, its fixed costs were low, and it had huge amounts of capital to play with. Consequently, it was able to attract customers from bricks-and-mortar bookstores by offering very low prices and a wide selection of titles.

To gain the loyalty of new customers it attracted, Amazon worked hard to constantly improve its customer service. It collected information from customers concerning their preferences, desires, and complaints and then launched a series of customer service innovations, such as one-click ordering and a popular best-seller list ranking sales on the site. More recently, it has invested hundreds of millions of dollars to build a network of company-owned distribution centers to better control order fulfillment and ensure quick and reliable delivery.

Finally, Amazon has greatly expanded its product lines over the years to include CDs, toys, electronics, tools, and even its own proprietory e-book reader, the Kindle. In part, this was accomplished by inviting independent suppliers to sell their wares through the Amazon website on a commission basis. This move was motivated by the company's desire to become a one-stop shopping venue and to increase average annual revenues per customer.

Amazon's mass-market strategy has been very successful so far. The firm made $631 million in net income on $48 billion of global sales in 2011. However, the future remains somewhat unsettled due to ongoing changes in the firm's competitive and technical environments. New challengers in internet retailing include both established bricks-and-mortar firms, such as Walmart and Tesco, and other web portals, such as Germany's Otto. To stay one step ahead of such rivals, Amazon has been investing heavily in new technology—particularly software development—to further personalize its website and improve the customer's shopping experience.

The company is also pursuing a new strategy aimed at leveraging those investments in technical infrastructure by selling internet services to other firms who want a sophisticated web presence but do not have the resources to develop it in-house. Amazon's web services include order processing, data storage, warehousing, and order fulfillment. Fulfillment by Amazon, for example, shipped more than 20 million items for clients in the last quarter of 2011 alone.

Some analysts and investors were concerned that Amazon would never be able to recoup the heavy investments inherent in its pursuit of the mass market. Consequently, the company's stock fell more than $50 a share and hit a low of $26 a few years ago. Recently, however, Amazon has emerged as the undisputed e-commerce champ. In spite of a technical glitch that shut down part of its server network for a couple of days, its web services are winning acceptance among both start-up firms and major corporations, and sales are booming in both the United States and much of Europe. As a result, the firm's stock price was flirting with $200 a share in the summer of 2012.

Sources: Fred Vogelstein, "Mighty Amazon," *Fortune*, May 26, 2003, pp. 60–74; Robert Hof, "Amazon's Costly Bells and Whistles," *BusinessWeek* Online, February 3, 2006; Peter Burrows, "Bezos: How Frugality Drives Innovation," *BusinessWeek*, April 28, 2008, pp. 64–66; and Amazon's 2011 annual report, archived at *www.amazon.com*.

provides less control than exporting. Further, if the contract is terminated, the licensor may have developed a competitor. It is appropriate, however, when the market is unstable or difficult to penetrate.

Franchising grants the right to use the company's name, trademarks, and technology. Also, the franchisee typically receives help in setting up the franchise. It is an especially attractive way for service firms to penetrate foreign markets at low cost and to couple their skills with local knowledge and entrepreneurial spirit. Host countries are reasonably receptive to this type of exporting since it involves local ownership. U.S. companies have largely pioneered franchising—especially such fast-food companies as

McDonald's, Pizza Hut, Burger King, and Kentucky Fried Chicken. In recent years, foreign franchisers have entered the United States—largely from Canada, Great Britain, and Japan—in a variety of fields, including food, shoe repair, leather furniture, and automobile dealerships.

Other contractual entry modes include **contract manufacturing,** which involves sourcing a product from a manufacturer located in a foreign country for sale there or elsewhere (e.g., auto parts, clothes, and furniture). Contract manufacturing is most attractive when the local market is too small to warrant making an investment, export entry is blocked, and a quality licensee is not available. A **turnkey construction contract** requires the contractor to have the project up and operating before releasing it to the owner. **Coproduction** involves a company's providing technical know-how and components in return for a share of the output that it must sell. **Countertrade** transactions include barter (direct exchange of goods—hams for aircraft), compensation packages (cash and local goods), counterpurchase (delayed sale of bartered goods to enable the local buyer to sell the goods), and a **buyback arrangement** in which the products being sold are used to produce other goods.

Overseas direct investment can be implemented in two ways: joint ventures or sole ownership. **Joint ventures** involve a joint ownership arrangement (e.g., one between a U.S. firm and one in the host country) to produce or market goods in a foreign country. Today, joint ventures are commonplace because they avoid quotas and import taxes and satisfy government demands to produce locally. They also have the advantage of sharing investment costs and gaining local marketing expertise. For example, Sir Richard Branson's Virgin Books Ltd. recently partnered with a group of Indian entrepreneurs, who were running a comic book distribution business, to form a new venture called Virgin Comics LLC. The joint venture plans to build India into a multibillion-dollar comic book market by combining Virgin's capital and production expertise with the Indians' distribution system to appeal to the country's 500 million teenagers with mythic tales and possibly animated movies and TV shows. There may also be opportunities to export some of the firm's offerings to the West via Virgin's established retail channels.[32]

A **sole ownership** investment entry strategy involves setting up a production facility in a foreign country. Direct investment usually allows the parent organization to retain total control of the overseas operation and avoids the problems of shared management and loss of flexibility. This strategy is particularly appropriate when the politics of the situation require a dedicated local facility. Firms using a direct investment strategy extensively include General Motors, Procter & Gamble, Nestlé, and General Electric.

Exporting has the advantage of lowering the financial risk for a pioneer entering an unfamiliar foreign market. Unfortunately, such arrangements also afford a pioneer relatively little control over the marketing and distribution of its product or service—activities that are critical for winning customer awareness and loyalty in a new market. At the other extreme, investing in a wholly owned subsidiary typically makes little sense until it becomes clear that the pioneering product will win customer acceptance. Consequently, intermediate modes of entry, such as licensing or forming a joint venture with a local firm in the host country, tend to be the preferred means of developing global markets for new products. Joint ventures are particularly appropriate in this regard because they avoid quotas and import restrictions or taxes and they allow a pioneer to share financial risks while gaining local marketing expertise.[33] Thus Bausch & Lomb established a joint venture with Beijing Optical as a basis for building contact lens factories in China and for gaining access to Chinese opticians. Consequently, the firm was able to develop and maintain a leading market share in the world's most heavily populated country with a modest investment of only about $20 million.

Strategic Issue

Licensing and joint ventures with local firms tend to be the preferred means of developing global markets for new products.

Marketing Program Components for a Niche Penetration Strategy

Because the objectives of a niche penetration strategy are similar to but more narrowly focused than those of a mass-market strategy, the marketing program elements are also likely to be similar under the two strategies. Obviously, however, the niche penetrator should keep its marketing efforts clearly focused on the target segment to gain as much impact as possible from its limited resources. This point is evident in the outline of program components in Exhibit 8.10. For example, although a niche strategy calls for the same advertising, sales promotion, personal selling, and trade promotion activities as a mass-market program, the former should use more selective media, call schedules, and channel designs to precisely direct those activities toward the target segment.

Luckily, the internet provides firms with a number of promotional tools that can reach specific segments at relatively low cost. For example, companies like Nantucket Nectars in the United States and Innocent Drinks in the United Kingdom have relied on quirky public relations efforts, internet ads, word of mouth on social networking sites like Facebook, and blogs to build their brands' identities among niche segments of younger consumers and build distribution specialty health-food retail outlets. Such efforts generated sufficient customer demand over time that some big retail chains began carrying their products.[34]

Marketing Program Components for a Skimming Strategy

As Exhibit 8.10 suggests, one major difference between a skimming strategy and a mass-market penetration strategy involves pricing policies. A relatively high price is appropriate for a skimming strategy to increase margins and revenues, even though some price-sensitive customers may be reluctant to adopt the product at that price.[35] This also suggests that introductory promotional programs might best focus on customer groups who are least sensitive to price and most likely to be early adopters of the new product. This can help hold down promotion costs and avoid wasting marketing efforts on less profitable market segments. Thus, in many consumer goods businesses, skimming strategies focus on relatively upscale customers, since they are often more likely to be early adopters and less sensitive to price.

Another critical element of a skimming strategy is the nature of the firm's continuing product development efforts. A pioneer that plans to leave a market when competitors enter should not devote much effort to expanding its product line through line extensions or multiple package sizes. Instead, it should concentrate on the next generation of technology or on identifying new application segments, in other words, preparing its avenue of escape from the market.

Now that we have examined some strategies a pioneer might follow in entering a new market, we are left with two important strategic questions. The pioneer is by definition the early share leader in the new market; hence, the first question is: What adjustments in strategy might be necessary for the pioneer to *maintain its leading share position* after competitors arrive on the scene? The second question is: What strategies might followers adopt *to take business away from the early leader and increase their relative share position* as the market grows? These two strategic issues are the focus of Chapter 9.

Marketing
Plan Exercise

Identify an appropriate marketing strategy consistent with the product's stage in its product life cycle and the market and competitive conditions it faces, drawing on Chapters 8, 9, and/or 10 as appropriate. Identify the strategies key competitors are using, and develop a rationale for the strategy you have chosen.

Discussion Questions

1. A few years ago, pet rocks were a fad and Nike Air Jordan basketball shoes were a fashion among younger customers in the United States. Graph the life-cycle curves of the two products on the same chart. How do the two curves differ from one another? What are the major marketing implications for each product?

2. Minnetonka, Inc., is a relatively small firm that pioneered the development of consumer health and beauty products, such as Softsoap and Check-Up plaque-fighting toothpaste. What potential advantages does being the pioneer in new product-markets provide a firm such as Minnetonka in an industry dominated by giants such as Procter & Gamble and Colgate-Palmolive?

3. Not all new market pioneers effectively take advantage of the potential benefits inherent in their early lead. What does the research evidence suggest that Minnetonka should do relevant to major elements of its marketing strategy to gain and maintain a leading share position in the new markets it enters?

4. Under what conditions do pioneer and follower strategies each have the greatest probability of long-term success?

Self-diagnostic questions to test your ability to apply the analytical tools and concepts in this chapter to marketing decision making may be found at this book's website at **www.mhhe.com/walker8e.**

Endnotes

1. This opening case example is based on information found in "Hard to Copy," *The Economist,* November 2, 2002, pp. 63–64; Clay Chandler, "Canon's Big Gun," *Fortune,* February 6, 2006, pp. 92–98; and Canon's 2012 Annual Report available at *www.canon.com.*

2. These results are reported in Myron Magnet, "Let's Go for Growth," *Fortune,* March 7, 1994, pp. 60–72.

3. For an interesting discussion of fads versus trends, see Martin G. Letscher, "How to Tell Fads from Trends," *American Demographics,* December 1994, p. 38.

4. For additional examples, see Dan Macsai, "Marketing to Milennials," *Businessweek Online/ SmallBiz,* August 22, 2008.

5. Hans B. Thorelli and Stephen C. Burnett, "The Nature of Product Life-Cycles for Industrial Goods Businesses," *Journal of Marketing* 45, Fall 1981, p. 108.

6. Frederick E. Webster, Jr., *Industrial Marketing Strategy* (New York: John Wiley & Sons, 1991), p. 128.

7. *New Products Management for the 1980s* (New York: Booz, Allen & Hamilton, 1982). More recent studies, though focusing on smaller samples of new products, suggest that the relative proportions of new-to-the-world versus less innovative product introductions have not changed substantially over the years. For example, see Eric M. Olson, Orville C. Walker Jr., and Robert W. Ruekert, "Organizing for Effective New Product Development: The Moderating Role of Product Innovativeness," *Journal of Marketing* 59 (January 1995), pp. 48–62.

8. Katrijn Gielens and Jan-Benedict E. M. Steenkamp, "Drivers of Consumer Acceptance of New Packaged Goods: An Investigation Across Products and Countries," *International Journal of Research in Marketing* 24 (June 2007), pp. 97–111.

9. For a more extensive review of the potential competitive advantages of being a first mover and the controllable and uncontrollable forces that influence a firm's ability to capitalize on those potential advantages, see Roger A. Kerin, P. Rajan Varadarajan, and Robert A. Peterson, "First-Mover Advantage: A Synthesis, Conceptual Framework, and Research Propositions," *Journal of Marketing* 56 (October 1992), pp. 33–52; and David M. Szymanski, Lisa M. Troy, and Sundar J. Bharadwaj, "Order-of-Entry and Business Performance: An Empirical Synthesis and Reexamination," *Journal of Marketing* 59 (October 1995), pp. 17–33.

10. Thomas S. Gruca and D. Sudharshan, "A Framework for Entry Deterrence Strategy: The Competitive Environment, Choices, and Consequences," *Journal of Marketing* 59 (July 1995), pp. 44–55.

11. Robert Berner, "There Goes the Rainbow Nut Crunch," *BusinessWeek,* July 19, 2004, p. 38; and Pierre Chandon, J. Wesley Hutchinson, Eric T. Bradlow, and Scott H. Young, "Does In-Store Marketing Work? Effects of the Number and Position of Shelf Facings on Brand Attention and Evaluation at the Point of Purchase," *Journal of Marketing* 73 (November 2009), pp. 1–17.

12. Carl Shapiro and Hal R. Varian, *Information Rules* (Boston: Harvard Business School Press, 1999), chap. 7.

13. Raji Srinivasan, Gary L. Lilien, and Arvind Rangaswamy, "First In, First Out? The Effects of Network Externalities on Pioneer Survival," *Journal of Marketing* 68 (January 2004), pp. 41–58. Also see Qi Wang, Yubo Chen, and Jinhong Xie, "Survival in Markets with Network Effects: Product Compatibility and Order-of-Entity Effects," *Journal of Marketing* 74 (July 2010), pp. 1–14.

14. Rajan Varadarajan, Manjit S. Yadav, and Venkatesh Shankar, "First-Mover Advantage on the internet: Real or Virtual?" *MSI Report # 05-100* (Cambridge, MA: The Marketing Science Institute, 2005).

15. Rob Walker, "The Guts of a New Machine," *The New York Times Magazine,* November 30, 2003, pp. 78–84.

16. For example, see William T. Robinson, "Market Pioneering and Sustainable Market Share Advantages in Industrial Goods Manufacturing Industries," working paper, Purdue University, 1984; and Robert D. Buzzell and Bradley T. Gale, *The PIMS Principles: Linking Strategy to Performance* (New York: Free Press, 1987), p. 183.

17. Peter N. Golder and Gerard J. Tellis, "Pioneer Advantage: Marketing Logic or Marketing Legend," *Journal of Marketing Research* 30 (May 1993), pp. 158–70.

18. William T. Robinson and Sungwook Min, "Is the First to Market the First to Fail? Empirical Evidence for Industrial Goods Businesses," *Journal of Marketing Research* 39 (February 2002), pp. 120–28.

19. Marvin B. Lieberman and David B. Montgomery, "First-Mover Advantages," *Strategic Management Journal* 9 (1988), pp. 41–59; and Michael J. Moore, William Boulding, and Ronald C. Goodstein, "Pioneering and Market Share: Is Entry Time Endogenous and Does It Matter?" *Journal of Marketing* 28 (February 1991), pp. 97–104.

20. Szymanski, Troy, and Bharadwaj, "Order-of-Entry and Business Performance."

21. Venkatesh Shankar, Gregory S. Carpenter, and Lakshman Krishnamukthi, "Late Mover Advantages: How Innovative Late Entrants Outsell Pioneers," *Journal of Marketing Research* 35 (February 1998), pp. 54–70.

22. Moore, Boulding, and Goodstein, "Pioneering and Market Share."

23. Michael Arndt, "McDonald's 24/7," *BusinessWeek,* February 5, 2007, pp. 64–72; and Beth Kowitt, "Why McDonald's Wins in Any Economy," *www.managment.fortune.cnn.com,* August 23, 2011.

24. Mary L. Coyle, "Competition in Developing Markets: The Impact of Order of Entry," unpublished doctoral dissertation, University of Toronto, 1986. Also see Kerin, Varadarajan, and Peterson, "First-Mover Advantage."

25. William T. Robinson and Jeongwen Chiang, "Product Development Strategies for Established Market Pioneers, Early Followers, and Late Entrants," *Strategic Management Journal* 23 (September 2002), pp. 855–66.

26. For a more detailed discussion of when it makes sense for a follower to invest in R&D in an attempt to leapfrog an established pioneer, see Elie Ofek and Ozge Turut, "To Innovate or Imitate? Entry Strategy and the Role of Market Research," *Journal of Marketing Research* 45 (October 2008), pp. 575–92.

27. Gerard J. Tellis, Eden Yin, and Rakesh Hiraj, "Does Quality Win? Network Effects Versus Quality in High-Tech Markets," *Journal of Marketing Research* 46 (April 2009), pp. 135–49.

28. Venkatesh Shankar, Gregory S. Carpenter, and Lakshman Krishnamukthi, "Late Mover Advantages: How Innovative Late Entrants Outsell Pioneers."

29. Mathew Ingram, "Why Most Startup Acquisitions Fail—and Always Will," *www.businessweek.com/technology,* February 23, 2011.

30. Michael Arndt, "3M's Rising Star," *BusinessWeek,* April 12, 2004, pp. 62–74; and Brian Hindo, "At 3M, a Struggle Between Efficiency and Creativity," *BusinessWeek–Indepth,* June 2007, pp. in8–in14.

31. Shapiro and Varian, *Information Rules,* chap. 2.

32. Steve Hamm, "Speed Demons," *BusinessWeek,* March 27, 2006, pp. 68–74.

33. Franklin R. Root, *Entry Strategy for International Markets* (Lexington, MA: D. C. Heath, 1987). Also see Jeremy Main, "Making Global Alliances Work," *Fortune,* December 17, 1990, pp. 121–26.

34. For additional examples, see Dan Macsai, "Marketing to Milennials," *www.businessweek.com/smallbiz,* August 22, 2008.

35. This assumes that demand is relatively price inelastic. In markets where price elasticity is high, a skimming price strategy may lead to lower total revenues due to its dampening effect on total demand.

Chapter Nine

Strategies for Growth Markets

The Global Battle for Jocks' Soles[1]

Nike athletic shoes began life in 1964—albeit under a different name—as a specialty product targeted at long-distance runners, a very narrow niche of the athletic footwear market. Phil Knight, a former distance runner at the University of Oregon, and his former coach Bill Bowerman believed that distance runners needed better shoes. With his wife's waffle iron and some latex, Bowerman developed the waffle outsole that would revolutionize the running shoe.

The company struggled for years to strengthen its foothold in an industry dominated by much larger global competitors such as Adidas. But in 1972 Nike finally gained the sporting world's attention when four of the top seven finishers in the Olympic marathon wore the firm's shoes. By 1974, Nike was America's best-selling brand of training shoe, and the Nike brand was on the way to stardom.

Nike's Drive for Share Leadership

Having become number one in training shoes, Nike set its sights on achieving share leadership in the entire industry. The company invested heavily in new product R&D and design efforts to expand its product line with offerings tailored to the needs and preferences of participants in a wide variety of other sports. It held down costs by outsourcing production of the new lines to a number of off-shore manufacturers. However, the firm maintained tight control over and was much less frugal with its marketing efforts. Nike spent heavily on endorsement deals with sport celebrities such as Michael Jordan and on a series of stylish but edgy mass-media ad campaigns to capture attention and build a strong brand image in its new target segments. It also constructed an extensive distribution network consisting largely of independent mass retailers and specialty chains such as Footlocker.

Over the years, Nike's aggressive competitive strategy has paid off. It is now the world's leading sportswear company in terms of sales volume. The firm generated $20.8 billion in revenue in the 2011 fiscal year, and more than half of those sales were outside North America.

The Attack of the Global Competitors

In recent years, however, Nike's overall market share has slipped a bit, both in the U.S. market and worldwide. This is because some of Nike's global competitors—such as Adidas, Puma, New Balance, K-Swiss, and Vans—have challenged it in a variety of specialized market segments and niche markets. Instead of copying Nike's emphasis on designing high-tech shoes to enhance performance in specific sports, they usually have appealed to different lifestyle segments by focusing on different product attributes and benefits.

For instance, shoes offered by Puma, Sketchers, and K-Swiss appeal to younger customers by emphasizing fashion, "coolness," and limited availability. On the other hand, New Balance targets older customers, emphasizes comfort and conservative design, and touts that it is "Endorsed by No One."

A few larger competitors, such as Adidas, have had some success going head-to-head with Nike in selected sport segments. Headquartered in Herzogenaurach, Germany, Adidas has long held a leading share of the world soccer market, and the firm has engaged in some aggressive marketing actions in recent years to further strengthen its position, such as sponsoring the global TV and web broadcasts of the 2010 World Cup.

One of the more unusual—and successful—challenges to Nike's dominance has been in the niche skateboarder segment from Vans, Inc., a tiny California start-up. Vans pioneered thick-soled, slip-on sneakers able to absorb the shock of a five-foot leap on wheels. It then nurtured a rebel, extreme-sports image with an offbeat marketing program that focused on sponsorships, events, and other "experience" activities that fit the skateboard culture.

Another recent challenge to Nike's dominance of the U.S. market was the introduction of a stylish but very low-priced basketball shoe, the Starbury One, priced at $14.98 (compared to Nike's Zoom LeBron IV priced at $150.00). Made and sold by the discount clothing chain Steve & Barry's, the sneaker was endorsed by New York Knicks guard Stephon Marbury. His endorsement helped to overcome the low-quality image typically associated with low-priced footwear and helped sell an estimated 1 million pairs in its first six months on the market.

Nike's Response

Nike managers believed it was necessary to meet the challenges of competitors pursuing lifestyle and price-sensitive market segments, but they did not want to tarnish the prestige image of the Nike brand nor cannibalize its high-margin sales. Consequently, the company launched a new product line named Tailwind aimed at fashion- and value-conscious women. The new line's prices ranged from $19.99 to $34.99 and it was distributed largely through the Payless discount retail chain. Unfortunately, Nike did not provide sufficient advertising and promotional support to build demand for the new line, sales were disappointing, and the line was eventually abandoned.

The company has been more successful acquiring and expanding other brands aimed at various life-style segments. For example, Nike's Converse brand offers more traditional but very fashionable sneakers at moderate prices, and it's Umbro unit offers sportswear targeted at international football (soccer) enthusiasts around the world.

Nike is also attempting to raise its profile as well as its revenue and market share in emerging markets like Brazil and China. Since football is by far the most popular sport in those countries, the company is expanding and heavily promoting its football apparel, shoe, and equipment lines. In 2010 about 25 percent of Nike's sales—$5 billion—were in developing countries, and the company plans to increase revenues in those market by another $3–$3.5 billion by the end of 2015.

A final part of Nike's strategy is to defend and strengthen its leading market share and strong profit margins in North America and other developed countries. Cutting-edge design continues to play a major role in this effort. For instance, celebrities like rapper Kanye West have been invited to design limited-edition shoes (the Nike Air Yeezy II sneakers West designed carry a price tag of $245). The firm also relies on new technology to differentiate its products from the competition. For example, it makes a line of sneakers, called Nike+ with built-in sensors that can communicate with a runner's iPod to track calories, consumption, and the like. And NikeiD, a service on the company's website that allows buyers to design their own customized shoes, generated more than $100 million in sales its first year. Technology is also transforming the firm's promotional programs. As we shall see later in this chapter, Nike is one of the pioneers at utilizing social networking as a promotional tool.

STRATEGIC CHALLENGES ADDRESSED IN CHAPTER 9

Although Nike was clearly not the pioneer of the athletic shoe industry, the firm's technical innovations, stylish designs, and savvy market segmentation strategy spurred a sustained period of market growth. Both conventional wisdom and the various portfolio models suggest there are advantages to be gained from a strategy of investing heavily to build and sustain a commanding share of a growing market, a strategy similar to Nike's.

But a market is neither inherently attractive nor unattractive simply because it promises rapid future growth. Not all competitors have the resources and capabilities necessary to dominate an entire market, as Vans and Steve & Barry's—with their limited marketing budgets—seem well aware. Consequently, managers must consider how customer desires and the competitive situation are likely to evolve as a market grows and determine whether their firms can exploit market growth to establish a sustainable advantage. Therefore, the next section of this chapter examines both the opportunities and competitive risks often found in growing product-markets.

The primary objective of the early share leader, usually the market pioneer, in a growth market is **share maintenance.** From a marketing perspective, the firm must accomplish two important tasks: (1) retain repeat or replacement business from its existing customers and (2) continue to capture the major portion of sales to the growing number of new customers entering the market for the first time. The leader might use any of several marketing strategies to accomplish these objectives. It might try to build on its early scale and experience advantages to achieve low-cost production and reduce its prices. Alternatively, the leader might focus on rapid product improvements, expand its product line to appeal to newly emerging segments, or increase its marketing and sales efforts, all of which Nike employed in building global leadership in the athletic footwear market.

The second section of this chapter explores marketing strategies—both defensive and offensive—that leaders might use to maintain a dominant market share in the face of continuing growth and increasing competition.

A challenger's strategic objective in a growth market is usually to build its share by expanding its sales faster than the overall market growth rate. Firms do this by stealing existing customers away from the leader or other competitors, capturing a larger share of new customers than the market leader, or both. Once again, challengers might use a number of strategies to accomplish these objectives. These include developing a superior product technology; differentiating through rapid product innovations, line extensions, or customer service; offering lower prices; or focusing on market niches where the leader is not well established, as Vans did in the skateboarding segment. The third section details these and other **share-growth** strategies that market challengers use under different conditions.

Strategic Issue

The growth stage is often short, and rapid technological change and market fragmentation are making it even shorter in many industries.

The success of a firm's strategy during the growth stage is a critical determinant of its ability to reap profits, or even survive, as a product-market moves toward maturity. Unfortunately, the growth stage is often short; one recent study of 30 product categories found that the growth stage lasted just a little over eight years.[2] Increasingly, rapid technological change and market fragmentation may be causing it to become even shorter in many industries.[3] The brief duration of the growth stage concerns many firms—particularly late entrants or those who fail to acquire a substantial market share—because as growth slows during the transition to maturity, there is often a shakeout of marginal competitors. Thus, when choosing marketing strategies for competing in a growing product-market, managers should keep one eye on building a competitive advantage that the business can sustain as growth slows and the market matures.

If you are working on the Marketing Plan Exercise and if your plan involves a product or service that is in the growth stage of its life cycle, you will be asked to detail your strategy for either maintaining your leading market share position or for challenging the share leader. As usual, you will need to justify that strategy in terms of your business's competencies and resources, potential customer characteristics, segments, and choice criteria. An analysis of current and potential competitors, their respective market shares, their relative strengths and weaknesses, and their current or likely competitive strategies will be particularly important.

OPPORTUNITIES AND RISKS IN GROWTH MARKETS⁴

Why are followers attracted to rapidly growing markets? Conventional wisdom suggests such markets present attractive opportunities for future profits because:

- It is easier to gain share when a market is growing.
- Share gains are worth more in a growth market than in a mature market.
- Price competition is likely to be less intense.
- Early participation in a growth market is necessary to make sure that the firm keeps pace with the technology.

Although generally valid, each of these premises may be seriously misleading for a particular business in a specific situation. Many followers attracted to a market by its rapid growth rate are likely to be shaken out later when growth slows because either the preceding premises did not hold or they could not exploit growth advantages sufficiently to build a sustainable competitive position. By understanding the limitations of the assumptions about growth markets and the conditions under which they are most likely to hold, a manager can make better decisions about entering a market and the kind of marketing strategy likely to be most effective in doing so.

Gaining Share Is Easier

The premise that it is easier for a business to increase its share in a growing market is based on two arguments. First, there may be many potential new users who have no established brand loyalties or supplier commitments and who may have different needs or preferences than earlier adopters. Thus, there may be gaps or undeveloped segments in the market. It is easier for a new competitor to attract those potential new users than to convert customers in a mature market. Second, established competitors are less likely to react aggressively to market-share erosion as long as their sales continue to grow at a satisfactory rate.

There is some truth to the first argument. It usually is easier for a new entrant to attract first-time users than to take business away from entrenched competitors. To take full advantage of the situation, however, the new entrant must be able to develop a product offering that new customers perceive as more attractive than other alternatives, and it must have the marketing resources and competence to effectively persuade them of that fact. This can be difficult, especially when the pioneer has had months or years to influence potential customers' decision criteria and preferences.⁵

The notion that established competitors are less likely to react to share losses so long as their revenues are growing at an acceptable rate is more tenuous. It overlooks the fact that those competitors may have higher expectations for increased revenues when the market itself is growing. Capital investments and annual operating budgets are usually tied to those sales expectations; therefore, competitors are likely to react aggressively when sales fall below expected levels, whether or not their absolute volumes continue to grow. This is particularly true given that increased competition will likely erode the leader's relative market share even though its volume may continue to increase. As illustrated by the hypothetical example in Exhibit 9.1, the leader's market share might drop from a high of 100 percent at the beginning of the growth stage to 50 percent by the maturity stage, even though the firm's absolute volume shows steady growth.

Industry leaders often react forcefully when their sales growth falls below industry levels or when the industry's growth rate slows. For example, when growth in the personal computer market slumped in 2000 due to the dot-com crash and other factors, Dell Computer did not adjust its aggressive sales growth objective. Instead, it launched a brutal price war aimed at taking more business away from competitors in order to achieve its goal.

EXHIBIT 9.1   **Market Shares of the Leader and Followers over the Life Cycle of a Hypothetical Market**

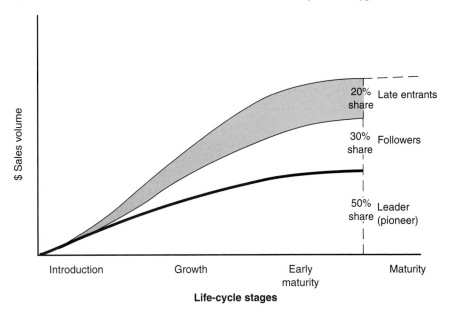

Source: From *Analysis for Strategic Market Decisions*, 1st edition, by G. S. Day, 1986. Reprinted by permission of South-Western, a division of Thomson Learning: www.thomsonrights.com. Fax: 800-730-2215.

Because Dell's focus on direct selling over the internet, its build-to-order manufacturing system, and its tightly integrated supply chain made it the undisputed low-cost producer in the industry, Dell was able to slash gross margins from 21.3 percent in mid-2000 to 17.5 percent in mid-2001 and still make money. As a result, Dell's leading share of the global PC market increased from 10 percent to 13 percent in 2001, rose another three points in 2002, and continued to grow until shortcomings in new-product development and customer service and support opened the door for competitors such as Hewlett-Packard, Lenovo, and Acer to challenge their lead.[6]

Share Gains Are Worth More

The premise that share gains are more valuable when the market is growing stems from the expectation that the earnings produced by each share point continue to expand as the market expands. The implicit assumption in this argument, of course, is that the business can hold its relative share as the market grows. The validity of such an assumption depends on a number of factors, including the following:

- *The existence of positive network effects.* As we saw in the previous chapter, pioneers in new product-markets enjoy several potential competitive advantages that they can—but don't always manage to—leverage as the market grows. For information-based products, such as computer software or internet auction sites, one of the most important such advantages is the existence of positive network effects, the tendency for the product to become more valuable to users as the number of adopters grows. Such network effects increase the likelihood that an early share leader can sustain, and even increase, its relative share as the market grows.[7] As Microsoft was able to license its Windows operating system to a growing number of computer manufacturers, for example, software developers created more and more applications to run on Windows, which made Windows even more attractive to later computer buyers and helped Microsoft expand its already commanding market share.

- *Future changes in technology or other key success factors.* On the other hand, if the rules of the game change, the competencies a firm relied on to capture share may no longer be adequate to maintain that share. For instance, Sony was the pioneer and early share leader in the videocassette recorder industry with its Betamax technology. But Matsushita's longer-playing and lower-priced VHS format equipment ultimately proved much more popular with consumers, captured a commanding portion of the market, and dethroned Sony as industry leader. Then along came digital recording, which made every manufacturer's videotape equipment obsolete.

- *Future competitive structure of the industry.* The number of firms that ultimately decide to compete for a share of the market may turn out to be larger than the early entrants anticipate, particularly if there are few barriers to entry. The sheer weight of numbers can make it difficult for any single competitor to maintain a substantial relative share of the total market.

- *Future fragmentation of the market.* As the market expands, it may fragment into numerous small segments, particularly if potential customers have relatively heterogeneous functional, distribution, or service needs. When such fragmentation occurs, the market in which a given competitor competes may shrink as segments splinter away.

In addition to these possible changes in future market conditions, a firm's ability to hold its early gains in market share also depends on how it obtained them. If a firm captures share through short-term promotions or price cuts that competitors can easily match and that may tarnish its image among customers, its gains may be short-lived.

Price Competition Is Likely to Be Less Intense

In some rapidly growing markets, demand exceeds supply. The market exerts little pressure on prices initially; the excess demand may even support a price premium. Thus, early entry provides a good opportunity for a firm to recover its initial product development and commercialization investment relatively quickly. New customers also may be willing to pay a premium for technical service as they learn how to make full use of the new product. In contrast, as the market matures and customers gain more experience, the premium a firm can charge without losing market share slowly shrinks; it eventually may disappear entirely.[8]

However, this scenario does not hold true in every developing product-market. If there are few barriers to entry or if the adoption process is protracted and new customers enter the market slowly, demand may not exceed supply—at least not for very long. Also, the pioneer, or one of the earliest followers, might adopt a penetration strategy and set its initial prices relatively low to move quickly down the experience curve and discourage other potential competitors from entering the market.

Early Entry Is Necessary to Maintain Technical Expertise

In high-tech industries, early involvement in new product categories may be critical for staying abreast of technology. The early experience gained in developing the first generation of products and in helping customers apply the new technology can put the firm in a strong position for developing the next generation of superior products. Later entrants, lacking such customer contact and production and R&D experience, are likely to be at a disadvantage.

There is substantial wisdom in these arguments. Sometimes, however, an early commitment to a specific technology can turn out to be a liability. This is particularly true when multiple unrelated technologies might serve a market or when a newly emerging technology might replace the current one. Once a firm is committed to one technology, adopting a new one can be difficult. Management is often reluctant to abandon a technology in which

---

EXHIBIT 9.2   *Slowness in Adopting New Technologies Costs Stent Makers Market Share and Profits*

In 1994, Johnson & Johnson introduced the first stent to be approved for cardiac patients in the United States. A stent is a cylinder of flexible wire mesh that looks a bit like a spring for a ballpoint pen. This metal device is designed to expand when inserted into a clogged artery, propping open the vessel so that blood can flow through unimpeded, thereby extending the effects of balloon angioplasty and greatly reducing the need for heart bypass surgery.

The stent was an immediate hit with cardiologists, and as the pioneer, J&J captured a commanding share of a huge and rapidly growing market, a market that reached $5.3 billion in global sales by 2006. The firm made only one misstep. It was so focused on keeping up with burgeoning demand that, as one executive admits, "we failed to develop a new generation of stents."

In October 1997, Guidant Inc. introduced a technically more advanced stent. Their device was designed to be much more flexible and therefore easier to snake through arteries. Within weeks Guidant had snared 70 percent of the market from J&J.

But Guidant's product had shortcomings, too. Many patients, particularly diabetics, experience aggressive scar tissue growth with bare metal stents, which soon reclogs the artery. While Guidant concentrated on harvesting the financial rewards of its successful new design, both J&J and Boston Scientific worked feverishly to develop a third generation of stents using a new technology that reduces scarring by coating the device in a polymer that gradually releases a drug.

J&J was first to release its new coated stent in April 2003. The firm built a huge initial demand for the product by aggressively promoting it before its release. Unfortunately, it then discovered that it was unable to produce enough stents to satisfy that demand. Boston Scientific released its new stent several months later and was careful to build production capacity and adequate inventories first. Consequently, Boston Scientific was estimated to hold about a 65 percent share of the stent market in 2004, whereas Guidant's share plummeted to around 7 percent.

Guidant's failure in the stent business, together with technical problems with some of its other products—such as heart defibrillators—severely weakened its competitive position; so severely, in fact, that the firm became an acquisition candidate and was ultimately purchased by Boston Scientific.

Sources: Shawn Tully, "Blood Feud," *Fortune*, May 31, 2004, pp. 100–17; and Shawn Tully, "The [Second] Worst Deal Ever," *Fortune*, October 16, 2006, pp. 102–19.

---

it has made substantial investments, and it might worry that a rapid shift to a new technology will upset present customers or kill a profitable product prematurely. As a result, early commitment to a technology has become increasingly problematic because of more rapid rates of technological change. This problem is dramatically illustrated by the experience of Guidant, Inc., as described in Exhibit 9.2.

GROWTH-MARKET STRATEGIES FOR MARKET LEADERS

For the share leader in a growing market, of course, the question of the relative advantages versus risks of market entry is moot. The leader is typically the pioneer, or at least one of the first entrants, who developed the product-market in the first place. Often, that firm's strategic objective is to maintain its leading share position in the face of increasing competition as the market expands. Share maintenance may not seem like a very aggressive objective because it implies the business is merely trying to stay even rather than forge ahead. But two important facts must be kept in mind.

Strategic Issue

The dynamics of a growth market—including the increasing number of competitors, the fragmentation of market segments, and the threat of product innovation from within and outside the industry—make maintaining an early lead in relative market share very difficult.

First, the dynamics of a growth market—including the increasing number of competitors, the fragmentation of market segments, and the threat of product innovation from within and outside the industry— make maintaining an early lead in relative market share very difficult. The continuing need for investment to finance growth, the likely negative cash flows that result and the threat of governmental antitrust action can make it even more difficult.

Second, a firm can maintain its current share position in a growth market only if its sales volume continues to grow at a rate equal to that of the overall market, enabling the firm to stay even in *absolute* market share. However, it may be able to maintain a relative share lead even if its volume growth is less than the industry's.

Marketing Objectives for Share Leaders

Share maintenance for a market leader involves two important marketing objectives. First, the firm must *retain its current customers,* ensuring that those customers remain brand loyal when making repeat or replacement purchases. This is particularly critical for firms in consumer nondurable, service, and industrial materials and components industries where a substantial portion of total sales volume consists of repeat purchases. Second, the firm must *stimulate selective demand among later adopters* to ensure that it captures a large share of the continuing growth in industry sales.

In some cases, the market leader might pursue a third objective: stimulating primary demand to help speed up overall market growth. This can be particularly important in product-markets where the adoption process is protracted because of the technical sophistication of the new product, high switching costs for potential customers, or positive network effects.

The market leader is the logical one to stimulate market growth in such situations; it has the most to gain from increased volume, assuming it can maintain its relative share of that volume. However, expanding total demand—by promoting new uses for the product or stimulating existing customers' usage and repeat purchase rates—is often more critical near the end of the growth stage and early in the maturity stage of a product's life cycle. Consequently, we discuss marketing actions appropriate to this objective in Chapter 10.

Marketing Actions and Strategies to Achieve Share-Maintenance Objectives

A business might take a variety of marketing actions to maintain a leading share position in a growing market. Exhibit 9.3 outlines a lengthy, though not exhaustive, list of such actions and their specific marketing objectives. Because share maintenance involves multiple objectives and different marketing actions may be needed to achieve each one, a strategic marketing program usually integrates a mix of the actions outlined in the exhibit.

Not all the actions summarized in Exhibit 9.3 are consistent with one another. It would be unusual, for instance, for a business to invest heavily in new product improvements and promotion to enhance its product's high-quality image and simultaneously slash prices, unless it was trying to drive out weaker competitors in the short run with an eye on higher profits in the future. Thus, the activities outlined in Exhibit 9.3 cluster into five internally consistent strategies that a market leader might employ, singly or in combination, to maintain its leading share position: a **fortress, or position defense, strategy;** a **flanker strategy;** a **confrontation strategy;** a **market expansion strategy;** and a **contraction,** or **strategic withdrawal, strategy.**

Exhibit 9.4 diagrams this set of strategies. It is consistent with what a number of military strategists and some marketing authorities have identified as common defensive strategies.[9] To think of them as strictly defensive, however, can be misleading. Companies can use some of these strategies offensively to preempt expected future actions by potential competitors, or they can use them to capture an even larger share of future new customers.

Which, or what combination, of these five strategies is most appropriate for a particular product-market depends on (1) the market's size and its customers' characteristics, (2) the number and relative strengths of the competitors or potential competitors in that market, and (3) the leader's own resources and competencies. Exhibit 9.5 outlines the situations

EXHIBIT 9.3   **Marketing Actions to Achieve Share-Maintenance Objectives**

Marketing Objectives	Possible Marketing Actions
Retain current customers by	
• Maintaining/improving satisfaction and loyalty.	• Increase attention to quality control as output expands. • Continue product modification and improvement efforts to increase customer benefits and/or reduce costs. • Focus advertising on stimulation of selective demand; stress product's superior features and benefits; reminder advertising. • Increase salesforce's servicing of current accounts; consider formation of national or key account representatives to major customers; consider replacing independent manufacturer's reps with company salespeople where appropriate. • Expand postsale service capabilities; develop or expand company's own service force or develop training programs for distributors' and dealers' service people; expand parts inventory; develop customer service hotline and website.
• Encouraging/simplifying repeat purchase.	• Expand production capacity in advance of increasing demand to avoid stockouts. • Improve inventory control and logistics systems to reduce delivery times. • Continue to build distribution channels; use periodic trade promotions to gain more extensive retail coverage and maintain shelf-facings; strengthen relationships with strongest distributors/dealers. • Consider negotiating long-term requirements contracts with major customers. • Consider developing automatic reorder systems or logistical alliances.
• Reducing attractiveness of switching.	• Develop a second brand or product line with features or price more appealing to a specific segment of current customers (*flanker strategy*—see Exhibits 9.4 and 9.5). • Develop multiple-line extensions or brand offerings targeted to the needs of several user segments within the market (*market expansion*). • Meet or beat lower prices or heavier promotional efforts by competitors—or try to preempt such efforts by potential competitors—when necessary to retain customers and when lower unit costs allow (*confrontation strategy*).
Stimulate selective demand among later adopters by	
• Head-to-head positioning against competitive offerings or potential offerings.	• Develop a second brand or product line with features or price more appealing to a specific segment of potential customers (*flanker strategy*). • Make product modifications or improvements to match or beat superior competitive offerings (*confrontation strategy*). • Meet or beat lower prices or heavier promotional efforts by competitors when necessary to retain customers and when lower unit costs allow (*confrontation strategy*). • When resources are limited relative to a competitor's, consider withdrawing from smaller or slower-growing segments to focus product development and promotional efforts on higher potential segments threatened by competitor (*contraction or strategic withdrawal strategy*).
• Differentiated positioning against competitive offerings or potential offerings.	• Develop multiple-line extensions or brand offerings targeted to the needs of various potential user applications or geographical segments within the market (*market expansion strategy*). • Build unique distribution channels to more effectively reach specific segments of potential customers (*market expansion strategy*). • Design multiple advertising and/or sales promotion campaigns targeted at specific segments of potential customers (*market expansion strategy*).

EXHIBIT 9.4   **Strategic Choices for Share Leaders in Growth Markets**

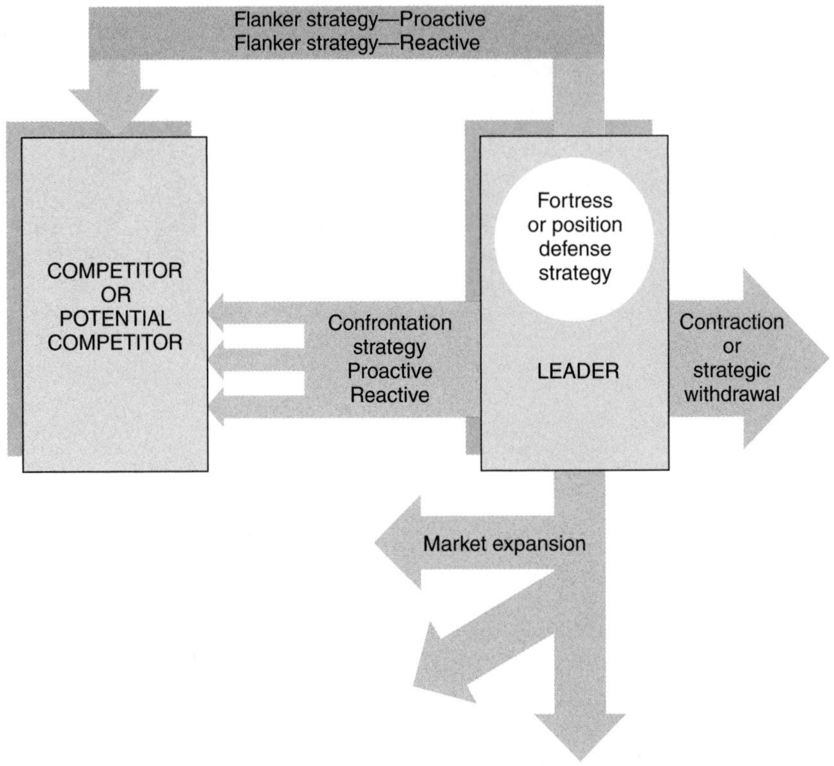

Flanker strategy—Proactive
Flanker strategy—Reactive

COMPETITOR
OR
POTENTIAL
COMPETITOR

Confrontation
strategy
Proactive
Reactive

Fortress
or position
defense
strategy

LEADER

Contraction
or
strategic
withdrawal

Market expansion

Source: P. Kotler and R. Singh Achrol. "Marketing Warfare in the 1980's," *Journal of Business Strategy*, Winter 1981. Reprinted with permission.

in which each strategy is most appropriate and the primary objectives for which they are best suited.

Fortress, or Position Defense, Strategy

The most basic defensive strategy is to continually strengthen a strongly held current position—to build an impregnable fortress capable of repelling attacks by current or future competitors. This strategy is nearly always part of a leader's share-maintenance efforts. By shoring up an already strong position, the firm can improve the satisfaction of current customers while increasing the attractiveness of its offering to new customers with needs and characteristics similar to those of earlier adopters.

Strategic Issue

The most basic defensive strategy is to continually strengthen a strongly held current position.

Strengthening the firm's position makes particularly good sense when current and potential customers have relatively homogeneous needs and desires and the firm's offering already enjoys a high level of awareness and preference in the mass market. In some homogeneous markets, a well-implemented position defense strategy may be all that is needed for share maintenance.

Most of the marketing actions listed in Exhibit 9.3 as being relevant for retaining current customers might be incorporated into a position defense strategy. Anything the business can do to improve customer satisfaction and loyalty and encourage and simplify repeat purchasing should help the firm protect its current customer base and make its offering more attractive to new customers. Some of the specific actions appropriate for accomplishing these two objectives are discussed below.

EXHIBIT 9.5 **Marketing Objectives and Strategies for Share Leaders in Growth Markets**

Situational Variables	Share Maintenance Strategies				
	Fortress or Position Defense	**Flanker**	**Confrontation**	**Market Expansion**	**Contraction or Strategic Withdrawal**
Primary objective	Increase satisfaction, loyalty, and repeat purchase among current customers by building on existing strengths; appeal to late adopters with same attributes and benefits offered to early adopters.	Protect against loss of specific segments of current customers by developing a second entry that covers a weakness in original offering; improve ability to attract new customers with specific needs or purchase criteria different from those of early adopters.	Protect against loss of share among current customers by meeting or beating a head-to-head competitive offering; improve ability to win new customers who might otherwise be attracted to competitor's offering.	Increase ability to attract new customers by developing new product offerings or line extensions aimed at a variety of new applications and user segments; improve ability to retain current customers as market fragments.	Increase ability to attract new customers in selected high-growth segments by focusing offerings and resources on those segments; withdraw from smaller or slower-growing segments to conserve resources.
Market characteristics	Relatively homogeneous market with respect to customer needs and purchase criteria; strong preference for leader's product among largest segment of customers.	Two or more major market segments with distinct needs or purchase criteria.	Relatively homogenous market with respect to customers' needs and purchase criteria; little preference for, or loyalty toward, leader's product among largest segment of customers.	Relatively heterogeneous market with respect to customers' needs and purchase criteria; multiple product uses requiring different product or service attributes.	Relatively heterogeneous market with respect to customers' needs, purchase criteria, and growth potential; multiple product uses requiring different product or service attributes.
Competitors' characteristics	Current and potential competitors have relatively limited resources and competencies.	One or more current or potential competitors with sufficient resources and competencies to effectively implement a differentiation strategy.	One or more current or potential competitors with sufficient resources and competencies to effectively implement a head-to-head strategy.	Current and potential competitors have relatively limited resources and competencies, particularly with respect to R&D and marketing.	One or more current or potential competitors with sufficient resources and competencies to present a strong challenge in one or more growth segments.
Firm's characteristics	Current product offering enjoys high awareness and preference among major segment of current and potential customers; firm has marketing and R&D resources and competencies equal to or greater than any current or potential competitor.	Current product offering perceived as weak on at least one attribute by a major segment of current or potential customers; firm has sufficient R&D and marketing resources to introduce and support a second offering aimed at the disaffected segment.	Current product offering suffers low awareness, preference, and/or loyalty among major segment of current or potential customers; firm has R&D and marketing resources and competencies equal to or greater than any current or potential competitor.	No current offerings in one or more potential applications segments; firm has marketing and R&D resources and competencies equal to or greater than any current or potential competitor.	Current product offering suffers low awareness, preference, and/or loyalty among current or potential customers in one or more major growth segments; firm's R&D and marketing resources and competencies are limited relative to those of one or more competitors.

Actions to Improve Customer Satisfaction and Loyalty

The rapid expansion of output necessary to keep up with a growth market often can lead to quality control problems for the market leader. As new plants, equipment, and personnel are quickly brought on line, bugs can suddenly appear in the production process. Thus, the leader must pay particular attention to quality control during this phase. Most customers have only limited, if any, positive past experiences with the new brand to offset their disappointment when a purchase does not live up to expectations.

Perhaps the most obvious way a leader can strengthen its position is to continue to modify and improve its product. This can reduce the opportunities for competitors to differentiate their products by designing in features or performance levels the leader does not offer. The leader might also try to reduce unit costs to discourage low-price competition.

The leader should take steps to improve not only the physical product, but also customers' perceptions of it as well. As competitors enter or prepare to enter the market, the leader's advertising and sales promotion emphasis should shift from stimulating primary demand to building selective demand for the company's brand. This usually involves creating appeals that emphasize the brand's superior features and benefits. The leader might also employ public relations efforts, internet ads, word-of-mouth on social networking sites such as Facebook, and blogs to build its brand's identity and customer loyalty—particularly among niche segments of younger consumers.[10] For example, Nike maintains a social networking site for serious runners, as described in Exhibit 9.6.

Although the leader may continue sales promotion efforts aimed at stimulating trial among later adopters, some of those efforts might be shifted toward encouraging repeat purchases among existing customers. For instance, it might include cents-off coupons inside the package to give customers a price break on their next purchases of the brand.

For industrial goods, some salesforce efforts should shift from prospecting for new accounts to servicing existing customers. Firms that relied on independent manufacturer's reps to introduce their new product might consider replacing them with company salespeople to increase the customer service orientation of their sales efforts. Firms whose own salespeople introduced the product might reorganize their salesforces into specialized

---

EXHIBIT 9.6 *Building Loyalty to the Nike Brand Via Online Social Networking*

The worldwide use of social networks as a marketing tool grew 38 percent in the year 2008 alone, according to market researcher comScore. But few company-sponsored networks have been as popular as Nike+.com, a website aimed at running enthusiasts. The key to attracting runners to the site was the development of a $29 Sport Kit sensor that can be synched with an iPod touch or nano to track a runner's speed, mileage, and calories burned. Nike+ .com launches when the runner docks his or her iPod, and the data are automatically uploaded and saved. The company has recently added additional types of sensors, including sports watches with GPS and Sportband bracelets. It has also added features to the website that allow runners to track their performance relative to daily goals and compare with their friends.

More importantly, the site is a virtual gathering place that connects runners from around the world.

For example, in 2008 Nike+ sponsored a 10K race run simultaneously in 25 cities around the world and 800,000 runners signed up. And as of this writing, participating runners have logged nearly 500 million miles on the site.

Although it is difficult to directly measure the impact of the Nike+ social network on the firm's bottom line, managers are convinced that the site has helped reinforce customer loyalty and attract new users to the Nike brand. The firm's share of the running shoe market in the United States has increased from 48 percent in 2006 to more than 60 percent since the launch of Nike+. Consequently, new Nike+ networks have been developed for basketball players and people who work out with the X Box Kinect system.

Sources: Jay Greene, "How Nike's Social Network Sells to Runners," www.businessweek.com/innovation, November 6, 2008; and the company's website at www.nike.com.

groups focused on major industries or user segments, or they might assign key account representatives, or cross-functional account teams, to service their largest customers.

Finally, a leader can strengthen its position as the market grows by giving increased attention to postsale service. Rapid growth in demand not only can outstrip a firm's ability to produce a high-quality product, but it also can overload the firm's ability to service customers. This can lead to a loss of existing customers as well as negative word of mouth that might inhibit the firm's ability to attract new users. Thus, the growth phase often requires increased investments to expand the firm's parts inventory, hire and train service personnel and dealers, expand customer call centers, improve the information content on the firm's website, and closely monitor and respond to any problems or complaints reported to the company's call center or on customer blogs.[11]

Actions to Encourage and Simplify Repeat Purchasing

One of the most critical actions a leader must take to ensure that customers continue buying its product is to maximize its availability. It must reduce stockouts on retail store shelves or shorten delivery times for industrial goods. To do this, the firm must invest in plant and equipment to expand capacity in advance of demand, and it must implement adequate inventory control and logistics systems to provide a steady flow of goods through the distribution system. The firm also should continue to build its distribution channels. In some cases, a firm might even vertically integrate parts of its distribution system—such as building its own warehouses, as Amazon.com and several other e-tailers have done—to gain better control over order fulfillment activities and ensure quick and reliable deliveries.

Some market leaders, particularly in industrial goods markets, can take more proactive steps to turn their major customers into captives and help guarantee future purchases. For example, a firm might negotiate requirements contracts or guaranteed price agreements with its customers to ensure future purchases, or it might tie them into a computerized reorder system or a tightly integrated supply-chain relationship. Such actions are all aimed at increasing customers' repeat purchases and loyalty in order to maximize their lifetime value. Although it makes good sense to begin building strong customer relationships right from the beginning, they become even more crucial as the market matures and competition to win over established customers becomes more intense. Consequently, we'll have more to say about building and managing customer relationships in Chapter 10.

Flanker Strategy

One shortcoming of a fortress strategy is that a challenger might simply choose to bypass the leader's fortress and try to capture territory where the leader has not yet established a strong presence. This can represent a particular threat when the market is fragmented into major segments with different needs and preferences and the leader's current brand does not meet the needs of one or more of those segments. A competitor with sufficient resources and competencies can develop a differentiated product offering to appeal to the segment where the leader is weak and thereby capture a substantial share of the overall market.

To defend against an attack directed at a weakness in its current offering (its exposed flank), a leader might develop a second brand (a **flanker** or **fighting brand**) to compete directly against the challenger's offering. This might involve trading up, where the leader develops a high-quality brand offered at a higher price to appeal to the prestige segment of the market. This was Toyota's rationale for introducing its Lexus brand of luxury automobiles, for instance.

More commonly, a flanker brand is a lower-quality product designed to appeal to a low-price segment to protect the leader's primary brand from direct price competition. Thus, Toyota introduced the Scion brand in the U.S. market in 2003, a line of cars that appeals to young car buyers looking for good quality, funky design, low prices, and no-hassle shopping. The Scion brand is an attempt to insulate Toyota cars from low-price competitors and to establish a presence among young first-time buyers who might "trade up" to more expensive Toyota models in the future. Similarly, Nike launched Tailwind—a low-priced flanker brand aimed at value-conscious women—though the firm's managers have been reluctant to introduce flankers in larger market segments, such as basketball shoes, for fear of cannibalizing the high-margin Nike brand.

A flanker strategy is always used in conjunction with a position defense strategy. The leader simultaneously strengthens its primary brand while introducing a flanker to compete in segments where the primary brand is vulnerable. This suggests that a flanker strategy is appropriate only when the firm has sufficient resources to develop and fully support two or more entries. After all, a flanker is of little value if it is so lightly supported that a competitor can easily wipe it out. Indeed, Nike's Tailwind line languished owing to a lack of promotional support and customer interest. Unfortunately, although a recent study using secondary sources indicates that offering a portfolio of brands at different price and quality levels has a significant impact on a firm's marketing and financial performance, the relationship between specific portfolio characteristics and performance outcomes is not yet well understood.[12]

Confrontation Strategy

Suppose a competitor chooses to attack the leader head to head and attempts to steal customers in the leader's main target market. If the leader has established a strong position and attained a high level of preference and loyalty among customers and the trade, it may be able to sit back and wait for the competitor to fail. In many cases, though, the leader's brand is not strong enough to withstand a frontal assault from a well-funded, competent competitor. For example, Nokia introduced the first mobile phone with full personal digital assistant (PDA) capabilities—the 9000 Communicator—in 1996, and it quickly captured the leading global market share among PDA devices. But PDA phones with greater functionality (e.g., RIM'S BlackBerry), more versatile smartphones (e.g., Apple's iPhone), and cheaper Android-based phones from Asia have all substantially reduced Nokia's share of the market.

In such situations, the leader may have no choice but to confront the competitive threat directly. If the leader's competitive intelligence is good, it may decide to move proactively and change its marketing program before a suspected competitive challenge occurs. A confrontational strategy, though, is more commonly reactive. The leader usually decides to meet or beat the attractive features of a competitor's offering—by making product improvements, increasing promotional efforts, or lowering prices—only after the challenger's success has become obvious.

Strategic Issue

Simply meeting the improved features or lower price of a challenger does nothing to reestablish a sustainable competitive advantage for the leader.

Simply meeting the improved features or lower price of a challenger, however, does nothing to reestablish a sustainable competitive advantage for the leader. A confrontation based largely on lowering prices creates an additional problem of shrinking margins for all concerned.[13] Unless decreased prices generate substantial new industry volume and the leader's production costs fall with that increasing volume, the leader may be better off responding to price threats with increased promotion or product improvements while trying to maintain its profit margins. Evidence also suggests that in product-markets with high repeat-purchase rates or a protracted diffusion process, the leader may be wise to adopt a penetration pricing policy in the first place. This would strengthen its share position and might preempt low-price competitors from entering.[14]

The leader can avoid the problems of a confrontation strategy by reestablishing the competitive advantage eroded by challengers' frontal attacks. But this typically requires additional investments in process improvements aimed at reducing unit costs, improvements in product quality or customer service, or even the development of the next generation of improved products to offer customers greater value for their dollars.

Market Expansion Strategy

A market expansion strategy is a more aggressive and proactive version of the flanker strategy. Here the leader defends its relative market share by expanding into a number of market segments. This strategy's primary objective is to capture a large share of new customer groups who may prefer something different from the firm's initial offering, protecting the firm from future competitive threats from a number of directions. Such a strategy is particularly appropriate in fragmented markets if the leader has the resources to undertake multiple product development and marketing efforts.

The most obvious way a leader can implement a market expansion strategy is to develop line extensions, new brands, or even alternative product forms utilizing similar technologies to appeal to multiple market segments. For instance, Nike captured and has sustained a leading share of the athletic shoe market by developing a series of line extensions offering technical, design, and style features tailored to the preferences of enthusiasts in nearly every sport. Nokia has become the leading seller of cellular phones in both India and China by developing phones with unique features tailored to those developing nations' customers, such as phones with dust covers and a slip-free grip for use in scorching summer weather, software in seven regional languages for non-Hindi speakers, phones that respond to Chinese characters written with a stylus, and phones that retail for as little as $30.[15]

A less expensive way to appeal to a variety of customer segments is to retain the basic product but vary other elements of the marketing program to make it relatively more attractive to specific users. Thus, a leader might create specialized salesforces to deal with the unique concerns of different user groups, or it might offer different ancillary services to different types of customers or tailor sales promotion efforts to different segments. Thus, performing arts groups often promote reduced ticket prices, transportation services, and other inducements to attract senior citizens and students to matinee performances.

Contraction, or Strategic Withdrawal, Strategy

In some highly fragmented markets, a leader may be unable to defend itself adequately in all segments. This is particularly likely when newly emerging competitors have more resources than the leader. The firm may then have to reduce or abandon its efforts in some segments to focus on areas where it enjoys the greatest relative advantages or that have the greatest potential for future growth. Even some very large firms may decide that certain segments are not profitable enough to continue pursuing. For example, Samsung has withdrawn from the most price-sensitive consumer electronics segments—and from discount retailers such as Wal-Mart—to concentrate on higher-margin products that take full advantage of the firm's strengths in cutting-edge technical R&D and hip design.

SHARE-GROWTH STRATEGIES FOR FOLLOWERS

Marketing Objectives for Followers

Not all late entrants to a growing product-market have illusions about eventually surpassing the leader and capturing a dominant market share. Some competitors, particularly those with limited resources and competencies, may simply seek to build a small but profitable business within a specialized segment of the larger market that earlier entrants have overlooked, as Vans did in the skateboarder segment of the athletic shoe market. As we have seen, this kind of *niche strategy* is one of the few entry options that small, late entrants can pursue with a reasonable assurance of success. If a firm can successfully build a profitable business in a small segment while avoiding direct competition with larger competitors, it often can survive the shakeout period near the end of the growth stage and remain profitable throughout the maturity stage.

But many followers, particularly larger firms entering a product-market shortly after the pioneer, have more grandiose objectives. They often seek to displace the leader or at least to become a powerful competitor within the total market. Thus, their major marketing objective is to attain *share growth,* and the size of the increased relative share such challengers seek is usually substantial. For instance, when Haier, the Chinese appliance manufacturer, started making refrigerators just two decades ago, it set its sights on becoming a global share leader even though the category was dominated by large international brands such as Whirlpool, Electrolux, and General Electric. Today, Haier is the world's number one refrigerator brand according to Euromonitor International.[16]

Marketing Actions and Strategies to Achieve Share Growth

A challenger with visions of taking over the leading share position in an industry has two basic strategic options, each involving somewhat different marketing objectives and actions. Where the share leader and perhaps some other early followers have already penetrated a large portion of the potential market, a challenger may have no choice but to *steal away some of the repeat purchase or replacement demand from the competitors' current customers.* As Exhibit 9.7 indicates, the challenger can attempt this through marketing activities that give it an advantage in a head-to-head confrontation with a target competitor, or it can attempt to leapfrog over the leader by developing a new generation of products with enough benefits to induce customers to trade in their existing brand for a new one. Secondarily, such actions also may help the challenger attract a larger share of late adopters in the mass market.

If the market is relatively early in the growth phase and no previous entrant has captured a commanding share of potential customers, the challenger can focus on *attracting a larger share of potential new customers* who enter the market for the first time. This also may be a viable option when the overall market is heterogeneous and fragmented and the current share leader has established a strong position in only one or a few segments. In either case, the primary marketing activities for increasing share via this approach should aim at *differentiating* the challenger's offering from those of existing competitors by making it more appealing to new customers in untapped or underdeveloped market segments.

Once again, Exhibit 9.7's list of possible marketing actions for challengers is not exhaustive, and it contains actions that do not always fit well together. The activities that do fit tend to cluster into five major strategies that a challenger might use singly or in combination to secure growth in its relative market share. As Exhibit 9.8 indicates, these five share-growth strategies are *frontal attack, leapfrog strategy, flanking attack, encirclement,* and *guerrilla attack.* Most of these strategies are basically mirror images of the share-maintenance strategies discussed earlier.

Which, or what combination, of these five strategies is best for a particular challenger depends on market characteristics, the existing competitors' current positions and strengths, and the challenger's own resources and competencies. The situations in which each strategy is likely to work best are briefly outlined in Exhibit 9.9 and discussed in the following sections.

EXHIBIT 9.7 Marketing Actions to Achieve Share-Growth Objectives

Marketing Objectives	Possible Marketing Actions
Capture repeat/replacement purchases from current customers of the leader or other target competitor by	

• Head-to-head positioning against competitor's offering in primary target market.	• Develop products with features and/or performance levels superior to those of the target competitor.
	• Draw on superior product design, process engineering, and supplier relationships to achieve lower unit costs.
	• Set prices below target competitor's for comparable level of quality or performance, but only if low-cost position is achieved.
	• Outspend the target competitor on promotion aimed at stimulating selective demand:
	    Comparative advertising appeals directed at gaining a more favorable positioning than the target competitor's brand enjoys among customers in the mass market.
	    Sales promotions to encourage trial if offering's quality or performance is perceptively better than target competitor's or induce brand switching.
	    More extensive and/or better-trained salesforce than target competitor's.
	• Outspend the target competitor on trade promotion to attain more extensive retail coverage, better shelf space, and/or representation by the best distributors/dealers.
	• Outperform the target competitor on customer service:
	    Develop superior production scheduling, inventory control, and logistics systems to minimize delivery times and stockouts.
	    Develop superior postsale service capabilities. Build a more extensive company service force or provide better training programs for distributor/dealer service people than those of target competitor.

• Technological differentiation from target competitor's offering in its primary target market.	• Develop a new generation of products based on different technology that offers superior performance or additional benefits desired by current and potential customers in the mass market (*leapfrog strategy*).
	• Build awareness, preference, and replacement demand through heavy introductory promotion:
	    Comparative advertising stressing product's superiority.
	    Sales promotions to stimulate trial or encourage switching.
	    Extensive, well-trained salesforce; heavy use of product demonstrations in sales presentations.
	• Build adequate distribution through trade promotions and dealer training programs.

Stimulate selective demand among later adopters by	
• Head-to-head positioning against target competitor's offering in established market segments.	• See preceding actions.
• Differentiated positioning focused on untapped or underdeveloped segments.	• Develop a differentiated brand or product line with unique features or prices that is more appealing to a major segment of potential customers whose needs are not met by existing offerings (*flanking strategy*).

(Continued)

EXHIBIT 9.7   (Continued)

> or
> - Develop multiple line extensions or brand offerings with features or prices targeted to the unique needs and preferences of several smaller potential applications or regional segments (*encirclement strategy*).
> - Design advertising, personal selling, and/or sales promotion campaigns that address specific interests and concerns of potential customers in one or multiple underdeveloped segments to stimulate selective demand.
> - Build unique distribution channels to more effectively reach potential customers in one or multiple underdeveloped segments.
> - Design service programs to reduce the perceived risks of trial and/or solve the unique problems faced by potential customers in one or multiple underdeveloped segments (e.g., systems engineering, installation, operator training, extended warranties, service hotline, or website).

EXHIBIT 9.8   Strategic Choices for Challengers in Growth Markets

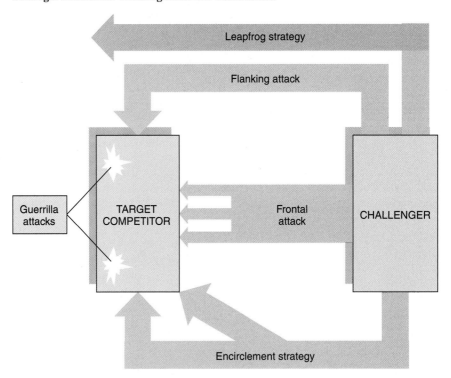

Source: P. Kotler and R. Singh Achrol, "Marketing Warfare in the 1980's," *Journal of Business Strategy*, Winter 1981. Reprinted with permission.

Deciding Whom to Attack

When more than one competitor is already established in the market, a challenger must decide which competitor, if any, to target. There are several options:

- *Attack the market-share leader within its primary target market.* As we shall see, this typically involves either a *frontal assault* or an attempt to *leapfrog* the leader through the development of superior technology or product design. It may seem logical to try to

EXHIBIT 9.9   **Marketing Objectives and Strategies for Challengers in Growth Markets**

Situational Variables	Share-Growth Strategies				
	Frontal Attack	**Leapfrog**	**Flank Attack**	**Encirclement**	**Guerrilla Attack**
Primary objective	Capture substantial repeat/replacement purchases from target competitor's current customers; attract new customers among later adopters by offering lower price or more attractive features.	Induce current customers in mass market to replace their current brand with superior new offering; attract new customers by providing enhanced benefits.	Attract substantial share of new customers in one or more major segments where customers' needs are different from those of early adopters in the mass market.	Attract a substantial share of new customers in a variety of smaller, specialized segments where customers' needs or preferences differ from those of early adopters in the mass market.	Capture a modest share of repeat/ replacement purchases in several market segments or territories; attract a share of new customers in a number of existing segments.
Market characteristics	Relatively homogeneous market with respect to customers' needs and purchase criteria; relatively little preference or loyalty for existing brands; no positive network effects.	Relatively homogeneous market with respect to customers' needs and purchase criteria, but some needs or criteria not currently met by existing brands.	Two or more major segments with distinct needs and purchase criteria; needs of customers in at least one segment not currently met by existing brands.	Relatively heterogeneous market with a number of small, specialized segments; needs and preferences of customers in some segments not currently satisfied by competing brands.	Relatively heterogeneous market with a number of larger segments; needs and preferences of customers in most segments currently satisfied by competing brands.
Competitors' characteristics	Target competitor has relatively limited resources and competencies, particularly in marketing and R&D; would probably be vulnerable to direct attack.	One or more current competitors have relatively strong resources and competencies in marketing, but relatively unsophisticated technology and limited R&D competencies.	Target competitor has relatively strong resources and competencies, particularly in marketing and R&D; would probably be able to withstand direct attack.	One or more competitors have relatively strong marketing, R&D resources and competencies, and/or lower costs; could probably withstand a direct attack.	A number of competitors have relatively strong marketing, R&D resources and competencies, and/or lower costs; could probably withstand a direct attack.
Firm's characteristics	Firm has stronger resources and competencies in R&D and marketing and/or lower operating costs than target competitor.	Firm has proprietary technology superior to that of competitors; firm has necessary marketing and production resources to stimulate and meet primary demand for new generation of products.	Firm's resources and competencies are limited, but sufficient to effectively penetrate and serve at least one major market segment.	Firm has marketing, R&D, and production resources and competencies necessary to serve multiple smaller segments; firm has decentralized and adaptable management structure.	Firm has relatively limited marketing, R&D, and/or production resources and competencies; firm has decentralized and adaptable management structure.

win customers away from the competitor with the most customers to lose, but this can be a dangerous strategy unless the challenger has superior resources and competencies that can be converted into a sustainable advantage. In some cases, however, a smaller challenger may be able to avoid disastrous retaliation by confronting the leader only occasionally in limited geographic territories through a series of *guerrilla attacks.*

- *Attack another follower who has an established position within a major market segment.* This also usually involves a *frontal assault,* but it may be easier for the challenger to gain a sustainable advantage if the target competitor is not as well established as the market leader in the minds and buying habits of customers.

- *Attack one or more smaller competitors who have only limited resources.* Because smaller competitors usually hold only a small share of the total market, this may seem like an inefficient way to attain substantial share increases. But by focusing on several small regional competitors one at a time, a challenger can sometimes achieve major gains without inviting retaliation from stronger firms. For example, by first challenging and ultimately acquiring a series of smaller regional manufacturers, Borden managed to capture the leading share of the fragmented U.S. pasta market.

- *Avoid direct attacks on any established competitor.* In fragmented markets in which the leader or other major competitors are not currently satisfying one or more segments, a challenger is often best advised to "hit 'em where they ain't." This usually involves either a *flanking* or an *encirclement strategy,* with the challenger developing differentiated product offerings targeted at one large or several smaller segments in which no competitor currently holds a strong position. Thus, Vans profited in the athletic shoe market by focusing on small alternative sports whose adherents did not find the "mainstream" image of Nike and other major brands very appealing.

Deciding which competitor to attack necessitates a comparison of relative strengths and weaknesses, a critical first step in developing an effective share-growth strategy. It also can help limit the scope of the battlefield, a particularly important consideration for challengers with limited resources.

Frontal Attack Strategy

Where the market for a product category is relatively homogeneous, with few untapped segments and at least one well-established competitor, a follower wanting to capture an increased market share may have little choice but to tackle a major competitor head-on. Such an approach is most likely to succeed when most existing customers do not have strong brand preferences or loyalties, the target competitor's product does not benefit from positive network effects, and the challenger's resources and competencies—particularly in marketing—are greater than the target competitor's. But even superior resources are no guarantee of success if the challenger's assault merely imitates the target competitor's offering.

To successfully implement a frontal attack, a challenger should seek one or more ways to achieve a sustainable advantage over the target competitor. As discussed earlier, such an advantage is usually based on attaining lower costs or a differentiated position in the market. If the challenger has a cost advantage, it can cut prices to lure away the target competitor's customers, as low-cost airlines like Ryanair and JetBlue have done in Europe and the United States.[17] Or it can maintain a similar price but engage in more extensive promotion.

Challenging a leader solely on the basis of low price is a highway to disaster, however, unless the challenger really does have a sustainable cost advantage. Otherwise, the leader might simply match the lower prices until the challenger is driven from the market. The problem is that initially a challenger is often at a cost *disadvantage* because of the experience-curve effects established competitors have accumulated. The challenger must have offsetting advantages such as superior production technology, established relations with low-cost suppliers, the ability to share production facilities or marketing efforts across multiple SBUs, or other sources of synergy before a low-price assault makes sense.

A similar caveat applies to frontal assaults based solely on heftier promotional budgets. Unless the target competitor's resources are substantially more limited than the challenger's, it can retaliate against any attempt to win away customers through more extensive advertising or attractive sales and trade promotions.

One possible exception to this limitation of greater promotional effort is the use of a more extensive and better-trained salesforce to gain a competitive advantage. A knowledgeable salesperson's technical advice and problem-solving abilities can give additional value to a firm's product offering, particularly in newly developing high-tech industries.

In general, the best way for a challenger to effectively implement a frontal attack is to differentiate its product or associated services in ways that better meet the needs and preferences of many customers in the mass market. If the challenger can support those meaningful product differences with strong promotion or an attractive price, so much the better, but usually the unique features or services offered are the foundation for a sustainable advantage. For example, until recently Dell was successful as a follower in the PC market by offering *both* superior customer service and low prices. Customers could design their own computers on the company's website, get exactly the features they wanted, and have the equipment delivered to their doors in two or three days. Such excellent service was possible, in large part, due to the close coordination between Dell and its suppliers, coordination that minimized inventories of parts and finished computers, thereby lowering costs and prices. Dell's competitive advantage proved sustainable, too, because its alliances with suppliers took years to develop and were hard for its competitors to match.

In recent years, however, Dell's aggressive cost cutting in order to pursue share growth via ever-lower prices caused the firm to reduce its investments in things such as R&D and technical training for customer support personnel. Subsequent shortcomings in Dell's new product development and customer service opened the door for competitors such as Hewlett-Packard, Lenovo, and Acer to challenge its lead.[18] The lesson once again is that low price alone is not a good way to capture or hold a leading share position unless customers also perceive they are receiving good value for that price.

Variables that might limit the competitor's willingness or ability to retaliate can also improve the chances for successful frontal attack. For instance, a target competitor with a reputation for high product quality may be loath to cut prices in response to a lower-priced challenger for fear of cheapening its brand's image, as is the case with Nike. A competitor pursuing high ROI or cash flow objectives may be reluctant to increase its promotion or R&D expenditures in the short run to fend off an attack.[19]

Leapfrog Strategy

A challenger stands the best chance of attracting repeat or replacement purchases from a competitor's current customers when it can offer a product that is attractively differentiated from the competitor's offerings. The odds of success might be even greater if the challenger can offer a far superior product based on advanced technology or a more sophisticated design. This is the essence of a leapfrog strategy. It is an attempt to gain a significant advantage over the existing competition by introducing a new generation of products that significantly outperform or offer more desirable customer benefits than do existing brands. For example, the introduction of reasonably priced video cameras by Sony and other Japanese electronics manufacturers largely took over the market for home movie equipment and a large share of the market for Polaroid's self-developing photography equipment as well. Now digital cameras are doing the same thing to the video market.

In addition, such a strategy often inhibits quick retaliation by established competitors. Firms that have achieved some success with one technology—or that have committed substantial resources to plant and equipment dedicated to a current product—often are reluctant to switch to a new one because of the large investments involved or a fear of disrupting current customers.

A leapfrog strategy is not viable for all challengers. To be successful, the challenger must have technology superior to that of established competitors as well as the product and process engineering capabilities to turn that technology into an appealing product. Also, the challenger must have the marketing resources to effectively promote its new products and convince customers already committed to an earlier technology that the new product offers sufficient benefits to justify the costs of switching.

Flanking and Encirclement Strategies

The military historian B. H. Liddell-Hart, after analyzing battles ranging from the Greek Wars to World War I, determined that only 6 out of 280 victories were the result of a frontal attack.[20] He concluded that it is usually wiser to avoid attacking an established adversary's point of strength and to focus instead on an area of weakness in his defenses. This is the basic premise behind flanking and encirclement strategies. They both seek to avoid direct confrontations by focusing on market segments whose needs are not being satisfied by existing brands and where no current competitor has a strongly held position.

Flank Attack

A flank attack is appropriate when the market can be broken into two or more large segments, when the leader and/or other major competitors hold a strong position in the primary segment, and when no existing brand fully satisfies the needs of customers in at least one other segment. A challenger may be able to capture a significant share of the total market by concentrating primarily on one large untapped segment. This usually involves developing product features or services tailored to the needs and preferences of the targeted customers, together with appropriate promotional and pricing policies to quickly build selective demand. Japanese auto companies, for instance, penetrated the U.S. car market by focusing on the low-price segment, where domestic manufacturers' offerings were limited. Domestic car manufacturers were relatively unconcerned by this flanking action at first. They failed to retaliate very aggressively because the Japanese were pursuing a segment they considered to be small and unprofitable. History proved them wrong. More recently, Steve and Barry's discount chain captured a significant share of the basketball shoe market by targeting the low-priced Starbury One to young players with limited incomes, and the Earth Friendly Products Company has succeeded in the household cleaning market by offering an environmentally friendly product line, as discussed in Exhibit 9.10.

EXHIBIT 9.10 *Earth Friendly Products versus Clorox*

How can a small, family-run business hold its own against a cleaning products giant? After arriving in the United States at age 18, Greek immigrant Van Vlahakis worked his way through Roosevelt University's chemistry program before becoming a chemist in the cleaning products industry. Laid off in 1967, he became inspired by Rachel Carson's 1962 bestseller *Silent Spring* started a company with the descriptive name Earth Friendly Products, and developed a line of environmentally safe household cleaners. Today the profitable 300-employee firm in Garden Grove, California, brings in a reported $100 million-plus in sales revenue. Lacking a big ad budget and facing much larger competitors like Clorox's Green Works line, Earth Friendly sparks sales through in-store demos at retailers like Costco. Vlahakis keeps his employees motivated by awarding the equivalent of as much as eight weeks' salary in bonuses, and they get Earth Day off.

Source: Elaine Pofeldt, "David vs. Goliath: Earth Friendly Products versus Green Works," www.money.cnn.com, March 21, 2012.

In some cases, a successful flank attack need not involve unique product features. Instead, a challenger can sometimes meet the special needs of an untapped segment by providing specially designed customer services or distribution channels. For instance, Apple's iTunes music store captured a substantial share of the global recorded music market by offering a convenient way for web-savvy consumers to locate and download songs for their personal music libraries.

Encirclement

An encirclement strategy involves targeting several smaller untapped or underdeveloped segments in the market simultaneously. The idea is to surround the leader's brand with a variety of offerings aimed at several peripheral segments. This strategy makes most sense when the market is fragmented into many different applications segments or geographical regions with somewhat unique needs or tastes.

Once again, this strategy usually involves developing a varied line of products with features tailored to the needs of different segments. Rather than try to compete with Coke and Pepsi in the soft drink market, for example, Cadbury-Schweppes offers a wide variety of flavors such as cream soda, root beer, and ginger ale—almost anything but cola—to appeal to small groups of customers with unique tastes. Similarly, Vans is trying to expand its foothold in the athletic shoe industry by targeting several niche segments of enthusiasts in other alternative sports—such as snowboarding—where the brand's youthful "outsider" image might be appealing and where the firm's larger competitors are not well established.

Guerrilla Attack

When well-established competitors already cover all major segments of the market and the challenger's resources are relatively limited, flanking, encirclement, or all-out frontal attacks may be impossible. In such cases, the challenger may be reduced to making a series of surprise raids against its more established competitors. To avoid massive retaliation, the challenger should use guerrilla attacks sporadically, perhaps in limited geographic areas where the target competitor is not particularly well entrenched.

A challenger can choose from a variety of means for carrying out guerrilla attacks. These include sales promotion efforts (e.g., coupon drops and merchandising deals), local advertising blitzes, and even legal action. Short-term price reductions through sales promotion campaigns are a particularly favored guerrilla tactic in consumer goods markets. They can target specific customer groups in limited geographic areas; they can be implemented quickly; and they are often difficult for a larger competitor to respond to because that firm's higher share level means that a given discount will cost it more in absolute dollars.

Because they are both geographically targeted and time limited, promotions offered over social couponing sites such as Groupon and LivingSocial can be very effective guerrilla marketing tools. For instance, Groupon partnered with The Gap to offer a 50 percent–off coupon in selected cities, which generated $11 million in sales in a single day. However, recent studies suggest such quick revenue blips—and the buzz they generate—tend not to last very long and may not be cost-effective. Consequently, one study found that 40 percent of the companies who had promoted their product or service via Groupon said they would not do so again.[21]

For similar reasons, carefully targeted direct mail, public relations, or internet marketing campaigns also can be an effective guerrilla tactic, particularly when they generate positive word of mouth between customers and potential customers. For example, when BMW rolled out the Mini Cooper—its small sporty car targeted at younger and less affluent customers than the typical BMW buyer—its ad agency Crispin Porter & Bogusky didn't bother with TV commercials. Instead, it put giant trash cans and pay phones in airports, and hung mini-billboards beside them reading "makes everything else seem a little too big."[22]

In some cases, the ultimate objective of a series of guerrilla attacks is not so much for the challenger to build its own share as it is to prevent a powerful leader from further expanding its share or engaging in aggressive actions to which it would be costly for the followers to respond. Lawsuits brought against the leader by several smaller competitors over a range of activities can effectively slow down the leader's expansionist tendencies by diverting some of its resources and attention.

Supporting Evidence

Several studies provide empirical support for many of the managerial prescriptions we have discussed.[23] These studies compare businesses that achieved high market shares during the growth stage of the product life cycle, or that increased their market shares over time, with low-share businesses. The marketing programs and activities of businesses that successfully achieved increased market share differed from their less successful counterparts in the following ways:

- Businesses that increased the quality of their products relative to those of competitors achieved greater share increases than businesses whose product quality remained constant or declined.
- Share-gaining businesses typically developed and added more new products, line extensions, or product modifications to their line than share-losing businesses.
- Share-gaining businesses tended to increase their marketing expenditures faster than the rate of market growth. Increases in both salesforce and sales promotion expenditures were effective for producing share gains in both consumer and industrial goods businesses. Increased advertising expenditures were effective for producing share gains primarily in consumer goods businesses.
- Surprisingly, there was little difference in the relative prices charged between firms that gained and those that lost market share.

These findings are consistent with many of our earlier observations. For instance, they underline the folly of launching a frontal attack solely on the basis of lower price. Unless the challenger has substantially lower unit costs or the leader is inhibited from cutting its own prices for some reason, the challenger's price cuts are likely to be retaliated against and will generate few new customers. On the other hand, frontal, leapfrog, flanking, or encirclement attacks based on product improvements tailored to specific segments are more likely to succeed, particularly when the challenger supports those attacks with substantial promotional efforts.

Regardless of the strategies pursued by market leaders and challengers during a product-market's growth stage, the competitive situation often changes as the market matures and its growth rate slows. In Chapter 10, we examine the environmental changes that occur as a market matures and the marketing strategies that firms might use to adapt to those changes.

Marketing
Plan Exercise

Identify an appropriate marketing strategy consistent with the product's stage in its product life cycle and the market and competitive conditions it faces, drawing on Chapters 8, 9, and/or 10 as appropriate. Identify the strategies key competitors are using, and develop a rationale for the strategy you have chosen.

Discussion Questions

1. Apple Computer's iPod holds a commanding share of the rapidly growing global market for digital music players. To maintain its lead as the market continues to grow, what strategic marketing objectives should Apple focus on and why?

2. Given your answer to question 1, which specific marketing actions would you recommend for accomplishing Apple's objectives? Be specific with regard to each of the 4 Ps in the firm's marketing program.

3. How would you characterize the strategies of the major Korean automakers (e.g., Hyundai, Kia) as they attempt to capture a larger share of developed markets such as Europe and the United States? What marketing variables do you think are critical to the ultimate success of their strategies?

4. If you were the top marketing executive at General Motors or Ford, what strategy would you recommended to defend your firm's market share against this competitive threat from South Korea?

Self-diagnostic questions to test your ability to apply the concepts in this chapter to marketing decision making may be found at this book's website at **www.mhhe.com/walker8e.**

Endnotes

1. Information to prepare this opening case was taken from Arlen Weintraub and Gerry Khermouch, "Chairman of the Board," *BusinessWeek,* May 28, 2001, p. 96; Christopher Palmeri, "Teach an Old Sneaker Enough New Tricks—and Kids Will Come Running," *BusinessWeek,* June 7, 2004, pp. 92–93; Stanley Holmes, "Adidas' World Cup Shutout," *BusinessWeek,* April 3, 2006, pp. 104–6; Rob Walker, "Chicer by the Dozen," *New York Times Magazine,* March 11, 2007, p. 22; "The Swoosh Heard Around the World," *The Economist*, July 3, 2010, pp. 62–63; Matt Townsend, "Is Nike's Flyknit the Swoosh of the Future?" www.businessweek.com, March 15, 2012; and the company's 2011 Annual Report at www.nike.com.

2. Peter N. Golder and Gerard J. Tellis, *Cascades, Diffusion, and Turning Points in the Product Life Cycle, Report # 03-120* (Cambridge, MA: Marketing Science Institute, 2003).

3. Neil Gross, Peter Coy, and Otis Port, "The Technology Paradox," *BusinessWeek,* March 6, 1995, pp. 76–84.

4. For a more extensive discussion of the potential opportunities and pitfalls of rapidly growing markets, see David A. Aaker and George S. Day, "The Perils of High-Growth Markets," *Strategic Management Journal* 7 (1986), pp. 409–21; and Myron Magnet, "Let's Go for Growth," *Fortune,* March 7, 1994, pp. 60–72.

5. Gregory S. Carpenter and Kent Nakamoto, "Consumer Preference Formation and Pioneering Advantage," *Journal of Marketing Research,* August 1989, pp. 285–98.

6. Andrew Park and Peter Burrows, "Dell, the Conqueror," *BusinessWeek,* September 24, 2001, pp. 92–102; Andrew Park and Peter Burrows, "What You Don't Know About Dell," *BusinessWeek,* November 3, 2003, pp. 76–84; Nanette Byrnes, Peter Burrows, and Louise Lee, "Dark Days at Dell," *BusinessWeek,* September 4, 2006, pp. 26–29; and Aaron Ricadela, "Dell: Scant Signs of Recovery," www.businessweek.com/technology, July 14, 2009.

7. However, the positive relationship between network effects and pioneering advantage does not always hold, especially in product/markets where incompatible technologies are competing with one another. See Qi Wang, Yubo Chen, and Jinhong Xie, "Survival in Markets with Network Effects: Product Compatibility and Order-of-Entry Effects," *Journal of Marketing* 74 (July 2010), pp. 1–14.

8. In some rapidly evolving high-tech markets, price premiums can disappear *very* quickly, as pointed out in Gross, Coy, and Port, "Technology Paradox."

9. For a detailed discussion of these strategies in a military context, see Carl von Clausewitz, *On War* (London: Routledge and Kegan Paul, 1908); and B. H. Liddell-Hart, *Strategy* (New York: Praeger, 1967). For a related discussion of the application of such strategies in a business setting, see Philip Kotler and Ravi Singh Achrol, "Marketing Warfare in the 1980's," *Journal of Business Strategy,* Winter 1981, pp. 30–41.

10. For additional examples, see Dan Macsai, "Marketing to Milennials," www.businessweek.com/smallbiz, August 22, 2008.

11. Jeff Jarvis, "Love the Customers Who Hate You," *BusinessWeek,* March3, 2008, p. 58.

12. Neil Morgan and Lopo L. Rego, "Brand Portfolio Strategy and Firm Performance," *Journal of Marketing* 73, January 2009, pp. 59–74.

13. Thomas T. Nagle, "Managing Price Competition," *Marketing Management* 2 (Spring 1993), pp. 36–45; Akshay R. Rao, Mark E. Bergen, and Scott Davis, "How to Fight a Price War," *Harvard Business Review,* March–April 2000, pp. 107–16; and Harald J. Van Heerde, Els Gijsbrechts, and Koen Pauwels, "Winners and Losers in a Major Price War," *Journal of Marketing Research* 45, October 2008, pp. 499–518.

14. Robert J. Dolan and Abel P. Jewland, "Experience Curves and Dynamic Demand Models: Implications for Optimal Pricing Strategy," *Journal of Marketing,* Winter 1981, p. 52.

15. Bruce Einhorn and Nandini Lakshman, "Nokia Connects," *BusinessWeek,* March 27, 2006, pp. 44–45; and Jack Ewing, "Mad Dash for the Low End," *BusinessWeek,* February 18, 2008, p. 30.

16. "Haier's Purpose," *The Economist,* March 20, 2004, p. 70; and Haier's 2012 Annual Report at www.haieramerica.com.

17. Carol Matlack, "Fare Wars: A Great Time to Be a Tourist," *BusinessWeek Online,* February 16, 2004; and Suzanne Kapner, "Flying the Unfriendly Skies," *Fortune,* July 7, 2008, p. 30.

18. Nanette Byrnes, Peter Burrows, and Louise Lee, "Dark Days at Dell," *BusinessWeek,* September 4, 2006, pp. 26–29; and Aaron Ricadela, "Dell: Scant Signs of Recovery."

19. For a more extensive discussion of factors that can limit a leader's willingness or ability to retaliate against a direct attack, see Michael E. Porter, *Competitive Advantage* (New York: Free Press, 1985), chap. 15.

20. Liddell-Hart, *Strategy,* p. 163.

21. Jeffery M. Stibel, "What Groupon and LivingSocial Cannot Offer," www.businessweek.com/managing, January 25, 2011.

22. Devin Leonard, "Nightmare on Madison Avenue," *Fortune,* June 28, 2004, p. 96.

23. Robert D. Buzzell and Federik D. Wiersema, "Successful Share-Building Strategies," *Harvard Business Review,* January–February 1981, pp. 135–43; Carl R. Anderson and Carl P. Zeithaml, "Stages in the Product Life Cycle, Business Strategy, and Business Performance," *Academy of Management Journal,* March 1984, pp. 5–25; and Robert D. Buzzell and Bradley T. Gale, *The PIMS Principles: Linking Strategy to Performance* (New York: Free Press, 1987), chap. 9.

Chapter **Ten**

Strategies for Mature and Declining Markets

Johnson Controls: Making Money in Mature Markets[1]

At first glance, Johnson Controls Inc. in Glendale, Wisconsin, appears to be the epitome of a staid, slow-growing, "old-economy" company. After all, the firm's success and future survival depend on several product and service categories that have not experienced very much growth in the domestic market in recent years. Johnson's major businesses include batteries, seats, and other internal components for automobiles; heating and cooling equipment for large commercial buildings and schools; and facilities management services.

But first glances can be deceiving. The firm's managers have developed a four-pronged strategy for making money in such mature markets. First, Johnson has acquired a number of weaker competitors in each of its product categories over the years in order to gain market share and remove excess capacity. Second, the firm has expanded sales volume by moving aggressively into global markets. The firm now operates in 500 different locations around the world.

Most important, the firm has nurtured close relationships with established customers such as Ford, Daimler, BMW, and Toyota. Those relationships, in turn, have enabled Johnson to maintain solid profit margins by improving customer retention and gaining operating efficiencies via logistical alliances, just-in-time delivery systems, and other process improvements. Finally, the firm's close customer relationships have provided it with market intelligence and facilitated joint development projects, both of which have helped the firm gain additional revenue from the introduction of new product and service offerings targeted at those customers.

A strong balance sheet and a long-term perspective have helped Johnson build market share—and expand into foreign countries—through the acquisition of competitors. In some cases, the firm has snapped up firms with product or service offerings that complement and extend Johnson's own product line in one of its established target markets. For instance, the firm spent $167 million to acquire Pan Am's World Services division, a facility management operation that does everything from mow the lawn to run the cafeteria. That acquisition, when combined with Johnson's existing heating and cooling systems business and some new products and services developed internally, turned the company into a full-service facilities operator. In addition, many of the new products and services the firm has developed in-house were born in response to changing customer desires or emerging environmental trends, such as a demand for "greener" commercial buildings with more sustainable energy systems and a smaller impact on the natural environment. Consequently, Johnson can now manage a client's entire building while offering highly customized heating and cooling systems and controls that minimize energy use. This combination of customized products and full service has both expanded the company's share of the commercial real estate market and enabled it to maintain relatively high margins in a highly competitive business.

In other businesses, Johnson has combined the economies of scale generated through savvy acquisitions with the knowledge gained from close customer relationships to both develop new products and drive down operating costs. For example, Johnson has become the leading worldwide supplier of automotive seating and interior systems, such as floor consoles and instrument panels, by assisting manufacturers with the design and development, as well as the manufacture, of such components. As one engineer at Chrysler pointed out, "Johnson is able to completely integrate the design, development, and manufacture of [our] seats," and do it for less than the auto companies could. On the design side, Johnson Controls has maintained its own industrial design department for many years. The firm's European design center in Cologne, Germany, alone has 70 staff members, more than the interior design teams of many car manufacturers. The center includes an in-house market research department to help identify trends in consumer tastes in European markets and pretest consumer reactions to possible design innovations.

On the manufacturing side, by closely coordinating inventories and production schedules, Johnson has reduced costs even further for both its customers and itself. For instance, by locating its plants close to a customer's production facility, Johnson is able to assemble seats to order, load them on a truck in a sequence that matches the cars coming down the assembly line, and deliver them to the customer all in as little as 90 minutes.

Despite the maturity of its markets, Johnson's strategy is paying off, in terms of both revenue growth and profits. While the firm's sales and profits took a hit during the global financial crisis of 2008–2010, they rebounded quickly. In the 2011 fiscal year, the company's revenues hit a record $40.8 billion and produced $1.6 billion in net income and a 15 percent return on shareholders' equity.

STRATEGIC CHALLENGES ADDRESSED IN CHAPTER 10

Many managers, particularly those in marketing, seem obsessed with growth. Their objectives tend to emphasize annual increases in sales volume, market share, or both. But the biggest challenge for many managers in developed nations in future years will be making money in markets that grow slowly, if at all. The majority of product markets in those nations are in the mature or decline stages of their life cycles. As accelerating rates of technological and social change continue to shorten such life cycles, today's innovations will move from growth to maturity—and ultimately to decline—ever faster.

A period of competitive turbulence almost always accompanies the transition from market growth to maturity in an industry. This period often begins after approximately half the potential customers have adopted the product and the rate of sales growth starts to decline. As the growth rate slows, many competitors tend to overestimate future sales volume and consequently end up developing too much production capacity. Competition becomes more intense as firms battle to increase sales volume to cover their high fixed costs and maintain profitability. As a result, such transition periods are commonly accompanied by a **shakeout** during which weaker businesses fail, withdraw from the industry, or are acquired by other firms, as has happened to some of Johnson Controls' competitors in the U.S. and European automotive seat and battery industries. In the next section of this chapter, we examine some strategic traps that can threaten a firm's survival during an industry shakeout.

Challenges in Mature Markets

Strategic Issue

A primary marketing objective of all competitors in mature markets is simply to hold their existing customers.

Businesses that survive the shakeout face new challenges as market growth stagnates. As a market matures, total volume stabilizes; replacement purchases rather than first-time buyers account for the vast majority of that volume. A primary marketing objective of all competitors in mature markets, therefore, is simply to hold their existing customers—to sustain a meaningful competitive advantage that will help ensure the continued satisfaction and loyalty of those customers. Thus, a product's financial success during the mature life-cycle stage depends heavily on the firm's ability to achieve and sustain a lower delivered cost or some perceived product quality or customer-service superiority.

Some firms tend to passively defend mature products while using the bulk of the revenues produced by those items to develop and aggressively market new products with more growth potential. This can be shortsighted, however. All segments of a market and all brands in an industry do not necessarily reach maturity at the same time. Aging brands such as Adidas, Johnson's baby shampoo, and Arm & Hammer baking soda experienced sales revivals in recent years because of creative marketing strategies. Thus, a share leader in a mature industry might build on a cost or product differentiation advantage and pursue a marketing strategy aimed at increasing volume by promoting new uses for an old product or by encouraging current customers to buy and use the product more often. Therefore, in this chapter we examine basic business strategies necessary for survival in mature markets and marketing strategies a firm might use to extend a brand's sales and profits, including the strategies that have been so successful for Johnson Controls.

If you are working on the Marketing Plan Exercise and if your plan involves a product or service that is in the mature stage of its life cycle, you will be asked to detail your strategy for maintaining its market share and profitability in the face of little or no future sales growth. Your strategy will likely focus on actions aimed at maintaining a lower-cost position or superior product benefits or customer service relative to competitors. You should also evaluate whether there is potential for generating additional sales growth by pursuing underserved market segments or encouraging existing customers to increase their purchases.

Challenges in Declining Markets

Eventually, technological advances; changing customer demographics, tastes, or lifestyles; and development of substitutes result in declining demand for most product forms and brands. As a product starts to decline, managers face the critical question of whether to divest or liquidate the business. Unfortunately, firms sometimes support dying products too long at the expense of current profitability and the aggressive pursuit of future breadwinners.

An appropriate marketing strategy, however, can produce substantial sales and profits even in a declining market.[2] If few exit barriers exist, an industry leader might attempt to increase market share via aggressive pricing or promotion policies aimed at driving out weaker competitors. Or it might try to consolidate the industry, as Johnson Controls has done in its automotive components businesses, by acquiring weaker brands and reducing overhead by eliminating both excess capacity and duplicate marketing programs. Alternatively, a firm might decide to harvest a mature product by maximizing cash flow and profit over the product's remaining life. The last section of this chapter examines specific marketing strategies for gaining the greatest possible returns from products approaching the end of their life cycle.

SHAKEOUT: THE TRANSITION FROM MARKET GROWTH TO MATURITY

Characteristics of the Transition Period

The transition from market growth to maturity typically begins when the market is still growing but the rate of growth starts to decline. This slackening of the growth rate either sparks or occurs simultaneously with other changes in the market and competitive environment. As mentioned earlier, such changes typically include the appearance of excess capacity, increased difficulty of maintaining product differentiation, increased intensity of competition, and growing pressures on costs and profits. Consequently, weaker members of the industry often fail or are acquired by larger competitors during this shakeout stage.

Strategic Traps during the Transition

A business's ability to survive the transition from market growth to maturity depends to a great extent on whether it can avoid some common strategic traps.[3] Four such traps are summarized in Exhibit 10.1.

The most obvious trap is simply the failure to recognize the events signaling the beginning of the shakeout period. The best way to minimize the impact of slowing growth is to accurately forecast the slowdown in sales and hold the firm's production capacity to a sustainable level. For both industrial and consumer durable goods markets, models can forecast when replacement sales will begin to outweigh first-time purchases, a common signal that a market is beginning to mature.[4] But in consumer nondurable markets—particularly those where growth slows because of shifting consumer preferences or the emergence of substitute products—the start of the transition period can be nearly impossible to predict.

A second strategic trap is for a business to get caught in the middle during the transition period without a clear strategic advantage. A business may survive and prosper during the growth stage even though it has neither differentiated its offering from competitors nor attained the lowest-cost position in its industry. But during the transition period, such is not the case.

A third trap is the failure to recognize the declining importance of product differentiation and the increasing importance of price or service. Businesses that have built their success on technological superiority or other forms of product differentiation often disdain aggressive pricing or marketing practices even though such differentiation typically erodes as markets mature.[5] As a result, such firms may delay meeting their more aggressive

---

EXHIBIT 10.1   Common Strategic Traps Firms Can Fall into during the Shakeout Period

1. Failure to anticipate transition from growth to maturity.
   - Firms may make overly optimistic forecasts of future sales volume.
   - As a result, they expand too rapidly, and production capacity overshoots demand as growth slows.
   - Their excess capacity leads to higher costs per unit.
   - Consequently, they must cut prices or increase promotion in an attempt to increase their volume.
2. No clear competitive advantage as growth slows.
   - Many firms can succeed without a strong competitive advantage during periods of rapid growth.
   - However, firms that do not have the lowest costs or a superior offering in terms of product quality or service can have difficulty sustaining their market share and volume as growth slows and competition intensifies.
3. Assumption that an early advantage will insulate the firm from price or service competition.
   - In many cases, technological differentials become smaller as more competitors enter and initiate product improvements as an industry approaches maturity.
   - If customers perceive that the quality of competing brands has become more equal, they are likely to attach greater importance to price or service differences.
   - Failure to detect such trends can cause an early leader to be complacent and slow to respond to competitive threats.
4. Sacrificing market share in favor of short-run profit.
   - A firm may cut marketing or R&D budgets or forgo other expenditures in order to maintain its historical level of profitability even though industry profits tend to fall during the transition period.
   - This can cause long-run erosion of market share and further increases in unit costs as the industry matures.

competitors head-on and end up losing market share, as Hewlett-Packard and many other computer firms discovered in the wake of Dell's aggressive pricing policies in the early years of this century.

Why should a firm not put off responding to the more aggressive pricing or marketing actions of its competitors? Because doing so may lead to a fourth trap—giving up market share too easily in favor of short-run profit. Many businesses try to maintain the profitability of the recent past as markets enter the transition period. They usually do this at the expense of market share or by forgoing marketing, R&D, and other investments crucial for maintaining future market position. Although some smaller firms with limited resources may have no choice, this tendency can be seriously shortsighted, particularly if economies of scale are crucial for the business's continued success during market maturity. Indeed, some analysts argue that a major reason for Dell's recent loss of market share in the global PC market is that the firm failed to invest adequate resources in new product development and customer support activities because it was trying to maintain its margins in the face of its aggressive pricing strategy.[6]

STRATEGIC CHOICES IN MATURE MARKETS

The maturity phase of an industry's life cycle is often depicted as one of stability characterized by few changes in the market shares of leading competitors and steady prices. The industry leaders, because of their low per-unit costs and little need to make any further investments, enjoy high profits and positive cash flows. These cash flows are harvested and diverted to other SBUs or products in the firm's portfolio that promise greater future growth.

Unfortunately, this conventional scenario provides an overly simplistic description of the situation businesses face in most mature markets. For one thing, it is not always easy to tell when a market has reached maturity. Variations in brands, marketing programs, and customer groups can mean that different brands and market segments reach maturity at different times.

Further, as the maturity stage progresses, a variety of threats and opportunities can disrupt an industry's stability. Shifts in customer needs or preferences, product substitutes, increased raw material costs, changes in government regulations, or factors such as the entry of low-cost foreign producers or mergers and acquisitions can threaten individual competitors and even throw the entire industry into early decline. Consider, for example, the competitive position of Kodak, a brand that dominated the world market for photographic film for decades. First, the appearance of high-quality foreign competitors such as Fuji film and then the development and consumer acceptance of digital cameras quickly eroded the size of the photographic film market and Kodak's share of that market.

On the positive side, such changes also can open new growth opportunities in mature industries. Product improvements, advances in process technology, falling raw materials costs, increased prices for close substitutes, or environmental changes all can provide opportunities for a firm to dramatically increase its sales and profits. An entire industry can even experience a period of renewed growth. Note, for example, how rising petroleum prices increased the demand for coal to power electricity-generating plants in Asia, Europe, and North America in spite of coal's environmental shortcomings.

Discontinuities during industry maturity suggest that it is dangerously shortsighted for a firm to simply milk its cash cows. Even industry followers can substantially improve volume, share, and profitability during industry maturity if they can adjust their marketing objectives

Strategic Issue

Success in mature markets requires a strategy to sustain a competitive advantage, customer satisfaction, and loyalty, and creative marketing programs to pursue growth or profit opportunities as conditions change.

and programs to fit the new opportunities that arise.[7] Thus, success in mature markets requires two sets of strategic actions: (1) the development of a well-implemented business strategy to sustain a competitive advantage, customer satisfaction, and loyalty and (2) flexible and creative marketing programs geared to pursue growth or profit opportunities as conditions change in specific product-markets.

Strategies for Maintaining Competitive Advantage

As discussed in Chapter 3, both *analyzer* and *defender strategies* may be appropriate for units with a leading, or at least a profitable, share of one or more major segments in a mature industry. Analyzers and defenders are both concerned with maintaining a strong share position in established product markets. But analyzers also do some product and market development to avoid being leapfrogged by competitors with more advanced products or being left behind in new applications segments. On the other hand, defenders may initiate some product improvements or line extensions to protect and strengthen their position in existing markets, but they spend relatively little on new product R&D. Thus, an analyzer strategy is most appropriate for developed industries that are still experiencing some technological change and may have opportunities for continued growth, such as the computer and commercial aircraft industries. The defender strategy works best in industries where the basic technology is not very complex or is unlikely to change dramatically in the short run, as in the food industry.

Both analyzers and defenders can attempt to sustain a competitive advantage in established product markets through *differentiation* of their product offering (either on the basis of superior quality or service or by maintaining a low-cost position). Evidence suggests the ability to maintain either a strongly differentiated or a low-cost position continues to be a critical determinant of success throughout both the transition and the maturity stage. One study examined the competitive strategies pursued by the two leading firms (in terms of return on investment) in eight mature industries characterized by slow growth and intense competition. In each industry, the two leading firms offered either the lowest relative delivered cost or high relative product differentiation.[8] Similarly, more recent observations by Treacy and Wiersema found that market leaders tend to pursue one of three strategic disciplines. They either stress operational excellence, which typically translates into lower costs, or differentiate themselves through product leadership or customer intimacy and superior service.[9]

Generally, it is difficult for a single business to pursue both low-cost and differentiation strategies at the same time. For instance, businesses taking the low-cost approach typically compete primarily by offering the lowest prices in the industry. Such prices allow little room for the firm to make the investments or cover the costs inherent in maintaining superior product quality, performance, or service over time.

Of course, improvements in quality—especially the reduction of product defects via improved production and procurement processes—can also reduce a product's cost, as advocates of "six sigma" programs point out. There is some evidence, however, that efforts aimed at improving quality in order to increase the benefits consumers associate with the product, and thereby generate increased sales and market share, generate greater financial returns for a firm than quality improvement efforts focused mainly on cost reduction.[10] Therefore, in the following sections we discuss quality improvement efforts aimed at differentiating a firm's offering and making it more appealing to customers separately from methods for reducing an offering's cost.

It is important to keep in mind, however, that pursuit of a low-cost strategy does not mean that a business can ignore the delivery of desirable benefits to the customer. Similarly, customers will not pay an unlimited price premium for superior quality or service, no matter how superior it is. In both consumer and commercial markets, customers seek good

EXHIBIT 10.2   **The Process of Customer Value Management**

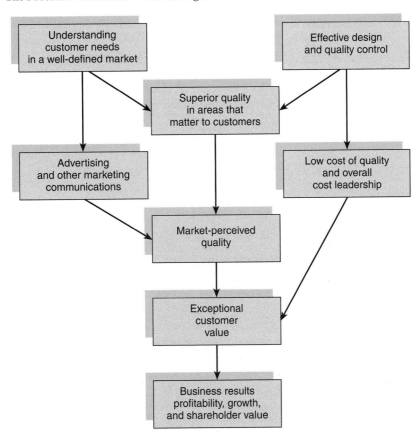

value for the money, either a solid, no-frills product or service at an outstanding price or an offering whose higher price is justified by the superior benefits it delivers on one or more dimensions.[11] Thus, even low-cost producers should continually seek ways to improve the quality and performance of their offerings within the financial constraints of their competitive strategy. Even differentiated defenders should continually work to improve efficiency without sacrificing product quality or performance. This point is clearly illustrated in the diagram of the customer value management process in Exhibit 10.2, which shows that actions to improve customers' perceptions of quality (whether of goods or service) and to reduce costs both impact customer value. The critical strategic questions facing the marketing manager are: How can a business continue to differentiate its offerings and justify a premium price as its market matures and becomes more competitive, and how can businesses, particularly those pursuing low-cost strategies, continue to reduce their costs and improve their efficiency as their markets mature?

Methods of Differentiation

Strategic Issue

Quality and service may be defined in a variety of different ways by customers.

At the most basic level, a business can attempt to differentiate its offering from competitors' by offering either superior product quality, superior service, or both. The problem is that *quality* and *service* may be defined in a variety of different ways by customers.

EXHIBIT 10.3 **Dimensions of Product Quality**

• Performance	How well does the washing machine wash clothes?
• Durability	How long will the lawn mower last?
• Conformance with specifications	What is the incidence of product defects?
• Features	Does an airline flight offer a movie and dinner?
• Reliability	Will each visit to a restaurant result in consistent quality?
	What percentage of the time will a product perform satisfactorily?
• Serviceability	Is the product easy to service?
	Is the service system efficient, competent, and convenient?
• Fit and finish	Does the product look and feel like a quality product?
• Brand name	Is this a name that customers associate with quality?
	What is the brand's image?

Source: Reprinted from "What Does 'Product Quality' Really Mean?" by David A. Garvin, *MIT Sloan Management Review,* Fall 1984, pp. 25–43, by permission of publisher. Copyright © 1984 by Massachusetts Institute of Technology. All rights reserved.

Dimensions of Product Quality[12]

To maintain a competitive advantage in product quality, a firm must understand what *dimensions customers perceive to underlie differences across products* within a given category. One authority has identified eight such dimensions of product quality. These are summarized in Exhibit 10.3 and discussed next.

European manufacturers of prestige automobiles, such as Mercedes-Benz and Porsche, have emphasized the first dimension of product quality—**functional performance.** These automakers have designed cars that provide excellent performance on such attributes as handling, acceleration, and comfort. Volvo, on the other hand, has emphasized and aggressively promoted a different quality dimension—**durability** (and the related attribute of safety). A third quality dimension, **conformance to specifications,** or the absence of defects, has been a major focus of the Japanese automakers. Until recent years, American car manufacturers relied heavily on broad product lines and a wide **variety of features,** both standard and optional, to offset their shortcomings on some of the other quality dimensions.

The **reliability** quality dimension can refer to the consistency of performance from purchase to purchase or to a product's uptime, the percentage of time that it can perform satisfactorily over its life. Tandem Computers has maintained a competitive advantage based on reliability by designing mainframe computers with several processors that work in tandem, so that if one fails, the only impact is the slowing of low-priority tasks. IBM had difficulty matching Tandem's reliability because its operating system was not easily adapted to the multiple-processor concept. Consequently, Tandem has maintained a strong position in market segments consisting of large-scale computer users, such as financial institutions and large retailers, for whom system downtime is particularly undesirable.

The quality dimension of **serviceability** refers to a customer's ability to obtain prompt and competent service when the product does break down. For example, Caterpillar has long differentiated itself with a parts and service organization dedicated to providing "24-hour parts service anywhere in the world."

Many of these quality dimensions can be difficult for customers to evaluate, particularly for consumer products. As a result, consumers often generalize from quality dimensions that are more visual or qualitative. Thus, the **fit and finish** dimension can help convince consumers that a product is of high quality. They tend to perceive attractive and well-designed products as generally high in quality, as witnessed by the success of Samsung's stylish consumer electronics products. Similarly, the **quality reputation of the brand name,** and the promotional activities that sustain that reputation, can strongly influence consumers' perceptions of a product's quality.[13] A brand's quality reputation together with psychological factors such as name recognition and loyalty substantially determine a brand's **equity**—the perceived value customers associate with a particular brand name and its logo or symbol.[14] To successfully pursue a differentiation strategy based on quality, a business must understand what dimensions or cues its potential customers use to judge quality, and it should pay particular attention to some of the less concrete but more visible and symbolic attributes of the product.

Dimensions of Service Quality

Customers also judge the quality of the service they receive on multiple dimensions. A number of such dimensions of perceived service quality have been identified by a series of studies conducted across diverse industries such as retail banking and appliance repair, and five of those dimensions are listed and briefly defined in Exhibit 10.4.[15]

The quality dimensions listed in Exhibit 10.4 apply specifically to service businesses, but most of them are also relevant for judging the service component of a product offering. This pertains to both the objective performance dimensions of the service delivery system, such as its **reliability** and **responsiveness,** as well as to elements of the performance of service personnel, such as their **empathy** and level of **assurance.**

The results of a number of surveys suggest that customers perceive all five dimensions of service quality to be very important regardless of the kind of service being evaluated. As Exhibit 10.5 indicates, customers of four different kinds of services gave reliability, responsiveness, assurance, and empathy mean importance ratings of more than 9 on a 10-point rating scale. Though the mean ratings for tangibles were somewhat lower in comparison, they still fell toward the upper end of the scale, ranging from 7.14 to 8.56.

The same respondents also were asked which of the five dimensions they would choose as being the most critical in their assessment of service quality. Their responses, which are shown in Exhibit 10.5, suggest that reliability is the most important aspect of service quality to the greatest number of customers.

Are the Dimensions the Same for Service Quality on the Internet?

Some of the researchers who identified the dimensions of service quality listed in Exhibit 10.4 have also studied whether service quality on the internet has the same or different underlying dimensions. They defined online service quality as the extent to which a website facilitates efficient and effective shopping, purchasing, and delivery. They identified 11 dimensions of perceived e-service quality: access, ease of navigation, efficiency, flexibility, reliability, personalization, security/privacy, responsiveness, assurance/trust, site aesthetics, and price knowledge.[16]

Although e-service quality obviously has more underlying dimensions, some of the most important of those dimensions are the same online as offline, such as reliability and responsiveness. This helps explain why e-tailers such as Amazon.com have spent millions building distribution centers geared toward improving the reliability of their order fulfillment activities.

EXHIBIT 10.4   Dimensions of Service Quality

• Tangibles	Appearance of physical facilities, equipment, personnel, and communications materials.
• Reliability	Ability to perform the promised service dependably and accurately.
• Responsiveness	Willingness to help customers and provide prompt service.
• Assurance	Knowledge and courtesy of employees and their ability to convey trust and confidence.
• Empathy	Caring, individualized attention the firm provides its customers.

Source: Adapted with the permission of The Free Press, A Division of Simon & Schuster Adult Publishing Group, from *Delivering Quality Service: Balancing Custom Perceptions and Expectations* by Valarie A. Zeithaml, A. Parasuraman, and Leonard L. Berry. Copyright © 1990 by The Free Press. All rights reserved.

EXHIBIT 10.5   **Perceived Importance of Service Quality Dimensions in Four Different Industries**

	Mean Importance Rating on 10-Point Scale*	Percentage of Respondents Indicating Dimension Is Most Important
Credit-card customers (*n* = 187)		
Tangibles	7.43	0.6%
Reliability	9.45	48.6
Responsiveness	9.37	19.8
Assurance	9.25	17.5
Empathy	9.09	13.6
Repair-and-maintenance customers (*n* = 183)		
Tangibles	8.48	1.2
Reliability	9.64	57.2
Responsiveness	9.54	19.9
Assurance	9.62	12.0
Empathy	9.30	9.6
Long-distance telephone customers (*n* = 184)		
Tangibles	7.14	0.6
Reliability	9.67	60.6
Responsiveness	9.57	16.0
Assurance	9.29	12.6
Empathy	9.25	10.3
Bank customers (*n* = 177)		
Tangibles	8.56	1.1
Reliability	9.44	42.1
Responsiveness	9.34	18.0
Assurance	9.18	13.6
Empathy	9.30	25.1

*Scale ranges from 1 (not at all important) to 10 (extremely important).

Source: Adapted with the permission of The Free Press, a Division of Simon & Schuster Adult Publishing Group, from *Delivering Quality Service: Balancing Customer Perceptions and Expectations* by Valarie A. Zeithaml, A. Parasuraman, and Leonard L. Berry. Copyright © 1990 by The Free Press. All rights reserved.

On the other hand, some dimensions that are important offline are not as crucial on the internet. Empathy, for example, does not appear to be a major concern for online customers, unless they are having problems on some of the other service dimensions.

The key to a differentiation strategy based on providing superior service is to meet or exceed target customers' service quality expectations and to do it more consistently than competitors. The problem is that sometimes managers underestimate the level of those customer expectations, and sometimes those expectations can be unrealistically high. Therefore, a firm needs to clearly identify target customers' desires with respect to service quality and to clearly define and communicate what level of service they intend to deliver. When this is done, customers have a more realistic idea of what to expect and are less likely to be disappointed with the service they receive.

Improving Customer Perceptions of Service Quality

The major factors that determine a customer's expectations and perceptions concerning service quality—and five gaps that can lead to dissatisfaction with service delivery—are outlined in Exhibit 10.6 and discussed next.

EXHIBIT 10.6 Determinants of Perceived Service Quality

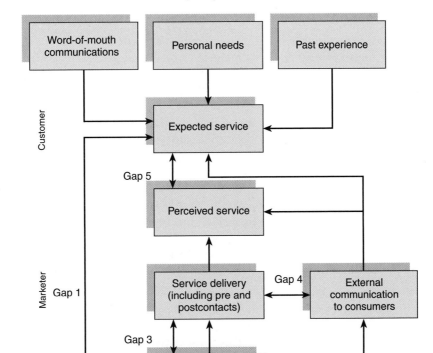

Source: Reprinted with permission from *Journal of Marketing*, published by the American Marketing Association, A. Parasuraman, Valerie A. Zeithaml, and Leonard L. Berry, "A Conceptual Model of Service Quality and Its Implications for Future Research," Fall 1985, p. 44.

1. **Gap between the customer's expectations and the marketer's perceptions.** Managers do not always have an accurate understanding of what customers want or how they will evaluate a firm's service efforts. The first step in providing good service is to collect information—through customer surveys, evaluations of customer complaints, ethnographic studies,[17] or other methods—to determine what service attributes customers consider important.

2. **Gap between management perceptions and service quality specifications.** Even when management has a clear understanding of what customers want, that understanding might not get translated into effective operating standards. A firm's policies concerning customer service may be unclear, poorly communicated to employees, or haphazardly enforced. Unless a firm's employees know what the company's service policies are and believe that management is seriously committed to those standards, their performance is likely to fall short of desired levels.

3. **Gap between service quality specifications and service delivery.** Lip service by management is not enough to produce high-quality service. High standards must be backed by the programs, resources, and rewards necessary to enable and encourage employees to deliver good service. Employees must be provided with the training, equipment, and time necessary to deliver good service. Their service performance must be measured and evaluated. Good performance must be rewarded by making it part of the criteria for pay raises or promotions, or by other more direct inducements, in order to motivate the additional effort good service requires.[18]

4. **Gap between service delivery and external communications.** Even good service performance may disappoint some customers if the firm's marketing communications cause them to have unrealistically high expectations. If the photographs in a vacation resort's advertising and brochures make the rooms look more spacious and luxurious than they really are, for instance, first-time customers are likely to be disappointed no matter how clean or well tended those rooms are kept by the resort's staff.

5. **Gap between perceived service and expected service.** This results when management fails to close one or more of the other four gaps. It is this difference between a customer's expectations and his or her actual experience with the firm that leads to dissatisfaction.

The preceding discussion suggests a number of actions management can take to close the possible gaps and improve customer satisfaction with a company's service. Achieving and sustaining high levels of service quality can present difficult implementation problems, however, because it usually involves the coordination of efforts of many employees from different functional departments and organizational levels.[19] Some of these coordination problems are examined in Chapter 12.

Methods of Maintaining a Low-Cost Position

Moving down the experience curve is the most commonly discussed method of achieving and sustaining a low-cost position in an industry. But a firm does not necessarily need a large relative market share to implement a low-cost strategy. For instance, Johnson Controls relies on close alliances with customers, as well as economies of scale, to hold down its inventory and distribution costs. Michael Dell, as a small follower in the personal computer industry, managed to achieve costs below those of much larger competitors by developing logistical alliances with suppliers and an innovative, internet-based direct distribution channel.

Some other means for obtaining a sustainable cost advantage include producing a no-frills product, creating an innovative product design, finding cheaper raw materials, automating or outsourcing production, developing low-cost distribution channels, and reducing overhead.[20]

A No-Frills Product

A direct approach to obtaining a low-cost position involves simply removing all frills and extras from the basic product or service. Thus, Tata cars, warehouse furniture stores, legal services clinics, discount airlines such as Southwest and Ryanair, and grocery stores selling canned goods out of crates all offer lower costs and prices than their competitors. This lower production cost is often sustainable because established differentiated competitors find it difficult to stop offering features and services their customers have come to expect. However, those established firms may lower their own prices in the short run—even to the point of suffering losses—in an attempt to drive out a no-frills competitor that poses a serious threat. Thus, a firm considering a no-frills strategy needs the resources to withstand a possible price war.[21]

Innovative Product Design

A simplified product design and standardized component parts also can lead to cost advantages. In the office copier industry, for instance, Japanese firms overcame substantial entry barriers by designing extremely simple copiers, with a fraction of the number of parts in the design used by market-leading Xerox.

Cheaper Raw Materials

A firm with the foresight to acquire or the creativity to find a way to use relatively cheap raw materials also can gain a sustainable cost advantage. For example, Fort Howard Paper achieved an advantage by being the first major papermaker to rely exclusively on recycled pulp. Although the finished product was not so high in quality as paper from virgin wood, Fort Howard's lower cost gave it a competitive edge in the price-sensitive commercial market for toilet paper and other such products used in hotels, restaurants, and office buildings.

Innovative Production Processes

Although low-cost defender businesses typically spend little on *product R&D,* they often continue to devote substantial sums to *process R&D.* Innovations in the production process, including the development of automated or computer-controlled processes, can help them sustain cost advantages over competitors.

In some labor-intensive industries, a business can achieve a cost advantage, at least in the short term, by gaining access to inexpensive labor. This is usually achieved by moving all or part of the production process to countries with low wage rates, such as China, India, or Mexico. Unfortunately, because such moves are relatively easy to emulate, this kind of cost advantage may not be sustainable.[22] Also, as developing nations become increasingly successful economically, wages and other operating costs tend to rise, thereby reducing the cost advantages of outsourcing to those countries.[23] Finaly, some firms have discovered that moving production offshore can reduce their control over labor practices, product quality, and distribution schedules.[24]

Low-Cost Distribution

When distribution accounts for a relatively high proportion of a product's total delivered cost, a firm might gain a substantial advantage by developing lower-cost alternative channels. Typically, this involves eliminating, or shifting to the customer, some of the functions performed by traditional channels in return for a lower price. In the consumer banking industry, for example, automated teller machines have helped reduce labor costs and investment in bricks-and-mortar branch banks. But they also have reduced the amount of personalized service banks provide to their customers, which contributed to a decline in customer satisfaction. That, in turn, helps to explain why Barclays Bank, Bank of America, and many other European and North American banks are developing and analyzing customer databases to identify the needs and preferences of different market segments, redesigning branches to make them more welcoming, and adding personal services—everything from free museum tickets to customer lounges and free coffee—to strengthen customer satisfaction and loyalty.[25]

Reductions in Overhead

Successfully sustaining a low-cost strategy requires that the firm pare and control its major overhead costs as quickly as possible as its industry matures. With increasing globalization in recent years, many companies have learned this lesson the hard way as the high cost of old plants, labor, outmoded administrative processes, and large inventories have left them vulnerable to more efficient foreign competitors and to corporate raiders.

Customers' Satisfaction and Loyalty Are Crucial for Maximizing Their Lifetime Value

Analyzer, and particularly defender, businesses are mostly concerned with protecting their existing positions in one or more mature market segments and maximizing profitability over the remaining life of those product markets. Thus, financial dimensions of performance, such as return on investment and cash flow, are usually of greater interest to such businesses than are more growth-oriented dimensions, such as volume increases or new product success. Businesses can achieve such financial objectives by either successfully differentiating their offerings or maintaining a low-cost position.

Although the primary emphasis in many businesses during the early years of the twenty-first century was on improving efficiency through downsizing and reengineering, there is substantial evidence that firms with superior quality goods and services also obtain higher returns on investment than do businesses with average or below average offerings.[26] The lesson to be learned is that the choice between a differentiation or a low-cost strategy is probably not the critical determinant of success in mature markets. What is critical is that a business *continually work to improve the value* of its offerings—by either improving product or service quality, reducing costs, or some combination—as a basis for maintaining its customer base as its markets mature and become increasingly competitive.

Measuring Customer Satisfaction

To gain the knowledge necessary to continually improve the value of their offerings to customers, firms must understand how satisfied existing and potential customers are with their current offerings. This focus on customer satisfaction has become increasingly important as more firms question whether all attempts to improve *absolute* quality of their products and services generate sufficient additional sales and profits to justify their cost. This growing concern with the economic "return on quality" has motivated firms to ask which dimensions of product or service quality are most important to customers and which dimensions customers might be willing to sacrifice for lower prices. For instance, Amazon discovered that many customers would like to receive their purchases more quickly than they usually arrived via the firm's standard delivery process. As a result, the firm created Amazon Prime, a service that guarantees delivery of products within two days for an annual fee of $79. While a relatively small segment of customers have signed up so far, Prime has been very successful at encouraging those buyers to concentrate more of their purchases with Amazon. Analysts estimate that Prime members increase their purchases by about 150 percent after signing up and may now be responsible for as much as 20 percent of Amazon's volume in the United States. Amazon has expanded Prime to Britain, France, Germany, and Japan, and is considering a move to guaranteed delivery within 24 hours.[27]

Because lengthy questionnaires often suffer from low response rates and can be subject to varying interpretations by different managers, some companies employ simple overall measures of customer satisfaction. Perhaps the most popular of these is the single question measure proposed by Fred Reichheld:[28] "On a scale of zero to ten, how likely is it that you would recommend us to your friends or colleagues?" Although such measures are simple for customers to answer and make it easy for managers to identify trends in satisfaction over time, they don't provide any information about *why* customers are either happy or disappointed with a firm's product or service. Indeed, if a substantial portion of respondents turn out to be "detractors" who would advise their friends against purchasing the product, the firm would need to conduct a second, more detailed survey to find the source of their dissatisfaction and how to dealt with it. For example, General Electric Healthcare's European services business, which maintains hospital imaging equipment, had to ask managers to follow up with dissatisfied customers in order to discover that a chief source of irritation was slow response times from GE engineers. Once the firm overhauled its call center and put more specialist engineers in the field, its satisfaction score on the "would you recommend us" measure jumped by 10 to 15 percent.

Useful measures of customer satisfaction should examine both (1) customers' *expectations and preferences* concerning the various dimensions of product and service quality (such as product performance, features, reliability, on-time delivery, competence of service personnel, and so on) and (2) their *perceptions* concerning how well the firm is meeting those expectations. Any gaps where customer expectations exceed their recent experiences may indicate fruitful areas for the firm to work at improving customer value and satisfaction. Of course, such measurements must be made periodically to determine whether the actions taken have been effective.[29]

Improving Customer Retention and Loyalty

Maintaining the loyalty of existing customers is crucial for a business's profitability. This is especially true as markets mature because loyal customers become more profitable over time. The firm not only avoids the high costs associated with trying to acquire replacement customers in an increasingly competitive market, but it also benefits because loyal customers (1) tend to concentrate their purchases, thus leading to larger volumes and lower selling and distribution costs; (2) provide positive word-of-mouth and customer referrals; and (3) may be willing to pay premium prices for the value they receive.[30]

Periodic measurement of customer satisfaction is important because a dissatisfied customer is unlikely to remain loyal over time. Unfortunately, the reverse is not always true: Customers who describe themselves as satisfied are not necessarily loyal. Indeed, one author estimates that 60 to 80 percent of customer defectors in most businesses said they were "satisfied" or "very satisfied" on the last customer survey before their defection.[31] In the interim, perhaps competitors improved their offerings, the customer's requirements changed, or other environmental factors shifted. Companies that measure customer satisfaction should be commended—but urged not to stop there. Satisfaction measures need to be supplemented with examinations of customer *behavior,* such as measures of the annual retention rate, frequency of purchases, and the percentage of a customer's total purchases captured by the firm.

Most important, any problems or complaints reported to the company's call center or on customer blogs should be closely monitored and dealt with. Indeed, recently developed software enables managers to engage in a continuous, real-time analysis of customers' perceptions about a brand and its various attributes by analyzing comments—both positive and negative—from millions of sites on the web, including personal blogs, Twitter tweets, and Facebook pages. This kind of **sentiment analysis** examines peoples' comments about the brand using statistical analysis and natural language processing, a software system designed to interpret written communications even when they include slang and abbreviations.[32]

Defecting customers should also be studied in detail to discover why the firm failed to provide sufficient value to retain their loyalty. Such failures often provide more valuable information than satisfaction measures because they stand out as a clear, understandable message telling the organization exactly where improvements are needed.

Are All Customers Equally Valuable?[33]

Although improving customer loyalty is crucial for maintaining market share and profitability as markets mature, an increasing number of companies are asking whether every customer's loyalty is worthy of the same level of effort and expense. In these firms, technology is creating a new business model that alters the level of service and benefits provided to a customer based on projections of that customer's value to the firm. With the development of extensive customer databases, it is possible for companies to measure what different levels of customer service cost on an individual level. They also can know how much business a particular customer has generated in the past, estimate what she or he is likely to buy in the future, and calculate a rate of return for that individual for different levels of service.[34]

The ability of firms to tailor different levels of service and benefits to different customers based on each person's potential to produce a profit has been facilitated by the internet. The web has made it easier to track and measure individual transactions across businesses. It also has provided firms with new, low-cost service options. People can now serve themselves at their own convenience, but they have to accept little or no human contact in return.

The end result of this trend toward individually tailored service levels could be an increased stratification of consumer society. The top tier may enjoy unprecedented levels of personal attention. But those who fall below a certain level of profitability for too long may face increased service fees or receive reduced levels of service and benefits. For example, some credit-card companies now charge higher annual fees to customers who do not rack up some minimum level of interest charges during the year. In other firms, call center personnel route customers to different queues. Big spenders are turned over to high-level problem solvers while less profitable customers may never speak to a live person. Finally, choice customers may get fees waived or receive promotional discounts based on the value of their business, whereas less valuable customers may never know the promotions exist.

The segmentation of customers based on projections of their value and the tailoring of different service levels and benefits to those segments raise both ethical and strategic questions, some of which are explored in Exhibit 10.7. One possible way for a firm to resolve some of the dilemmas involved in dealing with less profitable customers is to find ways to increase their lifetime value by increasing the frequency and/or volume of their purchases. This is one strategy examined in detail in the following section.

MARKETING STRATEGIES FOR MATURE MARKETS

Strategies for Maintaining Current Market Share

Since markets can remain in the maturity stage for decades, milking or harvesting mature product-markets by maximizing short-run profits makes little sense. Pursuing such an objective typically involves substantial cuts in marketing and R&D expenses, which can lead to premature losses of volume and market share and lower profits in the longer term. The business should strive during the early years of market maturity to *maximize the flow of profits over the remaining life of the product-market.* Thus, the most critical marketing objective is to *maintain and protect the business's market share.* In a mature market where few new customers buy the product for the first time, the business must continue to win its share of repeat purchases from existing customers.

In Chapter 9, we discussed a number of marketing strategies that businesses might use to maintain their market share in growth markets. Many of those same strategies continue to be relevant for holding on to customers as markets mature, particularly for those firms that survived the shakeout period with a relatively strong share position. The most obvious strategy for such share leaders is simply to continue strengthening their position through a *fortress defense.* Recall that such a strategy involves two sets of marketing actions: those aimed at improving customer satisfaction and loyalty and those intended to encourage and simplify repeat purchasing. Actions like those discussed earlier for improving the quality of a firm's offering and for reducing costs suggest ways to increase customer satisfaction and loyalty. Similarly, improvements to service quality, such as just-in-time delivery arrangements or computerized reordering systems, can help encourage repeat purchases.

EXHIBIT 10.7   *Pros and Cons of Varying Service Levels According to Customers' Profitability*

From a purely economic viewpoint, tailoring different levels of service and benefits to different customer segments depending on their profitability makes sense, at least in the short run. In an era when labor costs are increasing while many markets, especially mature ones, are getting more competitive, many firms argue they cannot afford to provide extensive hands-on service to everyone. Companies also point out that they're often delivering a wider range of products and services than ever before, including more ways for customers to handle transactions. Thanks to the internet, for example, consumers have better tools to conveniently serve themselves. Finally, service segmentation may actually produce some positive benefits for customers—more personalized service for the best customers and, in many cases, lower overall costs and prices for everyone else. For instance, Fidelity Investments gets more than 700,000 daily phone calls, three-quarters of which go to automated systems that cost the company less than a dollar each, including research and development costs. The rest are handled by human operators, at a cost of about $13 per call.

From an ethical standpoint, however, many people question the inherent fairness and potential invasion of privacy involved in using a wealth of personal information about individual consumers as a basis for withholding services or benefits from some of them, especially when such practices are largely invisible to the consumer. You don't know when you're being shuttled to a different telephone queue or sales promotion. You don't know what benefits you're missing or what additional fees you're being charged. Some argue that this lack of transparency is unfair because it deprives consumers of the opportunity to take actions, such as concentrating their purchases with a single supplier, switching companies, or paying a service fee, that would enable them to acquire the additional services and benefits they are currently denied.

From a strategic view, there are also some potential dangers in cutting services and benefits to customers who have not generated profits in the past. For one thing, past behavior is not necessarily an accurate indicator of a customer's future lifetime value. The life situations and spending habits of some customer groups—college students, for instance—can change dramatically over time. In addition, looking only at a customer's purchases may overlook some indirect ways that customer affects the firm's revenues, such as positive word-of-mouth recommendations and referrals to other potential buyers. Some customers may not be spending much with a company precisely because of the lousy service they have received as a result of not spending very much with that company. Instead of simply writing off low-volume customers, it may make more strategic sense to first attempt to convert them into high-volume customers by targeting them for additional promotions, trying to sell complementary goods and services, or instituting loyalty programs (e.g., the airlines' frequent-flier programs).

Finally, by debasing the satisfaction and loyalty of low-volume customers, firms risk losing those customers to competitors. In a mature industry, particularly one with substantial economies of scale, such a loss of market share can increase unit costs and reduce the profitability of those high-volume customers that do remain loyal. A creative competitor may find ways to make other firms' cast-off customers very profitable after all.

Sources: Diane Brady, "Why Service Stinks," *BusinessWeek*, October 23, 2000, pp. 118–28; and Christian Homburg, Mathias Droll, and Dirk Totzek, "Customer Prioritization: Does It Pay off and How Should It be Implemented?" *Journal of Marketing* 72 (September 2008), pp. 110–130.

Since markets often become more fragmented as they grow and mature, share leaders also may have to expand their product lines, or add one or more *flanker* brands, to protect their position against competitive inroads. Thus, Johnson Controls has strengthened its position in the commercial facilities management arena by expanding its array of services through a combination of acquisitions and continued internal development.

Small-share competitors also can earn substantial profits in a mature market. To do so, however, it is often wise for them to focus on strategies that avoid prolonged direct confrontations with larger share leaders. A *niche strategy* can be particularly effective when the target segment is too small to appeal to larger competitors or when the smaller firm can establish a strong differential advantage or brand preference in the segment. For instance, with fewer than 50 hotels worldwide, the Four Seasons chain is a small player in the lodging industry. But by focusing on the high end of the business travel market, the chain has grown and prospered. The chain's hotels differentiate themselves by offering a wide range of amenities, such as free overnight shoeshines, that are important to business travelers. Thus, although they charge relatively high prices, they also are seen as delivering good value.

Strategies for Extending Volume Growth

Market maturity is defined by a flattening of the growth rate. In some instances, growth slows for structural reasons, such as the emergence of substitute products or a shift in customer preferences. Marketers can do little to revitalize the market under such conditions. But in some cases a market only *appears* to be mature because of the limitations of current marketing programs, such as target segments that are too narrowly defined or limited product offerings. Here, more innovative or aggressive marketing strategies might successfully extend the market's life cycle into a period of renewed growth. Thus, *stimulating additional volume* growth can be an important secondary objective under such circumstances, particularly for industry share leaders because they often can capture a relatively large share of any additional volume generated.

A firm might pursue several different marketing strategies—either singly or in combination—to squeeze additional volume from a mature market. These include an *increased penetration strategy,* an *extended use strategy,* and a *market expansion strategy.* Exhibit 10.8 summarizes the environmental situations where each of these strategies is most appropriate and the objectives each is best suited for accomplishing. Exhibit 10.9

EXHIBIT 10.8   Situational Determinants of Appropriate Marketing Objectives and Strategies for Extending Growth in Mature Markets

Situation Variables	Growth Extension		
	Increased Penetration	Extended Use	Market Expansion
Primary objective	Increase the proportion of users by converting current nonusers in one or more major market segments.	Increase the amount of product used by the average customer by increasing frequency of use or developing new and more varied ways to use the product.	Expand the number of potential customers by targeting underdeveloped geographic areas or applications segments.
Market characteristics	Relatively low penetration in one or more segments (i.e., low percentage of potential users have adopted the product); relatively homogeneous market with only a few large segments.	Relatively high penetration but low frequency of use in one or more major segments; product used in only limited ways or for special occasions; relatively homogeneous market with only a few large segments.	Relatively heterogeneous market with a variety of segments; some geographic areas, including foreign countries, with low penetration; some product applications underdeveloped.
Competitors' characteristics	Competitors hold relatively small market shares; comparatively limited resources or competencies make it unlikely they will steal a significant portion of converted nonusers.	Competitors hold relatively small market shares; comparatively limited resources or competencies make it unlikely their brands will be purchased for newly developed uses.	Competitors hold relatively small market shares; have insufficient resources or competencies to preempt underdeveloped geographic areas or applications segments.
Firm's characteristics	A market share leader in the industry; has R&D and marketing competencies to produce product modifications or line extensions; has promotional resources to stimulate primary demand among current nonusers.	A market share leader in the industry; has marketing competencies and resources to develop and promote new uses.	A market share leader in the industry; has marketing and distribution competencies and resources to develop new global markets or applications segments.

EXHIBIT 10.9 **Possible Marketing Actions for Accomplishing Growth Extension Objectives**

Marketing Strategy and Objectives	Possible Marketing Actions
Increased Penetration	
Convert current nonusers in target segment into users	• Enhance product's value by adding features, benefits, or services. • Enhance product's value by including it in the design of integrated systems. • Stimulate additional primary demand through promotional efforts stressing new features or benefits: 　Advertising through selective media aimed at the target segment. 　Sales promotions directed at stimulating trial among current nonusers (e.g., tie-ins with other products). 　Some sales efforts redirected toward new account generation, perhaps by assigning some sales personnel as account development reps or by offering incentives for new account sales. 　Improve product's availability by developing innovative distribution systems.
Extended Use	
Increase frequency of use among current users	• Move storage of the product closer to the point of end use by offering additional package sizes or designs. • Encourage larger volume purchases (for nonperishable products): 　Offer quantity discounts. 　Offer consumer promotions to stimulate volume purchases or more frequent use (e.g., multipack deals, frequent-flier programs). • Reminder advertising stressing basic product benefits for a variety of usage occasions.
Encourage a wider variety of uses among current users	• Develop line extensions suitable for additional uses or applications. • Develop and promote new uses, applications, or recipes for the basic product. 　Include information about new applications/recipes on package. 　Develop extended use advertising campaign, particularly with print media. 　Communicate new application ideas through sales presentations to current customers. • Encourage new uses through sales promotions (e.g., tie-ins with complementary products).
Market Expansion	
Develop differentiated positioning focused on untapped or underdeveloped segments	• Develop a differentiated flanker brand or product line with unique features or price that is more appealing to a segment of potential customers whose needs are not met by existing offerings. 　　　　　　　　　　or • Develop multiple line extensions or brand offerings with features or prices targeted to the unique needs and preferences of several smaller potential applications or regional segments. • Consider producing for private labels. • Design advertising, personal selling, and/or sales promotion campaigns that address specific interests and concerns of potential customers in one or multiple underdeveloped segments to stimulate selective demand. • Build unique distribution channels to more effectively reach potential customers in one or multiple underdeveloped segments. • Design service programs to reduce the perceived risks of trial and/or solve the unique problems faced by potential customers in one or multiple underdeveloped segments (e.g., systems engineering, installation, operator training, extended warranties). • Enter global markets where product category is in an earlier stage of its life cycle.

then outlines specific marketing actions a firm might employ to implement each of the strategies, as discussed in more detail in the following paragraphs.

Increased Penetration Strategy

The total sales volume produced by a target segment of customers is a function of (1) the number of potential customers in the segment; (2) the product's penetration of that segment, that is, the proportion of potential customers who actually use the product; and (3) the average frequency with which customers consume the product and make another purchase. Where usage frequency is quite high among current customers but only a relatively small portion of all potential users actually buy the product, a firm might aim at increasing market penetration. It is an appropriate strategy for an industry's share leader because such firms can more likely gain and retain a substantial share of new customers than smaller firms with less well-known brands.

The secret to a successful increased penetration strategy lies in discovering why nonusers are uninterested in the product. Very often the product does not offer sufficient value from the potential customer's view to justify the effort or expense involved in buying and using it. One obvious solution to such a problem is to enhance the product's value to potential customers by adding features or benefits, usually via line extensions.

Another way to add value to a product is to develop and sell integrated systems that help improve the basic product's performance or ease of use. For instance, instead of simply selling control mechanisms for heating and cooling systems, Johnson Controls offers integrated facilities management programs designed to lower the total costs of operating a commercial building.

A firm also may enhance a product's value by offering services that improve its performance or ease of use for the potential customer. Since it is unlikely that people who do not know how to knit will ever buy yarn or knitting needles, for example, most yarn shops offer free knitting lessons.

Product modifications or line extensions, however, will not attract nonusers unless the enhanced benefits are effectively promoted. For industrial goods, this may mean redirecting some sales efforts toward nonusers. The firm may offer additional incentives for new account sales or assign specific salespeople to call on targeted nonusers and convert them into new customers. For consumer goods, some combination of advertising to stimulate primary demand in the target segment and sales promotions to encourage trial, such as free samples or tie-in promotions with complementary products that nonusers currently buy, can be effective.

Finally, some potential customers may be having trouble finding the product due to limited distribution or the product's benefits may simply be too modest to justify much purchasing effort. In such cases, expanding distribution or developing more convenient and accessible channels may help expand market penetration. For example, few travelers are so leery of flying that they would go through the effort of calling an insurance agent to buy an accident policy for a single flight. But the sales of such policies are greatly increased by making them conveniently available through the credit card companies travelers use to pay for their flights.

Extended Use Strategy

Some years ago, the manager of General Foods' Cool Whip frozen dessert topping discovered through marketing research that nearly three-fourths of all households used the product, but the average consumer used it only four times per year and served it on only 7 percent of all toppable desserts. In situations of good market penetration but low frequency of use, an extended use strategy may increase volume. This was particularly true in the Cool Whip case; the relatively large and homogeneous target market consisted for the most part of a single mass-market segment. Also, General Foods held nearly a two-thirds share of the frozen topping market, and it had the marketing resources and competencies to capture most of the additional volume that an extended use strategy might generate.

One effective approach for stimulating increased frequency of use is to move product inventories closer to the point of use. This approach works particularly well with low-involvement consumer goods. Marketers know that most consumers are unlikely to expend any additional time or effort to obtain such products when they are ready to use them. If there is no Cool Whip in the refrigerator when the consumer is preparing dessert, for instance, he or she is unlikely to run to the store immediately and probably will serve the dessert without topping.

One obvious way to move inventory closer to the point of consumption is to offer larger package sizes. The more customers buy at one time, the less likely they are to be out of stock when a usage opportunity arises. This approach can backfire, though, for a perishable product or one that consumers perceive to be an impulse indulgence. Thus, most superpremium ice creams, such as Häagen-Dazs, are sold in small pint containers; most consumers want to avoid the temptation of having large quantities of such a high-calorie indulgence too readily available.

The design of a package also can help increase use frequency by making the product more convenient or easy to use. Examples include single-serving packages of Jell-O pudding or salad to pack in lunches, packages of paper cups that include a convenient dispenser, and frozen-food packages that go directly into a microwave oven.

Various sales promotion programs also help move inventories of a product closer to the point of use by encouraging larger volume purchases. Marketers commonly offer quantity discounts for this purpose in selling industrial goods. For consumer products, multi-item discounts or two-for-one deals serve the same purpose. Promotional programs also encourage greater frequency of use and increase customer loyalty in many service industries. Consider, for instance, the frequent-flier programs offered by major airlines.

Sometimes the product's characteristics inhibit customers from using it more frequently. If marketers can change those characteristics, such as difficulty of preparation or high calories, a new line extension might encourage customers to use more of the product or to use it more often. Microwave waffles and low-calorie salad dressings are examples of such line extensions. For industrial goods, however, firms may have to develop new technology to overcome a product's limitations for some applications. For instance, Johnson Controls recently acquired Prince Automotive to gain the expertise necessary to develop instrument panels and consoles incorporating the sophisticated electronics desired by top-end manufacturers such as BMW and Mercedes-Benz.

Finally, advertising can sometimes effectively increase use frequency by simply reminding customers to use the product more often. For instance, General Foods conducted a reminder campaign for Jell-O pudding that featured Bill Cosby asking: "When was the last time you served pudding, Mom?"

Another approach for extending use among current customers involves finding and promoting new functional uses for the product. A recent success story involving an extended use program for a mature old brand is outlined in Exhibit 10.10.

Firms promote new ways to use a product through a variety of methods. For industrial products, firms send technical advisories about new applications to the salesforce to present to their customers during regular sales calls. For consumer products, new use suggestions or recipes may be included on the package, in an advertising campaign, or on the firm's web site. Sales promotions, such as including cents-off coupons in ads featuring a new recipe, encourage customers to try a new application.

In some cases, slightly modified line extensions might encourage customers to use more of the product or use it in different ways. For example, Australian, French, Chilean, and

---

EXHIBIT 10.10   *Philadelphia Cream Cheese's Spreading Appeal*

Until Irene Rosenfeld took over as Kraft Food's CEO in 2006, the firm was content to simply defend the leading market share—and $1.7 billion in revenue—of its Philadelphia brand cream cheese against other brands and private labels around the world. But then the firm's market researchers discovered that frequent users of cream cheese were using it as a cooking ingredient, not just as a spread for bagels. Consequently, the firm launched a marketing campaign in Britain and western Europe pointing out how cream cheese could be added to everything from Spanish tapas to spaghetti carbonara. Kraft's website soon hosted thousands of recipes submitted by consumers, some of which were incorporated in Philly's advertising and online videos. Kraft even persuaded British retailers, like Tesco, to display Philly next to main-dish staples, like salmon, to inspire recipe ideas.

A team of Kraft marketing and R&D people also got into the act by developing line extensions aimed at enhancing Philly's value as a cooking ingredient. For example, they recently introduced Philly cooking cream in nine varieties, such as savory garlic, in North America and Europe.

Kraft's extended use campaign has been extremely successful so far. Whereas the Philadelphia brand's revenues were stagnant when the campaign started in 2009, sales revenues grew 9 percent in the United States and 15 percent worldwide in 2011.

Source: Matthew Boyle, "Philly Cream Cheese's Spreading Appeal," *Bloomberg Businessweek*, December 18, 2011, pp. 32–33.

---

 even a few large U.S. winemakers have attempted to attract more young consumers and broaden the variety of occasions at which they drink wine rather than beer or other beverages. They have pursued these objectives by blending fruitier, less tannic wines, designing whimsical labels and logos—such as the Yellow Tail wallaby from Australia and Fat Bastard from France—and lowering prices to between $3 and $9 a bottle. Consequently, U.S. consumers drank a record 278 million cases of wine in 2005, and consumption has been growing at a brisk 3 percent annual rate.[35]

Market Expansion Strategy

Strategic Issue

In a fragmented and heterogeneous market where some segments are less well developed than others, a market expansion strategy may generate substantial additional volume growth.

In a mature industry with a fragmented and heterogeneous market where some segments are less well developed than others, a market expansion strategy may generate substantial additional volume growth. Such a strategy aims at gaining new customers by targeting new or underdeveloped geographic markets (either regional or foreign) or new customer segments. Once again, share leaders tend to be best suited for implementing this strategy. But even smaller competitors can employ such a strategy successfully if they focus on relatively small or specialized market niches.

Pursuing market expansion by strengthening a firm's position in new or underdeveloped **domestic geographic markets** can lead to experience-curve benefits and operating synergies. The firm can rely on largely the same expertise and technology, and perhaps even the same production and distribution facilities, it has already developed. Unfortunately, domestic geographic expansion is often not viable in a mature industry because the share leaders usually have attained national market coverage. Smaller regional competitors, on the other hand, might consider domestic geographic expansion a means for improving their volume and share position. However, such a move risks retaliation from the large national brands as well as from entrenched regional competitors in the prospective new territory.

To get around the retaliation problem, a regional producer might try to expand through the acquisition of small producers in other regions. This can be a viable option when (1) the low profitability of some regional producers enables the acquiring firm to buy their assets for less than the replacement cost of the capacity involved and (2) synergies gained by combining regional operations and the infusion of resources from the acquiring firm can improve the effectiveness and profitability of the acquired producers.

For example, Clear Channel Worldwide got its start in 1972 when the founders Lowry Mays and Billy Joe McCombs acquired an unprofitable country-music radio station in San Antonio, Texas. They then grew the station, first by buying out other radio stations in a variety of U.S. states, and then by acquiring small, struggling TV stations and outdoor advertising companies. Clear Channel's strategy was to buy radio, TV, and outdoor advertising properties with operations in many of the same local markets; share facilities and staff to cut costs; improve programming; and sell advertising to customers in packages incorporating all three media. As a result, the company achieved significant cost savings, boosted profit margins, and grew to become the fourth largest media company in the world by the early years of the twenty-first century.

In a different approach to domestic market expansion, the firm identifies and develops **new or underserved customer** or **application segments.** Sometimes the firm can effectively reach new customer segments by simply expanding the distribution system or promotional mix without changing the product's characteristics. A sporting goods manufacturer that sells its products to consumers through retail stores, for instance, might expand into the commercial market consisting of schools and amateur and professional sports teams by establishing a direct salesforce. Another recent example is provided by General Mills, Procter & Gamble, Verizon, and other consumer goods and services companies who have targeted America's 45.5 million Hispanics by shifting substantial portions of their promotional budgets into ads on Spanish-language TV. Even though Hispanic households were hit hard by the economic crisis of 2008, they continue to spend heavily on the basics—such as packaged foods and wireless phone services—they like to buy brands advertised on TV, and viewership of the major Hispanic TV networks was up 22 percent in 2008, compared to the stagnant audiences of the English-language networks. Consequently, the Hispanic segment offered a growth opportunity that did not require any major product modifications.[36] In most instances, though, developing new market segments requires modifying the product to make it more suitable for the application or to provide more of the benefits desired by customers in the new segment.

One final possibility for domestic market expansion is to produce **private-label brands** for large retailers such as Sears or Tesco. Firms whose own brands hold relatively weak positions and who have excess production capacity find this a particularly attractive option. Private labeling allows such firms to gain access to established customer segments without making substantial marketing expenditures, thus increasing the firm's volume and lowering its per-unit costs. However, since private labels typically compete with low prices and their sponsors usually have strong bargaining power, producing private labels is often not a very profitable option unless a manufacturer already has a relatively low-cost position in the industry. It also can be a risky strategy, particularly for the smaller firm, because reliance on one or a few large private-label customers can result in drastic volume reductions and unit-cost increases should those customers decide to switch suppliers.[37]

Global Market Expansion—Sequential Strategies

For firms with leading positions in mature domestic markets, less developed markets in foreign countries often present the most viable opportunities for geographic expansion. As discussed in previous chapters, firms can enter foreign markets in a variety of ways, from simply relying on import agents to developing joint ventures to establishing wholly owned subsidiaries—as Johnson Controls has done by acquiring an automotive seat manufacturer in Europe.

Regardless of which mode of entry a firm chooses, it can follow a number of different routes when pursuing global expansion.[38] By *route* we mean the sequence or order in which the firm enters global markets. Japanese companies provide illustrations of different global expansion paths. The most common expansion route involves moving from Japan to developing countries to developed countries. They used this path, for example, with automobiles (Toyota), consumer electronics (National), watches (Seiko), cameras (Minolta), and home appliances, steel, and petrochemicals. This routing reduced manufacturing costs and enabled them to gain marketing experience. In penetrating the U.S. market, the Japanese obtained further economies of scale and gained recognition for their products, which would make penetration of European markets easier.

This sequential strategy succeeded: By the early 1970s, 60 percent of Japanese exports went to developed countries—more than half to the United States. Japanese motorcycles dominate Europe, as do its watches and cameras. Its cars have been able to gain a respectable share in most European countries. Toyota, for instance, sells more than 750,000 cars in the European Union for nearly a 4.5 percent share of that market. Toyota's share of the U.S. market, where it sold 2.5 million cars and trucks, topped 15 percent by 2006, although quality control problems and product recalls have since flattened the firm's growth curve in North America[39]

A second type of *expansion path* has been used primarily for high-tech products such as computers and semiconductors. For the Japanese it consists of first securing their home market and then targeting developed countries. Japan largely ignored developing countries in this strategy because of their small demand for high-tech products. When demand increased to a point where developing countries became "interesting," Japanese producers quickly entered and established strong market positions using price cuts of up to 50 percent.

A home market—developed markets—to developing markets sequence is also usually appropriate for discretionary goods such as soft drinks, convenience foods, or cosmetics. Coca-Cola, for instance, believes that as disposable incomes and discretionary expenditures grow in the countries of South America, Asia, and Africa, those markets will drive much of the company's future growth. Unfortunately for Coke, Pepsi and other major competitors are targeting the same markets.[40] Similarly, firms such as the French cosmetics giant L'Oreal have positioned a number of different "world brands"—including Ralph Lauren perfumes, L'Oreal hair products, and Maybelline and Helena Rubinstein cosmetics—to convey the allure of different cultures to developing markets around the world.[41]

STRATEGIES FOR DECLINING MARKETS

Strategic Issue

The relative attractiveness of the declining product-market and the business's competitive position within it should dictate the appropriate strategy.

Most products eventually enter a decline phase in their life cycles. As sales decline, excess capacity once again develops. As the remaining competitors fight to hold volume in the face of falling sales, industry profits erode. Consequently, conventional wisdom suggests that firms should either divest declining products quickly or harvest them to maximize short-term profits. Not all markets decline in the same way or at the same speed, however, nor do all firms have the same competitive strengths and weaknesses within those markets. Therefore, as in most other situations, the relative attractiveness of the declining product-market and the business's competitive position within it should dictate the appropriate strategy.

Relative Attractiveness of Declining Markets

Although U.S. high school enrollment declined by about 2 million students from its peak in 1976 through the early 1990s, Jostens, Inc., the leading manufacturer of class rings and other school merchandise, achieved annual increases in revenues and profits every year during that period. One reason for the firm's success was that it saw the market decline coming and prepared for it by improving the efficiency of its operations and developing marketing programs that were effective at persuading a larger proportion of students to buy class rings.

Jostens's experience shows that some declining product-markets can offer attractive opportunities well into the future, at least for one or a few strong competitors. In other product-markets, particularly those where decline is the result of customers switching to a new technology (e.g., students buying personal computers instead of portable typewriters), the potential for continued profits during the decline stage is more bleak.

Three sets of factors help determine the strategic attractiveness of declining product-markets: *conditions of demand,* including the rate and certainty of future declines in volume; *exit barriers,* or the ease with which weaker competitors can leave the market; and factors affecting the *intensity of future competitive rivalry* within the market.[42] The impact of these variables on the attractiveness of declining market environments is summarized in Exhibit 10.11 and discussed as follows.

Conditions of Demand

Demand in a product-market declines for a number of reasons. Technological advances produce substitute products (such as electronic calculators for slide rules), often with higher quality or lower cost. Demographic shifts lead to a shrinking target market (baby foods). Customers' needs, tastes, or lifestyles change (the falling consumption of

EXHIBIT 10.11   **Factors Affecting the Attractiveness of Declining Market Environments**

	Environmental Attractiveness	
Conditions of Demand	**Hospitable**	**Inhospitable**
Speed of decline	Very slow	Rapid or erratic
Certainty of decline	100% certain, predictable patterns	Great uncertainty, erratic patterns
Pockets of enduring demand	Several or major ones	No niches
Product differentiation	Brand loyalty	Commodity like products
Price stability	Stable, price premiums attainable	Very unstable, pricing below costs
Exit Barriers		
Reinvestment requirements	None	High, often mandatory and involving capital assets
Excess capacity	Little	Substantial
Asset age	Mostly old assets	Sizable new assets and old ones not retired
Resale markets for assets	Easy to convert or sell	No markets available, substantial costs to retire
Shared facilities	Few, freestanding plants	Substantial and interconnected with important businesses
Vertical integration	Little	Substantial
Single-product competitors	None	Several large companies
Rivalry Determinants		
Customer industries	Fragmented, weak	Strong bargaining power
Customer switching costs	High	Minimal
Diseconomies of scale	None	Substantial penalty
Dissimilar strategic groups	Few	Several in same target markets

high-carbohydrate foods). Finally, the cost of inputs or complementary products rises and shrinks demand (the effects of rising gasoline prices on sales of recreational vehicles).

The cause of a decline in demand can affect both the rate and the predictability of that decline. A fall in sales due to a demographic shift, for instance, is likely to be gradual, whereas the switch to a technically superior substitute can be abrupt. Similarly, the fall in demand as customers switch to a better substitute is predictable, whereas a decline in sales due to a change in tastes is not.

As Exhibit 10.11 indicates, both the rate and certainty of sales decline are demand characteristics that affect a market's attractiveness. A slow and gradual decline allows an orderly withdrawal of weaker competitors. Overcapacity is less likely to become excessive and lead to predatory competitive behavior, and the competitors who remain are more likely to make profits than in a quick or erratic decline. Also, when most industry managers believe market decline is predictable and certain, reduction of capacity is more likely to be orderly than when they feel substantial uncertainty about whether demand might level off or even become revitalized.

Not all segments of a market decline at the same time or at the same rate. The number and size of enduring niches or pockets of demand and the customer purchase behavior within them also influence the continuing attractiveness of the market. When the demand pockets are large or numerous and the customers in those niches are brand loyal and relatively insensitive to price, competitors with large shares and differentiated products can continue to make substantial profits. For example, even though the market for cigars shrank for years, there continued to be a sizable number of smokers who bought premium-quality cigars. Those firms with well-established positions at the premium end of the cigar industry have continued to earn above-average returns.

Exit Barriers

The higher the exit barriers, the less hospitable a product market will be during the decline phase of its life cycle. When weaker competitors find it hard to leave a product market as demand falls, excess capacity develops and firms engage in aggressive pricing or promotional efforts to try to prop up their volume and hold down unit costs. Thus, exit barriers lead to competitive volatility.

Once again, Exhibit 10.11 indicates that a variety of factors influence the ease with which businesses can exit an industry. One critical consideration involves the amount of highly specialized assets. Assets unique to a given business are difficult to divest because of their low liquidation value. The only potential buyers for such assets are other firms who would use them for a similar purpose, which is unlikely in a declining industry. Thus, the firm may have little choice but to remain in the business or to sell the assets for their scrap value. This option is particularly unattractive when the assets are relatively new and not fully depreciated.

Another major exit barrier occurs when the assets or resources of the declining business intertwine with the firm's other business units, either through shared facilities and programs or through vertical integration. Exit from the declining business might shut down shared production facilities, lower salesforce commissions, damage customer relations, and increase unit costs in the firm's other businesses to a point that damages their profitability. Emotional factors also can act as exit barriers. Managers often feel reluctant to admit failure by divesting a business even though it no longer produces acceptable returns. This is especially true when the business played an important role in the firm's history and it houses a large number of senior managers.

Intensity of Future Competitive Rivalry

Even when substantial pockets of continuing demand remain within a declining business, it may not be wise for a firm to pursue them in the face of future intense competitive rivalry. In addition to exit barriers, other factors also affect the ability of the remaining firms to avoid intense price competition and maintain reasonable margins: size and bargaining power of the customers who continue to buy the product; customers' ability to switch to substitute products or to alternative suppliers; and any potential diseconomies of scale involved in capturing an increased share of the remaining volume.

Divestment or Liquidation

When the market environment in a declining industry is unattractive or a business has a relatively weak competitive position, the firm may recover more of its investment by selling the business in the early stages of decline rather than later. The earlier the business is sold, the more uncertain potential buyers are likely to be about the future direction of demand in the industry and thus the more likely that a willing buyer can be found. Thus, Raytheon sold its vacuum tube business in the early 1960s even though transistors had just begun replacing tubes in radios and TV sets and there was still a strong replacement demand for tubes. By moving early, the firm achieved a much higher liquidation value than companies that tried to unload their tube-making facilities in the 1970s when the industry was clearly in its twilight years.[43]

Of course, the firm that divests early runs the risk that its forecast of the industry's future may be wrong. Also, quick divestment may not be possible if the firm faces high exit barriers, such as interdependencies across business units or customer expectations of continued product availability. By planning early for departure, however, the firm may be able to reduce some of those barriers before the liquidation is necessary.

Marketing Strategies for Remaining Competitors

Conventional wisdom suggests that a business remaining in a declining product market should pursue a harvesting strategy aimed at maximizing its cash flow in the short run. But such businesses also have other strategic options. They might attempt to maintain their position as the market declines, improve their position to become the profitable survivor, or focus efforts on one or more remaining demand pockets or market niches. Once again, the appropriateness of these strategies depends on factors affecting the attractiveness of the declining market and on the business's competitive strengths and weaknesses. Exhibit 10.12 summarizes the situational determinants of the appropriateness of each strategy. Some of the marketing actions a firm might take to implement them are discussed below and listed in Exhibit 10.13.

Harvesting Strategy

The objective of a harvesting or milking strategy is to generate cash quickly by maximizing cash flow over a relatively short term. This typically involves avoiding any additional investment in the business, greatly reducing operating (including marketing) expenses, and perhaps raising prices. Since the firm usually expects to ultimately divest or abandon the business, some loss of sales and market share during the pursuit of this strategy is likely. The trick is to hold the business's volume and share declines to a relatively slow and steady rate. A precipitous and premature loss of share would limit the total amount of cash the business could generate during the market's decline.

A harvesting strategy is most appropriate for a firm holding a relatively strong competitive position in the market at the start of the decline and a cadre of current customers likely to continue buying the brand even after marketing support is reduced. Such a strategy also works best when the market's decline is inevitable but likely to occur at a relatively slow and steady rate and when rivalry among remaining competitors is not likely to be very intense. Such conditions enable the business to maintain adequate price levels and profit margins as volume gradually falls.

EXHIBIT 10.12   Situational Determinants of Appropriate Marketing Objectives and Strategies for Declining Markets

Situational Variables	Strategies for Declining Markets			
	Harvesting	Maintenance	Profitable Survivor	Niche
Primary objective	Maximize short-term cash flow; maintain or increase margins even at the expense of a slow decline in market share.	Maintain share in short term as market declines, even if margins must be sacrificed.	Increase share of the declining market with an eye to future profits; encourage weaker competitors to exit.	Focus on strengthening position in one or a few relatively substantial segments with potential for future profits.
Market characteristics	Future market decline is certain, but likely to occur at a slow and steady rate.	Market has experienced recent declines, but future direction and attractiveness are currently hard to predict.	Future market decline is certain, but likely to occur at a slow and steady rate; substantial pockets of demand will continue to exist.	Overall market may decline quickly, but one or more segments will remain as demand pockets or decay slowly.
Competitors' characteristics	Few strong competitors; low exit barriers; future rivalry not likely to be intense.	Few strong competitors, but intensity of future rivalry is hard to predict.	Few strong competitors; exit barriers are low or can be reduced by firm's intervention.	One or more stronger competitors in mass market, but not in the target segment.
Firm's characteristics	Has a leading share position; has a substantial proportion of loyal customers who are likely to continue buying brand even if marketing support is reduced.	Has a leading share of the market and a relatively strong competitive position.	Has a leading share of the market and a strong competitive position; has superior resources or competencies necessary to encourage competitors to exit or to acquire them.	Has a sustainable competitive advantage in target segment, but overall resources may be limited.

Implementing a harvesting strategy means avoiding any additional long-term investments in plant, equipment, or R&D. It also necessitates substantial cuts in operating expenditures for marketing activities. This often means that the firm should greatly reduce the number of models or package sizes in its product line to reduce inventory and manufacturing costs.

The business should improve the efficiency of sales and distribution. For instance, an industrial goods manufacturer might service its smaller accounts through telemarketing or a website rather than a field salesforce or assign its smaller customers to agent middlemen. For consumer goods, the business might move to more selective distribution by concentrating its efforts on the larger retail chains.

The firm would likely reduce advertising and promotion expenditures, usually to the minimum level necessary to retain adequate distribution. Finally, the business should attempt to maintain or perhaps even increase its price levels to increase margins.

Maintenance Strategy

In markets where future volume trends are highly uncertain, a business with a leading share position might consider pursuing a strategy aimed at maintaining its market share, at least until the market's future becomes more predictable. In such a maintenance strategy, the business continues to pursue the same strategy that brought it success during the

Marketing Strategy and Objectives	**Possible Marketing Actions**

Harvesting Strategy
 	
Maximize short-term cash flow; maintain or increase margins even at the expense of market share decline.
	• Eliminate R&D expenditures and capital investments related to the business.
	• Reduce marketing and sales budgets.
	  Greatly reduce or eliminate advertising and sales promotion expenditures, with the possible exception of periodic reminder advertising targeted at current customers.
	  Reduce trade promotions to minimum level necessary to prevent rapid loss of distribution coverage.
	  Focus salesforce efforts on attaining repeat purchases from current customers.
	• Seek ways to reduce production costs, even at the expense of slow erosion in product quality.
	• Raise price if necessary to maintain margins.

Maintenance Strategy Maintain market share for the short term, even at the expense of margins.	• Design service programs to reduce the perceived risks of trial and/or solve the unique problems faced by potential customers in one or multiple underdeveloped segments (e.g., systems engineering, installation, operator training, extended warranties, service hotline, or website). • Continue product and process R&D expenditures in short term aimed at maintaining or improving product quality. • Continue maintenance levels of advertising and sales promotion targeted at current users. • Continue trade promotion at levels sufficient to avoid any reduction in distribution coverage. • Focus salesforce efforts on attaining repeat purchases from current users. • Lower prices if necessary to maintain share, even at the expense of reduced margins.

Profitable Survivor Strategy
 	
Increase share of the declining market; encourage weaker competitors to exit.
	• Signal competitors that firm intends to remain in industry and pursue an increased share.
	  Maintain or increase advertising and sales promotion budgets.
	  Maintain or increase distribution coverage through aggressive trade promotion.
	  Focus some salesforce effort on winning away competitors' customers.
	  Continue product and process R&D to seek product improvements or cost reductions.
	• Consider introducing line extensions to appeal to remaining demand segments.
	• Lower prices if necessary to increase share, even at the expense of short-term margins.
	• Consider agreements to produce replacement parts or private labels for smaller competitors considering getting out of production.

Niche Strategy Strengthen share position in one or a few segments with potential for continued profit.	• Continued product and process R&D aimed at product improvements or modifications that will appeal to target segment(s). • Consider producing for private labels in order to maintain volume and hold down unit costs. • Focus advertising, sales promotion, and personal selling campaigns on customers in target segment(s); stress appeals of greatest importance to those customers. • Maintain distribution channels appropriate for reaching target segment; seek unique channel arrangements to more effectively reach customers in target segment(s). • Design service programs that address unique concerns/problems of customers in the target segment(s).

market's mature stage. This approach often results in reduced margins and profits in the short term, though, because firms usually must reduce prices or increase marketing expenditures to hold share in the face of declining industry volume. Thus, a firm should consider share maintenance an interim strategy. Once it becomes clear that the market will continue to decline, the business should switch to a different strategy that will provide better cash flows and return on investment over the market's remaining life.

Profitable Survivor Strategy

An aggressive alternative for a business with a strong share position and a sustainable competitive advantage in a declining product-market is to invest enough to increase its share position and establish itself as the industry leader for the remainder of the market's decline. This kind of strategy makes most sense when the firm expects a gradual decline in market demand or when substantial pockets of continuing demand are likely well into the future. It is also an attractive strategy when a firm's declining business is closely intertwined with other SBUs through shared facilities and programs or common customer segments.

A strong competitor often can improve its share position in a declining market at relatively low cost because other competitors may be harvesting their businesses or preparing to exit. The key to the success of such a strategy is to encourage other competitors to leave the market early. Once the firm has achieved a strong and unchallenged position, it can switch to a harvesting strategy and reap substantial profits over the remaining life of the product market.

A firm might encourage smaller competitors to abandon the industry by being visible and explicit about its commitment to become the leading survivor. It should aggressively seek increased market share, either by cutting prices or by increasing advertising and promotion expenditures. It also might introduce line extensions aimed at remaining pockets of demand to make it more difficult for smaller competitors to find profitable niches. Finally, the firm might act to reduce its competitors' exit barriers, making it easier for them to leave the industry. This could involve taking over competitors' long-term contracts, agreeing to supply spare parts or to service their products in the field, or providing them with components or private-label products. For instance, large regional bakeries have encouraged grocery chains to abandon their own bakery operations by supplying them with private-label baked goods.

The ultimate way to remove competitors' exit barriers is to purchase their operations and either improve their efficiency or remove them from the industry to avoid excess capacity. With continued decline in industry sales a certainty, smaller competitors may be forced to sell their assets at a book value price low enough for the survivor to reap high returns on its investment.

Niche Strategy

Even when most segments of an industry are expected to decline rapidly, a niche strategy may still be viable if one or more substantial segments will either remain as stable pockets of demand or decay slowly. The business pursuing such a strategy should have a strong competitive position in the target segment or be able to build a sustainable competitive advantage relatively quickly to preempt competitors. This is one strategy that even smaller competitors can sometimes successfully pursue because they can focus the required assets and resources on a limited portion of the total market. The marketing actions a business might take to strengthen and preserve its position in a target niche are similar to those discussed earlier concerning niche strategies in mature markets.

Marketing Plan Exercise

Identify an appropriate marketing strategy consistent with the product's stage in its product life cycle and the market and competitive conditions it faces, drawing on Chapters 8, 9, and/or 10 as appropriate. Identify the strategies key competitors are using, and develop a rationale for the strategy you have chosen.

Discussion Questions

1. Suppose you were the marketing manager for General Foods' Cool Whip frozen dessert topping. Marketing research indicates that nearly three-quarters of all households use your product, but the average user only buys it four times a year, and Cool Whip is used on only 7 percent of all toppable desserts. What marketing strategy (or strategies) would you recommend and why? What specific marketing actions would you propose to implement that strategy?

2. In recent years, McDonald's—which had attained decades of outstanding growth by selling burgers and fries to American families with young children—has aggressively sought franchisees in foreign countries, including Russia and China. The firm has also introduced a wide variety of new product lines and line extensions (breakfast items such as Egg McMuffin, Chicken McNuggets, McChicken sandwiches, low-carbohydrate salads, etc.). What was the strategic rationale for these moves?

3. The J. B. Kunz Corporation, the leading manufacturer of passbooks and other printed forms for financial institutions, saw its market gradually decline during the 1980s and 1990s because the switch to electronic banking was making its product superfluous. Nevertheless, the firm bought up the assets of a number of smaller competitors, greatly increased its market share within its industry, and managed to earn a very high return on investment. What kind of strategy was the company pursuing? Why do you think the firm was able to achieve a high ROI in the face of industry decline?

Self-diagnostic questions to test your ability to apply the analytical tools and concepts in this chapter to marketing decision making may be found at this book's website at **www.mhhe.com/walker8e.**

Endnotes

1. This example is based on material found in Rick Tetzeli, "Mining Money in Mature Markets," *Fortune,* March 22, 1993, pp. 77–80; Edmund Chew, "Johnson Controls Inc. Displays Interior Concepts at Frankfurt Auto Show," *Automotive News,* October 29, 2001, p. 18; Thomas Content, "Johnson Controls Completes Two European Acquisitions," www.jsonline.com. June 20, 2011; and Johnson Controls' 2011 Annual 10K Report, found on the company's website at www.jci.com.

2. Peter N. Golder and Gerard J. Tellis, *Cascades, Diffusion, and Turning Points in the Product Life Cycle, Report # 03-120* (Cambridge, MA: Marketing Science Institute, 2003).

3. For a more detailed discussion of these traps, see Michael E. Porter, *Competitive Strategy* (New York: Free Press, 1980), pp. 247–49.

4. Fareena Sultan, John U. Farley, and Donald R. Lehmann, "A Meta-Analysis of Application of Diffusion Models," *Journal of Marketing Research,* February 1990, pp. 70–77.

5. Ming Jer Chen and Ian C. MacMillan, "Nonresponse and Delayed Response to Competitive Moves: The Roles of Competitor Dependence and Action Irreversibility," *Academy of Management Journal* 35 (1992), pp. 539–70; Hubert Gatignon, Eric Anderson, and Kristiann Helsen, "Competitive Reaction to Market Entry: Explaining Interfirm Differences," *Journal of Marketing Research,* February 1989, pp. 45–55; and William T. Robinson and Sungwook Min, "Is the First to Market the First to Fail? Empirical Evidence for Industrial Goods Businesses," *Journal of Marketing Research* 39 (February 2002), pp. 120–128.

6. Nanette Byrnes, Peter Burrows, and Louise Lee, "Dark Days at Dell," *BusinessWeek,* September 4, 2006, pp. 26–29; and Aaron Ricadela, "Dell: Scant Signs of Recovery," www.businessweek.com/technology, July 14, 2009.

7. Cathy Anterasian and Lynn W. Phillips, "Discontinuities, Value Delivery, and the Share-Returns Association: A Re-Examination of the 'Share-Causes-Profits' Controversy," distributed working paper (Cambridge, MA: Marketing Science Institute, April 1988). Also see Robert Jacobson, "Distinguishing among Competing Theories of the Market Share Effect," *Journal of Marketing,* October 1988, pp. 68–80.

8. William K. Hall, "Survival Strategies in a Hostile Environment," *Harvard Business Review,* September–October 1980, pp. 75–85.

9. Michael Treacy and Fred Wiersema, *The Discipline of Market Leaders* (Reading, MA: Addison-Wesley, 1995).

10. Roland T. Rust, Christine Moorman, and Peter R. Dickson, "Getting Return on Quality: Revenue Expansion, Cost Reduction, or Both?" *Journal of Marketing* 66, October 2002, pp. 7–24.

11. Rahul Jacob, "Beyond Quality and Value," *Fortune,* Special Issue, Autumn–Winter 1993, pp. 8–11.

12. The following discussion is based on material found in David A. Garvin, "What Does 'Product Quality' Really Mean?" *Sloan Management Review,* Fall 1984, pp. 25–43; and David A. Aaker, *Strategic Market Management,* 5th ed. (New York: John Wiley & Sons, 1998), chap. 9.

13. Kathleen Kerwin, "When Flawless Isn't Enough," *BusinessWeek,* December 8, 2003, pp. 80–82.

14. For a more extensive discussion of brand equity, see David A. Aaker, *Brand Equity* (New York: Free Press, 1991).

15. Valarie A. Zeithaml, A. Parasuraman, and Leonard L. Berry, *Delivering Quality Service: Balancing Customer Perceptions and Expectations* (New York: Free Press, 1990). See also Valarie A. Zeithaml and Mary Jo Bitner, *Services Marketing* (New York: McGraw-Hill, 1996).

16. Valarie A. Zeithaml, A. Parasuraman, and Arvind Malhotra, *A Conceptual Framework for Understanding E-Service Quality: Implications for Future Research and Managerial Practice,* Report No. 00-115 (Cambridge, MA: Marketing Science Institute, 2000). Also see Mary Wolfinbarger and Mary C. Gilly, "E-TailQ: Dimensionalizing, Measuring, and Predicting E-Tail Quality," *Journal of Retailing* 79 (Fall 2003), pp. 183–98.

17. Spencer E. Ante, "The Science of Desire," *BusinessWeek,* June 5, 2006, pp. 98–106.

18. For a case example of how an employee training program might be designed to improve service performance, see Andrew J. Czaplewski, Eric M. Olson, and Stanley F. Slater, "Applying the RATER Model for Service Success," *Marketing Management,* January–February 2002, pp. 14–17. For a broader review of academic research on service, see Roland T. Rust and Tuck Siong Chung, "Marketing Models of Service and Relationships," *Marketing Science* 25 (November–December 2006), pp. 560–80.

19. Rita Di Mascio, "The Service Models of Frontline Employees," *Journal of Marketing* 74 (July 2010), pp. 66–80.

20. For a more detailed discussion of these and other approaches for lowering costs, see Aaker, *Strategic Market Management,* chap. 10.

21. Akshay R. Rao, Mark E. Bergen, and Scott Davis, "How to Fight a Price War," *Harvard Business Review,* March–April 2000, pp. 107–16; and Harald J. Van Heerde, Els Gijsbrechts, and Koen Pauwels, "Winners and Losers in a Major Price War," *Journal of Marketing Research* 45, October 2008, pp. 499–518.

22. Pete Engardio, "The Future of Outsourcing," *BusinessWeek,* January 30, 2006, pp. 50–64.

23. Pete Engardio, "Can the U.S. Bring Jobs Back From China?" *BusinessWeek,* June 30, 2008, pp. 39–43.

24. "The Trouble with Outsourcing," *The Economist,* July 30, 2011, p. 64.

25. Mara Der Hovanesian, "Coffee, Tea, or Mortgage," *BusinessWeek,* April 3, 2006, pp. 48–49.

26. Robert Jacobson and David A. Aaker, "The Strategic Role of Product Quality," *Journal of Marketing,* October 1987, pp. 31–44; Rust, Moorman, and Dickson, "Getting Return on Quality;" Gerard J. Tellis, Eden Yin, and Rakesh Niraj, "Does Quality Win? Network Effects Versus Quality in High-Tech Markets," *Journal of Marketing Research* 46 (April 2009), pp. 135–149; and Sundar G. Bharadwaj, Kapril R. Tuli, and Andre Bonfrer, "The Impact of Brand Quality on Shareholder Wealth," *Journal of Marketing* 75 (September 2011), pp. 88–104.

27. Brad Stone, "What's in the Box? Instant Gratification," *Bloomberg Businessweek,* November 29, 2010, pp. 39–40.

28. Frederick F. Reichheld, *The Ultimate Question: Driving Good Profits and True Growth* (Toronto: The University of Toronto Press, 2006). See also Jena McGregor, "Would You Recommend Us?" *BusinessWeek,* January 30, 2006, pp. 94–95.

29. For a discussion of various approaches to measuring customer satisfaction and models relating satisfaction to dimensions of financial performance, see Susan J. Devlin and H. K. Dong, "Service Quality from the Customer's Perspective," *Marketing Research* 6 (1994), pp. 5–13; Roland T. Rust, Katherine N. Lemon, and Valarie Zeithaml, "Return on Marketing: Using Customer Equity to Focus Marketing Strategy," *Journal of Marketing* 68 (January 2004), pp. 109–27; Vernna Vogel, Heiner Evanschitzky, and B. Ramaseshan, "Customer Equity Drivers and Future Sales," *Journal of Marketing* 72 (November 2008), pp. 98–108; and Paul W. Farris, Neil T. Bendle, Phillip E. Pfeifer, and David J. Reibstein, *Marketing Metrics,* 2nd ed. (Upper Saddle River, NJ: Pearson Education, 2010), pp. 56–62.

30. Frederick F. Reichheld, "Loyalty and the Renaissance of Marketing," *Marketing Management* 2 (1994), pp. 10–21. Also see Rahul Jacob, "Why Some Customers Are More Equal than Others," *Fortune,* September 19, 1994, pp. 215–24.

31. Reichheld, "Loyalty and the Renaissance of Marketing." See also Murali Chandrashekaran, Kristin Rotte, Stephen S. Tax, and Rajdeep Grewal, "Satisfaction Strength and Customer Loyalty," *Journal of Marketing Research* 44 (February 2007), pp. 153–63.

32. Rachael King, "Sentiment Analysis Gives Companies Insight into Consumer Opinion," www.businessweek.com, March 1, 2011.

33. The following discussion is largely based on Brady, "Why Service Stinks," pp. 118–28.

34. For examples, see Sunil Gupta, Donald R. Lehmann, and Jennifer Ames Stuart, *Valuing Customers, Report # 01-119* (Cambridge, MA: Marketing Science Institute, 2001); Rajkumar Venkatesan and V. Kumar, *Using Customer Lifetime Value in Customer Selection and Resource Allocation, Report # 03-112* (Cambridge, MA: Marketing Science Institute, 2003); and Michael D. Johnson and Fred Selnes, "Customer Portfolio Management: Toward a Dynamic Theory of Customer Exchange Relationships," *Journal of Marketing* 68, April 2004, pp. 1–17.

35. Julia Flynn, "In Napa Valley, Winemaker's Brands Divide an Industry," *The Wall Street Journal,* February 22, 2005, pp. A1 and A8; and David Kiley, "Winning Back Joe Corkscrew," *BusinessWeek,* April 24, 2006, pp. 82–83.

36. Ronald Grover, "The Payoff from Targeting Hispanics," *BusinessWeek,* April 20, 2009, p. 76.

37. For a more detailed discussion of private-label strategy see Nirmalya Kumar and Jan-Benedict E. M. Steenkamp, *Private Label Strategy: How to Meet the Store-Brand Challenge* (Boston: Harvard Business School Press, 2007); and Jan-Benedict E. M. Steenkamp, Harald J. Van Heerde, and Inge Geyskens, "What Makes Consumers Willing to Pay a Price Premium for National Brands Over Private Labels?" *Journal of Marketing Research* 47 (December 2010), pp. 1011–1024.

38. The following discussion of sequential strategies is based largely on material found in Somkid Jatusripitak, Liam Fahey, and Philip Kotler, "Strategic Global Marketing: Lessons from the Japanese," *Columbia Journal of World Business,* Spring 1985, pp. 47–53.

39. Brian Bremmer and Chester Dawson, "Can Anything Stop Toyota?" *BusinessWeek,* November 17, 2003, pp. 114–22; and Alex Taylor III, "America's Best Car Company," *Fortune,* March 19, 2007, pp. 98–104.

40. Bruce Einhorn and Nanette Byrnes, "Coke vs. Pepsi: The Slugfest in China," *BusinessWeek,* July 13 & 20, 2009, p. 70. For other examples, see "Fighting for the Next Billion Shoppers," *The Economist,* June 30, 2012, pp. 65–67.

41. Gail Edmonson, "The Beauty of Global Branding," *BusinessWeek,* June 28, 1999, pp. 70–75.

42. Kathryn Rudie Harrigan and Michael E. Porter, "End-Game Strategies for Declining Industries," *Harvard Business Review,* July–August 1983, pp. 111–20. Also see Kathryn Rudie Harrigan, *Managing Maturing Businesses* (New York: Lexington Books, 1988).

43. Harrigan and Porter, "End-Game Strategies," p. 114.

Chapter **Eleven**

Marketing Strategies for a Digitally Networked World

Opportunities in the App Economy[1]

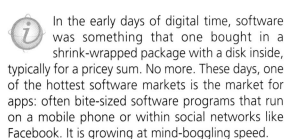 In the early days of digital time, software was something that one bought in a shrink-wrapped package with a disk inside, typically for a pricey sum. No more. These days, one of the hottest software markets is the market for apps: often bite-sized software programs that run on a mobile phone or within social networks like Facebook. It is growing at mind-boggling speed.

Apple's Apps Store, launched in the summer of 2009, was offering more than 100,000 apps for its hot-selling iPhone by year-end. By 2011, consumers had spent more than $4.3 billion on apps, upgrades, and the advertising that appears within them. Eddie Marks, who with some college friends at Stanford created a simple app, Shotgun, that lets iPhone users use their phone to simulate the sound of cocking and firing a shotgun, set out to make a little beer money. "We've made more than $1 million," from the ads that pop up on their app, says Marks. It beats taking a real job, say the duo's envious friends. Google's Google Play app store for Android devices has raced to get into the game, with more than 600,000 apps available by mid-2012, a figure similar to Apple's fast-growing total. Rival app stores have also sprung up, though none can match Apple's and Google's inventory.

But it's not just the number of apps and stores that sell them that is growing. It's also the volumes of revenue—and profit—that some apps enjoy. Zynga, with its hits like FarmVille, an app that runs inside the Facebook community, surpassed the $100 million mark in revenue in just two years. Zynga's success with FarmVille and other hot titles led to its billion-dollar IPO in December 2011, though its share price is down by nearly half as we write.

Games as Apps

While it is not entirely clear to us why tens of millions of people want to be online farmers—and pay real money for digital cattle, seeds, tractors, and more—there's clearly something powerful happening here. And it's profitable, too. When Zynga offered its new digital sweet potato seeds at $5 per packet, FarmVille players bought more than $400,000 worth of them in the first three days. Since the seeds are virtual, of course, they cost Zynga virtually nothing to produce, and the revenue drops directly to Zynga's bottom line. It's no wonder that London-based imitator Playfish and California-based Playdom have attracted both venture capital and players in droves.

More than Games

The hot app economy isn't just about games, however. Far from it. FedEx offers a mobile app for the iPhone that tracks shipments' status and provides updates of when the package arrives. Salesforce .com offers an app on a variety of platforms that lets salespeople monitor leads and account information while on the go. Proongo lets business travelers log their travel expenses and photos of receipts, then e-mails the data back to their desktop. Increasingly, thanks to apps, work that used to be done in the office on a PC can now be done on a tablet or mobile phone.

There's also a growing number of apps to suit just about anyone's lifestyle. With Flixster—a free app that works on your iPhone, Android device, Black-Berry, or Palm—you can check movie show times, read reviews, and even watch trailers so you can decide where to go with the hot date you have lined up for next weekend. With CNN Mobile—a $2 app for your iPhone or iPad—you can keep up to date with live video coverage of breaking news. With ESPN ScoreCenter, you can follow the play-by-play action and grab schedules and stats for your favorite team.

Business Models

But how—other than selling digital sweet potato seeds and tractors—you might ask, can the proliferation of app providers or the social networks that host some of them make any money? The reality is that most of them don't. But one way, aside from selling virtual goods, is to charge a small fee for downloading the app, such as the $2 that CNN charges for CNN Mobile. The $2.99 "I am T-Pain" app, which lets fans of the performer mimic his robot like voice, pulled in downloads worth a seven figure sum. Another way to make money is by placing ads inside your app, as the Shotgun founders did. AdMob, since its start-up in early 2006, has placed more than 200 billion ads—including ads for blue-chip clients like Ford and Coca-Cola—in websites appearing on mobile phones and in apps on iPhones and Android devices. Some researchers expect mobile advertising to grow into a $10 billion business by 2014.

Facebook, with $3.7 billion in revenue in 2011, of which $3.1 billion was from advertising, and its own hot—and then not so hot—IPO, appears to have begun to figure out how to generate meaningful amounts of revenue. For Twitter, now five years old, the jury is still out. As columnist Jessi Hempel noted in early 2009, "Twitter has no business model." By 2012, some observers saw progress, however, with companies as diverse as Nike, Disney, and General Motors testing ways to use Twitter effectively.

Is It Real, or Is It a Bubble?

All the phenomena we're discussing are rooted in today's reality that people are now digitally networked practically everywhere they go. They use LinkedIn to connect with business associates, Facebook to stay connected with family and friends, and their mobile phones to stay connected while on the go. Observers and investors wonder, however, whether there are enduring businesses here, or whether it's all just another internet bubble.

As the social networking phenomenon approaches market saturation—Facebook alone has some 900 million active users globally—its double-digit growth in users is slowing down. Noted investor Warren Buffett warns that valuations of social networking companies have become overvalued, and that investors should be wary as some of these companies prepare to sell their shares to the public in IPOs. True to Buffett's prediction, Facebook, Zynga, Groupon, and others have seen their share prices drop substantially post-IPO.

Whatever the valuations, though, it appears that digitally enabled social networks of many kinds and the apps that are developed to serve them are here to stay. Some will become real companies, making real money. Others, undoubtedly, will disappear as quickly as the morning dew on a warm summer day. For marketers of all kinds, however, the ubiquity and reach of the social networking phenomenon and the proliferation of apps means that these phenomena demand full attention.

STRATEGIC CHALLENGES ADDRESSED IN CHAPTER 11

As the vibrant market for apps and social networking sites shows, the quest for new, marketable ideas in today's digitally networked world hasn't run out of fuel. The rapid pace of change on the web, in mobile telephony, and in related technologies offers an abundance of opportunities to create new companies, and it can help transform stone-age companies and provide them with attractive opportunities for growth. But, for most companies, the optimal path through the digital maze is far from clear.

Thus, in Chapter 11, we address several timely and important questions that marketing managers in today's companies and entrepreneurs must ask. Does every company need a digital or social media strategy? Do recent technological advances represent threats or opportunities? Most important, how should marketers address the development of strategies to take advantage of—or defend against—the rapid pace of change inherent in today's digitally networked world? What marketing roles can the internet, social networking, and other recent and future technological developments play, and to which of these should significant resources be allocated?

We begin by reviewing several trends that highlight the growing importance of social networking and other related digital developments. We then identify the fundamental principles that underlie today's digital phenomena and the key advantages and disadvantages inherent therein, all of which every marketer must clearly understand. Next, we identify some of the roles that digital networking technologies can plausibly play in marketing strategies, and we articulate a decision framework for managers to use to decide which of the growing array of such tools their firms should employ—from web-based marketing research to advertising on mobile phones or tablets to the delivery of digitized information, goods, and services over the web. Finally, we take a brief look into what it is likely to take to effectively serve the dot-com and mobile markets of tomorrow.

DOES EVERY COMPANY NEED A DIGITAL OR SOCIAL MEDIA STRATEGY?

Like it or not, despite the scepticism of some early observers, the digital revolution and social networks like Facebook, LinkedIn, and some not yet conceived as we write in mid-2012, are here to stay. And it's not just teens and twenty-somethings who are getting on board. Though social networking penetration is highest among the 18-to-24 age group at 90 percent, more than half the online population aged 45 to 64 were expected to use social networks regularly in 2011, with further growth expected in future years (see Exhibit 11.1)[2]

EXHIBIT 11.1 Social Networking Demography

U.S. Social Network User Penetration, by Age, 2009–2013 (Historical and Forecast)

	% of internet Users in Each Group Who Use Social Networks				
Age	**2009**	**2010**	**2011**	**2012**	**2013**
0–11	12	14	15	16	17
12–17	75	78	81	84	85
18–24	83	88	90	92	93
25–34	70	77	82	84	85
35–44	52	65	72	75	77
45–54	42	53	58	63	65
55–64	35	48	52	55	57
65+	20	28	31	34	36
Total	**52**	**60**	**64**	**66**	**67**

Note: Internet users who use social networks via any device at least once per month.
Source: eMarketer, February 2011, "Days of Double-Digit Growth in Social Network Use Are Over," at *www.emarketer.com/Article.aspx?R=1008288.*

If you're in newspaper publishing, everyone knows that digital media are eating the lunch of their print brethren, though in some emerging markets that's not the case.[3] If you're in retailing, online (and now mobile) retailing is inexorably taking business from traditional bricks-and-mortar stores.[4] As a result, most newspaper publishers and retailers are working hard to develop digital strategies. At Macy's, the American department store chain internet sales at Macy's and Bloomingdale's jumped 40 percent in 2011.[5] Even Walmart has belatedly decided to "make winning e-commerce a key priority," says CEO Mike Duke.[6] But what about companies in other industries?

Ted Schadler, a Forrester analyst who surveyed 68,000 U.S. homes, says there are important implications in the rapidly changing digital world for nearly all marketers. "The rise of consumers' adoption of personal devices, home networking and broadband, combined with the increasing importance of the internet in media, retail, banking, and health care, means that every consumer-facing industry must better understand the intricacies of technology adoption and use. Missing from most marketers' tool boxes is an understanding that consumers' attitudes toward technology determine a lot about how they receive marketing messages, get service online, adopt new technologies, and spend their time."[7] Consumers having more than five years of online experience spend 24 percent less time reading newspapers and 23 percent less time in front of the TV, according to the Forrester report. And these marketing implications are confined neither to social media nor to the United States. The implications of these changes are equally dramatic virtually everywhere, even in China, and the growing penetration of smartphones and tablets—including the Apple iPad and its imitators—is exacerbating them.

Advertisers, too, are getting on board. Procter & Gamble, the world's largest advertiser, has made social media an integral part of its brand-building efforts, and all its major brands now include social media elements in their marketing plans. "For us, the real aha! was an incredible ability to listen to consumers much better, much faster, more broadly," says Alex Tosolini, head of e-business at P&G.[8] These efforts have led to Facebook campaigns that have delivered market share rises of 11 percent for Pepto-Bismol (as a reliever of Saturday night eating and drinking binges) and 5 percent for Secret, a deodorant targeted at teenage girls.[9] But measurement of the effectiveness of such campaigns remains difficult, observes Oliver Fleurot, CEO of MSL Groups, a global PR network owned by Publicis Groupe. "Measurement in social media is still in its very, very, early infancy," he says. "Advertisers are clearly intrigued by this space where 900 million people interact. They are not sure how to be part of the conversation."[10]

What should marketers conclude from these developments? Notwithstanding the mind-boggling stock market valuations of social networking companies, notwithstanding the difficulties many companies have had in developing business models that actually make money, and notwithstanding the so-called digital divide, in which some segments of the population are still underrepresented in the internet population, the long-term prospects for jumping into the digitally networked world with both feet are still enormous. The growing market acceptance of the internet and various digitally networked technologies—both software and hardware—and the inherent advantages that they bring suggest that nearly every company needs to examine how it will be affected by and can take advantage of these developments.

The outcome of such an examination might well be the development of the company's own digital or social media strategy. The fact that one's competitors will surely develop and deploy such strategies is a further argument for doing so. But care needs to be taken in doing so, not only in developing cost-effective strategies that deliver results, but also in addressing a variety of ethical issues that are likely to arise (see Ethical Perspective 11.1). Today's well-educated business students can bring up-to-date insights—as well as digital and social networking expertise—to the companies they join.

Ⓔ Ethical Perspective The Growing Risks of Information Ubiquity 11.1

As smartphones and their applications make it possible for users to tell the world where they are moment by moment—as they check in on Foursquare at their local Starbucks, for example—their whereabouts, if not properly protected, may become known to others, whether they like it or not. Even more dramatic are new wearable devices or apps that continuously detect and transmit a user's medical data. These devices are collecting what is, in many cases, extremely sensitive information. "We are all part of a brave new experiment in privacy whose outcome is unclear," says Alessandro Acquisti, a professor at Carnegie Mellon University.

What is a company considering the gathering or use of such information to do? Clear principles should be established, for example, indicating that it is the users who own their data and it is they who should decide what to do with the stuff. This means, among other things, that opt-in formats and easy opt-outs should be part of any such solution. Such firms also need to be transparent about exactly what information is being collected and how it is being used.

Source: Martin Giles, "Here Comes Anywhere," *The Economist Special Report, Personal Technology,* October 8, 2011, pp. 15–16.

THREATS OR OPPORTUNITIES? THE INHERENT ADVANTAGES AND DISADVANTAGES OF THE DIGITALLY NETWORKED WORLD FOR MARKETERS

What advantages do the new internet, telecommunication, and social networking technologies provide to marketers and their customers? Eight potentially attractive elements characterize them: the ability to optimize, the syndication of information, the increasing returns to scale of network products, the ability to efficiently personalize and customize market offerings, the ability to disintermediate distribution, global reach, round-the-clock access, and the possibility of instantaneous delivery. Collectively, these elements lie at the heart of **viral marketing,** wherein those who see something they like on the web or on their mobile phones share it with others. Viral marketing, of course, is a marketer's nirvana, as it makes it possible to gain widespread awareness, perhaps even adoption, at little cost. A recent study has examined how marketers can best "seed" and manage a viral marketing effort. The study found that the best seeding strategies can be eight times more effective than others, and it identified four key factors that are central to viral marketing success: message content, the structure of the social network that is targeted, the behavior of the recipients, and the incentives for them to share the message, and the seeding strategy.[11] Thus, taking best advantage of today's digital tools requires a keen understanding of what makes them possible, along with creative planning and effective implementation. We examine the eight fundamental elements next.

The Ability to Optimize

In many aspects of marketing practice, it can be difficult for marketers to understand what is working, what's not, and why. The beauty of today's digital technologies is that everything is measurable. Data—and data analytics—rules! Tools like Omniture's Test & Target or Google's web Optimizer enable marketers to dynamically change content aimed at different market segments and optimize what runs where to get the biggest bang for the buck. Whether it's paid search, banner ads, or even a social networking effort on Facebook (we address these tools and others later in this chapter), the ability to measure everything, while working at a scale that has not been possible before, and optimize spending is what sets today's digital marketing efforts apart from the rest of the marketing effort.

That said, however, as the digital landscape changes so fast, new companies with new metrics and techniques are fueling rapid innovation in the digital marketing and **big data** arenas, and attracting considerable amount of venture capital as well. Thus, while marketers are excited about—and even obsessed with—all the data that's now available to them, knowing exactly what to do with the data, and how to make the most of it, is not always clear.

The Syndication of Information

Syndication involves the sale of the same good—typically an informational good—to many customers, who may then combine it with information from other sources and distribute it. The entertainment and publishing worlds have long employed syndication, producing comic strips, newspaper columns, and TV shows that appear in many places at once. Without syndication, today's mass media would not exist as we know them. Though internet marketers rarely use the word *syndication* to describe what they do, it lies at the heart of many e-commerce business models. Inktomi, an **originator** of syndicated content, provides its search engine technology to many branded search engine sites. YellowBrix, a **syndicator,** provides news articles in electronic form and delivers them to other sites, each of which appeals to a different target audience. E*Trade, a **distributor** of syndicated information, brings together from many sources content relevant to its investor clientele and packages it in ways useful to these clients. iMode, the mobile telephone operator in Japan, syndicates an enormous variety of information—even cartoons.

Why is syndication important? First, because syndication delivers informational goods (digitized text, audio, music, photos, CAD/CAM files, even digital sweet potato seeds), rather than tangible goods, a person or company can syndicate the same informational goods or services to an almost infinite number of customers with little incremental cost. Variable costs approach zero. Producers of tangible goods and most services (from chocolate bars to haircuts) must spend money on sugar and chocolate or labor for each additional chocolate bar or haircut sold. Not so for information producers, where sending a digital copy of a photo or an internet news feature to one more recipient, or a Facebook posting of where you had lunch today, is essentially free. Second, the syndication process can be automated and digitized, enabling syndicated networks to be created, expanded, and flexibly adapted far more quickly than would be possible in the physical world. By using technology called **Really Simple Syndication (RSS),** syndicated content can be fed to users having preferences for such content (see Exhibit 11.2).

Syndication via the internet—and via mobile phones or tablets or other devices—opens up endless opportunities for marketers. It replaces scarcity with abundance. Information

---

EXHIBIT 11.2 *RSS Lets Expedia Send Customized Alerts for Hot Travel Deals*

You're planning your spring break holiday, and you know what you want, but you're tired of searching countless websites for the best deal to the sunniest destination. Now, thanks to Really Simply Syndication (RSS) technology, Expedia.com lets customers select alerts for exactly the sort of travel they are planning. A sunny beach in Mexico? No problem. A luxury villa in Italy? Easy. Expedia's Sally McKenzie says, "This is just another example of how Expedia (gives) travelers the travel intelligence and tools they want, when, where, and how they want it."

The power of RSS is that it lets consumers with newsreader facilities in their browsers specify the kind of syndicated information they want to see. Follow your stock portfolio? Track your favorite football team? RSS makes it simple. Or, if it's travel info you want, tell Expedia where you want to go at *www.expedia.com/rss*, and they'll watch the best deals for you.

Source: PR Newswire, "Expedia.com Introduces Most Comprehensive Service Providing Real-Time Travel Deal Alerts Leveraging RSS Technology," May 2, 2006.

can be replicated an infinite number of times and combined and re-combined in an infinite number of ways. It can be distributed everywhere, all at once, and be available all the time. At ChinesePod, a web 2.0–based language school founded in 2005 by Shanghai-based Irishman Ken Carroll, millions of students in more than 100 countries have downloaded free Chinese podcast language lessons, an example of the power of syndication. About 250,000 listen regularly, and some sign up for premium services, such as live conversations in Mandarin with a tutor in Shanghai, using Skype and their broadband connection. Carroll's 35 employees in Shanghai, including some of the city's best language teachers, together with ChinesePod's Apple and Android apps, serve customers from Alaska to the Vatican.[12]

Taking advantage of the full potential of syndication, however, requires new thinking. Companies need to identify and occupy the most important niches in syndication networks. These are the ones that maximize the number and strength of links to other companies and customers, though shifting market conditions inevitably mean that these links must change as markets evolve. Bloomberg, the ubiquitous provider of syndicated information to stock traders and analysts, is an example of a company that has positioned itself well; many of its clients now regard their Bloomberg terminals as indispensable. Thus, almost any company can think of itself as part of a larger, interconnected world and seek ways to occupy originator, syndicator, or distributor roles in an appropriate syndication network.

Increasing Returns to Scale of Network Products[13]

Any undergraduate economics student knows that an increased supply of a good leads to lower value, hence lower prices. But that was before fax machines, operating systems, and other products used in networks, where the second fax machine, for example, makes the first one more valuable, and so on. This characteristic of informational networks— a product becomes more valuable as the number of users increases—is often called a **positive network effect,** or **network externality.** When combined with the syndication of informational products, this characteristic has led to the seemingly crazy strategy of giving one's product away for free, often a strategy of choice for marketers! Facebook and other social networks offer potential value for advertisers and others in the large network that they have created, though Facebook users pay nothing to participate in the network.

Are the various networks a thing of the future, or will their "closed worlds," each walled off from the others, make them dinosaurs in the end? David Ascher, of Thunderbird, an open-source e-mail provider, says "E-mail in the wider sense is the most important social network." Charlene Li, an analyst with Forrester Research and author of *Groundswell,* a book on the social technology phenomenon, shares Ascher's doubts about their staying power. "We will look back to 2008 and think it archaic and quaint that we had to go to a destination like Facebook or LinkedIn to be social," she says. Future social networks "will be like air. They will be everywhere and anywhere we want them to be."[14] Four years later, however, as we write in 2012, the closed social networks are still going strong.

The network effects of today's digitally networked world have spawned considerable new thinking about the relative value of different kinds of media. Conventionally, there were two broad media categories: paid media—magazine, TV and radio ads and the like— and publicity, now referred to as earned media, which marketers coveted but did not pay for, at least directly. Today, the potential for social media like Facebook to deliver word-of-mouth conversations about a brand has moved to a front-and-center position in brand managers' deliberations about how to deliver truly integrated and cost effective marketing campaigns (see Exhibit 11.3).

EXHIBIT 11.3 *Paid Media, Earned Media, Owned Media: What's Your Company's Focus?*

No longer is what marketers used to call "publicity" an afterthought. Given the growing power of digital marketing, marketing professionals now think of media as divided into three categories: **owned media** (such as a brand's website, blog, or Twitter account), **paid media** (print and broadcast ads and the like, along with such things as paid search or online display ads), and **earned media** (places where customers themselves—and their Facebook pages or tweets, for example—become the medium). While the boundaries between the categories can be blurry (Is a Facebook fan page owned or earned, for example? What about a branded YouTube video?), for some marketers, paid media are now seen, to a significant degree, as catalysts for winning consumers' engagement via earned media like Facebook and Twitter.

A key challenge for marketers is how to integrate all three kinds of media for maximum—and cost-effective—results. Hallmark, the greeting card company, created a series of touchpoints for moms to connect with like-minded moms and with Hallmark itself. As a result, some moms created videos about Hallmark products, others wrote blog posts about Hallmark, and others then shared these videos or posts with their social networks.

As observer Curtis Hougland asks, "Why would a TV spot end and there be no URL or Facebook page? The conversation should be ongoing and cross-platform." Increasingly, earned media are the holy grail. You run a Super Bowl ad (paid), which gets the media talking about it (earned) and Twitterers (also earned) abuzz. But achieving success in earned media "often requires a paid spark," says Grant Owens, an account planning vice president at digital marketing agency Razorfish. "We have empirical evidence that a kick-start from paid media is often the difference between a cultural juggernaut and complete silence."

According to Forrester, more than half a billion word-of-mouth impressions were made online in the United States as long ago as 2009, a figure that is certainly far higher today. This kind of volume can build product or brand awareness very quickly, and it's why earned media is becoming so important to marketing campaigns.

Sources: Sean Corcoran, "Defining Earned, Owned, and Paid Media," Forrester Blogs at *http://blogs.forrester.com/interactive_marketing/2009/12/defining-earned-owned-and-paid-media.html*, December 16, 2009; Heather Whaling, "5 Ways Social Media Has Changed marketing Campaigns," Mashable.com, at *http://mashable.com/2011/05/12/social-media-change-marketing/*, May 12, 2011; Lauren Drell, "How Social Media Is Changing Paid, Earned, and Owned Media," Mashable.com, at *http://mashable.com/2011/06/23/paid-earned-owned-media/*, June 23, 2011. For more on Hallmark, see *www.hallmark.com*.

The Ability to Efficiently Personalize and Customize Market Offerings

Amazon tracks the books I buy and, using a technology known as **collaborative filtering,** is able to compare my purchases with those of others and thereby recommend to me books they think I would like, personalized to my taste and reading habits, as Amazon understands them. If they do this well, my purchases go up, and I become a happier customer because Amazon helps me find books I want to read. While collaborative filtering technology has a long way to go (the book I bought for my daughter when she was studying for a semester in Ecuador does not make me a Latin American culture buff), the potential of this and other similar technologies offers the promise of creating sharply targeted market segments—ultimately, market segments of one.

Collaborative filtering is but one way of personalizing a market offering to each customer. In addition, when formal decision rules can be identified in the way customers behave (for example, reminding customers of, or making special offers for, upcoming birthdays or offering supplementary items based on past purchases), **rules-based personalization** can be done. The most predictive rules, however, may require customers to divulge information that they do not want to take the time, or are not willing, to divulge.

Mass-customization techniques, which are user-driven instead of marketer-driven (as we have seen for personalization approaches), allow customers to specify the nature of what is offered to them, from T-shirts to coffee mugs and more.[15] Several office supply firms offer corporate users the ability to create customized office supply catalogs tailored to their company. Such catalogs simplify ordering procedures, save time and money in the purchasing department, and help control expenses by offering to perhaps far-flung employees only what the purchasing department has approved in advance. Similarly, some online music sellers offer consumers the opportunity to order customized CDs consisting of only the songs the customer chooses. In today's highly competitive markets, personalization and customization can help build customer loyalty and make it less likely that customers will switch to other suppliers.

Disintermediation and Restructuring of Distribution Channels

Many goods and services are sold through distribution channels. The internet makes it possible for marketers to reach customers directly, without the expense or complication of distribution channels, a phenomenon known as **disintermediation.** Burlington Industries, for example, makes dress socks I like, but they are harder and harder to find because of the demise of local apparel retailers and the growing reach of chain retailers marketing their own brands. The solution? Burlington now sells them directly to consumers at *www.burlingtonsocks.com.*

What's next in the disintermediation derby? The humble razor blade is now on the list. DollarShaveClub.com wants to break the industry duopoly—Gillette, owned by Procter & Gamble, and Wilkinson Sword and Schick, owned by Energizer Holdings, hold the majority of the market—by going straight to the consumer online with a low-priced monthly supply of razors and blades delivered to the consumer's door. Dollar Shave Club's YouTube video, starring cofounder Mike Dubin has surpassed 4 million hits to date.[16]

Deciding to disintermediate or restructure one's channel, however, should not be done lightly. Levi Strauss, the jeans manufacturer, angered its existing retailers by offering custom-fit jeans direct to consumers via the web. Ultimately, the company withdrew the offering due in part to the howls of protest it heard from its regular retail channel members. Similar concerns have arisen in the travel industry, as airlines and others have disintermediated travel agents by selling airline tickets and other travel services directly to consumers—as do web-based travel agents like Expedia .com and Travelocity.com—via the web. Someone must perform the functions normally performed by channel members—taking orders, delivering products, collecting payment, and so on—so those who consider disintermediating their channels and selling direct must determine how they will perform these functions and must evaluate whether doing so is more effective and efficient than using intermediaries. Companies that carry out all these functions on an outsourced basis are available to would-be web-based marketers.

> **Strategic Issue**
>
> *Deciding to disintermediate or restructure one's channel should not be done lightly.*

Somewhat paradoxically, however, as web-based disintermediation has grown, new kinds of intermediaries have appeared to fill new needs. The music industry is now rife with new kinds of intermediaries, from Apple's iTunes music store and Apps Store to subscription-based services such as Pandora Radio and Spotify, where subscribers can create their own personalized stations or playlists.

Other new intermediaries include aggregators and affiliate schemes. Aggregators such as Kayak.com, a travel aggregator, are a more evolved version of price comparison sites. These sites assist the customer in finding the best deal from hundreds of sites. Travel agency and tour operator sites cooperate with Kayak because of the vast amount of traffic Kayak attracts, as well as the fact that their competitors are likely to be on Kayak as well. Affiliate schemes, of which Commission Junction (*www.cj.com*) is one of the largest, are similar. CJ is an application service provider whose platform allows businesses with products to sell (advertisers) to interact with businesses (or individuals) with websites to populate (publishers). The publisher makes money from commissions from the advertiser when a purchase is made by a customer who was directed from the publisher's site. Why are aggregators and affiliate schemes growing? The aggregator sites can focus on improving the technologies that allow customers to find exactly what they want, and publishers can specialize in promotion and attracting customers, since they are not involved in managing the product that the customer is actually buying.

Even when channels are not disintermediated by digital technologies, as is the case with Amazon, which is still a retailer at heart, the overwhelming efficiency of doing business on the web or a mobile, and doing it with scale, instead of the old-fashioned way, can be overpowering. A recent study by investment bank William Blair found that Amazon's price advantage over other retailers ranged from 5 to 13 percent over Walmart and from 24 to 32 percent over nutrition retailer GNC.[17]

Global Reach, 24/7 Access, and Instantaneous Delivery

With the internet, typically there is no extra cost entailed in making information, digital goods, or services available anywhere one can gain access to the web—literally, **global reach,** making the offering available 24 hours per day, seven days per week, 52 weeks per year and, in some cases, providing instantaneous delivery. In our increasingly time-pressed world, access and service like this can be of great value to customers. Air Asia, the rapidly growing low-priced airline based in Singapore, sells most of its tickets on its own website, many of them to international travelers who reserve flights from afar, even from another continent. Flight confirmations are delivered instantly. Software vendors, like those selling apps as we saw at the beginning of this chapter, whose products may be purchased and instantaneously downloaded from the web, provide similar responsiveness. As mobile telephony and GPS technologies develop further, similar benefits are starting to be available to customers and marketers whose products are well suited to mobile media.

Despite the web's advantage of global reach, local logistical and other issues make doing business on the web a different cup of tea from one place to the other. In places like Vietnam and India, developing a system for collecting cash on delivery is essential, due to a paucity of credit cards and a reluctance to use them online.[18] In places like Belgium, where broadband penetration has yet to cross the 20 percent mark (compared to Sweden and South Korea, which exceed 80 percent), e-commerce is difficult to do at all.[19]

Are These Digital World Fundamentals Opportunities or Threats?

Most marketers can choose to take advantage of one or more of the fundamental attributes and benefits offered by today's digital and social networking technologies, including those we have identified above. To that extent, these technologies constitute opportunities available to marketers who employ them. Viewed differently, however, they raise complex ethical issues (see Ethical Perspective 11.2), and they also present potentially significant threats.

First, the fact that the variable cost for syndicated goods approaches zero sounds like a good thing, until one realizes that for most products, price, over the long run, usually is not far from variable cost. If variable cost is zero, will prices drop to near zero, too? If so, such an outcome might represent disaster for information producers. Fierce warfare—between Amazon, Apple, Google, and Barnes & Noble, as well as antitrust regulators in Washington—has broken out over control of the pricing and terms under which electronic books are sold. To make matters worse for publishers, Amazon has begun signing authors, such as the self-help guru Timothy Ferris, to deal with it directly, cutting publishers out of the game entirely.[20]

Amazon is also enraging brick-and-mortar retailers with its Price Check app, which enables consumers to scan a product's bar code while shopping in a store and price-check it against Amazon's probably lower price. Google Shopper, eBay's Red Laser, and others are offering similar applications.[21] Manufacturers that want to maintain the ability of brick-and-mortar retailers to achieve the gross margins they need to stay in business may start offering slightly different models to their online and offline retailers to make such comparisons more difficult.

Strategic Issue

The fact that the variable cost for syndicated goods approaches zero sounds like a good thing.

(E) Ethical Perspective   Are Web "Cookies" a Good Thing?   11.2

In 1993, early days in internet time, a cartoon in *The New Yorker* magazine showed two dogs using a computer. One of them said to the other, "On the internet, nobody knows you're a dog." These days, somebody probably does know you're a dog, who your master is, and whether you prefer Iams or Purina dog chow. So-called "cookies," digital codes placed on your computer to enable websites to remember who you are when you log on and to track the sites you visit, how long you linger, and other such data, are what makes such detailed customer knowledge possible.

Collection of online consumer data is a growing phenomenon, one some observers are concerned about. "When you start to get into the details, it's scarier than you might suspect," says Marc Rotenberg, executive director of the Electronic Privacy Information Center, a watchdog for privacy rights.

Companies that collect all this data argue that it's all in the consumer's interest because it makes the ads they see more relevant. Matt Simpson, chairman of the digital media group of the Institute of Practitioners in Advertising and digital media head at OMD, a UK-based media agency, says, "In a perfect world, you can deliver a more relevant message and spend less money."

In a study by research firm comScore, Yahoo! emerged as the cookie champion, collecting data 811 times each month for an average user. That doesn't count another 1,709 data collection instances on partner sites such as eBay and others, where Yahoo! places ads, bringing the total for Yahoo! users to more than 2,500 data collections each day.

Consumers have not been vocal about such practices, perhaps because such data collection is largely invisible. But just how much would you like Yahoo!, or any other internet company, to know about your shopping habits, what you view on the web, and so on? Web companies say their policies on such data collection and dissemination are clearly spelled out, and most say they have consumer protection policies in place.

But Rotenberg is not convinced that all this data collection is a good thing. Web companies are "recording preferences, hopes, worries, and fears," he says. Government authorities in the United States and Europe are joining the fray. The U.S. Federal Trade Commission has called for a "do not track" system that would enable consumers to avoid having their click-streams tracked online. New rules in Europe that took effect in 2012 require that first-time visitors to a site be asked for consent to collect cookies. Proposed additional rules in the European Union would give users the right to tell websites to permanently delete existing personal data. Will the regulators and privacy advocates prevail? Most online marketers are hoping they won't. Will that remain the case? Who knows?

Sources: Louise Story, "internet Firms Keeping Ever-Closer Tabs on You," *International Herald Tribune,* March 15, 2007, p. 15; and Maija Palmer, "A Deeper Peeper," *Financial Times,* April 15, 2009, p. 11, John W. Miller, "EU Floats More Rights for Online Privacy," *The Wall Street Journal* European Edition, November 5–7, 2010, p 19; and Julia Angwin and Jennifer Valentino-DeVries, "Web Privacy 'Inadequate'," *The Wall Street Journal* European Edition, December 2, 2010, p. B₂; Dave Lee, BBC News Technology, "Cookie Law: Websites Must Seek Consent from This Weekend," May 25, 2012, at *www.bbc.co.uk/news/technology-18194235.*

Selling music on the internet also seemed like a good idea to music publishers and even to artists. Imagine getting $12 to $15 for the music on a CD, with no retailers or distributors to take cuts of the revenue and no costs to pay for fancy packaging! Disintermediation sounds good if you are a music publisher, but it's a threat if you're a music retailer, even a web-based one such as Amazon! If you were Apple's Steve Jobs, however, disintermediation was music to your ears. The combination of Apple's iPod portable digital music player and its iTunes online music store followed by its iPhone and iPad, has transformed the company, with these lines of business growing to more than 86 percent of total revenue for Apple's six months ended March 31, 2012.[22] Internet distribution of music may also change how new bands are discovered and promoted (see Exhibit 11.4).

Another threat to today's digital technologies is that there are few barriers to entry, and many internet strategies are easily imitated. Apps of all kinds have proliferated, but few win traction with users and most get lost in the crowd.

Other threats include privacy and security issues, which can drive away customers rather than attract them if they are not handled with care. The most restrictive jurisdictions'

EXHIBIT 11.4 *Arctic Monkeys Say "No Thanks" to the A&R Crowd*

In January 2006, the Artic Monkeys sold more than 360,000 copies of their album, "Whatever People Say I Am, That's What I'm Not," in its first week of release, the United Kingdom's fastest-selling debut since records began. But who are they? The Arctic Monkeys, based in Sheffield in the United Kingdom, were one of the hottest new acts in years. Says a spokesman for music retailer HMV, "In terms of sheer impact . . . we haven't seen anything quite like this since The Beatles."

But the traditional route to musical success, being discovered by an A&R person, signing a contract, then going on tour, and so on, isn't the route the Arctic Monkeys followed. Instead, the quartet started gigging at small venues in 2003 and handed out demo CDs to the crowd, who in turn put the band's songs on the internet for others to hear. Despite alluring promises of fame and fortune, they resisted signing with a major record label, opting eventually for the independent Domino Records label.

The band members are quick to point out that they did not put the songs online themselves and were barely aware of what was happening at the time. "The only reason people have got into it [the music] is because they've listened to it and they like it, so it's something real," says Jarvis Cocker, another Sheffield-based singer.

Sources: BBC web site, *http://news.bbc.co.uk/1/hi/entertainment/4644214.stm* and *http://news.bbc.co.uk/1/hi/entertainment/4660394.stm*. For more on the Arctic Monkeys, see *www. arctic monkeys.com.*

privacy rules may eventually apply to internet marketers anywhere. Privacy laws in Europe, compared to the United States, are substantially more strict.

In the United States, internet privacy has been dealt with largely through market forces, whereby consumers are expected to avoid sites where privacy is not handled to their liking. As firms attempt to take advantage of the global reach afforded by the internet, will they run afoul of privacy laws in countries whose consumers they serve? In what jurisdictions will complaints be heard and dealt with? Will the most restrictive countries end up ruling the roost? These ethical and legal privacy questions are far from settled.

First-Mover Advantage: Fact or Fiction?

In the internet gold rush in the late 1990s, and again in the later rush to build social networking sites, the key to success was said to be **first-mover advantage.** The first firm to establish a significant presence in each market niche would be the one that succeeded. Thus, Amazon would win in books. eBay would win in auctions. Myspace would win in social networking, and so on. Later followers need not bother. But is first-mover advantage on the internet or elsewhere real?

Being the first mover can bring some potential advantages, but not all first movers are able to capitalize on those advantages. Thus, many are surpassed over time by later entrants, just as late-comer Facebook left Myspace in the dust by 2008. One thing a pioneer must do to hold on to its early leadership position is to continue to innovate in order to maintain a differential advantage over the many imitators likely to arrive late to the party but eager to get in. Easy to say, not so easy to do.

Jim Collins, author of the best sellers *Good to Great* and *Built to Last,* is more blunt about the supposed rule that nothing is as important as being first to reach scale. "It's wrong," he says. "Best beats first."[23] As Collins points out, VisiCalc was the first major personal computer spreadsheet. Where is VisiCalc today? It lost the battle to Lotus 1-2-3, which in turn lost to Excel. What about the once-ubiquitous Palm Pilot? It came to market years after early leader Sharp and the Apple Newton. Palm's designers found a better way to design personal digital assistants—using one reliable script, instead of everyone's own script—and sold more than 6 million units.[24] But Palm was then leapfrogged by Black-Berry, which has been further leapfrogged by Apple's iPhone and other smartphones based on Google's Android operating system. Even the mighty Google wasn't the first of the search engines.

Strategic Issue

Being first may help attract investors and may make some founders and venture capitalists rich, but it's hardly a recipe for building a great company.

In the bricks-and-mortar economy, Walmart didn't pioneer discount retailing. Nucor didn't pioneer the minimill for making steel from scrap. Starbucks didn't pioneer the high-end coffee shop. Yet all were winners, while the early leaders fell behind or disappeared. None of these entrants were first—they were *better*. Being first may help attract investors and may make some founders and venture capitalists rich, but it's hardly a recipe for building a great company.

DEVELOPING A STRATEGY FOR A DIGITALLY NETWORKED WORLD: A DECISION FRAMEWORK

Most companies of substantial size or scope, whatever their industry, will need to develop strategies to take advantage of new digital, mobile, and social networking technologies, but doing so is easier said than done. While we recognize that nonmarketing applications of these technologies may be compelling for many companies, our focus remains on marketing, Thus, in this section we focus on how the latest such tools can fruitfully be employed for marketing purposes.

Marketing Applications for a Digitally Networked World

Earlier in this book we pointed out that a number of activities have to be performed by somebody for an exchange transaction to occur between a selling firm and a potential customer. Retaining that customer for future transactions adds additional activities, such as providing effective and responsive customer service after the sale. From the customer's point of view, these necessary activities can be summarized in a six-stage **consumer experience process** that begins with communicating one's wants and needs to prospective sellers; moving through the awareness, purchase, and delivery processes; obtaining any necessary service or support after the purchase to support its use or consumption; and ultimately sometimes returning or disposing of the product (we identify the six stages in Exhibit 11.5).

Customers first provide information about their needs to sellers, whose **customer insight** permits them to develop goods or services intended to meet the customer's needs. This stage in the process requires that information flow from customer to seller, as shown in Exhibit 11.5. While there may be several back-and-forth iterations in the insight stage, as new product developers invent and refine their product ideas, ultimately some good or

EXHIBIT 11.5   A Customer Experience Model for Marketing Decision-Making

Stage in customer experience process	Direction of information flows	Direction of product flows (goods or services)	Direction of cash flows (revenue opportunities)
Customer insight	P←—C		
Production promotion, customer acquisition, and brand building	P—→C		
Transaction	P←→C		P←—C
Product delivery		P—→C	P←—C
Customer support and service	P←→C	P—→C	P←—C
Product return or disposal		P←—C	P—→C

P = Producer
C = Customer

service is developed, and information about the new product—**promotion, customer acquisition, and brand building**—then flows to customers to inform and encourage them to buy. If the customer likes what is offered, a **transaction**—an agreement to buy—ensues, requiring that information about pricing, terms, delivery, and so on flows to the customer, and cash—either now or upon delivery—flows the other way. With a transaction consummated, **delivery** of the good or service is made, with the product flowing to the customer and money or other compensation flowing to the seller. But the seller's job is not yet done for the customer may need some kind of **customer support or service** during use, in which case additional information may flow in either direction or additional goods or services may flow to the customer, possibly in exchange for additional revenue. Finally, the customer may need to **return, dispose** of, or discontinue use of the good or service, at which point the product may be returned to the seller, cash may flow back to the customer (as a result of the product's return or some kind of trade-in, perhaps), and another transaction—with this or another seller—may ensue, thereby repeating much of the process.

Social networking, the internet, and to an increasing extent, mobile telephony offer applications at some or all of these stages. We now explore some of these applications, though in this fast-moving arena, new ones will undoubtedly arise before the ink is dry on this book. Then, in the next section, we set forth a decision framework to assist marketers in deciding for which of these stages, and with which applications, resources should be allocated.

Applications for Customer Insight

In Chapter 5, we discussed the role of marketing research in understanding customers and developing products—whether goods or services—to meet their needs. Marketers rely on a flow of information from customers or prospective customers about their wants and needs, however latent these may sometimes be, to generate the insight essential to the development of compelling new products. How might today's digital and social networking technologies facilitate this process?

First, consider the trove of data posted daily on Facebook and other social networking sites. Sifting through such data—and providing it in an organized manner to customers willing to pay for it—is becoming a big business (see Exhibit 11.6). In some industries, keeping track of what customers are saying about your business can be crucial. Take hotels, for instance. These days, everybody checks out TripAdvisor, Yelp, or another website before booking a vacation, because user reviews are seen as more objective sources of information than the property's own site. Entrepreneurs Mark Heyneker and Jay Ashton saw an opportunity here, to alert hotels to potentially damaging posts on such sites. "We monitor fire hoses of Twitter content, all public Facebook content, YouTube, everything on Flickr," declares Ashton, who says that their company, Revinate, has about 1,000 clients, including hotels from the most widely recognized brands like Radisson, Hyatt, and Holiday Inn.

EXHIBIT 11.6 *Why Do Men Wear Stubble?*

Marketers have long wanted to be able to gather evidence of trends using data floating around on the web. NetBase, a social media analytics company, enables them to do just that. On one assignment, NetBase found 77,000 mentions of stubble online, in less than six seconds. Its analysts then sorted the positive comments into themes and built a chart inless than an hour, ranking the top reasons why men wear stubble. The top-ranked answer wasn't a surprise—men who wear stubble do so because they see it as sexy—and any hip urbanite could have told them that. But the ability to now quickly gather and mine the abundance of web data is.

Source: Ryann Flinn, "The Big Business of Sifting through Social Media Data," *Bloomberg Businessweek*, October 25–31, 2010, pp. 20–21. For more on NetBase, see *www.netbase.com*.

Pollsters and other marketing researchers are increasingly turning to the internet to conduct marketing research, due to its cost-cutting, time-saving advantages over traditional survey methods.[25] Why? Just as internet marketers see the potential for "easier, faster, and cheaper," so, too, do researchers when they consider the internet.

Among the online research techniques is the use of instant messaging (IM) to gather consumer data. "Clients are using the (IM) tools and liking what they get out of them," reports Joel Benenson, CEO of iModerate, an online market research firm. In IM-based focus groups, for example, researchers can use IM to probe respondents' answers more deeply in follow-up conversations.[26]

Nonetheless, using the web for research is not without controversy. Traditional researchers debate the web's merits on a number of dimensions: in terms of representativeness of the current makeup of the web audience, somewhat whiter, richer, younger, and more educated than the population as a whole; in terms of self-selection biases, where people volunteer to participate in web-based polls; and in terms of the randomness, or lack thereof, of web samples. Procter & Gamble, the world's largest user of marketing research, reported that two online surveys by the same provider, conducted two weeks apart, delivered diametrically opposite results.[27] But many of these problems are present in other forms of research, too, especially as more people refuse to answer mail or telephone surveys.

Strategic Issue

Using the web for research is not without controversy.

Regardless of its limitations, however, web-based research, for customer insight, both for qualitative studies and for large-scale quantitative studies, is here to stay and will undoubtedly grow.

Applications for Product Promotion, Customer Acquisition, and Brand Building

The basic tools for these activities have grown extensively over the past few years. The "if we build it they will come" mind-set that allowed companies to perceive their website as a mere marketing tool as opposed to a channel that required its own, specific marketing efforts has become obsolete. The tools that today's *au courant* web marketers use comprise a variety of time-tested tactics like banner ads, **search engine marketing** (SEM), **search engine optimization** (SEO), e-mail marketing, blogs, and promotional websites.

Perhaps the most fundamental of these tools over the past decade or so are SEM and SEO, which enable marketers to take best advantage of consumers' search efforts on Google or other search engines. We address SEM and SEO in some detail in Chapter 13. More recently, with the rising number of consumers spending time on social networks, Facebook has worked to earn the trust—and budgets—of advertisers. Doing so, and finding a way to monetize Facebook's 900 million user base, has not been easy, however. Facebook has been unwilling to allow banner ads, for fear of upsetting its users.[28] But as a now publicly held company, pressure to create more meaningful advertising revenues will grow. On the other side of the table, advertisers will have to find ways to take advantage of Facebook's large and potentially targetable audience. Companies like Wildfire (see *www.wildfireapp.com*) have sprung up to help marketers do just that.

Google and Facebook aside, the pace of innovation is so rapid that new applications are arising and sometimes growing explosively. Consider the daily deals marketer Groupon, for example. Groupon enables Thalia Spice, an Asian fusion restaurant in Chicago, to offer discounted meals to fill tables that would otherwise be empty during slow periods. Groupon junkies can find daily deals on everything from meals to massages from merchants in their city".[29]

From its modest presence in just 30 American cities in 2009, with 2 million subscribers, Groupon has exploded into a global phenomenon. Groupon's targeted location-based approach is getting even more precise with the testing of its app for mobile phones. Simply tell its Groupon Now application, "I'm hungry," and it will tell you which nearby restaurants have deals right now.[30] Advertising on mobile phones is beginning to skyrocket with the increasing penetration of smartphones in North America and Europe and, undoubtedly soon, everywhere. Analysts predict that mobile advertising will be a $10 billion business by 2014.[31]

Then there's the burgeoning number of so-called flash sales sites like Europe's Vente Privée and Gilt Group in the United States. These sites enable apparel makers and others to offload unwanted inventory in a classy manner, without disturbing their normal distribution channels. "It's a huge period of innovation for consumer-facing commerce, unlike anything we've seen in the past 10 years," says Josh Goldman, of Norwest Venture Partners, which has invested in a number of e-commerce startups.[32]

And what about online consumer reviews, whether by consumers or professionals? The growing clout of TripAdvisor for travel decisions, despite occasional concerns about whether all the reviews are fake or real, has made TripAdvisor one of the few success stories in the recent spate of dot-com IPOs. By July 2012, its stock price was up 77 percent since its 2011 IPO.[33] A recent study has shown that online reviews of less popular items have greater influence over purchase decisions than for those of more popular items.[34] Such reviews can affect the firm's value to its shareholders, too.[35]

Then there's product sampling, no longer just done by gray-haired ladies in a supermarket on Saturday. These days, outfits like Birchbox.com use the web to attract customers willing to receive boxes of new product samples—from cosmetics to children's clothing to tea—for a low monthly fee. "It's a business model we love," says Kent Goldman of First Round Capital, an investor in three such services. "You have regular subscribers; you have a direct relationship with them."[36]

Another arena that appears poised to grow rapidly is that brought about by the confluence of GPS technology and mobile phones. This confluence makes it possible for marketers such as retailers and restaurants to deliver promotional messages to customers who are nearby. Whether customers will want to receive such messages, and on what basis might they opt in to receive them, are issues that have not yet been fully resolved.

Finally, there's the newest form of search, one that may hold considerable potential to grow, video search (see Exhibit 11.7). Though its commercial potential has not yet been widely tapped, some observers believe that video search is a plausible candidate on the short list for the web's "next big thing."

Though all of these new wrinkles enable companies of various kinds to build their brands or promote product sales in a highly targeted manner, and most benefit from being

---

EXHIBIT 11.7 *Video Search Grows on the Web*

When 9-year-old Tyler Kennedy of Alameda, California, had to gather information for a school report on the platypus, he began his search on the web, of course. But he didn't use Google or Yahoo!. YouTube was his search engine of choice.

In November 2008, Americans conducted nearly 2.8 billion video searches on YouTube, which slipped past Yahoo! to become number two in the internet search derby, though still a long way behind Google's number one position. With so much video content now online, video search is a natural development. According to Suranga Chandratillake, CEO of Blink, a video search engine, "An increasing number of people . . . are doing video searches to supplement and improve what they do in their offline lives."

Do you need to regrout the tile in your bathroom? There's an online video to show you how. Are you thinking about buying one of the new tablets? Check out videos on YouTube of the weirdest, best, or even the most expensive models. As YouTube's director of product management Hunter Walk notes, "Video is part of the discovery process. Depending on the user and the type of content, users may want to start with video or text."

Will YouTube be the next Google? Blogger Alex Iskold, founder of internet start-up adaptiveblue.com, says that the "shift toward video will continue, and that young internet users would only accelerate it."

Source: Miguel Helft, "Video Search Opens New Frontier on internet." *International Herald Tribune,* January 19, 2009, p. 14.

highly measurable as well, there's a dark side. Shell's efforts to drill for oil in Alaska have been opposed by a group of environmental activists, who have run fake ads and videos intended to damage the company's image, even using the Shell logo, and circulated them virally on Facebook and YouTube. To make matters worse for Shell, some news outlets picked up the false reports.[37]

Applications for Conducting Transactions

If promotional activities do their jobs, the hoped-for consequence is that some customers will decide to buy. Can the internet or mobile telephony help transactions occur? Several web-based companies are in the business of enabling client websites to handle transactions. BroadVision Inc., for example, offers a wide range of software products that enable clients to conduct B2B or B2C commerce on their websites or via kiosks or mobile telephones. Such companies typically provide back-end systems and inventory control, prepare warehouse and shipping documents, and bill the customer for the sale. Some such systems now allow companies to engage in **dynamic pricing,** a controversial system that gauges a customer's desire to buy, measures his means, and sets the price accordingly.[38] In this respect, target markets of one are now here, to the chagrin of some consumers!

Another arena where internet and mobile transactions are growing in number is banking, with or without the banks! From online bill payment to moving money from one account to another, online banking seems here to stay, with its lower costs to handle a transaction (the banks like that) and 24/7 convenience that means the end of "bankers' hours" for consumers (they like that).

In Africa, where internet connections are not widespread, but mobile phones are everywhere, the mobile is fast becoming the banking instrument of choice. In Kenya, nearly 70 percent of Kenyan adults use Safaricom's M-PESA banking service for services ranging from paying a taxi driver to sending money to friends or family. These mobile banking accounts provide Africans, many of whom work in the informal economy and probably have never had a bank account before, with a safe place to keep their money and to transfer it as simply as sending a text message. There's lots of potential for bringing Africa's unbanked into the twenty-first century, banking-wise, since more than $1 trillion in cash currently resides—not very safely—under the mattress or, quite literally, in holes in the ground.[39]

In the developed world, mobile phones are taking over from banks in another way. With services like Google Wallet on an Android phone, the user simply taps her phone at a point of sale terminal, listens for the beep, and the transaction is done in seconds. With **near field technology** (NFT), there's no more swiping a credit card or scrawling your name at the terminal. Just touch and go. If such systems become more widespread, plastic cards and wallets may become relics of the past.[40]

Applications for Delivering Digital Products

Many companies probably don't give much thought to it, but an increasing array of goods and services can be digitized and thereby delivered to customers via any digital medium, including the internet, satellites, and mobile telephones. More than fifty years ago, the then-current technological miracle was the analog delivery of sounds and images to consumers via the newfangled invention called television. Today, as we have seen earlier in this chapter, books, music, language lessons, and more can be delivered digitally any time, at any digitally connected place. In 2, 5, or 10 years, what else will be digitally deliverable? Psychotherapy, with or without a live therapist, and legal advice are available online from numerous providers. Online postage is available at several websites, including that of the United States Postal Service. And audio books, such as Madonna's *Mr. Peabody's Apples* children's book—read by the author herself—and thousands of other downloadable titles, are available from Audible.com and from other sources such as Apple's iTunes on-line music site.

Health care appears to be an arena where digital delivery offers significant benefits. A fast-expanding array of telemedicine applications, some using two-way video, is bringing medical expertise to the most remote places, like oil rigs in the South China Sea. Telemedicine is already a $3.9 billion business that includes hundreds of monitoring applications for smartphones and monitoring devices in homes. It even saves taxpayers money and improves public safety by offering remote diagnosis in prisons.[41] For the story of how one Israeli entrepreneur is taking mobile health care one step further, see Exhibit 11.8.

Delivering products digitally is not confined to consumer marketing, of course. An entire industry, **software-as-a-service** (SaaS) has sprung up to deliver the benefits of software without the hassle involved in owning and maintaining the software itself. Salesforce.com, which enables salespeople to keep track of customer and other data, is but one B2B example.

Applications for Customer Service and Support

An increasingly important application on the internet is for various sorts of customer service, replacing more costly—and sometimes more inconsistent and error prone—human support. Companies from Dell to the Denver Zoo use the web to provide answers to frequently asked questions, from technical ones in Dell's case to how to arrange a children's birthday party at the zoo. Savvy marketers know that, for all the hoopla about acquiring new customers, the real driver of the bottom line is the ability to profitably retain existing ones and that effective, responsive customer service is a key ingredient in doing so. They also know that **customer retention** is a competitive necessity. In nearly every industry, some company will soon figure out new ways to exploit the potential of today's digital data to create value for customers. Without the ability to retain those customers, however, even the best-conceived business model on the web will collapse. So new companies such as Zendesk are sprouting up to address the customer retention issue. Zendesk, founded in Copenhagen and now headquartered in San Francisco, is integrating Facebook and Twitter into its SaaS-based customer service technology.

The growing number of web-based or app-based customer service applications—from tracking a FedEx parcel online to getting boarding passes on mobile phones to chat

---

EXHIBIT 11.8 *United Hatzalah's Fast Response Saves Lives*

Anyone in Israel who sees an auto accident or other incident creating a medical emergency can dial 1221. Within 2 to 3 minutes, United Hatzalah's (UH) nearest volunteer will arrive on the scene, most likely riding one of the charity's "ambucycles," which can dart and weave through traffic far quicker than any ambulance can. In such emergencies, the first few minutes can make the difference between life and death. UH volunteers treat more than 500 people each day throughout Israel, individually serving an average of nearly one call per day. Each UH volunteer is a trained EMT, medic, or doctor—who stops whatever he or she is doing to rush to stabilize the affected individual. When the ambulance arrives, the UH volunteer goes back to her day job.

UH founder Eli Beer, who was named a Young Global Leader by the World Economic Forum in 2012, aims to get the average response time down to 90 seconds, using his company's proprietary combination of GPS and mobile technology. Soon, a downloadable app for mobile phones will bypass the call center, making the faster response times possible.

Beer's model—a dispersed network of volunteers using mobile phones, a basic medical kit, and a motorbike—is simple, but ingenious. What Beer is doing is combining technology and people to meet a real human need. To what other applications and in what other places might such a system be employed?

Sources: "Scattered Saviours," *The Economist*, January 28, 2012, p. 56; the United Hatzalah website at *www.unitedhatzalah.org*.

functionality that can access a real person—offers the tantalizing combination of better service and significant cost savings. The trick is to focus on the customer service benefits first, rather than mere cost cutting. Customers are quick to discern when cost cutting takes precedence over genuine service responsiveness. Does anyone like the way call center software has changed the way consumers obtain phone numbers from directory assistance, or the fact that some banks won't provide bank-by-mail envelopes to those who prefer to do their banking the old-fashioned way?

One bank, Kazkommertsbank (KKB), Kazakhstan's largest, discovered in 2010 that its most profitable customers were those who did their banking from home. So it started a loyalty program for such customers, using Facebook and Twitter to update customers on new benefits. By helping KKB to cross-sell other services, the new program has increased the lifetime value of such customers.[42]

One myth some companies have bought into is that the internet is a self-service medium. They assume that they can let customers do all the work, but most customers really don't want to do more. One solution is **coproduction,** in which companies carefully consider which burdens they can remove from the customer, using digital technologies, and which customers can perform, assessing costs and benefits to both parties. Doing so can provide insights into new ways to serve customers better, as Charles Schwab has long done when it e-mails customers to alert them to big moves in their stocks.

Strategic Issue

One myth that some companies have bought into is that the internet is a self-service medium.

Applications for Product Return and Disposal

Customers' experiences with goods and some services do not end until the products are consumed, returned, or disposed of. Some companies have found ways to use digital technologies to facilitate these processes. Dell, for example, provides an internet space where Dell customers can sell their old computers when they upgrade to a new one. Many companies can avail themselves of similar applications. In retailing, many retailers with both online and offline stores accept returns at any location.

Developing Digital World Marketing Strategies: The Critical Questions

Strategic Issue

Knowing what marketing arrows are available in one's digital quiver is one thing. Deciding which of these applications will deliver the best return on investment is quite another.

Knowing what marketing arrows are available in one's digital quiver is one thing. Deciding which of these applications will deliver the best return on investment is quite another. Our flow model of the customer experience process (see again Exhibit 11.5) facilitates such decision making by raising six important questions that should be asked about whether to employ new digital and social networking tools at any or all stages of the process. These six diagnostic questions are shown in Exhibit 11.9. We address each of them in this section.

Can We Digitize Any or All of the Necessary Flows at Each Stage in the Consumer Experience Process?

At the heart of today's digitally networked world is the reliance on digital means of transmitting *information,* some of which is recomposed into *goods*—CDs, books, and more. In considering whether to employ new digital technologies at any stage of the consumer experience process, a company should ask whether any of the flows—information, goods or services, or cash—can be digitized.

For cash, the answer is an automatic yes, via credit cards, payments on M-PESA, with new touch and go technology, or through other forms of electronic payment, except where currency issues pose problems, such as in some international settings. New forms of electronic payment are already enhancing the security of cash flows over the web, and social

EXHIBIT 11.9 **Diagnostic Questions for Digital World Marketing Decisions**

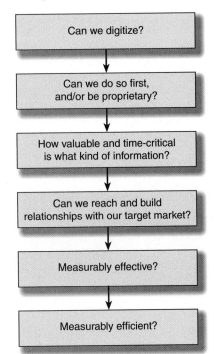

networks hold the potential to enhance trust in transactions. International remittances provider WorldRemit uses Facebook to help its happy users spread the word about its low-cost and efficient money-transfer services.[43]

For goods and services, the question is more difficult. Text, audio, and visual images (moving or still) can be digitized, as can books, music, photos, and, given enough bandwidth, movies and other videos. But what about the *soft hand* of a cashmere sweater? The *heft and balance* of a carpenter's hammer? The *taste* of fine European chocolate? The *fragrance* of a new cologne? The fit of a sweater offered by an online retailer? Today, these important informational attributes of goods cannot be readily digitized, though one new company is using robotics technology to address the "fit" problem (see Exhibit 11.10). At present, most tangible goods and many services cannot easily be transmitted digitally. For others, however, such as legal advice, therapy for mental health patients, and other goods or services that can adequately be represented in words, sounds, or images, the possibilities are endless. Will technology soon make possible the digital transmission of physical goods? Who knows? When it happens, the many sci-fi buffs around the world will not be surprised! Beam me up, Scotty?[44]

When any of the flows at any stage of the consumer experience process can be digitized, given sufficient information and ingenuity, the remaining questions in Exhibit 11.9 should then be considered to decide whether or not other such applications for a particular flow should be implemented.

Can We Do So First and/or in a Proprietary Way?

As we have seen, barriers to entry on the web and in social networking are low, and most good ideas can be quickly imitated. A key question in deciding whether or not to employ a new digital application is whether one can do so in a proprietary way, thereby deterring imitation, or do so with a sufficient head start so that competitive advantage can be established before others follow. Amazon was early in the internet retailing game and enjoyed

---

EXHIBIT 11.10   *Beer-Bellied or Toned: This Shirt's for You*

Two-thirds of all books and half of all PCs are sold on-line. For clothing, however, the number is only 8 percent. Why? It's obvious, right? Will the shirt fit? Will I like the fabric? Heikke Haldre and his team at Fits.Me, an Estonian start-up that hopes to take the online apparel business by storm, wants to solve the fit problem once and for all. The customer uncertainty translates into a huge problem for the retailers. Not only must they contend with a return rate that can be 25 precent or more, but many custormes simply don't buy if they aren't confident that the shirt will fit.

Haldre's solution? A robotic mannequin that shows the consumer what this particular garment will look like on *his/her* particular body. How? The robot can replicate 2,000 body shapes. When a retailer signs up with Fits .me, they first send in their clothes. Each size is placed on the robot, which then cycles through all the body shapes it knows, while a camera takes pictures of each

permutation. This photographic log is then stored in an online database. Once you go online and type your measurements into the retailer's site, it calls up the photo corresponding to your precise body type and clothing size. "It can be as beer-bellied or gym-toned as you are," says Haldre. "And we can show you how a small versus a medium fits on you, for example."

Getting the male mannequin right took persistence, says Haldre, more than three years of development. The women's version is more difficult, he says. But his engineers are undaunted. As Haldre tells it, "My engineers now have the best job in the world: Studying women's breasts."

Source: Cliff Kuang, "Fits.Me's Shape-Shifting Robot Lets You Try on Clothes, Online," *Fast Company Online,* September 27, 2010, *www.fastcodesign.com/1662372/fitsme.* For more on Fits.Me, see *http://fits.me/.*

---

a helpful head start. As we have seen, however, being first or early in today's digitally networked world rarely provides an advantage for long.

How Valuable and How Time Critical Are What Kinds of Information to the Recipient?

For the informational flows in Exhibit 11.5, a key question in making resource deployments is the importance of various kinds of information to the recipient, either the company or the customer, depending on the direction of the flow. The more valuable and time-critical the information, the more sensible it may be to invest in digital applications to provide easy, timely, and 24/7 access to those who can benefit from the information. Walmart puts on the web password-protected, up-to-the-minute, store-by-store, SKU-by-SKU sales information that its key suppliers can access, thereby enabling them to better ensure that Walmart's stores remain in stock on their merchandise.

Can Digital and Social Networking Tools Reach and Build Relationships with Customers in the Target Market?

Making information, goods, or services available on the web or on mobile devices is of little use if the people to whom those flows are directed lack web or smartphone access. As we have seen, some groups are underrepresented on the internet, a situation that's likely to remain, though smartphones are expected to dominate even most emerging markets very soon. In tomorrow's digitally networked world, the computer of choice will overwhelmingly be in our pockets, not on our desks.

Simply *reaching* customers with digital tools may not be enough, however, especially for marketers of commodity-like products. Going beyond reach to build mutually beneficial *relationships* may be what is needed. Facebook hopes to develop a significant role here. Amazon has built loyal relationships with its customer base by focusing its efforts on exceptional customer service. While book lovers may find books for lower prices elsewhere, many of them simply return to Amazon's site, with its easy 1-Click™ ordering, customer reviews, and other customer-friendly features. Using the latest tools for building customer relationships may be these tools' most important application in the long run.

Are Digital Tools Measurably Effective and Efficient Compared to Other Solutions?

Ultimately, given favorable answers to the first four questions in this section, deciding to invest in a particular digital or social networking strategy or application comes down to two final questions. Is the new solution effective, and is it more efficient than other solutions?

Marketers' concerns over the effectiveness and efficiency of their websites have led to the development of web analytics, software solutions that monitor and summarize website usage patterns (see Exhibit 11.11). Web analytics technology is the equivalent of having a team of marketing researchers follow customers through a bricks-and-mortar retail store. The technology can uncover a variety of problems that can plague websites: cumbersome navigation, content that can't be easily found, underperforming search engine strategies, and unprofitable online marketing partnerships. The results of these analyses can improve customer satisfaction and response to the website, strengthen the marketer's hand in negotiating terms of partnership deals, and even identify new market segments that might be better served with tailored sites. "Many organizations I have worked with are not exploiting their data," says Giles Warner, who specializes in data analytics at Deloitte.[45] Deciding what metrics are the most important—to assess customer behavior on the site or on their mobile devices, not just traffic—is key.

For companies transacting business on the web or on mobile devices, a particularly important issue is what Saul Klein of Index Ventures calls "the leaky bucket" issue. In Klein's view, at the top of the funnel is somebody visiting your site, while out the bottom end comes a completed transaction. The trick is to systematically measure the points where potential customers drop off without making a purchase, and then find ways to keep more of them in the funnel until they buy. Kevin Cornils, CEO of British spectacles e-tailer Glasses Direct discovered an even bigger benefit of tracking customer activity in his company's funnel. "The initial role was to try to save some of those customers, but it is actually making the business a lot better at being customer-focused for the long term," he says.[46]

In the final analysis, setting SMART objectives that the latest tools or activities are intended to meet—specific, measurable, attainable, relevant, and timebound—and running cost-benefit analyses to assess their likely performance are necessary for making go/no-go decisions and for prioritizing which initiatives should be pursued first. Fortunately, the inherent measurability of many of these tools often provides clear and compelling feedback on whether they are meeting the objectives. In addition, attention must be given to a variety

---

EXHIBIT 11.11 *Web Optimization Creates a Utah-Based High Flyer*

"Where," you probably wouldn't bother to ask, "is the fastest-growing publicly traded software company based?" Orem, Utah, might not come to mind. Omniture's web optimization software, which sits on the computers of more than 2,000 of the world's largest corporations—including Microsoft, Walmart, and Toyota—is revolutionizing how companies measure their websites' performance. Take Harrah's Hotels & Resorts, for example, long a measurement disciple. Harrah's used to pay an ad agency to manage the more than 70,000 keywords that it bids on every day from Yahoo!, Google, and other search engines. It needed several software programs to analyze the results. No more. Omniture shows Harrah's not only how many clicks each search ad generates, but also the conversion rate—the number of consumers who actually buy based on a search ad. "It has dramatically changed the funding for each of the keywords and categories we buy," says Greg Johnston, Harrah's e-commerce director. "We are saving hundreds of thousands of dollars."

Source: Spencer E. Ante, "A Radar Screen for E-biz," *Business-Week*, European Edition, April 30, 2007, pp. 68–70. For more on Omniture, see *www.omniture.com/en/.*

of business process issues that can get in the way of effective execution of even the best intentions for a digital world strategy in an old-economy company. Avoiding these errors is easier said than done, of course, but web analytics can help catch any errors that are made.

MANAGING DIGITALLY NETWORKED STRATEGIES: THE TALENT GAP

Setting out the opportunities that new digitally networked technologies provide—for almost any company, of any size, in any industry, anywhere—and the fundamental principles and forces driving these technologies is easy, relatively speaking, as is providing conceptual frameworks for thinking about the issues and trade-offs involved. A much more difficult challenge is finding the people to manage and lead the necessary efforts and initiatives in this complex and rapidly changing arena, especially when it comes to marketing, rather than purely technological issues. Observers note that the shelf life of chief marketing officers (CMOs) is short—a mere 26 months, on average, according to a recent study—much shorter on average than that for CEOs, CFOs, or CIOs.[47]

While marketers are confronted with a bewildering array of new media possibilities and consumers—thanks to the digital revolution—are better informed than ever, Wall Street wants results, quarter after quarter. "It makes for a deadly cocktail of high expectations, resistance, and complexity," says Mark Jarvis, CMO at Dell.[48] John Costello, a former CMO at Home Depot, Sears, and Yahoo!—adds, "CMOs have almost everyone second-guessing (them) and looking over their shoulder."[49]

As Sean Meehan, a marketing professor at IMD business school in Switzerland notes, "The marketing playbook is the same playbook it always was, it's just that there are new tools and they're very powerful tools in terms of reach. And if you use them well, you will learn more about your served community. But if you misuse it, you can blow it completely."[50]

Several years ago, the CMO's job was much more straightforward than it is today: develop the brand's positioning, hire an ad agency to create great ads, and manage the promotional budget. If the campaign hit the mark, it was bonus time. If not, out the door you went. But how does a typical senior marketing executive in his or her 40s or 50s know what do with today's dizzying array of new media—social and otherwise—and new tools, most of which didn't even exist when he or she was learning the business? Blogs, search engine optimization, social networking, mobile advertising, and more; and never mind figuring out what's cool in the mind of tomorrow's consumer, much less today's.

As Wharton marketing professor Patti Williams points out, "It's not clear how Crest should leverage search advertising. How many people are going online to search for toothpaste?"[51] But leveraging the power of social networking, as we've seen earlier in this chapter, is already within P&G's grasp. Then there's the difficulty of reaching a wide audience with many of today's highly targeted tools as well as figuring out how to buy the new media efficiently. A marketing executive at a large advertiser such as Procter & Gamble, Diageo, or Toyota might, as Wharton's Dave Reibstein notes, think all this sounds like great stuff, "but I would have to deal with 10,000 of you. I would need a manager to manage this interface and that becomes an overwhelming task. It takes a village of these (focused audiences) before we can have impact."[52] Thankfully, new technology-driven businesses will soon be up to this challenge.

Finally, there's the fact that changing habits is never easy, for marketers or anyone else. "In many cases, institutionalized cultures, agency relationships, and media relationships are still limiting them," says Donovan Neale-May, executive director of the CMO council, a trade group for marketing executives.[53] Thus, perhaps it is not surprising that younger companies without long histories of traditional advertising, as well as web-based businesses, are adopting these new digital and social networking strategies much faster than larger and older firms. Chris Moloney, CMO of Scottrade, an internet stock brokerage, thinks part of the problem is generational. He thinks about half of today's CMOs are extremely knowledgeable about the internet and what it offers.[54] Half are not. But Facebook, Twitter? And what about Pinterest and Instagram?

The good news in all of this is that today's web-savvy, well-educated marketing graduates have much to bring to the table in the companies they join. Getting a grasp of how the digitally networked world really works, along with some experience in an internship or other work setting, may be a great way to jump-start one's marketing career, and having grown up as a digital denizen surely doesn't hurt!

DEVELOPING STRATEGIES TO SERVE DIGITAL AND SOCIAL NETWORKING MARKETS

This chapter has, for the most part, addressed how companies of any kind, size, industry, or age can use digital and social networking tools and technologies for marketing purposes. No doubt, however, there are readers who see bigger fish to fry in the digital skillet. They see this arena as offering the prospect for starting an entrepreneurial venture, in a new firm or within an existing one, to serve a market created by the advent of social networking, the internet, mobile telephony, or other new or still-emerging digital technologies. Thus, we close the chapter with a brief look at some of the issues involved in serving the new markets created by the digital networking revolution.

Serving the Digitally Networked Markets of Tomorrow

What might tomorrow's entrepreneurs do to craft marketing strategies to serve new markets—like the one for apps or that for aggregating today's niche media to solve Dave Reibstein's problem—in our increasingly digitally networked world? For one, would-be internet or social networking entrepreneurs should consider the various ways in which revenue can be generated on the web or in other settings such as mobile phones. Unless someone, a business or a consumer, is eventually willing to fork over money for what a new business offers, its chances for success lie somewhere between slim and none. The rush to create new social networking sites, following the success of Facebook and YouTube in the United States, and others like them elsewhere, raises exactly this question. Thus, understanding one's **revenue model** and being willing to change it as market and technological conditions warrant are essential.

Next, such entrepreneurs must ask not what can I sell but what do today's and tomorrow's customers need, and how and where might they want to consume what I have to offer? From business-to-business (Grainger.com), to business-to-consumer (Amazon or LandsEnd .com), to consumer-to-consumer (eBay.com), to consumer-to-business-(Priceline.com) models, there's no limit to the ways in which companies can provide better, easier, faster, or cheaper solutions using these tools and technologies. If a particular business idea does not fill some real, though perhaps currently latent, need identified by these questions, however, there is likely to be no viable business, Twitter's history to date notwithstanding.

Finally, would-be entrepreneurs must realize that barriers to entry are incredibly low in this new world. For everyone who has the next latest and greatest web-based or social networking idea, there are dozens of other prospective entrepreneurs likely to be exploring similar ideas concurrently. It's not really the ideas that count. What matters is the team that will execute an idea to deliver the performance and value that customers, whether businesses or consumers, or even potential acquirers of the nascent business want and will pay for. Facebook wanted, and paid dearly for, Instagram. Is Pinterest next in the sights of Facebook, Google, or someone else? Or will it, like Twitter, build a large audience but struggle to develop a business model that works?[55]

Thus, execution is key, a truism we explore in greater depth in Chapters 12 and 13. As Intel's Andy Grove said at the turn of the twenty-first century about building the next wave of (it is hoped successful) internet businesses, "It's work. Very unglamorous work. . . . The heavy lifting is still ahead of us."[56] Grove's observation remains true today. Much of this work is of the kind set forth in the earlier chapters of this book: understanding customers and the markets they make up, understanding industries and the competitors that do battle in them each day, and developing marketing programs that can establish and maintain sustainable competitive advantage.

But there's also the work of developing marketing strategies well suited to the market and competitive conditions that currently prevail in one's industry and implementing those strategies. In this chapter, we've explored the digitally networked world and how both existing and new firms can find ways—measured in terms of effectiveness and efficiency—to take advantage of the promise it offers. In the chapters that remain, we examine how best to organize for the effective implementation of, and monitor the results generated by, these strategies. "Give me 'A' execution of a 'B' plan over 'B' execution of an 'A' plan" is a common refrain heard from venture capitalists and other investors. Planning is important. But effective execution delivers the results, and results are what count.

Marketing Plan Exercise

Develop a digitally networked strategy for your product(s) or company. Identify relevant digital tools that should be included in the marketing strategy you are preparing.

Develop the rest of your marketing mix, integrating your digital strategy therein, and prepare arguments why the product, pricing, promotion, and distribution decisions you've made are the best ones to make given the market and competitive conditions you face.

Discussion Questions

1. As director of marketing of a medium-sized Canadian sporting goods manufacturer that produces helmets for use in sports, such as cycling, skiing, hockey, and football, you have been considering using the internet as a marketing tool. Although your helmets are sold in retail stores and to schools and athletic programs across Canada, you believe the company could reach a bigger audience and sell more helmets if the company also sold the product online at the company's website. What arguments would you use to convince the CEO that online marketing is a good strategy?

2. In meeting with the CEO of the helmet manufacturer, you have been asked to outline the possible threats of selling the product online. Explain.

3. You have been hired to do some marketing research for a candy company that sells its products mainly to kids that represent all races and economic levels. The company is leaning toward using the internet to conduct the research. The company managers' reasoning is that web-based marketing research is easier, faster, and cheaper than more traditional methods. Why might you persuade the company executives to think otherwise?

4. What characteristics are common among industries that are highly susceptible to being revolutionized by digital technologies?

Additional self-diagnostic questions to test your ability to apply the analytical tools and concepts in this chapter to strategic decision making may be found at the book's website at **www.mhhe.com/walker8e.**

Endnotes

1. This material is drawn from Jessi Hempel, "web 2.0 Is So Over. Welcome to web 3.0," *Fortune* European Edition, January 19, 2009, p. 27; Douglas MacMillen, Peter Burrows, and Spencer E. Ante, "The App Economy," *BusinessWeek* European Edition, November 2, 2009, pp. 4–49; Peter Burrows, "Innovator: Omar Hamoui," *Bloomberg Businessweek* European Edition, May 3–9, 2010; Joseph Menn, Richard Waters, and Alan Rappeport, "Amazon Launches Android App Store," *Financial Times,* March 23, 2011, p. 24; Daya Baran, "Buffett Warns of Bubble in Social Networking IPOs," *www.webguild.org,* March 28, 2011 at *www.webguild.org/*

20110328/buffett-warns-of-bubble-in-social-networking-of-ipos; Peter Burrows and Adam Satariano, "How Apple Feeds Its Army of App Makers," *Bloomberg Businessweek* European Edition, June 13, 2011, pp. 39–40; Daya Baran, "Groupon Goes Public. Raises $700m. Shares Oversubscribed," *Webguild*, November 3, 2011, at *www.webguild.org/20111103/groupon-goes-public-share-oversubscribed*; Cotton Delo, "Facebook Files for IPO; Reveals $1 Billion in 2011 Profit," *Ad Age Digital,* February 1, 2012, at *http://adage.com/article/digital/facebook-files-ipo-reveals-1-billion-2011-profit/232484/*; Brad Stone, "Idiot Proof," *Bloomberg Businessweek* European Edition, March 5, 2012, pp. 61–67; and Jennifer Booton, "Bullish Zynga Analysts 'All In' on Game Maker's Gambling Prospects," *FoxBusiness.com*, July 3, 2102, at *www.foxbusiness.com/technology/2012/07/02/bullish-zynga-analysts-all-in-on-game-maker-prospects/*.

2. "Days of Double Digit Growth in Social Network Users Are Over," *eMarketer Daily Newsletter,* March 18, 2011.

3. Martin Giles, "Bulletins from the Future," *The Economist Special Report, Personal Technology,* October 8, 2011, pp. 1–16.

4. *The Economist,* "Making It Click," February 25, 2012, pp. 65–66.

5. Ibid.

6. Ibid.

7. "Broadband Users Spend More Money Online, Watch Less TV," CMP TechWeb, August 4, 2005.

8. Lauren Coleman-Lochner, "Social Networking Takes Center Stage at P&G," *Bloomberg Businessweek* European Edition, April 2, 2012, pp. 24–25.

9. Ibid.

10. April Dembosky and Tim Bradshaw, "Advertisers Uneasy as Facebook Goes Own Way," *Financial Times,* May 7, 2012.

11. Oliver Hinz, Bernd Skiera, Christian Barrot, and Jan U. Becker, "Seeding Strategies for Viral Marketing: An Empirical Comparison," *Journal of Marketing* 75 (November 2011), pp. 55–71.

12. "Mandarin 2.0: How Skype, Podcasts, and Broadband Are Transforming Language Teaching," *The Economist,* June 9, 2007, p. 75.

13. For more on the phenomenon of increasing returns to scale, see Thomas Petzinger, Jr., "So Long, Supply and Demand," *The Wall Street Journal,* January 1, 2000; and W. Brian Arthur, Increasing Returns and Path Dependence in the Economy (Ann Arbor, MI: University of Michigan Press, 1994).

14. "Everywhere and Nowhere: Social Networking Will Become a Ubiquitous Feature of Online Life, That Does Not Mean It Is a Business," *The Economist,* March 22, 2008, pp. 81–82.

15. For more on customization, see C. Page Moreau, Leff Bonney, and Kelly B. Herd, "It's the Thought (and the Effort) That Counts: How Customizing for Others Differs from Customizing for Oneself," *Journal of Marketing* 75 (September 2011), pp. 120–33.

16. *The Economist,* "Blade Runners," March 31, 2012, p. 73.

17. *The Economist,* "The Walmart of the web," October 1, 2011, pp 67–68.

18. Bruce Einhorn, K. Oanh Ha, and Diep Ngoc Pham, "Shopping on the web, Delivering on a Moped," *Bloomberg Businessweek* European Edition, January 23, 2012, pp. 38–39.

19. *The Economist,* "Going Local," July 16, 2011, p. 68.

20. Brad Stone, "Amazon's Hitman," *Bloomberg Businessweek* European Edition, January 30, 2012, pp. 55–59.

21. Sandra M. Jones, "Retailers Pay the Price," *The Denver Post*, December 12, 2011, p. 24A.

22. Apple, Inc., Form 10-Q for the quarterly period ended March 31, 2012.

23. Jim Collins, "Best Beats First," *Inc.*, August 2000, p. 48.

24. Ibid., p. 49.

25. Zoomerang.com is one commonly used provider, with over 2 million survey respondents in its database.

26. Deborah L. Vence, "In an Instant," *Marketing News,* March 1, 2006, p. 53.

27. Joel Rubinson, "Online Marketing Research: It Was the Best of Times, It Was the Worst of Times," *Fast Company,* October 8, 2009, at *http://www.fastcompany.com/blog/joel-rubinson/brave-new-marketing/online-marketing-research-it-was-best-times-it-was-worst-time*.

28. "Advertisers Uneasy as Facebook Goes Own Way," May 7, 2012.

29. Brad Stone and Douglas MacMillan, "Are Four Words Worth $25 Billion?" *Bloomberg Businessweek* European Edition, March 21–27, 2011.

30. "Groupon Anxiety," *The Economist*, March 19, 2011, p. 64; Brad Stone and Douglas MacMillan, "Are Four Words Worth $25 Billion?" *Bloomberg Businessweek* European Edition, March 21–27, 2011.

31. Peter Burrows, "Innovator: Omar Hamoui," *Bloomberg Businessweek* European Edition, May 3–9, 2010.

32. David Gelles, "Innovation Brings a Touch of Class to Online Shopping," *Financial Times*, June 14, 2010.

33. Dan Caplinger, "The S&P 500's Big Winners in 2012," *Motley Fool on MSNBC*, July 8, 2012, at *www.msnbc.msn.com/id/48110531/ns/business-motley_fool/#.T_tcMvVSTdc.*

34. Feng Zhu and Xiaoquan (Michael) Zhang, "Impact of Online Consumer Reviews on Sales: The Moderating Role of Product and Consumer Characteristics," *Journal of Marketing* 74 (March 2010), pp. 133–48.

35. Yubo Chen, Yong Liu, and Jurui Zhang, "When Do Third-Party Product Reviews Affect Firm Value and What Can Firms Do? The Case of Media Critics and Professional Movie Reviews," *Journal of Marketing* 76 (March 2012), pp. 116–34.

36. Olga Kharif, "A Surprise in Every Birchbox," *Bloomberg Businessweek*, February 20, 2012, pp. 39–40.

37. Emily Steel, "How Shell Was Hijacked by a New Style of Cyberprotest," *Financial Times*, June 22, 2012, p. 10.

38. David Streitfeld, "On the web, Price Tags Blur," *The Washington Post Online*, www.washingtonpost .com/wp-dyn/articles/A 15159-2000Sep25.html.

39. "The Meek Shall Inherit the web," *The Economist Technology Quarterly*, September 16, 2008, pp. 3–4; Brendan Greeley and Eric Ombok, "In Kenya, Keeping Cash Safe on a Cell Phone," *Bloomberg Businessweek*, September 12, 2011, pp. 55–56.

40. Brad Stone and Olga Kharif, "Pay As You Go," *Bloomberg Businessweek*, July 18, 2011, pp. 66–72.

41. Milt Freudenheim, "You Can't Get to a Doctor's Office? Now It's Only a Few Keystrokes Away," *International Herald Tribune*, May 31, 2010, p. 15.

42. Jane Bird, "How to Make web Shoppers Buy, Rather Than Move On," *Financial Times Special Report: The Connected Business*, March 16, 2011, p. 4.

43. See the WorldRemit website at *www.worldremit.com.*

44. From the science fiction movie *Star Trek*, in which it was routine to digitally transmit objects, including people, from place to place.

45. Stephen Pritchard, "Better Strategy Comes from a Dogged Approach to Your Data," *Financial Times Special Supplement: The Connected Business*, March 16, 2011, p. 4.

46. Jonathan Moules, "Observe, Measure, Respond: The Keys to web Selling," *Financial Times FT Weekend*, June 26–27, 2010, pp. 30–31.

47. David Kiley and Burt Helm, "The Short Life of the Chief Marketing Officer," *BusinessWeek*, European Edition, December 10, 2007, pp. 63–65.

48. Ibid.

49. Ibid.

50. Beth Gardiner, "Business Schools Tackle Social Media," *The Wall Street Journal* European Edition, December 7, 2010, p. 27.

51. "If Online Marketing Is the Future, Why Are Some CMOs Stuck in the Past?" *Knowledge@ Wharton*, February 26, 2008, *http://knowledge .wharton.upenn.edu/article.cfm?articleid=1892.*

52. Ibid.

53. Ibid.

54. Ibid.

55. Jessi Hempel, "Is Pinterest the Next Facebook?" *Fortune* European Edition, April 9, 2012, pp. 67–71.

56. Jerry Useem, "What Have We Learned?" *Fortune*, October 30, 2000, pp. 82–104.

Implementation and Control

Chapter **Twelve**

Organizing and Planning for Effective Implementation

Electrolux—Organizing to Rule the World of Household Appliances[1]

Electrolux, the Swedish household appliances giant, began selling Lux vacuum cleaners in a few European countries in 1919. The company soon undertook an aggressive growth strategy, largely via mergers and acquisitions. It grew by both acquiring other appliance lines—refrigerators in 1925, washing machines in 1951, dishwashers in 1959, food service equipment in 1962, and so forth—and by buying established local brands in many countries around the world, such as Frigidaire in North America, Zanussi and AEG in Europe, and Simpson in Australia. This strategy made Electrolux the world's number one household appliance company at the beginning of this century, until a merger between Whirlpool and Maytag in 2006 bumped it to number two.

Electrolux's aggressive acquisition strategy not only increased the firm's revenues, it also established its presence in more countries than many of its competitors. As Keith McLoughlin, the firm's CEO, points out, "We're the only one that has the distribution and local market presence in over 150 countries. You have to know the local consumer, and we do that globally more than anyone." Indeed, only about a third of the firm's revenues comes from the Scandinavian countries, Europe, and the Middle East. North America accounts for 27 percent of sales, Latin America for 18 percent, and the Asia Pacific region for another 8 percent.

Too Many Brands. Too Little Coordination

During Electrolux's decades of rapid growth, many of the firm's newly acquired brands retained a substantial amount of operational autonomy. While the parent company imposed financial goals and cost controls, the various brands were essentially managed as separate business units, each with its own R&D, manufacturing, and marketing departments. This gave the different brands substantial freedom to grow and compete in their regional markets as they saw fit.

Eventually, though, the proliferation of brands—more than fifty in all—and the lack of coordination among them, became a major problem. For one thing, different brands were targeted at different ends of the market—from super premium to discount—and had different levels of awareness and acceptance in different geographic regions. Thus, Electrolux did not have a strong, coherent brand image around the world, and it was wasting marketing dollars on many unrelated, and sometimes competing, product development projects and marketing campaigns. Similarly, the large number of autonomous brands and product lines limited the opportunities for synergy and economies of scale in purchasing and manufacturing. These inefficiencies became especially critical when low-cost Asian manufacturers such as LG and Haier emerged as major players in the global market. Electrolux's managers realized that without strong brands with a reputation for high quality and innovation, the company would have no defense against lower-priced competitors, and no way to differentiate themselves from other high-end manufacturers such as Bosch-Siemens, General Electric, or Samsung. Summarizing the firm's new competitive strategy, the CEO said, "Our aim is to become a reliable and trusted partner with our customers and retailers. That means we need a few strong brands. We can't support too many."

Consequently, the firm has pulled the plug on some of its weaker brands and licensed other regional brands to local manufacturers. While it continues to support a few strong regional brands like Frigidaire and AEG, its marketing efforts are currently concentrated on a single premium global brand—Electrolux. Strangely, in order to implement its new strategy, it first had to buy back the rights to the Electrolux name in North America, which it had sold in the 1960s to raise money for its global acquisition spree.

A New Structure to Implement the New Strategy

In order to coordinate its more focused brand strategy across countries around the world, the old company structure with its semi-autonomous brands obviously had to change. The new structure is a matrix organization (a form we will examine later in this chapter) with both product-market and functional components. First, the company's various product lines and remaining brands were collapsed into three main product sectors: (1) major appliances, (2) small appliances and floor care, and (3) professional products (equipment for restaurants and dry cleaners). The major Appliances sector was further subdivided into four geographic regions: (a) Europe, Middle East, and Africa, (b) North America, (c) Latin America, and (d) Asia Pacific—in order to respond to the differing consumer desires, distribution channels, and competitive environments across countries.

All seven of the product-market sectors are serviced by five group-level staff units: (1) finance, (2) human resources, (3) legal affairs, (4) corporate communications, and (5) branding (responsible for licensing activities). Finally, in order to gain economies of scale and synergy across the firm's product lines, three group-level global operations units are responsible for all (a) technical R&D, (b) purchasing, and (c) manufacturing activities.

Marketing decisions—including the design and introduction of new products, advertising and promotional campaigns, budgeting, internet utilization, and website design—are decentralized and largely left to the individual product-market sectors. Such decisions are the responsibility of sector boards made up of the top functional managers within the sector plus the company president and the chief financial officer. However, oversight and coordination of those sector decisions is provided by regular meetings of a group management committee consisting of the CEO, the sector heads, and top executives of the staff and global operations departments.

Preliminary Results

The global economic crisis has made it difficult to fully evaluate the performance of Electrolux's new corporate structure. But despite soft consumer spending in the developed economies and a weak Swedish krona, the firm performed relatively well in 2011 with an operating income of $437 million on global revenues of $14.7 billion, for a return on equity of nearly 11 percent.

STRATEGIC CHALLENGES ADDRESSED IN CHAPTER 12

Electrolux's recent history illustrates that a business's success is determined by two aspects of *strategic fit*. First, its competitive and marketing strategies must fit the needs and desires of its target customers and the competitive and technological realities of the marketplace. Thus, the entry of low-cost Asian manufactures in to the global major appliances market forced Electrolux to adopt a new strategy aimed at building a widely recognized global brand with a reputation for premium quality and innovative design.

Strategic Issue

A business's organizational structure, internal policies, procedures, and resources must fit its chosen strategy or else implementation will fall short.

But even if a firm's competitive strategy is appropriate for the circumstances it faces, it must be capable of implementing that strategy effectively. A business's organizational structure, internal policies, procedures, and resources must fit its chosen strategy or else implementation will fall short. For instance, the firm's old structure with multiple brands organized into largely autonomous business units would obviously not be effective for implementing the new strategy focused on strengthening the global image and customer appeal of the Electrolux brand.

In the next section, we examine several questions related to the second aspect of strategic fit—the issue of **organizational fit**—the fit between a business's competitive and marketing strategies and the organizational structures, policies, processes, and plans necessary to effectively implement those strategies.

- For companies with multiple business units or product lines, what is the appropriate administrative relationship between corporate headquarters and the individual SBUs? How much autonomy should business unit managers be given to make their own strategic decisions, how much control should they have over the SBU's resources and programs, and how should they be evaluated and rewarded?

- Within a given business unit, whether it's part of a larger corporation or a one-product entrepreneurial start-up, what organizational structures and coordination mechanisms are most appropriate for implementing different competitive strategies? Answering this question involves decisions about variables such as the desired level of technical competence of the various functional departments within the business, the manner in which resources are allocated across those functions, and the mechanisms used to coordinate and resolve conflicts among the departments.

- How should organizational structures and policies be adjusted, if at all, as an organization moves into international markets?

If you are working on the Marketing Plan Exercise, you will be asked to draw on the preceding discussion and prepare an organization chart that relates the various personnel, and their functional activities, necessary to implement your plan. You'll need to justify your proposed structure's appropriateness in view of the firm's product line, resources, and the market and competitive environments it faces. As part of that justification, you might demonstrate how your proposed organization meets the tests called for in the seven domains framework outlined in Chapter 4.

However, even if a business has crafted brilliant competitive and marketing strategies, and it has the necessary organizational arrangements and wherewithal to implement them, implementation is unlikely to be very effective unless all of the business's people are following the same plan. This fact underlines the importance of developing formal, written marketing plans to document all the decisions made in formulating the intended strategy for a given good or service so it can be clearly communicated to everyone responsible for its implementation and to firmly establish who is responsible for doing what and when. As we'll see in the next chapter, formal plans also establish the timetables and objectives that are the benchmarks for management's evaluation and control of the firm's marketing strategies. Thus, good planning is important.

Given the importance of formal plans as tools to aid implementation and control, we will return in the last part of this chapter to the planning framework we introduced briefly in Chapter 1. We will examine the content of effective marketing plans in more detail and review the many strategic decisions involved in formulating that content. The purpose of these strategic planning decisions is to lay a well-conceived foundation that permits effective implementation of the strategy. Although good planning is important, effective implementation is crucial.

DESIGNING APPROPRIATE ADMINISTRATIVE RELATIONSHIPS FOR THE IMPLEMENTATION OF DIFFERENT COMPETITIVE STRATEGIES

In Chapter 3, we pointed out that businesses, whether small independent firms or units within a larger corporation, compete in different ways depending on their intended rate of new product-market development (i.e., prospectors versus analyzers versus defenders) and whether they seek an advantage by differentiating themselves via superior product or service quality or by being the low-cost producer.

The chosen competitive strategy tends to influence the marketing strategies pursued by individual product offerings within the business unit, at least in the short term. The differentiated analyzer strategy of Electrolux's major appliances sector, for example, dictates an aggressive new product development program, as well as extensive advertising and social media campaigns to build awareness of the Electrolux brand and the stream of new products.

Because the competitive strategies seek to satisfy customers and gain a sustainable advantage in varying ways, different organizational structures, policies, and resources are necessary to effectively implement them.[2] For one thing, the administrative relationshipsbetween the unit and corporate headquarters influence the ability of SBU managers, including its marketing personnel, to implement specific competitive and marketing strategies successfully. This section examines three aspects of the corporate–business unit relationship that can affect the SBU's success in implementing a particular competitive strategy:

1. The degree of autonomy provided each business unit manager.
2. The degree to which the business unit shares functional programs and facilities with other units.
3. The manner in which the corporation evaluates and rewards the performance of its SBU managers.

Exhibit 12.1 summarizes how these variables relate to the successful implementation of different business strategies. Analyzer strategies are not included because they incorporate some elements of both prospector and defender strategies. The administrative arrangements appropriate for implementing an analyzer strategy typically fall somewhere between those best suited for the other two types. To simplify the following discussion, we focus only on the polar types—prospector, differentiated defender, and low-cost defender strategies.

EXHIBIT 12.1 Administrative Factors Related to the Successful Implementation of Business Strategies

Administrative Factor	Types of Business Strategy		
	Prospector	Differentiated Defender	Low-Cost Defender
SBU autonomy	Relatively high level	Moderate level	Relatively low level
Shared programs and synergy	Relatively little synergy— few shared programs	Little synergy in areas central to differentiation— shared programs elsewhere	High level of synergy and shared programs
Evaluation and reward systems	High incentives based on sales and share growth	High incentives based on profits or ROI	Incentives based on profits or ROI

Business-Unit Autonomy

Prospector business units are likely to perform better on the critical dimensions of new product success and increases in volume and market share when organizational decision making is relatively decentralized and the SBU's managers have substantial autonomy to make their own decisions. There are several reasons for this. First, decentralized decision making allows the managers closest to the market to make more major decisions on their own. Greater autonomy also enables the SBU's managers to be more flexible and adaptable. It frees them from the restrictions of standard procedures imposed from above, allows them to make decisions with fewer consultations and participants, and disperses power. All of these help produce quicker and more innovative responses to environmental opportunities.

Strategic Issue

High levels of autonomy and independence can lead to coordination problems across SBUs.

One caveat must be attached to the preceding generalization, however. High levels of autonomy and independence can lead to coordination problems across business units. This can have a negative effect on market performance in situations where a firm's business units are narrowly defined and focused on a single product category or technology, but the firm's customers want to buy integrated systems incorporating products or services from different units. This was the problem encountered by IBM, Hewlett-Packard, and other computer hardware manufacturers as the growing popularity of the internet caused customers to attach greater importance to system integration. One possible solution to this coordination problem is to redefine SBUs with a focus on customer or application segments rather than on narrowly defined product categories, as we discussed in Chapter 2. An alternative approach is to reduce the SBUs' autonomy somewhat by installing an additional level of managers responsible for coordinating the efforts of related business units. The risk inherent in this approach is that the essential flexibility and creativity of the individual business units may be compromised.

On the other hand, low-cost defender SBUs perform better on ROI and cash flow by giving their managers relatively little autonomy. For a low-cost strategy to succeed, managers must relentlessly pursue cost economies and productivity improvements. Such efficiencies are more likely to be attained when decision making and control are relatively centralized, or at least closely monitored.

The relationship between autonomy and the ROI performance of differentiated defenders is more difficult to predict. On the one hand, such businesses defend existing positions in established markets, and their primary objective is ROI rather than volume growth. Thus, the increased efficiency and tighter control associated with relatively low autonomy should lead to better performance. On the other hand, such businesses can maintain profitability only if they continue to differentiate themselves by offering superior products and services. As customers' wants change and new competitive threats emerge, the greater flexibility and market focus associated with greater autonomy may allow these businesses to more successfully maintain their differentiated positions and higher levels of ROI over time. These arguments suggest that the relationship between autonomy and performance for differentiated defenders (and probably for differentiated analyzers as well) may be mediated by the level of stability in their environments and by the proportion of offensive or proactive marketing strategies they employ. Units operating in relatively unstable environments and pursuing more proactive marketing programs (such as extended use or market expansion strategies) are likely to perform better when they have relatively greater autonomy.

Shared Programs and Facilities

Firms face a trade-off when designing strategic business units. A SBU should be large enough to afford critical resources and to operate on an efficient scale, but it should not be so large that its market scope is too broad or that it is inflexible and therefore cannot respond to its unique market opportunities. Some firms attempt to avoid this trade-off between efficiency and adaptability by designing relatively small, narrowly focused business units, but then having two or more units share functional programs or facilities, such as common manufacturing plants, R&D programs, or a single salesforce.

Sharing resources can pose a problem for prospector business units.[3] Suppose, for instance, a business wants to introduce a new product but shares a manufacturing plant and salesforce with other SBUs. The business would have to negotiate a production schedule for the new product, and it may not be able to produce adequate quantities as quickly as needed if other units sharing the plant are trying to maintain sufficient volumes of their own products. It also may be difficult to train salespeople on the new product or to motivate them to reduce the time spent on established products to push the new item. This is especially true if the salesforce is compensated largely by commissions or bonuses tied to overall sales volume, since new products typically generate less revenue and require more selling effort than established items in the firm's product line. This problem can be at least partially offset, however, by linking generous special incentives—such as bigger commissions, bonuses, or sales contests—directly to sales revenue generated by the new item.

One exception to this generalization may be sharing sales and distribution programs across consumer package goods SBUs. In such cases, a prospector's new product may have an easier time obtaining retailer support and shelf space if it is represented by salespeople who also sell established brands to the same retail outlets. Similarly, sharing, or at least coordinating, sales, distribution, and customer service functions may be a good idea for business units that produce complementary goods or services that customers want to purchase as integrated systems rather than stand-alone offerings. In general, however, functional independence usually facilitates good performance for prospector businesses.

On the other hand, the increased efficiencies gained through sharing functional programs and facilities often boost the ROI performance of low-cost defender SBUs. Also, the inflexibility inherent in sharing is usually not a major problem for such businesses because their markets and technologies tend to be mature and relatively stable. Thus, Heinz, the cost leader in a number of food categories, uses a single salesforce to represent a wide variety of products from different business units when calling on supermarkets.

The impact of shared programs on the performance of differentiated defenders is more difficult to predict because they often must modify their products and marketing programs in response to changing market conditions to maintain their competitive advantage over time. Thus, greater functional independence in areas directly related to the SBU's differential advantage—such as R&D, sales, and marketing—tends to be positively associated with the long-run ROI performance of such businesses. But greater sharing—or even outsourcing—of facilities and programs in less crucial functional areas, such as manufacturing or distribution, also may help improve their efficiency and short-run ROI levels.

Evaluation and Reward Systems

Increasingly, companies around the world are adopting some form of pay-for-performance compensation scheme. Some do it for individuals who meet specific goals (e.g., bonuses for salespeople who exceed their quotas); others on the basis of the performance of the SBU or the company as a whole (e.g., stock options). In either case, SBU managers are often motivated to achieve their objectives by bonuses or other financial incentives tied to one or more dimensions of their unit's performance. The question is: Which dimensions of performance should be rewarded?

For defender businesses in relatively mature markets, particularly those competing as low-cost defenders, operating efficiency and profitability tend to be the most important objectives, for reasons discussed in Chapter 3. Consequently, tying a relatively large portion of managers' incentive compensation to short-term profits seems sensible. This can be done either through bonuses based on last year's profit performance or economic value added (EVA) or through options keyed to increases in the firm's stock price. However, recent research suggests that such bonus system are most effective at motivating good performance when they are made available to all employees, not just top managers.[4]

In prospector businesses, on the other hand, basing too large a portion of managers' rewards on current profitability may cause problems. Such rewards may motivate managers to avoid innovative but risky actions or investments that may not pay off for some years into the future.[5] Even successful new product introductions can dramatically increase costs and drain profits early in the product's life cycle. By the time the new product starts contributing to the unit's profits, the manager who deserves the credit may have been transferred to a different business. Therefore, evaluation and reward systems that place relatively more emphasis on sales volume or market share objectives or on the percentage of volume generated by new products may be more appropriate for businesses pursuing prospector strategies.

DESIGNING APPROPRIATE ORGANIZATIONAL STRUCTURES AND PROCESSES FOR IMPLEMENTING DIFFERENT STRATEGIES

Different strategies emphasize varying ways to gain a competitive advantage. Thus, a given functional area may be key to the success of one type of strategy but less critical for others. For instance, competence in new product R&D is critical for the success of a prospector business but less so for a low-cost defender.

Successful implementation of a given strategy is more likely when the business has the **functional competencies** demanded by its strategy and supports them with substantial **resources** relative to competitors; is **organized** suitably for its technical, market, and competitive environment; and has developed appropriate **mechanisms** for coordinating efforts and resolving conflicts across functional departments. Exhibit 12.2 summarizes the relationships between these organizational structure and process variables and the performance of different business strategies.

Functional Competencies and Resource Allocation

Competence in marketing, sales, product R&D, and engineering is critical to the success of prospector businesses because those functions play pivotal roles in new product and market development and thus must be supported with budgets set at a larger percentage of sales than their competitors. Because marketing, sales, and R&D managers are closest to the changes occurring in a business's market, competitive, and technological environments, they should be given considerable authority in making strategic decisions. This argues that bottom-up strategic planning systems are particularly well suited to prospector businesses operating in unstable environments. Success here is positively affected by the extent to which customer orientation is an integral part of the unit's corporate culture.[6]

In low-cost defender businesses, on the other hand, the functional areas most directly related to operating efficiency, such as financial management and control, production, process R&D, and distribution or logistics, play the most crucial roles in enabling the SBU to attain good ROI performance. Because differentiated defenders need to attain high returns on their established products, functional areas related to efficiency are also critical for their success. Similarly, such units also seek to improve efficiency by investing in process R&D, making needed capital investments, and maintaining a high level of capacity utilization. But because they also must maintain their differential advantage over time, functional departments related to the source of that advantage—the salesforce and product R&D for

EXHIBIT 12.2   **Organizational and Interfunctional Factors Related to the Successful Implementation of Business Strategies**

Organizational Factor	Types of Business Strategy		
	Prospector	**Differentiated Defender**	**Low-Cost Defender**
Functional competencies of the SBU	SBU will perform best on critical volume and share-growth dimensions when its functional strengths include marketing, sales, product R&D, and engineering.	SBU will perform best on critical ROI dimensions when its functional strengths include sales, financial management and control, and those functions related to its differential advantage (e.g., marketing, product R&D).	SBU will perform best on critical ROI and cash flow dimensions when its functional strengths include process engineering, production, distribution, and financial management and control.
Resource allocation across functions	SBU will perform best on volume and share-growth dimensions when percentage of sales spent on marketing, sales, and product R&D are high and when gross fixed assets per employee and percent of capacity utilization are low relative to competitors'.	SBU will perform best on the ROI dimension when percentage of sales spent on the salesforce, gross fixed assets per employee, percent of capacity utilization, and percentage of sales devoted to other functions related to the SBU's differential advantage are high relative to competitors'.	SBU will perform best on ROI and cash flow dimensions when marketing, sales, and product R&D expenses are low, but process R&D, fixed assets per employee, and percentage of capacity utilization are high relative to competitors'.
Decision-making influence and participation	SBU will perform best on volume and share-growth dimensions when managers from marketing, sales, product R&D, and engineering have substantial influence on unit's business and marketing strategy decisions.	SBU will perform best on ROI dimension when financial managers, controller, and managers of functions related to unit's differential advantage have substantial influence on business and marketing strategy decisions.	SBU will perform best on ROI and cash flow when controller, financial, and production managers have substantial influence on business and marketing strategy decisions.
SBU's organizational structure	SBU will perform best on volume and share-growth dimensions when structure has low levels of formalization and centralization, but a high level of specialization.	SBU will perform best on ROI dimension when structure has moderate levels of formalization, centralization, and specialization.	SBU will perform best on ROI and cash flow dimensions when structure has high levels of formalization and centralization, but a low level of specialization.
Functional coordination and conflict resolution	SBU will experience high levels of interfunctional conflict; SBU will perform best on volume and share-growth dimensions when participative resolution mechanisms are used (e.g., product teams).	SBU will experience moderate levels of interfunctional conflict; SBU will perform best on ROI dimension when resolution is participative for issues related to differential advantage, but hierarchical for others (e.g., product managers, product improvement teams, etc.).	SBU will experience low levels of interfunctional conflict; SBU will perform best on ROI and cash flow dimensions when conflict resolution mechanisms are hierarchical (e.g., functional organization).

Source: Adapted from Orville C. Walker Jr., and Robert W. Ruekert, "Marketing's Role in the Implementation of Business Strategies," *Journal of Marketing*, July 1987, p. 31.

SBUs with a technical product advantage or sales, marketing, and distribution for SBUs with a customer service advantage—are also critical for the unit's continued success. For example, in an attempt to defend its leading share position, cement the loyalty of its growing customer base, and generate greater revenues from repeat purchases, Amazon.com has invested hundreds of millions of dollars to build its own distribution centers and improve the speed and reliability of its order fulfillment.[7]

Additional Considerations for Service Organizations

Given that service organizations pursue the same kinds of business-level competitive strategies as goods producers, they must meet the same functional and resource requirements to implement those strategies effectively. However, service organizations—and manufacturers that provide high levels of customer service as part of their product offering—often need some additional functional competencies because of the unique problems involved in delivering quality service.

This is particularly true for services involving high customer contact. Because the sale, production, and delivery of such services occur almost simultaneously, close coordination between operations, sales, and marketing is crucial. Also, because many different employees may be involved in producing and delivering the service—as when thousands of different cooks prepare Big Macs at McDonald's outlets around the world—production planning and standardization are needed to reduce variations in quality from one transaction to the next. Similarly, detailed policies and procedures for dealing with customers are necessary to reduce variability in customer treatment across employees. All of this suggests that personnel management—particularly the activities of employee selection, training, motivation, and evaluation—is an important adjunct to the production and marketing efforts of high-contact service organizations.[8] A good example of how well-trained service personnel can help improve sales and customer retention in even the most mundane businesses is provided by Wawa convenience stores, as discussed in Exhibit 12.3.

Strategic Issue

Personnel management—particularly the activities of employee selection, training, motivation, and evaluation—is an important adjunct to the production and marketing efforts of high-contact service organizations.

Competence in human resource development is more crucial for service businesses pursuing prospector strategies—and perhaps also for defenders and analyzers who differentiate their offerings on the basis of good service—than for those focused primarily on efficiency and low cost. In prospector service organizations, employees often play a critical role in identifying potential new service offerings and in introducing them to potential customers.

EXHIBIT 12.3 *Good Service Personnel Can Turn Customers into Fans*

Wawa is a chain of convenience stores with 550 locations in five states on the East Coast of the United States. Convenience stores, where employee turnover is often high and transactions impersonal, might seem like the perfect venue for indifferent service. But many Wawa customers are enthusiastic fans. The "I Love Wawa" group on MySpace.com grew to more than 5,000 members, and one couple even had their wedding at the Wawa store where they first met.

Wawa has been successful at making loyal fans among its clientele by focusing on repeat customers—some of whom stop by every day—and trying to provide satisfying customer-employee interactions via careful hiring and training practices. Although Wawa's wages are about the same

as those of its competitors, the firm does a better job of investing in the development of the people it hires: training them at its Wawa Corporate University and providing them with benefits that facilitate self-improvement—such as reimbursing tuition for college courses—and the like. Consequently, employee turnover rates are low, and the firm receives hundreds of applications for each job opening. If a lowly convenience store chain can turn customers into fans, perhaps many other service companies could benefit from increased investments in employee recruitment, training, and incentive rewards.

Source: Rob Walker, "Convenience Cult?" *New York Times Magazine*, July 30, 2006, p.15.

Consequently, the effective implementation of such a strategy requires employees with superior communication and social skills and necessitates frequent employee retraining and performance feedback. For instance, banks pursuing a prospector strategy not only have more branches and engage in more market scanning, advertising, and new service development than those with other types of competitive strategies, but also devote more effort to screening potential employees and providing training and support after they are hired.[9]

Organizational Structures

Three structural variables—formalization, centralization, and specialization—are important in shaping both a SBU's and its marketing department's performance within the context of a given competitive strategy. **Formalization** is the degree to which formal rules and standard policies and procedures govern decisions and working relationships. **Centralization** refers to the location of decision authority and control within an organization's hierarchy. In highly centralized SBUs or marketing departments, only one or a few top managers hold most decision-making authority. In more decentralized units, middle- and lower-level managers have more autonomy and participate in a wider range of decisions. Finally, **specialization** refers to the division of tasks and activities across positions within the organizational unit. A highly specialized marketing department, for instance, has a large number of specialists, such as market researchers, advertising managers, and sales promotion managers, who perform a narrowly defined set of activities often as consultants to product managers.

Highly structured business units and marketing departments are unlikely to be very innovative or quick to adapt to a changing evironmental circumstance. Adaptiveness and innovativeness are enhanced when (1) decision-making authority is decentralized, (2) managerial discretion and informal coordination mechanisms replace rigid rules and policies, and (3) more specialists are present. Thus, prospector business units and their marketing departments are likely to perform better when they are decentralized, have little formalization, and are highly specialized.[10]

Differentiated defenders perform best when their organizational structures incorporate moderate levels of formalization, centralization, and specialization. Those departments most directly related to the source of a differentiated defender's competitive advantage (sales, marketing, and R&D), however, should be less highly structured than those more crucial for the efficiency of the unit's operations (production and logistics).

Several common organizational designs incorporate differences in both the structural variables (formalization, centralization, and specialization) and the mechanisms for resolving interfunctional conflicts. These include (1) functional, (2) product management, (3) market management, and (4) various types of matrix organizational designs.

Functional Organizations

The functional form of organization is the simplest and most bureaucratic design. At the SBU level, managers of each functional department, such as production or marketing, report to the general manager. Within the marketing department, managers of specific marketing activity areas, such as sales, advertising, or marketing research, report to the marketing vice president or director, as shown in Exhibit 12.4. At each level the top manager coordinates the activities of all the functional areas reporting to him or her, often with heavy reliance on standard rules and operating procedures. This is the most centralized and formalized organization form and relies primarily on hierarchical mechanisms for resolving conflicts across functional areas. Also, because top managers perform their coordination activities across all product-markets in the SBU, there is little specialization by product or customer type.

EXHIBIT 12.4   Functional Organization of a SBU and Its Marketing Department

These characteristics make the functional form simple, efficient, and particularly suitable for companies operating in stable and slow-growth industries where the environments are predictable. Thus, the form is appropriate for low-cost defender SBUs attempting to maximize their efficiency and profitability in mature or declining industries. For example, Ingersol-Rand, a low-cost manufacturer of low-tech air compressors and air-driven tools such as jackhammers, uses a functional structure.

The simplicity of the functional organization also makes it the most common organizational form among entrepreneurial start-ups. Even though the functional form is very hierarchical, such firms can still be nimble and innovative provided that (1) the company remains small enough that the entrepreneur can personally supervise and coordinate the various functions, (2) the firm is focused on a single product or product line targeted at one customer segment, and (3) the entrepreneur's personal vision is an adequate source of innovation to differentiate the entire company. As the start-up grows, its product offerings expand, and its markets fragment, however, it is usually wise to adopt a more decentralized and specialized organizational form. Unfortunately, some entrepreneurs find it difficult to delegate decision-making authority to their subordinates.

Product Management Organizations

When a company or SBU has many product-market entries, the simple functional form of organization is inadequate. A single manager finds it difficult to stay abreast of functional activities across a variety of different product-markets or to coordinate them efficiently. One common means of dealing with this problem is to adopt a product management organizational structure. As Exhibit 12.5 illustrates, this form adds an additional layer of managers to the marketing department, usually called product managers, brand managers, or marketing managers, each of whom has the responsibility to plan and manage the marketing programs and to coordinate the activities of other functional departments for a specific product or product line.

A product management structure decentralizes decision making while increasing the amount of product specialization within the SBU. If the product managers also are given substantial autonomy to develop their own marketing plans and programs, this structure also can decrease the formalization within the business. Finally, although the product

EXHIBIT 12.5   A Marketing Department with a Product Management Organization

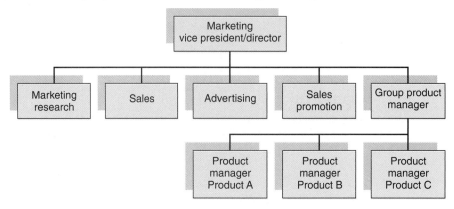

managers are responsible for obtaining cooperation from other functional areas both within and outside the marketing department, they have no formal authority over these areas. They must rely on persuasion and compromise—in other words, more participative methods—to overcome conflicts and objections when coordinating functional activities. These factors make the product management form of organization less bureaucratic than the functional structure. It is more appropriate for businesses pursuing differentiated defender and analyzer strategies, particularly when they operate in industries with complex and relatively unstable market and competitive environments. Thus, many large consumer goods companies with multiple brands competing in diverse segments—such as Nestlé, Unilever, and General Mills—incorporate a product management structure.

When a firm targets a number of brands at different market segments, a product management organization typically includes one or more "group" or "category" marketing managers, on the level immediately above the product managers, who allocate resources across brands. Category management also provides an opportunity for the involvement of more experienced managers in brand management, particularly those concerned with coordinating pricing and other marketing efforts.[11]

Product management organizations have a number of advantages, including the ability to identify and react more quickly to the threats and opportunities individual product-market entries face, improved coordination of functional activities within and across product-markets, and increased attention to smaller product-market entries that might be neglected in a functional organization. Consequently, about 85 percent of all consumer goods manufacturers use some form of product management organization.

Unfortunately, a product management organization also has shortcomings. The major one is the difficulty of obtaining the cooperation necessary to develop and implement effective programs for a particular product given that a product manager has little direct authority. Also, the environment facing product managers is changing drastically. They increasingly must face the fact that customers can quickly compare products and prices— and even suggest their own price—over the internet; that customers are becoming more price sensitive and less brand loyal; that competition is becoming more global; that rapidly changing technologies are providing new ways to improve production and distribution efficiency, but also shortening product life cycles; and that the power of large retailers and distributors has increased due in part to their ability to collect and control information about the marketplace. These environmental trends have led to an increase in the sales of private-label brands and more aggressive bargaining by distributors.[12] As a result of these trends and the inherent weakness of the product manager type of organization, many companies have undertaken two major types of modifications—market management and matrix organization—discussed next.

Market Management Organizations

In some industries, a SBU may market a single product to a large number of markets where customers have very different requirements and preferences. Pepsi-Cola, for example, is sold through restaurants, fast-food outlets, and supermarkets. The syrup needed to make Pepsi is sold directly to institutions such as Kentucky Fried Chicken and Taco Bell. But marketing Pepsi to consumers for home consumption involves the use of franchised bottlers who process and package the product and distribute it to a variety of retail outlets. The intermediaries and marketing activities involved in selling to the two markets are so different that it makes sense to have a separate market manager in charge of each. Such a company or SBU might organize itself along the lines shown in Exhibit 12.6. Some SBUs have adopted a combination of product and regional market management organizational structures. A product manager has overall responsibility for planning and implementing a national marketing program for the product, but several market managers are also given some authority and an independent budget to work with salespeople to develop promotion programs geared to a particular user segment or geographic market. This kind of decentralization or regionalization has become popular with consumer goods companies in their efforts to increase geographic segmentation and cope with the growing power of regional retail chains.

Matrix Organizations

A business facing an extremely complex and uncertain environment may find a matrix organization appropriate. The matrix form is the least bureaucratic or centralized and the most specialized type of organization. It brings together two or more different types of specialists within a participative coordination structure. One example is the product team, which consists of representatives from a number of functional areas assembled for each product or product line. As a group, the team must agree on a business plan for the product and ensure the necessary resources and cooperation from each functional area. This kind of participative decision making can be very inefficient; it requires a good deal of time and effort for the team to reach mutually acceptable decisions and gain approval from all the affected functional areas. But once reached, those decisions are more likely to reflect the expertise of a variety of functional specialists, to be innovative, and to be quickly and effectively implemented. Thus, the matrix form of organization particularly suits prospector businesses and the management of new product development projects within analyzer or differentiated defender businesses. Some examples are discussed in Exhibit 12.7.

EXHIBIT 12.6 **A Marketing Department with a Market Management Organization**

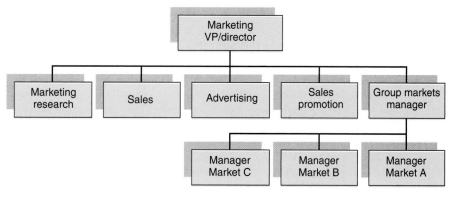

EXHIBIT 12.7 *Using Teams to Get the Job Done*

Pillsbury, which has recently merged with General Mills, replaced its traditional marketing department with multiple discipline teams centered around a product group (e.g., pizza snacks). Each involves managers from marketing, sales, and production. Lever Brothers restructured in a similar fashion. It reorganized its marketing and sales departments into a series of business groups and set up a separate customer development team responsible for retailer relations across all the various SBU brands. Large companies are increasingly relying on small interdisciplinary teams to launch new product or service initiatives in their attempts to improve innovativeness and reduce time to market.

Sources: "Death of the Brand Manager," *The Economist*, April 9, 1994, p. 67; and Steve Hamm, "Speed Demons," *BusinessWeek*, March 27, 2006, pp. 68–76.

Another form of matrix structure involves the creation of an additional organizational unit or managerial position responsible for coordinating the actions of other units within the firm. For example, nearly every business school has a MBA program director responsible for coordinating the courses offered by the functional departments in the hope of creating a tightly integrated and coherent curriculum.

Electrolux's new structure incorporates both of the above matrix types taken up to the corporate level. First product specialists and market specialist were combined in the four regional major appliances sectors (e.g., major appliances North America, Latin America, etc.). The ongoing operations of the various product-market sectors are managed by boards made up of the sector's functional managers plus representatives of the corporate staff departments. Finally, common activities with substantial potential for cross-country synergies and economies of scale, such as purchasing and manufacturing, are coordinated across the product-market sectors by global operations units.

Recent Trends in Organizational Design

As we have stressed throughout this book, the dynamics of the marketplace are forcing companies to respond more quickly to their opportunities and threats if they hope to survive and prosper. This has spurred a search for organizational structures that are flexible, responsive, able to learn, and market oriented.[13] Although we are only just beginning to gain insights into organizational structures of the future, certain aspects seem reasonably clear. We briefly discuss the more important of these.

Organizations will increasingly emphasize the **managing of business processes** in contrast to functional areas.[14] Every business has about six basic or core processes, such as, for example, new product development and supply chain management. The former would be staffed by individuals from marketing, R&D, manufacturing, and finance. The latter would contain people with expertise in purchasing, manufacturing, order delivery, and billing.

Managing processes will make the organization essentially horizontal—flat and lean versus a vertical or hierarchical model. Thus, executive positions may no longer be defined in terms of managing a group of functionally oriented people; instead, executives will be concerned with a process that strongly emphasizes the importance of customer satisfaction.[15] Process management is quite different from the management of a function because, first, it uses external objectives, such as customer satisfaction versus simple revenues. Second, people with different skills are grouped to undertake a complete piece of work; their work is done simultaneously, not in sequence. Third, information flows directly to where it is used. Thus, if you have an upstream problem, you deal with people involved directly rather than via your boss.

Next, the use of **self-managing teams** is increasing. Regardless of the form of worker self-management, all are based on the concept of *empowerment*—the theory that those doing the work should have the means to do what it takes to please the customer. In turn, this requires that performance objectives and evaluation of activities be linked to customer satisfaction. Successful teams can dramatically improve productivity; for example, Boeing used empowered teams to reduce the number of hang-ups by half on its 777 jet. But many teams have failed because management was not serious about its empowerment, team members were poorly selected, or the team was launched in isolation with little training or support.[16]

In the future, many companies will use teams as the basis for collaborative networks that link thousands of people together with the help of a variety of new technologies. Such networks enable businesses to form and dissolve relations quickly and to bring to bear on an opportunity or a threat the needed resources, regardless of who owns them.[17] For example, XM Satellite Radio formed an alliance with Samsung Electronics to develop the first portable satellite radio combined with a digital music player. The two companies created a virtual product development team jointly headed by one manager from each company. Samsung engineers focused on industrial design and manufacturing, whereas XM dealt with the user interface, the antenna, and performance features—such as the ability to "bookmark" a song playing on the radio and purchase it later online. Samsung and XM were able to introduce their co-branded Helix radio just nine months after forming their alliance.[18]

But not all such collaborative networks are successful, especially those involving **joint ventures.** Partnering is at best a difficult and demanding undertaking requiring considerable managerial skills as well as a great deal of trust.[19] A major difficulty, especially for those involving companies from different parts of the world, is that "they cannot be controlled by formal systems, but require a dense web of interpersonal connections and internal infrastructures that enhance learning."[20]

Organizational Adjustments as Firms Grow and Markets Change

Managers often think of the design of their organization as stable and not subject to change. In rapidly growing entrepreneurial companies and in changing markets, however, such thinking can be dangerous. As the number of customers and the range of product lines grow, the best way to organize the marketing and sales functions should be subject to change.

An entrepreneurial start-up may begin with a simple functional structure, perhaps even simpler than that diagrammed in Exhibit 12.4. As it grows and its product offerings become broader and more complex, it may assign specialized product managers to coordinate the marketing efforts for the various products or product lines. Eventually, the firm might even split into several product divisions, each with its own sales and marketing departments. Or the firm's customers might fragment into a number of diverse segments with unique needs and requirements, favoring the adoption of a market management or matrix structure.

With each of these adjustments to a company's organizational structure, however, comes added complexity and potential disadvantages. For instance, what if the new structure results in multiple salespeople, representing the company's different product lines, competing with each other for a customer's business? Such competition may be contrary to the company's self-interest as well as confusing and inconvenient for the customer. More importantly, such a lack of coordination would make it difficult to sell comprehensive solutions that cut across the firm's product or divisional boundaries.

How should managers decide when the time has come to restructure an organization, and what new structure should replace the old one? There are five key drivers with such decisions: (1) customer needs, (2) informational requirements of the sales and marketing personnel charged with meeting those needs, (3) ability of a given structure to motivate and coordinate the kinds of activities that market conditions require, (4) available competencies and resources, and (5) costs.

When customers all tend to use a narrow range of goods or services to satisfy similar needs, a simple functional structure may be sufficient. When customer segments use goods or services in different ways, either a product-focused or market-focused structure is likely to work well. If individual customers buy a broad range of the firm's goods or services, however, having multiple salespeople calling on those customers, unless they are organized into teams, is probably a bad idea. When a company's offerings are relatively simple and easy to understand, a single salesforce may be able to handle the entire line. But when products are technically complex or open to customization, each line may require its own specialized sales and marketing organization. When the firm is not well established or needs to educate potential buyers about the advantages of an innovative offering, it may need heavy incentives to encourage salespeople to expend the effort necessary to win new business. Under such circumstances, team-oriented selling arrangements are likely to be ineffectual. Finally, the fact that more highly specialized structures also tend to increase personnel and administrative costs should not be overlooked.

Thus, growing firms or those serving rapidly changing markets are likely to need to rethink—and perhaps change—the structure of their sales and marketing organizations frequently. Such changes can be disruptive to both internal and customer relationships, but failure to adjust in the face of changing market conditions can make it hard for the firm to implement its marketing strategy and maintain a leading position in its industry.

Organizational Designs for Selling in Global Markets[21]

An organization's complexity increases, often quite dramatically, as it "goes international," and especially so as overseas sales as a percentage of total sales increase. The issue is essentially one of deciding what organizational design is best for developing and implementing worldwide strategies while simultaneously maintaining flexibility with regard to individual markets. In evaluating the several types of international organizational structures discussed in this section, keep in mind two things: "first, that innovation is the key to success. An organization that relies on one culture for its ideas and treats foreign subsidiaries as dumb production-colonies might as well hire subcontractors."[22] Second, technology is making the world smaller.

Little or No Formal Organization

Early on in a firm's international involvement, the structure ranges from the domestic organization handling international transactions to a separate export department. The latter may be tied to the marketing department or may be a freestanding functional department.

An International Division

To avoid discriminating against international customers in comparison with domestic customers, an international division is often established to house all international activities, most of which relate to marketing. Manufacturing, engineering, finance, and R&D typically remain in their previous form to take advantage of scale effects. This type of organization serves best with a limited number of products that lack cultural sensitivity—for example, basic commodity types such as chemicals, metals, and industrial machinery.

Many Japanese firms historically emphasized low-cost manufacturing coupled with quality assurance as the essence of their international competitive strategy. Both of these require strong centralized control and, thus, the use of an export-based organizational structure. In recent years, though, Japanese firms have become more interested in global structures based on products or geographic areas.[23]

Global Structures

There are a variety of global types, of which the simplest replicates the firm's basic functional departments. A global company using the functional type of organization would have vice presidents (worldwide) for such areas as manufacturing, marketing, and finance—all reporting to the president.

By far the most common global structure is one based on products, which translates into giving SBUs worldwide control over their product lines. The main advantages of this type of structure are the economies derived from centralizing manufacturing activities and the ability to respond quickly to product-related problems originating in overseas markets. Marketing is localized at the country or regional level. This is essentially the structure that evolved at Electrolux during the decades of its merger and acquisitions spree. As the number of product lines and brands proliferated, however, this structure led to a lack of coordination and substantial duplication of effort.

The *area structure* is another popular global organizational type and is especially appropriate when there is considerable variance across markets regarding product acceptance and marketing activities. Firms typically organize on a regional basis (North America, Latin America, Europe, Far East, Middle East, and Africa) using a central staff that coordinates worldwide planning and control activities. In some cases, this kind of geographic structure is taken all the way down to individual countries. For example, in order to reach the millions of untapped consumers living in China's rural countryside, Procter & Gamble has established a nearly autonomous operation with the authority to develop new products and line extensions suited to the Chinese market (such as Morning Lotus Blossom Crest), an extensive network of wholesale subdistributors who service small rural retailers, and a substantial budget for market development within the country.[24]

Some companies use a hybrid organization that typically is some combination of the functional, product, or area types of structure. The global matrix is one such attempt. It has individual business managers reporting to both area and functional groups, or—as in the case of Electrolux—area managers who are responsible for marketing and product-development strategies, but who report to global functional managers for manufacturing and purchasing decisions. Such dual reporting can lead to conflicts and a lack of coordination across areas. Therefore, the firm created sector and group management boards to deal with such issues.

Decision-Making and Organizational Structure

Organizational structures can be centralized or decentralized in terms of decision making. In the case of the latter, controls are relatively simple, and relations between subsidiaries and headquarters are mainly financial. The logic here is that local management is closest to the market and can respond quickly to change. But multinationals faced with strong global competition require more centralization, which calls for headquarters to provide the overall strategy that subsidiaries (country units) implement within a range agreed upon with headquarters.[25]

MARKETING PLANS: THE FOUNDATION FOR IMPLEMENTING MARKETING ACTIONS

As we pointed out in Chapter 1, preparation of a written plan is a key step in ensuring the effective execution of a strategic marketing program because it spells out what actions are to be taken, when, and by whom. Written plans are particularly crucial in larger organizations because a marketing manager's proposals must usually be reviewed and approved by

Strategic Issue

A written plan is a key step in ensuring the effective execution of a strategic marketing program because it spells out what actions are to be taken, when, and by whom.

higher levels of management and because the approved plan then provides the benchmark against which the manager's and the marketing program's performances will be evaluated. Preparing formal, written marketing plans, however brief, is a useful exercise even in small firms because the discipline involved helps ensure that the proposed objectives, strategy, and marketing actions are based on rigorous analysis of the 4 Cs and sound reasoning. Marketing plans can vary a good deal in content and organization,[26] but they generally follow a format similar to the one outlined in Exhibit 1.10 and reproduced in Exhibit 12.8. To illustrate the kinds of information that might be included in each section of the plan, the contents of a marketing plan for a disguised Pillsbury refrigerated dough product in the U.S. market are summarized in Exhibit 12.9.

Much of this book has focused on the planning process, the decisions that must be made when formulating a marketing strategy and its various components, the development of strategic marketing plans, and the analytical tools managers can use in reaching those decisions.

EXHIBIT 12.8   Contents of an Annual Marketing Plan

Section	Content
I. Executive summary	Presents a short overview of the issues, objectives, strategy, and actions incorporated in the plan and their expected outcomes for quick management review.
II. Current situation and trends	Summarizes relevant background information on the market, competition and the macroenvironment, and trends therein, including size and growth rates for the overall market and key segments.
III. Performance review (for an existing product or service only)	Examines the past performance of the product and the elements of its marketing program (e.g., distribution, promotion, etc.).
IV. Key issues	Identifies the main opportunities and threats to the product that the plan must deal with in the coming year and the relative strengths and weaknesses of the product and business unit that must be taken into account in facing those issues.
V. Objectives	Specifies the goals to be accomplished in terms of sales volume, market share, and profit.
VI. Marketing strategy	Summarizes the overall strategic approach that will be used to meet the plan's objectives.
VII. Action plans	This is the most critical section of the annual plan for helping to ensure effective implementation and coordination of activities across functional departments. It specifies: • The target market to be pursued. • What specific actions are to be taken with respect to each of the 4 Ps. • Who is responsible for each action. • When the action will be engaged in. • How much will be budgeted for each action.
VIII. Projected profit-and-loss statement	Presents the expected financial payoff from the plan.
IX. Controls	Discusses how the plan's progress will be monitored: may present contingency plans to be used if performance falls below expectations or the situation changes.
X. Contingency plans	Describes actions to be taken if specific threats or opportunities materialize during the planning period.

EXHIBIT 12.9   Summary of an Annual Marketing Plan for a Refrigerated Bread Dough Product

I. Analysis of current situation

A. Market situation

- The total U.S. market for dinner breadstuffs is enormous, amounting to about 10.5 billion servings per year.
- Specialty breads, such as whole-grain breads, are growing in popularity, largely at the expense of traditional white breads.
- Pillsbury's share of the total dinner breadstuffs market, accounted for by several brands including Crescent rolls as well as refrigerated bread dough, is small, amounting to only about 2 percent of the total dollar volume.
- Since its introduction several years ago, refrigerated bread dough (RBD) has been able to achieve only low levels of penetration (only about 15 percent of all households have used the product) and use frequency (nearly two-thirds of the product's volume comes from light users who buy only one or two cans per year).
- RBD consumption is concentrated in the northern states and during the fall and winter months (about 75 percent of volume is achieved from September through February).
- Marketing research results suggest consumers believe RBD is relatively expensive in terms of price/value compared to alternative forms of dinner breadstuffs.

B. Competitive situation

- RBD's share of the total dinner breadstuffs category is likely to remain low because of the wide variety of competing choices available to consumers.
- The largest proportion of volume within the category is captured by ready-to-eat breads and rolls produced by supermarket chains and regional bakeries and distributed through retail grocery stores.
- RBD's major competition within the refrigerated dough category comes from other Pillsbury products, such as Crescent rolls and Soft Breadsticks.
- There are currently no other national competitors in the refrigerated bread dough category; but Merico, a small regional producer, was recently acquired by a major national food manufacturer. Evidence suggests Merico may be preparing to introduce a competing product line into national distribution at a price about 10 percent lower than Pillsbury's.

C. Macroenvironmental situation

- Changes in American eating habits may pose future problems for dinner breadstuffs in general, and for RBD in particular:

  More meals are being eaten away from home, and this trend is likely to continue.

  People are eating fewer starch foods.

  While total volume of dinner breadstuffs has not fallen over the past decade, neither has it kept pace with population growth.

- Increasing numbers of women working outside of the home, and the resulting desire for convenience, may reduce consumers' willingness to wait 30 minutes while RBD bakes, even though the dough is already prepared.
- Because RBD does not use yeast as a leavening agent, Food and Drug Administration regulations prohibit the company from referring to it as "bread" in advertising or package copy, even though the finished product looks, smells, and tastes like bread.

D. Past product performance

- Although sales volume in units increased only slightly during the past year, dollar volume increased by 24 percent due to a price increase taken early in the year.
- The improvement to gross margin was even greater than the price increase due to an improvement in manufacturing costs.
- The improvement to gross margin, however, was not sufficient to produce a positive net margin due to high advertising and sales promotion expenditures aimed at stimulating primary demand and increasing market penetration of RBD.
- Consequently, although RBD showed improvement over the last year, it was still unable to make a positive contribution to overhead and profit.

II. Key issues

A. Threats

- Lack of growth in the dinner breadstuff category suggests the market is mature and may decline in the future.
- The large variety of alternatives available to consumers suggests it may be impossible for RBD to substantially increase its share of the total market.
- Potential entry of a new, lower-priced competitor poses a threat to RBD's existing share and may result in lower margins if RBD responds by reducing its price.

B. Opportunities

- The largest percentage of RBD volume accounted for by light users suggests an opportunity of increasing volume among current users by stimulating frequency of use.
- Trends toward increased consumption of specialty breads suggest possible line extensions, such as whole wheat or other whole-grain flavors.

(continued)

EXHIBIT 12.9 (Continued)

C. Strengths
- RBD has a strong distribution base, with shelf-facings in nearly 90 percent of available retail outlets.
- RBD sales have proved responsive to sales promotion efforts (e.g., cents-off coupons), primarily by increasing volume among existing users.
- The fact that most consumers who try RBD make repeat purchases indicates a high level of customer satisfaction.

D. Weaknesses
- RBD sales have proved unresponsive to advertising. Attempts to stimulate primary demand have not been able to increase market penetration.
- Consumer concerns about RBD's price/value place limits on ability to take future price increases.

III. Objectives

A. Financial objectives
- Achieve a positive contribution to overhead and profit of $4 million in current year.
- Reach the target level of an average of 20 percent return on investment over the next five years.

B. Marketing objectives
- Maintain market share and net sales revenues at previous year's levels.
- Maintain current levels of retail distribution coverage.
- Reduce marketing expenditures sufficiently to achieve profit contribution objective.
- Identify viable opportunities for future volume and profit expansion.

IV. Marketing strategy
- Pursue a maintenance strategy aimed at holding or slightly increasing RBD volume and market share primarily by stimulating increased frequency of use among current users.
- Reduce advertising aimed at stimulation of primary demand/penetration and reduce manufacturing costs in order to achieve profit contribution objective.
- Initiate development and test marketing of possible line extensions to identify opportunities for future volume expansion.

V. Marketing action plans
- Improve the perceived price/value of RBD by maintaining current suggested retail price at least through the peak selling season (February). Review the competitive situation and the brand's profit performance in March to assess the desirability of a price increase at that time.
- Work with production to identify and implement cost savings opportunities that will reduce manufacturing costs by 5 percent without compromising product quality.
- Maintain retail distribution coverage with two trade promotion discount offers totaling $855,000: one offered in October–November to support peak season inventories and another offered in February–March to maintain inventories as volume slows.
- Reduce advertising to maintenance level of 1,100 gross ratings points during the peak sales period of September to March. Focus copy on maintaining awareness among current users.
- Encourage greater frequency of use among current users through three sales promotion events, with a total budget of $748,000, that will stimulate immediate purchase:
  - One freestanding insert (FSI) coupon for 15 cents off next purchase to appear in newspaper on September 19.
  - One tear-off refund offer (buy three, get one free) placed on the retailer's shelves during November.
  - A $1 refund with proof of purchase offer placed in women's service books (i.e., women's magazines such as *Good Housekeeping*) during March.

VI. Contingency plans
- Maintain the preceding marketing strategy and action plans without change during the planning period even if Merico (see item I.B) enters the market.
- If Merico enters, carefully monitor its pricing and promotion actions, sales results, consumer perceptions, and so forth, and prepare recommendations for next year's plan.

Consequently, we will say little here about the processes or procedures involved in putting together a marketing plan. Instead, our purpose is to summarize how the topics we've covered can be integrated with a coherent marketing plan and how the plan's content should be organized and presented to best ensure that the strategy will be effectively carried out.

The success of a marketing plan depends on effective communication with other parts of the organizations (such as production, engineering, and R&D) and a variety of marketing units, especially those concerned with sales, advertising, promotions, and marketing research. By using the experience of others (as consultants) in preparing the action programs (for instance, in-store promotions), the planner not only benefits from the expertise of specialists, but also increases their buy-in to the overall marketing plan, thereby increasing the likelihood of its success.

The action programs should reflect agreements made with other departments and marketing units as to their responsibilities over the planning period concerning the product. For example, if a special sale is to occur in a given month, the production department must commit to making sufficient product available and to the use of a special package; the promotion group agrees to develop and have available for use by the salesforce in-store displays; the salesforce must allocate the time necessary to do the in-store work; and so on. Thus, the annual plan serves as a means of allocating the firm's resources as well as a way of assigning responsibility for the plan's implementation.[27]

The Situation Analysis[28]

Although many marketing plans start with a brief executive summary of their contents, this is typically the first substantive section in which the marketing manager details his or her assessment of the current situation. It is the "homework" portion of the plan where the manager summarizes his or her analysis of current and potential customers, the competitive environment and the company's relative strengths and weaknesses, trends in the broader macroenvironment that may impact the product, and past performance outcomes for existing products. This section also typically includes estimates of sales potential, forecasts, and other assumptions underlying the plan. Based on these analyses, the manager may then call attention to one or more key issues, major opportunities, or threats that should be dealt with during the planning period.

Market Situation

Here data are presented on the target market. Total market size and growth trends should be discussed, along with any variations across geographic regions or other market segments. Marketing research information also might be presented concerning customer perceptions (perhaps, awareness of the brand) and buying-behavior trends (market penetration, repeat purchase rate, heavy versus light users). As Exhibit 12.9 indicates, for instance, information about the market situation presented in the plan for Pillsbury's refrigerated bread dough (RBD) not only includes data about the size of the total market for dinner breadstuffs and Pillsbury's market share, but also points out the low penetration and use frequency of RBD among potential users.

Competitive Situation

This section identifies and describes the product's major competitors in terms of their size, market share, product quality, marketing strategies, and other relevant factors. It also should discuss the likelihood that other potential competitors will enter the market in the near future and the possible impact of such entry on the product's competitive position. Note, for instance, that although other Pillsbury brands are the primary competitors for RBD in the refrigerated dough category, the potential entry of a new low-cost competitor could dramatically change the competitive situation.

Macroenvironmental Situation

This section describes broad environmental occurrences or trends that may have a bearing on the product's future. The issues mentioned here include any relevant economic,

EXHIBIT 12.10 **Historical and Projected Financial Performance of Refrigerated Bread Dough Product**

Variable	Last Year	This Year	Percent Change	Next Year	Percent Change
Sales volume (cases)	2,290M	2,350M	3%	2,300M	(2%)
Net sales ($)	17,078M	21,165M	24	21,182M	0
Gross margin ($)	6,522M	10,787M	65	11,430	5
Gross margin/net sales	38%	51%	—	54%	—
Advertising and sales promotion ($)	11,609M	12,492M	+6	6,100M	(51)
Advertising & sales promotion/gross margin	178%	116%	—	53%	—
Net margin ($)	(5,087M)	(1,725M)	—	5,330M	—
Net margin/net sales	—	—	—	25	—
Product contribution ($)	(6,342M)	(3,740M)	—	4,017M	—

technological, political/legal, or social/cultural changes. As Exhibit 12.9 indicates, for example, lifestyle trends leading to more meals being eaten away from home and increased desires for convenience pose a threat to future demand for Pillsbury's RBD.

Past Product Performance

If the plan is for an existing product, this part of the situation analysis discusses the product's performance on such dimensions as sales volume, margins, marketing expenditures, and profit contribution for several recent years. This information is usually presented in the form of a table, such as the one for RBD shown in Exhibit 12.10. As the table indicates, even though RBD showed an improvement in gross margin due in part to reduced manufacturing costs, high advertising and sales expenditures prevented the product from making a positive contribution to overhead and profit.

The data contained in Exhibit 12.9 do not answer the question of whether the company's RBD prices and costs are competitive. Such information is critical since if a product's costs are not in line, then the product's market position is in jeopardy. This is especially true with commodity-type products. Although even when products are differentiated, it is essential that costs be maintained at competitive levels and any price premium charged reflect a corresponding benefit to buyers. Some methods for measuring and monitoring costs and profitability are examined in Chapter 13.[29]

Sales Forecast and Other Key Assumptions

Finally, the assessment of the current situation also typically includes estimates of sales potential, sales forecasts, and other evidence or assumptions underlying the plan. As we discussed in Chapter 5, such market measurements are particularly critical as the foundation for marketing plans for new goods or services where there is no past history to draw on. Although the RBD plan does not explicitly report an estimate of total market potential, a sales forecast underlies the expected volume for next year, reported in the fourth column of Exhibit 12.10.

Key Issues

After analyzing the current situation, the product manager must identify the most important issues facing the product in the coming year. These issues typically represent either threats to the future market or financial performance of the product or opportunities to improve those performances. This section also should highlight any special strengths of the product or weaknesses that must be overcome in responding to future threats and opportunities. Some of the key threats and opportunities faced by Pillsbury's RBD, together with the product's major strengths and weaknesses, are summarized in Section II of Exhibit 12.9.

Objectives

Information about the current situation, the product's recent performance, and the key issues to be addressed now serve as the basis for setting specific objectives for the coming year. Two types of objectives need to be specified. **Financial objectives** provide goals for the overall performance of the brand and should reflect the objectives for the SBU as a whole and its competitive strategy. Those financial goals must then be converted into **marketing objectives** that specify the changes in customer behavior and levels of performance of various marketing program elements necessary to reach the product's financial objectives.

The major financial and marketing objectives for Pillsbury's RBD are summarized in Section III of Exhibit 12.9. Sales volume and market share are not expected to increase, but the product is expected to make a $4 million contribution to overhead and profit through additional cost reductions.

Marketing Strategy

Because there may be a number of ways to achieve the objectives specified in the preceding section, the manager must now specify the overall marketing strategy to be pursued. It is likely to be one, or a combination of several, of the strategies discussed earlier in Chapters 8, 9, 10, and 11. The chosen strategy should fit the market and competitive conditions faced by the product and its strategic objectives. It also should incorporate all of the necessary decisions concerning the 4 Ps.

The RBD product manager recommends that a **maintenance strategy** be pursued. The intense competitive situation, uncertainty over the possible entry of Merico, and the past inability of primary-demand advertising to increase market penetration all suggest that it would be difficult to expand RBD's market by simply doing more of the same. Consequently, the recommended strategy seeks to maintain or slightly increase RBD volume and share primarily by stimulating repeat purchases among current customers. Reductions in advertising expenditures and continued improvements in manufacturing costs will be relied on to help the brand achieve its profit contribution objective. In addition, it is recommended that development and test marketing of several line extensions (for example, whole wheat and a French-style loaf) be initiated in an attempt to identify viable opportunities for future volume expansion.

Action Plans

The action plan is the most crucial part of the annual marketing plan for ensuring proper execution. Here the specific actions necessary to implement the strategy for the product are listed, together with a clear statement of who is responsible for each action, when it will be done, and how much is to be spent on each activity. Of course, actions requiring the cooperation of other functional departments should be included, but only after the product manager has contacted the departments involved, worked out any potential conflicts, and received assurances of support.

Here is where specific timelines and milestones are set forth. A variety of planning and project management tools—such at Gantt charts, stage-gate development processes, and others—may be used to illustrate and orchestrate the action steps entailed in the plan. Some of the action programs specified for RBD are outlined in Section V of Exhibit 12.9.

Projected Profit-and-Loss Statement

The action plan includes a supporting budget that is essentially a projected profit-and-loss statement. On the revenue side, it forecasts next year's sales volume in units and dollars. On the expense side, it reflects manufacturing, distribution, and marketing costs associated with the planned actions. This budget is then presented to higher levels of management for review and possible modification. Once approved, the product's budget serves as a basis for the plans and resource allocation decisions of other functional departments within the SBU, such as manufacturing and purchasing, as well as other marketing units (e.g., marketing research). The projected financial results of RBD's annual plan are summarized in thesecond-to-last column of Exhibit 12.10.

Contingency Plans

Finally, the manager also might detail contingency plans to be implemented if specific threats or opportunities should occur during the planning period. The RBD product manager, for instance, recommended that no changes be made in the product's overall marketing strategy nor in its pricing or promotion tactics in the event that Merico entered the national market. The rationale was that time should be taken to carefully analyze Merico's market impact and the magnitude of its competitive threat before crafting a response.

Marketing Plan Exercise

Prepare an organizational chart that includes the various marketing people and functions necessary to implement your marketing plan and explain why such a structure is appropriate. Show why the team can meet the tests called for in the seven domains framework (see Chapter 4), and identify any gaps in the team that need to be filled in order to effectively implement your planned strategy.

Prepare pro forma forecasts and budgets of sales, gross margin, and marketing expenses, including people and programs.

Discussion Questions

1. Suppose you have been offered the job of developing and managing a new medical products unit for a major electronics manufacturer. The purpose of the new SBU will be to adapt technology from other parts of the company for medical applications (diagnostic equipment such as CAT scanners, surgical lasers, etc.) and to identify and build markets for the new products the unit develops. The new unit's performance over the next several years will be judged primarily on its success at developing a variety of new products and its rate of growth in sales volume and market share. Before accepting the job, what assurances would you seek from the company's CEO concerning the administrative relationships to be established between the new SBU and corporate headquarters? Why?

2. Now that you have accepted the job described in question 1, you have been given a $50 million operating budget for the first year. Your first task is to staff the new unit and to allocate your budget across its various functional departments. Although you obviously want to hire good people for every position, which departments require the most competent and experienced personnel, and which departments should receive relatively large shares of the available budget? Why?

3. As general manager, what type of organizational design would you select for the new SBU described in question 1? Justify your choice in terms of its ability to help the SBU implement its strategy and accomplish its primary objectives. What potential disadvantages—if any—might be associated with your chosen organizational structure?

Self-diagnostic questions to test your ability to apply the analytical tools and concepts in this chapter to marketing decision making may be found at this book's website at **www.mhhe.com/walker8e.**

Endnotes

1. This opening case is based on material found in "Electrolux: Brand Challenge," *The Economist*, April 4,2002, archived at www.economist.com; Ola Kinnander and Kim McLaughlin, "Electrolux Wants to Rule the Appliance World," *Bloomberg Businessweek*, March 28, 2011. pp. 33–34; and the *Electrolux Group's 2011 Annual Report* and supporting documents found at the company's website www.electrolux.com.

2. Eric M. Olson, Stanley F. Slater, and G. Thomas M. Hult, "The Performance Implications of Fit among Business Strategy, Marketing Organization Structure, and Strategic Behavior," *Journal of Marketing* 69 (July 2005), pp. 49–65. For more examples, also see George S. Day, *Aligning the Organization with the Market, Report #05-110* (Cambridge, MA: Marketing Science Institute, 2005).

3. Robert W. Ruekert and Orville C. Walker Jr., "The Sharing of Marketing Resources across Strategic Business Units: The Effect of Strategy on Performance," in *Review of Marketing 1990* (Chicago: American Marketing Association, 1990).

4. Vivek Wadhwa, "How To Fix Oversize Executive Compensation," www.businessweek.com, March 25, 2011.

5. Bernard J. Jaworski, "Toward a Theory of Marketing Control: Environmental Context, Control Types, and Consequences," *Journal of Marketing*, July 1988, pp. 23–39.

6. Subin Im and John P. Workman, Jr., "Market Orientation, Creativity, and New Product Performance in High-Technology Firms," *Journal of Marketing* 68 (April 2004), pp. 114–32.

7. Fred Vogelstein, "Mighty Amazon," *Fortune*, May 26, 2003, pp. 60–74. See also George S. Day, *Creating a Superior Customer-Relating Capability, Report #03-101* (Cambridge, MA: Marketing Science Institute, 2003).

8. For a more detailed discussion, see Jeffery F. Rayport and Bernard J. Jaworski, *Best Face Forward* (Boston: Harvard Business School Press, 2005); and Rita Di Mascio, "The Service Models of Frontline Employees," *Journal of Marketing* 74 (July 2010), pp. 66–80.

9. Daryl O. McKee, P. Rajan Varadarajan, and William M. Pride, "Strategic Adaptability and Firm Performance: A Market-Contingent Perspective," *Journal of Marketing*, July 1989, p. 19. For an interesting discussion of developments in the implementation of strategies for service organizations, see James L. Heskett, W. Earl Sasser Jr., and Christopher W. L. Hart, *Implementing Strategy: Service Breakthroughs: Changing the Rules of the Game* (Cambridge, MA: The Mac Group, n.d.).

10. For recent empirical evidence, see Douglas W. Vorhies and Neil A. Morgan, "A Configuration Theory Assessment of Marketing Organization Fit with Business Strategy and Its Relationship with Marketing Performance," *Journal of Marketing* 67 (January 2003), pp. 100–15; and Stanley F. Slater, Eric M. Olson, and Tomas M. Hult, "Worried About Strategy Implementation? Don't Overlook Marketing's Role," *Business Horizons* 53 (2010), pp. 469–79.

11. Michael J. Zenor, "The Profit Benefits of Category Management," *Journal of Marketing Research*, May 1994, p. 202.

12. Allen D. Shocker, Rajendra K. Srivastava, and Robert W. Ruekert, "Challenges and Opportunities Facing Brand Management," *Journal of Marketing Research*, May 1994, p. 149. Also see Donald R. Lehmann and Russell S. Winer, *Product Management* (Burr Ridge, IL: Richard D. Irwin, 1994), chap. 16; Jan-Benedict E. M. Steenkamp, Harald J. Van Heerde, and Inge Geyskens, "What Makes Consumers Willing to Pay a Price Premium for National Brands Over Private Labels?" *Journal of Marketing Research* 47 (December 2010) pp. 1011–24.

13. For a discussion of firms as learning organizations and hence better able to cope with change, see "The Knowledge Firm," *The Economist*, November 11, 1995, p. 63; Stanley F. Slater and John C. Narver, "Market Orientation and the Learning Organization," *Journal of Marketing*, July 1995, p. 63; and Michael Arndt and Bruce Einhorn, "The 50 Most Innovative Companies," www.businessweek.com, April 14, 2010.

14. Some analysts believe this may lead to a strategic advantage. See David A. Garvin, "Leveraging Processes for Strategic Advantage," *Harvard Business Review*, September–October 1995, p. 77.

15. Rahul Jacob, "The Struggle to Create an Organization for the 21st Century," *Fortune*, April 3, 1995, p. 90; Thomas A. Stewart, "Planning a Career in a World without Managers," *Fortune*,

March 20, 1995, p. 72; John A. Byrne, "Management by web," *BusinessWeek,* August 21, 2000, pp. 84–96; and Frederick E. Webster, "Marketing Management in Changing Times," *Marketing Management* 11 (January–February 2002), pp. 18–23.

16. Brian Dumaine, "The Trouble with Teams," *Fortune,* September 5, 1994, p. 86

17. Samuel E. Blucker, "The Virtual Organization," *The Futurist,* March–April 1994, p. 9; and Peter Coy, "The Creative Economy," *BusinessWeek,* August 21, 2000, pp. 76–82.

18. Steve Hamm, "Speed Demons," *BusinessWeek,* March 27, 2006, p. 74.

19. Rosabeth Moss Kanter, "Collaborative Advantage: The Art of Alliance," *Harvard Business Review,* July–August 1994, p. 97; Ravi S. Achrol and Phillip Kotler, "Marketing in the Network Economy," *Journal of Marketing* 63 (Special Issue 1999), pp. 146–63; and Corine S. Noordhoff, Kyriakos Kyriakopoulos, Christine Moorman, Pieter Pauwels, and Benedict G. C. Dellaert, "The Bright and Dark Side of Embedded Ties in Business-to-Business Innovation," *Journal of Marketing* 75 (September 2011), pp. 34–52.

20. Kanter, "Collaborative Advantage," p. 97.

21. The discussion that follows draws heavily from Michael R. Czinkota, Pietra Rivali, and Idkka A. Ronkausen, *International Business* (New York: Dryden Press, 1992), pp. 536–45.

22. "The Discreet Charm of the Multicultural Multinational," *The Economist,* July 30, 1994, p. 57.

23. Christopher A. Bartlett and Sumantra Ghoshal, *Transnational Management* (Burr Ridge, IL: Richard D. Irwin, 1992), p. 520.

24. Dexter Roberts, "Scrambling to Bring Crest to the Masses," *BusinessWeek,* June 25, 2007, pp. 72–73. Also see Lauren Coleman-Lochner, "Procter & Gamble Needs to Shave More Indians," *Bloomberg Businessweek* June 19, 2011, pp. 21–22; and "Fighting for the Next Billion Shoppers," *The Economist.* June 30, 2012, pp. 65–67.

25. Czinkota et al., *International Business,* p. 545.

26. For a more in-depth discussion of the contents and ways of organizing marketing plans, see Marian Burk Wood, *The Marketing Plan: A Handbook* (Upper Saddle River, NJ: Prentice Hall, 2003).

27. Donald R. Lehmann and Russell S. Winer, *Product Management* (Burr Ridge, IL: Richard D. Irwin, 1994), pp. 28–29.

28. Although this example is based on the material contained in an actual marketing plan for a Pillsbury product, the name of the brand and some of the specific numbers included in this example have been disguised in order to protect proprietary information.

29. Robin Cooper and Robert S. Kaplan, "Measure Costs Right: Make the Right Decisions," *Harvard Business Review,* September–October 1988, pp. 96–103; and Paul W. Farris, Neil T. Bendle, Phillip E. Pfeifer, and David J. Reibstein, *Marketing Metrics,* 2nd ed. (Upper Saddle River, NJ: Pearson Education, 2010), chaps. 3, 10.

Chapter **Thirteen**

Measuring and Delivering Marketing Performance

Metrics Pay for Walmart[1]

Walmart, the discount general merchandise and grocery retailer, generated sales of $444 billion and after-tax income of $15.8 billion in fiscal 2011–2012. It is America's largest, most profitable, and, in some circles but not others, one of its most admired companies.

As of January 2012, the company operated over 10,000 stores, of which more than 9,000 were in 26 countries outside the United States (in the Americas, Europe, and Asia). In the United States, Walmart operates stores in several different formats apart from its original stores—some are supercenters (a combination supermarket and general merchandise store), some are Sam's Clubs (a members-only warehouse store, selling high volumes, but at very low individual profit margins), and some are a smaller format, Neighborhood Markets, with a focus on groceries, in carefully chosen urban locations. Walmart stores serve more than 200 million customers per week, and the company employs more than 2 million people.

A major reason for Walmart's success is its ability to control costs. In 2011–2012, it was able to hold its operating, selling, and general administrative costs to 19.2 percent of sales. Year in, year out, Walmart holds these costs below those of its closest competitors in the United States, Kmart and Target, and this explains, in part, the company's excellent profitability record.

In the 1960s when he had only 10 stores, Walmart founder Sam Walton realized he couldn't expand successfully unless he could capture the information needed to control his operations. He became, according to one competitor, the best utilizer of management information in the industry. By the late 1970s, Walmart was using a company-wide computer-driven information system that linked stores, distribution centers, and suppliers. Kmart started using a similar system only in the early 1990s.

Today, the company can convert information into action almost immediately. As Walmart's U.S. chief marketing officer Stephen Quinn notes, Walmart's data advantage is central to its success. "The insights-driving machine at the core of retail is the ability to look at our data and bring some kind of meaning to that." Putting its world-class data system in place required a massive investment (over $700 million) in computer and satellite systems, which collectively generate the largest civilian database of its kind in the world. In addition to automated replenishment, the system provides up-to-the-minute sales of any item by region, district, and store. By looking at the computer screens in the satellite room, a manager can see systemwide data on the day's sales as they happen, the number of stolen bank cards retrieved that day, whether the seven-second credit card approval system is working properly, the number of customer transactions completed that day, and more.

Changing Metrics for a Changing Strategy

The combination of its nearly fanatical focus on keeping costs low and the availability of sophisticated and timely management information, which has enabled Walmart management at all levels to respond quickly to new opportunities as well as to performance problems, has served Walmart well. But in recent years, Walmart has struggled.

As the purchasing power of Walmart's mostly low-income core U.S. customers has been squeezed by a combination of low hourly wages and rising housing and energy costs, the company has sought to trade up in an effort to attract more selective middle-income shoppers. For these customers, quality, style, and store ambience are as important as—maybe more important than—price. New kinds of management tools and new metrics for the new merchandise mix may be in order.

But trading up has not been smooth sailing for Walmart, especially in a recession. Same-store sales in the U.S. fell for nine consecutive quarters before turning upwards in late 2010. And its stock price languished, up a meagre 5.8 percent over a decade, compared to 53 percent for arch-rival Target and 83 percent for Costco.

Can Walmart's Overseas Stores Plug the Gap?

Fortunately for Walmart, its expansion into international markets—which now deliver nearly one-quarter of the company's sales—has begun to pay dividends. In spite of the global economic downturn, Walmart's Brazilian business has delivered nearly double-digit sales increases, outpacing the overall 6 percent growth in Brazilian retailing overall. And Walmart's Todo Dia convenience store concept in Brazil has been translated in China as Smart Choice, where Walmart now has more than 250 stores, across this and other formats. As further evidence of Walmart's commitment to fast-growing emerging markets, a joint venture in India with the Bharti group is underway.

Will Walmart bounce back and return to its former glory? CEO Michael T. Duke, who took the leadership reins in 2009 after 15 years with the company, is bullish about Walmart's future. "We live at a time and in a world that I believe truly calls out for Walmart and the work that our 2 million associates do every day. We strongly believe that Walmart is the best-positioned global retailer and that we can continue to build on our momentum." Time will tell.

STRATEGIC CHALLENGES ADDRESSED IN CHAPTER 13

In Chapter 12, we said that planning is important and that effective implementation is crucial. The Walmart example demonstrates how effective planning and implementation can, over good times and bad, play out in the performance of a company. Together, these two activities constitute the heart of most business endeavors. In the end, however, it is neither planning nor implementation that really counts. What really counts? Results. Results are what managers and entrepreneurs are paid to deliver. Results are what attract investment capital to permit a company—whether a large public company such as Walmart or an emerging start-up—to grow. Just watch what happens to a public company's stock price when the results are not what Wall Street expects. The share price plummets and, sometimes, heads roll. Weak sales and profit performance at Nokia cut Nokia's stock price by 90 percent from 2007 to 2012 and led to a series of middle- and upper-management changes at the once high-flying cell phone maker.[2] The focus on results is not restricted to for-profit organizations either. Exhibit 13.1 shows how one nonprofit organization is adapting customer analytics to its own environment.

In Chapter 13, we address several critical questions that provide the link between a company's efforts to plan and implement marketing strategies and the actual results that those strategies produce. How can we design **strategic monitoring systems** to make sure

Strategic Issue

Results are what managers and entrepreneurs are paid to deliver. Results are what attract investment capital to permit a company to grow.

EXHIBIT 13.1   *Customer Analytics at the Red Cross*

When major disasters strike, generous donors respond in droves with gifts to the Red Cross and other nonprofit organizations. While such generosity in times of need is a very good thing, a key challenge for the Red Cross is retaining such donors after the disaster. Only 10 percent of those who give following a major disaster become repeat donors, according to Tony DiPasquale of the Red Cross, despite the fact that much of what the Red Cross does, such as responding to some 60,000 house fires annually in the United States, requires stable funding year after year.

To address this challenge, the Red Cross has teamed up with a consortium of researchers including the Wharton Customer Analytics Initiative to find ways to encourage one-time donors to remain on board. In its embrace of customer analytics, the Red Cross is following what has become clear to leading-edge companies in the for-profit world: leveraging data adds some rigor to the creativity of marketing. According to research firm Gartner, the market for business intelligence, analytics, and performance management software was more than $10 billion in 2010.

But there are psychological and other barriers to overcome in making use of such techniques, says Wharton marketing professor Peter Fader. "People are afraid to trust data too much. They often trust their gut more." Adds Gartner research director Gareth Herschel, "There is a lot of organizational inertia to be overcome."

Source: Knowledge@Wharton, "Customer Analytics: A New Lifeline for the Red Cross and Other Nonprofits?", February 1, 2012, at *http://knowledge.wharton.upenn.edu/article.cfm?articleid=2937.* For more on the Red Cross, see *www.redcross.org.*

our strategies remain in sync with the changing market and competitive environment in which we operate, such as the smartphone onslaught that has decimated Nokia? How can we design systems of **marketing metrics** to ensure that the marketing results we plan for are the results we deliver? In other words, if the ship gets off course during the journey, either strategically or in terms of execution of the marketing strategy, how can we make sure that we know quickly of the deviation so that midcourse corrections can be made in a timely manner? In today's rapidly changing markets, even the best-laid plans are likely to require changes as their implementation unfolds.

We begin by developing a five-step process for monitoring and evaluating marketing performance on a continuous basis. We then apply the process to the issue of **strategic control:** How can we monitor and evaluate our overall marketing strategy to ensure that it remains viable in the face of changing market and competitive realities? Next, we apply the process to tracking the performance of a particular product-market entry and to the marketing actions taken to implement its marketing plan, or **marketing performance measurement.** Are we meeting sales and margin targets in the aggregate and for various products and market segments? Is each element of the marketing mix doing its job? Which items in the product line are selling best, are the ads producing enough sales leads, is the salesforce generating enough new accounts, are our Internet marketing efforts working, and so on? Finally, we show how **marketing audits** can be used periodically to link the overall performance measurement process—that for both strategic control and for measuring current marketing performance—with marketing planning.

DESIGNING MARKETING METRICS STEP BY STEP

As the Walmart example and a recent empirical study demonstrate, a well-functioning performance measurement system is critical to the success of a business.[3] To be successful, it should be well integrated with the other steps in the marketing management process—setting objectives, formulating strategies, and implementing a plan of action. The performance measurement system monitors the extent to which the firm is achieving its objectives. When it is not, the firm determines whether the reason lies in the environment, the strategies employed, the action plans, the way the plans are being implemented, or

EXHIBIT 13.2   **The Performance Measurement Process**

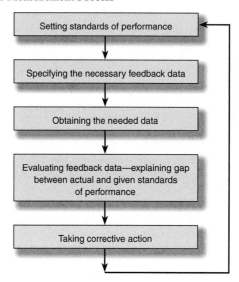

some combination thereof. Thus, reappraisal is diagnostic, serving to start the marketing management process anew.

Performance measurement processes differ at each organizational level. Thus, in a large diversified company, corporate management is concerned with how well its various SBUs are performing relative to the opportunities and threats each faces and the resources given them, a strategic issue. At the SBU level, or in smaller companies, concern is primarily with the unit's own strategy, especially as it pertains to its individual product-market entries. We will concentrate mainly on this latter organizational level since it constitutes the bulk of any performance measurement system.

Regardless of the organizational level involved, the performance measurement process is essentially the same. It consists of five steps: setting performance standards, specifying feedback, obtaining data, evaluating it, and taking corrective action (see Exhibit 13.2). Although the staff organization is typically responsible for reporting the performance data, the line organization administers the process. Certainly, this is the case with Walmart, as seen in the involvement of regional vice presidents, district managers, store managers, and department heads in obtaining and processing performance data as well as taking corrective action. More importantly, line managers need to be closely involved with the development of the performance measurement system, so that they can be assured of getting the performance data they need, on a timely basis and in a format they can easily use to support their long-term and day-to-day decision making.

Setting Standards of Performance

Performance standards derive largely from the objectives and strategies set forth at the SBU and individual product-market entry level. They generate a series of performance expectations for profitability (return on equity, return on assets managed, gross margins, or operating margins), market share, and sales. At the product-market level, standards of performance also include sales and market-share determinants such as percent effective distribution, relative shelf-facings, awareness, consumers' attitude change toward a given product attribute, customer satisfaction, and the extent of price parity.

Similarly, for every line item in a marketing budget—product development costs, advertising and promotional expenses, costs for salespeople, and so on—specific and measurable

Strategic Issue

For every line item in a marketing budget—product development costs, advertising and promotional expenses, costs for salespeople, and so on—specific and measurable standards of performance must be set.

standards of performance must be set so that each of these elements of marketing performance can be evaluated. We address the development of these standards later in this chapter. Without an appropriate set of performance standards, managers cannot know what results are being obtained, the extent to which they are satisfactory, or why they are or are not satisfactory.

Recent years have witnessed a shift from primarily using financially based performance measures to treating them as simply part of a broader array of marketing metrics. The now widely used balanced scorecard is one such approach (see Exhibit 13.3).[4] While the use of nonfinancial measures is not new, giving them greater emphasis is. Thus, more and more companies are turning to metrics they feel better reflect how their managers and customers think about issues that drive the firm's success, such as customer satisfaction, product quality, market share, and new product development. For Walmart store managers, no longer is profit the only thing that matters at bonus time. Scores on customer surveys now matter. To make managers more accessible to customers, their offices are now located at the front of the store.[5]

To be of any value, performance standards must be measurable; further, they must be tied to specific time periods, particularly when they concern a management compensation system. The SMART acronym (specific, measurable, attainable, relevant, and timebound) is a useful framework for setting performance standards. In recent years, the trend has been for performance measurement systems to operate over shorter periods (weekly and even daily) and for performance data to be more readily available. Walmart's inventory control system, for example, provides instantaneous up-to-date data. Strategic control tends to operate over longer periods.

Of particular importance is whether a business or business unit as a whole and its individual product-market entries have set forth milestone achievement measures based on the strategies that were originally developed. For example, in a venture capital backed start-up, a short-term **dashboard** will be set up to track such metrics as the cost of acquiring a customer, sales and gross margin by product or product line, and repeat purchase rates. Given the rampant uncertainty entailed in most early-stage ventures, disciplined attention to such metrics will assist the entrepreneurial team in determining whether the original plan is on track or whether midcourse pivots are called for.[6]

EXHIBIT 13.3 *Working ON the Business, Not IN the Business, with a Balanced Scorecard*

Karen Ponce, who runs Shat-R-Shield, a leading maker of plastic-coated shatter-resistant lamps for the food processing industry and others, was struggling. In 2005, her company had begun to put into place a series of key performance indicators (KPIs) to measure operational performance. But she wanted her company to grow faster, and the company's more than 20 different objectives seemed to be too many to manage. "We were successful because for the first time we were measuring things that were really important across the entire company. But it was way too much," Ponce recalls.

With the help of some training from the Balanced Scorecard Institute, she decided to start over on her KPIs, and build a measurement system that wasn't just operational. It would be based on a *strategic* balanced scorecard. The number of objectives was refined to eight.

Integrated teams were assembled to manage the transition and to cascade the scorecard throughout her company. "Implementing a cascaded and aligned balanced scorecard strategic planning and management system is time well spent working ON the business, because it gives clear direction and guidance to those I entrust and empower to work IN the business," says Ponce.

Her new system's results have spoken for themselves. After implementing the new balanced scorecard in 2010, her company delivered its best net income in its more than 30 years in business.

Source: Balanced Scorecard Institute, "A Balanced Scorecard Journey," at *www.balancedscorecard.org/LinkClick.aspx?fileticket=Qd7wk08IcWE%3d&tabid=57*. For more on Shat-R-Shield, see *www.shatrshield.com*.

In recent years, major multinationals such as Tata, DuPont, Roche, IBM, and others have used another performance measure—benchmarking. What this means is that the firm's performance in a given area is compared against the performance of other companies. Thus, Walmart regularly compares itself with its competitors on merchandise assortments, service quality, and out of stocks. The comparison does not have to be with companies in the same industry. For example, many years ago Xerox benchmarked its order filling/shipping performance against L. L. Bean (a mail-order retailer catering to the outdoor set), which has a well-deserved reputation for fulfilling orders both quickly and accurately.[7] Small companies also use benchmarking to find out how they can better serve their customers and thereby increase sales.

Return on Marketing Investment

Increasingly these days, investors, boards, CFOs, and others are insisting that marketing managers do a better job of measuring the returns their marketing programs deliver on the investment therein. Doing so is important for a variety of reasons, including demonstrating the overall and program-by-program effectiveness of marketing expenditures, choosing among various marketing tactics or media, and obtaining the financial resources necessary to support top-line sales growth. There is also evidence that marketing can strengthen a company's competitive position and enhance its long-term viability.[8]

Fortunately, as we saw in Chapter 11, the growing use of online promotional strategies, most of which are eminently measurable, is making this task more doable than it used to be. But for many kinds of marketing spending, including many brand-building efforts, it can be difficult to make clear connections between an advertising campaign, for example, and the short-term and long-term impact it has on revenue and brand equity, because a host of other variables—from the weather to competitor actions and more—can also play significant roles. In short, ensuring the accountability of marketing managers and their spending is a good idea. But turning that good idea into practice and doing so without incurring adverse consequences is a lot harder than it looks, as shown in Exhibit 13.4.

Profitability Analysis

In brief, **profitability analysis** requires that analysts determine the costs associated with specific marketing activities to find out the profitability of different market segments, products, customer accounts, and distribution channels. Walmart does this at the department and individual store levels as well as for individual lines of goods within a department. More and more managers are attempting to obtain profitability measures for individual products by market segments.

EXHIBIT 13.4   *Does ROI Add Up?*

These days, there's lots of interest in measuring ROI as a means of holding marketing accountable for its performance. A good idea, right? Not so fast, argues Tim Ambler, author of *Marketing and the Bottom Line*. Ambler agrees that accountability is essential. But "this focus on ROI is misguided for five reasons," he says. "First, very few can calculate ROI with any accuracy. Second, ROI ignores the longer term. Third, it is inconsistent with corporate financial goals. Fourth, marketers do not really mean 'ROI' anyway. Fifth, zealous application of ROI will bankrupt the business."

Like the old tale about improving a donkey's ROI by cutting its food rations and increasing its loads until what results is a dead donkey, Ambler argues that much of the talk about ROI for marketing is fashion rather than substance. Nonetheless, he argues that it does constitute a step "toward increasing accountability and the understanding of marketing by top management."

Sources: Tim Ambler, "Why ROI Doesn't Add Up," *Financial Times*, FT Creative Business, October 14, 2003, p. 15; and Tim Ambler, *Marketing and the Bottom Line: The Marketing Metrics to Pump Up Cash Flow*, 2nd ed. (Upper Saddle River, NJ: Prentice Hall, 2003).

EXHIBIT 13.5   *Good Profits or Bad Profits?*

Some retail banks have found a lucrative source of earnings—nuisance fees, as customers call them. Charges for bouncing a check are a whopping $25 or $30 at many banks. As if that were not bad enough, some banks process the largest checks first each day, potentially hitting customers with bad check fees for the greater number of small checks that follow and may bounce. Is this any way to earn long-term customer loyalty?

But it's not just banks that engage in customer-abusive behavior such as this. Cell phone operators offer such a confusing array of rate plans that it's nearly impossible for customers to know which plan is best for their pattern of calls. Putting customers on the plan that's best for them would cut profits by as much as 40 percent, according to one operator.

A book by Fred Reichheld, *The Ultimate Question: Driving Good Profits and True Growth*, argues that

accounting systems and incentive plans often fail to distinguish between profits that result from customer-abusive policies and those that arise from activities that enhance customer loyalty. Thus, as we'll see in this chapter, in some companies measures of customer satisfaction are taking their place alongside measures of profitability. Reichheld and his co-author James Allen argue that there's an undeclared war on customers raging in many companies, a war that companies cannot afford and cannot win. Thinking differently about performance metrics may offer an olive branch to end the fighting.

Sources: Fred Reichheld and James Allen, "How Companies Can End the Cycle of Customer Abuse," *Financial Times*, March 23, 2006, p. 43; and Fred Reichheld, *The Ultimate Question: Driving Good Profits and True Growth* (Cambridge, MA: Harvard Business School Press, 2006).

Strategic Issue

Profitability is probably the single most important measure of performance, but it has limitations.

Profitability (or cash flow) is probably the single most important measure of performance, but it has limitations. These are that (1) many objectives can best be measured in nonfinancial terms (e.g., customer satisfaction); (2) profit is a short-term measure and can be manipulated by taking actions that may prove dysfunctional in the longer term (reducing R&D expenses); and (3) profits can be affected by factors over which management has no control (the weather). Sometimes, a managerial obsession with profitability can prove counterproductive, leading to decisions that sap customer loyalty and can, over the long term, erode profits rather than enhance them. For one view of how obsession with profit targets leads to customer abuse, see Exhibit 13.5.

Analysts can use direct or full costing in determining the profitability of a product or market segment. In **full costing,** analysts assign both direct, or variable, and indirect costs to the unit of analysis. **Indirect costs** involve certain fixed joint costs that cannot be linked directly to a single unit of analysis. For example, the costs of occupancy, general management, and the management of the salesforce are all indirect costs for a multiproduct company. Those who use full costing argue that only by allocating all costs to a product or a market can they obtain an accurate picture of its value.

Direct costing involves the use of **contribution accounting.** Those favoring the direct costing approach argue there is really no accurate way to assign indirect costs. Further, because indirect costs are mostly fixed, a product or market may make a contribution to profits even if it shows a loss. Thus, even though the company must eventually absorb its overhead costs, the contribution method clearly indicates what is gained by adding or dropping a product or a customer. Exhibit 13.6 shows an example of full and direct costing. The difference in the results obtained is substantial—$370,000 using full costing versus $650,000 with the contribution method.

Contribution analysis is helpful in determining the yield derived from the application of additional resources (for instance, to certain sales territories). Using the data in Exhibit 13.7 we can answer the question: "How much additional profit would result from a marginal increase in sales of $300,000—assuming the gross margin remains at 29.62 percent and the only cost is $35,000 more in sales commissions and expenses?" As Exhibit 13.7 shows, the answer is a profit increase before taxes of $53,000.

EXHIBIT 13.6 **Finding Product or Market Profitability with Full Costing and Marginal Contribution Methods ($000)**

	Full Costing	Marginal Contribution
Net sales	$5,400	$5,400
Less: Cost of goods sold—includes direct costs (labor, material, and production overhead)*	3,800	3,800
Gross margin	$1,600	$1,600
Expenses		
Salesforce—includes direct costs (commissions) plus indirect costs (sales expenses, sales management overhead)†	510	450
Advertising—includes direct costs (media, production) plus indirect costs (management overhead)	215	185
Physical logistics—includes direct costs (transportation) plus indirect costs (order processing, warehousing costs)	225	190
Occupancy—includes direct costs (telephone) plus indirect costs (heat/air, insurance, taxes, building maintenance)	100	25
Management overhead—includes direct costs (product/brand manager and staff) plus indirect costs (salaries, expenses, occupancy costs of SBU's general management group)	180	100
Totals	$1,230	$ 950
Profit before taxes	$ 370	
Contribution to fixed costs and profits		$ 650

*Production facilities dedicated to a single product.
†Multiproduct salesforce.

EXHIBIT 13.7 **Effect of $300,000 Increase in Sales Resulting from Increased Sales Commissions and Expenses of $35,000 (same data as in Exhibit 13.6) ($000)**

Net sales	$5,700
Less: direct costs (70.38%)	4,012
	$1,688
Expenses	
Sales commissions and expenses	485
Advertising	185
Physical logistics	190
Occupancy	25
Management	100
	$ 985
Contribution to overhead and profits	$ 703
Increase in profit (before tax) = $703 − $650 =	$ 53

Companies are increasingly turning from traditional accounting methods, which identify costs according to various expense categories, to **activity-based costing** (ABC), which bases costs on the different tasks involved in performing a given activity. ABC advocates have used it to improve product costing, thereby improving pricing parameters, providing better service, trimming waste, and evaluating quality initiatives.[9]

Customer Satisfaction

So far, we have been discussing performance measures in essentially financial terms. But financial terms are insufficient since they fail to recognize the importance of customer satisfaction, which is an important driving force of the firm's future market share and profitability. As products and services become more alike in an already highly competitive marketplace, the ability to satisfy the customer across a variety of activities (of which the product is only one) will become an even greater success determinant. Thus, measures relating to customer preferences and satisfaction are essential as an early warning of impending problems and opportunities.

Developing meaningful measures of customer satisfaction can be done in various ways. One way involves understanding and measuring the criteria used by customers to evaluate the quality of the firm's relationship with them. Knowing the product/service attributes that constitute the customer's choice criteria as well as the relative importance of each should facilitate this task. Once these attributes are identified, they serve as the basis for developing expectation measures. Then, measures are taken of how well the firm is meeting the customer's expectations on an individual attribute as well as an overall basis.

Strategic Issue

Developing meaningful measures of customer satisfaction can be done in various ways.

For example, if the choice criteria of a cruise line's target market included such attributes as food, exercise facilities, and entertainment, then a performance measure would be developed for each. By weighting these by the relative importance of each, an overall performance measure can be obtained. These two measures collectively serve as the basis for evaluating the company's performance on customer satisfaction.

Another approach favored by some companies is far simpler. General Electric, Enterprise Car Rental, and others ask customers one simple question: How likely is it that you would recommend us to a friend or a colleague? Such a simple approach has some significant benefits. It gets high response rates—as much as 70 percent in some cases—and can be conducted often enough and inexpensively enough to give timely and granular information by product, by car rental branch, or whatever. GE adds the percentages of customers who are happiest (scores of 9 or 10 out of 10) and subtracts the percentage who are clearly unhappy (those scoring 6 or lower). The net score provides a clear and compelling—and actionable—indicator of customer satisfaction. At Enterprise, employees working at branches scoring below the company mean are ineligible for promotion. Not surprisingly, employees seeking to boost their branches' scores have developed many customer-friendly innovations at Enterprise.[10]

Face-to-face approaches to assessing customer satisfaction are also used, adding depth to the more cursory quantitative approaches. In recent years, more top-level executives are visiting their major accounts (whether they be end-use customers or intermediaries) to learn firsthand how to better serve them. Such visits frequently result in joint projects designed to reduce the costs incurred by both parties in the sale of a given set of products.

Finally, some companies are using the growing availability of customer relationship management (CRM) data to measure the lifetime value of customers. Doing so enables them to more effectively allocate marketing resources.[11]

Specifying and Obtaining Feedback Data

Once a company has established its performance standards, its next step is to develop a system that provides usable and timely feedback data on actual performance. In most cases, someone must gather and process considerable data to obtain the performance measures, especially at the product-market level. Analysts obtain feedback data from a variety of sources, including company accounting records and syndicated marketing information services such as Nielsen.

The sales invoice or other transaction records, such as those produced by retailers' point-of-sale systems, are often the basic internal source of data because they provide a

EXHIBIT 13.8 *It's Not about the Bananas*

Tesco, the largest supermarket chain in the United Kingdom, has pioneered the use of loyalty card information to better manage its pricing, product assortment, and store location decisions, along with a host of other crucial management issues. Tesco wanted to beat Asda's image for having the lowest prices. The question was how. The obvious first step was to cut the price of bananas, since nearly everyone buys bananas. But Tesco's targeted marketing director, Laura Wade-Gery, wouldn't buy it. Instead, she used Tesco's loyalty card data to carefully examine the segment of Tesco customers that was its most price-sensitive, as revealed by their shopping habits recorded on their Tesco ClubCard accounts.

She found cutting the price of a bunch of bananas is emphatically not the place to start because you are giving a discount to everyone, including lots of people who are not really looking for low prices. The solution?

Tesco Value Brand Margarine, along with a carefully targeted group of similar products bought largely by price-conscious shoppers. By cutting prices on these items, Tesco was able to buy a low-price image with the customers to whom such an image mattered most, for a lower net cost overall. Its ability to use customer data insightfully has been a powerful source of competitive advantage. According to Edwina Dunn, whose company Dunnhumby works with Tesco on its ClubCard program, "They obviously have to get the basics of grocery retailing right, and we are only part of the equation. But if you asked them how it would affect them, they'd say it is fundamental to their business."

Sources: Clive Humby, Terry Hunt, with Tim Phillips, *Scoring Points: How Tesco Is Winning Customer Loyalty* (London: Kogan Page, 2003), pp. 146–47; and "Marketing—Clubbing Together," *Retail Week*, November 8, 2002. For more on Tesco or Dunnhumby, see *www.tesco.com* or *www.dunnhumby.com*.

detailed record of each transaction. Invoices are the basis for measuring profitability, sales, and various budget items. They also provide data for the analysis of the geographic distribution of sales and customer accounts by type and size. Exhibit 13.8 gives an example of how Tesco, the British supermarket chain, uses customer purchasing data to strengthen its low-price image.

For many companies, tracking referrals, and who makes them, is a key element in h and managing marketing performance. According to a recent study, tracking the number of referred customers (which tend to be more valuable), how long they stay, and how referrers are incentivized to make referrals are key.[12] Careful measurement of post-sale service can also pay dividends in enhanced performance.[13]

Tesco's ClubCard data has informed numerous strategic decisions, including the company's move into smaller store formats, the launch of its Internet shopping business, the development of its up-market Finest food assortment, and others. "ClubCard has brought about a step-change in the size of the company," says Tim Mason, who heads Tesco's nascent but so far underperforming, business in the United States. In Mason's view, ClubCard has been the driver of Tesco's recent success. Retail analyst Mike Tattersall of Cazenove agrees. "Contrary to popular belief, Tesco's most significant competitive advantage in the U.K. is not its scale," he says. "We believe that ClubCard, which conveys an array of material benefits across virtually every discipline in its business, is Tesco's most potent weapon in the ongoing battle for market share."[14]

Another source, and typically the most expensive and time-consuming, involves undertaking one or more marketing research projects to obtain needed information. In-house research projects are apt to take longer and be more expensive than using an outside syndicated service. But there may be no alternative, for example, in determining awareness and attitude changes and obtaining data on customer service.

Evaluating Feedback Data

Management evaluates feedback data to find out whether there is any deviation from the plan and, if so, why. Walmart does this in a variety of ways, including sending its regional vice presidents into the field on a regular basis to learn what's going on and why.

Typically, managers use a variety of information to determine what the company's performance *should* have been under the actual market conditions that existed when the plan was executed. In some cases, this information can be obtained in measured form; examples include a shift in personal disposable income (available from government sources), a change in the demand for a given product type (obtained when measuring market share), the impact of a new brand on market share (reported by a commercial source), or a change in price by a major competitor. Often, however, the explanation rests on inferences drawn from generalized data, as would be the case in attributing poor sales performance to an improvement in a competitor's salesforce.

At the line-item level, whether for revenue or expenses, results are compared with the standards set in step one of the control process. A merchandise manager or buyer at an apparel retailer such as H&M, for example, would track sales results of each style or merchandise category in terms of its selling rate (how many weeks' supply is on hand overall and in which stores) and its gross margin performance. For a district sales team of an industrial goods manufacturer, salespeople might be measured on the number of sales calls they make per week, the number of new accounts they generate, their sales volume in revenue and units, their travel expenses, and a variety of other metrics. A stylist in a beauty salon might be measured in terms of the number of haircuts or the sales revenue she produces per day or per hour.

Taking Corrective Action

The last step in the control process concerns prescribing the needed action to correct the situation. At Walmart, this is partly accomplished at its various congresses held every Friday and Saturday when managers decide what actions to take to solve selected problems. Success here depends on how well managers carry out the evaluation step. When linkages between inputs and outputs are clear, managers can presume a causal relationship and specify appropriate action. For example, assume that input consisted of an advertising schedule that specified the frequency of a given TV message. The objective was to change attitudes about a given product attribute (the output). If the attitude change did not occur, remedial action would start with an evaluation of the firm's advertising effort, particularly the advertising message and how frequently it ran.

But in many cases it is difficult to identify the cause of the problem. Almost always, an interactive effect exists among the input variables as well as the environment. There is also the problem of delayed responses and carryover effects. For example, advertisers can rarely separate the effects of the message, media, frequency of exposure, and competitive responses in an attempt to determine advertising effects. Even if the company could determine the cause of a problem, it faces the difficulty of prescribing the appropriate action to take. The result of these difficulties is that marketers continue to struggle with quantifying the value of marketing efforts and with creating a culture of accountability for marketing performance.[15]

DESIGN DECISIONS FOR STRATEGIC MONITORING SYSTEMS

Strategic Issue

Strategic monitoring must provide some way of changing the firm's thrust if new information about the environment and/or the firm's performance so dictates.

While it's difficult to argue that managers can actually "control" anything they are asked to monitor, strategic monitoring is concerned with evaluating a firm's SBU-level strategies (see Exhibit 13.9 for the kinds of questions this type of system is designed to answer). Such a system is difficult to implement because there is usually a substantial amount of time between strategy formulation and when a strategy takes hold and results are evident. Since both the external and internal environments are constantly evolving,

EXHIBIT 13.9 **Examples of Questions a Strategic Monitoring System Should Be Able to Answer**

1. What changes in the environment have negatively affected the current strategy (e.g., demographic or social trends, interest rates, government controls, or price changes in substitute products)?

2. What changes have major competitors made in their objectives and strategies?

3. What changes have occurred in the industry in such attributes as capacity, entry barriers, and substitute products?

4. What new opportunities or threats have derived from changes in the environment, competitors' strategies, or the nature of the industry?

5. What changes have occurred in the industry's key success factors?

6. To what extent is the firm's current strategy consistent with the preceding changes?

strategic monitoring must provide some way of changing the firm's thrust if new information about the environment and/or the firm's performance so dictates. Inevitably, much of this intermediate assessment is based on information about the marketplace and the results obtained from the firm's marketing plan.

Identifying Key Variables

To implement strategic monitoring, a company must identify the key variables to monitor, which are usually the major assumptions made in formulating the strategy. The key variables to monitor are of two types:

- Those concerned with external forces.
- Those concerned with the effects of certain actions taken by the firm to implement the strategy.

Examples of the former include changes in the external environment such as changes in long-term demand, the advent of new technology, a change in governmental legislation, and actions by a competitor. Examples of the latter types (actions by the firm) include the firm's advertising efforts to change attitudes, the performance of the firm's website and its social networking efforts, and, for retailers, in-store merchandising activities designed to improve product availability.

The frameworks and analytical tools for market and competitive analysis that we discussed in Chapter 4 are useful in determining what variables to monitor in a strategic monitoring system. Deciding exactly which variables to monitor is a company-specific decision; in general, it should focus on those variables most likely to affect the company's future position within its industry group.

Tracking and Monitoring

The next step is to specify what information or measures are needed on each of the key variables to determine whether the implementation of the strategic plan is on schedule—and if not, why not. The firm can use the plan as an early-warning system as well as a diagnostic tool. If, for example, the firm has made certain assumptions about the rate at which market demand will increase, it should monitor industry sales regularly. If it has made assumptions about advertising and its effect on attitudes, it would be likely to use measures of awareness, trial, and repeat buying. In any event, the firm must closely examine the relevance, accuracy, and cost of obtaining the needed measures.

The advent of the Internet, social networks, **graphical information systems,**[16] and other digital tools for gathering and disseminating information has made it easier for sometimes far-flung managers to monitor strategic developments. Critical strategic information can now be monitored on a real-time basis anywhere in the world.

Strategy Reassessment

This can take place at periodic intervals—for example, quarterly or annually, when the firm evaluates its performance to date along with major changes in the external environment. A strategic monitoring system can also alert management of a significant change in its external or internal environment. This involves setting triggers to signal the need to reassess the viability of the firm's strategy. It requires a specification of both the level at which an alert will be called and the combination of events that must occur before the firm reacts.

In today's fast-changing world, strategy reassessment may happen much more quickly, as competitive and technological developments cause firms to quickly change their entire strategies and business models. Such developments enabled Amazon to grow from an online bookseller into a veritable online global shopping mall, with a huge assortment of merchandise categories and a local presence in several countries across the globe.

DESIGN DECISIONS FOR MARKETING METRICS

Designing systems to measure marketing performance at the product-market and line-item levels involves answering four essential questions:

- Who needs what information?
- When and how often is the information needed?
- In what media and in what format(s) or levels of aggregation should the information be provided?
- What contingencies should be planned for?

In essence, designing a marketing performance measurement system is like designing the dashboard of a car. Such a system needs to include the most critical metrics to assess whether the car or the business is progressing toward its objectives. Thus, for a car, the dashboard includes a speed gauge and odometer to measure progress toward the destination, a fuel gauge, warning lights for engine and braking system malfunction, and so on, but it typically does not indicate how much windshield wiper fluid remains, how much weight the car is carrying, or other relatively nonessential indicators. The same holds true for a business: The "drivers" who are managing the business need to know certain essential information while the "car"—or strategy—is running, whereas other less crucial indicators can be omitted or provided only when requested. Designing such an informational **dashboard** for the top management team is a good place to start, since it provides a clear signal about the kinds of data to which the rest of the organization should attend. We now address the four key questions, or **design parameters,** of marketing performance measurement systems.[17]

Strategic Issue

In essence, designing a marketing performance measurement system is like designing the dashboard of a car.

Who Needs What Information?

Marketing performance measurement systems are designed to ensure that the company achieves the customer image, sales, profits, and other objectives set forth in its marketing and strategic plans. In the aggregate, these plans reflect the outcomes of the company's or the SBU's planning efforts, which have specified how resources are to be allocated across markets, products, and marketing-mix activities. These plans, as we noted in Chapter 12, include line-item budgets and typically specify the actions expected of each organizational unit—whether inside or outside the marketing function or department—and deemed necessary to attain the company's customer, financial, and competitive positioning objectives. The first and foremost objective for marketing is often the level of sales the company or the product-market entry achieves.

Who needs sales information? Top management needs it. Functional managers in other parts of the organization—manufacturing, procurement, finance, and so on—need it. Marketing managers responsible for the various marketing-mix activities, from product design to pricing to channel management to selling and other promotional activities, need it. Even the ad agency needs it.

Sales Analysis

A sales analysis involves breaking down aggregate sales data into such categories as products, end-user customers, channel intermediaries, sales territories, and order size. The objective of such an analysis is to find areas of strength and weakness; for example, products producing the greatest and least volume, customers accounting for the bulk of the revenues, and salespersons and territories performing the best and the worst.

Sales analysis recognizes that aggregate sales and cost data often mask the real situation. Sales analysis not only helps to evaluate and control marketing efforts, but also helps management to better formulate objectives and strategies and administer such nonmarketing activities as production planning, inventory management, and facilities planning.

An important decision in designing the firm's sales analysis system concerns which units of analysis to use. Most companies analyze data in the following groupings:

- Geographical areas—regions, counties, and sales territories.
- Product, package size, and grade.
- Customer—by type and size.
- Channel intermediary—such as type and/or size of retailer.
- Method of sale—mail, phone, channel, Internet, or direct.
- Size of order—less than $10, $10–100, and so on.

These breakdowns are not mutually exclusive. Most firms perform sales analyses hierarchically, for example, by county within a sales territory within a sales region. Further, they usually combine product and account breakdowns with a geographical one, for example, the purchase of product X by large accounts located in sales territory Y, which is part of region A. Only by conducting sales analysis on a hierarchical basis using a combination of breakdowns can analysts be at all sure that they have made every reasonable attempt to locate the opportunities and problems facing their firms.

Sales Analysis by Territory

The first step in a sales territory analysis is to decide which geographical control unit to use. In the United States, the county is the typical choice since it can be combined into larger units such as sales territories, and it is also a geographical area for which many kinds of data are available, such as population, employment, income, and retail sales. Analysts can compare actual sales (derived from company invoices) by county against a standard such as a sales quota that takes into account such factors as market potential and last year's sales adjusted for inflation. They can then single out territories that fall below standard for special attention. Is competition unusually strong? Has less selling effort been expended here? Is the salesforce weak? Studies dealing with such questions as these help a company improve its weak areas and exploit its stronger ones. Category and brand development indices, such as those described in Chapter 5, (see Exhibit 5.4) are often used in assessing sales performance by territory.

Exhibit 13.10 illustrates a sales territory analysis. It shows that only one territory out of seven shown exceeded its 2012 quota, or standard of performance, and by just $18,112. The other six territories accounted for a total of $394,685 under quota. Territory 3 alone accounted for 55 percent of the total shortfall. The sales and the size of the quota in this territory suggest the need for further breakdowns, especially by accounts and products. Such breakdowns may reveal that the firm needs to allocate more selling resources to this territory. The company needs to improve its sales primarily in territories 3 and 5. If it can reach its potential in these two territories, overall sales would increase by $301,911, assuming that the quotas set are valid.

Without a standard against which to compare results, the conclusions would be much different. Thus, if only company sales were considered (column 1), White would be the best salesperson and Finch the worst. By using sales quotas as a performance standard, White was not the best but the worst salesperson, with a 77 percent rating.

Sales Analysis by Product

Over time, a company's product line tends to become overcrowded and less profitable unless management takes strong and continuous action to eliminate no-longer-profitable items. By eliminating weak products and concentrating on strong ones, a company can sometimes increase its profits substantially. An important element in Procter & Gamble's strong performance under former CEO A. G. Lafley was the company's renewed emphasis on its 17 billion-dollar brands.[18] Before deciding which products to abandon, management must study such variables as market-share trends, contribution margins, scale effects, and the extent to which a product is complementary with other items in the line.[19]

 A product sales analysis is particularly helpful when combined with account size and sales territory data. Using such an analysis, managers can often pinpoint substantial opportunities and develop specific tactics to take advantage of them. For example, one firm's analysis revealed that sales of one of its highest-margin products were down in all the Scandinavian sales territories. Further investigation showed that a regional producer was aggressively promoting a recently modified product with reduced prices. An analysis of the competing product revealed questionable reliability under certain operating conditions. The salesforce used this information to turn around the sales problem.

Sales Analysis by Order Size

Sales analysis by order size may identify which orders, in monetary size, are not profitable. For example, if some customers frequently place small orders that require salesforce

EXHIBIT 13.10 **Sales Analysis Based on Selected Sales Territories**

Sales Territory	Salesperson	(1) Company Sales 2012	(2) Sales Quota 2012	(3) Overage, Underage	(4) Percent of Potential Performance
1	Barlow	$552,630	$585,206	−$32,576	94%
2	Burrows	470,912	452,800	+18,112	104
3	White	763,215	981,441	−218,226	77
4	Finch	287,184	297,000	−9,816	96
5	Brown	380,747	464,432	−83,685	82
6	Roberts	494,120	531,311	−37,191	93
7	Macini	316,592	329,783	−13,191	96

attention and need to be processed, picked, and shipped, a problem of some importance may exist.

Analysis by order size locates products, sales territories, and customer types and sizes where small orders prevail. Such an analysis may lead to setting a minimum order size, charging extra for small orders, training sales reps to develop larger orders, and dropping some accounts. An example of such an analysis involved a nationwide needlework product distributor, which found that 28 percent of all its orders were $10 and under. A study revealed that the average cost of servicing such orders was $12.82. The analysis also showed that the company did not break even until the order size reached $20. Based on these findings, the company installed a $35 minimum order, charged a special handling fee of $7.50 on all orders below $35, and alerted its field sales reps and telephone salespeople to the problem. As a result, the company increased its profits substantially.

Sales Analysis by Customer

Analysts use procedures similar to those described earlier to analyze sales by customers. Such analyses typically show that a relatively small percentage of customers account for a large percentage of sales. For example, the needlework products distributor cited previously found that 13 percent of its accounts represented 67 percent of its total sales. Frequently, a study of sales calls shows that the salesforce spends a disproportionate amount of its time with the small accounts as compared with the larger ones. Shifting some of this effort to the larger accounts may well increase sales.

Tesco, using its ClubCard data, now categorizes its customers into various buckets, or market segments, based on the premise that "you are what you eat." It then tailors quarterly coupon mailings based on the customer's own shopping behavior. The "Loyal Low Spenders" get different coupons than the "High Spending Superstore Families," for example. Within these still broad segments, the quarterly offers are further tailored. Tesco mails more than 400,000 variations each quarter.[20]

The key to sales analysis by customer is to find useful decompositions of the sales data that are meaningful in a behavioral way. Three useful variables in doing so are recency (how recently did the customer last buy), frequency (how often), and monetary value (how much did the customer spend). These variables can lead to the development of metrics that can aid the marketer in defining market segments and in understanding the dynamics that underlie changes in sales.[21]

Line-Item Margin and Expense Analysis

Sales data are not the only marketing performance information needed. Gross and net margins must be tracked, and the effectiveness and efficiency of all line-item marketing expenses must be measured. The designers of marketing performance measurement systems must develop appropriate metrics to track the critical performance indicators for margins and expenses so that timely midcourse corrections can be made. Thus, the weeks-on-hand metric, which tells an H&M sweater buyer how quickly each style is selling, tells her whether to buy more of a particular style if it is selling well or mark it down if it is not moving. Making such decisions on a timely basis can have a profound effect on gross margins. A not-so-pretty sweater may be more salable at 25 percent off before Christmas than at 60 percent off after December 26. The same idea holds for swimsuits in summer, as shown in Exhibit 13.11.

Because budgets project revenues and expenses for a given time period, they are a vital part of the firm's planning and control activities. They provide the basis for a continuous evaluation and comparison of what was planned with what actually happened. In this sense, budgeted revenues and profits serve as objectives against which to measure performance in sales, profits, and actual costs.

EXHIBIT 13.11 *Web-Based Pricing Metrics Fatten Swimsuit Margins*

Steven Schwartz, senior vice president of planning at Casual Male, the 410-store U.S. clothing chain, knew that swimsuit prices had to fall after the Fourth of July holiday in the United States. But was the optimal timing the same in the lake country in Minnesota as at the beaches of Florida or New Jersey or California? Guesswork wasn't good enough, so Schwartz and his team loaded boatloads of the prior year's swimsuit sales data into a Web-based pricing system to get some answers. Northeasterners stopped dead in their tracks in July. Midwesterners kept buying into August. Sun Belt shoppers never stopped at all.

By making smarter pricing decisions, Casual Male improved its swimsuit gross margins by 25 percent over the prior year. Dillard's, the department store chain, saw 5 percent to 6 percent increases in gross margin across 17 departments using similar tools. Best of all, sales rose, too. Swimsuits may be getting skimpier, but their margins are moving the other way!

Source: Faith Keenan, "The Price Is Really Right," *BusinessWeek*, March 31, 2003, pp. 62–67. For more on Casual Male, see *www .casualmale.com*.

Budget analysis requires that managers continuously monitor marketing expense ratios to make certain the company does not overspend in its effort to reach its objectives. Managers also evaluate the magnitude and pattern of deviations from the target ratios. Managers of the various marketing units often have their own control measures. For example, advertising managers track advertising costs per 1,000 target audience, buyers per media vehicle, print ad readership, size and composition of TV audiences, and attitude change. Sales managers typically track number of calls per salesperson, costs per call, sales per call, and new accounts.

Recent advances in data gathering and analytics have led to a new breed of integrated marketing software such as Aprimo (*www.aprimo.com*). Such tools enable marketing managers to keep track of the varied kinds of activities that comprise any integrated marketing communications effort. They bring together data on all kinds of marketing projects and campaigns into a coherent and integrated platform, so that various elements of the marketing program—from e-mail marketing, to a new branding campaign still under development, to your media spend by region or by channel—can be tracked in a common manner.

SEO and SEM Analysis

In today's online world, where for many companies online traffic to the website is an important generator of leads, sales transactions, and more, the inherent measurability of the online world means that metrics to examine the effectiveness and efficiency of websites are essential.

Search engine optimization (SEO) refers to a set of techniques that helps ensure that a company's web pages are ranked highly when consumers search for information using Google, China's Baidu, or any other search engine. The search engines' **organic search,** as it is called, is driven by proprietary algorithms which vary from one search engine to another and are programmed to look for certain things. SEO's first job is to figure out what the algorithms are looking for, despite the fact that this is always a moving target. Then, job two is to optimize the company's web pages by, for example, ensuring that commonly searched-for **keywords** appear where the search engines are programmed to look for them. Doing so involves ensuring that the code is written so that the search engines can "read" it; ensuring that the right keywords are used in the site's content (and buried in its meta-data across the site); and influencing other authoritative sites to provide inbound links to one's own site. All in all, winning a superior organic ranking involves a highly technical set of tasks! The results of a company's effective use of SEO are that a company's web pages rank higher in the results returned from consumers' searches—the main left-hand side of a page on Google's search results, for example—than they would otherwise.

The Villa Poggiale, a lovely place for a family vacation in the heart of the Chianti region in Tuscany, would love it if its page would come up near the top of the listings when vacationers search for Tuscany or Chianti hotels, and might be tempted to use SEO to accomplish that goal. Because the Villa Poggiale is a small property, however, it is unlikely to rank nearly as high on the search engines as more widely visited sites offering more properties, such as TripAdvisor. Thus it might decide that **search engine marketing** (SEM) is a better way to go.

SEM is a related but fundamentally different activity from SEO. It involves buying keywords—AdWords, in Google-speak—for which consumers are likely to search so that one's **paid links,** on the right-hand side of a page of Google search results, come up at or near the top of the **paid search** listings. The good news—and the bad news—is that there's a market for keywords, with the more coveted terms commanding higher prices, of course. The catch is that paying a higher price to get to the top of the rankings only makes sense if doing so generates enough click-throughs that ultimately are converted into paying customers. Thus Villa Poggiale may choose to buy AdWords such as "Chianti hotels" or "Tuscany hotels" so that it ranks near the top of the paid search listings when consumers type either of those phrases into Google. Optimizing SEM means bidding a high enough price for your site to be highly ranked, but not so high that the cost of buying the AdWords is higher than their value as leads. AdWords are a main source of revenue for search engines like Google.

For marketers whose websites are intended to deliver completed transactions—booking a week's stay on the Villa Poggiale site, for example—there is a host of other metrics that the villa's **webmaster** should track to measure how effective each of its web pages is. The goal, of course, is that the consumer's journey from the Villa Poggiale **landing page** to its various other pages ultimately ends up on the book-

ing page with an inquiry at least, or a completed booking, at best. The attractiveness of the photos, the way copy is worded, and the design and mechanics of the overall website— Do pages load slowly or quickly, for example?—all play important roles in determining whether the consumer follows though and makes a booking, or whether she goes elsewhere. Savvy online marketers run experiments—Which photo works best, or what copy keeps the visitor hooked?—and use information on the dropout rates from page to page, in order to improve the productivity of the traffic that visits the site as a result of effective SEO or SEM efforts. There's nothing more wasteful than doing a great job on SEO or SEM and having users visit a set of pages that just don't work.

In the paragraphs above, we've only scratched the surface of a few of the analytical techniques that separate the best online marketers from the also-rans. The use of these and other kinds of **web analytics,** which take advantage of the inherent measurability of the web, opens a wide array of possibilities in an exciting new world in which marketing results can be clearly linked to marketing actions.

When and How Often Is the Information Needed?

Timeliness is a key criterion for the development of a marketing performance measurement system. As we have seen, Walmart's systems provide sales information at the store and item level on an up-to-the-minute basis. More commonly, managers attend to performance information—whether for sales, margins, or expenses—on a periodic basis, since they don't have time or the need to assess the performance of every item at every minute of every day. Buyers and merchandise managers in retailing firms typically assess item and category sales performance on a weekly basis. In fashion categories, such as women's apparel, where timeliness is especially important, having sales information a couple of days, or even hours, ahead of competitors can make the difference between obtaining more of a hot-selling item and being left in a faster-moving competitor's dust. For global retailers such as Mango, fast data is a crucial driver of the company's fast-fashion strategy (see Exhibit 13.12).

EXHIBIT 13.12 *Mango Breaks the Fashion Rules*

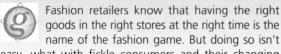

Fashion retailers know that having the right goods in the right stores at the right time is the name of the fashion game. But doing so isn't easy, what with fickle consumers and their changing tastes in everything from hemlines to colors to silhouettes. David Egea, merchandising director at Mango, the Barcelona-based fast-fashion chain with more than 1200 boutiques in 91 countries, says, "To react and have what people want, we have to break some rules."

Breaking the rules, in Mango's case, means that designs for new items can move from sketchpad to stores in as little as four weeks. By sourcing its styles close to home—instead of making big commitments to Asian suppliers with longer lead times—Mango can drop what's not selling and move quickly into what's hot, as it did in February 2004, when its collection of leather-trimmed black styles inspired by the movie *Matrix* weren't selling. Out went the black, and in came softer, more feminine styles.

Mango's fast-fashion system demands flexibility and speed, as well as up-to-the-minute sales data from the stores, all of which have paid big dividends for the young company, less than 30 years old. With fast data and fast fashion, "We know how to improvise," says Egan.

Sources: Erin White, "Speeding Up Fast Fashion," *The Wall Street Journal Europe*, May 28–30, 2004, p. A5. Mango.com website at *www.mango.com/web/pv/servicios/IN/franquicias/mangoMundo.htm*. For more on Mango, see *www.mango.com*.

Store payroll expense, another key performance criterion for retailers that impacts both customer service and profitability, is typically measured on a weekly basis, though store managers may be encouraged to send employees home if business is unexpectedly slow on a given day or call in extra help when more is needed. The performance of industrial salespeople—in terms of number of sales calls, sales volume, expense control, and other indicators—is typically done on a monthly basis, though some firms may do so more or less frequently as they see fit. Strategic control indicators, such as changes in market share, macro trends, and so on, are likely to be measured and reported less frequently because these kinds of longer-term issues may not be readily apparent or may give false alarms at more frequent intervals.

In What Media and in What Format(s) or Levels of Aggregation Should the Information Be Provided?

Strategic Issue

Having good and timely information and reporting it in such a manner that it is easy and quick to use are different things.

Advances in information technology have made possible the measurement and reporting of marketing performance information with previously unheard-of case of access and timeliness, without even printing the data! As we have seen, Walmart's sales information is available on its intranet on an up-to-the-minute basis. In other companies, salespeople around the world now log on to company intranets to see the latest order status of a customer before they walk in the door on a sales call. But *having* good and timely information and *reporting* it in such a manner that it is easy and quick to use are different things. Imagine a Mango buyer having to manually add up the performance of various styles to determine how the category or a particular vendor is performing. Reports should provide such aggregation, of course, but someone must decide what sort of aggregation is most useful for each information user.

The format or medium in which performance information is presented can make a big difference to the manager using the data. Weekly weeks-on-hand sales reports that retail buyers and merchandise managers depend on are most usefully reported in order of how fast the styles are selling, rather than alphabetically or some other way. The styles at the top of the report (those with little stock on hand, as measured by their weeks-on-hand sales rate) are candidates for reorders. Styles at the bottom of the report (the ugly wool sweater in mid-November with 25 weeks of inventory on hand) are candidates for markdowns. The ones in between may need little attention. Once a season ends, a different report, aggregating styles by vendor, perhaps, might be useful to determine which vendors have performed well and which have performed poorly across the assortment of styles they provide. Thoughtful attention to the format in which marketing performance information is reported, to the levels at which it is aggregated, for different kinds of decision purposes, and for different users can provide a company with a significant competitive advantage. As we noted earlier in this chapter, it took Kmart many years to come close to Walmart's system of tracking and reporting store and item sales performance.

Does Your System of Marketing Metrics Measure Up?

A key issue in developing a set of marketing metrics as part of an overall performance measurement system is getting the metrics aligned with the strategy. Just as professional athletes measure their performance in order to raise the bar, so too must marketing managers quantify and measure what they accomplish against what was planned. Doing so is particularly difficult if there's no explicit strategy or no culture of measurement that goes beyond summary financial performance.

As we've seen in this chapter, marketing metrics involve far more than simple analysis of the variances reported by the company's accounting system. So where should one start? A good first step is to identify the elements in a dashboard that the top management team can use to track marketing performance from period to period. Doing so will help gain top management involvement in marketing issues, and it will identify some of the data to which the rest of the organization should attend. Exhibit 13.13 lists 10 questions for

EXHIBIT 13.13   Do Your Marketing Metrics Measure Up?

Ten questions for your company's top executive team	
1. Does the exec regularly and formally assess marketing performance?	(a) Yearly (b) Six-monthly (c) Quarterly (d) More often (e) Rarely (f) Never
2. What does it understand by "customer value"?	(a) Don't know. We are not clear about this (b) Value of the customer to the business (as in 'customer lifetime value') (c) Value of what the company provides from the customer's point of view (d) Sometimes one, sometimes the other
3. How much time does the exec give to marketing issues?	—%
4. Does the business/marketing plan show the nonfinancial corporate goals and link them to market goals?	(a) No/no plan (b) Corporate no, market yes (c) Yes to both
5. Does the plan show the comparison of your marketing performance with competitors or the market as a whole?	(a) No/no plan (b) Yes, clearly (c) In between
6. What is your main marketing asset called?	(a) Brand equity (b) Reputation (c) Other term (d) We have no term
7. Does the exec's performance review involve a quantified review of the main marketing asset and how it has changed?	(a) Yes to both (b) Yes but only financially (brand valuation) (c) Not really
8. Has the exec quantified what "success" would look like 5 or 10 years from now?	(a) No (b) Yes (c) Don't know
9. Does your strategy have quantified milestones to indicate progress toward that success?	(a) No (b) Yes (c) What strategy?
10. Are the marketing performance indicators seen by the exec aligned with these milestones?	(a) No (b) Yes, external (customers and competitors) (c) Yes, internal (employees and innovativeness) (d) Yes, both

Source: Tim Ambler, *Marketing and the Bottom Line. The Marketing Metrics to Pump Up Cash Flow,* 2nd edition. (Copyright © 2003. Pearson Education Limited)

assessing any firm's system of marketing metrics and for identifying some of the elements that its dashboard might report. For many companies, these questions provide a useful wake-up call.

What Contingencies Should Be Planned For?

Because all strategies and the action plans designed to implement them are based on assumptions about the future, they are subject to considerable risk. Too often, assumptions are regarded as facts; and little attention is paid to what action or actions can be taken if any or all of the assumptions turn out to be wrong.

Managers, therefore, often follow a contingency planning process that includes the elements shown in Exhibit 13.14: identifying critical assumptions, assigning probabilities of being right about the assumptions, ranking the importance of each assumption, tracking and monitoring the action plan, setting the "triggers" that will activate the contingency plan, and specifying alternative response options. We discuss these steps briefly as follows.

Identifying Critical Assumptions

Because there are simply too many assumptions to track them all, contingency plans must cover only the more important ones. Assumptions about events beyond the control of the individual firm but that strongly affect the entry's strategic objectives are particularly important. For example, assumptions about the rate of market growth coupled with the entry's market share will strongly affect the entry's profitability objectives. The effect of a wrong assumption here can be either good or bad, and the contingency plan must be prepared to handle both. If the market grows at a rate faster then expected, then the question of how to respond needs to be considered. Too often contingency plans focus only on the downside.

Another type of uncontrollable event that can strongly affect sales and profits is competitive actions. This is particularly true with a new entry (when a competitor responds with its own new product), although it can apply with more mature products (competitor's

EXHIBIT 13.14 **The Contingency Planning Process**

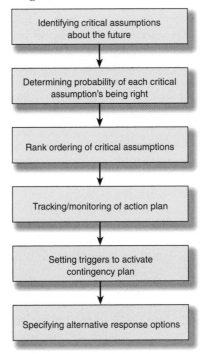

advertising is increased). Assumptions about industry price levels must be examined in depth because any price deterioration can quickly erode margins and profits.

Assumptions about the effects of certain actions taken by the firm to attain its strategic objectives also need to be considered in depth. Examples include the firm's advertising objectives, which are based on assumptions about an improvement or maintenance of consumer attitudes toward the product's characteristics compared with competing brands, or the monies allocated to merchandising to improve the product's availability. Further, once the targeted levels of the various primary objectives are reached, there are assumptions about what will happen to sales and share.

Determining Probabilities

This step consists of assigning to the critical assumptions probabilities of being right. These probabilities must be considered in terms of the consequences of being wrong. Thus, assumptions that have a low probability of being wrong but could affect the firm strongly need to be considered in depth (for automakers, for instance, political turmoil in oil-producing countries in the middle east).

Rank Ordering the Critical Assumptions

If assumptions are categorized on the basis of their importance, the extent to which they are controllable, and the confidence management has in them, then the basis for rank ordering the assumptions and drafting the contingency plan has been set forth. Ordinarily, these criteria will have screened out those assumptions that need not be included—those with a low impact and those about which there is a high confidence they will not occur. Assumptions that relate to uncontrollable events should, however, be monitored if they strongly affect the entry's strategic objectives since the firm can react to them. For example, if the assumption about the rate of market growth is wrong, then the firm can either slow or increase its investments in plant construction.

Tracking and Monitoring

The next step is to specify what information or measures are needed to determine whether the implementation of the action plan is on schedule—and if not, why not. The contingency plan is, therefore, an early warning system as well as a diagnostic tool. If, for example, the firm has made certain assumptions about the rate of market demand increase, then it would monitor industry sales on a regular basis. If assumptions were made about advertising and its effect on attitudes, then measures of awareness, trial, and repeat buying would be likely to be used. Relevance, accuracy, and cost of obtaining the needed measures must be examined in depth. Some of the information needed in the contingency plan might have been specified in the control plan, in which case it is already available.

Activating the Contingency Plan

This step involves setting the "triggers" to activate the contingency plan. It requires a specification of both the level at which an alert will be called and the combination of events that must occur before the firm reacts. If, for example, total industry sales were 10 percent less than expected for a single month, this might not be likely to trigger a response, whereas a 25 percent drop would. Or a firm may decide the triggering would occur only after three successive months in which a difference of 10 percent occurred. Triggers must be defined precisely and responsibility assigned for putting the contingency plan into operation.

Specifying Response Options

Actually, the term *contingency plan* is somewhat misleading. It implies that the firm knows in advance exactly how it will respond if one or more of its assumptions go awry. This implication is unrealistic because there are a great many ways for critical assumptions to turn out wrong. To compound the problem, the firm's preplanned specific responses can be difficult to implement, depending on the situation and how it develops. This can lead to a set of responses that build in intensity. Thus, most firms develop a set of optional responses that are not detailed to any great extent in an effort to provide flexibility and ensure further study of the forces that caused the alert.

Global Marketing Monitoring

Measuring the performance of global marketing activities is more difficult than with domestic marketing, primarily because of the number of countries involved, each presenting a unique set of opportunities and threats. This makes it difficult to monitor simultaneously a variety of environments and to prescribe corrective action on an individual country basis where appropriate. Differences in language and customs, accentuated by distance, further compound the control problem.

Nonetheless, global companies typically use essentially the same format for both their domestic and foreign operations, though report frequency and extent of detail can vary by the subsidiary's size and environmental uncertainties. The great advantage of using a single system is that it facilitates comparisons between operating units and communications between home office and local managers. If Mango didn't have uniform systems across its 1200-plus stores in 91 countries, it simply would not have been able to grow as it has. On the surface, the use of **electronic data interchange** and the Internet should simplify performance evaluation across countries. While this is true in terms of budget control, it leaves much to be desired in terms of understanding the reasons for any deviations.

A TOOL FOR PERIODIC ASSESSMENT OF MARKETING PERFORMANCE: THE MARKETING AUDIT

While marketing performance measurement systems are essential for tracking day-to-day, week-to-week, and month-to-month performance to see that planned results are actually delivered, it is sometimes useful to step back and take a longer view of the marketing performance of an SBU or of the entire company. Marketing audits are growing in popularity, especially for firms with a variety of SBUs that differ in their market orientation. They are both a control and planning activity that involves a comprehensive review of the firm's or SBU's total marketing efforts cutting across all products and business units. Thus, they are broader in scope and cover longer time horizons than sales and profitability analyses.

Strategic Issue

While marketing performance measurement systems are essential, it is sometimes useful to step back and take a longer view of the marketing performance of a SBU or of the entire company by using marketing audits.

Marketing audits generally focus on the individual SBU level or, for smaller or single-business firms, the entire company. Such an audit covers both the SBU's objectives and strategy and its plan of action for each product-market entry. It provides an assessment of each SBU's current overall competitive position as well as that of its individual product-market entries. It requires an analysis of each of the marketing-mix elements and how well they are being implemented in support of each entry. The audit must take into account any environmental changes that can affect the SBU's strategy and product-market action programs.

Types of Audits

Audits are normally conducted for such areas as the SBU's marketing environment, objectives and strategy, planning and control systems, organization, productivity, and individual marketing activities such as sales and advertising. These areas are shown in Exhibit 13.15

EXHIBIT 13.15   Some Major Areas Covered in a Marketing Audit and Questions Concerning Each for a Consumer Goods Company

Audit Area	Examples of Questions to Be Answered
Marketing environment	What opportunities and/or threats derive from the firm's present and future environment; that is, what demographic, social, technological, political, economic, and natural trends are significant? How will these trends affect the firm's target markets, competitors, suppliers, and channel intermediaries? Which opportunities/threats emerge from within the firm?
Objectives and strategy	How logical are the company's objectives, given the more significant opportunities/threats and its relative resources? How valid is the firm's strategy, given the anticipated environment, including the actions of competitors?
Planning and control system	Does the firm have adequate and timely information about consumers' satisfaction with its products? With the actions of competitors? With the services of intermediaries? Is the new product development process effective and efficient?
Organization	Does the organizational structure fit the evolving needs of the marketplace? Can it handle the planning needed at the individual product/brand level?
Marketing productivity	How profitable is each of the firm's products/brands? How effective and efficient is each of its major marketing activities?
Marketing functions	How well does the product line meet the line's objectives? How well do the products/brands meet the needs of the target markets? Does pricing reflect cross-elasticities, experience effects, and relative costs? Is the product readily available? What is the level of retail stockouts? What percentage of large stores carries the firm's in-store displays? Is the salesforce large enough? Is the firm spending enough on advertising?

with examples of the kinds of data needed and serve as the basis for the discussion that follows.

- The **marketing environment audit** requires an analysis of the firm's present and future environment with respect to its macro components, as discussed in Chapter 4. The intent is to identify the more significant trends to see how they affect the firm's customers, competitors, channel intermediaries, and suppliers.

- The **objectives and strategy audit** calls for an assessment of how appropriate these internal factors are, given current major environmental trends and any changes in the firm's resources.

- The unit's **planning and control system audit** evaluates the adequacy of the systems that develop the firm's product-market entry action plans and the control and reappraisal process. The audit also evaluates the firm's new product development procedures.

- The **organization audit** deals with the firm's overall structure (can it meet the changing needs of the marketplace), how the marketing department is organized (can it accommodate the planning requirements of the firm's assortment of brands), and the extent of synergy between the various marketing units (are there good relations between sales and merchandising).

- The **marketing productivity audit** evaluates the profitability of the company's individual products, markets (including sales territories), and key accounts. It also studies the cost-effectiveness of the various marketing activities.

- The **marketing functions audit** examines, in depth, how adequately the firm handles each of the marketing-mix elements. Questions relating to the *product* concern the attainability of the present product-line objective, the extent to which individual products fit the needs of the target markets, and whether the product line should be expanded or contracted. *Price* questions have to do with price elasticity; experience effects, relative costs, and the actions of major competitors; and consumers' perceptions of the relationship between a product's price and its value. *Distribution* questions center on coverage, functions performed, and cost-effectiveness. Questions about *advertising* focus on advertising objectives and strategies, media schedules, and the procedures used to develop advertising messages. The audit of the *salesforce* covers its objectives, role, size, coverage, organization, and duties plus the quality of its selection, training, motivation, compensation, and control activities.

- The company's **ethical audit** evaluates the extent to which the company engages in ethical and socially responsible marketing. Clearly this audit goes well beyond monitoring to make sure the firm is well within the law in its market behavior. If the company has a written code of ethics, then the main purpose of this audit is to make certain that it is disseminated, understood, and practiced.

- The **product manager audit,** especially in consumer goods companies, seeks to determine whether product managers are channeling their efforts in the best ways possible. They are queried on what they're doing versus what they *ought* to be doing. They are also asked to rate the extent to which various support units were helpful.

MEASURING AND DELIVERING MARKETING PERFORMANCE

As we've seen in this final chapter, the challenges entailed in measuring expenditures in marketing programs in relation to marketing performance in such a manner as to produce information that is timely, relevant, easy to use, cost-effective, useful to managers, and credible across the organization are daunting. But tackling these challenges head-on can make the difference when it comes to the sort of superior returns on investment that companies such as Walmart—at least in their glory days—deliver year after year. While marketing audits and various kinds of decision support systems do not guarantee strong performance, they help responsible, committed managers make decisions on the basis of current and valid information instead of hunches or uninformed guesses. It is for this reason that companies are paying increased attention to the development of information dashboards that provide people at all levels—from board members to top execs to line managers who deal with customers every day—the information they need to make timely, well-informed decisions about marketing, operational, and a host of other crucial decisions (see Exhibit 13.16). Whether Walmart's strengths in gathering and putting to use management information will enable the company to recover its mojo remains to be seen.

Even in entrepreneurial start-ups, the rampant uncertainty about consumers' needs, their responses to a new offering, competitor responses, and a host of other issues means that the best-laid strategies outlined in the company's business plan rarely pan out. For this reason, many early stage companies are avoiding the straight jacket that a business plan can be and turning to dashboards as their key tool for planning their entrepreneurial journey and tracking their progress. A dashboard comprised of the life-or-death metrics that can signal whether the company's "Plan A" is working and alert it to the need for mid-course pivots before it's too late can spell the difference between survival and extinction.[22]

At the end of the day, as a recent study points out, almost all positive cash flows in a firm of any size can be traced to customers that the firm's marketing and other efforts have delivered. Thus, measuring marketing performance well, both strategically and by product-market entry, is—to put it simply—essential. Further, the ultimate measure of firm value can arguably be said to be the firm's customer equity: the sum of the lifetime values of the firm's current and future customers.[23] If the adage "What gets measured gets done" holds some measure of truth, then measuring effectively, from a marketing performance point of

---

EXHIBIT 13.16   *Dashboards: The CEO's Killer App?*

Jerry Driggs, COO of Little Earth Productions, a marketer of funky, eco-fashion clothing and accessories such as handbags made out of recycled license plates, used to run his business by the seat of his pants. It showed. Without a good system to keep track of the amount of raw materials his Chinese suppliers needed, it used to take Little Earth six weeks to make and ship a handbag. Too much cash was tied up in trim pieces and closures that weren't really needed. To solve his problems, Driggs spent four months installing a dashboard from NetSuite, a fast-growing software company that specializes in this arena. Now he gets critical information displayed in easy-to-read graphics whenever and wherever he needs it.

Little Earth and many much larger companies including Verizon, Home Depot, and Microsoft swear by their dashboards, which some observers now regard as the CEO's killer app, making details that used to be buried deep inside the business available at a moment's notice. "The dashboard puts me and more and more of our executives in real-time touch with the business," says CEO Ivan Seidenberg of Verizon. While some critics worry that executives will spend too much time glued to their PCs and that the instant availability of data can add to the pressures that line managers already face, Driggs is a convert. As he puts it, "All of those things that used to drive us crazy are literally at our fingertips. Once you see it is so intuitive, you wonder how we ran the business before."

Source: Spencer E. Ante, "Giving the Boss the Big Picture," *BusinessWeek*, European Edition, February 13, 2006, pp. 48–51. For more on Little Earth or NetSuite, see *http://shop.littlearth.com* or *www.netsuite.com*.

---

view, is likely to bring about not only current profitability, but an enhancement in the value of the firm as well.

Thus, we close this book with one final message: measure early, measure often, and measure well.

Marketing Plan Exercise

Identify key milestones at which certain progress steps are to be met. Then, design strategic and operating "dashboards" that will provide the necessary information for the top management team to monitor—and if necessary, take steps to change—the marketing performance of the product or business once your plan is rolled out. For the operating dashboard, identify what information is to be provided, to whom, how often, and at what levels of aggregation. The operating dashboard should link to critical success factors identified earlier and should also measure any key variable costs subject to short-term control.

Discussion Questions

1. MTS Systems Inc. is a relatively small manufacturer of measurement instruments used to monitor and control automated production processes in a number of different industries, such as autos and aerospace. The firm has 12 salespeople, each of whom calls on companies in a particular industry. While the firm's sales have increased steadily in recent years, its profits have been relatively stagnant. One problem is that the firm has no information concerning the relative profitability of the various products it makes or the different customers to whom it sells. MTS Systems has hired you as a marketing consultant to design a *performance measurement system* that will enable the firm to evaluate its performance across the various items in its product line and the various segments of its market. As if you were a marketing consultant, outline the major *marketing metrics* you would recommend including in such a system.

2. What specific types of *information* would have to be collected and evaluated in order to implement the system you outlined in your answer to question 1? What sources could be used to obtain each necessary type of information?

3. After finishing your report, including the types of information needed (see question 2), you decide to develop a dashboard of performance metrics to be used by the top management team to evaluate the drivers of the firm's success. These measures would be used with the system you recommended. Outline the contents of this "addition," making sure you give examples of your individual recommendations.

4. You are a marketing manager in an SBU of a large consumer food manufacturer. The SBU's general manager has asked you to conduct a *marketing audit* of the SBU as a basis for evaluating its strategic and operations strengths and weaknesses. What issues or areas of concern should be covered by your audit? After completing your marketing audit, you are asked to develop a contingency plan for the SBU's major product line. Provide an outline of what the plan should cover.

Additional self-diagnostic questions to test your ability to apply the analytical tools and concepts in this chapter to strategic decision making may be found at the book's website at **www.mhhe.com/walker8e.**

Endnotes

1. Based on Sam Walton, *Sam Walton: Made in America* (New York: Doubleday, 1992), pp. 85–86, 118, 212–27; Bill Saporito, "What Sam Walton Taught America," *Fortune,* May 4, 1992, p. 104; "Remove Control," *The Economist,* May 29, 1993, p. 90; Patricia Sellers, "Can Walmart Get Back the Magic?" *Fortune,* April 29, 1996, p. 132; Anthony Blanco, "Walmart's Midlife Crisis," *BusinessWeek* European Edition, April 30, 2007, pp. 46–56; Miguel Bustillo, "Walmart Thinks Outside the Big Box," *The Wall Street Journal* European Edition, August 14–16, 2009, p. 1; Miguel Bustillo, "Walmart Tries to Recapture Mr. Sam's Winning Formula," *The Wall Street Journal* European Edition, February 23, 2011, p. 14; Geoff Colvin, "Walmart's Makeover," *Fortune* European Edition, December 26, 2011, pp. 44–49; and Walmart 2012 Annual Report and information from the company's website at *www.walmartstores.com.*

2. Reuters Helsinki, "Nokia Defends Ground, Plans for a Turnaround," *The Economic Times Hyderabad,* May 4, 2012, p. 18.

3. Don O'Sullivan and Andrew V. Abela, "Marketing Performance Measurement Ability and Firm Performance," *Journal of Marketing* 71 (April 2007), pp. 79–93.

4. Robert S. Kaplan and David P. Norton, "Putting the Balanced Scorecard to Work," *Harvard Business Review,* September–October 1993.

5. Matthew Boyle, "Walmart's Magic Moment," *BusinessWeek* European Edition, June 15, 2009, pp. 51–52.

6. John Mullins and Randy Komisar, *Getting to Plan B: Breaking Through to a Better Business Model* (Boston: Harvard Business Press, 2009).

7. Jeremy Mann, "How to Steal the Best Ideas Around," *Fortune*, October 19, 1992, p. 102.

8. K. S. Rao Ramesh and Neeraj Bharadwaj, "Marketing Initiatives, Expected Cash Flows, and Shareholders' Wealth," *Journal of Marketing* 72 (January 2008), pp. 16–26.

9. For more on activity-based costing, see any textbook in managerial accounting, such as Ray H. Garrison, Eric Noreen, and Peter C. Brewer, *Managerial Accounting* (Burr Ridge, IL: McGraw-Hill, 2011).

10. Fred Reichheld and James Allen, "How Companies Can End the Cycle of Customer Abuse," *Financial Times*, March 23, 2006, p. 43.

11. See Rajkumar Venkatesan and V. Kumar, "A Customer Lifetime Value Framework for Customer Selection and Resource Allocation Strategy," *Journal of Marketing,* October 2004, pp. 106–25; and Knowledge@Wharton, "The Customer Lifetime Value Equation: Will it Pay Off for Tech Companies?" December 7, 2011, at *http://knowlege.wharton.upenn.edu/printer_friendly.cfm?articleid=2890.*

12. Philipp Schmitt, Bernd Skiera, and Christophe Van den Bulte, "Referral Programs and Customer Value," *Journal of Marketing* 75 (January 2011), pp. 46–59.

13. Goutam Challagalla, R. Venkatesh, and Ajay K. Kohli, "Proactive Postsales Service: When and Why Does It Pay Off?" *Journal of Marketing* 73 (March 2009), pp. 70–87.

14. Elizabeth Rigby, "Eyes in the Till," *Financial Times FT Magazine*, November 11–12, 2006, pp. 16–22.

15. Deborah L. Vence, "Return on Investment," *Marketing News*, October 15, 2005, pp. 14–18.

16. For more on graphical information systems and their uses for marketing decision making, see Ana-Marija Ozimec, Martin Natter, and Thomas Reutterer, "Geographical Information

Systems-Based Marketing Decisions: Effects of Alternative Visualizations on Decision Quality," *Journal of Marketing* 74 (November 2010), pp. 94–110.

17. For two overviews of the measurement of marketing performance, see Donald R. Lehmann, "Metrics for Making Marketing Matter," *Journal of Marketing,* October 2004, pp. 73–75; and Roland T. Rust, Tim Ambler, Gregory S. Carpenter, V. Kumar, and Rajendra Srivastava, "Measuring Marketing Productivity: Current Knowledge and Future Directions," *Journal of Marketing*, October 2004, pp. 76–89.

18. From the *Procter & Gamble 2006 Annual Report.*

19. Activity-based costing is particularly helpful to managers in determining product profitability since it allocates costs to products more accurately than traditional methods by breaking down overhead costs more precisely.

20. Clive Humby, Terry Hunt, with Tim Phillips, *Scoring Points: How Tesco Is Winning Customer Loyalty* (London: Kogan-Page, 2003), pp. 148–49.

21. Bruce Hardie, "Metrics for Customer Base Analysis," presentation to a conference of the Marketing Science Institute, *Does Marketing Measure Up?* London, June 21–22, 2004.

22. John Mullins and Randy Komisar, *Getting to Plan B: Breaking Through to a Better Business Model* (Boston: Harvard Business Press, 2009).

23. Dominique M. Hanssens, Roland T. Rust, and Rajendra K. Srivastava, "Marketing Strategy and Wall Street: Nailing down Marketing's Impact," *Journal of Marketing* 73 (November 2009), pp. 115–18.

Name Index

Subject Index

Page numbers followed by f and t indicate figures and tables